PROOF *of* COLLUSION

How Trump Betrayed America

★ ★ ★ ★ ★ ★ ★

Seth Abramson

Simon & Schuster

NEW YORK · LONDON · TORONTO
SYDNEY · NEW DELHI

Simon & Schuster
1230 Avenue of the Americas
New York, NY 10020

Copyright © 2018 by Seth Abramson

First Simon & Schuster hardcover edition November 2018

For information about special discounts for bulk purchases,
please contact Simon & Schuster Special Sales at
1-866-506-1949 or business@simonandschuster.com.

The Simon & Schuster Speakers Bureau can bring authors to your
live event. For more information, or to book an event, contact
the Simon & Schuster Speakers Bureau at 1-866-248-3049
or visit our website at www.simonspeakers.com.

Interior design by Paul Dippolito

Manufactured in the United States of America

1   3   5   7   9   10   8   6   4   2

Library of Congress Cataloging-in-Publication Data has been applied for.

ISBN 978-1-9821-1608-8
ISBN 978-1-9821-1610-1 (ebook)

To all the public defenders

Mr. Trump's claims of "no collusion" are, in a word, hogwash.

—Former CIA director John Brennan, August 16, 2018

CONTENTS

PROOF *of*
COLLUSION

AUTHOR'S NOTE

The index for *Proof of Collusion* has been published online rather than in print, because of both its size and the likelihood some readers will want to search it electronically. You can find the book's index at www.sethabramson.net or http://proofofcollusionindex.com.

A THEORY OF THE CASE

THE TRUMP-RUSSIA INVESTIGATION MAY BE THE MOST MUL-tifaceted, wide-ranging, high-stakes federal criminal investigation in American history. It crosses continents and decades and has swept into its vortex more than four hundred people, millions of pages of financial records, and scores of unanswered questions about the state of our democracy. It has already resulted in dozens of indictments and a host of guilty pleas and prison sentences. If President Trump colluded with Kremlin agents to secure his election or to benefit his real estate empire down the road, or if he knows that any of his associates did so, it gives the Kremlin leverage over him in a way that endangers our national security and even our national sovereignty. Whatever your political views, and whatever your opinion of Donald Trump, you have a vested interest in finding out the truth about Trump-Russia collusion if you want America to be governed by the consent of the people and not the Kremlin.

In view of all this, you may be surprised to learn that, as a legal term, "collusion" is meaningless outside antitrust law. In lay terms, collusion is simply a clandestine agreement between two or more parties, implicit or explicit, to act in a mutually beneficial way. That collusion is always clandestine underscores that it is almost always a transgression, no matter the venue or the participants. That certain acts of collusion can violate criminal statutes means that collusive behavior is sometimes criminal behavior as well. The notion of an American politician colluding with a foreign power, let alone a hostile one, is antithetical to our values and has been since the nation declared its independence in 1776. Because foreign nationals are not permitted by U.S. law to interfere in our elections, foreign governments generally refrain from commenting on our electoral processes and certainly do not seek to contribute money or other benefits to our candidates. Doing so is a federal crime. In the few instances in which politicians have been caught receiving money or in-kind contributions from foreign entities, it's been regarded as a rare scandal. Should it also be discovered that the politician and his staff reached out to that foreign entity with the aim of securing a hard-money or in-kind contribution, the scandal would become generationally significant. And should that politician be running for president, and should the nation he sought contributions from be a hostile foreign power that was waging cyberwar on America's critical infrastructure, that generationally significant scandal would become unprecedented. In short, it is likely that the Trump-Russia story ends with Americans choosing a new archetype for "American traitor" besides Benedict Arnold.

Proof of collusion in the Trump-Russia case is in plain sight. When the president or his allies say "there was no collusion," what they mean is that the type of collusion the president undoubtedly engaged in does not constitute a criminal offense—whether or not it constitutes an impeachable one. This latter distinction is important: Trump attorney Rudy Giuliani has taken great pains in the latter half of 2018 to say that the Trump-Russia case is predominantly a political one, and to the extent most legal scholars believe a sitting president can't be indicted, he is correct. The House of Representatives has to vote to bring charges against a president, and the Senate has to preside over his trial and find him guilty. In this current climate, there is a chance that may not happen.

That said, it so happens that much of this president's collusion may in fact be criminal. The particular forms of collusion in which Trump, members of his family who are also political advisers, and his presidential campaign engaged may include aiding and abetting or conspiracy connected to electoral fraud, computer crimes, bribery, and money laundering, as well as acts of witness tampering, making false statements, obstruction of justice, and much more. Conspiracy occurs when two or more persons have a "meeting of the minds" and set as their ambition the commission of a criminal act; the federal conspiracy statute is violated when the parties take an "act in furtherance" of the commission of the intended crime. But the crime does not have to be committed for a violation of the conspiracy statute to be found.

In America's system of justice, those designated to prosecute a case are obligated by the rules of professional ethics to be relentlessly zealous advocates for their position. The system doesn't work, otherwise; without zealous advocates, we might as well adopt the so-called inquisitorial system of justice employed in most of Europe's courtrooms rather than the adversarial system we have here in America. To an outside observer, zealous advocacy often looks like radicalism; in fact, it's a civic duty for trial advocates, and one that's emotionally and intellectually exhausting to fulfill. That's certainly the case with my ongoing public accounting of the Trump-Russia investigation, though the work is made easier, I'll confess, by the almost historic absence—I say this advisedly—of *any* exculpatory evidence suggesting the president of the United States did *not* conspire with our enemies to violate federal law. I make that statement not as a political partisan but as an American citizen and legal professional who for many years pored over thousands of police reports, witness statements, lab results, and documentary and photographic evidence, looking for any trace of information that could exculpate my clients. I am trained, by years of experience and habit, to search for an alternative explanation besides the obvious one: that the defendant is indeed a criminal, responsible for either the charges as leveled against him or some lesser offense included in or ancillary to the ones he's currently facing. That roughly 95 percent of defendants in criminal cases in America accept responsibility for their actions and enter a guilty plea in exchange for a fair punishment is at times a testament to law enforcement and at times an indictment of our ability to give defendants the resources to adequately defend themselves; most commonly, though, it denotes a body of evidence that is overwhelmingly inculpatory.

It's within this framework of experience, principle, and philosophy that I say that I have never before encountered a criminal investigation in which the entirety of the evidence is as damning as it is in the Trump-Russia investigation. From a professional rather than partisan perspective, the conclusion of the Trump-Russia scandal is all but certain: an untold number of indictments, prison sentences, and dispiriting revelations about public figures, all of which will momentarily cast doubt on our ability to move forward as a functioning democracy. That the evidence against Trump and his associates is so thoroughly in one direction makes it all the more startling that there has yet to be any published defense of Trump or his allies *on the facts* whose contentions would be taken seriously in a court of law. I'm as surprised by that fact as anyone, especially given who the defendant is here and what is so conspicuously at stake in the investigation.

As a longtime criminal defense attorney, I have long sympathized most—philosophically, at least—with the role of defense counsel in our adversarial system of justice. Defense teams are commonly under-resourced, outgunned by a state or federal apparatus with a built-in investigatory arm, a judiciary systematically tilted toward the needs and values of the government, and well-trained prosecutors who are ruthlessly ambitious if not always efficient. But Donald Trump is a different type of defendant; his defense team is a different sort of defense team; and the defense he and his team have mounted so far is not recognizable to an attorney as any sort of legal defense at all.

From his Twitter feed, Trump launches daily baseless ad hominem attacks against prosecutors, investigators, and witnesses alike, and he does so with a seeming impunity from the allegations of witness tampering and obstruction of justice that any of my clients at public defender offices in Massachusetts, New Hampshire, or D.C. would have faced had they behaved similarly. His attorneys daily play semantic games that don't so much advance their client's interests as function as a pervasive campaign to misinform Americans about how our system of justice works and why. For instance, their contention that "collusion is not a crime" goes beyond mere rhetoric and into a profoundly unethical misrepresentation of the real state of affairs: within the umbrella term "collusion" there are dozens of federal criminal statutes that federal law enforcement can and does routinely enforce. As for the broader defense strategy Trump and his attorneys have fashioned against his critics, the strategy seems to be a political, not a legal, one. Every time I see Giuliani or Jay Sekulow on television implying, if not outright alleging, a "deep state" conspiracy to frame this president, I do not see a fellow "brother at the bar" but a high-priced political operator.

While several chapters of this book contain original reporting, the bulk of *Proof of Collusion* aggregates and curates information rather than reporting it. The book is a compilation, at times in summary form and at times in minute detail, of not just the evidence of collusion between the Trump campaign (now administration) and Russian nationals, but also of the criminality born of that collusion. The book's subchapters are drawn from major-media news stories linked to on my Twitter feed since January 2017 and supplementary news stories and factual updates supporting and expanding upon the materials available on my feed. Taken in sum, these articles and analyses compose the current state of affairs in the Trump-Russia investigation—at least that part of the investigation that is open to public view. My hope is that readers will not only benefit from this presentation but also find many opportunities to discover new connections within the curated pieces of evidence.

An accounting of this evidence is made necessary not just by the frenetic pace of Trump-Russia news and the gravity of the investigation behind it, but the fact that Americans are likely to remain in the dark for months. What originally was six investigations in Congress—the House Permanent Select Committee on Intelligence, the Senate Select Committee on Intelligence, the House Judiciary Committee, the Senate Judiciary Committee, the House Oversight and Government Reform Committee, and the Senate Judiciary Subcommittee on Crime and Terrorism—is now just one: the Senate Select Committee on Intelligence. The other investigations have either been shut down or turned their attention toward harassing, impeaching, and in some cases even seeking criminal charges against the law enforcement officials and U.S. intelligence partners who have been, and in many cases still are, investigating the president and his team. While a separate congressional investigation of Russian interference in the 2016 presidential

election—better classified as a "hot" cyberwar than "interference"—
is ongoing, it has yet to lead to new election safeguards by the Trump
administration or to new funding for election security. Meanwhile, the
one professional, nonpartisan investigation of Trump-Russia ties, conducted by Special Counsel Robert Mueller at the Justice Department,
is at once virtually leak-free and under constant assault and threat of
termination by Trump, his allies in Congress, and his advocates in the
media.

The result of all this chaos is that Americans are either misled by
partisan evidentiary summaries released by Trump allies in Congress;
disheartened by the Senate Select Committee on Intelligence and its
lack of progress and odd unwillingness to subpoena critical witnesses;
or bewildered by the lack of information forthcoming from the Office
of the Special Counsel under the direction of the Department of Justice.
Every few weeks or months a new indictment or plea hits the news, or
a leak from the White House by an attention-seeking staffer gives the
public some insight into what might be going on behind the scenes. But
it's never enough; nothing ever seems to get resolved. This is the state
of America in 2018: we wait for news on the possibility that our president may be beholden to a foreign power and the final verdict never
arrives, despite feeling tantalizingly close.

America deserves and demands an accounting of the evidence compiled by media outlets, congressional investigators, and law enforcement in advance of a final, comprehensive special counsel report that
might not arrive until mid- to late 2019 or even 2020. Deputy Attorney
General Rod Rosenstein, who is currently overseeing the investigation,
isn't obligated to make that report public once he receives it—though
as a fellow attorney I certainly hope and expect he will, for the good of
the nation. So the public might never get the full details of what went
on between the Kremlin and Donald Trump, the Republican Party, and
allies of Trump in and out of government.

Proof of Collusion aims to move forward the public discussion of
the most significant criminal investigation of our lives. But readers
should know that there is one type of evidence that is absent from this

book entirely: financial records. Breaking a forty-year tradition, Trump refused to release his tax returns prior to Election Day, and we've since come to learn that they will never be released. And, breaking a tradition much longer than forty years, the U.S. Congress has refused to subpoena or otherwise force the disclosure of any financial records through any of its investigations, even though they may well hinge on the flow of money into shell corporations and hidden bank accounts. Even the Treasury Department has recently been accused of failing to turn over documents that might have informed America much sooner of suspicious transactions involving accused Russian spy Maria Butina (also spelled "Mariia") and her boyfriend, GOP operative and NRA member Paul Erickson.[1]

Unfortunately, these are derelictions of duty and lapses of honor that no public investigation can remedy—we in the public do not have the subpoena power and can only encourage those who do to do their jobs by how we vote every two years and during special elections. So while the Trump-Russia investigation may end up revealing one of the most audacious money-laundering schemes in the last century, perhaps involving one or more European banks or banks in Cyprus under investigation for Russian money laundering, this book cannot go there yet.[2]

That said, the investigatory model my Twitter feed and this book uses to contribute to public discussion of the Trump-Russia case relies on the development of a "theory of the case"—a narrative that connects all other narratives. A good "theory of the case" must be dynamic as well as encompassing; it must adapt as new facts emerge and must quickly supplant old presuppositions with fresh analyses. To develop a theory, a criminal investigator must first know all the facts of a case—a task that, with a fact pattern as complex and wide-ranging as that of the Trump-Russia investigation, can feel daunting or even impossible. Nevertheless, a committed investigator builds a timeline of events, a mental gallery of major witnesses and suspects, and a compendium of hard and circumstantial evidence. In doing so, the investigator is able to author a grand narrative that works in concert with, rather than against, the presently available evidence.

In the case of the ongoing Trump-Russia probe, the only plausible theory of the case that coordinates with all the existing evidence is that Donald Trump and a core group of ten to twenty aides, associates, and allies conspired with a hostile foreign power to sell that power control over America's foreign policy in exchange for financial reward and—eventually—covert election assistance. This theory doesn't contend that anyone in the president's sphere participated in any hacking or even knew about Russia's cyber-intrusions in advance; it doesn't allege that the conspiracy many members of the Trump team were involved in was finely wrought, as opposed to chaotic, amateurish, and quickly capable of producing a mountain of incriminating evidence; it doesn't require that all elements of its grand narrative take place in private, as indeed many of them occurred in the plain sight of millions of Americans; and it doesn't allege that any of the actions involved rose to the level of statutory treason—a federal criminal statute that applies only if America is in a declared state of war. What this theory of the case *does* do is explain decades of suspicious behavior by Donald Trump, his family, and his closest associates, behavior that suggests that these bad actors expected and received a massive financial reward for taking policy positions friendly to the Kremlin and adverse to the interests of the United States. The theory further maintains that once Trump had sufficient knowledge of Russian crimes to be legally responsible for not aiding and abetting them with promises of policies unilaterally beneficial to the Kremlin—a point Trump reached on August 17, 2016, at the very latest—any additional actions taken to advance Russian interests were criminal. The theory organizes a clear and discrete roster of those Trump aides, associates, and allies who were complicit in Trump's financially motivated appeasement of a hostile foreign power, and in so doing it explains why nearly every name on that list attaches to a Trump campaign, transition, or administration figure who has lied about his associations with Russian nationals.

In a criminal investigation, even a single significant lie can signal a witness's or suspect's guilty conscience; in the Trump-Russia investigation, the combined half-truths and outright falsehoods spread by ten to twenty "Team Trump" coconspirators now number in the doz-

ens. Right now, the inaction of congressional Republicans—a failure
to prosecute those who have lied to Congress or to subpoena those who
won't speak to Congress at all—enables these lies to continue.

Proof of Collusion aims to provide a careful, comprehensive, and
compelling presentation of the evidence supporting the only theory
of the case that answers the question of what's happening in America
right now and how we can stop it.

CHAPTER ONE

RUSSIA AND THE TRUMPS

1987–2012

Summary

AFTER FIFTEEN YEARS OF FINANCIAL FAILURES IN RUSSIA—
failures born not of a lack of desire to succeed but a lack of access to
the people in Russia who make wealth creation possible—the Trumps
discover that the key to making a fortune in real estate in Russia is
greasing the skids with influential Russian officials.[1] When the Trumps
finally learn this lesson in the early 2000s, the result is the Russian
riches that the family, particularly its patriarch, Donald Trump Sr.,
has long sought. The family gains, too, a new set of Russian, Russian-
American, and Soviet-born allies who will in time rescue the family from its business struggles in the recession of the late 2000s and
early 2010s, when many U.S. banks are declining to lend to the Trump
Organization.[2] Many of these new allies have criminal histories, dubious business practices, close ties to the Kremlin, or all three.

But the Trumps' many years of candor about their fondness for
Russia, as well as their boasts of the money their many business ties
to that nation have brought them over the years, will dissipate instantly
once Donald Trump decides to run for president of the United States
not long after the 2012 presidential election.[3]

The Facts

UP UNTIL 1987, DONALD TRUMP IS NOT REGARDED AS A PAR-
ticularly political public figure. However, in 1987 he publishes *The Art
of the Deal* and takes a trip to Moscow—one or both of which send him
in the direction of a political career.[4]

Trump's trip to Moscow in 1987 comes at the invitation of Russia's
ambassador to the United States, Yuri Dubinin. In Moscow, Trump
stays in the Lenin Suite of the Hotel National, which, as Jonathan Chait
of *New York Magazine* notes, "certainly would have been bugged" in
1987.[5] Trump holds meetings on the possible construction of a Trump
hotel with Soviet officials, coming away from the meetings certain that
the officials are "eager" to do business with him.[6]

On returning to the United States, Trump spends nearly $100,000
on politically charged newspaper ads, attacking American allies like
Japan and Saudi Arabia for spending too little on their own defense.[7]
He urges America to "tax these wealthy nations" and shortly thereafter makes a high-profile trip to New Hampshire—the sort of trip that is
often considered a prelude to a presidential bid.[8]

Trump's 1987 bid for a Trump hotel in Moscow falls through, according to the *Washington Post*, only because Trump was "preoccupied
with other business projects."[9]

Once Trump's companies recover from a string of bankruptcies
in 1991 and 1992, he returns his attention to the Russian market.[10] In
1996, he returns to Moscow with Howard Lorber, "one of his two closest friends," according to the *Post*.[11] Together they scout locations for
an office tower and eventually find both a location for the tower and
a prospective Russian partner for the project. Trump announces plans
for a Trump International–branded building in November 1996; the
deal will see him investing $250 million and licensing his name to two
buildings.[12] "We have an understanding we will be doing it," Trump
says.[13] At the press conference promoting the deal, he says he doesn't
think he's ever been "as impressed with the potential of a city as I have
been with Moscow."[14]

However, Trump has a problem: American banks will no longer lend to him, citing his track record for paying back only "pennies on the dollar"—what the banks call "the Donald risk." [15]

By 1997, though no construction has begun on Trump's hoped-for Moscow projects, the *New Yorker* is writing of "the breadth of Trump's hopes for Moscow investment and business connections." [16] Trump's plans for the expansion of his real estate portfolio into Russia go well beyond a single Trump International Hotel; Trump envisions a much larger series of investments. He tells the *New Yorker*, "[I]t would be skyscrapers and hotels. . . . [W]e're working with the local government, the mayor of Moscow, and the mayor's people. So far, they've been very responsive." [17]

As Trump's 1996 plans finally fall through for good, Russia begins a period of political upheaval that sees the nation led by five successive prime ministers appointed by Boris Yeltsin over a fifteen-month period in 1998 and 1999. The last of these prime ministers is a man by the name of Vladimir Putin. [18]

Putin, the former first deputy chairman (the equivalent of a deputy mayor) of St. Petersburg, develops a fondness for Miss St. Petersburg, Oxana Fedorova, sometime before she is crowned Miss Russia in 2001. [19] It is widely known that he has a picture of her in his office. [20] After Fedorova wins the 2001 Miss Russia pageant, rumors abound—spurred in part by the presence of Putin's domestic intelligence service, the FSB, acting as security at the competition—that the pageant has been rigged so that Fedorova will win. [21] Local media say that either the pageant was corrupt or its organizers knew instinctively it would be unwise—not "politically correct," according to the *Telegraph*—to let anyone but Fedorova win. [22]

In winning the Miss Russia pageant, Fedorova becomes Russia's entrant to the 2002 Miss Universe pageant, an international competition owned by Donald Trump. Though the 2002 pageant is scheduled to take place in Puerto Rico, anticipation for the event is high in Russia because of Putin's admiration for Fedorova and because no Russian woman has ever won the Miss Universe pageant in its then half century of continuous operation. [23]

At the time of the 2002 Miss Universe pageant, Fedorova's publicly acknowledged boyfriend is Vladimir Golubev, a St. Petersburg crime boss heavily involved in the construction industry.[24] But the scuttlebutt in Moscow is that Fedorova is actually with a different Vladimir; a May 2002 article published immediately after the 2002 Miss Universe pageant calls Fedorova "Putin's girl."[25] There is substantial press attention on the pageant in Moscow as Fedorova wins the competition and makes pageant history as the first Miss Universe from Russia.

On November 2, 2017, an eyewitness to the judging process at the 2002 Miss Universe contest will contact this author to say that the contest was "rigged."[26] After the eyewitness's identity has been verified, the eyewitness recounts the following: after there are only ten contestants left in the 2002 Miss Universe pageant—an elimination process that Trump directly participates in at this point in the pageant's history—Trump addresses the pageant's celebrity judges and indicates that he wants Miss Russia crowned Miss Universe.[27] The source reports Trump saying, "There's definitely, clearly one woman out there who's head and shoulders above the rest. She's the one I'd vote for."[28] Given the context of the statement—Trump issuing his formal instructions to the judges as they prepared for the conclusion of the pageant—as well as his demeanor while speaking, the eyewitness asserts that Trump "told the judges who to vote for," adding that a subsequent conversation among the celebrity judges revealed that several had had the same impression.[29]

The judges vote for Miss Russia, who thereby becomes Miss Universe until her dethroning 120 days later for failure to faithfully execute the duties of her office.[30] The contest's celebrity judges are later told by parties affiliated with the pageant that Fedorova has been dethroned because of unspecified criminal conduct by her boyfriend, Vladimir Golubev.[31]

In the forty-eight months following the 2002 Miss Universe pageant, Trump's fortunes in Russia change dramatically. After fifteen years of failed attempts to break into the Russian market—the Moscow market specifically—Trump finds that Russia is suddenly a critical component of the Trump Organization's investment portfolio, as Donald Trump Jr. will explain in a 2008 speech to investors at a Manhattan conference.[32] While this is partly attributable to the fact that "the push to sell units in Trump World Tower to Russians expand[s] in 2002"— when Sotheby's International Realty begins partnering with Kirsanova Realty, a Russian company—another reason is that a matter of months after the Miss Universe pageant, a Russian émigré associated with the Russian criminal underworld, accompanied by his Soviet-born business partner Tevfik Arif, approaches Trump about a business partnership.[33] The émigré, Felix Sater, will for the next few years deliver a large number of Russian clients to Trump and be instrumental in finding Russia-born partners for the biggest Trump construction project of the 2000s, Trump SoHo.[34]

Sater's access to the highest levels of the Russian government is made evident when, in 2006, he arranges for Ivanka Trump to sit in Putin's office chair during a tour of the Kremlin.[35] According to Daniel Treisman, a professor of political science at UCLA and an expert on Russian politics, anyone able to get a visitor to the Kremlin into Putin's chair would have to have "the highest [Russian] security clearances and [be] personally trusted by Putin."[36]

The same year, Paul Manafort moves into a forty-third-floor apartment in Trump Tower, paying $3.6 million for it at a time when he is making millions working for pro-Russian politicians in Ukraine.[37] Just a year earlier, "Manafort proposed in a confidential strategy plan . . . that he would influence politics, business dealings and news coverage inside the United States, Europe and former Soviet republics to benefit President Vladimir Putin's government."[38] Manafort's proposal is eventually accepted, and he is paid $10 million in 2006 by "close Putin ally" Oleg Deripaska—the same year he buys his apartment in Trump Tower.[39]

Down on the twenty-fourth floor of Trump Tower, Sater and his company, the Bayrock Group, have become critical to Trump's business success—especially with Russian investors and business partners.[40] Yet when asked at a civil deposition in November 2013 whether he knows who Felix Sater is, Trump, under oath, says he has seen Sater only a "couple of times" and that he "wouldn't know what [Sater] look[s] like."[41] At a deposition six years earlier, in 2007, *Bloomberg* reported that Trump had testified under oath that Sater's Bayrock "brought Russian investors to his Trump Tower office to discuss deals in Moscow . . . and he [Trump] was pondering investing there."[42] "It's ridiculous that I wouldn't be investing in Russia," Trump says at the time. "Russia is one of the hottest places in the world for investment."[43] Indeed, Trump had signed a one-year development deal with Bayrock for a Trump Tower Moscow in 2005; though the deal fell through, a site had been selected.[44]

In 2006, Trump's partners on a real estate project in Panama go on an investor-recruiting trip to Moscow.[45] In 2007, Trump again, through Bayrock, "line[s] up with Russian investors . . . a deal for a Trump International Hotel and Tower in Moscow."[46] According to Trump, "[i]t would be a nonexclusive deal, so it would not have precluded me from doing other deals in Moscow, which was very important to me."[47] After this deal falls through as well, Trump says—in the same 2007 deposition in which he speaks glowingly of Sater's real estate development company—"We're going to do [another Moscow deal] fairly soon. [Moscow] will be one of the cities where we will be."[48]

That year, Trump attends the Moscow Millionaire Fair, at which he unveils Trump Vodka for the Russian market.[49] He also partners with Russian Alex Shnaider to salvage an ailing project, Toronto's Trump International Hotel and Tower.[50] In 2005, *Forbes* had written a profile on Shnaider referencing his participation in the "shadowy," "murky," violent Ukrainian steel business, where to get along with other steel traders and avoid death ("at least seven steel executives were assassinated in Ukraine in the 1990s") you had to "hire their relatives, give them gifts—whatever could be done."[51] Trump would "[claim] to have a financial stake [in the Trump International Hotel and Tower in Toronto], only later to admit that it was a licensing deal. . . . Trump family members [also] presented inflated sales figures when the towers, in reality, stood nearly empty."[52]

In 2010, when the Toronto project falters yet again, it is rescued with nearly a billion dollars in new investment by the Kremlin-owned development bank Vnesheconombank, or VEB.[53] In December 2016, during the presidential transition, Trump's son-in-law, Jared Kushner, will meet secretly at Trump Tower with VEB's chairman, Sergei Gorkov, who graduated from the academy of Russia's chief intelligence agency, the FSB.[54] Observing that VEB is "known for advancing the strategic interests of Russian President Vladimir Putin," the *Washington Post* will report that VEB called the meeting with Kushner "part of a new business strategy" and that its chairman met with Kushner "in his role as the head of his family's real estate business."[55] Hope Hicks, a White House spokesperson, will insist instead that it was merely a "diplomatic" meeting.[56]

In 2008, Trump strikes a deal with Russian heavyweight mixed martial artist Fedor Emelianenko—who *Rolling Stone* will note in May 2018 "has very close ties to Vladimir Putin"—for a reality show in Russia that never materializes.[57] Trump even forms a company with Emelianenko, Affliction Entertainment, to manage and promote their joint venture; he makes his attorney Michael Cohen Affliction's COO.[58]

All of this helps to explain how, by 2008, Donald Trump Jr., speaking to a group of investors on the topic of emerging overseas markets, could boast that "Russians make up a pretty disproportionate cross-section of a lot of our [Trump Organization] assets."[59] He adds that the Trump Organization "primarily" looks for new real estate in Russia.[60]

Trump Jr.'s comments are striking for both their clarity and boldness. eTurboNews (eTN), the global travel industry news website that reports on Trump Jr.'s address, writes that, per Trump Jr., "[i]f he were to choose his top A-list for investments in the emerging world . . . his firm [the Trump Organization] would choose China and Russia."[61] eTN quotes the eldest Trump son as saying, "Given what I've seen in Russia's real estate market as of late relative to some of the emerging markets, [Russia] seems to have a lot more natural strength [than China], especially in the high-end sector where people focus on price per square-meter. In Russia, I really prefer Moscow over all cities in the world."[62]

Trump Jr. reveals to the investors that he has made "half a dozen trips to Russia" in the preceding eighteen months—one trip every ninety days—and that on these trips he brings clients to the Trump Organization's "projects" in Moscow; his travel partners are, he says, "buyers [who] have been attracted to our projects there."[63] In September 2017, Trump Jr. will testify before the Senate Judiciary Committee and say that he has been to Russia only "four or five" times in his life.[64]

Trump Jr. does, however, note to investors in 2008 some potential obstacles for those who want to invest heavily in Russia. He explains that, based on his significant experience seeking investments in Russia, investor concerns about the Russian market are "not an issue of [not] being able to find a deal—but . . . 'can I actually trust the person I am doing the deal with?' "[65] He explains that success in the Russian market is finally attributable to "who knows who" and "whose brother is paying off who."[66]

eTN describes Trump Jr.'s depiction of Trump Organization activities in Moscow this way: "Despite a current [Russian] government that projects a ramrod posture, to Trump the current leaders [of Russia] make the scene more scary. Holding back his grin, he said, 'It's so transparent—everything's so interconnected that it really does not matter what is supposed to happen as *what it is they want to happen* is ultimately what happens' " (emphasis added).[67] It is unclear from eTN's coverage of the Trump Jr. speech who the "they" is that the young Trump Organization executive is referring to.

Trump Jr. also discusses the Trump Organization's reliance on Russian investors investing in the United States. "We see a lot of money pouring in from Russia," he says, adding that the soon-to-be-completed Trump SoHo is also specifically targeting investors in the United Arab Emirates.[68] Trump Jr.'s boast is not an empty one; from sixty-five Russians buying units in a single Trump building in the late 1990s to a *Bloomberg* report finding that by 2004 fully one-third of units on floors seventy-six through eighty-three in Trump World Tower involved "people or companies connected to Russia or neighboring states," the Trump Organization has for years counted Russian clients among its most enthusiastic customers.[69] The *New Republic* describes how Trump International Beach Resort in Florida was so popular among Trump's

Russian clientele that the area, Sunny Isles Beach, came to be known as "Little Moscow."[70]

One of the deals Trump Jr. may be referring to in saying the Trump Organization "see[s] a lot of money pouring in from Russia" is a deal his father is working on the very summer Trump Jr. makes his claim. In November 2004, Trump had bought for $41 million a parcel of land in Florida that—despite the improvements he thereafter made to it—he couldn't unload.[71] In 2006, it was on the market for $125 million, more than three times what Trump paid for it; by the time the Great Recession begins in the latter half of 2007, Trump has had to drop the price by 20 percent, to around $100 million.[72]

In the summer of 2008, a Russian billionaire named Dmitry Rybolovlev offers nearly the full asking price for the property—$95 million—despite Trump's having no competing offers.[73] Trump thereby makes $54 million in forty-eight months. Rybolovlev immediately destroys the structures on the property that Trump had renovated and divides the land into three parcels; by 2018, he is hoping to make a mere $18 million profit—one-third of Trump's—in over a decade of holding the land.[74]

The *Charlotte Observer* will note in March 2017 that Rybolovlev's plane was parked next to Trump's in Charlotte, not briefly but for hours, five days before Election Day in 2016.[75] The two men—whose planes likewise "met" at a Las Vegas airport four days prior to their second meeting in Charlotte—claim that they've never met each other.[76] A representative for Rybolovlev "declined to say whether the oligarch had been aboard the plane when it landed in Charlotte," according to the *Observer*.[77] The representative also declined to say "whether anyone associated with Trump was a passenger [on Rybolovlev's plane] or whether its arrival was in any way connected with Trump's campaign."[78] As the *Observer* concluded, "If Rybolovlev were somehow assisting the campaign, it would constitute an illegal foreign donation."[79]

The same questions raised by the Trump-Rybolovlev transaction—both at the time and in the ten days before Election Day—can likewise be asked for a number of payments Trump has received from Russian oligarchs in recent years. In March 2017, Reuters reports that just sixty-three Russians have invested a total of nearly $100 million in Trump's Florida properties, adding,

> The tally of investors from Russia may be conservative. The analysis found that at least 703—or about one-third—of the owners of the 2044 units in the seven Trump buildings are limited liability companies, or LLCs, which have the ability to hide the identity of a property's true owner. And the nationality of many [other] buyers could not be determined. Russian-Americans who did not use a Russian address or passport in their purchases were not included in the tally.[80]

The influence Putin wields over his billionaire acolytes is such that if he wanted to turn off the spigot of their money flooding to Trump Organization properties in America he could do so—and quickly. Says Thomas Graham, codirector of the Russian studies program at Yale University, if you're a Russian oligarch, "You can lose your property overnight if you run afoul of the government."[81]

In 2010, Trump SoHo is sued for deceptive sales practices. The building is partly financed by Soviet-born Alexander Mashkevitch, an Israeli citizen who owns homes in Belgium and London.[82] Mashkevitch has been accused at various points, writes *Bloomberg*, of "laundering a $55 million bribe by purchasing property outside Brussels" (the case has since been settled for an undisclosed fine and no admission of fault), "[paying] hundreds of millions of dollars in potential bribes . . . to acquire mines in Africa," and "corruption in Kazakhstan."[83] The investigation of Trump SoHo involves two of Trump's children, Don Jr. and Ivanka, and mirrors the investigation of the Trump Tower in Toronto a year earlier, with the new claims contending the Trumps "made misleading statements as to what percentage of the units had been sold."[84]

The Trump family's candor is called into question again in 2014, when Eric Trump tells a reporter for *Golf* magazine, James Dodson, that the Trumps' golf courses are all financed by Russian banks—and that the Trump Organization has "all the money we need from Russia." Dodson will report the quote in 2017, after Trump's election; Eric will contend that Dodson "completely fabricated" it.[85]

In the 2010s, the New York Police Department arrests twenty-nine people suspected of having connections to a Russian money-laundering scheme headquartered in a Trump Tower condo right below one owned by Trump himself.[86] The alleged ringleader of the scheme is notorious Russian organized crime boss Semion Mogilevich—a man who has repeatedly been on the FBI's Ten Most Wanted list.[87] In the decade's early years Trump pursues numerous projects in the former Soviet republics, including a deal announced in 2011 to build "Trump Tower Batumi" in Georgia, a 2012 signed contract to build "Trump International Hotel & Tower Baku" in Azerbaijan, and a failed bid to build an "obelisk-shaped tower" near the presidential palace in Astana, Kazakhstan.[88] As McClatchy writes in June 2017, "Trump dreamed of his name on towers across the former Soviet Union."[89]

Craig Unger, a former editor for both the *New York Observer* and *Boston Magazine*, argues in his book *House of Trump, House of Putin* that, based on his own research and additional investigation by a former federal prosecutor, Trump was, through Felix Sater's Bayrock Group, "indirectly providing Putin with a regular flow of intelligence on what the [Russian] oligarchs were doing with their money in the United States."[90] Unger's research suggests "Putin wanted to keep tabs on the [Russian] billionaires—some of them former mobsters—who had made their post–Cold War fortunes on the backs of industries once owned by the state. The oligarchs . . . were stashing their money . . . beyond Putin's reach. Trump, knowingly or otherwise, may have struck a side deal with the Kremlin . . . secretly rat[ting] out his customers to Putin, who would allow them to keep buying Trump properties."[91]

On January 11, 2017, just nine days before his inauguration as president of the United States, Trump will tweet the following: "Russia has never tried to use leverage over me. I HAVE NOTHING TO DO WITH RUSSIA—NO DEALS, NO LOANS, NO NOTHING!"[92]

Annotated History

Trump's trip to Moscow in 1987 comes at the invitation of Russia's ambassador to the United States, Yuri Dubinin. In Moscow he stays in the Lenin Suite of the Hotel National, which, as Jonathan Chait of *New York Magazine* notes, "certainly would have been bugged" in 1987. Trump holds meetings on the possible construction of a Trump hotel with Soviet officials, coming away from the meetings certain that the officials are "eager" to do business with him.

In March 2018, the *New York Times* reported that Mueller's "investigation into Russian meddling in the 2016 election has expanded to include President Trump's family business, with the special counsel subpoenaing the Trump Organization for documents related to Russia.[93] "For more than 30 years, Mr. Trump has repeatedly sought to conduct business in Russia," the *Times* wrote, adding, "[H]is children and associates have met with Russian developers and government officials on multiple occasions in search of joint ventures." [94]

By 1997, though no construction has begun on Trump's hoped-for Moscow projects, the *New Yorker* is writing of "the breadth of Trump's hopes for Moscow investment and business connections." Trump's plans for the expansion of his real estate portfolio into Russia go well beyond a single Trump International Hotel; Trump envisions a much larger series of investments. He tells the *New Yorker*, "[I]t would be skyscrapers and hotels. . . . [W]e're working with the local government, the mayor of Moscow, and the mayor's people. So far, they've been very responsive."

The *Washington Post* quotes America's then ambassador to Russia, John Beyrle, as saying of Moscow's then mayor, Yuri Luzhkov, "Corruption in Moscow remains pervasive with Mayor Luzhkov at the top of the pyramid. Luzhkov oversees a system in which it appears that almost everyone at every level is involved in some form of corruption or criminal behavior."[95]

Russia begins a period of political upheaval that sees the nation led by five successive prime ministers appointed by Boris Yeltsin over a fifteen-month period in 1998 and 1999. The last of these prime ministers is a man by the name of Vladimir Putin.

Trump's answers on whether he has ever spoken to or developed a relationship with Vladimir Putin—in the 2000s or anytime after—run the gamut. The closest he came to contradicting Putin's claim that the two men never spoke before, during, or in the immediate aftermath of the 2002 Miss Universe pageant was in a 2015 interview with radio personality Michael Savage, well before Trump's relationship with Russian nationals had become controversial. Trump told Savage, in response to a question asking whether he'd ever met Putin, "Yes—one time, yes. Long time ago. Got along with him great, by the way."[96] Trump did not specify how long before 2015 he met Putin.

At various points Trump has said he knows Putin, while at other times he has denied it. According to a July 2017 Associated Press report, ever since the Russia investigation began, Trump has categorically denied having ever met Putin.[97] At a July 2016 press conference, Trump said, "I never met Putin. I don't know who Putin is. . . . I never met Putin. Never spoken to him. I don't know anything about him. . . ."[98] Shortly thereafter, Trump told ABC's George Stephanopoulos, "I have no relationship with [Putin] . . . I've never met him."[99] Pressed by Stephanopoulos on his prior statements to the contrary, Trump said,

> I have no relationship with Putin. I don't think I've ever met him. I never met him. I don't think I ever met him. . . . I don't think I've ever met him. I mean if he's in the same room or something. But I don't think so. . . . I don't have a relationship

with him. I didn't meet him. I haven't spent time with him. I
didn't have dinner with him. I wouldn't know him from Adam
except I see his picture and I would know what he looks like.[100]

Even Trump's pre-campaign statements about meeting and knowing Putin exhibit an unusual evasiveness for a man known to brag about
inconsequential encounters with famous people. In November 2015,
Time described an incident in which Trump said, "I got to know [Putin]
very well" because "we were stablemates" on the television program
60 Minutes; in fact, the two men had appeared via satellite from different continents and had never spoken.[101]

As noted by the Associated Press in its compilation of Trump's
contradictory statements about his relationship with Putin, in a 2013
NBC News interview Trump said—twice, in fact—"I do have a relationship [with Putin]." [102] In October of that year, he said to talk show
host David Letterman, of Putin, "He's a tough guy. I met him once"—
implying the two men had met prior to 2013.[103] After his alleged speakerphone conversation with Putin on November 9, 2013 (see chapter 2),
but before his relationship with the Russian leader had become controversial, Trump maintained his claim to have had contact with Putin in
the past, while adding a new wrinkle: "I spoke *indirectly* and *directly*
with President Putin [during the 2013 Miss Universe pageant]," he told
the National Press Club in May 2014, "[and he] could not have been
nicer" (emphasis added).[104] It is unclear what speaking with someone
"indirectly" could mean; certainly, a speakerphone conversation is one
possibility. Notable across all of these statements is that not only does
Trump insist he has met Putin, but that the two men have established
enough of a connection for it to be characterized: "I can tell you that
he's very interested in what we're doing here today," Trump said in his
2013 NBC News interview at the Miss Universe pageant in Moscow;
"[Putin] couldn't have been nicer [to me]," he said the next year; "got
along with him great," he said the year after that.[105]

On November 2, 2017, an eyewitness to the judging process at the 2002 Miss Universe contest will contact this author to say that the contest was "rigged."

Trump has enormous influence over which Miss Universe contestants will advance at the annual pageant. In 2009, TMZ secured an audio recording of Trump that revealed the pageant had since 1996 operated under the "Trump Rule," pursuant to which Trump himself got to choose the pageant's semifinalists.[106] On the recording Trump can be heard saying, "We get to choose a certain number [of contestants who will be guaranteed to make it through the first round]. You know why we do that? Because years ago when I first bought it [in 1996], we chose ten people, I chose none and I get here and the most beautiful people were not chosen. And I went nuts. So we call it the 'Trump Rule.'"[107] In September 2009, the *New York Daily News* called the pageant's annual winners "hand-picked [by Trump]," quoting the pageant's then choreographer, who said that "Donald Trump hand picks six of the fifteen finalists in the pageant" and that he does so "single-handedly."[108]

In March 2018, *Newsweek* reported that Trump applied the "Trump Rule" with two considerations: whether a contestant was "too ethnic" (meaning whether her skin tone strayed too far from white) and whether she had "snubbed his [sexual] advances."[109] The magazine cited multiple pageant staffers. The accounts of these whistle-blowers erase any confusion about whether Trump was joking when, as reported by *Rolling Stone*, he said on *The Howard Stern Show* in 2009 that he couldn't say if he'd ever slept with any contestants, because "it would be a conflict of interest," adding, "[B]ut you know, it's the kind of thing you worry about later—you tend to think about the conflict a little bit later on."[110] He finished the thought by arguing that a pageant owner in fact has an "obligation" to sleep with contestants.[111]

> The judges vote for Miss Russia, who thereby becomes Miss Universe until her dethroning 120 days later for failure to faithfully execute the duties of her office.

Trump's most extensive comments on Oxana Fedorova's dethroning, which came in New York on the day Fedorova was replaced by Justine Pasek of Panama, saw him admit that his organization had conducted an investigation to determine if Fedorova was secretly married to Golubev. The notoriously spiteful Trump—who Miss Universe 1996, Alicia Machado, said repeatedly called her "fat" and "ugly" and was "scary" to her, according to a September 2016 *Washington Post* report—was unusually gracious as he dethroned a Miss Universe for the first time in 2002.[112] "We worked hard with Oxana," he said of the object of Putin's fascination, according to a September 2002 report by the *Sydney Morning Herald*.[113] "But a lot of these events are for charity and you just have to be there. She wasn't able to be there, so we had no choice but to terminate."[114] Trump added—surprisingly, given his public penchant for firing contestants in his competitions—that he gave Fedorova a chance to resign so that everything could be "done nicely," but she refused (though he added that she "graciously" returned her tiara).[115] Besides Trump going out of his way to note that Fedorova was a "very nice person," perhaps Trump's most unusual comment regarding Fedorova was his reference to her home country during the press conference. "Was she homesick?" the *Herald* reports Trump asking rhetorically. " 'Well, she certainly enjoyed being in Russia,' he said, adding quickly that he had 'great respect' for Russia as a country."[116]

Sater's access to the highest levels of the Russian government is made evident when, in 2006, he arranges for Ivanka Trump to sit in Putin's office chair during a tour of the Kremlin. According to Daniel Treisman, a professor of political science at UCLA and an expert on Russian politics, anyone able to get a visitor to the

Kremlin into Putin's chair would have to have "the highest [Russian] security clearances and [be] personally trusted by Putin."

As *Business Insider* reported in August 2017, in November 2015 Sater wrote to Trump's then attorney Michael Cohen to simultaneously boast about getting Ivanka access to Putin's office in 2006 and his present ability to get Putin to agree to a Trump Tower Moscow deal for Ivanka's father.[117] The confluence of the two claims is striking. The former claim received a nonconfirmation confirmation from Ivanka, who wouldn't say if she'd sat in Putin's chair, but simply stated that she'd "never met President Vladimir Putin."[118]

Sater and his company, the Bayrock Group, have become critical to Trump's business success in the 2000s—especially with Russian investors and business partners. Yet when asked at a civil deposition in November 2013 whether he knows who Felix Sater is, Trump, under oath, says he has seen Sater only a "couple of times" and that he "wouldn't know what [Sater] look[s] like."

The question should have been an easy one for Trump, given that Sater, "the moving force behind Trump SoHo," according to *New York Magazine*, had by then, as noted by the *Nation* in September 2017, been "work[ing] on and off for a decade with the Trump Organization," sending Russian and other businessmen looking for luxury properties in Trump's direction.[119] Yet when asked about Sater just days before he headed off to Moscow for the 2013 Miss Universe pageant (see chapter 2), Trump said, "I've seen him a couple of times. I have met him. [But] if he were sitting in the room right now, I really wouldn't know what he looked like."[120] Trump maintained that story into December 2015, when, per a *Chicago Tribune* report, in response to a question from an Associated Press reporter about whether he knew Sater he responded, "Boy, I have to even think about it."[121]

Trump's denials and obfuscation on the question of whether he knows Sater is particularly notable given the role Sater has played in Trump's life since 2002. As *Forbes* wrote in October 2016, "[Sater] has said under oath that he represented Trump in Russia." But the timing of Sater's entrance into Trump's orbit is also notable—it coincided with Trump's selection of a Russian mobster's girlfriend as Miss Universe in 2002.[122] As *Forbes* recounts, from the time Sater joined Bayrock, the Trump Tower–housed entity that often sent property-seeking clients to the Trump Organization, Sater would pitch business ideas directly to Trump ("just me and him") "on a constant basis."[123] And as detailed by *Guardian* journalist Luke Harding in his book *Collusion*, Sater "worked on various licensing deals for Trump properties" and had a Trump Organization–issued business card that called him a "senior advisor" to Trump himself.[124]

What Trump presumably didn't know about Sater when the former Russian underworld operator entered his corporate milieu was that Sater had just finished up a federal cooperation deal that allowed him to escape jail on racketeering and fraud charges.[125] Harding notes that Sater's decision to begin working for the Bayrock Group in 2000 was either an attempt to "efface his past sins by returning from Moscow and working diligently for the FBI" or Sater "exploiting the fact that his fraud record was under seal . . . to make a lot of money."[126] Regardless of Sater's intentions, in mid-2002, the year "Putin's girl" was crowned Miss Universe by Donald Trump, Bayrock's founder, Tevfik Arif, made the decision to move Bayrock's offices into Trump Tower—just two floors below Trump's office.[127] The Soviet-born Arif had worked for seventeen years in the Soviet Ministry of Commerce and Trade. His decision to move himself inside Trump's perimeter both literally and financially, and so soon after Trump had himself come into the orbit of Vladimir Putin and Russian mobster Vladimir Golubev, seems significant. Together, Arif and Sater were central to the Trump Organization's recruitment of Soviet-born Tamir Sapir into the Trump SoHo project. According to *Washington Monthly*, Sapir had "ties to Russian intelligence."[128] By 2013, Tamir's son Alex and Rotem Rosen—CEO of Tamir's Sapir Organization—were running the Trump SoHo project and, according to both men, receiving numerous inquiries from Russian "oil and gas" oligarchs about when Trump would construct a new tower in Moscow.[129] They passed these entreaties on to Trump, who took them to heart by signing a letter of intent for Trump Tower Moscow soon after (see chapter 2). In this way, Sater became essential not only to numerous Trump licensing deals but also to Trump's two most ambitious corporate projects in this century: Trump SoHo and Trump Tower Moscow.

Trump SoHo was announced in mid-2006, after a lengthy buildup in 2005; plans for Trump Tower Moscow were announced in 2013. According to *Forbes*, Sater received in 2005—perhaps in recognition of his work recruiting the Russian intelligence-connected Tamir Sapir to the Trump SoHo project—"an exclusive deal to develop a project in Russia."[130] Sater referred to this as "the Moscow deal" and said in a 2008 deposition that the "deal" had a site already selected; he was still working on the deal when he gave Ivanka a special-access tour of the Kremlin.[131] According to Professor Treisman of UCLA, that coincidence of facts suggests Sater had intimate access to Putin—and a high security clearance at the Kremlin—at the same time he was hard at work running point on a "Moscow deal" for Trump.[132]

While we don't know why Sater and Arif entered Trump's business network between 2002 and 2003, Trump associate Michael Cohen—who the *Washington Post* says met Trump in the "late 1990s"—may be one explanation.[133] Cohen and Sater are childhood friends, bonding at a time when the young Cohen was trying to "emulate" the gangs of Soviet immigrants then ubiquitous in his hometown, Brighton Beach.[134]

There is evidence that Sater has at times jumped the fence to the "right" side of the law—albeit under duress and only intermittently. As reported by ABC News in March 2018, "Sater . . . says that for the past two decades he has served as a high-level intelligence asset for the DIA, CIA and the FBI. . . . help[ing] bust mafia families, capture cybercriminals and pursue top terrorists—including Osama bin Laden—and earning praise from some of the country's top law enforcement officials."[135] And, ABC adds, while "he won't say whether he's been interviewed by the special counsel, it's almost certain that Mueller knows his body of work well. [Mueller] served as FBI Director for much of Sater's clandestine career." [136]

---

eTN describes Trump Jr.'s depiction of Trump Organization activities in Moscow this way: "Despite a current [Russian] government that projects a ramrod posture, to Trump the current leaders [of Russia] make the scene more scary. Holding back his grin, he said, 'It's so transparent—everything's so interconnected that it really does not matter what is supposed to happen as *what it is they want to happen* is ultimately what happens'" (emphasis added). It is unclear from eTN's coverage of the Trump Jr. speech who the "they" is that the young Trump Organization executive is referring to.

Putin was Russia's president (the first time) from May 7, 2000, to May 7, 2008, and is widely reported to have exercised tight control over the Kremlin during that period. The *Guardian* wrote, in May 2015, that Putin spent his first two terms in office "mov[ing] toward greater consolidation of his own power." [137]

When Putin first ascended to power in Russia in 2000, he ushered in an era of brutality, corruption, and fear in a nation whose landmass is the world's largest.[138] Since Putin assumed control of the former Soviet Union—minus its many breakaway republics—it has come to be ranked 180 out of 199 nations in press freedom; *PolitiFact* notes that "[Putin's] regime began to commandeer the press" the very year Putin came to power.[139] As of 2015, when Trump announced his presidential run and immediately began praising Putin and his leadership, the rate at which journalists were being killed in Russia was 34 times that of the United States.[140] Putin has married this hostile environment for journalists with a deeply unsettling romanticizing of the Soviet era, publicly decrying Soviet repression while, according Kremlin critics inside Russia, "attempt[ing] to whitewash the image of Soviet dictator

Josef Stalin" by printing "government-sponsored school textbooks that [paint] Soviet dictator Stalin in a largely positive light." These critics call such actions part of Putin's deliberate, systematic "rollback on democracy."[141]

Putin's conspicuously deliberate retreat from democratic processes and rights has given rise to the term "Putinism" to describe the system of government in Russia. Putinism was decribed by Putin critic Boris Nemtsov, prior to his assassination 100 days before Trump announced his presidential campaign, as "a one-party system, with censorship, a puppet parliament, the ending of an independent judiciary, firm centralization of power and finances, [and a] hypertrophied role of special services and bureaucracy, in particular in relation to business."[142] Nemtsov's killers were paid a quarter of a million dollars to assassinate him, with the *New York Times* noting the evidence suggests a close ally of Putin was behind the payments.[143]

But Putin has done more than neutralize his opponents and arrest protesters and opposition leaders. In February 2014, his forces invaded Ukraine's Crimean peninsula just one day after its Kremlin-backed president, Viktor Yanukovych, fled the country. Yanukovych was the leader Trump campaign manager Paul Manafort worked for from 2005 to 2016.[144] Putin's unilateral military aggression in Europe deeply unnerved America's longtime European allies and resulted in sanctions in July 2014, leveled by a broad coalition of nations, including the United States, Canada, and all the nations of the European Union.[145] Since their initial imposition, the sanctions, which have been increased and enhanced multiple times, have devastated the Russian economy, with CNBC crediting the restrictions on Russia's international trade and business operations for having "taken a big bite out of Russia's economy." The sanctions have had a crippling effect on Russian oil revenues in particular, "help[ing] spark a collapse in Russia's currency, the ruble, sending the prices of Russian consumer goods soaring."[146]

Meanwhile, CNBC notes that the effect of U.S. sanctions against Russia on *American* businesses has been negligible, as "Russia makes up less than 1 percent of U.S. exports."[147]

Trump Jr. also discusses the Trump Organization's reliance on Russian investors investing in the United States. "We see a lot of money pouring in from Russia," he says.

A March 2017 Reuters investigation of Trump properties found twenty units in Trump Towers I, II, and III purchased by customers with Russian passports or addresses. This figure is sixteen for Trump Palace, twenty-seven for Trump Royale, and thirteen for Trump Hollywood.[148]

In the summer of 2008, a Russian billionaire named Dmitry Rybolovlev offers nearly the full asking price for the property—$95 million—despite Trump having no competing offers. Trump thereby makes $54 million in forty-eight months. Rybolovlev immediately destroys the structures on the property that Trump had renovated and divides the land into three parcels; by 2018, he is hoping to make an $18 million profit—one-third of Trump's—in over a decade of holding the land.

By January 2018, artnet News had reported that Rybolovlev had sold two of the three lots for a total of $71.34 million, with the final lot still listed at $42 million.[149] If Rybolovlev earns his asking price, he will have made an $18 million profit on the property in ten years.

After Fedorova wins the 2001 Miss Russia pageant, rumors abound—spurred in part by the presence of Putin's domestic intelligence service, the FSB, acting as security at the competition— that the pageant has been rigged so that Fedorova will win.

Putin's fixation on Fedorova, whether reciprocated or not, was both conspicuous and infamous in 2001. An April 2001 article in the *Telegraph*, a British media outlet, was entitled "Putin 'Rigged Miss Russia Contest as Policewoman's Secret Admirer.'"[150] The article, written by the *Telegraph*'s Moscow correspondent, referenced not just "whispers that [President Putin] personally intervened in the [Miss Russia] contest," but "accusations" in local media that the Kremlin had actually "dictat[ed] the result of this year's . . . beauty contest."[151] At a minimum, Oxana Fedorova's victory in that national competition—which sent her to the 2002 Miss Universe pageant—was "hailed . . . as 'politically correct' [because] Mr. Putin has been described as a secret admirer of Oksana Fyodorova and is said to possess a photograph of her. The contest organisers allegedly picked her as winner in a feudal display of loyalty to the head of state."[152] That these rumors were so ubiquitous in Moscow in 2001 that they were repeated by a media outlet in the United Kingdom is an indication that major investors in the Moscow real estate market could easily have come across them.

There is substantial press attention on the pageant in Moscow as Fedorova wins the competition and makes pageant history as the first Miss Universe from Russia.

Fedorova had to be removed from her post almost immediately. As the *New York Post* detailed in September 2002, Fedorova's was a tumultuous reign that lasted only 120 days—making her the first Miss Universe to be fired in the then fifty-year history of the pageant.[153] According to the *Post*, Fedorova had a "tangled love life, mysterious links to Russian President Vladimir Putin, a seemingly endless supply of cash and diamond jewelry and an attitude that tested even the most seasoned officials of the Miss Universe Organization."[154] Fedorova, from St. Petersburg, had a publicly acknowledged boyfriend—a "notorious" "Russian gangster" (per *Pravda*) named Vladimir Semenovich Golubev, commonly known as "Barmaley"—who also lived in St. Petersburg. Even so, she "insisted on spending most of her time in Moscow," wrote the *Post*, which likely helped fuel rumors about her and Putin.[155]

Lest it seem unlikely that Trump would fire a Miss Universe pageant winner he'd rigged a pageant to crown, a September 2002 CBS News report clarified that the Miss Universe Organization didn't actually *fire* Fedorova—it merely found that she "was unable to fulfill her duties," as Miss Universe Organization president Paula Shugart put it at the time.[156] "[Fedorova] needed to spend a lot of time in Russia," Shugart said. "I believe her mother was ill at one point."[157] For her part, Fedorova said "she gave up the title herself," because while "the duties of a world beauty are wonderful . . . my prime goal is my studies and career in Russia."[158] The notoriously loquacious Trump was muted, saying that it was "too bad it didn't work out better with Oxana."[159] Meanwhile, rumors on both sides of the Atlantic—rumors spread, even, by CBS News—held that Fedorova had had to give up her crown because she was pregnant; the *Daily Mail* noted in November 2009 that pageant officials were concerned because she suddenly "put on weight."[160] While those rumors were never confirmed or denied, Fedorova was at the time connected romantically—whether you believe her, Russian media, or both—to only two men: Vladimir Putin and Vladimir Golubev, both strongmen no woman could cheat on, one imagines, without repercussions.

What makes these allegations of a pregnancy worth noting here, however, is another, related allegation spread by Fedorova herself: that she quit her position because, as *International Business Times* put it in September 2011, "she was forced [by Trump's Miss Universe Organization] to go on *The Howard Stern Show*."[161] It was during that June 25, 2002, interview with longtime Trump friend Howard Stern that Oxana was asked the following question: "At what point during the contest did you have sex with Mr. Trump?"[162] When Fedorova said that she had not slept with Trump and added that he had a beautiful girlfriend (the then Melania Knauss), Stern replied, "Mr. Trump likes *everybody*."[163] A cohost added, "Could you repeat that question to her?"[164] Rumors that Fedorova had indeed slept with Trump were so persistent that fourteen years later Fedorova would report to the *Express*, a British media outlet, that "she became annoyed and frustrated during Trump's presidential campaign because Western media pestered her for information to defame the billionaire."[165] The *Express* noted that Trump had "[taken] an interest in Ms. Fedorova," and that after her victory he "took care of her" as her handler.[166]

Trump's interest in Fedorova could just as easily have been finan-cial instead of political or romantic, however. Fedorova's boyfriend, Golubev, was, according to *Forbes Russia*, a silent partner in a holding company known as Adamant that in the 2000s boasted $540 million in annual profits.[167] Adamant's business included restaurants, jewelry businesses, an industrial glass manufacturer, an advertising agency, a medical center, and—most significant to Trump, surely—a massive real estate construction and management operation.[168] While noting that there were "many reports [in the 1990s] of [Golubev's] links with organized crime," *Forbes Russia* reported in 2013 that Golubev had since gone straight and was helping Adamant ensure its "operations were conducted without collisions with or participation in the well-known St. Petersburg crim[inal community]. . . . [P]articipants in the real estate market of St. Petersburg believe that it was Golubev who helped [Adamant] in the 1990s successfully resolve issues with crimi-nal structures."[169] As with any Russian business, Adamant also had to stay on the right side of local government officials; in the mid-1990s, the first deputy chairman of St. Petersburg was a man named Vladimir Putin. Perhaps it's little surprise, then, that when local beauty Oxana Fedorova won Miss St. Petersburg in 1999, just thirty-six months after Putin moved from St. Petersburg to Moscow to take up his new post there, she became a favorite of his.

Trump's business profile suggests that business with Adamant—partly controlled by the new Miss Universe's boyfriend—was a possi-ble motive for attempting to rig the 2002 pageant. At the time, Adamant was building the first large-scale shopping center in St. Petersburg, which history suggests is the sort of real estate project that would draw Trump's attention.[170] Eleven years later, when Trump signed a letter of intent to build a Trump Tower Moscow, it was for a site in Moscow's Crocus City complex—whose centerpiece is a shopping mall built by Aras Agalarov.

While *Forbes Russia* may be right that, by 2013, Golubev had de-cided to leave organized crime, as late as October 2002—just days after Fedorova's reign as Miss Universe ended—Golubev was being called a "criminal boss in St. Petersburg" by *Pravda*.[171] The Russian news outlet added at the time that Golubev was "involved in the construction business" but also "sometimes extorts money from oligarchs with the help of his allegedly powerful links in the criminal world."[172] Trump becoming Fedorova's handler put him immediately within hailing distance of Golubev's orbit as well as Putin's, apart from any interest he may have had in Fedorova. By 2002, Trump had learned that building in Russia is about who one knows, not the capital one has.

The eyewitness asserts that Trump "told the judges who to vote for," adding that a subsequent conversation among the celebrity judges revealed that several had had the same impression. The judges vote for Miss Russia, who thereby becomes Miss Universe until her dethroning 120 days later for failure to faithfully execute the duties of her office. The contest's judges are subsequently told by parties affiliated with the pageant that Fedorova has been dethroned because of unspecified criminal conduct by her boyfriend, Vladimir Golubev.

In a September 2009 statement published by CNN and other media outlets, Paula Shugart told the media that Trump's involvement in the Miss Universe selection process ends before the final phase of the competition; the Miss Universe Organization does not appear to have ever acknowledged Trump's involvement in the selection process beyond that point.[173] However, Shugart indicated that the current pageant rules were put in place in 2005, suggesting that Trump had carte blanche to intervene prior to that year.[174] Trump's co-ownership of the pageant with NBC didn't begin until 2003, raising the distinct possibility that NBC instituted a new judging policy in 2005 in part because it had, by then, seen how Trump comported himself at his pageants.

Rigging televised contests is a crime under both state and federal statutes. The applicable federal statute, 47 U.S.C. § 509 (prohibited practices in contests of knowledge, skill, or chance) carries a maximum penalty of one year in prison per count.[175] Trump, who allegedly committed the crime while in Puerto Rico—where federal law applies—

would have faced two counts, the first for "engaging in any artifice or scheme for the purpose of prearranging or predetermining in whole or in part the outcome of a purportedly bona fide contest," and another for "participating in the production for broadcasting of" a contest tampered with under 47 U.S.C. § 509.[176] Also in question is whether Trump's actions would have contravened state or federal statutes protecting advertisers from being defrauded by the organizers of a purportedly "bona fide" broadcast competition.

Whether or not Trump can still be charged with these offenses, they are relevant to the Russia probe as crimes possibly committed to please the Russian president. Much has been made of Putin's pride at bringing the 2014 Winter Olympics and the 2018 World Cup to Russia, so his being the boyfriend—in reality or by reputation only—of the first-ever Miss Universe from Russia could not fail to have flattered him.[177]

A Russian émigré associated with the Russian criminal underworld, accompanied by his Soviet-born business partner Tevfik Arif, approaches Trump about a business partnership. The émigré, Felix Sater, will for the next few years deliver a large number of Russian clients to Trump and be instrumental in finding Russia-born partners for the biggest Trump construction project of the 2000s, Trump SoHo.

That Felix Sater has substantial ties to the mafia and to Russian intelligence officers is uncontested. In June 2018, *Newsweek* said he was "linked to the mob," adding that in the 1990s "he had done business with a number of high-ranking former Soviet intelligence officers. He eventually came back to New York but . . . stayed in touch with some of them."[178] In September 2017, the *Nation* said that Sater had a "decades-long record . . . outside the law," describing "his past record" as including "a conviction for lacerating a man's face with a broken margarita glass" and "his involvement in a multimillion-dollar stock fraud and money-laundering scheme."[179] In August 2017, *New York Magazine*, in addition to calling Sater "the moving force behind Trump

SoHo," said that "Sater introduced the future president to a byzantine world of oligarchs and mysterious money," calling it "verifiably true" that Sater was "tied to organized crime."[180] In the *Washington Post* in May 2016, Sater was "mafia-linked"; in the *Guardian* in August 2017, he was the son of "a local crime boss in Brighton Beach" who had been "involved in a mob-run stock exchange scam" and had "contacts in the Russian underworld."[181] In March 2018, ABC News reported on how, in his youth, Sater discovered at a Moscow dinner party that he had "gained access to a group of high-level Russian intelligence operatives who had valuable information about Russian defense technology."[182] Such is the man Trump partnered with on some of his biggest real estate deals in the 2000s and was still working with on business deals in Russia for the first year of his presidential run in 2015 and 2016 (see chapter 4).

Paul Wood, a BBC correspondent who has repeatedly broken news on the Trump-Russia story, wrote in August 2017 that, according to his sources, "Sater may have already flipped [begun cooperation with Mueller] and given prosecutors the evidence they need to make a case against Trump."[183] In the same story, Wood revealed the quality of his sourcing, noting that at least one source was in contact with and receiving information from a member of Robert Mueller's team.[184] That source gave Wood a key piece of corroborating information on the claim that Sater was now a "CI" (meaning, variously, a "confidential informant," a "cooperating individual," or a "cooperating informant") for Mueller. According to Wood, "Sater has told family and friends he knows he and [Trump] are going to prison."[185] Wood noted in his story that he received this information at a time when he had been hearing "for weeks" "rumors that Sater is ready to rat again."[186]

Wood's sources, he explained in the article, believed that Sater was ready to rat "again" because Sater had previously been a confidential informant in an FBI probe. But in fact we know more than this—we know that Sater is specifically willing to act as a confidential informat for Mueller in his *current* investigation. Sater, through his attorney, has offered to cooperate with Mueller; per his lawyer, Sater "intends to be fully cooperative with any and all government investigations in this matter." [187] Given that, at the time Sater's attorney issued his statement, Sater was being asked to cooperate only with the Senate Select Committee on Intelligence, his attorney's use of the word "fully" and the phrase "any and all" is notable.

In the summer of 2017, as Mueller was interviewing now cooperating witness George Papadopoulos following his arrest in late July, Sater discussed becoming a confidential informant in an interview with *New York Magazine*. At the time, he also made a startling claim that could have been an allusion to an upcoming FBI cooperation deal. He told the magazine, "In about the next 30 to 35 days, I will be the most colorful character you have ever talked about. Unfortunately, I can't talk about it now, before it happens. . . . [But] it ain't anything as small as whether or not they're gonna call me to the Senate committee." [188]

The Trump family's candor is called into question again in 2014, when Eric Trump tells a reporter for *Golf* magazine, James Dodson, that the Trumps' golf courses are all financed by Russian banks—and that the Trump Organization has "all the money we need from Russia." Dodson will report the quote in 2017, after Trump's election; Eric will contend that Dodson "completely fabricated" it.

As recounted by *Vanity Fair* in May 2017, while speaking to *Golf* journalist James Dodson in 2014, Trump's second son blurted out, apropos of nothing, that the Trump Organization had access to "$100 million" for golf courses.[189] When Dodson pressed Eric to explain the comment—in light of the difficulty most developers had in finding golf course funding from banks during the Great Recession—Eric replied, "[W]e don't rely on American banks. We have all the funding we need out of Russia. . . . We've got some [Russian] guys that really, really love golf, and they're really invested in our programs. We just go there all the time." [190] Though Dodson—whose beat is golf, not politics—had no reason to lie about Trump Organization financing, Eric responded on Twitter to Dodson's claim by saying that Dodson had "completely fabricated" the conversation. Eric later told the *New York Post* that Dodson's account was "a recollection from some guy three years ago through a third person. . . . We own our courses free and clear." [191] *Vanity Fair* observed at the time that Dodson fabricating a conversation with Trump was unlikely, in part because the substance of the conversation, as reported by Dodson, was extremely likely: "It wouldn't be the first time that the Trumps have been connected to Russian money," wrote the magazine. "A number of reports have indicated the Trump Organization received substantial funding from Russia when the business was struggling in the mid-1990s and again during the Great Recession, since major U.S. banks had refused to loan money to [Trump]." [192] The article added that, according to Reuters, a group of sixty-three Russian billionaires had invested nearly $100 million—an average of $1.6 million per Russian—in Trump's Florida properties alone. [193]

CHAPTER TWO

TRUMP AND THE AGALAROVS

2013

Summary

TRUMP INVITES A POWERFUL, KREMLIN-LINKED DEVEL-oper to go into business with him while he is dramatically increasing his political profile—and after he's conducted exploratory polling to test a 2016 White House bid.

During a November 2013 trip to Moscow to put on the Miss Universe pageant with his new business partner, Trump signs a letter of intent to build a "Trump Tower Moscow." After Trump leaves Moscow, he maintains a strong relationship with his new Russian business associates—having left a clear impression on his Moscow hosts that he will not only run for the presidency but on a platform opposing all sanctions on Russia.

Given the opportunity to be forthcoming as to his financial and personal dealings in Moscow in late 2013, Trump dissembles, telling voters false stories about his actions that suggest he has something significant to hide.

The Facts

IN JUNE 2013, DONALD TRUMP INVITES ARAS AND EMIN AGA-
larov to join him at the Miss USA pageant in Las Vegas.[1] Aras is a billionaire developer who does building projects for the Kremlin; Emin
is an aspiring pop star. Aras's favor with the Kremlin is demonstrated
in part by the Kremlin's sending a senior official, Vladimir Kozhin, to
a party at Agalarov's Crocus City complex.[2] Kozhin is the Kremlin's
"chief manager" and called "a top government official and member of
Putin's inner circle" by *Mother Jones*.[3]

Aras and Emin have gotten onto Trump's radar screen by selecting
the 2012 Miss Universe, Olivia Culpo, to star in one of Emin's music
videos.[4] A trip by Miss Universe pageant officials to Moscow ensues,
and discussions begin about the possibility of Miss Universe going to
Moscow in 2013.[5] The Miss USA pageant is an opportunity for Trump
to speak to the Agalarovs in person about the idea. The group that gath-
ers in Las Vegas includes the Agalarovs, Trump, Trump's attorney Michael Cohen, Emin's publicist Rob Goldstone, Trump's bodyguard
Keith Schiller, and Ike Kaveladze, a vice president at the Agalarovs'
company, the Crocus Group—called by the *Guardian* "one of the biggest corporations in Russia, carrying out government building contracts
worth hundreds of millions of dollars from Putin's administration."[6]
The *Guardian* will later write that Kaveladze "has in fact been an associate of some of Russia's richest and most powerful people for the past
three decades. . . . [He] was involved in the $341 m[illion] takeover
of a US company by a Russian mining firm belonging to an associate
of Putin, and was a business partner to two former senior officials at
Russia's central bank."[7] The transaction, overseen by Kaveladze, was
"the first time a Russian company had ever taken a majority stake in
a publicly traded US company. . . . Putin was reported at the time to
have personally advocated for the deal's approval by U.S. regulators."[8]
In 2000, the *New York Times* reported that Kaveladze helped "an unknown number of Russians . . . [move] more than $1.4 billion through
accounts at Citibank of New York and the Commercial Bank of San

Francisco. . . . Kaveladze, who immigrated to the United States from Russia in 1991. . . . set up more than 2,000 corporations in Delaware for Russian brokers and then opened the bank accounts for them, without knowing who owned the corporations."[9] According to the *Guardian*, "U.S. authorities said [the $1.4 billion] may have been used for money laundering."[10]

On the day of the Miss USA pageant, Yulya Alferova—a popular Russian blogger, the wife of Russian billionaire Artem Klyushin, and later the organizer of the 2013 Miss Universe pageant for the Agalarovs—posts nine candid pictures of Trump, the Agalarovs, Kaveladze, and the other members of Trump's entourage dining in Las Vegas the night before; it is unclear whether Alferova or Klyushin was in Las Vegas also.[11]

Trump and the Agalarovs bond immediately. "Look who's come to see me! It's the richest man in Russia!" Trump bellows just minutes after meeting Aras Agalarov for the first time.[12] The *Guardian* reports that Trump "quickly" agreed to Agalarov's offer of $20 million to bring the Miss Universe pageant to Moscow; Emin will later say that Paula Shugart, "Trump's top Miss Universe executive," confessed to him of the pageant, "We have a lot of debts."[13] Later on the night before the pageant, Trump tells Emin that he trusts him and that the Trump Organization and the Crocus Group will have an excellent business relationship going forward.[14] On the day of the pageant, Trump brings Aras Agalarov onstage to announce the 2013 Miss Universe pageant will be in Moscow.[15] Trump thus chooses Russia as the next pageant site approximately twenty-four hours after meeting the Agalarovs for the first time and over seventeen other nations.[16] The *Daily Mail* will note in February 2018 that not only does Trump pick pageant sites based on business considerations, but he also uses the same measure to select the competition's finalists, titling its report on the subject "Donald Trump hand-picked finalists for Miss Universe from countries he targeted to swing deals and hosted the contest in cities where he already had a financial stake, former contestants claim."[17] According to the *Mail*, it isn't just contestants who have accused Trump of using his pageants as a front for his business interests: "preliminary judges tasked with

selecting the finalists said they were shocked when their votes were
tallied and some women who advanced to the final stage weren't selected by *any* of the judges" (emphasis added).[18] Kerrie Baylis, a former Miss Jamaica, tells the *New Yorker*, of the list of finalists in the
year she participated in the Miss Universe pageant, "[T]he list looked
like the countries Donald Trump did business with, or wanted to do
business with."[19]

In Las Vegas in 2013, the Agalarovs promise Trump not only
$20 million but also, more important, an opportunity to meet with
Vladimir Putin and the prospect of building a Trump Tower Moscow
on the site where the 2013 Miss Universe pageant will be held.[20]

The day after the pageant is announced, Trump tweets, "Do you
think Putin will be going to The Miss Universe Pageant in November
in Moscow—if so, will he become my new best friend?"[21] He also,
per the *Washington Post*, writes a personal letter to Putin—now in the
hands of the special counsel—saying, among what else is as yet unknown, that he looks forward to seeing Russia's "beautiful women"
once he gets to Moscow.[22] Asked by *Washington Post* reporters in
March 2018 to give more information about Trump's private letter to
Putin in 2013, Trump's then attorney John Dowd will respond simply,
"It's all nonsense," and say no more on the subject.[23]

In Moscow in the summer of 2013, "a meeting with Trump [is] indeed penciled into Putin's diary by aides, but [falls] off his schedule a
few days beforehand."[24]

Trump arrives in Moscow in early November 2013 with two U.S.
business partners in tow, Alex Sapir and Rotem Rosen, whose ties to
powerful Russians are substantial. He immediately begins conducting business meetings with bankers and other influential Russians who
can help him and Aras Agalarov move forward with their Trump Tower
Moscow project.[25]

After promising that he will attend the pageant, Putin suddenly
chooses not to do so. He does, however, send Trump, according to Aras
Agalarov, a handwritten note—the contents are unknown—and "a traditional decorative lacquered box."[26] In March 2014, at the annual
Conservative Political Action Conference, Trump will tell the assem-

bled GOP activists that "Putin even sent me a present, beautiful present, with a beautiful note. I spoke to all of his people."[27] After Trump returns from Moscow, Agalarov's daughter will deliver a "polished black box" and a "sealed letter from the Russian president himself." It is unclear if this is the same box and letter as Agalarov says Trump received at the pageant, but Agalarov implies it is not: in March 2018 he tells the *Washington Post* that Trump "was leaving [the 2013 pageant in Moscow] with very warm feelings . . . very happy," because, Agalarov says, he had *already* received, at the pageant, a letter from Putin (in a "Russian lacquered box," says Agalarov) whose contents Agalarov could confirm were "friendly."[28]

Prior to the 2013 pageant, Trump speaks by phone with "an oligarch close to Putin," Dmitry Peskov, during which Peskov says Putin wants to invite Trump to attend the 2014 Winter Olympics in Sochi scheduled for February 7–23, 2014.[29] According to some accounts—including Trump's own—Trump does speak to Putin on the day of the pageant: "I spoke indirectly and directly with President Putin, who could not have been nicer," Trump will say in a May 27, 2014, appearance at the National Press Club.[30] A longtime friend of Trump's, actor Tom Arnold, bolsters Trump's claims of having spoken to Putin "indirectly and directly," saying he has knowledge of a speakerphone call between Trump and Putin on November 9 at the Ritz-Carlton Moscow because it was witnessed, he will say repeatedly on social media, by NBC executive Chuck LaBella and others. Per Arnold, "Putin called Trump at [the] Moscow Ritz [in] Nov[ember] 2013. Trump put [it] on speakerphone for everyone to hear. Putin congratulated Trump on Trump Tower Moscow & encouraged Trump to run for President & offered Russia's support. It's all on tape."[31]

According to a retrospective in the *Guardian*, Trump "certainly claimed" to have met "associates of Putin in lieu of the president himself," saying, "I was with the top-level people, both oligarchs and generals, and top-of-the-government people. I can't go further than that, but I will tell you that I met the top people, and the relationship was extraordinary."[32] One of those who attends the pageant and after-party in Putin's stead is Vladimir Kozhin, who had previously attended a

Crocus Group event and "from 2000 until 2014 was head of the Kremlin property department," according to Reuters—meaning he was one of the officials in the Kremlin with the authority to pave the way for new building projects in the city like Trump Tower Moscow.[33] In their book *Russian Roulette*, David Corn and Michael Isikoff note that Kozhin, a "senior Putin aide," was "a high-level emissary" sent to Trump by Putin himself.[34] The message of welcome to Trump—and, more particularly, to Trump Tower Moscow—would have been, based on Trump's experience in the Moscow real estate market, unmistakable. In a 2017 interview, then Trump attorney Michael Cohen, who was for years an executive vice president at the Trump Organization, will say of Trump Organization forays into the Russia real estate market, "Their system is different from ours. The Kremlin has to approve buildings in Moscow. That's not undue influence. That's just the way it is."[35] According to a 2013 Miss Universe pageant official, even beauty pageants were approved by Putin: "We all knew that the event was approved by Putin," said the official, "[as] you can't pull off something like this in Russia unless Putin says it's okay."[36]

Another VIP guest at the pageant is a Russian who lives in Trump Tower in New York City named Alimzhan Tokhtakhounov. According to *Mother Jones*, Tokhtakhounov is a "*vor*—a Russian term for a select group of the highest-level Russian crime bosses. . . . [A boss who] receives tributes from other criminals, offers protection, and adjudicates conflicts among other crooks."[37] The U.S. attorney for the Southern District of New York, Preet Bharara, had previously indicted Tokhtakhounov in 2013 for operating an international sportsbook that laundered more than $100 million, alleging that, as the indictment was described by *Mother Jones*, the Russian was using "his 'substantial influence in the criminal underworld' to protect a high-stakes illegal gambling ring operating out of Trump Tower" in New York City.[38] More significant to Trump's desire to meet Russian oligarchs while in Moscow is that, per Bharara's indictment, Tokhtakhounov and others ran "an international gambling business that catered to oligarchs residing in the former Soviet Union and throughout the world."[39] As of late 2016, Tokhtakhounov was wanted by Interpol on charges including conspiracy to commit wire fraud and bribery.[40]

During the pageant, Trump and Agalarov announce their plans to build Trump Tower Moscow, and ten days later more than $2 billion in funding is announced by a state-owned Russian bank, Sberbank, whose CEO, Herman Gref, is both a close associate of Putin's and has met directly with Trump during his trip to Moscow.[41] Gref will later tell *Bloomberg* he was impressed by Trump's "attitude toward Russia"; both Gref and Agalarov will subsequently refuse to reveal who attended any of Trump's meetings while he was in Moscow.[42]

During one of Trump's meetings on his first day in Moscow, either Emin Agalarov or a Russian associate of his tells Trump's bodyguard, Keith Schiller, that five prostitutes can be sent to Trump's hotel suite at the Ritz-Carlton that night if he so desires.[43]

On the day he returns from Moscow—November 10, 2013—Trump tweets, "I just got back from Russia—learned lots and lots. Moscow is a very interesting and amazing place! U.S. MUST BE VERY SMART AND VERY STRATEGIC."[44] The next day he adds to his prior tweet about American foreign policy by tweeting about the deal he announced in Moscow: "Aras Agalarov, I had a great weekend with you and your family. . . . TRUMP TOWER MOSCOW is next."[45]

In December 2013, just over a month after his return from Moscow, Trump begins formally reaching out to influential Republicans on the subject of a presidential run, which he predicts in conversations with politicians in New York will begin in 2015.[46] In August 2018, a top Trump adviser back in 2012 and 2013, Sam Nunberg, will tell Michael Isikoff of Yahoo News, "In 2013 I knew he was running for president. I knew he was running for president the minute Obama won Virginia [in 2012]."[47] On January 22, 2014, Yulya Alferova, an agent of the Agalarovs, tweets, atop a picture of her and Trump in Moscow, "I'm sure Donald Trump will be [a] great president! We'll support you from Russia! America needs [an] ambitious leader!"[48] On March 22, 2014, Alferova retweets Trump four times in succession, including this tweet from the then businessman: "The situation in Russia is much more dangerous than most people may think—and could lead to World War III. WE NEED GREAT LEADERSHIP FAST." [49] On March 29, 2014, the Agalarov employee retweets Trump three times in succession, with all three tweets on the subject of the Agalarovs' new business partner running for president.[50] According to both Emin Agalarov and Donald Trump Jr., the Agalarovs and Trumps are still planning a Trump Tower Moscow at this point. Indeed, in early February 2014, less than two weeks after the first of Alferova's flurry of tweets about a Trump presidential run in 2016, Ivanka Trump arrives in Moscow to scout possible locations for an Agalarov-built Trump Tower Moscow.[51] Meanwhile, Trump is telling the media that he had contact with Putin as he was negotiating and finalizing the Trump Tower Moscow deal in Moscow. He tells Fox News on February 10, 2014, that Putin "contacted him" when "he went to Russia with the Miss Universe pageant" and that during that "contact" Putin was "so nice." [52] Soon afterward, Russia's effort to annex Crimea leads to sanctions from the United States, which forces Trump to put plans for Trump Tower Moscow on hold because the project's funder, Sberbank, is one of the sanctioned entities.[53]

Three months later, in May 2014, Trump speaks at the National Press Club and tells the assembled reporters that when he was in Moscow for the Miss Universe pageant he spoke, both "indirectly and directly, with President Putin, who could not have been nicer, and we had a tremendous success." [54] Trump adds some detail on the content of the conversation, saying, "[T]o do well, you have to get the other side to respect you, and he [Putin] does not respect our president, which is very sad." [55]

In the fall of 2015, a *Politico* reporter contacts an unnamed Trump adviser to ask him "about memos saying the New York businessman was involved in an orgy in Russia"; the reporter explains that "the information [is] from a document made by Fusion GPS that [is] floating around." [56]

The Fusion GPS document is being financed, per the *New York Times*, by "a wealthy Republican donor who strongly oppose[s] Mr. Trump." The Republican donor hires a journalist-owned and -operated D.C. research firm to "compile a dossier about the real estate magnate's past scandals and weaknesses."[57] The Republican-funded allegation of Russian *kompromat* against Trump (see chapter 3) will be republished in mid-2016 by Christopher Steele, a former MI6 agent who had been the head of the agency's Russia desk.[58] When Fusion GPS's new client is later discovered to be a law firm under contract with the DNC, Trump will tweet on October 19, 2017, about the "discredited and Fake" dossier and ask whether it was "paid for" by "Russia, the FBI or the Dems (or all)?"[59]

When the dossier is released in January 2017, Americans read for the first time the allegations from 2015—based on research funded by a Republican Trump opponent—that someone sent prostitutes up to Trump's room in Moscow on November 8, 2013.[60] The dossier alleges, based on multiple sources, that what happened in Trump's room at the Ritz-Carlton was recorded for the purposes of maintaining, in secret, substantial leverage over Trump for the foreseeable future—including for the entirety of his political career (see chapter 3).[61] The dossier also includes raw intelligence—meaning intelligence that hasn't been confirmed—on Putin using proposed real estate deals in Russia to seal Trump's loyalty.[62]

The Trump-Agalarov letter of intent will remain active, according to Aras Agalarov, for three and a half years—a period covering the entirety of the presidential campaign.[63] It expires only on Trump's inauguration, according to a February 2017 statement to a Russian construction website by the elder Agalarov.[64] However, in a mid-2017 *Forbes* interview, Agalarov's son throws even this expiration date into doubt, revealing that the Agalarovs are still in negotiations with Trump's sons to do additional business—possibly including the building of a tower in Moscow.[65] Because Trump has not fully divested himself from the Trump Organization, he will benefit directly should the Agalarovs and his sons perform on the letter of intent he signed in 2013.[66]

Annotated History

Trump invites a powerful, Kremlin-linked developer to go into business with him while he is dramatically increasing his political profile—and after he's conducted exploratory polling to test a 2016 White House bid.

On May 27, 2013, just days before Trump invited Aras Agalarov and his son to Las Vegas for the Miss USA pageant, the *New York Post* announced, in an article entitled "Trump Researches 2016 Run," that the notoriously frugal Trump had just spent $1 million on pre-election research.[67] The same day, *Politico* reported that "Trump is musing about running for president," noting that Trump had just told a GOP county dinner in Michigan that "everybody" was telling him to "run for president."[68] Trump's May 2013 polling expenditures studied all fifty states to determine his popularity in each. When asked about this substantial financial outlay, Trump lawyer Cohen underscored that Trump was serious about a potential run. "We didn't spend $1 million on this research for it to sit on my bookshelf," said Cohen. "Trump is exactly what this country needs."[69]

Trump's preoccupation with politics before and during his Moscow trip has been confirmed by one of the members of his entourage, Agalarov employee and 2013 Miss Universe pageant organizer Yulya Alferova. A November 9, 2013, tweet from Alferova reads, "I'm tweeting, Donald Trump is talking . . . again and again about Obama."[70] The picture below the tweet shows Alferova, Trump pal Phil Ruffin, and Trump himself lounging in chairs as Trump talks on a cell phone. That Trump would be discussing politics on the phone while in Moscow—despite being in the city for only forty-eight hours and responsible for overseeing an international beauty pageant during that time—is noteworthy. In a January 2017 interview with the *Daily Beast*, Alferova added a new gloss to Americans' understanding of what was on Trump's mind while he was in Moscow for a couple of days, working on a beauty pageant and a real estate deal: "[Trump] calculated every little detail coming to Moscow, knowing that our countries had serious tensions."[71] Alferova's comment and earlier tweet seem to confirm that Trump's preoccupations during his Moscow trip were as much political as financial.

Trump knew who and what Aras Agalarov was when he entered into a letter of intent with him in November 2013. The *Daily Mail* has referred to Agalarov as an "oligarch who brings Putin 'solutions not problems'" and as the "Russian leader's go-to for tough projects (like wooing Trump)."[72] The *Mail* called Agalarov a Kremlin "insider" who is "Putin's main property developer" and the "liaison between Putin and Trump."[73] Agalarov is known as "Putin's right-hand man when it comes to carrying out development projects," wrote the *Mail*, and the Russian president is reportedly "fond" of him.[74] The *Washington Post*, on July 21, 2017, called Agalarov "a trusted executor for the Kremlin," noting also that "[t]he Kremlin expects the country's wealthiest business executives to take on, when asked, large-scale infrastructure projects, sometimes at a loss, to . . . promote Russia's national interests. The fortunes of Russia's rich can rise and fall precipitously based on the outcome of these prestige projects."[75]

These claims are substantiated by Putin's twice using Agalarov or his family to send gifts to Trump and choosing Agalarov for the Kremlin's grandest and most difficult land-development projects, including, as the *New York Times* has noted, Far Eastern Federal University, "a stretch of superhighway ringing Moscow," and "two troubled stadiums for the 2018 World Cup, including one in a Baltic swamp."[76] After the last of these, reported the *Times*, "Mr. Putin pinned a blue-ribboned state medal, the Order of Honor, on Mr. Agalarov's chest at a dazzling Kremlin ceremony."[77] In view of all this, the *Times* called Agalarov "a fixer for the Kremlin's toughest jobs."[78]

Not only did Putin award Agalarov Russia's Order of Honor—one of the highest honors any Russian civilian can receive—but the Kremlin builder received the medal, Putin's clearest possible imprimatur, just ten days before Trump went into business with him.[79]

In June 2013, Donald Trump invites Aras and Emin Agalarov to join him at the Miss USA pageant in Las Vegas. Aras is a billionaire developer who does building projects for the Kremlin; Emin is an aspiring pop star.

Emin was married, at the time, to the daughter of Azerbaijan's president, which had already put him in Trump's orbit, for Azerbaijani government officials are so notoriously corrupt that they habitually become deeply engaged in large domestic building projects.[80] Trump had signed a big deal in Azerbaijan—for an edifice to be called "Trump International Hotel and Tower Baku"—in 2012.[81] So when Trump met Aras and Emin in June 2013, the Agalarovs were implicitly able to help Trump bring not one but two dream deals to fruition: the completion of self-branded towers in both Moscow and Baku. Trump knew, too, that if hosted by the Agalarovs in Moscow, the pageant would be held in the same development for which his new tower was slated. This juxtaposition of the pageant and Trump's ambitions in real estate—and his ambitions in politics—was evident in Trump's tweet announcing the Trump-Agalarov deal to bring the 2013 Miss Universe to Moscow. "A big deal that will bring our countries together!" Trump wrote on Twitter.[82] In Trump's press conference, he added that "Moscow right now in the world is a very, very important place. We wanted Moscow all the way. One of the great families in Russia is our partner."[83] Trump also quickly and quite publicly invited Putin to his pageant, seemingly confirming that in his mind this would be, in the flurry of activity surrounding his presidential exploratory phase, a Trump-Putin political event.[84]

Trump and the Agalarovs bond immediately.

An unnamed veteran Western diplomat in Moscow told the *Daily Mail*, for an article dated July 13, 2017, that "[i]f there are skeletons in Trump's dealings with Russia, Aras knows where they are. And if Aras Agalarov knows Donald Trump's skeletons, you wouldn't bet on Vladimir Putin not also knowing."[85] In March 2018, *Mother Jones* painted a vivid picture of the Trump-Agalarov weekend in Las Vegas. At an intimate twenty-person VIP dinner the night before the Miss USA pageant, Trump talked business with Michael Cohen, Aras and Emin Agalarov, Emin's British publicist Rob Goldstone—who would later set up and attend the now infamous June 9, 2016, meeting at Trump Tower—and Ike Kaveladze, an Agalarov employee who would join Goldstone at Trump Tower in June 2016.[86] After dinner, the group headed to a nightclub to watch performances featuring semi-nude women; while there is no public record of the specific acts performed that night, popular acts at the club include one in which "naked college girls simulate urinating on a professor" and another in which "one female stands over the other female and simulates urinating while the other female catches the urine in two wine glasses."[87] According to Goldstone, Trump said to Emin, as the two men watched provocatively attired women dance for them, "When it comes to doing business in Russia, it's very hard to find people in there you can trust. We're going to have a great relationship."[88]

On another night less than five months later, either Emin or an associate (depending on whether you believe a source who spoke to the *Daily Caller* or Trump bodyguard Keith Schiller's Congressional testimony) would tell Schiller that prostitutes could be sent up to Trump's room at the Ritz-Carlton Moscow if he wanted.[89] And Christopher Steele's dossier reports that that nocturnal visit did in fact come to pass—and that Trump requested the women sent to him perform acts of urination.[90]

Pictures on social media confirm that Trump maintained his relationship with the Agalarovs throughout 2014, with Emin boasting to *Forbes* in July 2017 that after November 2013 "every time I was in America—in New York, in Miami—I performed at one of [Trump's] events. . . . I visited his office, and we stayed in touch. He stayed in touch with my father as well. They've exchanged numerous letters. It's been a great relationship so far."[91]

In Las Vegas in 2013, the Agalarovs promise Trump not only $20 million but also, more important, an opportunity to meet with Vladimir Putin and the prospect of building a Trump Tower Moscow on the site where the 2013 Miss Universe pageant will be held.

The *Washington Post* wrote on March 9, 2018, of Trump's 2013 trip to Moscow that when Putin didn't appear at the 2013 pageant, his absence created, in Aras Agalarov's words, "a very complicated situation . . . because I promised Trump he would meet Putin."[92]

Trump arrives in Moscow in early November 2013 with two U.S. business partners in tow, Alex Sapir and Rotem Rosen, whose ties to powerful Russians are substantial. He immediately begins conducting business meetings with bankers and other influential Russians who can help him and Aras Agalarov move forward with their Trump Tower Moscow project.

Trump later said of the pageant after-party that "almost all of the oligarchs were in the room," but he would not name them.[93] He also said in a 2015 interview with Fox News's Sean Hannity that he "doesn't want to say" if he spoke to Putin in Moscow.[94] This was out of character for Trump, who drops names when boasting about people with whom he has spent time. Trump has even been evasive about how long he was in Moscow, telling radio host Hugh Hewitt on Monday, September 21, 2015, that he spent a "weekend in Moscow," but telling the *New York Times* on July 19, 2017, by the time the trip had become controversial, "I went there for one day for the Miss Universe contest, I turned around, I went back."[95] In a 2017 press conference he went even further in insisting on the brevity of his contacts with Russia and Russians: "I have no deals that could happen in Russia because we've stayed away," he said.[96]

Trump went to Moscow prepared in 2013. He brought with him Alex Sapir and Rotem Rosen, two New York–based developers who'd previously worked with Trump on Trump SoHo in New York City. According to *Washington Monthly*, Alex's then living Soviet-born father, Tamir, had "ties to Russian intelligence."[97] Rosen, then CEO of the Sapir Organization—of which Tamir had been the founder—was also known as the right-hand man of Soviet-born Lev Leviev, whom the Israeli daily *Haaretz* has called "a close friend of Putin."[98] Just two days after the pageant, Sapir and Rosen reported to *Real Estate Weekly* that "a lot of [Russian] people from the oil and gas businesses have come to us asking to be partners in building a product like Trump SoHo [in Moscow]."[99] In Trump's own discussion with *Real Estate Weekly*, he claimed that he was simultaneously in serious negotiations with not just one or two but *four* Russian developers—only one of which was Agalarov—to build a Trump-branded tower in Moscow.[100]

In addition to meeting with Putin's permits man, Vladimir Kozhin, Trump also met with Herman Gref, CEO of a state-owned Russian bank, Sberbank. The result was that on November 8 and 9, 2013, Trump had the developer (Agalarov), permits (Kozhin), and money (Gref) he needed for Trump Tower Moscow all in one place. This enabled him to announce the Trump Tower Moscow deal prior to the pageant on November 9.

Trump's excitement over the agreement had hardly diminished by the time he returned to the States on November 10. His first tweet post-Moscow, on November 11, reads as follows: "I just got back from Russia. Learned lots and lots. Moscow is a very interesting and amazing place. UNITED STATES MUST BE VERY SMART AND VERY STRATEGIC."[101] Once again, Trump was seamlessly conjoining corporate and political rhetoric, his own interests and those of America. Trump also had a public message for the Agalarovs on November 11, which he likewise delivered by tweet: "I had a great weekend with you and your family. You have done a FANTASTIC job. TRUMP TOWER MOSCOW is next."[102]

> The dossier also includes raw intelligence—meaning intelligence
> that hasn't been confirmed—on Putin's using proposed real estate
> deals in Russia to seal Trump's loyalty.

The dossier of raw intelligence that the FBI's investigation of Trump-
Russia ties now in part relies upon does discuss Aras Agalarov, though
not by name. The dossier details Russian efforts to entice Trump toward pro-Russia policies through promises of future Russian land-
development deals, noting on its second page that "[t]he Kremlin's
cultivation operation on Trump also had comprised offering him various lucrative real estate development business deals in Russia, especially in relation to the ongoing 2018 World Cup soccer tournament.
However, so far, for reasons unknown, Trump had not taken up any
of these." [103] Agalarov was named on a *Forbes* list of the fifteen Russian billionaires tied to the World Cup, noting that "his Crocus Group
was awarded $580 million in state contracts to erect two stadiums in
host cities Kaliningrad and Rostov-on-Don." [104] As for Trump's not ac-
cepting the offers referenced in the dossier—keeping in mind that he
did indeed sign letters of intent in 2013 and 2015 to build a Trump
Tower Moscow—one explanation for Trump's lack of engagement can
be found in one of his earlier disengagements from a Russia deal. As
reported by the Associated Press in 2017, Trump declined a chance to
build a tower in Moscow in 1997 because "[he] said he did not have
enough money to renovate the property. Trump told [Alexander Kho-
menko, then assistant to Moscow's deputy mayor]: 'I'm really interested in this project but I don't have enough funds and I will need to
look for outside investment.' " [105] In the 2000s (see chapter 1), Trump
began licensing his name rather than becoming directly involved in new
building projects—while at least once, in Toronto, claiming to be involved in building a tower when in fact he was only licensing his name
to it—so any decision to turn down Kremlin-proffered opportunities in
Russia in the 2010s could have been the result of Trump being a licen-
sor rather than a builder because of a lack of capital. *Forbes* also noted
five additional Trump-linked Russian billionaires who had World Cup

projects: Viktor Vekselberg, who reportedly is tied to an investment firm that paid Trump's attorney Michael Cohen $500,000 between January and August 2017 (specifically, into an account Cohen used to pay off Trump's former girlfriends and mistresses), and Mikhail Fridman, German Khan, Alexei Kuzmichev, and Pyotr Aven, who, per *Forbes*, citing the Steele dossier, "worked with the Kremlin to influence the 2016 presidential elections." [106] Fridman, Khan, Kuzmichev, and Aven control Alfa Bank—a member of whose advisory board, Richard Burt, cowrote Donald Trump's first foreign policy speech (now known as the "Mayflower Speech") and thereafter "continue[d] to work with the bank's co-founder, Mikhail Fridman," according to *Politico*.[107]

According to the *Washington Post*, after the pageant there was a "glitzy after-party in a Moscow nightclub."[108] Trump, "energized," worked the room.[109] Trump would later claim that "all of the oligarchs" attended, which wasn't true—but the room was certainly packed with influential Russian nationals.[110] And the day before he had indeed been with powerful Russian businessmen, including Sberbank's Gref, called "a longtime ally of President Vladimir Putin" by *Bloomberg*.[111]

A longtime friend of Trump's, actor Tom Arnold, bolsters Trump's claims of having spoken to Putin "indirectly and directly," saying he has knowledge of a speakerphone call between Trump and Putin on November 9 at the Ritz-Carlton Moscow because it was witnessed, he will say repeatedly on social media, by NBC executive Chuck LaBella and others. Per Arnold, "Putin called Trump at [the] Moscow Ritz [in] Nov[ember] 2013. Trump put [it] on speakerphone for everyone to hear. Putin congratulated Trump on Trump Tower Moscow & encouraged Trump to run for President & offered Russia's support. It's all on tape."

On November 11, 2013, Yulya Alferova, then wife of well-connected Russian billionaire Artem Klyushin, posted on Twitter a picture of herself standing behind Donald Trump as Trump, seated at a small table, looked at something on a computer screen. To Trump's left was Emin

Agalarov, son of Trump's billionaire business partner Aras Agalarov—already well known for being Vladimir Putin's go-to real estate developer. To Trump's right was billionaire casino mogul and Trump friend Phil Ruffin, while over Trump's left shoulder, Trump bodyguard Keith Schiller hovered. Over his right shoulder were Alferova and an unidentified man. It is unknown what (or, given allegations made by Trump friend Tom Arnold, *who*) was on the computer screen. Alferova's tweet was captioned, "Waiting for your business in Russia to start, Mr. Trump!" She added hashtags for "Russia" and "Moscow" and directed the tweet to Trump's and Emin's attention by using their Twitter handles, @realdonaldtrump and @eminofficial, respectively.[112]

In January 2017, Arnold made the startling accusation that Trump spoke with Putin via speakerphone—whether through an actual phone or via a desktop computer application is unknown—at the 2013 Miss Universe pageant, that others had heard the call, and that the call was incriminating. On January 9, 2017, Arnold tweeted "at" Trump that "Chuck LaBella [NBC talent development executive] was not only listening on speakerphone when Putin called (you lied to *60 Minutes*, by the way) but he knows everything else, and just in case, Putin filmed it all."[113] In mid-2018, *VICE News*, convinced that Arnold has substantial knowledge of Trump's private dealings from his years of friendship with him and *Apprentice* producer Mark Burnett, announced that Arnold would star in a program entitled *The Hunt for the Trump Tapes*, to premiere in September 2018.[114] Arnold has since been pictured with Trump fixer Michael Cohen, now known to have a large number of audio recordings of the president.[115]

Arnold argued in his January 2017 tweets that his intention was not to harm Trump's political career, stating, as noted by the *International Herald Tribune*,

> There is a sex tape of him from Moscow in 2013 from when he was over there for the Miss Universe pageant. I wish that he would release it because I don't care. I wish he would say, "Putin has this over me, here's what it is. Okay, now it's out, now he [Putin] can't talk about me. Okay, I'm going to do what's best

for America." Because something is up, something happened there. I want to help him so he can do what's best for our country and the men and women who serve our country.[116]

LaBella has not discussed Arnold's allegations with the media, for reasons that may be connected to Trump's onetime fixer and attorney, Michael Cohen. In April 2018, CNN reported that Cohen, then Trump's attorney, had directed LaBella to retain Keith M. Davidson as an attorney in response to Arnold's claims.[117] Davidson is best known for helping adult film actor Stormy Daniels negotiate a "hush money" payment from Trump when she had information Trump did not want disclosed.[118] Whether LaBella plans to speak out about what he saw in Moscow is uncertain. LaBella has told the *Irish Examiner*, however, that "Donald is an incredible man, and I mean that sincerely in a positive way. He has been very good to me over the past 10 years personally and professionally. I've learned a lot of unique lessons from him."[119]

Trump has given different accounts of the reported speakerphone call with Putin, telling journalists at the National Press Club on May 27, 2014, that he spoke to Putin "directly" and "indirectly." However, it is LaBella who could state unequivocally whether the phone call took place.[120] Arnold has kept the pressure up on both Trump and LaBella, tweeting on October 16, 2017, "Trump *loves* Chuck LaBella. I'd kill if a reporter asked DJT about him. Chuck can confirm the [existence of the] 'pee pee tape' & Putin call and *Apprentice*/Miss U[niverse pageant] filth."[121] Arnold had previously alleged, in public tweets, that *Apprentice* producer Mark Burnett was in possession of tapes from *Apprentice* recording sessions on which Trump could be heard using racist and misogynistic language. This allegation of Trump using racist language has since been repeated by former Trump adviser Omarosa Manigault Newman.[122]

Beyond Aras Agalarov's promise to Trump that he could meet Putin, Trump's summer 2013 letter to Putin and tweet about Putin prepageant, and Trump's subsequent claims to have spoken to Putin indirectly and directly, his interest in meeting the Russian president is underscored by his choice of entourage in Moscow in November 2013.

One compatriot during the trip was Bob Van Ronkel, an American ex-patriate who has lived in Moscow for many years and specializes in getting Hollywood talent to travel to Russia.[123] Van Ronkel's specific skill is selling Hollywood stars on the idea that they can get rich by doing business in and with Russia; that Van Ronkel is good at his job is underscored by the fact that the front page of his website features several photos of him with Vladimir Putin.[124] Van Ronkel and Putin became friendly in part because the former does a great service for Russia by bringing the world's biggest celebrities there.[125] He also sought to make a TV show about the KGB in 2001; on August 13, 2001, the website of the Association of Former Intelligence Officers noted that

> producer Bob Van Ronkel is currently putting together a multimillion-dollar television series tentatively titled "Files From the KGB." The series is planned to be filmed in Russia and it will use an almost all-Russian cast to show the world the swashbuckling adventures of one of the world's most feared intelligence agencies. This time, however, they won't be the cruel psychopaths of Cold War movies or the megalomaniacs of James Bond films. . . . [The series will be] in the style of television series such as "La Femme Nikita." [126]

On his website, Van Ronkel lists, among his November 2013 accomplishments, the following four: "attended a private event with Steven Seagal"; "drinks with Donald Trump during the Miss Universe Competition in Moscow"; "entertained owners of Dick Clark Productions and Mandalay Entertainment, Allen Shapiro and Peter Guber, who were in Russian [sic] for the Miss Universe Competition they were producing"; and "dinner with Chuck LaBella, Vice President [of] Talent Relations at NBCUniversal[,] and the partners of Miss Universe." [127] The latter three events occurred at the 2013 Miss Universe pageant. It's unclear if Van Ronkel met with his client Seagal at the pageant or elsewhere; in either case, Seagal, a friend of Putin's, is now both a Russian citizen—an honor bestowed upon him by Putin at a widely publicized Moscow ceremony—and, as of 2018, Putin's "Special Envoy" to the Trump administration.[128]

In 2013, LaBella was an NBC talent development executive. He'd also been involved as producer in several Miss Universe pageants (2010, 2011, and 2012) and a judge in several others (particularly Miss Teen USA pageants).[129] LaBella's role with respect to the 2013 Miss Universe pageant is unclear; IMDB doesn't list it at all for him, but other sites say he was a producer for the 2013 edition of the show just as he was from 2010 to 2012.[130] Per IMDB, he worked on five episodes of *The Apprentice* with Trump in 2013.[131] Arnold claims LaBella was also NBC's liaison to Trump during the pageant—NBC co-owned the Miss Universe pageant with Trump at the time—and was therefore, Arnold alleges, with him for any incriminating behavior that may have occurred during the trip. "Chuck LaBella was there and knows all," Arnold tweeted out on October 16, 2017.[132]

In 2015, *BuzzFeed* published significant details about Van Ronkel's Moscow operation, establishing that his job was not just to get stars like Trump to Russia but to be certain they understood that doing so could lead to business deals with Russians and lots of money. *BuzzFeed* described Van Ronkel as "tak[ing] credit for bringing numerous celebrities to Russia" and mentioning in interviews with American media "large sums of money flowing to the celebrities whose trips he facilitates."[133] Speaking of Steven Seagal in particular, Van Ronkel bragged to *BuzzFeed* that "Steven has been offered commercials, film roles, and is working on all kinds of other interesting business deals in Russia and with very many interesting people."[134] Van Ronkel, *BuzzFeed* noted, even runs his own acting school in Moscow.[135]

Van Ronkel didn't just attend the 2013 Miss Universe pageant, but he also had drinks with Trump and had a meeting with him. Pictures available online show him sitting just six seats from Trump during the pageant, immediately beside Yulya Alferova and Artem Klyushin. At one point he had his picture taken with Trump; that picture, of the two men side by side and smiling, is also available online (as the "splash page" photograph on Van Ronkel's professional website).[136] Other celebrities photographed with one of Hollywood's chief conduits to Russian audiences include Katy Perry, Kanye West, Russell Crowe, Angelina Jolie, Jack Nicholson, Arnold Schwarzenegger, Kevin Costner, Snoop Dogg, Jared Leto, and "NBC/Universal executive Chuck LaBella." [137] If Trump didn't see any of these photos prior to connecting with Van Ronkel in Moscow, he may have since seen a July 14, 2017, article in the *Financial Times* crediting Van Ronkel with having "introduced several Hollywood celebrities to Mr. Putin." The British media outlet not only added that Van Ronkel had attended the 2013 Miss Universe pageant as a VIP, but that he had even "worked on the pageant" itself.[138] In speaking to *Financial Times*, Van Ronkel said that Trump "looked bored" at the 2013 pageant after-party in Moscow.[139] Yet Van Ronkel told *VICE News* something quite different; according to *VICE*, "When Russian pop star Emin Agalarov hit the stage at the 2013 Miss Universe pageant in Moscow, Bob Van Ronkel sat watching his longtime acquaintance [Emin] from the front row. . . . There, a few seats away, sat the pageant co-owner: Donald Trump. Later that night, Van Ronkel wound up at a vodka-soaked afterparty with Trump, Emin, and Emin's billionaire father, Aras. Trump was 'shaking hands and meeting anyone he could and trying to do business,' Van Ronkel says." [140]

After promising that he will attend the pageant, Putin suddenly chooses not to do so.

Why didn't Putin go to the pageant? There are as many answers offered to that question as there are reporters who've pursued it. The *Daily Mail* said Trump arrived in Moscow too late for the anticipated meeting with Putin because his plane was delayed in North Carolina.[141] The *Guardian* wrote that the Trump-Putin meeting mysteriously "fell off" Putin's schedule a few days before Trump arrived in Moscow.[142] *Mother Jones* said a "Moscow traffic jam" was to blame, while the *Washington Post* said it was a meeting between Putin and the king of the Netherlands that ran long.[143] Trump himself would later claim to Fox News that the meeting *did* in fact happen—though he was light on the details—and Putin, for his part, has claimed he didn't even know Trump was in Moscow that month.[144]

In December 2013, just over a month after his return from Moscow, Trump begins formally reaching out to influential Republicans on the subject of a presidential run, which he predicts in conversations with politicians in New York will begin in 2015.

Within forty-five days of returning to the United States from Moscow, Trump had already met with influential Republicans "to discuss a possible run for governor of New York [in 2014]," according to the *New York Times*.[145] During one such event he was given a four-page document by an upstate assemblyman that had a section entitled "Springboards to the Presidency." The *Times* noted that that document section was written with "the particular interests of Mr. Trump in mind," given that, per "an examination by The New York Times of contemporaneous documents and emails, as well as interviews with people who met with Mr. Trump during that period . . . he . . . measure[d] whether the governor's office was a necessary steppingstone to his long-held goal: the White House. His calculations [in December 2013] . . . run contrary to the seat-of-the-pants image he projects on the campaign trail, and offer a look at a formative stage of his presidential ambitions."[146] The *Times* added that Trump's intentions were serious, inasmuch as he actually "discussed with state Republican leaders the idea of using the governorship as a platform to run for president, a situation in which he would serve for a year" before running for the 2016 Republican nomination. "He made it clear [in December 2013] he wanted to run for president," said Manhattan's Republican Party chairman when contacted by the *Times*.[147] In another meeting that December, this time at Trump Tower, Trump told Republican leaders "he did not think the country could withstand eight years of Hillary Clinton," and that he wanted to "save the country."[148]

At one point in December 2013, Trump boosters met with him with the necessary documents to register a presidential exploratory committee in hand; they also brought a notary public to the meeting. Trump has said that "even then [in December 2013] . . . what I really wanted to do was run for president." [149]

In February 2018, Trump tweeted that "I didn't know I was going to run [in 2014]." [150]

The Trump-Agalarov letter of intent will remain active, according to Aras Agalarov, for three and a half years—a period covering the entirety of the presidential campaign. It expires only on Trump's inauguration, according to a February 2017 statement to a Russian construction website by the elder Agalarov.

On February 2, 2017, Agalarov announced that the Trump Tower Moscow project he and Donald Trump had signed a letter of intent to pursue in 2013 was dead. Popular Russian online journal *Construction.RU* announced the project's death in an article entitled "Russians Abandon Plan for Trump Tower Construction in Moscow Region." The article quoted Agalarov as saying his letter of intent with Trump had expired not because Trump had been elected president but because, as Agalarov put it, Trump had decided that as president he "couldn't do any deals." [151] Agalarov's statement confirmed that Trump had operated under one letter of intent for the entirety of his presidential run (Trump-Agalarov) and a second letter of intent (Trump-Rozov) from October 2015—three months into his presidential run—until May 2016 at the earliest (see chapter 4). As Yahoo News would report in May 2018 of the Trump-Rozov letter of intent, "Prosecutors and congressional investigators have obtained text messages and emails showing that. . . . as late as May 2016, around the time Trump was clinching the Republican nomination, Cohen was considering a trip to Russia to meet about the [Trump Tower Moscow] project with high-level government officials, business leaders and bankers." [152] Given statements, across multiple decades, by Donald Trump and Donald Trump Jr. about how real estate deals get done in Moscow, both of these tower deals would have depended upon the generosity of Russian officials.

However, in a mid-2017 *Forbes* interview, Agalarov's son throws even this expiration date into doubt, revealing that the Agalarovs are still in negotiations with Trump's sons to do additional business—possibly including the building of a tower in Moscow.

Emin told *Forbes* that "during our discussions . . . [Trump] ran for president, so we dropped the idea [of a Trump Tower Moscow]."[153] However, Emin was also so candid with *Forbes* about both what those discussions entailed and whether they in fact survived Trump's announcement of his presidential candidacy that he later tried to retract the portion of his interview referencing a 2013 letter of intent between his father and Trump. Pre-retraction, the younger Agalarov told *Forbes* that "we [Trump and the Crocus Group] had actually signed some nondisclosure documents at the time [in 2013] just to establish the relationship on a different level. . . . But if [Trump] hadn't run for president, we would probably be in the construction phase today, because he's a great person, very trusted on our side."[154] Echoing his father's implication in 2017 that the Trump-Agalarov Trump Tower Moscow letter of intent was still active in 2015, Emin, when asked by *Forbes*, "Do you think there's any possibility you might pick up those conversations [about Trump Tower Moscow] with Eric or Donald Jr.?," responded, "Yeah, we are in contact with both."[155] The response suggested that Trump had instructed neither Donald Trump Jr. nor Eric Trump that they were in fact prohibited from doing any foreign deals while he was in office. Indeed, according to Emin, the Trump boys' delay in responding to several post–June 2015 proposals by the Agalarovs—for instance, working with "a manufacturer of furniture in Turkey" and "building a building together [in Moscow]"—was only because, after their father's 2016 election, Don Jr. and Eric "[hadn't] realized who is handling what, how and when."[156]

On March 29, 2014, Yulya Alferova retweets Trump three times in succession, with all three tweets on the subject of the Agalarovs' new business partner running for president. According to both Emin Agalarov and Donald Trump Jr., the Agalarovs and Trumps are still planning a Trump Tower Moscow at this point.

By Trump's own public admission, as late as Election Day he didn't believe he would win the presidency. He thought that as of November 9, 2016—the day after Election Day—he'd return to being a nonpolitician private citizen free to do big international business deals without hindrance.[157] According to Michael Wolff's *Fire and Fury*, a week before the election Trump told the former head of the Fox News Channel Roger Ailes that "losing [the election] . . . isn't losing. We've totally won."[158] Wolff wrote that Trump appeared to his aides to be "horrified" when things started breaking his way on election night, almost certainly thinking that his grand plans for a Trump Tower Moscow would have to be put on hold.[159] Former congressman, current MSNBC host, and longtime Trump friend—now Trump enemy—Joe Scarborough said in August 2017, after having been in contact with Trump for much of the 2016 campaign, "Donald Trump never thought he was going to win the presidency. This was all a money-making scam. . . . [He was going to] take the money and run. 'Let me use the position I'm in right now and try to get that tower in Moscow.'"[160]

When Trump won on November 8, 2016, in addition to publicly expressing his surprise, he for weeks resisted any attempt to shut down his business dealings at home or abroad.[161] To this day, he has not divested himself of his business interests, almost certainly aware that the commitments he made to Agalarov prior to the election can be restarted more readily if he takes no appreciable steps to distance himself from the business entity—the Trump Organization—that made those commitments.[162]

CHAPTER THREE

KOMPROMAT

November 2013

Summary

WHEN DONALD TRUMP ARRIVES IN MOSCOW FOR THE MISS Universe pageant in November 2013, he checks into the presidential suite of the Ritz-Carlton Moscow. That night he is allegedly surreptitiously recorded asking multiple women to urinate on the presidential suite bed President Barack Obama and First Lady Michelle Obama had slept in on their trip to Moscow. Multiple active-duty CIA officers responsible for the case file on this incident, speaking to the BBC's Russia correspondent through an intermediary, say that the recording does indeed exist. BBC reporter Paul Wood reports that at least one allied European intelligence agency has the same information.[1] These officers also tell the BBC that there is at least one other recording of Trump "of a sexual nature" from a different location (St. Petersburg) and a different time. Any such recording would be considered national security–endangering *kompromat*—potential blackmail material—if it is now in the possession of the Kremlin.

Numerous witnesses in contact with British media confirm individual elements of the Ritz-Carlton allegation, which was originally published by *BuzzFeed* in January 2017 as part of a thirty-five-page dossier of raw intelligence now known as the "Steele dossier."

The Facts

DONALD TRUMP ARRIVES IN MOSCOW ON NOVEMBER 8, 2013, for a full day of business meetings.[2] A number of Russian businessmen attend the meetings; among them is Artem Klyushin, a Russian billionaire whose close friend Konstantin Rykov will post on social media the day after the 2016 election that he and Klyushin were part of a campaign to get Trump elected.[3] Rykov runs Dosug, a website that functions as Moscow's largest brothel.[4]

At one of Trump's first meetings, a Russian attendee—possibly Emin Agalarov, possibly Artem Klyushin or a third person—tells Keith Schiller, Trump's bodyguard, that if Trump wants, a group of prostitutes can be sent to his room at the Ritz-Carlton that night.[5] According to Schiller's testimony to Congress in November 2017, he declines the offer and tells Trump about it immediately; the two men laugh about it, Schiller testifies.[6] That night Schiller, as he normally does, stands outside Trump's door; after a few minutes, however, he goes to bed.[7] Trump is aware—by his own subsequent admission at a January 2017 news conference—that his room is likely filled with clandestine recording equipment and that he must be "careful" about what he does there.[8] Schiller tells Congress that he "could not say for sure what happened during the remainder of the night."[9]

According to the dossier compiled by former MI6 agent Christopher Steele—using Russian intelligence sources he developed during his time as head of the Russia desk at the British intelligence agency, as well as local Moscow sources and American sources alleged to be close to Trump—prostitutes were sent to Trump's room on November 8, 2013, and the room was being recorded.[10] The dossier cites for this intelligence "several of the staff [at the Ritz-Carlton Moscow]," as well as "Sources D and E."[11] The dossier sources allege that, to show disrespect to President Obama and his wife, Michelle, Trump asked a group of women to urinate on the bed in the presidential suite that the Obamas had slept in during a prior official visit to Russia.[12]

Over the course of the next year there will be reports of witnesses who saw a row in the Ritz-Carlton Moscow lobby between hotel staff and a group of women who wanted to go up to Trump's room without signing in.[13] Paul Wood of the BBC, in an article for the *Spectator*, will say he was told by an unnamed source that a hotel employee and an American tourist saw the row happen.[14] In October 2017, an editor at the *Guardian* will contact this author to say that the *Guardian* has heard "there are witnesses to a confrontation in the hotel lobby, when security wanted the girls to sign in and DJT [Donald Trump] objected. . . . [O]ne [witness] is [a] former Trump Organization [employee]." The editor adds that the *Guardian* source is a trusted one but "two layers away. She talked to a top Republican who talked to the witness. Her understanding is that the witness had talked to the FBI and given an interview to a local paper that never printed it."[15]

There is speculation, after the Steele dossier is published by *BuzzFeed* in January 2017, that Belarusian businessman Sergei Millian (born Siarhei Kukuts) is both Source D and Source E, a claim made unlikely by the dossier's contention that Source E "confirmed" raw intelligence provided by Source D as to the incident in Trump's hotel room.[16]

Shortly after the dossier's publication, Paul Wood reports that a retired spy told him in August 2016 that an eastern European intelligence agency had confirmed the existence of a tape of the Ritz-Carlton incident.[17] "Later," Wood writes, "I used an intermediary to pass some questions to active duty CIA officers dealing with the case file," to determine whether the intelligence community credits the allegations. According to Wood, he received a response through that intermediary that there was "more than one tape" of the then president-elect, with "audio and video," on "more than one date" and in "more than one place"—specifically, Moscow and St. Petersburg—and that the material in all instances was "of a sexual nature."[18]

The day after *BuzzFeed* publishes the dossier, the Kremlin calls the dossier's findings "a complete fabrication and utter nonsense." Trump cites the Kremlin's response nearly word for word, calling the dossier "A COMPLETE AND TOTAL FABRICATION, UTTER NONSENSE," and adds, "I HAVE NOTHING TO DO WITH RUSSIA—NO

DEALS, NO LOANS, NO NOTHING!"[19] He then compares America to Nazi Germany and himself to a victim of Nazi oppression, writing on Twitter, "Intelligence agencies should never have allowed this fake news to 'leak' into the public. One last shot at me. Are we living in Nazi Germany?"[20]

Defending himself against the allegations, Trump claims that it would be impossible for him to watch a third party urinate on a bed because he is a germaphobe.[21] Yahoo News reports in April 2018 that Trump told FBI director James Comey, at a January 27, 2017, dinner, that he never slept overnight in Moscow—a claim that is later found to be false.[22] The *Washington Post* reports, in January 2017, Trump's contention that he would never have acted inappropriately in his hotel room, writing, "[T]he president-elect professed an awareness that the hotel rooms he visits overseas may be bugged with tiny cameras."[23] At a press conference the day after the dossier is released, the president says, "When I leave our country. . . . I am extremely careful. I'm surrounded by bodyguards. I'm surrounded by people. And I always tell them . . . 'Be very careful, because in your hotel rooms and no matter where you go, you're gonna probably have cameras.'"[24] He adds, "I would certainly put [Russia] in that category."[25] Addressing specifically the possibility of being caught on camera doing something compromising, Trump says, "I always tell [my bodyguards and entourage]. . . . 'I hope you're gonna be good anyway. . . . [But you] better be careful, or you'll be watching yourself on nightly television.' I tell this to people all the time."[26]

Trump's claims of cautious behavior in Moscow are challenged by a pre-dossier interview on Hungarian television in which a former Miss Hungary, Kata Sarka, says that Trump approached her shortly before the 2013 Miss Universe pageant and propositioned her for sex in his hotel room at the Ritz-Carlton.[27] Another of Trump's defenses against the allegations is that he would never sleep with a prostitute; Karen McDougal, a former Playboy Playmate, says that the first time she slept with Trump he tried to pay her afterward.[28]

According to a January 2017 *Daily Caller* report, an unnamed former Trump adviser's initial defense of Trump contended that it was

Emin Agalarov who raised the matter of prostitutes and did not offer them so much as tell Schiller they would be sent; the same former adviser said that there were multiple "people" guarding Trump's door all night.[29] In his testimony to Congress, however, Schiller will say that it was a "Russian or Ukrainian" person, not Emin Agalarov, who made the offer, and that the only person assigned to Trump's door that night was Schiller himself, who left the door unguarded for much of the night.[30] Emin Agalarov himself denies the allegation that he arranged for prostitutes and claims that Trump could not have been with prostitutes at 1:00 or 2:00 a.m. on November 9, 2013, because at 7:00 a.m. that day he was filming part of a music video for Emin as a favor.[31] However Trump himself says he sometimes sleeps as few as three hours a night.[32]

In January 2017, Stanislav Belkovsky, a Muscovite who is the director of the National Strategy Institute in Moscow, a sometime freelancer for publications such as the *Guardian* and the *Moscow Times*, and a host at independent Russian network TV Rain, tells the *Daily Beast* that "[p]rostitutes around [Moscow] say the 'golden shower' orgy story is true."[33] In July 2017, independent journalist and surveillance expert Andrei Soldatov, while accompanying CBS's Stephen Colbert on a sweep of the presidential suite bedroom in which the Steele-reported recording was allegedly made, tells the *Daily Beast* that "Colbert and I look[ed] for surveillance cameras behind the large mirror [in the presidential suite] and to our astonishment we discovered an electric cable, which could not have any clear purpose, as the mirror had no electronic illumination."[34]

According to the *New York Times*, "Russia has a long and well-documented record of using kompromat to discredit the Kremlin's foes and to lean on its potential friends. For decades [at least sixty years following the end of World War II], hotels across the former Soviet Union visited by foreigners were equipped with bugging devices and cameras by the K.G.B."[35] Experts on Russian hospitality-industry tradecraft say that, historically, " 'interesting' . . . foreign businessmen" are put in a "handful of rooms" in the hotel in which they are staying that are wired for sound and video.[36]

In March 2018, the former CIA director John Brennan tells MSNBC that the Kremlin "may have something on [Trump] personally": "The Russians, I think, have had long experience with Mr. Trump, and may have things that they could expose."[37]

In April 2018, former FBI director James Comey, one of the original recipients of the Steele dossier in 2016, tells CNN, "I don't know whether the current President of the United States was with prostitutes peeing on each other in Moscow in 2013. It's possible."[38]

When Vladimir Putin is asked in Helsinki, Finland, whether the Kremlin has a tape of Trump from his November 2013 stay at the Ritz-Carlton Moscow, he does not deny the existence of such a tape; instead, he says that he was unaware Trump was in Moscow at the time.[39] Noting that there are too many "high-level, high-ranking" businessmen coming to Russia to try to collect compromising material on all of them, he adds that "when [Trump] was a private individual, a businessman, nobody informed me that he was in Moscow [in November 2013]. . . . Please disregard these issues and don't think about this anymore again."[40]

On August 10, 2018, Robert Baer, a former CIA case officer and an intelligence columnist for *Time*, tells a crowd at an event in Colorado that prior to the release of the Steele dossier in January 2017 he spoke to a former KGB officer who told him, "We have a tape of Donald Trump."[41] While, according to Baer, the Russian didn't say when the tape was recorded or what it depicted, Baer concluded, after the Steele dossier was published, that whether the tape referenced by the ex-KGB agent was from 2013 or not, based on the dossier's allegations and his own familiarity with Russian intelligence operations, "the Agalarovs are KGB [FSB] agents."[42]

Annotated History

Donald Trump arrives in Moscow on November 8, 2013, for a full day of business meetings. A number of Russian businessmen attend the meetings; among them is Artem Klyushin, a Russian billionaire whose close friend Konstantin Rykov will post on social media the day after the 2016 election that he and Klyushin were part of a campaign to get Trump elected. Rykov runs Dosug, a website that functions as Moscow's largest brothel.

Konstantin Rykov is a member of Putin's political party (previously serving in the Duma), is one of the Russian leader's most trusted confidants, and is widely considered by journalists and Kremlinologists as a member of the "propagandist arm of the Putin government machine," according to *Washington Monthly*.[43] Public Radio International noted his expertise in click-bait messaging, viral communication, and digital technology and referred to him in May 2018 as "the man who taught the Kremlin how to win the internet."[44] He also, according to a 2016 *Daily Dot* article entitled "This Dark Net Brothel Makes Finding Sex as Easy as Hailing an Uber," founded Dosug, now the largest brothel in Moscow.[45]

Rykov created a pro-Trump website, Trump2016.ru, in 2015 and published a pro-Trump endorsement just a few weeks after Trump's surprise announcement of his candidacy for president that June; pictures and text from Klyushin's Twitter account suggest Klyushin attended a Trump rally in Iowa later that year.[46] In a March 2016 Reuters article, Rykov, who is well known in Russia and among American journalists as a "pro-Kremlin blogger" and "Putin supporter," is quoted as saying, "Trump is the first member of the American elite in twenty years who compliments Russia. Trump will smash America as we know it, we've got nothing to lose. Do we want the grandmother Hillary? No. Maybe it's time to help the old brigand [Trump]."[47]

The dossier sources allege that, to show disrespect to President Obama and his wife, Michelle, Trump asked a group of women to urinate on the bed in the presidential suite that the Obamas had slept in during a prior official visit to Russia.

At one hotel in former Soviet republic Estonia, according to the *New York Times*, during the Soviet era "60 of the hotel's 423 rooms were bugged and reserved for 'interesting persons' like foreign businessmen. Guests who were judged vulnerable to blackmail were put in a handful of rooms with holes in the walls through which special cameras would film dalliances with prostitutes. All the prostitutes . . . worked for the K.G.B."[48] In a conversation with FBI director James Comey in early 2017, Trump allegedly said that Putin told him in Moscow in 2013 that "[Russia had] some of the most beautiful hookers in the world."[49] The comment echoes a letter Trump sent to Putin in the months before he went to Moscow, in which Trump had added a postscript indicating that "he looked forward to seeing 'beautiful' women during his trip," according to the *Washington Post*.[50]

As noted by CBS's Stephen Colbert when he traveled to the Ritz to investigate the allegations in the Steele dossier, Trump stayed in the nicest room in the hotel—the presidential suite—while in Moscow. In July 2017, Colbert rented out the room Trump had stayed in and videotaped his discovery of "an unexplained power cable . . . dangling from a section of the bedroom wall that was hidden behind a non-illuminated mirror."[51] Colbert would later recount for Conan O'Brien, on the latter's show *Conan*, how "I actually looked behind the mirrors of the presidential suite room where they supposedly had filmed this happening, and there were electrical wires going into a mirror."[52]

As for the motivation behind the acts Trump allegedly observed and/or engaged in at the Ritz-Carlton, reports suggest that Trump has hated Obama ever since Obama made fun of him at the White House Correspondents' Association Dinner in 2011 in front of the most powerful and influential figures in American media. According to a September 2015 article by Adam Gopnik in the *New Yorker*, "Trump's humiliation was as absolute, and as visible, as any I have ever seen: his head set in place, like a man in a pillory, he barely moved or altered his expression as wave after wave of laughter struck him. There was not a trace of feigning good humor about him. . . . No head-bobbing or hand-clapping or chin-shaking or sheepish grinning—he sat perfectly still, chin tight, in locked, unmovable rage."[53] According to the *Washington Post*, "reporters for major news organizations say Trump was so humiliated that it triggered a deep, previously hidden yearning for revenge."[54]

Over the course of the next year there will be reports of witnesses who saw a row in the Ritz-Carlton Moscow lobby between hotel staff and a group of women who wanted to go up to Trump's room without signing in.

Per Paul Wood—a Russia correspondent for the BBC at the time he filed his report—an American Ritz-Carlton Moscow guest alleged that prostitutes went up to Trump's room. As Wood wrote in an August 2017 article for the *Spectator*, "Steele is not the only source [on the Ritz-Carlton Moscow tape]. I heard of Russian kompromat—compromising material—on Trump from two sources months before the Steele dossier came to light. . . . There are . . . reports of witnesses in the hotel who corroborate Steele's reporting. These include an American who's said to have seen a row with hotel security over whether the (alleged) hookers would be allowed up to Trump's suite."[55]

Besides the (minimum) two hotel witnesses he referenced, Wood also directly or indirectly received information from intelligence agency contacts who confirmed Steele's reporting. As Wood wrote for the BBC on January 12, 2017, in an article entitled "Trump 'Compromising' Claims: How and Why Did We Get Here?":

Steele is not the only source for the claim about Russian kompromat on the president-elect. Back in August, a retired spy told me he had been informed of its existence by "the head of an East

European intelligence agency." Later, I used an intermediary to pass some questions to active duty CIA officers dealing with the case file. . . . I got a message back that there was "more than one tape," "audio and video," on "more than one date," in "more than one place"—in the Ritz in Moscow and also in St. Petersburg—and that the material [in the tapes] was "of a sexual nature."[56]

Steele's dossier offers us another person who could corroborate the alleged events of November 8, 2013. According to Steele, a Trump friend described as being in his early forties—either Felix Sater, Russian-born Republican strategist Boris Epshteyn, or (most likely of the three) Sergei Millian—knows that a "pee tape" exists.[57] Steele doesn't allege this witness spoke directly to him about the existence of a tape; rather, he wrote in his dossier that a man in Trump's 2013 Miss Universe pageant entourage spoke out of turn to a Russian source Steele had reason to trust.

Another possible corroborator is Aras Agalarov, father of Emin. A Western diplomat in Moscow, speaking to the *Daily Mail*, observed that "if there are skeletons in Trump's dealings with Russia, Aras is the man who will know where they are."[58]

Just three days after Steele's dossier was published, NBC News called Steele a "real-life James Bond," quoting tradecraft expert Nigel West.[59]

Multiple active-duty CIA officers responsible for the case file on this incident, speaking to the BBC's Russia correspondent through an intermediary, say that the recording does indeed exist. BBC reporter Paul Wood reports that at least one allied European intelligence agency has the same information. These officers also tell the BBC that there is at least one other recording of Trump "of a sexual nature" from a different location (St. Petersburg) and a different time. Any such recording would be considered national security–endangering *kompromat*—potential blackmail material—if it is now in the possession of the Kremlin.

Keith Darden, an international-relations professor at American University who "has studied the Russian use of *kompromat*," described to the *New Yorker* in July 2018 the political environment in Russia as being one where "*kompromat* is routinely used . . . to curry favor, improve negotiated outcomes, and sway opinion. Intelligence services, businesspeople, and political figures everywhere exploit gossip and damaging information."[60] Darden even coined the term "blackmail state" to describe the "uniquely powerful role" *kompromat* has in the former Soviet Union and how "pervasive" it is.[61] In September 2017, a Russian hotel industry source told the *Guardian*, "If you are in their field of interest then the FSB will absolutely attempt to carry out surveillance. . . . In the bigger hotels you also definitely have a number of people on the staff who work on the side for the FSB, so they would have had absolutely no problem getting into the room if necessary."[62] Added the source, "I'm pretty sure Trump would have been of a sufficient level to warrant [surveillance]. I've seen people of lower levels than him watched [in their hotel rooms] for sure."

If Trump has been caught up in Russia's "blackmail state," the implications for America's national security are significant. Whether the material is of a personal or financial nature or both, it throws into doubt the authenticity of Trump's Russia policy—which includes characterizing Putin in glowing terms, refusing to denounce the Russian strongman's role in the murder of journalists, opposing sanctions on Russia, challenging the authority and viability of NATO in a manner that echoes Kremlin propaganda, advocating Russia's immediate return to the G7, and remaining open to acknowledging Russia's illegal annexation of Crimea.

CHAPTER FOUR

THE CAMPAIGN BEGINS

2013 to 2015

Summary

NOT LONG AFTER THE 2012 PRESIDENTIAL ELECTION, THE Russians begin preparations for 2016, dispatching two spies to the United States with the goal of infiltrating the right-wing National Rifle Association (NRA) and ultimately creating a back channel between the Kremlin and top leaders in the Republican Party. At the same time, the Kremlin becomes more aggressive in its efforts to reach out to Donald Trump, as the signs that he is going to run for president are, by mid-2013, unmistakable.

The Kremlin is successful in its plans to infiltrate the NRA, as well as in its efforts to push Trump toward a foreign policy more favorable to Russia, by dangling Moscow land-development deals in front of him. It is unclear as of 2015 whether the Kremlin plans to simply influence NRA brass into contributing a record amount of money to Trump's 2016 presidential campaign or whether it wants to funnel illegal campaign contributions directly to Trump through the organization. In 2018, Special Counsel Robert Mueller will investigate both possibilities. What will be clear by Election Day is that an unprecedented amount of NRA money was essential to the success of Trump's presidential run.

As soon as Trump announces his candidacy on June 16, 2015, at Trump Tower in New York City, he begins lauding Putin, denigrating sanctions on Russia, and harping on the need for better relations with the Kremlin—even as a longtime business partner of his with ties to both the Kremlin and the Russian mafia is trying to help him parlay his pro-Russia foreign policy into a sizable payday in the Russian real estate market. Meanwhile, both Trump and his son Donald Trump Jr. strengthen their bonds with the NRA, which will, in May 2016, issue an unusually early endorsement of Trump—a full six months before Election Day.[1]

As the *Weekly Standard* will note in February 2017, "There are many claimants to the honor of having nudged Donald Trump over the top in the presidential election. But the folks with the best case are the National Rifle Association and the consultants who made their TV ads."[2]

The Facts

FROM 2013 THROUGH THE END OF 2017, ALEXANDER Torshin (Russian name: Aleksandr Porfiryevich Torshin), a Russian politician with ties to Putin's intelligence services, and Maria Butina, a twentysomething Russian student who will eventually be charged with conspiracy and acting as a foreign agent, seek to infiltrate the NRA as part of a plot to create a back channel between the Kremlin and top leaders in the Republican Party.[3] The tripartite plot involves making a social connection with powerful NRA members and GOP operatives; creating a bogus "gun rights" organization in Russia to create sympathy of purpose with American gun owners; and, finally, encouraging the NRA to give generously to one candidate in particular: Donald Trump.[4]

As related by *Rolling Stone* in April 2018, Torshin is a member of Putin's political party with "close ties to Russia's internal security service, the FSB, which awarded him a medal in 2016."[5] According to the CIA's former Russian operations chief Steven Hall, "[Putin] decided Mr. Torshin [was] going to be the guy to do it for him"—"it" being, as *Rolling Stone* phrases it, "exploit[ing] the American gun lobby."[6] That exploitation involves "forg[ing] a quick friendship" between NRA president David Keene and a Russian sister organization to the NRA, despite the fact that, as Hall puts it, "the idea of private gun ownership is anathema to Putin."[7] As Torshin is working on connecting the Kremlin to powerful NRA members and, later on, Republican politicians, prosecutors in Spain—who, according to *Bloomberg*, refer to Torshin as a Russian mafia "boss"—are investigating him for money laundering.[8] In May 2018, Spanish officials, still suspecting Torshin of "involvement in money laundering and organized crime," will turn over wiretaps from their investigation to the FBI, saying publicly of the recordings—on which Torshin is referred to by Alexander Romanov, a mob-linked former Russian banker, as "El Padrino," meaning "godfather"—that "Mr. Trump's son [Donald Trump Jr.] should be concerned." Prosecutors eventually decide not to charge Torshin, not for lack of evidence but because they do not believe the Kremlin would extradite him to Spain.[9]

In 2013, the then twenty-four-year-old Maria Butina begins a romantic relationship with the then fifty-four-year-old Paul Erickson, an influential GOP operative and NRA member.[10] According to a July 2018 *Mother Jones* summary of NRA-Russia collusion and subsequent indictments against Butina, Butina was hoping, through Erickson, to establish a back channel between the Kremlin and the Republican leadership.[11] In short order, she is cohabiting with Erickson, and Erickson has begun paying many of her expenses through a company established for this exclusive purpose called "Bridges, LLC."[12]

By the fall of 2013, Erickson has assisted Butina in getting close to NRA president David Keene; in November, Butina and Torshin host Keene in Moscow.[13] In January 2014, Keene publishes an essay by Torshin in the *Washington Times*, where Keene is editor of the opinion pages. Torshin and Butina "join Keene for meetings" at the 2014 NRA convention in Indianapolis, Indiana, and in the fall of 2014, Erickson travels to Moscow with Butina for a gun-rights event.[14]

In February 2015, Trump declines to renew his contract with the NBC reality show *The Apprentice*, confirming something that has been an open secret in GOP circles since 2013—that he plans a run for the presidency.[15] The assumption that Trump will seek the White House in 2016 is predicated in part on statements made by Trump to Republican leaders in New York in December 2013, at which point he "predicted he would begin [his presidential run] in 2015."[16] In March 2015, both Trump and Torshin attend the annual NRA conference in Nashville, Tennessee, and have a "jovial exchange," according to Torshin. Butina is also at the conference and has a "private meeting" with a "political candidate"; it is not known if the candidate was Trump.[17] Torshin leaves the 2015 NRA conference considering himself now an "acquaintance" of Trump's.[18] On November 8, 2015, he will tweet from his personal Twitter account, in response to allegations of racism against Trump, "I know Donald Trump (through NRA). [He is] a decent person."[19] In 2017, Torshin will secure an invite to the National Prayer Breakfast and a spot on the president's schedule afterward for a private audience. According to five sources who spoke to Yahoo News, Trump's team cancels the post–Prayer Breakfast Trump-Torshin meeting because Torshin is suspected of being a "godfather" in the Russia mafia.[20] The White House will later say that no such meeting was ever scheduled.[21] Trump will deny having ever met Torshin.[22]

From the moment Trump formally announces his presidential candidacy on June 16, 2015, he tends to discuss two topics with great regularity: first, how good he will be at "getting along" with the Russians and "making deals" with them; second, how well he knows Vladimir Putin and, moreover, Putin's perspective on whom he can (and whom he wants to) "make deals" with.[23]

On July 11, 2015, less than a month after he announces his candidacy, Trump is at a libertarian event in Las Vegas called "Freedom-Fest" conducting a Q&A session. He calls on a young woman from Russia—Maria Butina—who says she'd like to know Trump's position on sanctions and also what sort of relationship he would like to have with Putin and Russia if he is elected president.[24] The press conference is being recorded. Trump answers her question by saying, "I know Putin, and I'll tell you what, we get along with Putin. Putin has no respect for President Obama. Big problem. Big problem. . . . I believe I would get along very nicely with Putin. . . . I don't think you'd need the sanctions. I think that we would get along very, very well. I really believe that."[25] Trump also expresses the view that the United States "has driven [Russia and China] together with the big oil deals that are being made"—the implication being that it would be better for Russian oil to flow westward rather than eastward, and that the anti-Russia policies of the Obama administration have engendered greater Russian-Chinese cooperation.[26]

Ten days after he says at a televised event that he opposes sanctions on Russia, Trump receives an invitation to come to Moscow from Aras Agalarov. The invitation, communicated by Emin Agalarov's publicist Rob Goldstone to Trump's secretary, is ostensibly for Aras's birthday party in November 2015—but contains a promise that Trump can meet with Putin in person if he comes to the party. Goldstone tells Trump's secretary that Emin will set up the meeting with Putin if Trump agrees to it.[27]

Within sixty days of Trump's telling Butina at FreedomFest that he doesn't see the need for sanctions on Russia, longtime Trump business partner and Russian mafia-linked fixer Felix Sater approaches Trump's attorney Michael Cohen with a new business opportunity.[28] Sater has been promising Trump a new Moscow tower deal since 2005 but has been unable to deliver; now, he has a willing investor by the name of Andrei Rozov.[29] Sater and Rozov have both been on the executive board of a Moscow real estate company called Mirax Group since 2008, but until Trump announces he is running for president, Rozov betrays no interest in partnering with Trump.[30] Now, he agrees to let Sater approach Cohen with the idea. Sater follows a September email proposing the idea to Cohen and Trump with an October email that contains both a signed letter of intent from Rozov and a note from Sater saying that Trump's agreeing to build a Trump World Tower Moscow would "possibly fix relations between the countries [Russia and the United States]."[31] It appears that at least the September communication between Sater and Cohen was kept from everyone at the Trump Organization but Trump; on September 30, 2015, Alan Garten, the chief legal officer of the Trump Organization, tells ABC News that "there's really no direct relationship" between Sater and the Trump Organization and "I don't know that he ever brought any deals." [32] The statement is false.

In October 2015—while Cohen is communicating with Sater on a Trump Tower Moscow deal even as his client, Donald Trump, runs for president—Cohen receives yet another offer from Russia (Trump's third since 2013, at a minimum) to build a Trump Tower in Moscow. The proposal comes from Russian billionaire Sergei Gordeev, whom the *Washington Post* calls a "Moscow real estate mogul who served through 2010 as a Russian legislator." [33] Gordeev indicates, through an intermediary—"an international financier [Gordeev] had worked with in the past, Giorgi Rtskhiladze," according to the *Post*—that the deal he's offering Trump would involve a "Trump-branded residential development." [34] In October 2015, Gordeev and Rtskhiladze send Cohen a thirteen-page proposal and pictures of the prospective site. Cohen turns down the request only because, as he explains to Rtskhiladze, Trump is already working on a deal for a Trump Tower in Moscow. [35]

Sater tells Cohen in his note in October that "we" (Sater and Cohen) "will help [Putin] agree on [the] message" the construction of the tower is intended to embody: "that commerce & business are much better and more practical than politics." [36] Sater tells Cohen and Trump that the goal of this deal is to "help world peace and make a lot of money." [37] What exactly Trump must do to "help world peace" in order to "make a lot of money" is not specified in Sater's note—but when Trump mentions Russia on the campaign trail, much of the time he emphasizes the need to get along with Moscow and, more particularly, to make deals with Putin that would include eliminating sanctions against Russia. It is the fifth month of his presidential campaign.

On November 3, Sater writes Cohen to say, "I know how to play it, and we will get this done. Buddy, our boy can become President of the United States of America and we can engineer it. I will get all of Putin's team to buy in on this." [38] By the time he sends this note, Sater has lined up financing for the Trump-Rozov tower with VTB—a then sanctioned Kremlin-owned bank. [39] The next month, however, new sanctions are leveled against VTB, meaning that unless Trump wins the presidency and removes U.S. sanctions on Russia, he will not be able to get the money that Sater has secured for him.[40] Sater, knowing the connection between Trump's Russia policy and his ability to get a Trump Tower Moscow approved by the Kremlin, adds in his November 2015 email to Cohen that he is "eager to show video clips to his Russian contacts of instances of Mr. Trump speaking glowingly about Russia, and . . . he would arrange for Mr. Putin to praise Mr. Trump's business acumen." "If he [Putin] says it we own this election," Sater writes Cohen. "America[']s most difficult adversary agreeing that Donald is a good guy to negotiate [with]."[41] Sater's view is that Trump announcing— and Putin implicitly blessing—a Trump Tower Moscow in late 2015 or early 2016 will help propel Trump's presidential campaign forward. It is the most explicit juxtaposition of politics and business that any of Trump's business associates have proposed to date.

In January 2016, however, that mark will be bested—as Cohen contacts Dmitry Peskov, the Kremlin's spokesman, to directly ask for the Kremlin's help with Trump's Trump Tower Moscow deal with Rozov.[42] That Cohen is seeking Kremlin assistance on a financial transaction even as Trump is pushing his pro-Russia foreign policy with voters— and that Trump has chosen to hide this transaction not only from voters but even from many at his own company—is an indication that Trump and his team are working on two tracks with the hope that each will reinforce the other.

By late 2015, Torshin is hosting two dinners in Moscow for a high-level NRA delegation that includes NRA president David Keene, top NRA donor Joe Gregory, NRA board member Pete Brownell, and Sheriff David A. Clarke, a Trump supporter who will later become a key Trump surrogate.[43] They are joined at one of their dinners by Dmitry Rogozin, a "hardline deputy to Putin" who is at the time (and still is) under U.S. sanctions.[44] During the delegation's visit, members are also introduced, according to reporting by McClatchy, to other "influential Russian government and business figures."[45]

In December 2015, retired U.S. Army lieutenant general Michael Flynn, who has been advising Donald Trump and four other GOP candidates on national security issues for at least two months, goes to a gala in Moscow in celebration of the Kremlin's media outlet, RT— for whom Flynn works as an analyst.[46] He is seated immediately to the right of Putin. Former U.S. ambassador to Russia Michael McFaul will later tell NBC News, "Of course, it is not coincidence that General Flynn was placed next to President Putin. Flynn was considered a close Trump advisor. . . . Why else would they want him there?"[47] Flynn will subsequently fail to report any of his income from the event— approximately $40,000.[48]

One of the other candidates Flynn is advising is Ben Carson; one of Carson's national security advisers is George Papadopoulos.[49] Papadopoulos will be hired as a member of Trump's national security team, after an interview with Trump campaign cochair Sam Clovis, at a time when Flynn and a just-hired Jeff Sessions (R-AL) constitute the entirety of the Trump campaign's national security apparatus.[50]

In 2016, the annual NRA conference is held in Louisville, Kentucky, and once again Torshin and Butina attend. A few days before the conference, Butina's boyfriend, Erickson, writes Trump campaign aide Rick Dearborn to inform the Trump campaign that the Kremlin is "quietly but actively seeking a dialogue with the United States that isn't forthcoming under the current administration," adding that "the Kremlin believes that the only possibility of a true reset in this relationship would be with a new Republican in the White House."[51] Erickson notes that Torshin will attempt to make "first contact" with the Trump campaign at the NRA convention.[52] Erickson adds, "Putin is deadly serious about building a good relationship with Mr. Trump. He wants to extend an invitation to Mr. Trump to visit him in the Kremlin before the election."[53]

At the same time that Torshin approaches Dearborn through Erickson, he also uses Rick Clay, whom the *New York Times* describes as "an advocate for conservative Christian causes," to get the same message to Dearborn: Putin wants to meet with Trump, and Torshin wants to meet with Trump first to set up the meeting.[54] Dearborn sends the email from Clay on to Jared Kushner, who nixes the idea, according to two sources interviewed by the *New York Times*.[55] It is unknown whom else, if anyone, Dearborn or Kushner pass the email to after reading it, but in fact Torshin does end up dining with Donald Trump Jr. at the NRA convention several days later.[56]

Per *Vanity Fair*, Trump Jr.'s attorney Alan Futerfas says the two men engaged in no more than "gun-related small talk," but according to McClatchy and the *New York Times*, Torshin was in fact trying to set up a one-on-one meeting with candidate Trump at an event honoring wounded veterans being hosted at a location near the convention; he even told the campaign he was bringing a gift to the event for Melania.[57]

NRA expenditures on the 2016 presidential primaries and general election were far higher than the NRA initially reported—and eventually reach and exceed $70 million, according to a McClatchy report in January 2018.[58] The figure is a record-shattering one for the NRA.[59] Trump, who had originally promised voters he would spend $1 billion of his own money on his campaign, by the end of the primary season has spent only about 6.5 percent of that total—while paying his own companies $12 million from his campaign coffers in reimbursements for travel, lodging, meals, and other services.[60] In May 2016, upon clinching the nomination, he announces that he will not be financing his general election campaign and will take funds from the Republican National Committee (RNC) instead.[61] Massive spending by the NRA and the RNC on Trump's behalf make it possible for him to abandon his self-funding promise from the primary and nevertheless be adequately funded for the November election. In the end, the NRA spends more than the billionaire Trump does on his own election.

The FBI and Special Counsel Robert Mueller will eventually reveal they have initiated an investigation into whether Torshin and Butina had any effect on the NRA's remarkable outlay of funds on Trump's behalf; Torshin will later be sanctioned by the U.S. Treasury Department and Butina will be indicted. As noted by *Vanity Fair* in June 2018, "The FBI and special counsel Robert Mueller are investigating meetings between NRA officials and powerful Russian operatives, trying to determine if those contacts had anything to do with the gun group spending $30 million [in direct support] to help elect Donald Trump—

triple what it invested on behalf of Mitt Romney in 2012. The use of foreign money in American political campaigns is illegal."[62]

On October 4, 2016, just a month before the presidential election, Paul Erickson writes an email to an acquaintance that reads, "Unrelated to specific presidential campaigns, I've been involved in securing a VERY private line of communication between the Kremlin and key [GOP] leaders through, of all conduits, the NRA."[63]

Annotated History

From the moment Trump formally announces his presidential candidacy on June 16, 2015, he tends to discuss two topics with great regularity: first, how good he will be at "getting along" with the Russians and "making deals" with them; second, how well he knows Vladimir Putin and, moreover, Putin's perspective on whom he can (and whom he wants to) "make deals" with.

In an interview with Fox News host Bill O'Reilly in June 2015, Trump remarked, "I was over in Moscow two years ago and I will tell you—you can get along with those people and get along with them well. You can make deals with those people. Obama can't."[64] It is unclear how Trump knew, in June 2015, the ease with which he personally could "make deals" with the Russians and that Obama could not. One explanation comes in an interview with Sean Hannity three days after Trump's conversation with O'Reilly. When asked if he's ever had contact with Vladimir Putin, Trump answers "yes" and adds, "I was there two years ago. . . . And I got to meet everybody."[65] When Hannity pressed Trump to confirm that he'd spoken to Putin during the pageant, Trump replied, cryptically, "I don't want to say," repeating that answer twice.[66] He also guaranteed that Putin hated Obama, though once again he wouldn't confirm whether the information had come from Putin himself.[67] The next month—the same month as FreedomFest—Trump told CNN's Anderson Cooper, with respect to Putin, "I get along with him fine. . . . He hates Obama. He doesn't respect Obama. . . . [H]e has no respect for Obama. Has a hatred for Obama."[68] Perhaps most telling was a comment Trump made to Cooper about how, as president, he would work to terminate former NSA contractor Edward Snowden's continued asylum in Russia: "If I'm president, Putin says [to Snowden], hey, boom, you're gone [from Russia]. I guarantee you this."[69]

Trump's 2015 comments assuring American voters that he *had* met with Putin and indeed knew his mind on presidential politics—at a time when Trump was himself running for president—are so voluminous that only a few of them can be compiled here. On July 15, 2015, Trump told Hannity, "Putin has no respect for President Obama."[70] On July 26, 2015, he wrote on Twitter, "Putin knows that Obama is a danger to the world. Putin will respect President Trump."[71] At a July 30, 2015, presser at his golf course in Scotland, he observed that "[Putin] hates Obama."[72] A March 2017 CNN compendium of Trump-Putin quotes also reveals that Trump assured American voters he would get along with Putin during events on June 16 and 29 (telling the City Club of Chicago, "I had the Miss Universe over there [in Russia] two years ago; I got to know these guys well. We can get along with them well. We can get along with them well"); July 8, 26, and 30; August 12, 14, 20, 23, and 29; and September 23.[73]

As related by *Rolling Stone* in April 2018, Torshin is a member of Putin's political party with "close ties to Russia's internal security service, the FSB, which awarded him a medal in 2016."

According to a May 2018 NPR article, Torshin had spent "years of travel [dating] back to 2009 . . . cultivat[ing] ties with American conservatives."[74] The article quotes Steve Hall, a retired CIA chief of Russian operations:

> [Vladimir] Putin and probably the Russian intelligence services saw [Torshin's connections] as something that they could leverage in the United States. They reach out to a guy like Torshin and say, "Hey, can you make contact with the NRA and some other conservatives . . . so that we can have connectivity from Moscow into those conservative parts of American politics should we need them?" And that's basically just wiring the United States for sound, if you will, in preparation for whatever they might need down the road.[75]

NPR reported that Torshin took a trip to Alaska in 2009 seeking an audience with Sarah Palin, a request he communicated to the Alaska governor's office through Russian ambassador Sergey Kislyak. While Palin did not meet with Torshin, government records indicate that Alaska's lieutenant governor, Sean Parnell—now the state's governor—was slated to meet with Torshin in her stead. He now says that he does not recall the meeting.[76]

Some of Torshin's U.S. activities puzzle observers. In March 2015, he gave a speech in Washington, D.C., in his capacity as the deputy governor of the Bank of Russia, and one attendee, a former U.S. official, told NPR that "for anyone at the lunch who's remotely familiar with finance or the world of central banking, Torshin demonstrated no significant expertise in either realm."[77]

Within sixty days of Trump's telling Butina at FreedomFest that he doesn't see the need for sanctions on Russia, longtime Trump business partner and Russian mafia-linked fixer Felix Sater approaches Trump's attorney Michael Cohen with a new business opportunity. Sater has been promising Trump a new Moscow tower deal since 2005 but has been unable to deliver; now, he has a willing investor by the name of Andrei Rozov. Sater and Rozov have both been on the executive board of a Moscow real estate company called Mirax Group since 2008, but until Trump announces he is running for president, Rozov betrays no interest in partnering with Trump. Now, he agrees to let Sater approach Cohen with the idea.

Cohen and Sater are childhood friends from Brighton Beach, also known as "Little Odessa," in the southern portion of the New York City borough of Brooklyn, where Sater's father was a small-time crime boss and Cohen a boy who admired the area's many Russian émigré gangs from afar.[78] By 2015, Cohen had become Trump's most loyal foot soldier. As reported by *Business Insider* in April 2018, Cohen once said, "If you do something wrong [to Mr. Trump], I'm going to come at you,

grab you by the neck, and I'm not going to let you go until I'm finished."[79] It's no surprise, then, that Cohen has been called Trump's "pit
bull," and told *Vanity Fair* in a September 2017 article that "I'm the
guy who would take a bullet for the president. I'd never walk away."[80]

Cohen, who attended what *Politico* calls "the worst law school in
America," was found by a judge reviewing his client records to have
only three clients: Sean Hannity, GOP fund-raiser Elliott Broidy, and
Donald Trump.[81] The Republican National Committee named Broidy a
deputy finance chair of the RNC alongside Cohen in April 2017, while
Hannity acted as a Trump adviser during the 2016 campaign and has
continued to advise him throughout Trump's presidency. Broidy would
eventually be caught in a "hush money" payoff of a former mistress
almost identical in its mechanism and its secrecy to the one Cohen
pleaded guilty to orchestrating on Donald Trump's behalf in August
2018—with Broidy's mistress using the same Cohen-recommended
attorney to negotiate her payment from Broidy that one of Trump's
mistresses used to get a $130,000 payment from Trump.[82] According
to a March 2018 *New York Times* article, a witness cooperating with
Robert Mueller in the Trump-Russia investigation, George Nader, has
revealed to the special counsel a yearlong effort to turn Broidy "into
an instrument of influence at the White House for the rulers of Saudi
Arabia and the United Arab Emirates." The article says, "Hundreds of
pages of correspondence between the two men reveal an active effort
to cultivate President Trump on behalf of the two oil-rich Arab monarchies. . . . High on the agenda of the two men. . . . [is] repeatedly pressing the president to meet privately outside the White House with the
leader of the UAE."[83] The *Times* further reports Nader offering Broidy
more than $1 billion in contracts for the latter's private security com-
pany in exchange for preferred access to Trump by the UAE and its
agents, including Nader. It is not yet known what if any conversations
Trump's attorney, Cohen, had with Broidy about the UAE when Cohen
was representing Broidy and both men were Trump-appointed deputy
finance chairs at the Republican National Committee.

Cohen's tiny client roster is partly explained by the fact that he was, for a long time, also an executive vice president at the Trump Organization. In testimony before the House Intelligence Committee in December 2017, Donald Trump Jr. explained his belief that, in conversations among executives at Trump Tower, as long as one of the people in the room is a lawyer—or, as applicable, also a lawyer in addition to being a Trump Organization executive—anything said in the room is covered by attorney-client privilege. All that is required, per Trump Jr.'s testimony, is that there be "a lawyer in the room during the discussion."[84] This is, of course, incorrect.

In September 2015, per an ABC News report from August 2017, Felix Sater approached Cohen with what he called a "signature development opportunity": a chance to build a Trump Tower in Moscow separate from the one Trump had previously agreed to build (and was still under a letter of intent to build) in Moscow's Crocus City complex with the Agalarovs.[85] At the end of that September, reported ABC, "Trump Organization officials told ABC News that Sater inflated his connections to the company. Alan Garten, a senior Trump Organization attorney, told ABC that 'there's really no direct relationship' between Sater and [the Trump Organization]. 'To be honest, I don't know that he ever brought any deals,' Garten said."[86] Garten's statement was inaccurate at best and dishonest at worst: not only had Sater helped secure partners for Trump's Trump SoHo project—one of the most important projects of Trump's career—but he'd also sent a number of Russian oligarchs in Trump's direction. Whoever told Garten to deny Sater's long-standing relationship with the Trump Organization and his ongoing value to Trump's bottom line was presumably anxious to forestall public discovery of that arrangement should Sater's long-awaited "Moscow deal" finally bear fruit—as looked to be the case by September 2015. According to ABC, Cohen kept Sater's proposal from everyone at the Trump Organization but Trump.[87]

Several weeks later, on October 13, 2015, Sater emailed Cohen, saying that he'd secured an investor for his proposal and was enclosing, for Trump's signature, a letter of intent. Sater had appended a note to the letter of intent that read, in full, according to a September 8, 2017, story by *New York Times* reporter Maggie Haberman:

Dear Michael,

Attached is the signed LOI (Letter of Intent) by Andrey
Rozov. Please have Mr. Trump counter-sign, signed and sent
back. Lets make this happen and build a Trump Moscow.
And possibly fix relations between the countries by showing
everyone that commerce & business are much better and more
practical than politics. That should be Putins message as well,
and we will help him agree on that message. Help world peace
and make a lot of money, I would say thats a great lifetime goal
for us to go after.

Sincerely,

Felix Sater[88]

Trump signed the letter of intent almost immediately, according
to Cohen's statement to ABC News.[89] By signing a document already
signed by a Russian investor, Trump thereby agreed in principle to
"make [Trump World Tower Moscow] happen" by commingling business and politics. Building the tower, said Sater, would "fix relations
between [Russia and the United States]," implying, moreover, that
politics was improved, rather than compromised, when overlaid with
"commerce & business"—which Sater called "better and more practical" than politics on its own. Trump's signature authorized Sater to
begin trying to (as he had said in his note) convince Vladimir Putin
to "agree on" a political message that would gloss over the quid pro
quo implicit in the Trump-Rozov deal. As Trump had for months been
advocating better relations with Putin, Sater's proposal that Trump simultaneously "help world peace and make a lot of money" was consistent with the juxtaposition of ambitions the businessman had long
ago embraced. The "peace" Sater proposed was to be won by Trump
capitulating to the Kremlin on foreign policy as a political candidate
and—if he won—president of the United States. What would follow
was "mak[ing] a lot of money."

On November 3, Sater writes Cohen to say, "I know how to play it, and we will get this done. Buddy, our boy can become President of the United States of America and we can engineer it. I will get all of Putin's team to buy in on this."

As reported by Natasha Bertrand for *Business Insider* on September 8, 2017, "Trump World Tower Moscow" was to be built in "Moscow City," the Russian capital's nominal financial district.[90]

Sater's November 3 email is notable in several respects: first, in it a Trump business partner claimed ready access to the president of Russia and his top aides; second, Sater connected, for reasons unclear at the time, Putin's patronage of Trump and the probability of Trump being able to win the presidency; and third, Sater committed to paper that a single real estate deal—with Trump on one end and, it appears, "Putin's team" on the other—would allow a presidential election's outcome to be "engineered."

In an August 2017 interview with the *Huffington Post*, Cohen claimed to have spoken with Trump about the Trump World Tower Moscow deal only three times, despite the fact that his friend Sater had, by then, been working on such a deal, with Trump's knowledge, for twelve years.[91] More puzzlingly, Cohen told the *Huffington Post* that Trump was "barely aware" of the details of the project from its inception to its termination, a period of time we now know, from a May 2018 Yahoo News report, was nine months—from the fourth month of Trump's presidential run to the month he clinched the Republican nomination.[92] As Yahoo News noted at the time, Cohen had previously said, in a statement to Congress, that he'd given up on the project in January 2016; only once prosecutors and congressional investigators acquired Cohen's text messages and emails did they discover that he'd made false statements on that score. Sater confirmed to Yahoo News that he had provided all of his texts and emails to and from Cohen to Special Counsel Robert Mueller's team, as well as to the House Permanent Select Committee on Intelligence and the Senate's Intelligence and Judiciary Committees.[93] But perhaps the most unlikely fact

Cohen fed to the *Huffington Post* in his August 30, 2017, interview was that, in the many months he'd been working on the Trump World Tower Moscow project for Trump, he'd spoken with Trump about it for a total of only "four minutes"—and that in the first and third of the three conversations the businessman had said a total of four words, all monosyllabic.[94] Investigators are unlikely to find either claim plausible, particularly in light of Cohen's widely professed loyalty to Trump during the period the statements were made and the confirmation, by 2018, that Cohen had provided inaccurate testimony to Congress on the same subject.

By November, Sater has lined up financing for the Trump-Rozov tower with VTB—a then sanctioned Kremlin-owned bank. The next month, however, new sanctions are leveled against VTB, meaning that unless Trump wins the presidency and removes Russian sanctions, he will not be able to get the money that Sater has secured for him.

Sater's use of VTB for the funding of Trump World Tower Moscow brings an entirely new perspective to NBC News's reporting, in June 2017, that "[t]he Trump administration was gearing up to lift sanctions on Russia when the president took office," and that, having been given no prior warning of Trump's intentions, the unilateral ending of sanctions on Russia was only avoided by "career diplomats [at the State Department] ginn[ing] up pressure in Congress to block the move."[95] Had Trump's long-secret plans on Russian sanctions been successful— and while voters knew Trump opposed such sanctions, they didn't know he was prepared to unilaterally lift them upon taking office— VTB would eventually have been freed to release its promised funding for Trump World Tower Moscow. While perhaps Donald Trump Jr. would have managed the project instead of his father, the fact remains that the tower would have been financially feasible and that any returns from the deal would have—in due time, following his presidency— gone to Trump himself.

By late 2015, Torshin is hosting two dinners in Moscow for a high-level NRA delegation that includes NRA president David Keene, top NRA donor Joe Gregory, NRA board member Pete Brownell, and Sheriff David A. Clarke, a Trump supporter who will later become a key Trump surrogate. They are joined at one of their dinners by Dmitry Rogozin, a "hardline deputy to Putin" who is at the time (and still is) under U.S. sanctions. During the delegation's visit, members are also introduced, according to reporting by McClatchy, to other "influential Russian government and business figures."

It wasn't just the NRA that the Kremlin wanted to invite to Moscow in 2015. Yulya Alferova, the organizer of the 2013 Miss Universe pageant and an agent of the Agalarovs—themselves Kremlin agents—tweeted at Trump on November 12, 2015, "Donald Trump, are you going to visit Moscow? Many thing [sic] to discuss!"[96] Alferova did not follow up her tweet with another, and Trump did not reply to her via Twitter, so what needed to be discussed between Trump and the Agalarovs is unclear. The picture Alferova posted with her tweet, however, was the same one she had posted two years earlier, on November 11, 2013: a picture of herself, Trump, Keith Schiller, Emin Agalarov, Phil Ruffin, and another man looking with great interest at something on a computer screen.[97] "Waiting for your business to start in Russia, Mr. Trump," she'd tweeted to Trump at the time, with the hashtags "Russia" and "Moscow," and tagging Emin Agalarov.[98] The implication was that she wanted Trump to come to Russia in 2015 to discuss the very same "business" he'd been reviewing with Emin Agalarov in 2013: the Trump-Agalarov deal for a Trump Tower Moscow in the Crocus City complex in Russia's capital. Just a few weeks after Alferova's tweet to Trump, Michael Flynn, a Trump adviser, went to Moscow and met with Vladimir Putin.[99]

That Flynn is now cooperating with Special Counsel Robert Mueller following a guilty plea for having made false statements in December 2017 may help explain why Trump suddenly knows Flynn far less well than he once did.[100] In a May 2017 interview with NBC News, Trump said, "I don't know that I knew [Flynn] in 2015."[101] Yet Flynn told the *Washington Post* in 2016 that it was *Trump* who had requested their August 2015 meeting and who instructed his staff to arrange it.[102] And a *New Yorker* article notes that the two men connected almost immediately: "In August 2015, Flynn went to New York to meet Trump for the first time. They were scheduled to talk for thirty minutes; the conversation lasted ninety. Flynn was deeply impressed."[103] Indeed, Flynn said to his interviewer, of Trump, "I knew [in August 2015] he was going to be President of the United States."[104] But in fact Flynn had more than just one 2015 conversation with Trump. He told the *Washington Post* in August 2016 that well prior to his official hire by the Trump campaign in February 2016, he "consciously made a decision once I felt the country was at such risk" to begin "advising five of the [GOP] candidates running for president. They all reached out to me . . . [including] Donald Trump. . . . They would ask me about national security, what's happening in the world, my thoughts on particular issues. I met with all of them. Some of them I met with more often."[105]

Flynn's advice to the GOP candidates, especially on the subject of Russia, is unknown. However, Flynn had a long history of exhibiting a special affinity for Russia. As the *New Yorker* outlined in its February 2017 feature on the retired U.S. Army lieutenant general, in 2013, while still the Defense Intelligence Agency (DIA) director, Flynn received permission to meet in Moscow with a group of officers from Russia's largest foreign intelligence agency, the GRU.[106] Despite forces within the U.S. government pressuring him not to go to Moscow, Flynn not only insisted on making the trip but asked to go to Moscow a second time upon his return.[107] His request was denied.[108] According to Steven Hall, the chief of Russia operations at the CIA at the time, "[Flynn] wanted to build a relationship with his counterparts in the G.R.U., which seemed, at best, quaint and naïve. Every time we have tried to have some sort of meaningful cooperation with the Russians, it's almost always been manipulated and turned back against us."[109]

If indeed Trump reached out to Flynn because of his reputation for seeking cooperation with the Russians—including Russian intelligence—Hall's concern was prescient in this instance as well. Per a March 31, 2017, *Guardian* article, Flynn went to work for the Kremlin's propaganda outlet, RT, as soon as he left the DIA in 2014. As if that were insufficient to underscore Flynn's unusual affinity for Russia, the lieutenant general had, while still with the DIA in 2014, been in secret communication—a communication the DIA required him to report—with a Russian-British graduate student, Svetlana Lokhova, whom he met in February 2014.[110] While no links between Lokhova and Russian intelligence have yet been found, the young woman is nevertheless considered a "leading expert" on Soviet espionage and was one of "two or three" non-GRU personnel in the world granted special access to the military intelligence unit's archives.[111] She would therefore have appealed to Flynn on the basis of his seeming obsession with the GRU, whether or not Lokhova was a Russian asset seeking to seduce or recruit him. The two were close enough that in one 2014 email he signed off as "General Misha"—Russian for "Michael."[112] All this had occurred by the time Trump asked his staff to contact Flynn and set up a meeting in August 2015, after which Trump asked Flynn to advise him on national security issues and foreign policy.

As the *Guardian* detailed, Flynn's intersections with Russia were highly unusual for an American general; in 2015 alone he was paid for two speaking engagements in D.C. sponsored by Russian entities, one of them Kaspersky Lab—a cybersecurity company linked to the Kremlin.[113]

Just days after Flynn returned from his dinner with Putin, Putin issued what a May 2017 documentary by Dutch television program *Zembla* termed "almost an endorsement" of Trump: at a December 17, 2015, news conference, Putin volunteered that "Donald Trump is a talented person" and "the absolute leader of the presidential race. He wants to move to a different level of relations—to more solid, deeper relations with Russia—and how can Russia not welcome that? We welcome that."[114] Trump responded immediately, telling ABC News in a statement, "It is always a great honor to be so nicely complimented by a man so highly respected within his own country and beyond. I have always felt that Russia and the United States should be able to work well with each other towards defeating terrorism and restoring world peace, not to mention trade and all of the other benefits derived from mutual respect."[115]

Publicly available Trump-Russia documents and reporting do not tell us whether Flynn being seated next to Putin at the RT gala was the work of Felix Sater's outreach to "Putin's team" or a by-product of Flynn's known association with Trump—or both. But we do know that American politics was very much on the Russian president's mind during this period: he also invited and sat with at the gala a fringe American politician, Green Party presidential candidate Jill Stein, who would be in a position to spoil a Hillary Clinton victory in a very close 2016 election.[116]

CHAPTER FIVE

THE NATIONAL SECURITY ADVISORY COMMITTEE

January to March 2016

Summary

IN THE FIRST THREE MONTHS OF 2016, TRUMP ASSEMBLES A National Security Advisory Committee whose members surprise experts with their absence of qualifications. Several have no relevant national security experience; others do but are unknown to professionals in the field; and at least one Trump national security adviser expected to be named to the committee—retired U.S. Army lieutenant general Michael Flynn—is not named at all. A number of Trump's national security advisers are the subject of puzzling contacts with the Russians: one was recruited to be a Russian spy by the SVR RF (Russia's foreign intelligence service) in 2013; another had been part of a secret plot to sell Russian arms to Syrian rebels in 2013; another worked as an analyst for Kremlin-funded propaganda outlet RT in 2015; another will be approached by a Kremlin agent in Italy just two weeks after his engagement on the committee and be asked to serve as an intermediary between the Kremlin and the Trump campaign, an offer to which the Trump adviser will immediately agree; and yet another Trump national security adviser, Erik Prince—who, like Flynn, is a "shadow" adviser never formally recognized by Trump—will secretly meet with a source close to the Kremlin in the Seychelles in 2017. At the first meeting of the committee, one of its members intimates to campaign officials that he is "acting as an intermediary" for the Kremlin, and he will thereafter be promoted to Trump's speech-writing team.[1] The committee's chairman will be accused of giving false and misleading statements about secret meetings with the Russians, while its director will be accused of giving false statements about changes he made to the GOP platform to benefit the Kremlin.[2]

As the committee's director, J. D. Gordon, will tell CNN in 2017, at the first meeting of Trump's National Security Advisory Committee on March 31, 2016, at the Trump International Hotel in D.C., Trump orders the committee to change the GOP platform at the July Republican National Convention in Cleveland in a way that, per the *Washington Post*, "guts [its] anti-Russia stance on Ukraine"; after Gordon successfully changes the party's Ukraine plank at the convention he will say to CNN's Jim Acosta that "this was the language Donald Trump himself wanted and advocated for back in March [at the Trump International Hotel]."[3] At the same meeting, the Kremlin's new "intermediary," George Papadopoulos, reveals to the group—including Trump—that he is working with the Russians to effectuate a Kremlin-Trump back channel.[4] Reports of what happens next vary wildly, but three attendees at the meeting will later tell Special Counsel Robert Mueller and congressional committees that neither Sessions nor Trump offered any objections to Papadopoulos's continuing to conduct back-channel negotiations with the Kremlin.[5] When asked in 2017 about the March 31, 2016, meeting and his response to Papadopoulos identifying himself as an agent for the Kremlin, Trump, "who recently boasted of having 'one of the great memories of all time,'" according to the *Washington Post*, will say, "I don't remember much about that meeting."[6]

The Facts

IN THE THREE MOST CRITICAL MONTHS OF THE REPUBLI-
can primary season—after which all Republican presidential contend-
ers except Donald Trump, Texas senator Ted Cruz, and Ohio governor
John Kasich are eliminated—Trump puts together a national security
team he calls his National Security Advisory Committee.[7] The overwhelming majority of pre-election back-channel contacts between the
Trump campaign and the Kremlin will involve at least one member
of the National Security Advisory Committee, Paul Manafort, or both.
The pressure on Trump to build a national security advisory apparatus had increased exponentially once he won ten of the first seventeen
GOP primaries and caucuses—coming in second in four of the remaining seven, and in two of those (Alaska and Iowa) missing the top spot
by only 3 percent.[8]

In mid-February, however, at a time when only two states have
voted—Iowa, won by Ted Cruz, and New Hampshire, won by Trump—
billionaire Thomas Barrack, a good friend of Donald Trump and of
Ivanka Trump and Jared Kushner, has lunch with an old friend of his,
Paul Manafort.[9] Manafort has spent years making millions "working
for a corrupt pro-Russian political party" and "promot[ing] Russian
interests" in former Soviet republics like Ukraine and Kyrgyzstan.[10]
Manafort tells Barrack that "I really need to get to [Trump]" and makes
an unusual offer to convince Barrack to help him: he says he will work
for Trump for free, and even though Trump has no particular reason to
believe then that he will become the nominee, Manafort offers to become Trump's convention manager for the Republican National Convention, which is still four months away.[11] In October 2017, the *New
York Times* will publish the "talking points" Manafort used in convincing Trump to hire him. They include: "I am not looking for a paid job,"
"Position me as coming into the Trump campaign as 'your [Trump's]
guy,'" "I live in Trump Tower," and "When Black Manafort and Stone
[Manafort's old lobbying firm] worked for Trump, I managed the Mar

a Largo [*sic*] FAA [Federal Aviation Administration] problem Trump had." 12

Though Trump has known Manafort for many years, and knows him to be a well-paid lobbyist and consultant with clients around the world, Trump accepts Manafort's unusual offer to work for free on a delegate-counting operation still months in the future—at a political convention his campaign may never reach. Trump's comfort with Manafort, along with his friend Barrack's recommendation, may have carried the day: the *New York Times* reports that Trump and Manafort "had some business in the 1980s" and since then "had brushed shoulders over the years," with Manafort not only being one of Trump's tenants but at one point doing work for Trump "clear[ing] noisy airspace over Mr. Trump's Florida resort, Mar-a-Lago." 13 The *Times* also notes that Manafort "touted his overseas work"—work he did for a pro-Russia political party in Ukraine—in convincing Trump to bring him aboard the campaign.14

After joining Trump's team on March 28, 2016, Manafort becomes the de facto campaign manager for the entire Trump operation in well under three weeks.15 By April 6, CNN is reporting that "Trump met . . . with GOP strategist Paul Manafort, a huddle that suggests campaign changes could be in the works. . . . Two knowledgeable sources say Manafort, who was recently hired by Trump to lead his delegate operation, is taking on an expanded role." 16 By April 16, Manafort is already "[laying] out a vision for the Trump campaign" at a campaign meeting.17 By April 18, just three weeks after Manafort's hire, the campaign's former campaign manager, Corey Lewandowski, has been reduced to a "body man and scheduler," according to NBC News.18 How and why Manafort's takeover of Trump's presidential campaign happened as quickly as it did has never been fully explained, but *Politico* will report that Lewandowski was the victim of a "whisper" campaign by Manafort's former lobbying partner Roger Stone.19

Manafort's initial entreaties to Trump arrive at Trump Tower around February 29, 2016, the same day Trump receives an email from Rob Goldstone, Emin Agalarov's publicist, on behalf of Aras Agalarov—

as well as a letter from Agalarov himself.[20] Goldstone's note on behalf of Agalarov wishes Trump luck on Super Tuesday and lets him
know that his campaign has not only the elder Agalarov's "support" but
also "that of many of his important Russian friends and colleagues—
especially with reference to U.S./Russian relations."[21] The letter from
Aras says, in part, "many people in this country who appreciated your
statement that U.S. and Russia should work together more closely . . .
follow with great interest your bright electoral campaign. . . . [And] we
would like to wish you success in winning this major ballot and further
reinforcing your undisputed status as the front-runner for the Republican nomination for [the] U.S. Presidential Election."[22]

In March 2017, five months before Manafort is indicted on "charges
that he laundered millions of dollars through overseas shell companies,"
White House spokesman Sean Spicer will say that Manafort played a
"very limited role for a very limited amount of time" before walking
back his comments two days later.[23] In August 2017, Trump himself will
say of Manafort that he was with the campaign for a "very short period of time, relatively short period of time."[24] By August 2018, as the
jury is deliberating after the close of evidence in the first of Manafort's
two federal trials, Trump will eliminate the word "relatively" and say
Manafort "worked for me for a very short period of time."[25] In Spicer's
2018 book, *The Briefing*, he will contradict Trump on Manafort's role:

> Paul brought a much-needed maturity to the Trump cam-
> paign when it needed an experienced political professional
> operative. . . . [Before Manafort] there was no semblance of a
> campaign structure. . . . Paul immediately set up and staffed the
> political and communications operations necessary to take on
> the Clinton machine. The Manafort message was clear: Trump
> will be our nominee and our next president, and anyone who
> didn't want to work to that end could spend the next four years
> in political Siberia.[26]

The period between Manafort's hire by Trump and the day he quits
the campaign over his ties to pro-Russia politicians in Ukraine—

August 19, 2016—lasts nearly five months; after Manafort leaves the campaign, he has multiple additional conversations with Trump by telephone and continues to advise the White House on the Russia investigation as late as January 2017.[27]

Trump will repeatedly say that Manafort's charges have nothing to do with his work as an adviser to Trump's presidential campaign and then its chairman. But at Manafort's August 2018 federal trial in Virginia, "[a] Chicago bank CEO who thought he was being considered for positions in President Donald Trump's Cabinet" will testify under oath that he "helped facilitate $16 million in loans to Manafort during and after the campaign."[28] The *Washington Post* will call Manafort's trial "the prequel to the story of the Trump campaign's multiple contacts with Russia," given that Manafort worked somewhat suspiciously for "free" after years of working for millions on behalf of pro-Russian interests and given that the bulk of the campaign's contacts with Russian nationals came after his March 2016 hire.[29] It will later be revealed that Manafort was, at the time of his hire by Trump, "in debt to pro-Russia interests" by as much as $17 million, which may explain why in July 2016 he writes his old client, Russian oligarch Oleg Deripaska, through an intermediary to find out how he can use his work for Trump to "get whole."[30]

Around the time Trump begins discussions with Manafort about hiring him, he decides on March 3, 2016, to make Alabama senator Jeff Sessions, an early supporter, the chairman of his National Security Advisory Committee.[31] The committee already has one member, Carter Page, who in March 2016, unbeknownst to him or to anyone on the campaign, is being monitored by the FBI under a FISA warrant stemming from his 2013 interactions with Kremlin agents.[32]

Page, who at the time works in a building connected to Trump Tower by an atrium (and is consequently a "regular presence in Trump Tower," per CBS News), "volunteers" to work for Trump in December 2015—the same month Trump's unofficial or "shadow" national security adviser Michael Flynn dines with Vladimir Putin in Moscow.[33] In early January 2016, Page meets with Sam Clovis, who hires him after a simple Google search—which, presumably, fails to reveal that Page was under suspicion of being a Russian spy in 2013 as part of a highly publicized 2015 case involving Putin's foreign intelligence service, the SVR RF.[34] Page thereby becomes the first member of Trump's national security team and is soon joined by Flynn, acting as an informal adviser to the national security team, in February 2016.[35]

Page's brush with the FBI in 2013 involved suspicions that he was an unwitting or even witting Russian agent, having been identified by Russian intelligence agents in the United States as ripe for recruitment by the Kremlin.[36] In a 2015 court filing, a transcribed recording of a spy in Putin's SVR intelligence unit included discussions of Page: "[Page] got hooked on Gazprom [the Russian natural gas giant] thinking that if they have a project, he could rise up . . ." the spy said. "I also promised him a lot. . . . This is intelligence method to cheat, how else to work with foreigners? You promise a favor for a favor. You get the documents from him and tell him to go fuck himself." Court documents allege that Page agreed to and did provide documents about the U.S. energy business to the SVR.[37] In August 2013, Page would boast in a letter to a publisher, "I have had the privilege to serve as an informal advisor to the staff of the Kremlin"—despite having already been informed by the FBI that the Kremlin was actually seeking to recruit him as a spy.[38]

Page will testify before the House Permanent Select Committee on Intelligence that he was a volunteer with an "unpaid informal [Trump] committee" from his January interview with Clovis until his late March announcement as a member of Trump's National Security Advisory Committee, making him the senior member of the latter committee by tenure—over the committee's chairman, Jeff Sessions—by nearly two months.[39] According to the *Washington Post*, "As part of its broader investigation into potential collusion between the Trump campaign and the Russian government, the FBI continues to examine how Page joined the campaign and what conversations he may have had with Russian officials about the effort to interfere with the election—with or without the knowledge of Trump and his team—according to people familiar with the matter."[40] Investigators are asking, given that the SVR-linked Page appeared at Trump Tower asking for a job shortly after Flynn went to Moscow and dined with Putin, "Were Trump's connections to multiple Russia-friendly advisers mere coincidence, or evidence of a coordinated attempt to collude with a foreign government?"[41]

By late February 2016, as Manafort is preparing his pitch to Trump, and Sessions is days from being hired, Flynn has joined Trump's national security team—with a focus on U.S.-Russia relations. Reuters writes in February that "Donald Trump is receiving foreign policy advice from a former U.S. military intelligence chief who wants the United States to work more closely with Russia to resolve global security issues, according to three sources."[42] Almost immediately after the Sessions hire, Trump national cochair Sam Clovis hires a young and inexperienced George Papadopoulos to be the third official member of Trump's National Security Advisory Committee. According to Papadopoulos's October 2017 plea documents, on March 6, 2016, Clovis told Papadopoulos that "a principal foreign policy focus of the Campaign was an improved U.S. relationship with Russia"—echoing Flynn's position on that question.[43] Papadopoulos will stay with the campaign through the 2017 inauguration, working directly with Flynn during the presidential transition period.[44]

Papadopoulos's wife, Simona Mangiante, tells CNN that after his March 6, 2016, hire Papadopoulos "didn't take any initiative on his own without campaign approval."[45] If so, it is likely that Papadopoulos's mid-March trip to Italy, while ostensibly taken as part of his work with the London Center of International Law Practice (LCILP), was campaign-approved.[46] This is the trip he will later lie about to the FBI when questioned about it in January 2017, according to his October 2017 plea.[47] On his Italy trip, Papadopoulos is approached by Joseph Mifsud—a Kremlin agent who is affiliated, like Papadopoulos, with the LCILP—on March 14, 2016.[48] Papadopoulos thereafter meets, on March 24, with Mifsud; a deputy from the Russian Foreign Ministry, Ivan Timofeev; and a woman introduced to him—falsely—as "Putin's niece," Olga Polonskaya, née Vinogradova.[49] He emails Clovis immediately after this meeting to say that "Russian leadership [wants] to discuss U.S.-Russia ties under President Trump. They are keen to host us in a 'neutral' city, or directly in Moscow. They said the leadership, including Putin, is ready to meet with us and Mr. Trump. . . . Waiting for everyone's thoughts on moving forward with this very important issue."[50] Clovis emails him back, "Great work."[51]

Papadopoulos's Russian contact, Joseph Mifsud, is a Maltese professor who had become interested in Papadopoulos when he "discovered" Papadopoulos was working for the Trump campaign. Mifsud "did not exhibit any special interest or expertise in Russia until 2014," the *New York Times* has noted.[52] That year he hired a twenty-four-year-old Russian intern, Natalia Kutepova-Jamrom, who "introduced Mr. Mifsud to senior Russian officials, diplomats and scholars. Despite Mr. Mifsud's lack of qualifications, she managed to arrange an invitation for him to join the prestigious Valdai Discussion Club, an elite gathering of Western and Russian academics that meets each year with Mr. Putin."[53] Within a short time, Mifsud had become a regular pundit on state-run Russian television and was publicly arguing against Russian sanctions. The *Times* quotes him as saying to the Valdai Discussion Club in 2014, "Global security and economy needs partners, and who is better in this than the Russian Federation."[54]

Papadopoulos says that after he was hired by the campaign on March 6—but before his trip to Italy—he had a one-on-one phone call with Trump that neither Trump nor the campaign has ever disclosed.[55] Papadopoulos later meets with Trump one-on-one on March 21, 2016—between his first meeting with Mifsud and his second—another contact between Trump and Papadopoulos that Trump and the campaign have never disclosed.[56] At this March 21, 2016, meeting, Papadopoulos tells Trump about "his ongoing efforts to set up a meeting between Trump and Russian President Vladimir Putin," per *Newsweek*.[57] After the meeting, Trump announces Papadopoulos as part of his National Security Advisory Committee, calling him an "excellent guy"—the only compliment he affords any of his five new picks for the committee that day.[58]

Also named to the National Security Advisory Committee on March 21, 2016, is former Department of Defense inspector general Joseph Schmitz, who in 2013 had participated in an illicit, extra-governmental scheme to sell Russian arms to Syrian rebels.[59] Trump also names to the committee Walid Phares, a man who claims the Muslim Brotherhood infiltrated the Obama administration, lectures on the danger of "Sharia law" spreading across the United States, and is connected to the Center for Security Policy—which the Southern Poverty Law Center has designated a hate group for its anti-Islamic positions.[60] The final member of the team's first wave of appointees is retired lieutenant general Keith Kellogg, who at the time is best known for being the chief operating officer of the failed Coalition Provisional Authority in Iraq from 2003 to 2004. When Michael Flynn is fired as National Security Advisor nearly a year later, Kellogg will take his place temporarily until H. R. McMaster is appointed to the post.[61]

Two men who have been advising Trump on national security behind the scenes, Flynn and Erik Prince—the latter the former head of infamous private security company Blackwater—are not named to the first iteration of Trump's National Security Advisory Committee, nor will they be named to any iteration of it until Flynn is named National Security Advisor during the presidential transition.[62] Trump's first-ever appointment of Flynn to an official position, nearly sixteen months after the retired general began advising the New York businessman, is an event made possible by Jared Kushner and Ivanka Trump's involvement in the firing of transition chief Chris Christie—who had warned Trump about hiring Flynn and had refused to do so himself.[63] Both Flynn and Prince will later be accused of secretly and illegally negotiating U.S. foreign policy with agents of the Russian government.[64]

On March 31, 2016, Trump convenes what he will later call a "very unimportant" meeting: the first-ever meeting of his National Security Advisory Committee.[65] A picture of the gathering reveals twelve attendees besides Trump, with several new members of the committee who had not previously been announced.[66] With the exception of retired major general Bert Mizusawa and retired Navy rear admiral Charles Kubic, none of the new members will thereafter be reported as having significantly contributed to, or even actively participated in, the committee. Carter Page is absent from the meeting because, he says, he "had a previously scheduled meeting with some of the top U.S. military commanders many thousands of miles away from Washington"; a

photograph from that day suggests that Page was at a Council on Foreign Relations meeting in Hawaii.[67]

At the Trump International Hotel meeting, Papadopoulos tells
Trump and his fellow committee members what he previously told
Trump directly: that he is a Kremlin intermediary, and that he has been
in contact with the Russians to try to create a Trump-Putin back channel and set up a Trump-Putin summit.[68] There are at least five different
stories of what happens next. Committee director J. D. Gordon will
say that Sessions shut down Papadopoulos immediately and told him
never to raise the issue again.[69] Committee chairman Sessions will say
he "pushed back" on the suggestion and then the conversation moved
on.[70] Another attendee will say that Sessions said "Okay, interesting,"
and then moved on.[71] Two other attendees will largely concur with that
attendee, though instead of "Okay, interesting," they will report hearing something along the lines of "Well, thank you. And let's move on
to the next person."[72] Gordon gives an alternate version of the meeting
in which not only did Papadopoulos get to speak for a "few minutes"
about his Russian contacts, but there was then a wide-ranging discussion involving multiple members of the committee about the wisdom
of Papadopoulos's plan.[73] The *Daily Caller* reports a slightly different
version of the same events, with the wide-ranging discussion resulting
in the unanimous decision of "attendees . . . not to revisit Papadopoulos' suggestion."[74] What is certain is that at least three witnesses insist
Papadopoulos was never reprimanded, silenced, or rebuked by either
Sessions or Trump.[75] Trump's exact reaction is also disputed, however:
one attendee says the now president had "no reaction," while another
says he "seemed flattered"; Gordon's description of his reaction suggests simply—as CNN will later describe it—that Trump "did not dis-
miss the idea"; and the *New York Times* will report that not only did
Trump "not say 'yes,' and . . . not say 'no,'" but he actually "listened
with interest" to Papadopoulos and "asked questions."[76] Papadopoulos
himself will say that Trump "nodded his approval."[77]

What all agree on is that no one at the table contacts the FBI to inform the Bureau that the Russians may be trying to infiltrate the Trump
campaign. And neither does Trump, even after he is warned, in his first

national security briefing as a candidate in August 2016, that the Russians are trying to do just that. Athough Trump had information on Russian efforts to infiltrate his campaign to offer his CIA and FBI briefers on that date, and may well have been asked by his briefers if he had any relevant information to report, there is no evidence Trump volunteered any such knowledge or truthfully answered any queries on the subject he may have faced.[78] Nor is Papadopoulos fired by Trump on March 31; rather, Trump promotes him by giving him new responsibilities. First, Trump grants Papadopoulos the authority to act as a Russia policy adviser and spokesperson, despite Papadopoulos's having expertise only in Middle Eastern energy markets; second, Trump gives Papadopoulos the opportunity to help edit Trump's first-ever foreign policy speech, with the date of that speech just four weeks away.[79]

In August 2016, Papadopoulos will propose to the Trump campaign—specifically to the man who hired him, Sam Clovis—that he travel to Moscow to meet with Kremlin officials on Trump's behalf. Clovis will tell him that, if he determines the trip is feasible, he should "make the trip."[80] The *Washington Post* will summarize the exchange this way: "[Trump's] national campaign co-chairman urged a foreign policy adviser to meet with Russian officials [in August 2016] to foster ties with that country's government."[81]

At the time of the Papadopoulos-Clovis email exchange, there was no doubt that Russian hackers were attacking America's infrastructure. On June 14, 2016, the *Washington Post* had run a story whose headline read, in part, "Russian government hackers penetrated DNC."[82] By July 2016, public discussion had already moved to accusations by the Clinton campaign that Russian government hackers were specifically working to help elect Trump, as evidenced by WikiLeaks releasing hacked emails only from the DNC and doing so during the Democratic National Convention.[83]

Trump tells the *New York Times* his National Security Advisory Committee is made up of "very good" people "recommended" to him by "people I respect." But the group, including its "shadow" adjunct Michael Flynn, includes three individuals who at some point will be suspected of being foreign agents: George Papadopoulos, suspected by

Mueller's investigators of being an Israeli agent in 2016; Carter Page, suspected by the FBI of being a Russian agent in 2013; and Flynn, a confirmed unregistered Turkish agent throughout much of the presidential campaign—which the campaign knew pre-inauguration and did not reveal to anyone.[84] What they have in common, as summarized by the *New York Times*, is that "many on the team embraced a common view: that the United States ought to seek a rapprochement with Russia after years of worsening relations during the Obama administration. Now, however, their suspected links to Russia have put them under legal scrutiny and cast a shadow over the Trump presidency."[85]

Though not a member of the committee, Paul Manafort is sent many of the most sensitive emails produced by committee members, including emails from Papadopoulos about setting up a Trump-Putin meeting in Moscow or the United States.[86] In the two years before Manafort joins the Trump campaign, for part of his time on the campaign, and for many months afterward, the FBI uses a FISA warrant to conduct surveillance on Manafort because of his suspected activities as a foreign agent for Russian and Russia-allied interests.[87] As CNN reports, "Some of the intelligence collected [from the Manafort wiretap] sparked concerns among investigators that Manafort had encouraged the Russians to help with the campaign, according to three sources familiar with the investigation."[88]

Annotated History

Almost immediately after the Sessions hire, Trump national co-chair Sam Clovis hires a young and inexperienced George Papadopoulos to be the third official member of Trump's National Security Advisory Committee. According to Papadopoulos's October 2017 plea documents, on March 6, 2016, Clovis told Papadopoulos that "a principal foreign policy focus of the Campaign was an improved U.S. relationship with Russia"—echoing Flynn's position on the question.

During the same two-week period that Michael Flynn became an official Trump adviser and Manafort told Barrack he had to "get to" Trump so he could offer his services for free as a convention manager, the Internet Research Agency, a Russian troll farm, finalized its plans to support Trump's candidacy by spreading discord and misinformation on American social media.[89] In the two weeks after that, Trump hired Jeff Sessions; Manafort and Trump entered into discussions about Manafort coming aboard the campaign; and Clovis hired Papadopoulos and then—it appears—sent him off to Italy.

In late October 2017, Clovis, then serving as the Department of Agriculture's senior White House adviser, withdrew his pending nomination to become the agency's chief scientist. One ostensible reason was that the *Washington Post* had published the fact that he "has no academic credentials in science or agriculture," but it is widely believed the real reason had to do with his role in the ongoing Russia investigation.[90]

In May 2018, Clovis told the *Washington Examiner* that he had testified to the grand jury convened by the special counsel, been interviewed by Mueller's investigators, and answered questions for the two congressional intelligence committees investigating Trump-Russia ties for a total of nineteen hours.[91] He implied that one of the primary lines of questioning in each instance focused on his role as the liaison between the National Security Advisory Committee and the Trump campaign—as well as being the man who supervised the construction and composition of the committee. He denied any wrongdoing, however. "As far as I know," he told the *Examiner*, "no one in the campaign lifted a finger to get to the 30,000 [Clinton] emails [Trump said were 'missing']. I don't think it was in their interest. Anytime anybody approached me about oppo, I deleted it. Oppo research against Hillary Clinton? We had plenty of material. It's not like it's not a target-rich environment."[92]

Clovis's comment confirmed that he was approached multiple times via email or another method about pursuing "oppo" (opposition research) on Clinton that involved her "missing" emails. But Clovis's alleged lack of interest in the hunt for Clinton's emails is in question. When Peter W. Smith, a GOP researcher and operative, was looking for assistance in finding Clinton's emails, he listed Clovis—along with Steve Bannon, Kellyanne Conway, and Michael Flynn—as one of four Trump campaign officials who had explicitly endorsed and were supporting his effort.[93] Jonathan Safron, a former Smith assistant, said Smith "spoke to him of knowing Clovis . . . and that he had seen Smith email Clovis about matters unrelated to Clinton's emails. . . . [But] he does not know whether Clovis . . . ever replied."[94]

As of October 2017, Clovis was considered a "cooperative witness" in the Mueller investigation.[95] Court documents released by the Department of Justice in October 2017 confirmed that Clovis hired Papadopoulos in March 2016 and thereafter knew Papadopoulos was talking to the Russians—yet took no action to change Papadopoulos's status with the Trump campaign.[96] Speaking to *Politico*, administration and campaign officials justified Clovis's actions by saying Clovis had no foreign policy connections in early 2016, was under pressure to build a national security team for Trump, and therefore did virtually no vetting of his selections. They offered no explanation for Clovis's failure to fire Papadopoulos when it was discovered he was having clandestine communications with people connected to the Kremlin, or for his statement to Papadopoulos that Russia was going to be a top national security topic for Trump, or for his note of congratulations to Papadopoulos

NATIONAL SECURITY ADVISORY COMMITTEE 117

after the young adviser reported back to Clovis that he had advanced a clandestine negotiation with Kremlin agents.[97]

In November 2017, *Buzzfeed News*, trying to determine "how [Papadopoulos] was brought into the Trump camp's orbit," noted that Papadopoulos in 2016 appeared on an Israeli energy conference panel alongside Yigal Landau, the CEO of Ratio Oil Exploration, an Israeli company then in a business partnership with Kamil Ekim Alptekin, one of Michael Flynn's clients at the now-defunct Flynn Intelligence Group.[98] Alptekin was in 2016 a member of the European Council on Foreign Relations, a think tank with several hundred members—one of whom, Josef Mifsud, eventually became Papadopoulos' primary Russian contact.[99] *Buzzfeed News* further reported that Ratio denied any association with Alptekin, even though there were "numerous documents, emails, photographs and bank statements showing a business relationship."[100] Papadopoulos is also linked to Flynn by the involvement of both men with Ben Carson's 2016 presidential campaign as national security advisers.

Clovis's attorney Victoria Toensing released a statement to the press on October 30, 2017, noting that, Clovis's inaction on Papadopoulos notwithstanding, "Clovis did not believe an improved relationship with Russia should be a foreign policy focus of the campaign. Dr. Clovis always vigorously opposed any Russian trip for Donald Trump or staff. However, if a volunteer made any suggestions on any foreign policy matter, Dr. Clovis, a polite gentleman from Iowa, would have expressed courtesy and appreciation."[101] Toensing's statement was in response to *Washington Post* reporting that Clovis had indeed not just failed to oppose Papadopoulos's proposed trip to Russia as a Trump surrogate in the summer of 2016, but in fact "urged [him] to make the trip," saying to Papadopoulos that if he determined the trip was feasible, "Make the trip."[102]

Also named to the National Security Advisory Committee on March 21, 2016, is former Department of Defense inspector general Joseph Schmitz, who in 2013 had participated in an illicit, extra-governmental scheme to sell Russian arms to Syrian rebels.

Trump's March 2016 decision to tap Joseph Schmitz to advise him on national security "confounded top experts" in the field, according to a report that month by the *New York Times*.[103] Along with the appointments of Page, Papadopoulos, retired U.S. Army lieutenant general Keith Kellogg, and Walid Phares ("regularly accused by Muslim civil rights groups of being Islamophobic and of fear-mongering about the spread of Sharia law [into the United States]"), Schmitz's designation as a top Trump national security adviser "left some of the country's leading experts in the field scratching their heads as they tried to identify [Trump's] choices."[104] The *Times* used the phrase "identify his choices" advisedly; most of Trump's picks were so far off the radar of top national security experts that the experts simply had no idea who they were. Mike Green, a foreign policy expert at the Center for Strategic and International Studies, told the *Times* that everyone in his orbit had to resort to Google to "see what they [could] find" on Trump's selections.[105] As noted in a March 2016 CNN article, at a news conference the day Trump announced his picks, he called them a "very good team" and "a top-of-the-line team."[106]

A year before Trump announced his run, and a little more than two years before Trump named Schmitz to his National Security Advisory Committee, Schmitz spearheaded a secret plot to use seventy thousand Russian military weapons to arm Syrian rebels; as reported by the *Wall Street Journal* in May 2014, the CIA had to intervene directly to put a stop to it.[107] As part of Schmitz's Russian-arms plot, he told American officials that Erik Prince—a future Trump "shadow" national security adviser, as well as Schmitz's former boss at Blackwater, where Prince was CEO and Schmitz COO—could assist the United States in getting Russian arms to Syria.[108] Schmitz's close ties to Prince, who lives in

Abu Dhabi in the United Arab Emirates, offer some insight into why Trump selected Schmitz for his national security team (and may explain how Prince could be kept abreast of what was happening on that team). Jeremy Scahill of the *Intercept* called Schmitz an "enthusiastic fan" of Prince's in a March 2016 interview with *Democracy Now!*[109] Schmitz also had a tie to another member of Trump's National Security Advisory Committee, Walid Phares; Schmitz was a senior fellow at the Center for Security Policy (CSP). CSP notes on its website that Phares has "spoken at several events organized by the CSP." [110]

But the group, including its "shadow" adjunct Michael Flynn, includes three individuals who at some point will be suspected of being foreign agents: George Papadopoulos, suspected by Mueller's investigators of being an Israeli agent in 2016; Carter Page, suspected by the FBI of being a Russian agent in 2013; and Flynn, a confirmed unregistered Turkish agent throughout much of the presidential campaign—which the campaign knew pre-inauguration and did not reveal to anyone.

In the summer of 2016, Special Counsel Mueller threatened to charge George Papadopoulos with being an Israeli agent, according to Papadopoulos's wife, Simona Mangiante.[111] The allegation that Papadopoulos was working as an unregistered Israeli agent stemmed from events that occurred before Clovis selected him for the Trump campaign, Mangiante claimed.[112] After his hire by the campaign and his revelation to the National Security Advisory Committee on March 31, 2016, that he was acting as a Kremlin intermediary, the campaign immediately sent him to Israel to discuss Trump's Russia policy and other matters.[113] Papadopoulos had long been in communication with Eli Groner, then a top aide to current Israeli president Benjamin Netanyahu. But Mueller's investigators have made no statement on the Papadopoulos case besides their public filings and they do not implicate Papadopoulos as an Israeli agent, so Mangiante's claims can't be further substantiated.[114] The

Washington Post noted that Papadopoulos "attended a series of energy conferences in Israel, including one held in April 2016, just days after he was named to Trump's campaign."[115]

According to coverage of Papadopoulos's April 2016 visit to Israel in the *Jerusalem Post*, Papadopoulos told the Begin-Sadat Center for Strategic Studies (BESA) that

> Donald Trump would "overtly seek" serious engagement with Russia on a range of common concerns. Trump, says Papadopoulos, sees Russian President Vladimir Putin as a responsible actor and potential partner. . . . In particular, the US and Russia share a strong interest in combating the export of radical and violent Islam from the Middle East; to stop its spread into the Muslim republics on the borders of Russia, into Europe, and into the Baltics. Papadopoulos believes that Trump can ally with Putin this regard.[116]

Given that Papadopoulos had joined the Trump campaign the month before as a nominal expert in Middle Eastern energy issues, and given that Trump's National Security Advisory Committee had held only one meeting as of Papadopoulos's trip to Israel, it's unclear where his understanding of the Trump platform on Russia had come from by the first week of April.[117] J. D. Gordon would later tell CNN's Jim Acosta that Trump had laid out his vision for (at a minimum) the Russia-Ukraine crisis at the March 31, 2016, meeting of his National Security Advisory Committee, which Trump later called a "very unimportant" meeting.[118]

Papadopoulos's first April 2016 meeting with Israeli nationals was held at BESA.[119] There is at least some overlap between BESA and Joel Zamel's Wikistrat—Zamel being the Israeli national who offered Donald Trump Jr. clandestine assistance, in the form of a domestic disinformation campaign, at an August 2016 meeting in Trump Tower attended by adviser to the UAE crown prince George Nader and Erik Prince and set up by Prince.[120] For instance, a BESA publication on the ties between Israel and former Soviet republic Azerbaijan, by Alexander Murinson, notes that Murinson is both a senior researcher at

BESA and a senior analyst for Wikistrat.[121] The *Daily Beast* now says that Wikistrat is "in Mueller's sights," in part because of Zamel's attempts to recruit Trump national security adviser Michael Flynn in 2014 or 2015 for a position on his firm's advisory board and in part for other reasons: for instance, because Wikistrat's clients are governments and the firm is involved in "intelligence collection," Wikistrat uses "in country" "informants" for its work. The *Daily Beast* says it has "incredible access to top U.S. military and intelligence officials," and the environment within Wikistrat has been described by a former employee, James Kadtke, as "more . . . than meets the eye," "mysterious," and "clear . . . these guys had intelligence backgrounds [and were] intelligence professionals, not academics or analysts. . . . They were using their experts for tacit information going on [*sic*] in various parts of the world."[122]

While in Israel, Papadopoulos was also on a panel with Ratio CEO Yigal Landau, whose close business associate, Kamil Alptekin, is a member of the European Council on Foreign Relations (an organization with a membership in the dozens or low hundreds, depending on which level of engagement one considers: "expert," "associated researcher," "research group member," or general member). Papadopoulos had met another ECFR member, Joseph Mifsud, just three weeks earlier in Italy.[123]

Simona Mangiante claimed in 2018 that while she was with Papadopoulos in Greece during one of their trips there in 2016 or 2017, "an Israeli person who came—flew to Mykonos just to discuss business—much money was offered to George in many directions . . . and everything was highly suspicious."[124] Following the Israeli's offer of money to Papadopoulos, said Mangiante, he "invited [Papadopoulos] to Cyprus and Israel to discuss business."[125] Papadopoulos had been attending conferences in Cyprus annually and writing editorials about cooperation among Israel, Greece, and Cyprus on exploitation of the Leviathan gas field in the Mediterranean Sea a few dozen miles off Israel's coast. Landau's Ratio Oil Exploration is, according to *Buzzfeed News*, "one of several Israeli and US firms that are part of the consortium exploiting Leviathan.[126] Mangiante claimed Papadopoulos didn't take any money from the Israeli; however, in its recommendation for Papadopoulos's September 7, 2018, federal sentencing, the Office of the Special Counsel revealed that Papadopoulos had received $10,000 from someone he believed was a foreign (non-Russian) intelligence agent and had kept it.[127]

In a video of Papadopoulos published by the *Times of Israel* in June 2018, taken at a celebration the week of Trump's inauguration, Papadopoulos is seen meeting and discussing policy with a well-known right-wing activist in Israel, Yossi Dagan, and apparently doing so as a representative of the Trump campaign. *Haaretz* later confirmed that Papadopoulos was indeed speaking on Israel policy, post-inauguration, as a Trump representative.[128] "We are looking forward to ushering in a new relationship between the United States and all of Israel, including the historic Judea and Samaria," Papadopoulos says in the video.[129]

Since Papadopoulos pleaded guilty to making false statements in October 2017, his wife, acting as his spokeswoman, has said Papadopoulos has "reassessed his role" in aiding the Trump-Russia investigation. This development came after revelations that his drunken comment about Russia being in possession of stolen Clinton emails, made to Australian diplomat Alexander Downer in a London pub, initiated the FBI's counterintelligence investigation of the Trump campaign ("Operation Crossfire Hurricane") and after allegations that a Cambridge University professor named Stefan Halper, who reached out to Papadopoulos in the summer of 2016, was connected to the Bureau.[130] In June 2018, Mangiante publicly asked Trump to pardon Papadopoulos; in August 2018, she claimed that Papadopoulos planned to retract his guilty plea.[131] On September 8, 2018, Papadopoulos was sentenced to 14 days in prison by Judge Randy Moss, who found Papadopoulos to be contrite.[132] Prior to the sentence's being handed down, Papadopoulos' attorney, Thomas Breen, opined to Moss that "The President of the United States hindered this investigation more than George Papadopoulos ever did."[133] In the sentencing memo Papadopoulos submitted prior to his sentencing hearing, he accused Trump of "nodd[ing] in approval" when Papadopoulos informed him that Putin wanted to set up a private meeting with him using Papadopoulos as an intermediary;

according to the memo, Jeff Sessions also "appeared to like the idea and stated that the campaign should look into it." In a September 2018 interview with CNN, Papadopoulos said Sessions was "enthusiastic" about the possibility of a Trump-Putin meeting during the 2016 campaign, saying to Papadopoulos and Trump on March 31, 2016—as well as to the assembled National Security Advisory Committee—"this is a good idea."[134]

CHAPTER SIX

THE MAYFLOWER HOTEL

April 2016

Summary

WITHIN TWO WEEKS OF SEEING HIS ROLE IN THE TRUMP
campaign expanded, Paul Manafort announces that Trump will be giving his first foreign policy speech at the National Press Club, a traditional venue for big political launches. Less than forty-eight hours
before the speech is scheduled to occur, Manafort cancels it and moves
it to a new location in Washington, D.C.: the Mayflower Hotel. Prior to
the speech at the Mayflower, the event's hosts, the pro-Kremlin Center for the National Interest, sponsor a twenty-four-person VIP cocktail hour.[1] The event includes Trump's top aides, Russian ambassador
Sergey Kislyak, and ambassadors from Italy and Singapore, two nations that are major players in the upcoming sale of a stake in Russia's state-owned oil company, Rosneft.[2] Trump and his aides do not
disclose the presence of the Russian ambassador at the event or the
names of any of the VIP attendees, which include Robert "Bud" McFarlane, an Iran-Contra figure convicted of four counts of withholding
information from Congress.[3] McFarlane is an advocate for strengthened U.S.-Russia cooperation on energy issues, having called Russia
an "integral partner [of the United States] in ensuring the energy security of the Western world."[4] Trump meets the Russian ambassador at
the pre-speech reception.

In his speech, with Kislyak and McFarlane sitting in front-row VIP
seats, Trump says, "We must only be generous to those that prove that
they are indeed our friends. We desire to live peacefully and in friend-

ship with Russia. . . . [W]e are not bound to be adversaries. We should seek common ground based on shared interests."[5] He further calls for an "easing of tensions, and improved relations with Russia . . . [which] is possible, absolutely possible. Common sense says this cycle, this horrible cycle of hostility must end and ideally will end soon."[6] He expresses his intention of seeking a "good deal" for Russia that is "great" for the United States.[7]

One of the men who helps edit the speech, George Papadopoulos, is in regular contact with Kremlin agents for the four weeks leading up to the Mayflower event.[8] Two of the speech's authors are longtime Kremlin allies.

The Facts

ON MARCH 14, 2016, TRUMP'S SON-IN-LAW, JARED KUSHNER, is invited to discuss a détente with Russia by a think tank called the Center for the National Interest.[9] Kushner meets the center's president, Russian-born Dimitri Simes, who was raised in Moscow and is now publisher of the center's magazine, the *National Interest*. In June 2015, the month Trump announced his presidential candidacy, Simes published an article by Maria Butina (now an accused Russian spy) that began with this sentence: "It may take the election of a Republican to the White House in 2016 to improve relations between the Russian Federation and the United States."[10] In 2015, Simes had introduced Butina and her alleged intelligence handler, Alexander Torshin—called by *Bloomberg* "an ally of Vladimir Putin"—to the then Federal Reserve vice chairman; Butina felt comfortable enough with the center's staff that she also asked the center's then chairman, Maurice R. "Hank" Greenberg, to invest in a struggling Russian bank.[11]

In the weeks following his first meeting with Simes, Kushner agrees to coordinate with the Center for the National Interest on a Trump campaign event that will feature Trump's first big foreign policy speech.[12] The think tank is "more pro-Russia than most in Washington."[13] The Trump campaign tells Simes he will have "writing input" on Trump's April 27, 2016, speech, as well as the opportunity to provide the campaign with an invite list for the event.[14] Simes is assisted in writing Trump's speech by Richard Burt, one of the center's directors and an important figure at two major Russian institutions.[15] Burt is on the advisory board of Alfa Capital Partners, a private equity fund in which Russia's Alfa Bank is an investor, and is a lobbyist, like Carter Page, for Russian gas company Gazprom.[16] One of the editors of the speech is George Papadopoulos; Trump has known for over a month that Papadopoulos is in secret negotiations with the Kremlin over a Trump-Putin summit in Moscow or D.C.[17]

By April 21, just twenty-four days from his date of hire as a delegate counter, Manafort is not only Trump's de facto campaign manager but is addressing one hundred members of the Republican National Committee in Florida about what they can expect from the Trump campaign, and Trump himself, going forward.[18] The campaign will never explain how Manafort rises from being an outsider seeking to "get to" Trump—and willing to work for free—on February 14, 2016, to getting hired in late March and taking over the entirety of Trump's political operation almost immediately. What is clear is that one of Manafort's first acts in the "expanded role" he is given on April 6 is to begin detailed preparations for Trump's first foreign policy speech.

On April 11, several days after Manafort's power increases, the longtime lobbyist for pro-Russia politicians in Ukraine emails his old Russian-Ukrainian protégé, Konstantin Kilimnik, who has been called by *Politico* a "Kiev-based operative with suspected ties to Russian intelligence."[19] Kilimnik will "[consult] regularly with Manafort . . . while Manafort [is] running Donald Trump's presidential campaign."[20] In his April 11 email to Kilimnik, Manafort asks if Russian oligarch and Putin ally Oleg Deripaska ("among the two or three oligarchs Putin turns to on a regular basis," according to a 2006 U.S. diplomatic cable) is aware that Manafort has joined the Trump campaign. He further asks Kilimnik for advice on how he can "use" being Trump's new de facto campaign manager to "get whole" with Deripaska.[21] Manafort and Deripaska have business dealings that amount to as much as $60 million.[22] Manafort and Kilimnik meet in person shortly thereafter, just before Trump's "Mayflower Speech."[23] Over the ensuing weeks and months Manafort "discusses an array of subjects related to the presidential campaign [with Kilimnik], including the hacking of the DNC's emails."[24] In August 2016, a private jet belonging to Deripaska will land in New York City shortly after a known meeting there between Manafort and Kilimnik.[25]

The same week Manafort contacts Kilimnik to make sure Kremlin agents are aware of his newfound ability to "get whole" with them through his work with Trump, Sergey Kislyak invites longtime Kremlin ally Congressman Dana Rohrabacher (R-CA) to visit Moscow to meet with a friend of Vladimir Putin's, Vladimir Yakunin.[26] The California congressman also meets with Russian lawyer Natalia Veselnitskaya, who will in two months participate in the infamous Trump Tower meeting on June 9, 2016.[27] Rohrabacher is so popular with the Russian government, and considered such a valuable intelligence source by the Kremlin, that it has even given him his own code name; CNN, along with many other media outlets, calls Rohrabacher "Putin's favorite congressman."[28] While in Moscow, Rohrabacher and his aide Paul Behrends meet multiple times with Yakunin and Veselnitskaya to discuss the lifting of U.S. sanctions on Russia.[29] One of Rohrabacher's former congressional aides is Erik Prince, a "shadow" national security adviser to Trump.[30] Prince regularly sends national security white papers to Trump during the campaign and is "confident" they are taken seriously—as they are delivered (in at least one instance by Prince personally) to Steve Bannon.[31] It is unknown whether Rohrabacher or Behrends uses Prince or another intermediary to communicate Putin's sanctions-relief demands to the Trump campaign prior to Trump's speech at the Mayflower Hotel.

In May 2017, seven current and former U.S. officials will tell Reuters that Kushner spoke to Russian ambassador Sergey Kislyak on the phone in April; despite the substantial sourcing on the claim, Kushner will say through his attorney that he has no memory of any such call.[32]

Reuters concludes, by virtue of the April call and another undisclosed Kushner-Kislyak call from November 2016, that "[Kushner's] contacts with Russian envoy Sergey Kislyak were more extensive than the White House has acknowledged."[33] In his July 2017 statement to Congress, Kushner will imply that the first time he ever spoke to Kislyak was at the Mayflower Hotel, when the two men were introduced by Simes.[34]

In the days leading up to Kislyak attending the VIP cocktail hour with Trump and getting a front-row seat for the candidate's first foreign policy address, Papadopoulos communicates frequently with Kremlin agents—having been given no indication by Trump on March 31 that he should stop and every indication by Trump's national cochair Sam Clovis that he should continue. Per the *Washington Post*, during the first week of April 2016 Papadopoulos emails the National Security Advisory Committee "to update them about ongoing discussions with the professor [Joseph Mifsud] and Putin's 'niece' [Olga Polonskaya, née Vinogradova] . . . [and to detail] his 'outreach to Russia.' "[35] During this same period, Russian hackers attack and access the Democratic National Committee's servers for the first time since mid-2015. During the second week of April, Papadopoulos—now part of the editing team for Trump's first major address on foreign policy, including Russia policy—emails back and forth with Polonskaya "trying to set up a 'potential foreign policy trip to Russia,'" to which Mifsud eventually replies that such a trip "has already been agreed [to]" on the Russian end, as is confirmed by Polonskaya when she, too, replies to Papadopoulos, writing, "I have already alerted my personal links to our conversation and your request. . . . [W]e are all very excited by the possibility of a good relationship with Mr. Trump. The Russian Federation would love to welcome him once his candidature [as the confirmed GOP nominee] . . . [is] officially announced."[36] In the third week of April, Papadopoulos has a lengthy email conversation with Ivan Timofeev, a man Mifsud had described to Papadopoulos as a deputy with the Ministry of Foreign Affairs but who is, more important, the director of programs for the Russian International Affairs Council, which describes itself as a "partner" of the Russian Institute for Strategic Studies. The Institute is busy planning the Russian election interference operation

for Putin.[37] At the beginning of the fourth week of April, Manafort announces that Trump will be giving a foreign policy speech at an event
hosted by the Center for the National Interest; the same day, Papadopoulos speaks to Timofeev about Trump going to Moscow to meet with
Putin, or else having the two men meet in London.[38] Papadopoulos ultimately spends the fourth week of April 2016 "hav[ing] multiple conversations over Skype and email" with his "MFA [Russian Ministry of
Foreign Affairs] connection" about a meeting between the Trump campaign and Kremlin officials.[39]

The day before Trump's big speech at the Mayflower, Mifsud
tells Papadopoulos at an in-person meeting in London that he has
just learned, at a meeting of the Valdai Discussion Club in Moscow
the week before, that the Kremlin has "dirt" on Clinton in the form
of "thousands of [her] emails"—referred to by Mifsud as "emails of
Clinton."[40] The day of the speech, Papadopoulos emails campaign senior policy adviser Stephen Miller to say that he has "some interesting
messages coming in from Moscow about a [Trump] trip [to Moscow]
when the time is right"; he also emails Trump's then campaign manager, Corey Lewandowski, to confirm that Putin still wishes to host
Trump in Moscow.[41]

Just seventy-two hours after Trump's speech, Papadopoulos emails
Mifsud to thank him for his help in connecting the Kremlin to Trump
and notes that a Putin-Trump summit would be "history making."[42] The
same week, Papadopoulos emails Timofeev to tell him that Trump's
"Mayflower Speech" was intended as "the signal to meet"—meaning
the Trump campaign's indication that the time is right for Putin and
Trump to hold a summit in D.C. or Moscow.[43] Timofeev responds to
Papadopoulos on May 4, writing, "I have just talked to my colleagues
from the MFA [Ministry of Foreign Affairs]. The[y] are open for cooperation. One of the options is to make a meeting for you at the North
America Desk, if you are in Moscow."[44] Papadopoulos forwards the
email to Lewandowski, who by now has lost his authority to Manafort;
Papadopoulos also sends the Timofeev email to Clovis, who replies
that the campaign will have to figure out how to mitigate the "legal issues" inherent in private citizens meeting with foreign officials.[45]

Trump's "Mayflower Speech" was originally slated for the National

Press Club (NPC), a venue often used for maiden political speeches; just forty-eight hours before the event, however, Manafort switches the venue from the NPC, which seats seven hundred people. He asserts that the room in the Mayflower Hotel he has booked offers more seating, which it does not. The hotel's main ballroom seats six hundred people. The room where Trump is scheduled to speak seats 280.[46] Moving the event to the Mayflower allows, however, for a private, VIP-only cocktail hour to be held prior to the speech, at which time Trump aides hobnob with the four invited ambassadors, three of whom are from nations (Russia, Italy, and Singapore) that will shortly be involved in Russia's mysterious and largest-ever oil-stock sale.[47]

The Steele dossier alleges Trump campaign foreign policy adviser Carter Page met with the president of Rosneft about trade sanctions on Russia. The Rosneft president, reports Steele, "was so keen to lift personal and corporate western sanctions imposed on the company, that he offered PAGE/TRUMP's associates the brokerage of up to a 19 per cent (privatised) stake in Rosneft in return."[48] And indeed, consistent with the dossier, in December 2016 Rosneft will announce an estimated $11 billion private purchase of 19.5 percent of the state-owned oil giant— the 19 percent previously anticipated by Steele, plus an unexplained 0.5 percent that could well be a "brokerage" fee for Trump—by Glencore, a Swiss multinational trading and mining company, and by Qatar Investment Authority (QIA), Glencore's largest shareholder."[49]

Bloomberg will later write that the Trump campaign wanted the event to be held at the Mayflower so it could be televised.[50] Years earlier, Trump had implied to MSNBC's Thomas Roberts that Putin watches Trump whenever he's at a televised event: "He's probably very interested in what you and I are saying today," Trump said to Roberts at the time, "and I'm sure he's going to be seeing it in some form. . . ."[51]

When asked by Congress, in the spring of 2017, about his contacts with Russians during the presidential campaign, Jeff Sessions will fail to mention the Mayflower event—even after he has updated his originally inaccurate testimony to note two other meetings with Russian ambassador Sergey Kislyak that he failed to disclose under congressional questioning.[52] In June 2017, former FBI director James Comey will testify before the Senate Intelligence Committee, in classified session, that Russia-to-Russia intercepts indicate that Kislyak and Sessions met privately on the sidelines of the Mayflower Hotel event.[53] Comey will explain to the Intelligence Committee that he hadn't publicly testified about the third 2016 meeting between the chairman of Trump's National Security Advisory Committee and the Russian ambassador because he thought the information was too sensitive to be aired in open session.[54]

Sessions's position on what he did or did not do at the Mayflower has changed over time. In his opening statement before his June 2017 testimony, he says, "I did not have any private meetings nor do I recall any conversations with any Russian officials at the Mayflower Hotel. I did not attend any meetings at that event."[55] Moments later, he implies there might have been an exchange: "If any brief interaction occurred in passing with the Russian Ambassador during that reception, I do not remember it."[56] Not long after that, under questioning by Senator Roy Blunt (R-MO), he changes his position yet again: "I didn't have any formal meeting with him. I'm confident of that. But I may have had an encounter during the reception."[57] None of these answers explains, however, why Sessions, when asked under oath on January 10, 2017, by Senator Al Franken (D-MN) if he had "communicated with the Russian government" in 2016, had answered, "I'm not aware of any of those activities," and "I did not have communications with the Russians."[58] A day after the *Washington Post* reveals, in March 2017, the inaccuracy of that response, Sessions recuses himself from the Russia investigation.[59]

At the VIP cocktail hour before Trump's April 2016 speech, Kushner meets Kislyak in person for the first time—a fact he leaves off his disclosure forms when he applies for his job in the Trump administration seven months later.[60]

In his speech, Trump discusses finding a "good deal" for Russia that also works for the United States. Though he doesn't mention the subject of the "deal" he imagines making with Russia, his prior statements on Putin, Russia, and U.S. policy strongly imply he is talking about revisiting the United States' sanctions on Russia after its annexation of Crimea in 2014. It is unknown whether Papadopoulos has communicated to Trump by the time his speech begins—or whether Stephen Miller or Sam Clovis, both of whom have recently been in contact with Papadopoulos about his Russian contacts, communicates to Trump—Putin's most recent entreaty to Trump to meet face-to-face in Moscow, or the fact that there has been recent "interesting news" on this front. Also unclear is whether and when Papadopoulos communicates to the rest of the campaign Mifsud's revelation that Russia has incriminating Clinton emails. In the sentencing memo for his September 2018 sentencing hearing, Papadopoulos will claim that while he told the Greek Foreign Minister in May 2016 about the Russians' being in possession of stolen Clinton emails, he does not believe he ever told anyone from the presidential campaign he was then working for—though he later tells Jake Tapper of CNN that he "can't guarantee" his memory on this latter point is accurate and that he "might have" told someone on the campaign about Mifsud's April 2016 statements. In late March 2018, Trump campaign policy director John Mashburn will testify to the Senate Judiciary Committee that "he had received an email in the first half of 2016 alerting the Trump campaign that Russia had damaging information about Hillary Clinton. . . . [and] he remembered the email coming from George Papadopoulos."[61]

Reviewing the Mayflower event afterward, the European bureau of *Politico* will write, "That Trump would choose the Center for the National Interest as the place to premier[e] his new seriousness on foreign policy has Manafort's fingerprints all over it. For Manafort and the Center have something very important in common: both have ties to the Russian regime of President Vladimir Putin."[62] As part of a detailed analysis of the center and its attendant policy publication, the *National Interest*, *Politico Europe* writes,

> [These] are two of the most Kremlin-sympathetic institutions in the nation's capital. . . . Center director Dmitri Simes [*sic*] . . . for decades has used his connections to the Kremlin—real or perceived—to cultivate a reputation in Washington as one of the few Russia hands who intimately knows that country's politics.

For years, the Center for the National Interest partnered with the Russian government-funded Institute for Democracy and Cooperation . . . whose head, Andranik Migranyan, was personally appointed by Russian Foreign Minister Sergei Lavrov, according to a State Department cable released by Wikileaks. In May 2014 [after the Russian annexation of Crimea], the two think tanks held a press conference defending Russia's position in Ukraine. In 2013, Simes graced the stage alongside Putin at the Valdai International Discussion Club . . . frequented almost exclusively by Putin apologists. At Valdai, Putin referred to Simes as his "American friend and colleague" and Simes stated "I fully support President Putin's tough stance [on Syria]." This deference towards Russia extends to the *National Interest*, which . . . includes on its board Alexey Pushkov, . . . chairman of the Russian Duma's international affairs committee.[63]

After the speech, CNN will get the Russian reaction to Trump's speech by quoting Russians on the street in Moscow as well as several prominent Russians. The most high-profile response published by CNN, taken from Russia's TASS news agency, happens to be from Pushkov—the Center for the National Interest board member—who says, "[Trump] expresses readiness to come to terms with the Russian President instead of making conflicts with us, the way today's administration is doing."[64] CNN notes that Russian politicians are also happy that Trump has made no mention of Ukraine or Crimea in discussing better relations with the Kremlin.[65]

Trump's choice of sponsor for his first foreign policy speech is therefore a powerful statement of comity with Russia; the same speech given at a venue owned by a professional organization of American journalists, the National Press Club, would not send the same message—even putting aside who had authored and edited it.

Yet it isn't merely the sponsor of Trump's first foreign policy speech that is intended to send the Russians a signal: it's the speech itself. Papadopoulos, who the *Times* notes was "trusted enough to edit the outline" of the speech, also "flagged the speech to his newfound Russia contacts, telling Mr. [Ivan] Timofeev [an agent of the Russian Foreign Ministry] that [the speech] should be taken as 'the signal to meet.' "[66] Given that Putin "friend" Simes had been invited to contribute to Trump's speech and had also, within the previous three years, been an honored guest of Putin himself at the pro-Putin discussion club directed by Timofeev, what Papadopoulos is communicating to Timofeev is that Trump's willingness to deliver a speech directly influenced by Timofeev's associate—to the Russian ambassador, no less—can be taken as a sign that Trump is willing to surrender a portion of his foreign policy to the authorship of Kremlin allies. Olga Polonskaya, Papadopoulos's third Russian contact after Mifsud and Timofeev, responds to Trump's speech by saying that she is pleased Trump's "position toward Russia is much softer" than the other Republican candidates'.[67]

Besides Simes and Papadopoulos, Trump's other ghost speechwriter is Richard Burt.[68] Burt had participated in an April 14 panel discussion at the Center for the National Interest entitled "Does America Need Allies?"[69] That sentiment will show up less than two weeks later in Trump's speech at the Mayflower: "America First will be the major and overriding theme of my administration," Trump announces on April 27, later adding, "We're rebuilding other countries while weakening our own. . . . [O]ur allies are not paying their fair share. . . . The countries we are defending must pay for the cost of this defense, and if not, the U.S. must be prepared to let these countries defend themselves."[70] What Trump here describes—using the words of a man, Burt, recruited by Paul Manafort to help compose Trump's speech—is the end of the indefatigable Western alliance that won World Wars I and II and the Cold War. The prospect of America shirking its allies in April 2016 is surely music to the ears of Manafort's old boss, Russian oligarch Oleg Deripaska, as well as Deripaska's friend Vladimir Putin. *New York Magazine* has called "splitting the Western alliance" the core component of "Russia's dream."[71]

Whatever signal it was that Papadopoulos—or Trump—intended to send at the Mayflower Hotel, less than forty-eight hours after Trump's speech, on April 29, 2016, the DNC is attacked in a "serious way" by Russian hackers.[72]

Annotated History

Trump's "Mayflower Speech" was originally slated for the National Press Club (NPC), a venue often used for maiden political speeches; just forty-eight hours before the event, however, Manafort switches the venue from the NPC, which seats seven hundred people. He asserts that the room in the Mayflower Hotel he has booked offers more seating, which it does not.

As of April 21, 2016, news outlets were planning on sending crews to the National Press Club, as evidenced by stories about the upcoming speech in the *New York Times* and *Newsweek*.[73] The venue was still the NPC on April 25.[74] The *Hill* reported that "the day before the event [April 26], the campaign announced that the venue had been changed from the National Press Club to the Mayflower Hotel due to 'overwhelming interest' "—but in fact, the ballroom in which the event was held at the Mayflower holds fewer people than the NPC does.[75] The change of venue, first published by the *Hill* at 3:45 p.m. on April 26, risked confusing prospective media attendees of the event, as it came less than twenty-four hours before what was intended to be not only Trump's first major foreign policy address, but also a centerpiece in the redesign of his campaign and the reshaping of his image. Indeed, on the same day the Mayflower event was announced, Manafort addressed the Republican National Committee in Florida with the intention, as the *New York Times* wrote at the time, to inform the Republican establishment that "Trump recognized the need to reshape his persona and that his campaign would begin working with the political establishment that he has scorned to great effect."[76]

Reaction to Trump's speech was mixed. *Politico* wrote that "the speech was notable more for the atmospherics and presentation than for its substance."[77] In critiquing the speech's cadence, *Politico* noted that "Paul Manafort, a senior Trump adviser who wrote primary night remarks for Trump's victory in New York last Tuesday, told reporters that he did not write this one"; that Manafort had not only been promoted twice in his first two weeks with the Trump campaign but was also writing Trump's speeches was not widely known at that point.[78] Taking a contrary view on the quality of the speech was conservative commentator Ann Coulter, who tweeted after it had concluded that Trump's address from the Mayflower was the "GREATEST FOREIGN POLICY SPEECH SINCE WASHINGTON'S FAREWELL ADDRESS."[79] If Coulter knew at the time that the speech had been shaped *by* Russian interests *for* an audience of Russian interests and to be critiqued in the press by the *same* Russian interests that participated in its writing, her tweet betrayed none of that knowledge.

When asked by Congress, in the spring of 2017, about his contacts with Russians during the presidential campaign, Jeff Sessions will fail to mention the Mayflower event—even after he has updated his originally inaccurate testimony to note two other meetings with Russian ambassador Sergey Kislyak that he failed to disclose under congressional questioning.

Sessions's defense for not disclosing these contacts was that he thought he was being asked only about meetings he took—in his own understanding and classification of matters—as a surrogate for the Trump campaign rather than as a U.S. senator. However, as the *Atlantic* noted, in the first two months of 2016 Sessions met with zero foreign diplomats; his meetings with foreign diplomats began as soon as he became a Trump surrogate.[80]

Sessions also dissembled on the subject of his contacts with Papadopoulos. Sessions's right-hand man on the National Security Advisory Committee, J. D. Gordon, has said that—despite Sessions' and Gordon's being the chairman and director of the committee, respectively—neither of them ever saw any emails from Papadopoulos about Russia after March 31, 2016.[81] Gordon contends that, for unknown reasons, Sam Clovis conspired with Manafort and others to keep any such emails from both Sessions and Gordon. According to *Busi-*

ness Insider, Gordon said he was "surprised to learn" that Papadopoulos had gone outside "his direct chain of command" to try to schedule a Trump-Putin meeting.[82] Gordon's insistence that Papadopoulos and others on the Trump campaign deliberately kept the campaign's contacts with Russian nationals a secret from both he and Sessions is complicated by the fact that Sessions and Gordon themselves had meetings and contacts with Russians that they did not disclose—both at the Republican National Convention and thereafter. Sessions and Gordon met with Russian ambassador Sergey Kislyak at the convention in Cleveland; Sessions thereafter met with Kislyak in his Senate office to discuss (contrary to his initial claims) "campaign-related matters," while Gordon was in contact with now-accused Russian spy Maria Butina in September and October 2016—and never revealed it to anyone after the Russia investigation became national news.[83] That Papadopoulos sat next to Sessions at an hours-long Trump campaign dinner in the midst of his spring 2016 communications with Russian nationals—and that he revealed those communications to both an Australian diplomat, a Greek politician, and a British official during the same period—also calls into question why he would have kept the most critical information he was then holding from his boss on the National Security Advisory Committee.[84]

As for Papadopoulos's ongoing importance—in the view of top Trump officials—to the Trump campaign, it was underscored by two events that occurred around the time of Trump's "Mayflower Speech." First, despite Papadopoulos's ongoing contacts with Russian nationals, and his communications with Stephen Miller about those contacts, Miller became one of Papadopoulos's chief advocates within the campaign. As the *New York Times* wrote, even after learning of Papadopoulos's meetings with Mifsud, "Miller, then a senior policy adviser to the campaign and now a top White House aide, was eager for Mr. Papadopoulos to serve as a surrogate."[85] Then, just a week after the Mayflower Speech, Papadopoulos, now back in London, spoke out of turn to the *Times of London* by demanding that British prime minister David Cameron apologize to Trump for calling Trump's comments about Muslims "divisive, stupid, and wrong."[86] Papadopoulos implied that if Cameron failed to apologize it would put any chance he had of having a special relationship with Trump at risk. Clovis, who had not fired Papadopoulos after he revealed to the campaign that he was conducting ongoing negotiations with Kremlin agents, also took no action against Papadopoulos for causing an international incident with a U.S. ally besides "severely reprimand[ing]" him.[87] After the incident, Papadopoulos's back-channel outreach to Kremlin agents—and his regular notification of campaign advisers and officials on the particulars of his actions—did not abate.

CHAPTER SEVEN

THE BACK CHANNELS

May to June 2016

Summary

THE KREMLIN TAKES THE "MAYFLOWER SPEECH" AS THE signal it is intended to be, an invitation to move forward with a Trump-Putin meeting. George Papadopoulos now urges the Russians to move forward with back-channel negotiations, which they do. At the same time, Russian hackers and propagandists redouble their efforts with the creation, in June 2016, of the DCLeaks website, the "Guccifer 2.0" persona, and two election interference plans authored by the Russian Institute for Strategic Studies.

The Kremlin explores new clandestine approaches to Trump campaign aides. In May, Kremlin agent Alexander Torshin reaches out to a top Trump staffer, Rick Dearborn, through Maria Butina's boyfriend, Paul Erickson; in June, Torshin uses Rick Clay, a conservative activist from West Virginia, to get a message to Dearborn. Papadopoulos continues his regular communications with Kremlin agents Mifsud, Timofeev, and Polonskaya; he also makes contact with Kremlin allies in Athens, Greece. Carter Page is invited by Kremlin agents to give a speech at a university in Moscow, and Donald Trump Jr. dines with Torshin at an NRA conference that the latter had attended with the intention of speaking to Trump himself. Manafort continues his communications with Kilimnik; Felix Sater invites Michael Cohen to attend a business conference in Moscow; and Emin Agalarov's publicist emails Donald Trump Jr. with an offer that sounds almost too good to be true: the Kremlin will deliver to the Trump campaign incriminating information about Hillary Clinton. The proffered materials sound a lot like the Clinton emails Mifsud had discussed with Papadopoulos in late April.

On June 3, 2016, Rob Goldstone—Emin Agalarov's publicist, but also a frequent emailer on behalf of Emin's father, Aras—contacts Trump's son Don Jr. with a message from both Agalarovs: the Kremlin wants to set up a meeting. Goldstone has been authorized to send the information the Kremlin wants to share with Trump directly to the candidate himself, but he has decided to go to Trump's son first and to make the exchange in person rather than electronically. Goldstone informs Don Jr. that the Kremlin's interest in giving the Trump campaign incriminating information on Clinton is to actively support Trump's candidacy and to see it through to victory. Trump Jr. eagerly agrees to the proffered support, the proffered documents, and the requested meeting, telling Goldstone via email, "I love it." According to Trump's attorney Michael Cohen, Trump Jr. tells his father of the upcoming Trump Tower meeting immediately. One of Cohen's attorneys, Lanny Davis, will later attempt to revert his claim that Cohen will testify to Trump's prior knowledge of the June 9, 2016, meeting; Davis will now say he is "not certain" one way or another what Cohen knows. But *Vox* observes Davis may simply be trying to solve Cohen's "perjury problem."[1] As the digital media outlet explains, Cohen "testified to Congress last year that he personally did not know anything about Don Jr.'s Trump Tower meeting beforehand, and that he had no idea whether Trump did. If this was in fact a lie, Cohen could be charged for lying to Congress."[2] Meanwhile, CNN, the first outlet to report on Cohen's claim that Trump knew of the June 2016 Trump Tower meeting in advance, will stand by its reporting by Jim Sciutto, Pulitzer Prize winner Carl Bernstein, and Marshall Cohen, writing in a follow-up article after Davis's non-retraction retraction, "We stand by our story, which had more than one source, and we are confident in our reporting of it."[3]

Trump Jr., Jared Kushner, and Paul Manafort—the last of these Trump's formally designated campaign manager as of May 19—attend the June 9 meeting with several Kremlin agents. After the meeting is discovered by the media more than a year later, in July 2017, the Trump campaign will lie about its purpose via a false public statement dictated by Trump himself. Eventually, the meeting's Trump campaign attendees will admit to having been looking for Clinton "dirt" at the meeting and will say that they were disappointed to discover that no such dirt was forthcoming.

Their disappointment should have been short-lived, however. Two Russian hacking operations bring their websites online during the same seven-day period the Kremlin promises the Trump campaign materials that will damage Clinton, and in short order these two sites dump reams of stolen emails damaging to not just the Clinton campaign but the Democratic National Committee—a haul quite close in its scope and purpose to what at least Trump Jr. and Kushner had been expecting to get in hand on June 9. Even so, agitation on the part of the campaign that the Kremlin has not delivered on its implicit promise of supplying the campaign with Clinton's "missing" emails leads to formulation of a plan to locate these emails in the short term by clandestine means.

Several days after the "Mayflower Speech," Papadopoulos makes the first of two May 2016 trips to Greece, one of the seven European Union (EU) countries that opposes Russian sanctions and home to a host of Putin allies—particularly the Greek defense minister Panos Kammenos, who runs a think tank that is in a memorandum of understanding with the Russian Institute for Strategic Studies. While Papadopoulos is in Greece for the first time in May, Greek media outlet *To Vima* writes about Papadopoulos's trip and notes that he is "incognito," having "targeted" meetings, and "trying to make contacts." These efforts to make contact with powerful figures in Greek politics are successful, as Papadopoulos meets not only with Kammenos but also a number of other influential Greek politicians. According to *To Vima*, the list of Papadopoulos's Athens meetings includes "Secretary General Dimitrios Paraskevopoulos, Political Director Petros Mavroidis, and the head of three nodal addresses: A3 dealing with Balkan affairs, A4 monitoring Greek-Turkish [relations], and A7 handling the Greek-American relations. He then went to the Defense Ministry where, according to some information, he even had a meeting with National Defense Minister Panos Kammenos."[4]

In June, Jared Kushner contracts with British firm Cambridge Analytica to institute a domestic "microtargeting" scheme for Trump's general election campaign; the data compiled will be left open by Cambridge Analytica for Russian actors to steal and weaponize. That same month, the Russian Institute for Strategic Studies (RISS), a partner of Kammenos's think tank, drafts two documents outlining Russia's plans for interfering in the 2016 U.S. general election. Papadopoulos has by now made a second trip to Athens, this time one scheduled to coincide with a visit to Athens by Putin himself—the only trip Putin makes to an EU country in 2016. Papadopoulos once again meets with the RISS-connected Kammenos. Meanwhile, Nastya Rybka, girlfriend of Russian oligarch and close Putin ally Oleg Deripaska, posts on social media that she too is in Athens; she is known to travel regularly with Deripaska on his yacht, though whether Deripaska is with her in Athens is unclear.[5] Immediately after Rybka leaves Greece, she posts on Instagram that she is now in the United Arab Emirates—a country whose crown prince will offer his assistance to the Trump campaign approximately sixty days later.[6]

As the two Russian websites intended to aid the release of documents and emails stolen from the Democrats launch, Russia's attacks on America's electoral infrastructure begin in earnest. In Washington, the top three Republicans in the House of Representatives talk about Donald Trump and Dana Rohrabacher getting "paid" by Putin to take the policy positions they do; the three men do not realize their comments have been recorded.[7] In London, Christopher Steele begins writing what will become known as the "Steele dossier." The first pages of his compilation of raw intelligence—which is drawn in part from Russian HUMINT (human intelligence) Steele developed while working for MI6—describe some of the *kompromat* the Kremlin holds on Trump and begin outlining the size and scope of the international Trump-Russia conspiracy.

By late June, the "Brexit" vote is occurring in the United Kingdom—a Kremlin-backed push for the citizens of that nation to vote to leave the EU in a nationwide referendum. It is in part a trial run for the sort of election meddling the Kremlin is planning in the

United States. With the assistance of "Leave" backer and Trump ally Nigel Farage, the Kremlin strikes a significant blow against the future of Western democracy when the United Kingdom narrowly votes to leave the EU.

Despite all the advancements in the Trump-Russia network in May and June 2016, a Trump campaign adviser also makes a critical error in this period that will eventually threaten to topple the ever-expanding Trump-Russia enterprise: Papadopoulos, drunk in a London bar, leaks to an Australian diplomat, Alexander Downer, that the Russians have dirt on Clinton in the form of thousands of emails—and that the Russians have been in contact with the Trump campaign about passing those emails on. This confession will make its way to Australia and eventually, in two months, back to the United States, where it will initiate one of the largest, most complex, most politically significant federal criminal investigations in American history.

When, on June 15, 2016, the *Washington Post* reports that the Democratic National Committee has been hacked, the Trump campaign will immediately issue a statement in response: "We believe it was the DNC that did the 'hacking' as a way to distract from the many issues facing their deeply flawed candidate and failed party leader."

The Facts

Almost immediately after he receives Sam Clovis's email mentioning potential "legal issues" with a private citizen meeting with foreign officials, George Papadopoulos gets on a plane and goes on a campaign-approved trip to Athens, Greece—just the sort of "neutral city" his Russian contacts had previously told him the Russians prefer to meet in.[8]

Greece is one of the seven EU countries that, in spring 2016, stands in opposition to sanctions against Russia. As Papadopoulos touches down in Athens, Vladimir Putin is just a few weeks away from arriving in the city for his first and only trip to an EU nation of 2016, during which his explicit plan is to discuss U.S. sanctions with Greek officials.[9] Papadopoulos gives an interview to *Kathimerini*, an Athens newspaper, during his first May 2016 trip to Athens, telling his interviewer, Marianna Kakaounaki, that he is in Greece to make "contacts."[10] *To Vima* will report, however, that Papadopoulos is making his trip in "secret," "incognito," and "almost with absolute secrecy."[11] Papadopoulos is traveling with Seth Cropsey, a member of the Foreign Policy Initiative alongside Bud McFarlane and a senior fellow at the Hudson Institute— where Papadopoulos had worked from 2011 to 2015, according to *Time* magazine. He is also a former assistant to President Reagan's secretary of defense Caspar Weinberger.[12] Cropsey's immediate successor as Weinberger's chief speechwriter was future Trump deputy National Security Advisor (and Bud McFarlane mentee) K. T. McFarland.[13]

Despite the secret nature of his early May trip to Greece, Papadopoulos nevertheless gives interviews with local media, and will do so again both when he returns to Athens in late May and when he travels to Greece for a third time in 2016 during the presidential transition. According to these Greek media interviews, in late May Papadopoulos meets with—or, rather, is willing to acknowledge meeting with— Greek president Prokopis Pavlopoulos, Defense Minister Panos Kammenos, Foreign Minister Nikos Kotzias, and former prime minister Kostas Karamanlis.[14] In December, he again meets with Kammenos and, among others, Kyriakos Mitsotakis, called by Greek media "the chief of the conservative opposition" in Greece.[15]

The *Washington Post* later confirms that, in late May 2016, Papadopoulos and Putin were in Athens at the same time. According to the *Post*, "[J]ust as Putin arrived, [Papadopoulos] was in Athens, quietly holding meetings across town and confiding in hushed tones that he was there on a sensitive mission on behalf of his boss, Donald Trump."[16] Putin was in Athens to discuss with Greek officials the very issue Russian agents like Maria Butina had been so keen to discuss with Trump and his national security advisers: the lifting of sanctions against Russia for its annexation of Crimea.[17] Putin and Papadopoulos, who are both interested in the lifting of sanctions against Russia, meet with Kammenos.[18]

According to a November 2017 *Newsweek* article, in 2016 Papadopoulos told Greek media that Trump himself "knew that he [Papadopoulos] intended to meet with foreign nationals [in Athens]" in May 2016.[19] Papadopoulos said, moreover, that he had had both a one-on-one phone call and a one-on-one meeting with Trump in the midst of his March 2016 back-channel contacts with the Russians.[20] In February 2018, NPR will confirm with Papadopoulos's wife, Simona Mangiante, that her husband's official position is "everything [he] did was authorized by the top levels of the campaign."[21]

When Papadopoulos returns to Greece in December, he will "[brag] that he had helped Trump win the presidency" and, according to the *Washington Post*, "many here [in Athens] believed it."[22] During his December visit to Athens, Papadopoulos also tells those he meets with that he has "a 'blank check' to choose whatever role he want[s] in the administration."[23] The chief opposition politician, Mitsotakis, and his staff are "skeptical" of his claims, while Kammenos—still in a memorandum of understanding with the Russian think tank that drafted Russia's intricate plans for 2016 U.S. election interference—is "excited."[24] And Kammenos is right to be excited: at Trump's inauguration he will meet again with Papadopoulos, but this time the two men will be joined by the president-elect's chief of staff, Reince Priebus.[25] Kammenos will say afterward that Trump has "some very important Greek-Americans by his side who maintain their ties with our country. . . . We are certain that when the time comes for them to help their homeland . . . they will do so to the best of their ability."[26] On Election Day, Kammenos had congratulated Trump on Twitter, stressing the "important role" of Trump national security adviser George Papadopoulos.[27]

Just a few days after Papadopoulos returns from his second May 2016 trip to Greece, Emin Agalarov's manager, the British publicist Rob Goldstone, reaches out to Donald Trump Jr. An excerpt of his email from June 3, 2016, 10:36 a.m.:

Emin [Agalarov] just called and asked me to contact you with
something very interesting. The Crown prosecutor of Russia
met with his father Aras this morning and in their meeting offered to provide the Trump campaign with some official documents and information that would incriminate Hillary and her
dealings with Russia and would be very useful to your father.
This is obviously very high level and sensitive information but
is part of Russia and its government's support for Mr. Trump—
helped along by Aras and Emin. What do you think is the best
way to handle this information and would you be able to speak
to Emin about it directly? I can also send this info to your father
via Rhona [Graff], but it is ultra sensitive so wanted to send to
you first.[28]

The timeline Goldstone provides confirms that by early June 2016
connections between the Kremlin and Trump Tower are so well established that it takes only a matter of hours—at most—for a message to
get from the "Crown prosecutor of Russia," Yuri Chaika, to the Trump
campaign. The *Financial Times* will say of Chaika, in July 2017, that
he "has remained steadfastly loyal to President Vladimir Putin for more
than a decade."[29] Goldstone is transparent and forceful about the significant in-kind value to the Trump campaign of the material the Kremlin is offering: it is "very interesting," "very useful," "very high level,"
"sensitive," and "ultra sensitive." Goldstone underscores that the material is "official" and "incriminat[ing]," suggesting it is nonpublic information. He confirms that the Kremlin specifically wants the Trump
campaign to have this information and is willing to use both Aras and
Emin as agents to ensure the transfer of the material. Most important,
Goldstone is clear that the information is intended for Trump himself
and that it is being given to Trump's son as part of a coordinated campaign of support for his father orchestrated by the Kremlin.

Under 52 U.S.C. § 30121 (contributions and donations by foreign
nationals), the mere offering of this material by a foreign national—
including, in this case, according to the federal conspiracy statute, Yuri
Chaika, Aras Agalarov, Emin Agalarov, and Rob Goldstone—is an in-

dictable offense due to the "official information and documents" being offered to the Trump campaign constituting a "thing of value."[30] Likewise, under 52 U.S.C. § 30121 it is a federal crime to solicit, accept, or receive anything of value from a foreign national.[31]

Seventeen minutes after Goldstone emails Trump's son, at 10:53 a.m., Don Jr. replies: "Thanks Rob I appreciate that. I am on the road at the moment but perhaps I just speak to Emin first. Seems we have some time and if it's what you say I love it especially later in the summer."

Trump Jr. here acknowledges that he understands the general nature of what is being offered and its value, and he communicates clearly that he wants it, even giving some directions as to *when* he wants it. According to experts, Trump Jr. "may well have committed a federal crime" with this email.[32]

Trump Jr. will testify about his conduct on September 7, 2017 (see chapter 13).

On June 6, the exchange between Goldstone and Trump Jr. continues as they seek to set up a phone call for that day between Trump Jr. and Emin.[33] By the next day, June 7, Goldstone is referencing an upcoming Trump Tower meeting for the handover of "Hillary info" in a way that suggests Emin and Don Jr. had discussed such a meeting the day before.[34] "I believe you are aware of the meeting," Goldstone writes to Trump Jr. on June 7.[35]

June 7 is a busy day for candidate Trump, as he wins the final five GOP primaries in California, Montana, New Jersey, New Mexico, and South Dakota—and announces that night that he will be giving a "major" speech six days later, on June 13, about "all of the things that have taken place with the Clintons."[36] He tells his supporters, "I think you're going to find [the speech about the Clintons] very, very interesting."[37] Earlier that day, Trump Jr. had scheduled his meeting to receive dirt on Clinton from the Kremlin for June 9 at 3:00 p.m., telling Goldstone that his brother-in-law, Jared Kushner, and the "campaign boss," Paul Manafort, would likely be coming to the meeting also.[38] After Trump Jr. unsuccessfully attempts to bring the meeting forward to June 8, a final date and time is set: June 9 at 4:00 p.m.[39] Trump's

June 13 speech is later rescheduled to June 22 because of the mass shooting at Orlando's Pulse nightclub. However, the original date of the speech had been just four days after the Kremlin was to send agents to Trump Tower with "incriminating Clinton documents."[40] And on the rescheduled date, Americans will nevertheless learn that Trump wants to talk about Clinton's deleted emails. On June 22, he calls on Clinton's emails "to be found" and adds that they "[s]hould be able to be found . . . I've always heard you can never really delete an email. So it should be able to be found if they really want to find them."[41]

On the afternoon of June 9, Donald Trump is at Trump Tower, working on "prepar[ing] [a] charge sheet against Clinton," according to *Politico*.[42] One floor below him, his son, son-in-law, and campaign manager are working on the very same issue by meeting with a group of Russian nationals and Russian-Americans. But Trump wasn't slated to work on the "Clinton dirt" issue alone on June 9; in fact, *Politico* writes that he was scheduled to work with his top aides on that very issue that very day.[43] Per the digital media outlet,

> Donald Trump's team is hunkering down [on June 9] to draft the charge sheet the presumptive GOP nominee will unveil against Hillary Clinton on Monday, intent on laying out a credible general election argument that leads voters to question her trustworthiness. Senior campaign advisers [are] beginning to focus on the speech. . . . As Trump's inner circle begins to deliberate on what to say, the more salacious, headline-worthy attacks against Clinton, however dated, are never far from the candidate's mind. And he's already drawn on some of the most sordid allegations against the Clintons. . . . "Trump's advisers believe Hillary has three major vulnerabilities," a Trump insider said Wednesday, referring [in part] to [the] alleged "epic corruption of the Clinton foundation" . . . [and] "payoffs and bribes. . . ."[44]

Even so, when attorney and Kremlin "informant" Natalia Veselnitskaya, Agalarov agent Ike Kaveladze, and former Soviet counterintelligence operative Rinat Akhmetshin come to Trump Tower on June 9 to discuss precisely what the Trump team was meeting that day just one floor above to discuss—corruption centered around Clinton's donors—Trump Jr. will testify that he was thoroughly befuddled.[45] Indeed, though Trump Jr. says Veselnitskaya began the meeting by discussing "individuals connected to Russia supporting or funding Democratic presidential candidate Hillary Clinton," he will later testify before Congress, in September 2017, that his reaction to Veselnitskaya's discussion of Clinton corruption was that "it was quite difficult for me to understand what she was saying or why" and "[it] didn't seem all that relevant to me."[46]

Per his congressional testimony, Trump Jr. says he understood Veselnitskaya to be saying that certain individuals—possibly Russian—were donating to Clinton's campaign and the Democratic National Committee using a fraudulent tax scheme to avoid reporting their transfers in Russia or the United States.[47] Having offered up information on criminal activity among Clinton's donor class—implying Clinton had accepted illegal foreign contributions—Veselnitskaya next discussed what Russian interests would want in exchange for more details about such allegations: the lifting of sanctions. Trump Jr.'s response to the mention of U.S. sanctions on Russia was, according to his 2017 testimony, that the lifting of U.S. sanctions on Russia was "not a campaign issue."[48] He will add, in responding to questions by the Senate Judiciary Committee, that everything the Russian attorney said in Trump Tower was "vague, ambiguous, and made no sense," which is why he cannot recall almost any of it.[49] According to Trump Jr.'s testimony, he never told his father anything about his meeting with the Russians—even the fact of its occurrence.[50] Yet after the meeting Trump's team continues "huddling" on the subject of misconduct by Hillary Clinton, and twenty minutes after the meeting ends, Donald Trump Sr. tweets about Clinton's emails for the first time in 2016, writing to Clinton via Twitter, in part, "[W]here are your 33,000 emails that you deleted?"[51]

In July 2018, the *Washington Post* will report that Trump's attorney Michael Cohen is prepared to tell investigators that not only did Trump know of the June 9 meeting in advance but explicitly authorized it during a conversation with his son for which Cohen was present.[52]

The *Los Angeles Times* will report that Ivanka Trump spoke to Veselnitskaya and Akhmetshin after their meeting with Trump Jr., Kushner, and Manafort ended.[53] Ivanka will not voluntarily reveal her contact with the Russians on June 9 at any point, despite the significant media, law enforcement, and congressional attention on the meeting. Steve Bannon will tell journalist Michael Wolff, of the June 9 meeting, "Even if you thought that this [meeting] was not treasonous, or unpatriotic, or bad . . . and I happen to think it's all of that, you should have called the FBI immediately," adding, "The chance that Don Jr. did not walk these jumos [*sic*] up to his father's office on the twenty-sixth floor is zero."[54] In the summer of 2017, Trump's spokesman Mark Corallo will quit, "privately confiding," according to Wolff's 2018 book, *Fire and Fury*, "that he believed the meeting on Air Force One [to compose a statement about the June 9 meeting] represented a likely obstruction of justice."[55] Another reason Corallo quits, according to *Politico*, is that he "was concerned about whether he was being told the truth about various matters."[56]

Twenty days after the June 9, 2016, meeting between the Trump campaign and several Russian nationals, Rob Goldstone again sends an email to Trump's secretary Rhona Graff. Also on the email recipient list are Dan Scavino, the Trump campaign's director of social media, and Konstantin Sidorkov, the director of partnership marketing for a website the *New York Times* calls "Russia's equivalent to Facebook."[57] Goldstone's email references the content of the June 9 Trump Tower meeting:

> I am following up . . . [on] something I had mentioned to Don [Jr.] and Paul Manafort during a meet recently. There are believed to be around 2 million Russian-American voters living in the USA and more than 1.6 million of these use the Russian "Facebook". . . . As I mentioned to you guys . . . they want to create a Vote Trump 2016 promotion aired directly at these users, people who will be voting in November. At the time [of the June 9 meeting] Paul had said he would welcome it. So I had the VK folks mock up a basic sample page which I am resending for your approval now.[58]

Don Jr. will claim to have no recollection of either he or Manafort discussing this subject with Goldstone on June 9.[59]

Contacts between the Trump campaign and Russian nationals are legion in May and June 2016. Just forty-eight hours after Manafort is formally named Trump's campaign manager on May 19, Papadopoulos emails him about a Putin-Trump meeting and alerts him to his ongoing contacts with the Russians.[60] Papadopoulos's email to Manafort is bookended, on May 14 and May 21, by additional correspondence between the young national security adviser and Maltese professor Joseph Mifsud.[61] By May 25, Papadopoulos has returned to where he first met Mifsud—Italy—and indeed is pictured on a visit to Link Campus University, where Mifsud not only works but also is "part of the management."[62] Less than two days after traveling to Mifsud's workplace, Papadopoulos is in Athens, Greece, as Vladimir Putin's plane touches down there.[63]

The same month, accused spy Maria Butina's boyfriend, GOP operative and NRA member Paul Erickson, writes the following in an email titled "Kremlin Connection" to top Trump campaign staffer Rick Dearborn:

> I'm now writing to you and Sen. Sessions in your roles as Trump foreign policy experts/advisors. . . . Happenstance and the (sometimes) international reach of the NRA placed me in a position a couple of years ago to slowly begin cultivating a back-channel to President Putin's Kremlin. Russia is quietly but actively seeking a dialogue with the U.S. that isn't forthcoming under the current administration. And for reasons that we can discuss in person or on the phone, the Kremlin believes that the only possibility of a true re-set in this relationship would be with a new Republican White House.[64]

Erickson's email, when published in full by *Rolling Stone* in April 2018, will be significant in several ways: it will confirm that Jeff Sessions gave inaccurate testimony in January 2017 about his receipt of communications from the Russians, even considering his defense of never having been so approached in his role as a Trump adviser; it will confirm that the NRA was not just instrumental but essential to the establishment of a clandestine back channel between the Kremlin and top Republican leaders, as will be alleged in the indictments against Erickson's girlfriend; it will put in writing something long implicit, namely, that Trump-Russia communications are largely being conducted "in person or on the phone" so as not to leave a paper or digital trail; it will gravely undercut claims by the chairman (Sessions) and director (Gordon) of Trump's National Security Advisory Committee that they were unaware of Russian attempts to communicate with the committee after Sessions allegedly "shut down" Papadopoulos's proposal to converse with Russian agents on March 31, 2016; and it will confirm for Sessions, one of the top officials in the Trump campaign—well before June's revelation of massive Russian hacking of the Clinton campaign and the Democratic National Committee—that the Russian government not only supports Trump's campaign but deems it mission critical that Trump be elected instead of Clinton.

The Trump campaign will later report that Dearborn forwarded Erickson's email to Jared Kushner, who thereafter nixed the idea of responding to Erickson's outreach on behalf of Torshin.[65] Yet within five days, Trump's son Don Jr. will be dining with Torshin at the NRA conference in Kentucky.[66] Torshin expresses his hope that he can renew his "old acquaintance" with Trump at an offsite event for wounded veterans, where he also plans to bring a gift for Melania.[67] It is unknown whether that meeting ultimately occurs, but Trump Jr. will later issue a statement through his attorney that nothing passed between him and Torshin but "gun-related small talk."[68]

In early June, Trump National Security Advisory Committee member Carter Page will "[stun] a gathering of high-powered Washington foreign policy experts . . . [by] going off topic with effusive praise for Russian President Vladimir Putin and Trump. . . . hail[ing] Putin as stronger and more reliable than President Obama . . . and then tout[ing] the positive effect a Trump presidency would have on U.S.-Russia relations."[69] The *Washington Post* will further report that, as had been boasted about by secretly recorded Kremlin agents in 2013, "many [foreign policy experts] . . . say that Page's views may be compromised by his investment in Russian energy giant Gazprom."[70] It is during this period that Page receives an invitation to speak in Moscow; according to his congressional testimony, he informs Jeff Sessions, J. D. Gordon, Corey Lewandowski, and Hope Hicks, Trump's personal assistant, about his planned trip, and none of them offers any objection.[71] Indeed, Page recounts that Lewandowski said, of the trip, "that's fine," though he told Page that the trip would have to be "unaffiliated with the campaign."[72] Page says he informed Sessions of his upcoming trip to Moscow at a dinner at the Capitol Hill Club; this was the same dinner at which Papadopoulos, who had been wanting to take a trip to Moscow to continue his clandestine negotiations with the Kremlin, sat beside Sessions the entire night.[73] This dinner also appears to be one of those to which Sessions invited Alfa Bank advisory board member and Gazprom lobbyist Richard Burt; according to *Politico*, it was at these dinners the Russian agent "was invited to discuss issues of national security and foreign policy [and] white papers" that he then gave to Sessions.[74] Asked about contact between Burt and Sessions and the other members of the National Security Advisory Committee, such as Papadopoulos and fellow Gazprom lobbyist Carter Page, Trump spokeswoman Hope Hicks will say, "I don't believe Mr. Trump or our policy staff has ever met Mr. Burt."[75]

Annotated History

In June, Kushner contracts with British firm Cambridge Analytica to institute a domestic "microtargeting" scheme for Trump's general election campaign; the data compiled will be left open by Cambridge Analytica for Russian actors to steal and weaponize.

Kushner's hiring of Brad Parscale was what led to the Trump campaign contracting with British firm Cambridge Analytica, which "microtargeted" U.S. voters by creating "psychographic" profiles to predict whom any individual voter would be most likely to vote for.[76] Cambridge Analytica now stands accused of having helped the Trump campaign spread automated news in the United States in the lead-up to the 2016 election. As *Vox* wrote, by the time of Election Day 2016, "Trump's bots . . . outnumbered Clinton's five to one. Pro-Trump programmers carefully adjusted the timing of content production during the debates, strategically colonized pro-Clinton hashtags, and then disabled activities after Election Day."[77] *Vox* quoted Martin Moore, the director of the Centre for the Study of Media, Communication and Power at King's College in London, as observing that "[Trump's campaign] was using 40,000 to 50,000 variants of ads every day that were continuously measuring responses and then adapting and evolving based on that response."[78]

While unconventional, Cambridge Analytica's methods may have remained uncontroversial had not four things been discovered after the election: that Michael Flynn was secretly consulting for SCL Group, the parent company of Cambridge Analytica, during the campaign and had failed to disclose this on his financial disclosure forms; that Russia's propaganda and fake-news campaigns prior to the 2016 election were so carefully targeted to locales where Trump needed assistance that, according to Sean Illing at *Vox*, "congressional and DOJ investigators believe that Trump's campaign might have helped guide Russia's voter targeting scheme," perhaps with Flynn's help; that Facebook user data quietly compiled by Cambridge Analytica employee Aleksandr Kogan—a professor associated with a Russian university who made multiple trips to Russia between 2014 and Election Day 2016—was (at best) negligently left accessible to remote users, with the result that Cambridge Analytica's microtargeting data was "accessed from Russia" during the election; and that Cambridge Analytica CEO Alexander Nix, in an undercover video, said that not only had he met personally with Trump many times, but in fact Cambridge Analytica was responsible for "all the research, all the data, all the analytics, all the targeting, . . . all the digital campaign, the television campaign and . . . all the strategy" of Trump's presidential run.[79] Nix's claims were alarming because, in the same undercover video in which he all but took credit for Trump's victory, he also revealed that Cambridge Analytica was willing to "encourage[e] sting operations involving bribes and paid sex in an effort to swing a campaign," and that the firm's opposition research was often leaked to "proxy organizations," of which Nix (who admitted to reaching out directly to WikiLeaks during the 2016 presidential campaign) said, "[You] feed them the material, and they do the work. . . . And so this stuff infiltrates the online community and expands but with no branding—so it's unattributable, untrackable."[80]

The *Washington Post* reported that the original impetus behind the campaign's use of Cambridge Analytica was to secure the unlimited financial support, through an independent pro-Trump group called "Make America Number 1 PAC," of mysterious billionaires Robert and Rebekah Mercer.[81] Robert Mercer not only created Cambridge Analytica, but he and his daughter Rebekah have been longtime backers of Steve Bannon's *Breitbart*, which was often used by the Trump team to spread misinformation during the presidential campaign (see chapter 10). Bannon was the cofounder of Cambridge Analytica.[82]

By late June, the "Brexit" vote is occurring in the United Kingdom—a Kremlin-backed push for the citizens of that nation to vote to leave the EU in a nationwide referendum. It is in part a trial run for the sort of election meddling the Kremlin is planning

in the United States. With the assistance of "Leave" backer and Trump ally Nigel Farage, the Kremlin strikes a significant blow against the future of Western democracy when the United Kingdom narrowly votes to leave the EU.

The parallels between the Brexit vote and the Trump-Russia scandal are uncanny. While not connected to the official "Leave" campaign, one of the primary proponents of the United Kingdom's exit from the EU—a man who committed significant funds to that aim—was millionaire businessman Arron Banks, and in June 2018, the *Guardian* reported that Banks "met Russian officials multiple times before the Brexit vote" and that these officials were "high-ranking." [83] Moreover, just as the Russians, according to the Steele dossier, dangled not just real estate deals but oil and gas opportunities before Trump, Banks was reportedly offered a "multibillion dollar opportunity to buy Russian goldmines." [84] The *Washington Post* reported that the Russians also "dangled a diamond mine" as a possible prize for the top "Leave" bankrollers and organizers.[85] And just as Putin's support for Trump's "America First" agenda suggests a hostility to NATO's continued ascendance in Europe, the *Guardian* reported that the Kremlin sought to coordinate with the "Leave" campaign because "Putin has long seen the eastward expansion of European Union influence as a threat." [86] As with the Trump campaign, Russian outreach to the leaders of the "Leave" campaign involved invitations to meetings and events, as well as the persistent involvement of Russia's ambassador (in this case its ambassador to the United Kingdom).

One of the "Leave" figureheads, Nigel Farage, met and campaigned with Trump and was accused of acting as a back channel to both Putin and WikiLeaks founder Julian Assange, who for years has been holed up in the Ecuadorian embassy in London as an asylum seeker.[87] The Farage-Assange allegation, leveled by Glenn Simpson of Fusion GPS, has Farage meeting several times with Assange at the Ecuadorian embassy and at least once bringing him a USB memory stick filled with data; Farage is known to have visited Assange at least once, in March 2017.[88] When asked by a reporter who saw him leaving the embassy why he was there, Farage replied that he "couldn't remember." [89]

The Farage-Putin allegation comes from Guy Verhofstadt, a Belgian politician and member of the European Parliament (EP) who acted as the chief representative for the EP in the Brexit negotiations. Verhofstadt considers Farage, according to the *Independent*, "[a] pro-Putin 'fifth [columnist]' who want[s] to destroy Europe from within. . . . 'They're doing only one thing: they take Kremlin money, they take Kremlin intelligence.' "[90]

Trump has been described as "friends" with the now-controversial Farage, taking the unusual step of publicly calling for him to be named Britain's ambassador to the United States.[91] During his July 2018 visit to England, the British government had to explicitly forbid Trump from meeting with Farage.[92]

Almost immediately after he receives Sam Clovis's email mentioning potential "legal issues" with a private citizen meeting with foreign officials, Papadopoulos gets on a plane and goes on a campaign-approved trip to Athens, Greece—just the sort of "neutral city" his Russian contacts had previously told him the Russians prefer to meet in.

On March 24, 2016, Papadopoulos had emailed "Trump campaign officials, including the Campaign Supervisor [Clovis] and several members of the campaign's foreign policy team," saying that his Russian contacts wanted "to arrange a meeting between us and the Russian leadership to discuss U.S.-Russia ties under President Trump. . . . in a 'neutral' city, or directly in Moscow."[93] Two days before the "Mayflower Speech," Papadopoulos returned to the idea of meeting the Russians in a "neutral" city, writing to Stephen Miller, "The Russian government has an open invitation by Putin for Mr. Trump to meet him when he is ready. . . . [T]hese governments tend to speak a bit more openly in 'neutral' cities."[94]

> Despite the secret nature of his early May trip to Greece, Papado-
> poulos nevertheless gives interviews with local media, and will do
> so again both when he returns to Athens in late May and when he
> travels to Greece for a third time in 2016 during the presidential
> transition.

Papadopoulos's behavior in late May 2016 mirrored his behavior in
Athens earlier in the month. As reported by Athens newspaper *Kathimerini*, during Papadopoulos's first trip "he would lower his voice so
as not to be overheard or drop hints of major contacts. . . . It was obvious that he didn't know a lot of people in Athens at the time, but
was eager to make important acquaintances."[95] The same reporter who
interviewed Papadopoulos in early May interviewed the Trump adviser again when he returned to Athens in late May. "He came back
to Athens a few weeks later," wrote Alexis Papachelas for *Kathimerini*. "By then he had met everyone he needed to know and spoke
very comfortably about the Greek president, the ministers of foreign
affairs and defense, and the head of the main opposition and important businessmen. He 'revealed' that [the campaign] had been secretly
planning a pre-election trip by Trump to Greece and Israel, which he
saw taking place that July. His contacts with the Greek government,
he claimed, were quite advanced and he appeared confident the visit
would happen. . . ."[96]

That the campaign was aware of Papadopoulos's trip is confirmed
in part by an event that happened a week after Papadopoulos arrived
in Athens for the second time in May. On June 3, Papadopoulos forwarded to Papachelas of *Kathimerini* an email from Trump's personal assistant, Hope Hicks, agreeing to an interview with the Greek
newspaper—though she noted to Papachelas, through Papadopoulos,
that she "needed a bit of time."[97] In late September, Papadopoulos contacted Papachelas to direct his attention to his recent interview with
Russia media outlet Interfax, in which he decried sanctions on Russia.[98] Greek media reported that same month that Papadopoulos met
in New York with an adviser to Greek foreign minister Nikos Kotzias,

George Tzitzikos.[99] The Papadopoulos-Tzitzikos meeting is the third time that Papadopoulos met with either the Greek foreign minister or one of his aides prior to the 2016 election—a significant number, given that, in September 2018, Papadopoulos confessed to having told the Greek foreign minister in May 2016 of the Kremlin possessing stolen Clinton emails.[100]

Papachelas's assessment of Papadopoulos's status in Greece during the Trump adviser's December 2016 trip to Greece is telling. "He had acquired a new status in Athens and was widely regarded as being the key to having Trump's ear. He was bestowed with awards, wined and dined by prominent Athenians and even appointed to the judging committee of a beauty pageant on a Greek island. I had expected him to get a job at the State Department," wrote the *Kathimerini* reporter in 2017.[101] Papadopoulos told another *Kathimerini* reporter that he was "actively involved" in the presidential transition. It is unclear whether the "Greek island" the beauty pageant was held on was Mykonos, where Simona Mangiante will say that Papadopoulos was contacted under "highly suspicious" circumstances by an Israeli who thereafter offered him "much money" to discuss Cyprus- and Israel-related "business" in Tel Aviv. Cyprus is another one of the seven EU nations that opposes Russian sanctions.[102] In August 2018, the special counsel's office reported that at some point in the months or years before his arrest in mid-2017 Papadopoulos received money from someone "he believed was likely an intelligence officer of a foreign country (other than Russia)."[103]

In June 2017, Vassilis Kikilias, the shadow minister for defense of the Greek political party New Democracy—then in the midst of an investigation into whether Greek defense minister Panos Kammenos broke the law with a military procurement agreement with Saudi Arabia—said that "he [Kikilias] will also be seeking answers regarding reports in foreign media that in 2016 Kammenos had secretly acted as a mediator to arrange a meeting between Trump's foreign policy adviser, George Papadopoulos, and Russian President Vladimir Putin."[104]

Twenty days after the June 9, 2016, meeting between the Trump campaign and several Russian nationals, Rob Goldstone again sends an email to Trump's secretary Rhona Graff. Also on the email recipient list are Dan Scavino, the Trump campaign's director of social media, and Konstantin Sidorkov, the director of partnership marketing for a website the *New York Times* calls "Russia's equivalent to Facebook."

The European bureau of *Politico* wrote an article titled "Need to reach Trump? Call Rhona," noting, "When longtime friends and associates of President Donald Trump want to reach him, they don't go directly to the White House. Instead, they call the woman who's been the gatekeeper at Trump Tower for a quarter century: Rhona Graff."[105] The news outlet called Graff "a conduit for those who want to quietly offer advice [to Trump], make personnel suggestions [to Trump] or get on the president's calendar" when Trump is in Florida instead of Washington.[106] Under questioning by Congress in September 2017, Donald Trump Jr. testified that, during the campaign, "a lot" of the communications sent to Trump went through Graff.[107]

But writing Graff instead of Trump wasn't just the accepted way to contact Trump when he was away from his office, *Politico* noted.[108] "POLITICO spoke to seven associates of Trump who still pass on messages to the president through Graff, most of whom requested anonymity so as not to risk their access. 'If I really wanted to whisper something in his ear, I would probably go to Rhona,' said [a] New York grocery billionaire . . . [who] has known Trump for decades."[109]

Just forty-eight hours after Manafort is formally named Trump's campaign manager on May 19, Papadopoulos emails him about a Putin-Trump meeting and alerts him to his ongoing contacts with the Russians.

Manafort, according to the *Washington Post*, prohibited any such Trump-Putin meeting in May 2016.[110] At the time, Manafort said via email to his deputy Rick Gates that the Russians needed to be informed of Manafort's decision "by someone low level in the campaign so as not to send any signal."[111] Some of Trump's allies have taken this as an indication that Manafort intended for *no one* involved in the Trump campaign to meet with any Russian agents, while acknowledging that that prohibition then needed to be respectfully conveyed to the Kremlin; in fact, Manafort's email covered only Trump himself and only prospective Trump trips to Moscow or Putin visits to America. In October 2017, *Slate* observed that Manafort's reference to a "signal" was likely not about decorum: "It's more plausible," wrote William Saletan, "that Manafort was trying not to alert nosy Americans—perhaps the same ones [in the intelligence community] who, on behalf of our government, might have monitored a Trump-Putin meeting more easily in the United States than in London."[112]

CHAPTER EIGHT

THE REPUBLICAN NATIONAL CONVENTION

July 2016

Summary

JULY 2016 SEES THE TRUMP CAMPAIGN BEGINNING ITS frantic search of the dark web for the Russian hackers holding Clinton's "missing" emails (see chapter 9), increasing the pace and boldness of its attempts at making direct contact with and receiving direct assistance from Russian nationals, and permitting not just its foreign policy but the Republican Party platform to be guided in part by the input of known Kremlin agents.

As the month begins, it is clear that America's electoral infrastructure is under significant, sustained attack; by the last week of the month, it is nearly certain that the Russians are behind this attack. The certainty that these attacks are benefitting only the Trump campaign encourages Trump's team to draw itself still closer to the Russians. In this effort, campaign staffers are emboldened by the candidate himself, who toward the close of the month will openly ask a hostile foreign nation to attack America. Even two years later many of those who heard Trump say, "Russia, if you're listening, I hope you're able to find the 30,000 [Clinton] emails that are missing," refuse to accept that they heard—live—collusion between a U.S. presidential candidate and a geopolitical foe.

In Rome, a former MI6 agent shares with an FBI agent the first pages of a dossier of raw intelligence he will be compiling through the end of the year. The actions of the Trump campaign in July 2016 will seem to confirm a good deal of the dossier's intelligence. For instance, Carter Page indeed meets with Kremlin officials in Moscow, as the dossier indicates, and Michael Cohen takes a suspicious trip to Italy just before the Republican National Convention that dovetails with the allegations about the extent of his collusive activities made in the dossier. And at the Republican National Convention in Cleveland, Jeff Sessions discusses sanctions with Sergey Kislyak and J. D. Gordon amends the GOP platform to benefit the Kremlin in ways that suggest the unifying conspiracy described by Steele's dossier—a traitorous policy-for-aid quid pro quo between Trump and the Kremlin—is accurate.

The Facts

AS TRUMP PREPARES TO ACCEPT THE REPUBLICAN NOMINAtion for president in Cleveland, many long-simmering Trump-Russia plans come to fruition, with Trump aides, allies, and associates finally making the direct contact with their Russian counterparts they have long planned—while simultaneously delivering on past promises of a reliably pro-Russia foreign policy. These intense exchanges come in the shadow of a national realization: that the Russians are attacking America's electoral infrastructure and seeking to interfere in the 2016 presidential election. This knowledge not only doesn't slow the pace of Trump-Russia interactions, it speeds them to a frenetic pace.

On May 16, 2016, Carter Page proposes in an email to Walid Phares and J. D. Gordon that Trump make a trip to Moscow that summer in place of Page himself, who has been invited to speak at the New Economic School in Moscow in July.[1] Page writes, in part, "As discussed, my strategy in order to keep in sync with the media relations guidelines of the campaign has been to make my key messages as low-key and apolitical as possible. But after seeing the principal's [Trump's] tweet . . . I got another idea. If he'd like to take my place and raise the temperature a little bit, of course I'd be more than happy to yield this honor to him."[2] The tweet Page is referring to, according to *Vox*, is one in which Trump calls Barack Obama "the worst president in U.S. history," because "in politics, and in life, ignorance is not a virtue."[3] In November 2017, Page will confirm that "take my place" indeed referred to Page's intention, at the time, of traveling to Moscow to give a lecture; Page's suggestion, therefore, was that he coordinate with his Russian contacts for Trump to make a trip to Russia during the campaign to "raise the temperature a little bit."[4]

This mid-May proposal from Page, along with a similar one from Papadopoulos around the same time, will eventually prompt new campaign manager Paul Manafort to write an email to his deputy Rick Gates, saying, "We need someone to communicate [to the Russians] that DT [Donald Trump] is not doing these trips [to Moscow]. It should be someone low level in the campaign so as not to send any signal."[5] The *Washington Post* will refer to Manafort's use of the term "signal"—a term also used by Papadopoulos in an email to one of his Russian contacts, Ivan Timofeev—as significant, noting that "some see that as a potential tell when it comes to a larger effort to coordinate with the Russians."[6] Indeed, at the time, Manafort is engaged in regular clandestine contact with his old business associate Konstantin Kilimnik, a Soviet-born businessman whom Robert Mueller's team will describe as having "active ties to Russian intelligence through the 2016 presidential election" in a 2017 court filing.[7] Kilimnik, according to the *Atlantic*, came to the United States shortly after Manafort ascended to the position of Trump's campaign manager; "He told his friends that he had come to the United States for 'very significant meetings,'" the *Atlantic* writes. "It wasn't hard for his friends to intuit what he meant. They had read the news reports that Paul Manafort had engineered his own comeback, procuring a top job in the Trump campaign. Just like in the good old days, Manafort had summoned Kilimnik to trail after him."[8]

Around the same time Manafort sends the message that someone "low level" needs to "communicate" to the Russians on Trump's behalf that he cannot make a trip to Moscow himself, Page will get a some-what contradictory message from the campaign's recently ousted campaign manager, Corey Lewandowski, who allegedly tells Page that it is fine for him to travel to Moscow in July: "if you'd like to go on your own, not affiliated with the campaign . . . that's fine."[9] In March 2017, Lewandowski will deny ever giving permission to Page to go to Moscow, telling Fox News's Jeanine Pirro, "I've never met or spoken to Carter Page in my life."[10] Eight months later, he will declare that his "memory has been refreshed" on the question and that he did indeed give Page permission to go to Moscow.[11] J. D. Gordon will say in November 2017 that he tried to "dissuade" Page from going to Moscow in July 2016 and that Page "went around me" to get permission to go; it will subsequently be revealed that not only did Page email Gordon alongside Lewandowski at the time he received permission for the trip, but that he contacted Gordon immediately after his return to report on the results of his visit to Moscow.[12] On being confronted with this evidence, Gordon will reply, "[I don't] recall all of Carter Page's emails. I was getting thousands of emails on the campaign and didn't read all of them."[13] Page will note that Hope Hicks, Trump's personal assistant, was also on the recipient list of his May email to Lewandowski and Gordon.[14]

In late August, Page will say that he is going "on leave" from the Trump campaign, a somewhat different account from what the Trump campaign will give via Sean Spicer in January 2017. Spicer will say Page was "put on notice months ago by the campaign."[15] During a December 2016 speech in Moscow, however, Page will refuse to say what sort of involvement he still has with Donald Trump and his team.[16]

Between January and November 2017, Page will maintain that he spoke "not one word" to anyone from the Kremlin when he was in Moscow in July 2016.[17] However, when the ranking Democrat on the House Permanent Select Committee on Intelligence, Adam Schiff, confronts him, during his November 2017 congressional testimony, with a July 2016 email he sent to Gordon and Tera Dahl—an "ally of Steve Bannon's," according to CNN—in which he discussed the "incredible insights and outreach" from "Russian legislators" and "senior members of the Presidential administration [in Moscow]" that had resulted from his trip to Moscow, Page will concede that he did indeed have contact with both the Kremlin and Rosneft (Russia's state-owned oil company) in Moscow.[18] The latter admission is significant, because the Steele dossier alleges that not only did Page meet with a Rosneft executive in Moscow, but while doing so he received an offer from Rosneft's CEO, Igor Sechin, that, if accepted, would potentially provide Trump hundreds of millions of dollars from the then upcoming sale of a stake in the state-owned oil giant to Glencore, a Swiss multinational trading and mining company, and Qatar Investment Authority, a Qatari state-owned holding company that is Glencore's largest shareholder.[19] In November 2017, Schiff will further confront Page with a memo Page wrote to campaign officials after his Moscow trip in which he alerts them to the fact that "in a private conversation, [Russian deputy prime minister Arkady] Dvorkovich expressed strong support for Mr. Trump and a desire to work together toward devising better solutions in response to the vast range of international problems."[20] Page's explanation of the memo will be that he was not being forthright—that there was no "private conversation" with Dvorkovich, only Page "listening to Dvorkovich's speech and public statements, and . . . reading the Russian press and watching Russian television" in order to triangulate what he thought Dvorkovich's reaction to the Trump campaign might be.[21] Page's "incredible insights and outreach" were, he told Congress, taken from television, newspapers, and lectures that Page consumed without any contact with Dvorkovich beyond what he described as some "pleasantries."[22] In June 2018, Congressman Schiff will write the chairman of the House intelligence committee, Devin Nunes, of his concern that "certain witnesses may have testified untruthfully before our committee. . . . [and] Mr. Mueller should consider whether perjury charges are warranted in light of the additional evidence in his possession."[23]

While Page is in Moscow, Manafort is preparing for the convention in part by contacting Oleg Deripaska, his old boss and one of Putin's two or three closest allies, via Kilimnik; Manafort's offer to Deripaska is a simple one: private briefings for the Russian oligarch on the internal workings and goings-on of the Trump presidential campaign.[24] As more of Manafort's spring and summer 2016 emails are released, it is discovered that he referenced Deripaska—and his significant debts to Deripaska—in code when writing to Kilimnik.[25] Manafort's spokesman will call the emails "innocuous"; Deripaska's spokesman "dismisse[s] the email exchanges as scheming by 'consultants in the notorious "beltway bandit" industry,'" referring to the defense contractors operating along the Capital Beltway, Washington's outer ring expressway.[26]

A month before the convention, Trump business associate Felix Sater—the Russian mafia–linked rainmaker for the Trump Organization who is, in June 2016, still trying to help Trump and his attorney Michael Cohen advance a Trump Tower deal with Andrei Rozov—emails Cohen to suggest that Cohen attend a business conference in Russia "that would be attended by top Russian financial and government leaders, including President Vladimir Putin."[27] Sater's suggestion isn't a casual one, as the *Washington Post* will later observe; Sater had put a lot of thought, time, and effort in setting up this opportunity for Cohen. According to the *Post*,

> Sater encouraged Cohen to attend the St. Petersburg International Economic Forum, with Sater telling Cohen that he could be introduced to Russian Prime Minister Dmitry Medvedev, top financial leaders and perhaps Putin. . . . At one point, Sater told Cohen that Putin's spokesman, Dmitry Peskov, could help arrange the discussions, according to a person familiar with the exchange. . . . The correspondence included a formal invitation to the conference from the Russian leader of the event. . . . The invitation included a letter signed by a conference official designed to help Cohen get a visa from the Russian government. The St. Petersburg forum is a premiere [*sic*] government-hosted economic conference held annually under Putin's auspices. Business leaders from Russia and other countries convene in

what is designed to allow high-level conversation similar to the
international business conference held each year in Davos, Swit-
zerland, and at the same time to show off Russian investment
opportunities.28

Peskov's involvement in the plan to bring Cohen to Moscow is noteworthy, as Cohen had emailed Peskov asking for his help on the
Trump-Rozov tower prior to any Americans voting in the 2016 GOP
primaries. Peskov never responded to that email, according to statements by the two men, though he would later admit to having seen it.29
But now, with Trump scheduled to assume leadership of the Republican Party at the party's national convention in Cleveland, Peskov offers
to introduce Cohen to many of the most powerful Russians in business
and government, perhaps including Putin himself. It is an offer that
would have given Trump and Cohen much of what they had wanted
since the mid-2000s: immediate, facilitated access to the corridors of
power in Moscow. Whereas Trump had once boasted, falsely, that "all
of the oligarchs" came to his 2013 beauty pageant in Moscow, in this
instance Cohen really would have the opportunity to hobnob with those
oligarchs and politicians Trump had once hoped to meet in Russia.

Yet Cohen tells Sater no.

Cohen's reason for declining Sater's offer is worth additional consideration. According to the *Washington Post*, "Cohen declined the invitation to the economic conference, citing the difficulty of attending
so close to the GOP convention."30 On its face, Cohen's reply is reasonable, given how important the attorney was to Trump at the time
(and vice versa) and the fact that Cohen had only three clients on his
client roster in mid-2016, with Trump being far and away the most
time-consuming. Moreover, the convention was a landmark event in
Trump's life, and Cohen was, after all, Trump's loyal foot soldier.

As it turned out, Cohen was indeed busy in the twelve days immediately prior to the 2016 Republican National Convention: he was on
"vacation."31

According to Cohen, his pre-convention vacation saw him sunning
in Italy with actor and E Street Band guitarist Steven Van Zandt. Per

BuzzFeed, "[Cohen] said credit card receipts would prove he stayed in Capri, an island off the Italian coast, but he declined to make those receipts available."[32]

Roger Friedman, a longtime Fox News journalist and the founder of the entertainment news website *Showbiz 411*, says that Cohen is not telling the truth about his whereabouts in early July 2016. "I can tell you exclusively that Cohen lied," writes Friedman. "Sources tell me that Maureen van Zandt, Steve's wife, has confirmed that even though she was in Rome with her husband at the time for work, they know nothing about Cohen or his statement. They weren't in Capri."[33] *BuzzFeed* calls Cohen's claim that he was in Italy when the Steele dossier says he went to Prague in the summer of 2016 "intriguing," because flying into Italy—as it appears Cohen did, based on the stamps in his passport—immediately "places [him] in what's known as the Schengen Area: a group of 26 European countries, including the Czech Republic, that allows visitors to travel freely among them without getting any additional passport stamps. Upon entering the Schengen Area, visitors get a rectangular stamp with the date, a country code, their port of entry, and a symbol showing how they entered—such as an airplane or a train."[34] Cohen's passport is a topic of speculation in the media after he goes on Sean Hannity's television show and waves it about, saying it clearly has no stamps from Prague; Hannity mentions wanting to look inside it but never does.[35] Journalists will later uncover that Hannity is one of Cohen's three clients, a fact Hannity has never disclosed in any of his interviews with the attorney.[36]

Apropos of the mystery of Cohen's European vacation, the *Guardian* reports that British intelligence "became aware in late 2015 of suspicious 'interactions' between figures connected to Trump and known or suspected Russian agents. . . . This intelligence was passed to the US. . . . Over the next six months, until summer 2016, a number of western agencies shared further information on contacts between Trump's inner circle and Russians. . . . The European countries that passed on electronic intelligence—known as SIGINT—included Germany, Estonia and Poland. Australia . . . also relayed material."[37] *Politico* augments this reporting by noting that the Steele dossier "said the Kremlin used 'operationally soft' cities in Europe such as Prague for meetings with Trump associates in order to evade detection and provide both sides with plausible deniability. . . . Russia's intelligence services—known informally as the FSB, the GRU and the SVR—have for decades used such a tactic in Europe. Current and former U.S. intelligence officials [say] . . . Kremlin spies are trained to hold their meetings in neutral and inconspicuous locations."[38] Certainly, Papadopoulos had met Mifsud in Italy in March 2016 and then traveled again to Italy to Mifsud's place of employment in May 2016; whether Cohen was in Italy, Prague (the Czech Republic), or both, he was in a location conducive to meetings with Russian intelligence, according to their standard operating procedures.

On April 13, 2018, McClatchy will break the news that Special Counsel Robert Mueller has evidence Cohen did indeed go to Prague in the time frame alleged in the Steele dossier—August or September— entering the Czech Republic via Germany.[39] The mystery of why Cohen went to Italy—a repeated Trump-Russia meeting spot in the 120 days before the Republican National Convention—and then gave the media a false alibi has not yet been resolved. According to *BuzzFeed*, "The [Steele] dossier claims that Cohen was dispatched to Prague to 'clean up the mess' left behind by two revelations: that Trump's former campaign manager Paul Manafort had a financial relationship with a politically toxic Ukrainian president and that campaign adviser Carter Page visited top Russian officials [in Moscow in July]."[40] While information about Manafort's ties to Ukraine would indeed not become public knowledge until mid-August, Cohen entered Italy just a day after Page left Moscow.[41]

At the convention in Cleveland, Jeff Sessions, chairman of Trump's National Security Advisory Committee, meets with Russian ambassador Sergey Kislyak; in June 2017, Sessions, while testifying before Congress, will agree with the late senator John McCain (R-AZ) that he raised "Russia['s] invasion of Ukraine or annexation of Crimea" when he spoke to Kislyak in Cleveland.[42] After what Sessions later calls a "short and informal" conversation with Kislyak, the two men agree to continue their discussion in Sessions's office on September 8.[43]

Sessions will fail to disclose either meeting in his Senate confirmation hearing in January 2017.[44] Even when he does reveal that these conversations occurred, he will not disclose that he and Kislyak also discussed—as he had originally assured Congress he had not—the presidential campaign. The truth is revealed only by subsequent U.S. intelligence intercepts of Kislyak reporting back to Moscow.[45] Instead of admitting to this topic of discussion, Sessions will dissemble before Congress by saying that he took both the Republican National Convention and September 2016 meetings with Kislyak exclusively in his role as a member of the Senate Armed Services Committee.[46]

During a pre-convention subcommittee meeting, J. D. Gordon, Sessions's right-hand man and the director of Trump's National Security Advisory Committee, insists that the GOP change a plank of its platform to eliminate proposed language on giving lethal weaponry to anti-Russia rebels in Ukraine.[47] When Diana Denman, the sponsor of the platform language on lethal weaponry in Ukraine, resists, Gordon persists, telling her across several conversations that he has called Trump Tower and spoken to Trump personally multiple times and that Trump wants the language changed. He says, moreover, that the language he is pushing for was not only "cleared" by Trump but explicitly laid out by him at a meeting at Trump International Hotel in D.C. on March 31. Gordon succeeds in blocking the language.[48] Afterward, Manafort will say he had no involvement in the change; when asked about the change, Trump will likewise say he was in no way involved in it.[49] Asked by CNN to explain his comments indicating Trump's involvement, Gordon will suddenly change his story and say that in fact neither Manafort nor Trump was involved in the platform change.[50] Meanwhile, Manafort's protégé, Kilimnik, will later boast to political operatives in Ukraine "that he had played a role in gutting a proposed amendment to the Republican Party platform that would have staked out a more adversarial stance towards Russia."[51]

Shortly after the platform is changed, Carter Page, recently returned from Moscow, sends an email to Gordon and several other members of the National Security Advisory Committee, including former Department of Defense inspector general Joseph Schmitz and Bannon associate Tera Dahl, congratulating them on the change to the platform.[52] Page, Gordon, Phares, and Sessions will all engage with Kislyak at the Global Partners in Diplomacy event in Cleveland, an event also attended by Schmitz. Gordon will say that Phares was present when Gordon "stressed to the Russian envoy [Kislyak] that he would like to improve relations with Russia"; for his part, Phares will emphatically deny ever meeting the Russian ambassador.[53] *USA Today*, reporting on the story in March 2017, will note that in November 2016 Trump's personal assistant, Hope Hicks, told the media, "There was no communication between the campaign and any foreign entity during the campaign," and "The campaign had no contact with Russian officials."[54] Several days after the convention, ABC News's George Stephanopoulos will ask Manafort if there are any connections between the Trump campaign and Russia or its president. "No, there are not," Manafort will say, "and you know, there's no basis to it."[55] Some of the Trump team's late-summer denials on the Russia front will be even more bewildering; in September 2016, spokesman Jason Miller will say of Carter Page, "Mr. Page is not an advisor and has made no contribution to the campaign. He's never been part of our campaign. Period."[56]

On July 20, 2016, Papadopoulos is asked to sit on an American Jewish Committee panel at an event connected to the Republican National Convention. He appears alongside U.S. congressmen Tom Marino (R-PA) and Ted Yoho (R-FL), Senator Bob Corker (R-TN), and several others, and is introduced as the "director of the Center for International Energy & Natural Resources Law at the London Centre of International Law Practice."[57] Papadopoulos is also contacted, in July, by Sergei Millian, a man "claiming to have worked with the Trump organization to sell real estate in Russia," according to a July 2016 interview with ABC News.[58] Papadopoulos will tell CNN in a September 2018 interview that Millian asked him to "work for him for $30,000 a month as some sort of P.R. [public relations] consultant for an energy firm in Russia. . . . the qualifier was that I had to work for Trump at the same time."[59]

As the Trump campaign begins in earnest its hunt for Clinton's "missing" emails (see chapter 9), the data firm Jared Kushner just hired, the Bannon-founded Cambridge Analytica, reaches out to WikiLeaks in an attempt to see if Russian hackers have deposited Clinton's emails with Julian Assange's outfit—which has just released twenty thousand emails and eight thousand files stolen from the Democratic National Committee.[60] It will later be revealed that a Cambridge Analytica director, Brittany Kaiser, met directly with Assange in February 2017 to "discuss [the] U.S. election" and that she "channeled payments and donations to WikiLeaks" post-election.[61]

As Cambridge Analytica—called "Steve Bannon's baby" by longtime employee and eventual whistle-blower Christopher Wylie—is "reaching out" to Assange in late July, Bannon is just three weeks from being named the chief executive of Trump's presidential campaign.[62] Meanwhile, Manafort is approximately three weeks from being ousted from his role as campaign manager—a campaign shake-up that occurs almost immediately after Trump receives his first classified national security briefing.

Unbeknownst to the media, the Trump campaign's hunt for the Clinton emails—marked by attempts to reach out to Russians on the dark web to locate any tranche of Clinton documents it can find—is in full swing by the time of the Republican National Convention in mid-month. Indeed, by July 27, 2016, the date of Trump's "Russia, if you're listening" comment in Florida, a GOP operative named Peter W. Smith, who says in documents signed by his hand that he is working with Michael Flynn, Steve Bannon, Sam Clovis, and Kellyanne Conway, claims to have already connected with Russian hackers on the dark web and received a stockpile of Clinton emails.[63] Smith had by then already reached out to Matt Tait, a cybersecurity expert at the University of Texas at Austin, to try to authenticate the emails, but had been unable to do so because Tait refused to sign a nondisclosure agreement.[64]

On July 25, the FBI begins investigating the hack of the DNC; on July 26, U.S. intelligence officials tell the White House that they have "high confidence" that Russia was behind the hack; on July 27, Trump, having heard the by then universal speculation that Russia has hacked the DNC, publicly invites the Russians to continue committing cybercrimes against American citizens.[65]

On July 29, the Democratic Congressional Campaign Committee announces that it also has been hacked.[66]

Annotated History

At the convention in Cleveland, Jeff Sessions, chairman of Trump's National Security Advisory Committee, meets with Russian ambassador Sergey Kislyak; in June 2017, Sessions, while testifying before Congress, will agree with the late senator John McCain (R-AZ) that he raised "Russia['s] invasion of Ukraine or annexation of Crimea" when he spoke to Kislyak in Cleveland. After what Sessions calls a "short and informal" conversation with Kislyak, the two men agree to continue their discussion in Sessions's office on September 8. Sessions will fail to disclose either meeting in his Senate confirmation hearing in January 2017. Even when he does reveal that these conversations occurred, he will not disclose that he and Kislyak also discussed—as he had originally assured Congress he had not—the presidential campaign. The truth is revealed only by subsequent U.S. intelligence intercepts of Kislyak reporting back to Moscow. Instead of admitting to this topic of discussion, Sessions will dissemble before Congress by saying that he took both the Republican National Convention and September 2016 meetings with Kislyak exclusively in his role as a member of the Senate Armed Services Committee.

In March 2017, Sessions's spokeswoman told the media that Sessions's omissions under oath were justified by Sessions having been asked by Congress only about "communications between Russia and the Trump campaign—not about meetings he took as a senator and a member of the Armed Services Committee."[67] In responding to questions from Senator John McCain during his June 13, 2017, congressional testimony, Sessions said that he "may" have discussed "Russia-related security issues."[68] He then said to McCain, "I just don't have a real recall of the meeting," and "I just was basically willing to meet and see what he discussed."[69] This last comment indicates that, counter to what he would later contend, Sessions was not clear with Kislyak before their

September 8 meeting that only certain topics appropriate to his Senate role could be discussed. Moreover, while Sessions claimed that his discussion of Ukraine with Kislyak got "testy," Sessions, as a Trump surrogate on national security, was obligated to hew closely to Trump's pro-Russia, anti-sanctions policy—which would have been highly unlikely to anger Kislyak.[70] Nor would Sessions have been likely to speak extemporaneously on the subject; during Sessions's 2017 testimony, McCain had drily observed, in response to the notion that the Alabama senator had discussed "Russia-related security issues with Kislyak," "I don't recall you as being particularly vocal on such issues."[71]

The Sessions-Kislyak meetings in 2016 were irregular in other ways as well. In March 2017, *Vox* contacted all twenty-six members of the Senate Armed Services Committee and not one had met with Russia's ambassador in 2016; meanwhile, Sessions had encountered the Russian ambassador three times: at the Mayflower Hotel, at the Republican National Convention, and in his office in the Capitol.[72] And when the *Atlantic*'s Julia Ioffe asked a senior Republican Senate staffer in June 2017 whether Sessions "was known as a foreign-policy specialist who met regularly with ambassadors during his 20 years in the Senate," the staffer's incredulous response was, "Is that a serious question? He's clueless."[73]

During a pre-convention subcommittee meeting, J. D. Gordon, Sessions's right-hand man and the director of Trump's National Security Advisory Committee, insists that the GOP change a plank of its platform to eliminate proposed language on giving lethal weaponry to anti-Russia rebels in Ukraine. When Diana Denman, the sponsor of the platform language on lethal weaponry in Ukraine, resists, Gordon persists, telling her across several conversations that he has called Trump Tower and spoken to Trump personally multiple times and that Trump wants the language changed. He says, moreover, that the language he is pushing for was not only "cleared" by Trump but explicitly laid out by him at a meeting at Trump International Hotel in D.C. on March 31.

**Gordon succeeds in blocking the language. Afterward, Manafort
will say he had no involvement in the change; when asked about
the change, Trump will likewise say he was in no way involved
in it.**

Business Insider reported in March 2017 that on March 2 Gordon had
told CNN's Jim Acosta that he "advocated for the GOP platform to include language against arming Ukrainians against pro-Russian rebels
[because] this was in line with Trump's views, expressed at a March
[2016] national security meeting at the unfinished Trump hotel [in
D.C.]."[74] According to Gordon, "this was the language Donald Trump
himself wanted and advocated for back in March [2016]."[75] At that
March 31, 2016, National Security Advisory Committee meeting—
which Trump in November 2017 called "very unimportant"—Gordon
said that the candidate had laid out a sufficient vision of his Russia-
Ukraine policy for his assembled team to understand how he would
want a highly technical plank in the GOP platform handled nearly four
months later.[76] But Gordon's summary of Trump's March 2016 remarks ("he didn't want to go to 'WWIII' over Ukraine") does not explain his confidence that in seeking a pro-Russia platform change in
Cleveland he was doing the then candidate's bidding.[77] Gordon told
Business Insider in January 2017 that he "never left" his "assigned side
table" or "spoke publicly" at the RNC committee meeting in which
the platform change on Ukraine was discussed.[78] He said also, again
contradicting what he would later tell Acosta, that "neither Mr. Trump
nor Mr. Manafort were involved in those sort of details [of the GOP
platform], as they've made clear."[79]

NPR reported in December 2017 that Gordon told Denman that
"Trump [had] directed him to support weakening that position [on
Ukraine] in the official platform."[80] Denman said that Gordon was
quite specific about his orders, "inform[ing] her he had phoned 'New
York' about the Ukraine proposal" and "had discussed the issue with
Trump."[81] Denman later indicated that another "Trump campaign rep-
resentative" was with Gordon when he protested her amendment, and
that Gordon himself later disclosed, unexpectedly, that he had run the

amendment by John Mashburn and Rick Dearborn—the former of whom later told Congress that he already knew (from Papadopoulos) that the Kremlin had stolen Clinton emails, and the latter of whom had been in contact in both May and June with Alexander Torshin, the Russian banker now alleged to be accused spy Maria Butina's handler.[82]

That the platform change was a substantial topic of conversation within Trump's National Security Advisory Committee is evidenced by the July 14, 2016, email read aloud by Congressman Schiff during Carter Page's House Intelligence Committee testimony—"As for the Ukraine amendment, excellent work." That email was sent to a much wider group of Trump national security advisers than originally supposed, including Joseph Schmitz, Walid Phares, Bert Mizusawa, and Chuck Kubic, as well as J. D. Gordon and Tera Dahl.[83]

In March 2017, *USA Today* reported that it wasn't just Page, Gordon, Sessions, Phares, and Schmitz who attended the Global Partners in Diplomacy event in Cleveland—with the first four of those five meeting with Kislyak—but also future Trump deputy National Security Advisor K. T. McFarland.[84] Whether McFarland met with Kislyak in July is unknown, but five months later she would advise Flynn during his clandestine negotiations with Kislyak over U.S. sanctions on Russia.[85]

These repeated overlaps between Gordon, Page, and Schmitz are also noteworthy. Given the trips to Hungary taken by Page and Schmitz in the summer of 2016, it's significant that Gordon, too, was a "frequent visitor" to that country, according to *Hungarian Spectrum*, which noted Gordon had a "long-standing relationship with Hungarian government figures." According to an interview Gordon gave to Hungarian media outlet *Mandiner*, the Trump adviser visited Hungary six times between 2013 and 2016—most recently just after the 2016 election.[86] Not long after Schmitz and Page returned from Hungary, GOP activist and NRA member Paul Erickson introduced Gordon to Maria Butina. The two would later attend a Styx concert together.[87]

CHAPTER NINE

THE HUNT FOR HER EMAILS

July to September 2016

Summary

HAVING NOT RECEIVED ANY STOLEN "CLINTON DIRT" FROM Kremlin agent Joseph Mifsud when the Maltese professor first revealed to George Papadopoulos that the Kremlin had such information in April 2016, and having failed to get any such information from Kremlin agents at Trump Tower in June 2016, the Trump campaign continues nonetheless its efforts to appease the Kremlin through policy proposals and begins a clandestine effort to finally find what it has long sought: Clinton's "missing" emails.[1,2]

The Facts

FROM JULY TO SEPTEMBER 2016, TRUMP'S NATIONAL SECU-rity Advisory Committee coordinates the majority of the campaign's back-channel appeasement efforts. George Papadopoulos, one of the first men appointed to Trump's National Security Advisory Committee, gives an interview with Russian media in which he underscores that Trump will eliminate sanctions on Russia if elected.[3] Carter Page, another of the first five appointees to the National Security Advisory Committee, is cleared to travel to Moscow for a conference, during which he meets with both Kremlin officials and an executive from Rosneft. The Steele dossier says Trump is offered the brokerage of a 19 percent stake in Rosneft if the Russian sanctions are lifted when he is elected.[4] Page fails to disclose his Kremlin and Rosneft contacts in subsequent interviews with media and even denies such meetings took place until emails show they did.[5] He does report his activities to the Trump campaign, however.[6] In September, Page travels to Hungary and discusses U.S.-Russia policy with several Hungarian government officials; while there, he meets with a Russian whose name he will not divulge, even to Congress.[7]

During the summer of 2016, Joseph Schmitz—like Carter Page, one of the first five appointees to Trump's National Security Advisory Committee—travels to Hungary for unknown reasons.[8] Whether in Hungary for this purpose or not, Schmitz is at the time engaged in an effort to track down Clinton dirt on the dark web in the form of stolen emails.[9] He finds a trove of supposed Clinton emails from an unspecified source and takes it to a congressional committee, the FBI, and the State Department; the emails are presumed to be fake by an outside cybersecurity expert, and his request to transfer custody of the emails to the State Department and to the inspector general for the intelligence community is denied.[10] During his meetings with government officials, Schmitz says that he is working to find Clinton's emails with a "client" who, like him, has an ongoing security clearance from prior employment.[11] The description of his client Schmitz provides could fit many people, one of whom is Michael Flynn—the "shadow" head of Trump's national security team, as he has never been formally named to Trump's National Security Advisory Committee. CNN will report in April 2018 that "in the fall of 2016 . . . U.S. intelligence officials picked up chatter likely between Russian hackers hoping to steal Clinton's emails and possibly get them to foreign policy adviser Michael Flynn and Trump's team through an intermediary."[12] Of the possibility that Schmitz's unspecified dark web source for the presumptively fake Clinton emails he attempted to transfer to U.S. government officials was Russian, CNN writes, quoting Peter Clement, a retired top CIA analyst, "that it is 'extremely plausible' that [Schmitz's] penchant for conspiracy theories could have made him a target for various foreign influencers, including Russia. 'There's a lot we don't know, but Russians during the campaign were clearly targeting specific groups and parts of the country,' Clement said . . . [and] Schmitz's business ties 'would have made him stand out.' His small law firm represents a major Russian airline previously sanctioned by the US State Department for arms deals with Iran." [13]

Whether working with Schmitz or not, during this period Flynn is engaged in the very same effort as Schmitz is: seeking Clinton's emails on the dark web, in his case with the assistance of a cutout, GOP operative Peter W. Smith.[14] Smith receives a tranche of emails from sources he believes to be Russian hackers but cannot get the emails authenticated.[15] As Smith tries to recruit additional people to his cause in September, he reveals in a recruitment document that not only is he working with Michael Flynn but also with Steve Bannon, Sam Clovis, and Kellyanne Conway.[16] In May 2017, Smith will commit suicide in a Minnesota hotel room, leaving behind a note that says to investigators, among other things, "NO FOUL PLAY WHATSOEVER."[17]

At least six members of Trump's national security team are engaged in outreach to Russian nationals during this period, with two of them also part of the effort to find Clinton's "missing" emails. Trump expresses his frustration with the failure thus far of the latter effort by publicly asking Russia to find and turn over Clinton's "30,000" deleted emails to American nationals.[18] Within twenty-four hours, Russian hackers have begun cyber-intrusions intended to find the very documents Trump requested.[19] Three weeks later, on August 17, Trump receives his first classified security briefing as a presidential candidate.[20] Less than a month before, on July 26, top intelligence officials had determined with "high confidence" that the Russians were involved in the DNC breach.[21] At his classified briefing in August, Trump is told that Russia is likely seeking to interfere with the 2016 election and indeed wants specifically to infiltrate his campaign.[22] But there is no abatement in the Trump team's outreach to Russia. In fact, Trump becomes, in the ensuing weeks, quite publicly enamored with WikiLeaks, a non-state hostile intelligence service that has made contact with both Trump's son (September 20) and Trump adviser Roger Stone (August 8) and is engaged in an ongoing effort to publish reams of damaging information stolen by Russian hackers from the Democratic National Committee and the Clinton campaign.[23]

By comparison, the intelligence community is so concerned about Russian actions that CIA director John Brennan warns Putin's FSB, his domestic intelligence service, to immediately cease all meddling in the U.S. election.[24] The one change Trump makes after his August 17 classified briefing is that, within forty-eight hours of being told that Russia is behind the hacking of the DNC, he fires campaign manager Paul Manafort.[25] The reason given for the firing is that Manafort has become a distraction after the news, four days earlier, that he received secret payments from Putin allies in the Ukraine.[26]

In London, Alexander Nix, the head of Cambridge Analytica, which has been hired by the Trump campaign for its data services and at which top Trump adviser Steve Bannon had served as a vice president, reaches out to WikiLeaks founder Julian Assange to try to track down Clinton's emails.[27] Trump's campaign is by now engaged in a three-front battle to acquire stolen materials from the Russians: Trump asks for them directly and publicly; Schmitz, Flynn, Bannon, Clovis, Conway, and once-removed Trump agent Peter W. Smith hunt for them on the dark web; and Trump's son Don Jr., Trump's friend Roger Stone, and the Trump campaign's data firm, Cambridge Analytica, communicate directly with Russian hackers (Stone) or WikiLeaks (Don Jr. and Cambridge Analytica), the organization releasing the materials the Russian hackers stole.

Throughout this period, a server at Russia's Alfa Bank is "pinging" a Trump Tower server thousands of times for reasons that are unclear, though one possible explanation is that data is being transmitted.[28] According to computer scientists who gained access to the internet server records, 99 percent of all pings of Trump Tower during this period come from either Russia's Alfa Bank or a server controlled by the brother-in-law of Erik Prince,[29] like Michael Flynn a "shadow" national security adviser never formally recognized by the campaign. Russian cyber activities ramp up in other spheres as well, as Russian operatives launch a "spear-phishing operation" on VR Systems, an election-software company.[30] Elsewhere, Russian hackers begin their attack on election systems in twenty-one states.[31]

Trump's then campaign manager Paul Manafort emails an intermediary to offer Putin ally Oleg Deripaska—Manafort's former boss—clandestine briefings on the internal workings of the Trump campaign and the campaign's recent progress.[32] This occurs three weeks before the FBI initiates an investigation of the hacking of the Democratic National Committee (July 25) and then opens up a counterintelligence operation investigating covert Trump-Russia communications (July 31)—the FBI's counterintelligence operation having been prompted by a drunken George Papadopoulos telling an Australian diplomat in a London bar in May 2016 that the Russians have been peddling "dirt" on Clinton.[33]

At the first presidential debate, despite having received a classified national security briefing forty days earlier stating with "high confidence" that the Russians were hacking Americans and American organizations with the aim of interfering in the 2016 election, Trump tells a national audience that no one knows who is doing the hacking and that it could well be "somebody sitting on their bed that weighs 400 pounds."[34]

Annotated History

George Papadopoulos, one of the first men appointed to Trump's National Security Advisory Committee, gives an interview with Russian media in which he underscores that Trump will eliminate sanctions on Russia if elected.

Papadopoulos's September 30, 2016, interview with Russian media outlet Interfax, which the *Washington Post* reported on in March 2018, was directly authorized by Trump's deputy communications director Bryan Lanza. In the interview, Papadopoulos communicated to a Russian audience that "[U.S.] sanctions [on Russia] have done little more than turn Russia towards China"—a statement that became the interview's headline—and "unfortunately for the U.S., sanctions on Russia have resulted in massive energy deals between Russia and China." [35] The interview came in the final six weeks of the presidential campaign, at a time when WikiLeaks was releasing digital materials stolen by Russian hackers and threatening to continue doing so through Election Day. In fact, according to a December 2017 CNN report, Lanza authorized Papadopoulos's media statements to a Russian audience not long after Donald Trump Jr. had received, on September 14, an email with the website address for documents given to WikiLeaks by—as was understood at the time—Russian hackers. [36]

Carter Page, another of the first five appointees to the National Security Advisory Committee, is cleared to travel to Moscow for a conference, during which he meets with both Kremlin officials and an executive from Rosneft. The Steele dossier says Trump is offered the brokerage of a 19 percent stake in Rosneft if the Russian sanctions are lifted when he is elected. Page fails to disclose his Kremlin and Rosneft contacts in subsequent interviews with media and even denies such meetings took place until emails show they did. He does report his activities to the Trump campaign, however. In September, Page travels to Hungary for reasons that remain unclear; while there, he meets with a Russian whose name he will not divulge, even to Congress.

In his November 2 testimony to the House Permanent Select Committee on Intelligence, Carter Page gave evasive answers on the question of whether he'd met a Russian in Budapest during the same trip in which he met with Hungary's ambassador to the United States, Réka Szemerkényi. Those answers include "not that I can recall," "there may . . . at a hotel . . . there were a few people passing through there," "I have no recollection because it was totally immaterial and nothing serious was discussed," and "I vaguely recall that, you know, there may have been someone."[37] The possibility that Page met a Russian in Budapest is of interest to congressional, FBI, and Department of Justice investigators because, as has been noted by the *Hungarian Free Press*, Budapest is "the European Headquarters of Putin's FSB."[38]

During the summer of 2016, Joseph Schmitz, like Carter Page one of the first five appointees to Trump's National Security Advisory Committee, travels to Hungary for unknown reasons.

The *Guardian* reported in April 2017 that U.S.-allied spy agencies in France, Germany, the Netherlands, Australia, Poland, and Estonia had all told American intelligence in mid-2016 about communications between Trump campaign officials and Russian operatives. Was Budapest one of the locales for these meetings, whose number and secrecy caused John Brennan to go directly to eight senior members of Congress in late August and early September 2016?[39] According to a May 2017 *New York Times* article, at the time Brennan called the members "over secure phone lines while they were on recess. . . . [to tell them] there was evidence that Russia was working to elect Mr. Trump president."[40] Or perhaps Schmitz was taking the advice given by fellow Trump national security adviser George Papadopoulos, who wrote in an April 25, 2016, email to a senior Trump campaign official—just two days before Trump's "Mayflower Speech"—that if Trump were to accept Putin's "open invitation" to a pre-election summit, choosing a meeting place other than D.C. or Moscow would be wise because "these governments tend to speak a bit more openly in 'neutral cities' "?[41] Certainly, Brennan's intelligence—and Papadopoulos's—matched the information that Christopher Steele was contemporaneously recording in his thirty-five-page dossier, which said that at least one proposed meeting between Trump's and Putin's respective agents scheduled for Moscow was moved to "what was considered an operationally 'soft' EU country when [a Moscow meet] was judged too compromising." According to the Association of Accredited Public Policy Advocates to the European Union, the seven countries in the EU that oppose sanctions on Russia include Italy, Greece, and Hungary—all countries that Trump's national security advisers traveled to, in some cases more than once, in 2016.[42]

Trump expresses his frustration with the failure thus far of the effort to find Clinton's "missing" emails by publicly asking Russia to find and turn over Clinton's "30,000" deleted emails to American nationals. Within twenty-four hours, Russian hackers have begun cyber-intrusions intended to find the documents Trump requested.

The emails in question were never found, but that didn't stop Trump advisers from pretending they had been. In a November 4, 2016, *Breitbart* interview, Erik Prince claimed to have learned the content of certain "missing" Clinton emails, even though his accounting was declared false by Clinton campaign officials and was never substantiated, even in part, by any statement from either federal law enforcement or the New York Police Department.

Because of Weinergate and the sexting scandal, the NYPD started investigating it. Through a subpoena, through a warrant, they searched [Weiner's] laptop, and sure enough, found those

650,000 emails. They found way more stuff than just more information pertaining to the inappropriate sexting the guy was doing. They found State Department emails. They found a lot of other really damning criminal information, including money laundering, including the fact that Hillary went to this sex island with convicted pedophile Jeffrey Epstein. Bill Clinton went there more than 20 times. Hillary Clinton went there at least six times. The amount of garbage that they found in these emails, of criminal activity by Hillary, by her immediate circle, and even by other Democratic members of Congress was so disgusting they gave it to the FBI, and they said, "We're going to go public with this if you don't reopen the investigation and you don't do the right thing with timely indictments." I believe—I know, and this is from a very well-placed source of mine at 1PP, One Police Plaza in New York—the NYPD wanted to do a press conference announcing the warrants and the additional arrests they were making in this investigation, and they've gotten huge pushback, to the point of coercion, from the Justice Department, with the Justice Department threatening to charge someone that had been unrelated in the accidental heart attack death of Eric Garner almost two years ago. That's the level of pushback the Obama Justice Department is doing against actually seeking justice in the email and other related criminal matters. There's five different parts of the FBI conducting investigations into these things, with constant downdrafts from the Obama Justice Department. So in the, I hope, unlikely and very unfortunate event that Hillary Clinton is elected president, we will have a constitutional crisis that we have not seen since, I believe, 1860.[43]

Prince's false account of Clinton's emails drew heavily from "Pizzagate" lore—Pizzagate being a conspiracy theory that saw Clinton and several of her friends accused of running a human-trafficking and pedophilia ring from the basement of pizza restaurant Comet Ping Pong in Washington, D.C. In 2016, the theory was popular among one other election-savvy group besides Trump's cadre of national security advisers: Russian propagandists. A November 2017 *Rolling Stone* exposé found that, among others, "Russian operatives . . . manufactured the 'news' that Hillary Clinton ran a pizza-restaurant child-sex ring." The magazine discovered, more particularly, that "the claim that Hillary Clinton was a pedophile started in a Facebook post, spread to Twitter and then went viral with the help of far-right platforms like Breitbart and Info-Wars. . . . It took the better part of a year . . . to sift through the digital trail. We found ordinary people, online activists, bots, foreign agents and domestic political operatives. Many of them were associates of the Trump campaign. Others had ties with Russia."[44]

In his testimony before Congress on November 30, 2017, Prince admitted to being the fourth Trump national security adviser who traveled to Hungary in 2016—adding to the possibility he and Schmitz were coordinating on their 2016 Clinton email hunt. Moreover, in his testimony before the House, Prince said that he met with Schmitz ("a lawyer that used to work for me") twice during the 2016 campaign.[45] Whether either of those meetings was in Hungary is unclear. Schmitz's trip to Hungary was taken right in the middle of his summer 2016 search for Clinton's deleted emails; Prince flatly refused to tell Congress when he was in Hungary.[46]

Three weeks later, on August 17, Trump receives his first classified security briefing as a presidential candidate. Less than a month before, on July 26, top intelligence officials had determined with "high confidence" that the Russians were involved in the DNC breach. At his classified briefing in August, Trump is told that Russia is likely seeking to interfere with the 2016 election and indeed wants specifically to infiltrate his campaign. But there is no abatement in the Trump team's outreach to Russia. In fact, Trump becomes, in the ensuing weeks, quite publicly enamored with WikiLeaks, a non-state hostile intelligence service that has made contact with both Trump's son (September 20) and Trump adviser Roger Stone (August 8) and is engaged in an ongoing effort to publish reams of damaging information stolen by Russian

hackers from the Democratic National Committee and the Clinton campaign.

Trump's August 17, 2016, classified briefing irrevocably changed his legal status with respect to Russian cyber-aggression: the Republican nominee was now obligated to act as a "reasonable person" under federal law in evaluating the likelihood that Russian actors were, as of August 2016, committing crimes against America.

The federal statute that covers what is commonly known as "aiding and abetting," 18 U.S.C. § 2(a), dictates that anyone who aids or abets a crime is punishable as though he had committed the crime himself. Specifically, the statute prohibits aiding, abetting, counseling, commanding, inducing, or procuring a federal crime. Because many crimes incorporate not just a planning and execution phase but also a lengthy phase in which incriminating evidence is concealed, it's possible to aid and abet a crime "after the fact" by assisting the "principals"—those who committed the criminal act itself—in obscuring the fact of their guilt by any means, be it destuction of evidence, false statements to investigators, or obstruction of justice and witness tampering.

If one doesn't have a basis to believe a third party has committed a crime, one almost certainly won't be charged for taking actions that have the inadvertent effect of aiding or abetting that crime. Just so, if one knows someone has committed a crime but does nothing that materially aids or abets the commission or concealment of that crime, one is unlikely to be charged under this statute. If, however, one has reason to believe, under what the law calls the "reasonable person" standard, that there is a "high likelihood" a federal crime has been committed, and if one thereafter engages in behavior that a reasonable person would know was likely to have the effect of aiding or abetting a federal crime before, during, or after its commission, the statute is violated.

Once Trump left his classified briefing on August 17, 2016, both he and any aide who was in the room with him during the briefing, and any aide with whom he shared the classified intelligence he'd received in the briefing, were immediately required to act as "reasonable persons" under the law and accept that there was a "high likelihood" Russian nationals were committing crimes against the United States. That "high likelihood" would be predicated on a number of facts: that Trump received a consensus judgment from one, several, or all U.S. intelligence agencies on the question of Russian interference; that those agencies, while not infallible, are known to have access to the best signals intelligence (SIGINT), human intelligence (HUMINT), and financial intelligence (FININT) in the world; that as president of the United States, and having taken an oath of office, the "reasonable person" standard incorporates Trump's self-acknowledged duty to safeguard the nation; and the opportunity Trump had to question his briefers, follow up with them, receive subsequent briefings, and be apprised of their credentials. A legal assessment of Trump's responsibilities under 18 U.S.C. § 2(a) might also take into account that Trump had no experience in the field of national security; a reasonable person in his position would therefore presume a "high likelihood" of the Russians' being engaged in criminal activity not on the basis of gut instinct or personal experience but from the information that person had received from the U.S. intelligence community. I note here "the U.S. intelligence community" because Trump isn't legally entitled to rely on claims or intelligence originating from Russia in meeting the law's "reasonable person" standard, nor could he follow his instincts and thereby remain willfully ignorant. The aiding and abetting statute has no exception for willful ignorance.

18 U.S.C. § 2(b) further prohibits any person from "willfully"—which the law takes to mean "purposefully"—causing a crime against the United States to be committed. So if by July 27, 2016, Trump had received sufficient information from his national security advisers or members of his family to believe with reasonable certainty that the Russians favored his campaign over Clinton's, were looking to assist him in securing victory on November 8, and were engaged in an ongoing effort to illegally access emails or other materials stored in the United States, him saying what he said on July 27, 2016, would be a crime committed in public.

In the context of his full remarks on July 27, 2016, it's clear that Trump was discussing and addressing, as he said at the time, Russian hackers specifically. His now infamous "Russia, if you're listening" comment immediately followed a reference to those Russians who "hack into a major party and get everything." What Trump here is describing is known as "computer crimes," which can involve hacking, fraud, theft, and even espionage. So Trump's invitation to those Russian cybercriminals—saying he'd find it personally "interesting" to see any materials Russian hackers were able to steal and that he "hoped" those hackers could pull off their crimes successfully so that he and the media could see such "interesting" documents—was almost certainly criminal, given what Trump knew at the time.

Trump's criminal intent is further underscored by the fact that his entreaty to the Russian hackers was preceded by a series of deliberate lies about his ties to Russia. Most notably, as part of his response to CNN's Jim Acosta, he said, "I have nothing to do with Putin. I've never spoken to him. I don't know anything about him." Later in the exchange, when Trump says, "[I]f it is Russia [hacking the DNC]—which it's probably not, nobody knows who it is,"[47] Trump was hiding back-channel information he could well have received from his national security advisers or his own family: specifically, in April 2016 the Russians had told one of his aides, George Papadopoulos, that they were engaged in efforts to steal Clinton's emails, and in June 2016 his son and son-in-law were told that the Russians had come into possession of "official documents and information" that could incriminate Clinton. Likewise, if Trump was aware of the effort being made throughout the month of July by Peter W. Smith—in conjunction, Smith claimed, with Michael Flynn, Steve Bannon, Sam Clovis, and Kellyanne Conway, all top Trump advisers—to track down Russian hackers and get from them Clinton's "missing" emails, Trump's statement to Acosta in Florida would be untrue. Moreover, if during his August 17, 2016, classified national security briefing his FBI and CIA briefers asked him if the Russians had made any effort to infiltrate his presidential campaign and he responded in the negative—despite what he then knew about Papadopoulos's acting as an intermediary for the Kremlin—he may have run afoul of the federal statute prohibiting making false statements to federal law enforcement officers who are in the midst of an investigation (18 U.S.C. § 1001).

That Trump began his infamous remark in Florida by speaking about Russians' "hack[ing] into a major party" but ended by asking those same hackers to find "the 30,000 [Clinton] emails that are missing" underscores that he was aware of these hackers' past crimes and wanted them to now commit new and different ones. As noted by *Quartz* in July 2017, "one could . . . consider Trump's public request that Russia find and release Clinton's emails as an illegal [campaign donation] solicitation."[48] This is particularly true given that Trump had spoken publicly, not only on July 27, 2016, but as early as June 7, about how "interesting" information about Clinton's emails would be to voters and the media alike. That's a clear confirmation that, in Trump's view, derogatory information about Clinton would have cognizable value if provided to him, to the media, or to anyone else, for that matter.

In July 2018, Robert Mueller indicted twelve Russian intelligence officers for their roles in hacking the Democratic National Committee and the Clinton presidential campaign. A reading of the indictment would cause one to conclude that Trump's willful attempts to "induce" (18 U.S.C. § 2(a)) or "cause" (18 U.S.C. § 2(b)) crimes against the United States by Russian hackers had been successful—just as he'd publicly said he "hope[d]" they would be—as less than twenty-four hours after his remarks the very people he'd been addressing executed a cyberattack to access the very information he was requesting.

Trump's August 17, 2016, security briefing and henceforth requirement to act as a "reasonable person" under 18 U.S.C. § 2 also required him to cease and desist offering the Kremlin unilateral financial benefits under the guise of a détente with the Russian government. As NBC News reported in June 2017, "The Trump administration was gearing up to lift sanctions on Russia when the president took office." It was, said NBC, "the latest evidence that President Trump moved to turn his favorable campaign rhetoric into concrete action when he took power."[49] Under the "reasonable person" standard, Trump was required to understand that a person in his position arguing for a *unilateral* dropping of sanctions on Russia—with no preconditions or benefits to American interests offered in return—would be materially benefiting Russia, not the United States, and that such an action would be seen in those terms by Russia at a time it was expending money to commit crimes against the United States and presumably looking to offset or justify those expenditures.

In April 2017, PolitiFact, the nonpartisan political and media watchdog, found that Trump mentioned WikiLeaks—which his own CIA director, Mike Pompeo, called a "non-state hostile intelligence service"—between 140 and 160 times in the final month of his presidential campaign. PolitiFact found no evidence that Trump had ever spoken disparagingly of WikiLeaks in October 2016 and indeed quoted him as saying "I love WikiLeaks" during an October 10, 2016, speech. At the time, WikiLeaks was in the process of releasing stolen documents that, according to his August 2016 classified briefing, had a high likelihood of having been stolen by the Russians. And because Rob Goldstone had told Donald Trump Jr. that Russian actors were surreptitiously seeking dirt on Clinton—and because, per a July 2018 CNN story, Trump's attorney Michael Cohen says Trump was aware of the Goldstone-Trump Jr. emails—it's fair to say that by October 2016 Trump had reason to believe that praising WikiLeaks was likely to "induce" or "cause" both more cyber-intrusions against Democratic targets and more illegal releases of the evidence stolen during those intrusions. So here, too, Trump was committing crimes in plain sight— simultanously encouraging Russian transgressions while obscuring from U.S. voters the real state of his knowledge about Russia's actions.

CHAPTER TEN

THE OCTOBER SURPRISE

October 2016

Summary

TRUMP ALLIES CONTINUE TO SQUEEZE POLITICAL VALUE out of the "Clinton email" issue: they push the claim that the emails contain incriminating evidence against Hillary Clinton without specifying what that incriminating evidence is. But in the weeks before the 2016 election, made-up incriminating evidence in the form of a conspiracy theory called "Pizzagate" begins circulating on the internet, along with the suggestion that more evidence may be contained in the so-called missing Clinton emails. The widely debunked Pizzagate conspiracy theory says Clinton is running a sex-trafficking ring from the basement of a pizza restaurant in the D.C. area. *Rolling Stone* and the *New York Times* report that the effort to spread that conspiracy theory is backed in part by Russian operatives and Russian-influenced networks and involves some of Trump's top advisers and surrogates, including Steve Bannon, Erik Prince, Michael Flynn, Rudy Giuliani, and Donald Trump Jr.[1] The operation meets with unexpected success when Trump campaign disinformation about incriminating evidence, coupled with illegal leaks to the Trump camp from the NYPD and the FBI, help convince FBI director James Comey to reopen the Clinton server investigation, which he'd previously closed—via a controversial public statement on the matter—in July.

As Election Day looms, figures once thought to no longer be part of Trump's orbit reemerge. Paul Manafort is secretly advising Trump—with an emphasis, predictably, on leveraging the Clinton email issue into an Election Day victory. Roger Stone, officially gone (but never unofficially gone) from his role as a critical campaign adjunct, appears to have inside knowledge of WikiLeaks's and Guccifer 2.0's intentions with respect to last-minute election interference. Campaign surrogate Rudy Giuliani darkly intimates that leaks from the NYPD and the FBI office in New York City will produce a major surprise in late October that could tip the election to Trump. Ultimately, the reopening of the Clinton case—prompted, far more than is understood at the time, by the collusive actions of the Trump campaign—contributes to a collapse in Clinton's support in the month before the election. The Democratic candidate goes from leading Trump by more than seven points in a "poll of polls" three weeks before Election Day to losing the election in the Electoral College 304 to 227.[2]

Popular polling analysis website FiveThirtyEight will report, in May 2017, that "the Comey letter probably cost Clinton the election."[3]

The Facts

AN HOUR AFTER THE *ACCESS HOLLYWOOD* TAPE IS RELEASED to the public—featuring Trump bragging about serially sexually assaulting women—Trump has a secretary contact his old friend Roger Stone, the man *Politico* calls a "political dark-arts operative."[4] Trump had fired Stone in August 2015—or, to hear Stone tell it, Stone quit at that point—but the correspondence between the two men hasn't abated as of October 2016, a fact that will eventually lead Special Counsel Mueller to assert in his July 2018 indictment of twelve Russians that Stone stayed much more involved in the pro-Trump movement after his departure from the Trump campaign proper might have suggested.[5] He will interview at least eight people close to Stone to try to track his movements from 2015 onward, and in late August 2018 Stone himself will take to Instagram to declare that a *New Yorker* source is about to falsely accuse him of telling Trump about WikiLeaks data dumps in advance.[6] What Trump and Stone discussed immediately after the release of the *Access Hollywood* tape is unknown.

Stone, "known universally in political circles as a Nixon-era 'dirty trickster,'" according to *Politico*, never really disappears from the Trump campaign's milieu after his firing, in part because of his long relationship with Trump and in part because of his even longer relationship with Paul Manafort, with whom he ran a lobbying firm in the 1980s and 1990s.[7] According to *New York Magazine*, when Stone leaves the Trump campaign in August 2015, he does so, in his own words, on "excellent terms," a contention that will seemingly be confirmed by his post-departure statements about his relationship with the campaign: in late August 2015, he refuses to say if he's stayed in touch with the campaign after leaving it; in September 2015, he admits that since leaving the campaign he and Trump "talk on the phone from time to time"; in April 2016, he speaks glowingly of Trump's Manafort hire, noting that "by turning to Paul Manafort, who's a former partner of mine, a very skilled guy . . . I think that Donald has made an excellent selection"; the next month, in May 2016, he tells CNN that he speaks with Trump "now and then"; and in August 2016, as he begins to have contact with a Russian hacker and a non-state hostile intelligence service, WikiLeaks, he will tell C-SPAN, "I do have access to all the right people [in the Trump campaign]."[8] Weeks before Election Day, notes *New York Magazine*, Stone will brag about being able to "fir[e] off long memos to the Donald once or twice a week" with the expectation they will be read by the candidate.[9]

So when Stone met with a Russian national who called himself "Henry Greenberg" in May 2016—a meeting set up by Michael Caputo, a former adviser to Russian president Boris Yeltsin and, in May 2016, a communications adviser to Trump—he was in a position to pass on any information he learned to the candidate himself.[10] Greenberg (who also called himself "Henry Oknyansky") offered Clinton dirt to Trump, via Stone, for $2 million, an offer Stone will say—when the meeting is finally made public in 2018—he turned down only because he knew Trump would have wanted the dirt for free.[11] While the nature of the information Greenberg offered to Stone is as yet unknown, a clue about its topic can be gleaned from the man Greenberg showed up with when he met Stone: a Ukrainian named "Alexei" who claimed he had worked for the Clinton Foundation.[12] The 2018 revelation of the Stone-Greenberg meeting will reveal as inaccurate Stone's previous contention that "I didn't talk to anybody who was identifiably Russian during the two-year run-up to this campaign. I very definitely can't think of anybody who might have been a Russian without my knowledge. It's a canard."[13] When asked why they withheld information about the meeting with Greenberg in their separate congressional testimonies, both Stone and Caputo will claim to have forgotten the incident entirely.[14] Yet Caputo's alacrity in turning to Stone when his Russian business partner, Sergey Petrushin, comes to him with news that Greenberg has information of value for Trump underscores that in May 2016—nine months after his firing (or resignation) from the Trump campaign—Stone is still felt to have ready access to Trump officials and possibly Trump himself. As the *Washington Post* notes, "In the spring of 2016, Stone . . . remained in touch with Trump and some in his orbit."[15] Indeed, in April 2017 the *Daily Beast* will report that Stone was instrumental in convincing Trump to hire Paul Manafort in March 2016.[16]

Seen in this light, Stone's ongoing public association with WikiLeaks in the late summer and early fall of 2016 is troubling—especially when added to Trump Jr.'s late-summer communication with WikiLeaks, the Kushner-hired/Bannon-founded Cambridge Analytica's outreach to WikiLeaks, and Trump's own public fixation on the organization in his October 2016 speeches. An April 2017 PolitiFact assessment will concur with a Democratic congresswoman's claim that Trump mentioned WikiLeaks approximately 160 times in the final month before the election.[17]

On August 8, 2016, Stone says at a Republican conference in Florida, "I actually have communicated with Assange. I believe the next tranche of his documents pertain to the Clinton Foundation. . . ."[18] On August 12, he says Assange has Clinton's "missing" emails—the very materials the Trump campaign has been hunting for throughout the summer of 2016.[19] On August 21, he claims prior knowledge of the content of WikiLeaks's next release of stolen documents, tweet-ing that "it will soon the Podesta's [*sic*] time in the barrel"; the fact that WikiLeaks has Clinton campaign chairman John Podesta's emails won't become public information for another forty-five days.[20] In mid-September 2016, he says in a radio interview that he expects "Julian Assange and the WikiLeaks people to drop a payload of new docu-ments on a weekly basis fairly soon. And that [payload] of course will answer the question of exactly what was erased on that [Clinton] email server."[21]

Amid these comments, Stone boasts of his access to Assange and is secretly in contact with one of the very hackers who is leaking sto-len documents to the WikiLeaks founder. On August 14, Stone has a back-channel exchange via Twitter with Russian hacker Guccifer 2.0; the next day, he tells *WorldNetDaily* that he has communicated with Assange and knows from these communications that information on the Clinton Foundation will soon be released by WikiLeaks.[22] The day after that, Stone tells radio host Alex Jones that he has been having "backchannel communications" with WikiLeaks and knows Assange has "political dynamite" regarding Bill and Hillary Clinton."[23] Two days later, he tells C-SPAN he has an intermediary who has been act-ing as an interlocutor between him and Assange, and three days after *that* he repeats the claim yet again on Glenn Beck's TheBlaze Radio.[24] The intermediary Stone references is now believed to be former come-dian and current radio host Randy Credico, who will be subpoenaed to testify before a grand jury by Special Counsel Mueller on August 10, 2018.[25]

Credico, a longtime Stone friend, spends much of the 2016 presi-dential campaign loudly denouncing Bernie Sanders as insufficiently progressive, until suddenly he declares, on May 10, 2016—once it's clear that Trump will win the Republican nomination—that he is founding a "Sanders Supporters for Trump" group. It is an about-face that makes no sense, *Washington Monthly* observes, without the further knowledge that Credico and Stone are both seasoned political opera-tives "with a history of ratfucking their political opponents"—in this case, Sanders's primary opponent Hillary Clinton.[26] Despite his partnership with Stone during the presidential campaign, Credico will say, in June 2018, that he will honor any subpoena sent to him by Mueller. "I'm not going to go to jail for Roger Stone," he tells CNN.[27]

While Stone retreats, in late October 2016, from his prior claims of having special access to Assange, by early March 2017 he is once again claiming a "backchannel to Assange" and asserting that Assange "indeed had the goods on #CrookedHillary."[28] When a cache of Stone's private Twitter messages is published by the *Atlantic* in February 2018, however, it is revealed that Stone was in fact telling the truth in the beginning: he had direct contact with WikiLeaks before and after the 2016 election.[29] Indeed, the day after Trump's victory in November, WikiLeaks messaged Stone privately on Twitter to say, "Happy? We are now more free to communicate."[30]

Throughout all his late-summer and early-fall 2016 statements about WikiLeaks, Stone contends—as Trump is doing the same across three televised presidential debates—that the Russians are not behind the hack of the DNC or the Clinton campaign, calling that claim "a canard."[31]

Of all his WikiLeaks tweets, Stone's October 2016 tweets on the subject of the hacked and stolen Democratic National Committee and Clinton campaign emails are particularly troubling because of their specificity and how they dovetail with Trump's concurrent campaign rhetoric praising WikiLeaks. On October 1, Stone tweets (from an account since suspended by Twitter), "Wednesday @HillaryClinton is done. #Wikileaks."[32] On October 12, Stone says he and Assange have a "good mutual friend" with whose assistance he has been conducting a "backchannel communication" with Assange; he adds that "[my] friend travels back and forth from the United States to London and we talk. I had dinner with him last Monday."[33]

An August 2017 report by *Foreign Policy* will reveal that not only did Assange leak documents he received from the Russians, but he also *declined* to leak information in his possession that he apparently considered damaging to the Kremlin.[34]

Stone's foreknowledge of the release of Russia-hacked materials tracks with foreknowledge demonstrated in the last ninety days of the campaign by someone even closer to Trump than Stone: Trump's son. As the *Nation* explains,

> A series of e-mail exchanges—first reported by *The Atlantic* and then released, on Twitter, by Don Jr. himself—reveal that Trump Jr. queried WikiLeaks about damaging Clinton material. "What's behind this Wednesday leak I keep reading about?" Don Jr. wrote in one exchange. After WikiLeaks e-mailed him asking if he would persuade his father to promote WikiLeaks via the candidate's own account, just 15 minutes later Trump Sr. tweeted: "Very little pick-up by the dishonest media of incredible information provided by WikiLeaks. So dishonest! Rigged system!"[35]

This attempt to coordinate with and indeed placate WikiLeaks is rewarded later on in October 2016, when it becomes clear that WikiLeaks will not be releasing information damaging to Trump. Assange's political intentions will be further underscored when journalists get access to some of his private Twitter messages, which include calling Clinton a "bright, well connected, sadistic sociopath" and writing that "We [WikiLeaks] believe it would be much better for GOP to win [the election]."[36] On Russia, Assange will write sympathetically of the Kremlin's plight in the face of American military might: "Russia is absolutely terrified," he asserts in a Twitter direct message to a "low-security" internal WikiLeaks discussion group. "Kalingrad, Crimea, and its only foreign naval base, Syria[,] are all under threat and are not protected by Russia's strategic depth. . . . Consequently the Kremlin is deeply paranoid of everyone. . . ."[37] While Assange also levels criticisms of authoritarianism in Moscow, his focus is squarely on keeping Clinton from power, writing to his WikiLeaks discussion group after Super Tuesday of his desire that Clinton suffer a stroke.[38]

In October 2016, Stone's old business partner Manafort reemerges. It has never been clear what Manafort spends his time doing, and it is even less so during this period. Hired to organize the Republican National Convention in late March 2016, Manafort had made no effort to do so by June; according to *Politico*, "by mid-June, less than one month before the convention would be gaveled in, there was no program. No celebrity acts had been booked. No known GOP leaders or elders had asked for a speaking slot. Organizers were concerned enough that they decided to bring in [a new convention planner]."[39] Nevertheless, in October Manafort contacts Trump to offer "the GOP nominee pointers on how to handle the Clinton email news and urging him to make a play in Michigan"—the latter being a surprisingly, perhaps suspiciously prescient remark about where Trump must focus his energies if he wants to win the election.[40] During the presidential transition, Manafort calls Reince Priebus to counsel the administration on handling the publication of the Steele dossier by *BuzzFeed*.[41] In September 2017, CNN will report that, because Manafort was under an FBI wiretap for part of his time on the Trump campaign and thereafter, the fact that following Trump's inauguration Manafort continued to "talk to President Donald Trump" could become problematic for the president—as those conversations occurred against a backdrop of FBI intercepts that "sparked concerns among investigators that Manafort had encouraged the Russians to help with the campaign, according to three sources familiar with the investigation."[42] In January 2018, NBC News will report that Trump believes the investigation of him can be "crushed" in part because "he has decided that a key witness in the Russia probe, Paul Manafort, isn't going to 'flip' and sell him out."[43]

Trump's concern about whether Manafort might flip on him appears to grow after Manafort is convicted of eight felonies by a Virginia jury in August 2018 and Trump's personal attorney, Michael Cohen, pleads guilty to eight felonies on the same day—with Cohen saying during his in-court allocution that Trump personally directed him to pay hush money to multiple ex-mistresses.[44] Shortly after the Manafort and Cohen convictions, Trump will tweet angrily about "flippers"—witnesses who commit crimes, then cooperate with prosecutors in later cases against their co-conspirators—referring to them as individuals for whom "everything's wonderful and then they get ten years in jail and they flip on whoever the next highest one is, or as high as you can go." Trump unfavorably compares "flippers" to his "brave" former campaign manager and chairman, Manafort, who, unlike Cohen, "refused to break."[45]

As the campaign enters its final stretch, Trump aids Russia's hackers after the fact by casting doubt on their responsibility for the attacks against America's political and voting infrastructure—despite his legal responsibility, following his August 17, 2016, security briefing, not to take any action that might assist a Russian cover-up. This legal responsibility is underscored when, in July 2018, the Department of Justice indicts twelve Kremlin-backed hackers and includes in its indictments allegations that the hackers deliberately put out misinformation about who was responsible for their cyber-intrusions—exactly what Trump did, repeatedly, after his security briefing in August 2016.[46] Per the indictments, the indicted Russian hackers variously claimed to be American or Romanian "to undermine the allegations of Russian responsibility for the intrusion."[47] Few credited the hackers' claims at the time—giving little reason to believe their false claims affected the presidential election. However, many voters and Trump supporters appeared to believe Trump's persistent claims that Russia had not been involved in hacking U.S. persons and institutions.[48] That the claims were made by a GOP presidential nominee who was known to be receiving classified security briefings made them more plausible.

On October 10, in the second presidential debate, Trump picks up on an argument he made in the first presidential debate—that the DNC hacker could have been, rather than a Russian government agent, "somebody sitting on their bed who weighs 400 pounds"—and expands it substantially, arguing, "Maybe there *is* no hacking."[49] Ten days later, during the third presidential debate, Trump says—two months removed from having been told with "high confidence" by the U.S. intelligence community that Russia is hacking American citizens and institutions—"[We have] no idea whether it is Russia, China or anybody else."[50] Trump makes this argument even though, in between the first and second debate, the FBI has announced that "Russian hackers were behind cyberattacks on a contractor for Florida's election system that may have exposed the personal data of Florida voters."[51]

Even after the election, Trump's attempts to vindicate Russia from any responsibility for hacking America's infrastructure continue un-abated. In January 2017, he tweets out a defense of WikiLeaks to his tens of millions of social media followers, saying of WikiLeaks's founder, "Julian Assange said 'a 14 year old could have hacked Podesta'. . . . Also said Russians did not give him the info!"[52]

On October 26, two days before Comey reopens the Clinton case, Giuliani tells Fox News's Martha MacCallum that Trump has "a sur-prise or two that you're going to hear about in the next two days. I'm talking about some pretty big surprise [*sic*]."[53] On October 28, Giuliani goes on the Lars Larson radio program and says that current agents in the FBI have been leaking information to him about the ongoing Clinton investigation—a Hatch Act violation, as federal employees are not permitted to participate in political campaigns or political activ-ity in this way. On November 4, Giuliani tells *Fox & Friends* that he "heard about" what Director Comey was going to do—reopen the FBI investigation into Hillary Clinton's private email server—before it hap-pened.[54] "This has been boiling up in the FBI," he says. "I did nothing to get it out. I had no role in it. Did I hear about it? Darn right I heard about it."[55]

When Giuliani's comments become a source of controversy, he in-sists that the "pretty big [October] surprise" he referenced in speaking to MacCallum on October 26 was just a new Trump ad campaign.[56] He will hedge somewhat in a subsequent interview with CNN, however, saying that Comey reopening the Clinton case "came as a complete surprise to me, except to the extent that maybe it wasn't as much of a surprise to me because I had been hearing for quite some time that there was . . . debate and anger within the FBI about the way they [ac-tive FBI agents] were being treated by the Justice Department."[57] Wolf Blitzer, the CNN anchorman, extensively dissects Giuliani's Larson in-terview, however, noting that "the former mayor said he was in contact with former agents 'and a few active agents, who obviously don't want to identify themselves.'"[58] In a later CNN interview, Giuliani will say he hasn't spoken to an active FBI agent in eight to ten months.[59]

Giuliani's insistence that "I did nothing to get it out" and "I had no role in it"—with respect to the story that FBI agents were then (in

Giuliani's words) in a state of "revolution"—is particularly telling, as indeed it is *another* man who will in the future be a legal adviser to Donald Trump who *is* responsible for that information getting to the media. That man, well-known Republican attorney Joseph diGenova, was, with Giuliani, one of the most vocal opponents of Comey's decision not to prosecute Clinton when Comey announced that final judgment in July 2016.[60] DiGenova's firm—comprising him and his wife, Victoria Toensing—now represents Sam Clovis and Mark Corallo, as well as ("informally," they say) Donald Trump.[61]

Calling FBI director Comey a "dirty cop," a liar, and "worse than a criminal," diGenova says on *The Laura Ingraham Show* on October 13, 2016, that "his law firm will represent any FBI agent who comes forward and wants to testify before Congress about Comey's [Clinton] investigation."[62] That an attorney who would say, in April 2018, that he and his wife "[play] the role of lawyers on television and in real life" for Donald Trump would go on-air less than thirty days before a general election offering to assist FBI agents in undermining Trump's opponent—by way of testifying against the prosecutors who dropped her case—underscores how close to Trump's orbit the effort to pressure Comey into reopening Clinton's case finally was.[63] It appears diGenova did not stop there, either; after *LifeZette* (founded by Laura Ingraham) reports on diGenova's offer, the *Daily Caller* (founded by fellow Fox News personality Tucker Carlson) reports just ninety-six hours later that a group of FBI agents looking to blow the whistle on Comey has indeed found an "intermediary" to assist them.[64] Moreover, the agents' "intermediary" appeared to assist them within twenty-four hours of diGenova's offering to do just that: "FBI agents say the bureau is alarmed over Director James Comey urging the Justice Department to not prosecute Hillary Clinton over her mishandling of classified information," the *Daily Caller* writes. "According to an interview transcript given to *The Daily Caller*, provided by an intermediary who spoke to two federal agents with the bureau last Friday, agents are frustrated by Comey's leadership."[65] The story, a *Daily Caller* "exclusive," cites one person other than the FBI agents: Joe diGenova.[66] The *Daily Caller* notes that "more FBI agents will be talking about the problems at the bureau. DiGenova notes the agents will specifically point to the handling of the Clinton case by Comey when Congress comes back in session."[67] The agents spoken to and aided by diGenova had repeated to the *Daily Caller* false claims about Clinton's emails, saying "all the trained investigators [in the New York field office of the FBI] agree that there is a lot to prosecute [Clinton for] but he [Comey] stood in the way. The idea that [the Clinton email case] didn't go to a grand jury is ridiculous."[68]

What the *Daily Caller* does not disclose at the time is that it is, according to the *New York Observer*, "secretly" being paid "$150,000 . . . [or] even higher" by the Trump campaign in the form of advertising revenue—as the Trump campaign between September 2016 and Election Day is paying the *Daily Caller* for use of its email list.[69] That diGenova has in fact been planning to bring pressure to bear on Comey through FBI leaks to the media is evident from an interview he gives to WMAL 105.9 FM in Washington, D.C., the same week he speaks to Laura Ingraham, in which he reveals that he's already been in touch with active FBI agents: "People [in the FBI] are starting to talk," he tells his WMAL interviewer. "They're calling their former friends outside the bureau asking for help. We were asked today to provide legal representation to people inside the bureau and agreed to do so. . . . Comey thought this was going to go away. It's not. People inside the bureau are furious. . . . [T]hey think he's a crook. They think he's fundamentally dishonest. They have no confidence in him. . . . The most important thing of all is that the agents have decided that they are going to talk."[70] That after advising these agents, diGenova goes on to advise Trump—and is still doing so well into the summer of 2018—is confirmed by another Trump attorney, Rudy Giuliani, who tells *Politico* in June 2018, "[Trump] will call four or five people like Joe [diGenova] and say, 'What do you think? So and so says this. Who's right?' "[71] It is unclear for how long Trump has been advised by diGenova, though the question is a critical one; for instance, in March 2017, diGenova will be a vocal proponent of the fake news that former president Obama had tapped Trump Tower during the presidential transition in order to unmask transition officials involved in sensitive conversations.[72] It's a conspiracy theory lacking any evidence, and it will later be linked to an Israeli government-connected business intelligence firm—Black Cube, the chief competitor to Joel Zamel's Wikistrat—but it is nevertheless quickly adopted by Trump in the early weeks of his administration.[73]

That Trump shares "informal" legal counsel with the FBI agents who pressured Comey into reopening the Clinton case has not been widely discussed—but that the agents' illegal leaks to the media helped convince Comey to reopen the Clinton investigation, thereby costing Clinton the election, is clear. On October 30, 2016, just two days after Comey reopens the Clinton case, the *New York Times* reports that he did so because "he believed that if word of the new [Clinton] emails leaked out—*and it was sure to leak out, he concluded*—he risked being accused of misleading Congress and the public ahead of an election" (emphasis added).[74] Further evidence of Comey's certainty his own agents were leaking to the media is found in late October emails he and his deputy Andrew McCabe exchanged, uncovered through a FOIA request by the conservative watchdog group Judicial Watch.[75] In the Judicial Watch tranche of Comey-McCabe emails is an email from McCabe to Comey from October 25, 2016, alerting the latter to an article from the day before published on the website *True Pundit*, which reports that "Democratic factions controlled by a Hillary Clinton insider" paid almost $700,000 in campaign funds to Jill McCabe, Andrew McCabe's wife, who was a Virginia state senate candidate in 2015. Andrew McCabe, *True Pundit* noted, was a senior FBI agent who advised Comey against criminally charging Clinton.[76]

McCabe believed the article had used an FBI leaker as a source, telling Comey it was a "heavyweight [FBI] source."[77] While Comey disagreed that the leaker was a "heavyweight" in the FBI, he agreed it was someone within the Bureau leaking details of an internal investigation.[78] Forty-eight hours later, he and McCabe meet in person and he decides to reopen the Clinton case, partly, per the *New York Times*, because of his fear of continued FBI leaks—the same leaks Trump surrogate Rudy Giuliani had been discussing publicly on Fox News and Trump supporter and future legal counsel Joe diGenova had personally facilitated.[79] Indeed, the June 2018 Inspector General's report on Comey's decision to reopen the Clinton case will repeatedly cite Comey's concern about internal leaks as influencing his decision-making—both leaks of information concerning Attorney General Loretta Lynch and leaks of information concerning the "new" Clinton emails.[80] As the Inspector General (IG) will conclude, "several FBI officials told us that the concern about leaks played a role in the decision [to reopen the Clinton case]."[81] The IG will note also that "[t]he harm caused by leaks, fear of potential leaks, and a culture of unauthorized media contacts . . . influenced FBI officials who were advising Comey on consequential investigative decisions in October 2016."[82] The IG will quote one of the prosecutors in the Clinton case as indicating to him that "leaks undermine investigations and that 'unfair leaks' were an 'added' consideration in the [Clinton] investigation"; per the IG, "Laufman [a second prosecutor] told us that the [Clinton] prosecution team's goal was to . . . [be] mindful that leaks 'could be used by political actors in furtherance of political agendas.' "[83] The IG will find that Comey's concern touched equally on credible leaks and "leaks of . . . non-credible information"—the latter sort of leak being the kind facilitated by diGenova. Comey's pre-election review of the "new" Clinton emails on former congressman Anthony Weiner's computer will find no incriminating information, contrary to what diGenova's clients in the FBI told the *Daily Caller* to expect.[84]

When Comey reopens the Clinton case, the Republican National Committee will immediately declare that this "shows how serious this discovery [of 'new' Clinton emails] must be."[85] However, in August 2018 it will be revealed that the *True Pundit* story that concerned Comey and McCabe was written by a former employee of Republican National Committee finance chair Steve Wynn, who was appointed to his position by Trump in 2017.[86] As it happens, diGenova is also a former employee of the Republican Party, having been, before entering private practice, "chief counsel and staff director of the Senate Rules Committee and counsel to the Senate Judiciary, Governmental Affairs, and Select Intelligence committees."[87]

The effect of the leaks facilitated by Trump surrogates and

supporters—and aided by former employees of the Republican Party and their associates—is not just the reopening of the Clinton case but the mass dissemination of the fake news that Clinton's "new" emails contain incriminating evidence, including, supposedly, proof that—as alleged by Erik Prince—"Hillary went to this sex island with convicted pedophile Jeffrey Epstein. . . . at least six times." The convergence of Comey's decision and the supposed content of Clinton's "new" emails produces a vivid display of the influence and danger of viral alt-right conspiracy theories fueled in part by Russian disinformation and fake social media accounts. This display starts online a day after the Comey announcement and ten days before the November election. It ends in a pizza restaurant in Washington.

Indeed, the strangest Trump-Russia connection of October 2016 involves the "Pizzagate" conspiracy theory, which first appears in a Facebook post on October 29. That post comes just a day after FBI director Comey reopens the Clinton email investigation and a day after then Trump surrogate Rudy Giuliani finishes a three-day spree of radio and television interviews teasing an October surprise that will harm Clinton's campaign. Calling it a "fake news scandal," *Rolling Stone* will describe Pizzagate more particularly as the surprisingly widespread belief that Hillary Clinton was "sexually abusing children in satanic rituals . . . in the basement of a Washington, D.C., pizza restaurant." [88] The magazine notes that this conspiracy theory—for which no evidence ever emerges, indeed not even a basement in the suspect pizza parlor—is born and disseminated during the presidential campaign through the work of, among others, "Russian operatives [and] Trump campaigners." [89] "The claim that Hillary Clinton was a pedophile started in a Facebook post, spread to Twitter and then went viral with the help of far-right platforms like Breitbart and Info-Wars," *Rolling Stone* writes, name-checking a media outlet run by Steve Bannon and a podcast, radio show, and YouTube program frequented and sometimes even anchored by Trump adviser Roger Stone.[90] After nearly a year of investigative reporting, *Rolling Stone* concludes that, along with average Americans and social media "bots," "foreign agents and domestic political operatives"—"[m]any of them . . . associates of the Trump cam-

paign" and "[o]thers . . . tie[d] with Russia"—are the progenitors of the
Pizzagate fake-news operation.[91]

The Facebook post that launches the conspiracy theory will be
traced to a Cynthia Campbell in Joplin, Missouri, a woman, *Rolling
Stone* speculates—with supporting evidence, including a significant
overlap in social media accounts—is the "Carmen Katz" who posted
the October 29 allegations regarding the computer owned by former
congressman Weiner that was seized by the NYPD in late September
2016.[92] Because Weiner's then wife, Huma Abedin, was a top Clinton
staffer, when the NYPD found Clinton emails on Weiner's laptop there
was speculation that the emails might contain new information relevant
to the FBI's investigation of Clinton's private email server; the NYPD
subsequently turned the laptop over to the FBI, which had possession
of it by October 3 at the latest.[93] Though the Clinton investigation had
been closed by the FBI in July 2016, "Katz" insisted that "[m]y NYPD
source said its [the contents of Weiner's laptop] much more vile and serious than classified material on Weiner's device. The email DETAIL
[*sic*] the trips made by Weiner, Bill and Hillary on their pedophile
billionaire friend's plane, the Lolita Express. Yup, Hillary has a well
documented predilection for underage girls. . . . We're talking an international child enslavement and sex ring."[94]

Because the FBI had possession of Weiner's laptop but had not yet
conducted any significant analysis of its content, the fake news that
top officials at the FBI—particularly Comey and his deputy McCabe—
were deliberately hiding incriminating Clinton emails quickly spread
across the internet.[95] The claim dovetailed with longstanding claims
by Russian agents, dating back to Joseph Mifsud's conversations with
Trump adviser George Papadopoulos in April 2016, that there were
Clinton emails still waiting to be released. In June 2016, the Russians were intimating to Donald Trump Jr. that the Clinton materials
in Russia's possession were "incriminating." The Pizzagate conspiracy
thus seemed to coincide with a long-running narrative with which the
Trump campaign had been enamored, by October 2016, for six months.

The investigation conducted by *Rolling Stone* ultimately sets the
birth of Pizzagate much earlier than October 2016, however—and

THE OCTOBER SURPRISE 209

much closer to Russia, too. According to the magazine's November 2017 exposé, a "possible [seed] of Pizzagate" appears on July 2, 2016, when "someone calling himself FBIAnon, who claimed to be a 'high-level analyst and strategist' for the bureau, hosted an Ask Me Anything [AMA] forum on [the internet website] 4chan. He claimed to be leaking government secrets . . . out of a love for country, but it wasn't always clear which country he meant. At various times, he wrote, 'Russia is more a paragon of freedom and nationalism than any other country' and 'We [America] are the aggressors against Russia.'"[96] FBIAnon seemed particularly interested in the Clinton Foundation, as the Russians who had visited Trump Tower a month earlier also had been; "Dig deep," wrote FBIAnon. "Bill and Hillary love foreign donors so much. They get paid in children as well as money."[97] A 4chan reader following the AMA asked FBIAnon if Hillary had sex with kidnapped girls; "Yes," replied FBIAnon.[98]

In October, writes *Rolling Stone*, the claim that FBI brass might be engaged in a "cover-up" of the content of the "new" Clinton emails on Weiner's laptop shows up on a discussion board geared toward NYPD officers called "TheeRANT"—then quickly makes its way to a Facebook group focused on law enforcement, then in short order ends up on Twitter thanks to an account ("Eagle Wings," or @NIVIsa4031) whose followers include Trump advisers Michael Flynn and Sebastian Gorka.[99]

According to Samuel Woolley, the research director of the Institute for the Future in Palo Alto, California, the tweeting pattern established by Eagle Wings over many months confirms that, "[w]ithout a shadow of a doubt, Eagle Wings is a highly automated account [and] part of a bot network"—which, as *Rolling Stone* explains, is a "centrally controlled group of social-media accounts."[100] Another high-traffic Twitter account that immediately backs up Katz's claims—writing, "I have been hearing the same thing from my NYPD buddies too"—also looks to be "highly automated," per Woolley.[101] According to *Rolling Stone*,

> Pizzagate was shared roughly 1.4 million times by more than a quarter of a million accounts in its first five weeks of life. . . .

[and] more than 3,000 accounts in our [sample] set tweeted about Pizzagate five times or more. Among these were dozens of users who tweet so frequently—up to 900 times a day—that experts believe they were likely highly automated. Even more striking: 22 percent of the tweets in our sample were later deleted by the user. This could be a sign, Woolley says, of "someone sweeping away everything so that we can't follow the trail." [102]

The magazine cross-referenced a list of the 139 most Pizzagate-focused Twitter accounts. It found 14 that were linked to Russia, including one (@Pamela_Moore13) that had been retweeted by both Donald Trump Jr. and Roger Stone.[103] Noteworthy here is that, according to the *New York Times*, Donald Trump Jr. had in August 2016 been offered by Wikistrat's Joel Zamel—at a meeting set up and attended by Trump national security adviser Erik Prince—a "multimillion dollar . . . social media manipulation effort to help elect Mr. Trump." [104] According to the *Times*, Trump Jr. "did not appear bothered by the idea of [election] cooperation with foreigners"—despite the fact that such cooperation would be a federal crime.[105] The *Times* adds, "It is unclear whether such a proposal was executed." [106]

The possibility of both Russian and Trump campaign involvement in a conspiracy theory that spread quickly across the internet in the ten days before the 2016 presidential election—constituting an "October surprise" of the sort Giuliani had hinted at days earlier—is underscored by what *Rolling Stone* finds when it looks for intersections between the Trump campaign and the pre-election fake-news operation. "The [Trump] campaign's engagement [with Pizzagate] went far deeper," writes the magazine. "We found at least 66 Trump campaign figures who followed one or more of the most prolific Pizzagate tweeters. Michael Caputo, a Trump adviser who tweeted frequently about Clinton's e-mails, followed 146 of these accounts; Corey Stewart, Trump's campaign chair in Virginia, who lost a tight primary race for governor in June, followed 115; Paula White-Cain, Trump's spiritual adviser, followed 71; Pastor Darrell Scott, a prominent member of

Trump's National Diversity Coalition, followed 33. Flynn's son, Michael Flynn Jr. . . . followed 58 of these accounts. . . ."[107]

Some of the most popular Pizzagate accounts are ultimately traced to a Macedonian fake-news farm run by a Macedonian media attorney, Trajche Arsov. In July 2018, *BuzzFeed* will reveal that two American conservatives "worked closely" with Arsov, and that at least two writers for the American fake-news website *Gateway Pundit* wrote for the Macedonian attorney's fake-news operation.[108] Moreover, at least one member of Russia's Internet Research Agency visited Macedonia shortly before Arsov's first American-politics website was registered.[109] Arsov meets the two American conservatives—with whom, according to *BuzzFeed*, he engaged in "extensive cooperation"—via Facebook in 2016; one of the men, Paris Wade, at first denies even knowing Arsov until he is confronted by the *BuzzFeed* reporter with his messages to the Macedonian.[110] Wade's partner, Ben Goldman, will later admit the connection as well.[111] Wade is found to have written 40 articles for the Macedonian's American-politics website; his brother Alex, 670. Another American, Alicia Powe—who now writes for *Gateway Pundit*—is given a job by Arsov and allowed to write "as many articles as I wanted" for his sites.[112] A second *Gateway Pundit* author, Oliver Dollimore, also writes "news" for Arsov.[113] According to the *Las Vegas Review-Journal*, Paris now "boasts about getting Donald Trump elected."[114]

The *Washington Post* notes in November 2016 that shortly after the election the group website PropOrNot, "a nonpartisan collection of researchers with foreign policy, military and technology backgrounds," issued a list of the two hundred websites in the world that "echoed Russian propaganda" and were doing so during the 2016 campaign; Paris Wade's website, Liberty Writers News, made the list.[115] According to the *Post*, "The [PropOrNot] researchers used Internet analytics tools to trace the origins of particular tweets and mapped the connections among social-media accounts that consistently delivered synchronized messages."[116]

As for the member of Russia's Internet Research Agency who visited Macedonia just before Arsov got his first American-politics site off the ground—an operation that former FBI agent Clint Watts told *Buzz-Feed* would have required some start-up capital—her name is Anna Bogacheva, and Special Counsel Robert Mueller will indict her in February 2018 along with twelve of her IRA compatriots.[117] Bogacheva traveled to Macedonia right as Trump was announcing his presidential campaign in mid-2015, and during the same trip she appears to have also visited Greece and possibly Italy—two of the three nations (the other being the United Kingdom) in which Trump national security adviser George Papadopoulos will have face-to-face contact with Russian agents or allies, at least one of whom is peddling what turn out to be fake Clinton emails.[118]

In an interview with *Rolling Stone*, one of the Macedonians who disseminated fake news into the U.S. market during the presidential campaign said that he often just amped up existing articles from right-wing websites instead of concocting his own news stories; "Breit-bart [*sic*] was best" for this, he told the magazine, naming the website run for years by Steve Bannon, the CEO of Trump's 2016 presidential campaign.[119]

The Macedonians are right to be reading *Breitbart* and other pro-Trump websites in the days leading up to Election Day. When self-described private investigator Douglas Hagmann goes on Alex Jones's *Infowars* program four days after the "Carmen Katz" Facebook post to say, "Based on my source, Hillary did in fact participate on some of the junkets on the Lolita Express," the Pizzagate story is transformed from an obscure conspiracy theory to a mainstream phenomenon. According to *Rolling Stone*, "Google Trends measures interest in topics among the 1.17 billion users of its search engine on a 0–100 scale. . . . On October 29th, the day Katz posted the story on Facebook, searches for 'Hillary' and 'pedophile' ranked zero. . . . [But] when Hagmann 'broke' the story on InfoWars, they scored 100."[120] During his November 2 appearance on Jones's program, Hagmann implies, citing an NYPD source, that Clinton may have committed "treason" by allowing Huma Abedin to transfer classified intelligence to her "relations" or "associates"—Hagmann's intimation being Muslim terrorists—adding that "many of the higher-ranking NYPD investigators" have been pushing for the FBI to reveal this information about Clinton and her emails.[121] Whether he is one of the "higher-ranking NYPD investigators" Hagmann is referring to or not, NYPD deputy chief Michael Osgood—the man in charge of the Weiner investigation for the NYPD in October 2016—will be found in April 2018 to have donated thousands of dollars to Trump's 2016 presidential campaign in the final six weeks before Election Day.[122]

Hagmann tells Jones that there is a "group that [has] banded together" at the NYPD and FBI that's decided that "we're not going to allow this [the 'new' Clinton emails] to be pushed under the carpet."[123] He alleges that "a group of FBI agents" in the bureau's New York field office has secretly refused to destroy the hardware and data incriminating Clinton that it has been ordered to destroy.[124] Most important, Hagmann says to Jones, of Trump surrogate Rudy Giuliani, that "[p]eople better be looking at him really close and listening to what he's saying, because he's behind—he's *responsible*, I would say—for a lot of this information coming from the NYPD segment of this group of [NYPD and FBI] patriots that we see forming."[125]

The same day as the Hagmann-Jones interview, Michael D. Moore—a former employee of Trump's eventual RNC finance chair, Steve Wynn—publishes the sum and substance of the Pizzagate conspiracy on *True Pundit* in an article entitled "BREAKING BOMBSHELL: NYPD Blows Whistle on New Hillary Emails: Money Laundering, Sex Crimes with Children, Child Exploitation, Pay to Play, Perjury."[126] The article is retweeted almost immediately by Trump "shadow" national security adviser (and future National Security Advisor) Michael Flynn, who thereafter deletes his retweet for unknown reasons.[127] Flynn's deletion will effectuate the deletion of a Trump Jr. tweet—as Trump Jr. had retweeted Flynn's original link to *True Pundit*.[128]

Two days later, another of Trump's "shadow" national security advisers, Erik Prince, recounts on Steve Bannon's *Breitbart* radio station a conspiracy theory similar in its contours to Pizzagate (see chapter 9). Clinton's emails, Prince says, contained "a lot of other really damning criminal information, including money laundering, including the fact that Hillary went to this sex island with convicted pedophile Jeffrey

Epstein. Bill Clinton went there more than 20 times. Hillary Clinton went there at least six times." [129]

This piece of fake news will *also* be retweeted by Michael Flynn—but this time without any subsequent deletion. [130] On November 8, 2016, Trump invites Prince—whose importance to his campaign will never be acknowledged, either in 2016 or at any time afterward—to his election-night party, and he will name Prince's sister Betsy DeVos his secretary of education. [131]

When Prince testifies before Congress in November 2017, he will present himself as having had no formal or even informal role in Trump's 2016 campaign. [132]

Annotated History

Trump fired Stone in August 2015—or, to hear Stone tell it, Stone quit at that point—but the correspondence between the two men hasn't abated as of October 2016, a fact that will eventually lead Special Counsel Mueller to assert in his July 2018 indictment of twelve Russians that Stone stayed much more involved in the pro-Trump movement after his departure than his exit from the Trump campaign proper might have suggested.

As of August 2018, the likelihood of Roger Stone's being indicted by Special Counsel Mueller appears high. Stone protégé and former Trump adviser Sam Nunberg said on MSNBC, following his appearance before Mueller's grand jury—and basing his opinion on the questions Mueller's prosecutors asked of him—"I expect Roger Stone to be indicted."[133] Shortly afterward, another one of Stone's aides, Andrew Miller, repeatedly refused to honor a grand jury subpoena from Mueller, moved to "quash" (invalidate) it after two months of ignoring it, and finally was found in contempt of court for defying it—all, Stone said when asked about Miller, because Miller had refused "to bear false witness against me."[134] Stone's friend Michael Caputo likened his appearance before the grand jury to "a proctology appointment with a very large-handed doctor."[135] And on August 27, 2018, Stone himself predicted that he would be the next person indicted in the Mueller probe; "[Mueller] may frame me for some bogus charge in order to silence me or induce me to testify against the president," Stone told the *Guardian*.[136]

The intermediary Stone references is now believed to be former comedian and current radio host Randy Credico, who will be subpoenaed to testify before a grand jury by Special Counsel Mueller on August 10, 2018.

Mueller's interest in Credico appears to focus on threatening emails Stone allegedly sent him in spring 2018. According to *Mother Jones*, to which Credico forwarded a number of emails he said were from Stone, an email Stone wrote to Credico on April 9, 2018, said, "I am so ready. Let's get it on. Prepare to die cock sucker." [137] According to the magazine, "Stone was responding to a message from Credico that indicated Credico would release information contradicting Stone's claims about the 2016 election and that 'all will come out.' " [138]

Stone defended his "prepare to die" email as a response to news that Credico had "terminal prostate cancer." [139] Stone added that most, if not all, other messages Credico might show *Mother Jones* would "probably [be] fabricated." [140]

For his part, Credico said that he does not have prostate cancer and did not act as an intermediary between Stone and Julian Assange as Stone claims—implying that Stone's contact with Assange was direct, just as the former Nixon aide and longtime Trump and Manafort associate had originally claimed.[141] According to *Mother Jones*, "Credico also claims that around the time Stone was interviewed by the House Intelligence Committee in September [2017], Stone told him to 'just go along with' his story." [142] Nevertheless, in May 2018 Credico represented to four Democratic House Intelligence Committee staffers that he was in contact with Assange through a "WikiLeaks associate" and that he wanted to pass a message from Assange to Congressman Adam Schiff—the ranking member of the committee—to the effect that Assange wanted to meet with Schiff face-to-face.[143]

In August 2018, *Mother Jones* reported that Assange had called into Credico's radio program.[144] It noted, too, that Stone's lawyer had told a congressional committee that "Mr. Stone concedes that describing Credico as a go-between or intermediary is a bit of salesmanship." [145] The truth of the Stone-Credico-Assange relationship is still unknown.

Shortly after the Manafort and Cohen convictions, Trump will tweet angrily about "flippers"—witnesses who commit crimes, then cooperate with prosecutors in later cases against their co-conspirators—referring to them as individuals for whom "everything's wonderful and then they get ten years in jail and they flip on whoever the next highest one is, or as high as you can go." Trump unfavorably compares "flippers" to his "brave" former campaign manager and chairman, Manafort, who, unlike Cohen, "refused to break."

In August 2018, the *New York Daily News* reported that Trump was so eager to pardon Manafort—even before Manafort's upcoming trial in D.C.—that he was considering firing White House Counsel Don McGahn because McGahn was trying to dissuade him from the pardon.[146] Multiple aides told *Politico* they expected Trump would ultimately pardon Manafort, and a *Vanity Fair* article released the same week said that Trump's reaction to the convictions of Manafort and Cohen was to "spen[d] the weekend calling people and screaming."[147] *Vanity Fair* noted that an additional contributing factor to Trump's ire was the news, hard on the heels of the Cohen and Manafort guilty findings, that the longtime Chief Financial Officer of the Trump Organization (Allen Weisselberg) and one of Trump's friends at *The National Enquirer* (*Enquirer* publisher David Pecker) had both been granted immunity by Special Counsel Mueller in order to secure their assistance in his investigation.[148] *The Los Angeles Times* thereafter noted that Pecker allegedly has a "vault" full of documents and other materials that could damage Trump—even incriminate him—if they are disclosed to the Special Counsel.[149]

CHAPTER ELEVEN

THE TRANSITION

November 2016 to January 2017

Summary

WHILE NOT YET IN POWER, TRUMP, HIS FAMILY, AND HIS aides begin acting as though they are as soon as Trump wins the 2016 presidential election. Beginning less than two days after the final returns come in, several Trump aides and family members working on the transition team will call, meet, and negotiate with Russians and other foreign nationals. The last of these actions may well violate the federal Logan Act, which prohibits private citizens from negotiating U.S. foreign policy with foreign governments.[1] Most of those in Trump's orbit who surreptitiously meet with Russian or other foreign nationals will thereafter fail to disclose or else lie about their actions.

Meanwhile, a cadre of aides, associates, and family members—including Jared Kushner, Erik Prince, Michael Flynn, Tom Barrack, Rick Gates, and Bud McFarlane—are playing a dangerous political game. The game involves seven nations (the United States, Saudi Arabia, the United Arab Emirates, Qatar, Syria, Iran, and Russia) and seven seemingly unrelated subjects: Kushner's worsening money troubles; Saudi-Qatari tensions; the Saudis' desire for nuclear power and, eventually, the right to build a nuclear weapon; the Emiratis' own nuclear ambitions; Saudi and Emirati hostility toward Iran, and particularly Iranian involvement in the war in Syria; Russian construction firms' opposition to U.S. sanctions, which are hindering them from making tens of billions of dollars building new nuclear reactors in Saudi Arabia and the United Arab Emirates; and Russian actions relative to the war in

Syria, which are ostensibly being coordinated with Russia's ally, Iran. These issues engage parties that don't at first appear connected to one another, but at least part of their correlation involves the United States dropping sanctions against the Kremlin in exchange for the promise of a big financial windfall for Trump and his relatives.

In the midst of these transition-team attempts to illegally negotiate with Russian nationals and other foreign actors, two complicating events occur: the American intelligence community releases a report confirming there was a coordinated Russian campaign to interfere in the 2016 presidential election on Trump's behalf, and *BuzzFeed*, on January 10, 2017, publishes a thirty-five-page dossier of raw intelligence claiming that Donald Trump has been compromised by the Kremlin since at least 2013.

The Facts

LESS THAN FORTY-EIGHT HOURS AFTER THE ELECTION, RUSsian deputy foreign minister Sergei Ryabkov confirms that there were many undisclosed contacts between the Trump campaign and Kremlin agents during the 2016 presidential campaign—exactly the sort of clandestine communications European intelligence agencies had warned the CIA of in the summer of 2016.[2] According to an interview with Ryabkov by Russian news agency Interfax (the same outlet George Papadopoulos granted an interview to, with campaign permission, in September 2016), "There were contacts. We are doing this and have been doing this during the election campaign. Obviously, we know most of the people from his [Trump's] entourage. . . . I cannot say that all of them, but quite a few have been staying in touch with Russian representatives."[3]

The response to Ryabkov's comments from the Trump campaign is immediate and categorical: the Trump campaign had "no contact with Russian officials" before Election Day, Trump's personal assistant Hope Hicks says.[4] Hicks will later tell congressional investigators that she sometimes told "white lies" for Trump during the presidential campaign, adding that none of these "white lies" involved Russia.[5]

As American media report on Ryabkov's and Hicks's comments, Putin's right-hand man, Dmitry Peskov, announces that he will be coming to the United States—in under ninety-six hours—to attend a "chess tournament" a few blocks from Trump Tower.[6]

In the immediate aftermath of the election, President Obama issues two critical warnings. The first he offers in a face-to-face conversation with Facebook creator Mark Zuckerberg, who seventy-two hours after the election says that there is no possibility that material posted on Facebook in 2016 had any impact on the presidential election and that any suggestion otherwise is "crazy."[7] Obama urges him to take the problem of fake news and propaganda seriously, which Zuckerberg ultimately does when he admits, in July 2018, that instead of the "no [election] impact" he spoke of in November 2016, he now recognizes that material posted on Facebook during the campaign—including Russian fake news and propaganda—was in fact influential.[8]

The second warning, sent via emails from the Obama administration to Trump transition team members, unambiguously tells them not to "send conflicting signals [on U.S. foreign policy] to foreign officials before the inauguration, and to include [Obama] State Department personnel when contacting them."[9] A former Trump administration official will tell the *New York Times*, in December 2017, that the incoming administration explicitly agreed to honor President Obama's "pointed request."[10]

Nevertheless, within forty-eight hours of Trump's November 8, 2016, election, Michael Flynn—who has no official role in the transition and has been denied a White House position by transition head Chris Christie—is cleared to contact Syrian president Bashar al-Assad's government without involvement by the State Department. It is unknown who gave him permission to make the contact.[11] By the next day, at the direction of Jared Kushner and Ivanka Trump, Christie has been fired from the presidential transition team; he will openly speculate that his objection to Flynn's participation in the transition was a primary cause of his dismissal.[12] Vice President–elect Mike Pence immediately replaces Christie as the head of the transition team, even as Steve Bannon and Michael Flynn toss in the trash all the binders profiling potential administration nominees that Christie had been compiling.[13] Pence will later say that he had no knowledge of what Flynn was planning to do, and ultimately did, with respect to covertly negotiating U.S. foreign policy with the Russians.[14] This is how *Politico* will summarize Pence and his team's defense to allegations that, as head of Trump's transition team, he must have known something about that team's clandestine activities: "Donald Trump's No. 2 knew nothing at all. . . . their man was out of the loop, blissfully ignorant of contacts between the Trump campaign and various foreign actors, from the Russian ambassador to WikiLeaks."[15]

Shortly after he helps engineer Christie's ouster from and Flynn's emergence onto the presidential transition team, Kushner calls Russian ambassador Sergey Kislyak. Kushner will not disclose the call on his SF-86 federal security clearance form, and when challenged he will say that he does not remember speaking to Kislyak in November.[16] Nevertheless, Kislyak appears at the back door of Trump Tower on December 1 or 2 to discuss with Kushner and Flynn crafting a secure back channel between the White House and the Kremlin that is untraceable by the U.S. intelligence community.[17] The purpose of the line—its proponents will contend, when their actions are discovered many months later—is to allow Flynn to speak directly to the Russian military about America's Syria policy as well as "other security issues."[18] As Carrie Cordero, a ten-year Department of Justice national security expert, will write for *Politico* of the Kushner-Flynn-Kremlin pipeline,

> The issue is not so much that the White House wanted to establish a back-channel with a foreign government on a particular matter—the issue is with *whom* they wanted to establish the channel (Russia), and *how* they reportedly wanted the channel to operate (using Russian facilities and secure communications). . . . Did Kushner and Flynn realize that using

Russian communications channels would either evade or appear to evade the U.S. intelligence community's own foreign intelligence surveillance activities? It's hard to believe they didn't.[19]

Another question is whether it was Kushner, Flynn, another party, or a number of parties including Kushner and Flynn who were concerned about domestic surveillance of their communications. Ninety days after the Kushner-Flynn-Kislyak meeting in Trump Tower—a meeting whose other attendees, if any, are unknown—Donald Trump will accuse the Obama administration of using U.S. intelligence services to conduct surveillance of meetings held at Trump Tower during the presidential campaign, writing on Twitter, "How low has President Obama gone to tap my phones during the very sacred election process. This is Nixon/Watergate. Bad (or sick) guy!"[20]

If the surveillance Trump accused President Obama of in March 2017 had been in place in December 2016, it might have picked up Kushner and Kislyak discussing having the Trump administration use a sensitive compartmented information facility (SCIF) controlled by the Russians to contact Russian generals securely.[21] By negotiating U.S. policy with the Russians pre-inauguration using a SCIF, Kushner and Flynn would be violating the federal Logan Act, which prohibits unauthorized persons from negotiating U.S. foreign policy with agents of foreign governments; Kushner and Flynn won't join the government for seven more weeks after their meeting with Kislyak.[22] Because Kushner and Flynn have snuck Kislyak in the back door of Trump Tower, the media doesn't discover what they've been doing until well after Trump takes office.[23]

On December 5, K. T. McFarland visits Trump Tower with her mentor, Bud McFarlane, to see Flynn, with whom she will develop a "close working relationship" during the transition, particularly on the subject of negotiations with the Russians.[24] McFarland had been selected, on November 25, to act as Trump's deputy National Security Advisor under Flynn.[25] One of the main proponents of her getting the job was Paul Erickson, boyfriend of now-accused Russian spy Maria Butina; another was McFarlane, a VIP invitee of the pro-Kremlin Center for the National Interest when Trump delivered his "Mayflower Speech" in D.C. in April 2016 (see chapter 6).[26]

A year later, in December 2017, McFarland will be accused of lying to Congress about her knowledge of Flynn's secret negotiations with Kislyak during the transition.[27] After Flynn's firing in February 2017 and Trump's subsequent nomination of McFarland to be ambassador to Singapore (one of the Rosneft-deal nations whose ambassador was present at the Mayflower), Congress asks McFarland in a written interrogatory whether she ever spoke to Flynn about his 2016 contacts with Kislyak. McFarland will answer in the negative; her leaked emails later reveal, however, that not only did she know about the late December 2016 Flynn-Kislyak contacts in advance, but she advised Flynn as they were happening and indeed did so from Mar-a-Lago, where Trump and many of his top aides were huddled at the time.[28] McFarland's emails will reveal, too, that the discussion of Flynn's negotiations with the Russians at Mar-a-Lago involved many of Trump's top aides, including Trump's future chief of staff Reince Priebus, his future press secretary Sean Spicer, and the CEO of his 2016 campaign, Steve Bannon.[29] Moreover, while the emails will not resolve whether Trump knew of the Flynn-Russia sanctions discussions—"It is uncertain how involved Mr. Trump was," the New York Times will note—reporters will observe that Trump was scheduled to meet with his national security team on the very day members of that team were being kept in the loop about Flynn's calls with Kislyak.[30] Trump was also scheduled that day to have a phone call with nearly all the aides who had received McFarland's emails about Flynn and Kislyak: Flynn, McFarland, Priebus, and Bannon were all slated to take part in the call, which was due to happen "shortly" after McFarland sent an email to that group (plus Spicer) about Flynn's ongoing talks with the Russians.[31] Another December 2016 K. T. McFarland email uncovered in 2017 notes that "[i]f there is a tit-for-tat escalation [on sanctions], Trump will have difficulty improving relations with Russia, which has just thrown U.S.A. election to him."[32]

Sergey Kislyak is not the only Russian trying to contact Trump and his team during the transition period. On November 28, Emin

Agalarov's publicist Rob Goldstone once again writes Rhona Graff, the key "conduit" to Trump, according to *Politico*.[33] What Goldstone sends to Graff in late November is a message from Aras Agalarov urging Trump to eliminate the Magnitsky sanctions on Russia. In making the request, Agalarov initiates at least the second "follow-up" on the June 2016 meeting at Trump Tower he had arranged, the first being Goldstone's late June email to Trump aide Dan Scavino about a new, Russia-oriented social media push for the Trump campaign.[34] Members of Trump's campaign have long insisted, including under oath, that the June 2016 meeting was never followed up on in any fashion. Indeed, on July 8, 2017, a statement issued by Donald Trump Jr. about the June 2016 meeting—which was later found to have been dictated by Trump himself—will say that the Magnitsky Act "was not a campaign issue at the time [in June 2016] and there was no follow up."[35] That Trump dictated these words will not be discovered until June 2018, after many months of the Trump administration's denying that Trump had anything to do with the statement and a shorter period of time in which the administration said Trump may have "weighed in . . . like any father would do," but did not ultimately write the statement himself.[36]

The Magnitsky sanctions on which Agalarov lobbied Trump during the transition were leveled in mid-December 2012 against forty-four "suspected human rights abusers"—many of whom are "Russian government officials and businessmen"—to punish the apparent state-sanctioned murder of a lawyer who accused the Putin government of corruption.[37] Agalarov alleges, in his letter to Trump in November 2016, a series of facts identical to those raised by Kremlin agent Natalia Veselnitskaya at the June 2016 Trump Tower meeting, specifically allegations of a fraudulent tax scheme involving major Clinton donors.[38] Agalarov's letter then references Veselnitskaya by name, as well as her arguments for ending the sanctions.[39] Trump Jr., testifying before the Senate Judiciary Committee on September 7, 2017, will agree that what Goldstone sent Trump's secretary on Agalarov's behalf was "generally speaking" the same as what was presented to him by Veselnitskaya in June 2016.[40] Goldstone further offers to have a lawyer working to overturn the Magnitsky sanctions meet with Trump's transition team.[41]

After his early December meeting with Kushner and Flynn, Kislyak subsequently arranges for Kushner to meet, on either December 13 or 14, with Sergei Gorkov, a former FSB agent and the head of Russian bank VEB, which is on the U.S. sanctions list.[42] According to *Foreign Policy*, Gorkov "runs a major state entity that is nearly a century old and effectively serves as a slush fund for the Kremlin's pet projects. . . . Any decision to send Gorkov to serve as an intermediary with the Trump transition team would have been considered deliberately at the highest levels [in the Kremlin]."[43] After the meeting, Gorkov and VEB issue a statement maintaining, as summarized by the *Washington Post*, that "the session was held as part of a new business strategy and was conducted with Kushner in his role as the head of his family real estate business"; meanwhile, Kushner takes the position that "the meeting was unrelated to business" and was, instead, "diplomatic" in nature.[44] The *New York Times* notes that as Trump's son-in-law and Gorkov meet, Kushner's company is in the midst of "seeking financing for its troubled $1.8 billion purchase of an office building on Fifth Avenue in New York."[45] Gorkov leaves New York and, according to flight records, goes directly to Japan, where Vladimir Putin is making a visit on December 15 and 16.[46]

Having joined the transition team due to Kushner's intervention, and having met with Kislyak alongside Kushner, in late December Michael Flynn makes at least five calls to Kislyak to discuss both a pending UN resolution condemning Israeli settlements and the question of whether the United States will maintain its sanctions on Russia. Kushner is allegedly the "very senior member" of the Trump transition team who gives Flynn the order, on December 22, to make the calls to Kislyak.[47] As the *Washington Post* will report, however, "The talks were part of a series of contacts between Flynn and Kislyak that began *before the Nov. 8 election* and continued during the transition. In a recent interview, Kislyak confirmed that he had communicated with Flynn by text message, by phone and in person, but declined to say whether they had discussed sanctions" (emphasis added).[48]

On December 12, 2016, "former" Trump national security adviser Carter Page makes his second trip of the year to Moscow. While there, he is asked by a Russian journalist during a public Q&A whether he has—or plans to have—any influence on Trump's transition team or administration and whether he has any back channels to connect "Moscow and Team Trump."[49] Page does not answer any of the questions asked. Instead he says,

> The biggest influence is the process of helping to advance the objectives of the president-elect. . . . One of the biggest areas of impact is in terms of various research projects, which I've been involved in with some of the most prominent leaders in the United States and in Russia. So, it's absolutely accurate that I was limited in terms of what I can do, because I think that had a lot to do with the huge challenges and the misperceptions and fake news. As I told to the team as I was leaving, unfortunately, in September [2016], I did not want to be a distraction. . . . But I couldn't be more excited and happy as to the new opportunities that are not only for a number of the companies I've worked with here [in Russia], but really people across the United States. I think, particularly given my focus in the energy sector, the level of enthusiasm about some of the changes that are under way is really hard to overstate.[50]

According to the Steele dossier, Page is still secretly working for Trump at this point.[51]

Asked about his reasons for coming to Moscow, Page replies, "My main objective when I first moved over here in 2004 and when I've been coming back and forth throughout my life is really to have a positive impact with improving the situation with U.S.-Russia relations."[52] Asked about (a) whether he is, while in Moscow, carrying out his pre-trip plans to discuss "business contracts" and hold "negotiations" with Russian nationals; (b) whether any such negotiations have been successful, if already held; (c) whether he has had any contact with Rosneft executives while in Moscow; and (d) whether he knows who in the incoming Trump administration will be put in charge of negotiating the Ukraine crisis, Page makes reference to a just-closed deal in which Russian oil giant Rosneft sold a 19.5 percent stake of its ownership to a joint Swiss-Qatari venture. This is the deal the Steele dossier alleges Page helped Trump benefit from financially by means of a "brokerage" fee from Rosneft.

> I did have the opportunity to meet with an executive from Rosneft, and I think, unfortunately, it's a great example of where the recent deal which Glencore and Qatar were able to move forward with [was one that] unfortunately, United States actors were constrained [from being part of], and I think there's a lot of ways where a lot of the impact of sanctions has really affected individuals from the U.S. side much more so than we've seen with Russia.[53]

Page does not clarify who the "United States actors" are who had been hoping to profit from the Rosneft sale. As Page's questioner finishes asking him whether he has met with anyone from Rosneft and begins asking who will be handling the Ukraine crisis for the Trump administration, an unusually loud English-language, Russian-accented voiceover not native to the audio or video of the Q&A takes over the official RT YouTube clip of the event, making it difficult to hear Page's response. The unexplained audio distortion ends ten seconds after Page says he has met with Rosneft executives during his December trip.[54]

According to the Steele dossier, which cites a "close associate" of Rosneft CEO Igor Sechin, on July 7 or 8, 2016, during one of the two days of his first 2016 trip to Moscow, Page speaks face-to-face with Sechin.[55] During the conversation, Sechin allegedly tells Page that Sechin will offer Trump a "brokerage" windfall layered atop the upcoming Rosneft sale of a 19 percent stake in the company, but only if Trump agrees to lift U.S. sanctions on Russia should he become president.[56] Per the dossier, Page expresses interest in the offer and assures Sechin that Trump will end all sanctions on Russia if elected.[57] The dossier adds that Sechin later reports to his associate that, while Page never said so explicitly, he feels that Page does speak "with the Republican candidate's authority."[58]

Five months later, in December 2016, Page is once again in Moscow as the Rosneft deal—Russia's largest ever oil deal—closes. Rosneft sells a 19.5 percent stake in the company for $10.2 billion; the purchasers of the stake, in a fifty-fifty venture, are Swiss oil trading firm Glencore and the Qatar Investment Authority (QIA).[59]

As the transition team does its work in December 2016, a small (if overlapping) group of additional Trump aides, associates, and allies—including Michael Flynn, Tom Barrack, Rick Gates, and Bud McFarlane—do a different sort of work: they lobby Trump to give nuclear technology to Saudi Arabia so that Russian companies and others can get billions of dollars in contracts to build nuclear reactors in the Middle East.[60] The proposal would "require lifting sanctions on Russia," according to Reuters, to allow currently sanctioned Russian companies to partner with American entities to build reactors in Saudi Arabia and the United Arab Emirates—the latter nation, too, because, under the terms of a deal signed many years ago by the United States, if the American government relaxes nuclear-weapon safeguards on Saudi Arabia, a "gold standard" clause from a past U.S.-UAE nuclear deal would ultimately entitle the UAE to enrich uranium as well.[61] As explained by ProPublica, "Saudi Arabia needs approval from the U.S. in order to receive sensitive American technology. Past negotiations broke down because the Saudi government wouldn't commit to certain safeguards against eventually using the technology for weapons. Now the Trump administration has reopened those talks and might not insist on the same precautions."[62]

On December 15, Jared Kushner, Michael Flynn, Steve Bannon, George Nader, and the crown prince of Abu Dhabi, Mohammed bin Zayed (MBZ), meet secretly at Trump Tower.[63] Kushner never discloses the meeting on his SF-86 federal security clearance form, and MBZ breaches diplomatic protocol by not alerting the Obama administration to his presence in the United States.[64] Over the next few months, Nader will come to the White House several times to meet with administration officials, and one of these times he will bring Joel

Zamel—who was present at the August 3, 2016, meeting Nader had with Donald Trump Jr.—and meet with Bannon and Kushner.[65]

After the December 15, 2016, meeting, Erik Prince reaches out to MBZ "on behalf of Trump" and asks him to set up a back-channel meeting with a close Putin associate.[66] According to ABC News, Prince contacted MBZ through an agent of his, Nader, and Nader thereafter set up a January 2017 meeting between Prince and Kirill Dmitriev of the Russian Direct Investment Fund (RDIF).[67] Leon Black, a friend of Jared Kushner's with whom he was spotted at the U.S. Open just a few months before the 2016 election, is both the CEO of Apollo Global Management, which in 2017 will loan Kushner $184 million, and an RDIF board member; the parent company of the RDIF is VEB, the same sanctioned Russian bank whose chief executive Kushner had just met with a few weeks earlier.[68]

ABC News will report in August 2018 that Special Counsel Mueller has now accessed Erik Prince's phone and computer. This is "a sign," says ABC, "that Mueller could try to squeeze Prince, as he has others, probing potential inconsistencies in his sworn testimony."[69] According to ABC, "earlier this year . . . [Mueller] obtained evidence that calls [Prince's] testimony into question. Lebanese-American businessman George Nader, a key witness given limited immunity by Mueller, told investigators that he set up the meeting in the Seychelles between Prince and Dmitriev. . . . [Also,] before and after Prince met Nader in New York a week before the trip, Nader shared information with Prince about Dmitriev."[70] ABC suggests that Prince could therefore be in legal jeopardy, not just because of his testimony about Dmitriev, about whom he indicated to Congress he knew virtually nothing when he met him, but also because of other statements he made under oath that also appear to be untrue, including his claim he has "zero" " 'investments' or 'business partnerships with Russian nationals.' " According to ABC, multiple Prince associates have been contacted by Special Counsel Mueller and have told Mueller's investigators of Prince's partnership, through his Frontier Services Group, with "Dimitriy Streshinskiy, a former Russian special forces soldier turned arms dealer and manufacturer." ABC says Streshinskiy "acted as Prince's partner in an effort to

secure a possibly illegal private security contract with Azerbaijan. . . .
For the proposed contract, named 'Project Zulu,' Prince and Streshinskiy, a dual Russian-Israeli citizen, each stood to make $21 mil-
lion, or 20 percent of the proposed $216 million deal."[71] ABC also
found evidence that Prince "deal[t] with the Russian state-owned energy firm Rostec. According to [a] former associate [of Prince], Rostec asked Prince's Frontier Services Group to work on logistics for a
proposed refinery operation in Tanzania and Uganda. . . . Work began,
the associate said, but the deal fell through when the United States imposed sanctions on the Kremlin-run firm in 2014. . . . [The associate
said] there was no 'business' because the deals weren't finalized, . . .
but Prince provided manpower and resources in both projects. . . ."[72]
Prince thus joins Flynn as another "shadow" national security adviser
to Trump who discussed sanctions with a Russian national during the
presidential transition—a fact he failed to disclose and indeed misled
investigators about. And Prince stood to benefit personally if Russian
sanctions were lifted; like Flynn, who met with Russian ambassador
Sergey Kislyak before as well as after the election, Prince met with
foreign nationals both before and after Election Day who were in a position to assist him in securing business deals with the Russians going
forward—as long as Trump ended U.S. sanctions on Russia.

Michael Flynn's first recorded payment as a lobbyist working to
convince the U.S. government to sell nuclear reactors to Saudi Arabia came in 2014 from a company called ACU Strategic Partners.[73]
By 2015, he was partnering in his lobbying effort with the British-
American Alex Copson, who "was telling people he had a group of
U.S., European, Arab and Russian companies that would build as many
as 40 nuclear reactors in Egypt, Jordan and Saudi Arabia." Meanwhile,
"[i]n his role with ACU, Flynn flew to Egypt [in 2015] to convince officials there to hold off on a Russian offer . . . to build nuclear power
plants."[74] Given the association between Flynn and George Papadopoulos, it is noteworthy that just two months before the 2016 presidential election, Papadopoulos was in New York City, arranging a meeting
between Trump and President Abdel Fattah el-Sisi of Egypt.[75] Papadopoulos's academic specialization—one that dovetails with Flynn's

lobbying interests, as well as with the general-turned-lobbyist's own interest in Egypt—is Middle Eastern energy issues.[76]

By 2016, Flynn's lobbying efforts had transitioned into new entities and partnerships, and he was working with Bud McFarlane in a new iteration of ACU called IP3 International. By early 2017, Tom Barrack had joined them in lobbying Trump to sell nuclear technology to the Saudis.[77]

Jared Kushner's activities in 2016 and 2017 suggest an alignment between his business and professional interests and those of Flynn, McFarlane, Prince, Barrack, and Papadopoulos. In October 2017, Kushner will take a sudden trip to Riyadh, Saudi Arabia, where, according to Saudi crown prince Mohammed bin Salman, "Kushner . . . discusse[s] the names of Saudis disloyal to the crown prince"—including highly classified information from his father-in-law's president's daily brief (PDB).[78] Soon after, the crown prince tells friends that Kushner is "in his pocket."[79] Kushner is said to regularly use WhatsApp Messenger (an encrypted messaging app for smartphones) to text the crown prince, against the advice of his attorneys and in possible violation of the Presidential Records Act.[80] His use of WhatsApp means his communications with the Saudi Arabian prince are likely invisible to outside requests for review.[81]

In early November 2017, Kushner advises his father-in-law to support Saudi Arabia's blockade of Qatar—one of Trump's only advisers to do so. According to NBC News, "some top Qatari government officials believe the White House's position on the blockade may have been a form of retaliation driven by Kushner, who was sour about the failed [December 2016] deal" with the QIA to save his property at 666 Fifth Avenue in New York City with a massive investment from Qatar.[82] Later that month, Leon Black's Apollo Global Management, one of whose largest investors is the QIA, lends Kushner $184 million after Apollo cofounder Joshua Harris has several meetings with Kushner in the White House.[83] According to the *New York Times* in February 2018, "Even by the standards of Apollo, one of the world's largest private equity firms, the previously unreported transaction with the Kushners was a big deal: It was triple the size of the average property loan made

by Apollo's real estate lending arm. . . . [and] one of the largest loans
Kushner Companies received [in 2017]."[84] The concurrence of all these
events raises the suspicion, among several media outlets, that Kushner
has used his father-in-law's support of the Saudi blockade of Qatar to
squeeze the Qataris for money.[85] As *Vanity Fair* will sarcastically observe, "there's no way to know whether the Trump administration's decision to rain hell on Qatar was the result of Jared not getting his way.
Certainly, neither the Kushners nor the Trumps are known for holding
grudges, or for retaliating against people they believe have wronged
them. But the timing is interesting. . . . one could almost say a pattern
is emerging[.]"[86]

In August 2018, a QIA-backed firm loans Kushner money *again*,
when a company the QIA partly owns, Brookfield Asset Management,
invests $700 million in the Kushner-held property at 666 Fifth Avenue,
thereby allowing Kushner to pay off the entirety of the debt owed on
it.[87] According to *Slate*, because the QIA was one of the two purchas-
ers of the 19.5 percent stake in Rosneft discussed in the Steele dossier, Special Counsel Mueller is now investigating all QIA-Kushner
transactions. "[T]he stories of Kushner's loans line up remarkably well
with one of the Steele dossier's core allegations of Russian bribery . . ."
writes *Slate*. "[N]ew stories suggest that [Kushner] may have orchestrated a foreign policy crisis to pressure Qatar to bail him out. Months
later, a firm linked to Qatar gave him a staggeringly large loan. All
of these events suggest how Russia might have delivered a possible
quid—a potential payment from a huge oil sale through back channels
[a QIA-connected 'loan' to Kushner]—in return for a Trump administration quo—a reported promise of reduced sanctions [on Russia]."[88]
Importantly, Saudi Arabia's blockade of Qatar began in June 2017; the
Qataris loaned Kushner money almost immediately after Trump, on
Kushner's advice, tweeted that he supported the blockade in November
2017.[89]

Should Kushner not be required to pay back any portion of the $884
million loaned to him (in total) by the two QIA-linked outfits, it could
constitute the "brokerage" of the QIA/Glencore purchase of $10.2 bil-
lion in Rosneft that Sechin promised Trump. Trump's lifting of sanc-

tions on Rosneft—his intended plan upon entering the White House, as has since been reported—would so substantially raise Rosneft's profits that any such brokerage would be worth it for the Qataris. For instance, if U.S. sanctions on Russia are dropped, ExxonMobil can once again partner with Rosneft in the world's northernmost oil field, the Pobeda (Victory) field; a 2012 deal between Exxon and Rosneft to drill in it had earned then Exxon CEO Rex Tillerson the Russian Order of Friendship from Putin's own hand.[90] The Pobeda oil field was estimated in 2014 to hold at least 130 million tons of oil, which in 2018 would be worth approximately $60 billion—about six times what Glencore and QIA paid to own 19.5 percent of Rosneft.[91]

Two days after Kushner, Flynn, Bannon, Nader, and the crown prince of the United Arab Emirates meet secretly at Trump Tower, on December 13, 2016, Trump nominates Rex Tillerson for secretary of state—doing so while Carter Page is in Moscow meeting with Rosneft executives and on the same day Jared Kushner meets with the chief executive of VEB.[92]

By March 2018, "the Trump administration is . . . considering allowing Saudi Arabia to enrich uranium," a decision that could lead to the Middle Eastern nation handing out over $80 billion in construction contracts to build sixteen nuclear reactors over the next twenty-five years.[93] The United States, Russia, and China are slated to compete for these construction contracts; the Saudis could also seek the nuclear technology they need, however, from France, the United Kingdom, or even Russia instead of the United States.

In the end, that's exactly what the Saudis do: in August 2018, *Haaretz* writes, "Russia has staged a comeback in the Mideast, big time, to the extent that it may replace the United States as the leading foreign power in the region. Russia's success results from a combination of both deft diplomacy and weapons and nuclear reactor sales to states throughout the region."[94] *Haaretz* adds, "Putin's fundamental strategic objective is to restore Russian global leadership."[95]

Improving diplomatic relations with Russia is important to both Saudi Arabia and the United Arab Emirates not merely because Russian construction firms may end up building any new nuclear reactors in the two countries; far more important, both Saudi Arabia and the UAE are hoping that better relations with Russia will lead to a softening of Russia's support for two entities considered a potential threat to both Saudi and Emirati security: Iran and the Syrian regime of Bashar al-Assad, which is propped up by Iranian human, military, and financial resources.[96] The Saudis and Emiratis are joined in their enmity for Iran and its puppet regimes by Israel. This fact helps explain why George Nader, representing the interests of the crown princes of both Saudi Arabia and the UAE, and Joel Zamel, an Israeli business intelligence entrepreneur with Israeli government connections, tell Trump Jr. on August 3, 2016, that all three nations have a vested interest in seeing Trump elected president. Influential Saudis, Emiratis, and Israelis offer assistance to the Trump campaign because they believe Trump, not Clinton, is willing to do the one thing that will bring Putin back to the table in the Middle East: drop all sanctions on Russia.[97] The *New Yorker* will write in July 2018 that "before the November, 2016, election, Mohammed bin Zayed, the crown prince of Abu Dhabi, floated to a longtime American interlocutor what sounded, at the time, like an unlikely grand bargain. The Emirati leader told the American that Vladimir Putin, the Russian President, might be interested in resolving the conflict in Syria in exchange for the lifting of sanctions imposed in response to Russia's actions in Ukraine."[98] The magazine adds that while the idea of a rapprochement between Russia and the United States has long deeply unnerved America's European allies, "three countries that [in November 2016] enjoyed unparalleled influence with the incoming Administration—Israel, Saudi Arabia, and the U.A.E.—have repeatedly encouraged their American counterparts to consider ending the Ukraine-related sanctions in return for Putin's help in removing Iranian forces from Syria."[99]

It is in the midst of this years-long saga involving Saudi Arabia, the United Arab Emirates, Qatar, Russia, Syria, and Iran that Erik Prince flies to the Seychelles to meet with representatives from the United Arab Emirates and, at George Nader's orchestration, on behalf of Saudi crown prince Mohammed bin Salman, with Kirill Dmitriev from the Russian Direct Investment Fund. The QIA has just declined to loan

Kushner hundreds of millions in much-needed money, allegedly angering Kushner; in the coming months Kushner will convince Trump to support Saudi Arabia's blockade on the tiny Middle Eastern nation. The Saudi blockade will, by the end of 2017, help Kushner pressure Qatar into loaning him nearly a billion dollars.

In January 2017, however, what the Saudis (and Emiratis) most want from Trump is nuclear technology—specifically, sales of same without a Section 123 Agreement prohibiting the Saudis from ever weaponizing their uranium.[100] The opportunity exists, should the United States assent to these sales, for all parties to get what they want: the Trumps, as much as a billion dollars; the Russians, an end to sanctions; the Saudis and the UAE, nuclear reactors, an easing of Russian support for Iran, and the right to enrich uranium without prohibitions on its subsequent weaponization; Qatar, an end to the Saudi blockade, the favor of the Trump administration, and a very large—and likely to grow, should sanctions on Russia end—private stake in Russia's state-owned oil company.

In the Seychelles, Prince, acting as a Trump representative, meets with the UAE's MBZ and Dmitriev, the latter not just the manager of Russia's $10 billion sovereign wealth fund, but also a man "close to Vladimir Putin."[101] The purpose of the meeting is to set up a back channel between President-elect Trump and Putin, roughly the same effort that Kushner and Kislyak had been working on in early December.[102] Prince will say to CNN of the meeting that he was already in the Seychelles on unrelated business with Emirati officials when he met "some fund manager—I can't even remember his name."[103] Prince will tell CNN the meeting "probably lasted about as long as one beer."[104] In November 2017 testimony before the House Intelligence Committee, a confident, combative Prince—appearing without a lawyer—will say he had no official or unofficial role in the Trump campaign, though he will concede regularly sending and sometimes delivering in person national security and foreign policy white papers to campaign CEO Steve Bannon at Trump Tower. He will also say that, while in the Seychelles, the Emiratis he was already scheduled to meet with merely "mentioned a guy I should meet who was also in town to see them" and who also "ran some sort of hedge fund."[105] He will agree, when asked, that the two men did discuss U.S.-Russia relations.[106]

As Trump fills out his cabinet, Prince's sister Betsy DeVos is nominated to be secretary of education, despite her being called "uniquely unprepared," "unqualified," and "dangerous" by *U.S. News & World Report*; "manifestly unqualified" and "woefully ignorant" by the *Washington Post*; and "unprepared and unqualified" by the *Los Angeles Times*.[107] In the end, DeVos is confirmed only when Vice President Pence casts the tie-breaking vote in the U.S. Senate, two Republicans having bolted from their caucus to vote against the nomination alongside Senate Democrats.[108] Tillerson is successfully nominated for and confirmed as secretary of state, despite the *New York Times* noting "bipartisan concerns that the globe-trotting leader of an energy giant has a too-cozy relationship with Vladimir V. Putin, the President of Russia."[109] And Jeff Sessions, the chairman of Trump's National Security Advisory Committee, which included among its roster Carter Page, George Papadopoulos, J. D. Gordon, and Joseph Schmitz, is nominated to the post of attorney general, in part, Trump will later admit, because he assumed Sessions would "protect him" from any investigation into his, his family's, or the campaign's dealings with Russia.[110] Sessions will run into problems after his successful confirmation, however, as he will be found to have provided inaccurate testimony under oath regarding his work as the National Security Advisory Committee's chairman.[111] His controversial answers before the Senate Judiciary Committee, deliberately evasive at best and perjury at worst, will lead to his recusal from the Trump-Russia investigation in March 2017.[112]

On December 29, the Obama administration levels new sanctions on Russia. Putin's decision not to retaliate against the new sanctions— his usual practice in such situations—raises concerns within the Obama administration that Russia has been promised an end to sanctions under the Trump presidency.[113] Trump's immediate reaction to Putin's decision on Twitter—"Great move on delay (by V. Putin)," he tweets, adding, "I always knew he was very smart!"—does nothing to allay these concerns.[114] The administration's fears soon prove justified, not only because Flynn was in fact holding policy discussions—possibly negotiations—with Sergey Kislyak before Election Day, and thereafter began (or continued) negotiating sanctions with Kislyak during the presidential transition, but also because, as is revealed in June 2017, Trump did indeed have a "secret" plan to drop all sanctions on Russia after his inauguration. On the day President Obama issues new sanctions on Russia, Flynn speaks to Russia's ambassador no fewer than five times by telephone, keeping in contact with K. T. McFarland at Mar-a-Lago between the calls. According to his December 2017 guilty plea for making false statements to the FBI, Flynn successfully convinces the Russians to refrain from retaliating against either Obama's imposition of new sanctions or the outgoing president's expulsion of thirty-five Russian diplomats from the United States.[115]

Just after the first of the year, a group of CIA officers meet with their counterparts from Mossad, Israel's primary intelligence agency, at Langley in Virginia. The CIA agents tell the Israelis that Trump is compromised by a foreign power, suffering under "leverages of pressure." They warn the Israelis to "be careful" with intelligence sharing once Trump is in power.[116]

On January 6, the U.S. intelligence community releases a joint FBI/CIA/NSA report, which concludes that "Russian President Vladimir Putin ordered an influence campaign in 2016 aimed at the U.S. presidential election. Russia's goals were to undermine public faith in the U.S. democratic process, denigrate Secretary Clinton, and harm her electability and potential presidency. We further assess Putin and the Russian Government developed a clear preference for President-elect Trump. We have high confidence in these judgments."[117] In a statement that day, Trump refuses to accept the findings of the FBI, CIA, and NSA that Russia, uniquely and discretely, attacked the 2016 presidential election, saying in part, "While Russia, China, other countries, outside groups and people are consistently trying to break through the cyber infrastructure of our governmental institutions, businesses and organizations including the Democrat National Committee, there was absolutely no effect on the outcome of the election including the fact that there was no tampering whatsoever with voting machines."[118]

On January 9, 2017, eleven days before Trump's inauguration,

BuzzFeed publishes a now famous thirty-five-page dossier of raw intelligence compiled for a succession of anti-Trump Republicans and
Democrats. The curator of the intelligence, an Englishman named
Christopher Steele, is a former Russia-desk head of the MI6; numerous intelligence sources in England will vouch for his credibility and the
quality of his sources when his work comes under fire, almost immediately, from Trump.[119] Steele's dossier alleges that Trump aides coordinated with Kremlin agents throughout the 2016 general election season
in a sanctions-relief-for-money quid pro quo coupled with active assistance from the Russians in attacking and undermining Hillary Clinton.[120]
Trump first learns of the dossier from his FBI director, James Comey, on
January 6. Comey tells Trump that he is not the subject of an open counterintelligence investigation, despite the dossier's allegations.[121]

On January 11, less than forty-eight hours after *BuzzFeed* publishes
the Steele dossier's allegations, Trump says—one of the only times he
ever does so—"As far as hacking, I think it was Russia."[122] He quickly
adds, however, "But I think we also get hacked by other countries and
other people,"[123] and then blames the Democrats for the hacking, saying, "I have to say this also, the Democratic National Committee was
totally open to be hacked. They did a very poor job. They could've had
hacking defense, which we [Republicans] had."[124]

On the eve of Trump's inauguration, the *New York Times* reports
that Comey's Trump-Russia investigation is much deeper and broader,
and uses more varied forms of evidence, than had previously been suspected, noting that

> American law enforcement and intelligence agencies are exam-
> ining intercepted communications and financial transactions as
> part of a broad investigation into possible links between Russian
> officials and associates of President-elect Donald J. Trump, in-
> cluding his former campaign chairman Paul Manafort. The con-
> tinuing counterintelligence investigation means that Mr. Trump
> will take the oath of office on Friday with his associates under
> investigation and after the intelligence agencies concluded that
> the Russian government had worked to help elect him.[125]

The *Times* will also forecast logistically sensitive times ahead for both Trump and the nation, observing that Trump will "oversee" the very agencies that have concluded he benefitted from Russian assistance and will therefore "have the authority to redirect or stop at least some of those efforts." [126] This prescient comment presages and summarizes a central drama of the early months of the Trump presidency.

Annotated History

Nevertheless, within forty-eight hours of Trump's November 8, 2016, election, Michael Flynn—who has no official role in the transition and has been denied a White House position by transition head Chris Christie—is cleared to contact Syrian president Bashar al-Assad's government without involvement by the State Department. It is unknown who gave him permission to make the contact. By the next day, at the direction of Jared Kushner and Ivanka Trump, Christie has been fired from the presidential transition team; he will openly speculate that his objection to Flynn's participation in the transition was a primary cause of his dismissal.

According to the *Washington Examiner*, Jared Kushner's involvement in the firing of Christie was partly motivated by Christie's role in the prosecution of Jared's father, Charles Kushner.[127]

Trump went to extraordinary lengths to have Kushner named as one of his top advisers; to avoid anti-nepotism laws, Trump had to get an advisory opinion from the Department of Justice declaring the White House exempt from such regulations.[128] Kushner spent the transition period building up his political capital in preparation for his new White House role, and his "purge" of the transition team, as the *New York Times* called it, was one of his first steps in further solidifying his position within Trump's political orbit.[129] The *Times* wrote in November 2016, "Both [former congressman Mike Rogers and defense and foreign policy adviser Matthew Freedman] were part of what officials described as a purge orchestrated by Jared Kushner. Mr. Kushner, a transition official said, was systematically dismissing people like Mr. Rogers who had ties with Mr. Christie."[130] It was Christie's successful prosecution of Charles Kushner that had led indirectly to Jared Kushner's disastrous, nearly financially ruinous decision to purchase 666 Fifth Avenue in New York City; the purchase was Kushner's first major one after his father was incarcerated and Kushner took over Kushner Companies.[131] According to NBC News, ever since the purchase of the property at 666 Fifth Avenue, Kushner Companies had been "bleeding money."

Several months after Trump's inauguration, around the time that Saudi Arabia's blockade on Qatar began, Charles Kushner met with the Qatari finance minister to discuss funding for 666 Fifth Avenue, a decision he later said was the "wrong thing to do." Kushner defended his decision to attend the meeting, however, by saying that he met with the Qatari simply to tell him that he couldn't accept any funding from Qatar while his son was assisting with U.S.-Qatar policy in the White House. When asked by *Business Insider* why he didn't simply refuse the meeting in the first instance if he didn't intend to take any money from the Qataris, Kushner had no answer—except to agree that doing so would have been the right thing to do.[132]

Vice President Mike Pence immediately replaces Christie as the head of the transition team, even as Steve Bannon and Michael Flynn toss in the trash all the binders profiling potential administration nominees that Christie had been compiling. Pence will later say that he had no knowledge of what Flynn was planning to do, and ultimately did, with respect to covertly negotiating U.S. foreign policy with the Russians.

On January 15, 2017, five days before Trump's inauguration, Pence told CBS's *Face the Nation* that Flynn and Kislyak had not discussed sanctions in December 2016. "It was strictly coincidental that they had a conversation," said Pence, the head of the presidential transition team. "They did not discuss anything having to do with the United States' decision to expel diplomats or impose censure against Russia."[133] Pence's statement was ultimately found to be untrue, which forced the White House to say that either Flynn had lied to Pence or Pence had lied to the nation. It chose the former and thereafter fired Flynn.[134]

Kushner, Flynn, Bannon, Nader, and the crown prince of the United Arab Emirates meet secretly at Trump Tower. Two days later, on December 13, 2016, Trump nominates Rex Tillerson for secretary of state—doing so while Carter Page is in Moscow meeting with Rosneft executives and on the same day Jared Kushner meets with the chief executive of VEB.

Something else Trump did on December 13 was to tell the *Wall Street Journal* he wanted to end all sanctions on Russia. Trump's campaign manager–cum–presidential counselor Kellyanne Conway repeated that sentiment two weeks later, just before Trump's first phone call with Vladimir Putin as president of the United States.[135]

On January 6, the U.S. intelligence community releases a joint FBI/CIA/NSA report concluding that "Russian President Vladimir Putin ordered an influence campaign in 2016 aimed at the U.S. presidential election. Russia's goals were to undermine public faith in the U.S. democratic process, denigrate Secretary Clinton, and harm her electability and potential presidency. We further assess Putin and the Russian Government developed a clear preference for President-elect Trump."

The "new" information in the report, which Trump was briefed upon several hours before it was published, was that Russia preferred Trump to Clinton. Trump had already been briefed on August 17, 2016, on the fact that U.S. intelligence had seen "direct links" between the Russian government and systemic interference with the 2016 presidential election.[136]

Three days before the January 6, 2017, briefing, Trump took to Twitter to falsely claim that the briefing had originally been scheduled for January 3; he used the occasion of the briefing allegedly being moved back, which it was not, to try to discredit it in advance, tweeting, "The 'Intelligence' briefing on so-called 'Russian hacking' was delayed until Friday, perhaps more time needed to build a case. Very strange!" [137] This was one of the earliest instances of Trump's casting doubt on U.S. law enforcement not merely for its handling of the Clinton investigation but its handling of the ongoing Russia investigation. It is a political strategy that would shortly become a hallmark of the new Trump presidency.

CHAPTER TWELVE

THE FIRINGS OF FLYNN AND COMEY

February to May 2017

Summary

AS DONALD TRUMP ENTERS OFFICE, THE COLLUSION QUES-
tion no longer centers on Trump's securing the White House through
a clandestine quid pro quo but something altogether different: a col-
laborative effort by Trump and his aides, allies, and associates to obscure what has been done and by whom, mostly by seeking to control
or derail federal law enforcement's fast-expanding investigation into
the matter.

For Trump, the most immediate dilemma is National Security Advisor (and one-time VP short-lister) Michael Flynn, who was acting on
orders from Jared Kushner—and possibly others—in negotiating with
Russian ambassador Sergey Kislyak during the transition, but now
must be removed from his job before the scandal over his actions deepens.[1] From the moment Flynn is fired, Trump is engaged in an effort to
convince or compel FBI director James Comey to end the Flynn investigation and to clear Trump himself of any wrongdoing relating to Russia. The new president fires Sally Yates—the Obama-holdover acting
attorney general, and also the attorney who brought Flynn's actions to
the attention of law enforcement—and seeks to maintain Flynn's loyalty to him through a clandestine outreach.

Meanwhile, the December 9, 2016, handoff of the Steele dossier
from Senator John McCain to James Comey—McCain having received

it from a retired British diplomat, Sir Andrew Wood, at an annual security conference in Nova Scotia in mid-November 2016—has launched a new phase of the FBI's counterintelligence investigation of Russian election meddling.[2] This new phase puts Trump and several of his aides and associates in the crosshairs of federal law enforcement as chief figures in the dossier. When a man strongly suspected by investigators of being one of Steele's sources is apparently murdered in Moscow, U.S. and foreign journalists suggest that this lends credence to some of the intelligence Steele has compiled.[3]

When Comey refuses to publicly clear Trump of any wrongdoing, his job is immediately placed in jeopardy; he is fired by Trump on May 9, less than ninety days after Flynn is removed from his position. During those ninety days an event occurs, however, that will make Trump's firing of Comey the most problematic decision of his presidency: facing accusations of lying to Congress, Trump's attorney general, Jeff Sessions, recuses himself from the ongoing Trump-Russia investigation in early March. Sessions's recusal from the Russia probe, followed by Comey's firing, opens the door for Rod Rosenstein, the acting attorney general for the Russia investigation, to appoint Robert Mueller as special counsel. Rosenstein's appointment of Mueller—authorizing the former FBI director to investigate any coordination or links between the Russian government and individuals associated with the Trump campaign, as well as any crimes that might arise from the investigation of that question—comes under new Department of Justice regulations. The old ones had lapsed when the independent counsel statute expired after the last major investigation of a president (Kenneth Starr of Bill Clinton).[4] Mueller moves quickly to continue the work Comey had started, even as a series of sluggish and highly partisan congressional investigations begin interviewing a few of the key witnesses in the Trump-Russia case.

In Washington, D.C., Trump exhibits increasingly unusual behavior: urging the White House counsel to lobby Sessions to "un-recuse" himself; disclosing classified Israeli intelligence to Kremlin agents in the Oval Office; accusing President Obama, without any proof, of wiretapping his Trump Tower office; and finally firing Comey, an act he

brags about to Kremlin agents and then admits, in an interview with
NBC's Lester Holt, was an attempt to stifle the Russia investigation.
This fuels speculation that far more of the Steele dossier may be accurate than anyone had previously realized. While media will point out
that the dossier is "unverified," and Trump will call it "fake" and "sick,"
as the first 120 days of the Trump presidency comes to a close there is
substantial evidence to suggest the FBI is using Christopher Steele's
compilation of human intelligence as a road map for understanding
Trump-Russia collusion prior to Election Day.

The Facts

FBI DIRECTOR JAMES COMEY BRIEFS TRUMP ON THE STEELE
dossier two weeks before Trump's inauguration. He will later testify
before Congress that he immediately memorialized his briefing of
Trump, based on the president-elect's reaction to hearing the information in the dossier and because, as he later said, "I was honestly concerned that he might lie about the nature of our meeting."[5] Two days
after his inauguration, Trump will single out Comey during a public
event and attempt to embrace him in front of a bank of cameras; according to a friend of Comey's who was told the story later on by the former FBI director, "Comey was disgusted. He regarded the episode as a
physical attempt to show closeness and warmth in a fashion calculated
to compromise him before Democrats who already mistrusted him."[6]
Five days later, Trump invites Comey to dinner at the White House; according to former director of national intelligence James Clapper, who
spoke to Comey before the dinner, Comey was "uneasy with it, both
from a standpoint of the optic of compromising his independence and
the independence of the FBI."[7] At dinner, Trump does several things
that communicate a preoccupation with the Russian collusion allegations he knows the FBI is then investigating: for instance, he asks

Comey, who is working under a long-term, cross-administration appointment, whether he wants to remain the FBI director, which Comey will later say seemed like "an effort to have me ask for my job and create some sort of patronage relationship"; Trump demands an oath of loyalty from Comey immediately after Comey tells him the FBI needs to remain independent, saying, "I need loyalty, I expect loyalty," and then repeating, "I need loyalty," at the end of the dinner; and Trump is so attentive to the details of the Steele dossier, which he claims is both false and offensive, that, per Comey, "He said he was considering ordering me to investigate the alleged incident [at the Ritz-Carlton Moscow in 2013] to prove it didn't happen," though he never follows up on the idea.[8] In a May 2017 interview on Fox News, Trump will use the sort of vacillatory, self-exculpating phrasing he had previously used with respect to Michael Flynn—"I didn't direct him [to discuss sanctions with the Russian ambassador], but I would have directed him because that's his job," he'd declared on the Flynn matter—by saying to Jeanine Pirro, "I didn't [ask Comey for his loyalty], but I don't think it would be a bad question to ask."[9]

As Trump is attempting to build a relationship with Comey that would make continued investigation of him by the FBI less likely, he is also dealing with a growing crisis involving his National Security Advisor. Four days after Trump's inauguration, Michael Flynn is interrogated by the FBI on suspicion of having illegally negotiated U.S. foreign policy with a hostile foreign power prior to Trump taking office.[10] That Flynn had spoken to Kislyak around the time Putin decided not to retaliate for the new sanctions imposed by Obama was clear by January 12; however, Vice President–elect Mike Pence, who was the transition head, had told CBS three days later that "[Flynn and Kislyak] did not discuss anything having to do with the United States' decision to expel diplomats or impose censure against Russia."[11] When Flynn dissembles with the FBI on January 24, telling agents he never discussed sanctions with the Russians—which the FBI knows is untrue, as it has telephonic intercepts indicating otherwise—Acting attorney general Sally Yates, an Obama holdover fulfilling her role until Sessions is confirmed, will go to the White House to tell White House counsel Don

McGahn that the nation's National Security Advisor may be compromised by a foreign power.[12]

Yates's fear is that if the Russians know Flynn hasn't told the FBI the truth, they can exert leverage over him via a threat to disclose to federal law enforcement what he really said and did. Yates also wants McGahn to know that Flynn has been dishonest with White House officials about his calls to Kislyak—an assumption she makes because the White House has said publicly that no one on the transition team discussed sanctions with the Russians.[13] Instead of treating Flynn's potential compromising by Russia as an emergency, McGahn asks Yates why the Department of Justice cares about the issue. When Yates repeats that Flynn is now susceptible to blackmail by a foreign power, McGahn demands to see all the evidence the Department of Justice has compiled on Flynn.[14] Yates agrees to provide the evidence by January 30; Trump fires her that day.[15] According to subsequent comments by White House press secretary Sean Spicer, at the time Trump fired Yates he had been fully briefed on the fact that she was correct—Flynn had indeed lied about his discussions to the FBI and, ostensibly, to certain officials in the Trump administration.[16]

It is later revealed that then president Obama warned Trump against hiring Flynn two days after the 2016 election, the same forty-eight-hour span in which Chris Christie was issuing his own warning on Flynn.[17] Trump instead hired Flynn as his National Security Advisor on November 17, less than a week after both Obama and Christie had strongly advised him not to do so.[18] Within twenty-four hours, a Democratic congressman, Representative Elijah Cummings (D-MD), had written transition head Mike Pence demanding more details on Flynn's unregistered lobbying for both Turkey and Russia—the latter of which Flynn had been working for through the Kremlin-funded propaganda network, RT.[19] Cummings will later discover, and make public, that Flynn did not disclose on his federal security clearance forms a trip he took to the Middle East to lobby for nuclear power plant sales the very month Trump announced his presidential run. He will find, too, that Flynn failed to report several contacts with Israeli and Egyptian governmental officials—two nations with whom George Papadopoulos also had substantial contact during the campaign.[20] Notably, Flynn will be the next Trump campaign adviser charged with a crime after Papadopoulos becomes a cooperating government witness in July 2017.

In the final few days of Flynn's tenure as National Security Advisor, the Kremlin attempts to pass a sanctions relief proposal to Flynn—framed as a "peace deal" for Ukraine—through a Kremlin-allied Ukrainian politician, Andrii V. Artemenko.[21] Artemenko meets with Trump business partner Felix Sater and Trump attorney and fixer Michael Cohen. At the meeting, he hands them an envelope with the Kremlin-approved anti-sanctions proposal inside. The envelope later ends up on Flynn's desk. Cohen at first acknowledges bringing the envelope to the White House and giving it to Flynn, and then changes his story and says he had no interest in what Artemenko was "selling" and told the Ukrainian to mail his proposal to the White House by regular mail if he wanted to contact President Trump.[22]

For reasons that are never made clear, after Trump is told in late January by his White House counsel that Flynn has had conversations about sanctions with the Russian ambassador, he—according to the White House version of events—waits two weeks to tell Pence that Flynn lied to him.[23] Throughout this two-week period, Trump knows that his National Security Advisor has been compromised by the Russians, but he allows him to maintain his security clearance.[24] When questions are raised in the months ahead about why Flynn's security clearance wasn't revoked on January 27, Trump will blame Obama for having given Flynn a security clearance in the first instance.[25] Flynn resigns or is fired—depending upon whom one asks—ninety-six hours after Pence is officially informed (if he did not already know) that Flynn lied about his calls to Kislyak.[26] On March 9, when Flynn's lobbying for Turkey becomes national news, Pence will say he is hearing about it for the first time.[27] As for the date on which Trump first heard about the Flynn-Kislyak calls, that fact has not yet been established; it is confirmed by Fox News, however, that at some point prior to Flynn's firing, Trump is fully briefed on what his National Security Advisor said to Kislyak—including Flynn's statement to the Russian ambassador, in contravention of the Logan Act, that "the Kremlin could expect a reprieve from the sanctions" announced by then president Obama on December 29, 2016.[28] Nevertheless, on February 16, just seventy-two hours after Flynn's firing, Trump will say at a press conference, "Mike was doing his job. . . . I would have directed him to do it if I thought he wasn't doing it. I didn't direct him, but I would have directed him because that's his job."[29] Trump's claim that he believed Flynn was discussing sanctions policy with the Russians in late December, coupled with his denial that he specifically ordered the negotiations, does not include a concurrent denial that he had knowledge of the negotiations as they were happening.

A key issue for Trump, following Flynn's exit, is the question of how many of his former aides, allies, and associates will cooperate with the quickly evolving FBI probe of potential Trump-Russia collusion. On March 30, Flynn takes the extraordinary step of publicly offering to testify before Congress in exchange for immunity from prosecution.[30] His attorney will tell the media that Flynn "certainly has a story to tell."[31] Congress rebuffs his offer in under a day; it cannot, in any case, immunize him against possible prosecution by the special counsel.[32] Shortly thereafter, Trump calls Flynn and tells him to "stay strong."[33] Almost immediately, Flynn ceases to cooperate with congressional investigators, ignoring a subpoena in mid-May.[34] The same month, Carter Page reveals that he is cooperating with Senate investigators and is "eager" to continue doing so.[35] By then, it has already been revealed that Jared Kushner has volunteered to be questioned by Congress.[36] Meanwhile, Trump's son Don Jr. gives an interview in which he is asked whether he had any campaign-related meetings with Russian nationals pre-election. "Did I meet with people that were Russian? I'm sure," Trump Jr. responds, then adds, "but none that were set up, none that I can think of at the moment, and certainly none that I was representing the campaign in any way, shape, or form."[37]

On May 8, former acting attorney general Yates, under questioning from Senator Richard Blumenthal (D-CT), repeatedly refuses to publicly rule out Trump as a potential target of the FBI's ongoing counterintelligence investigation into Russian interference in the 2016 presidential election.[38]

At his testimony in June, James Comey—fired by Trump on May 9, six days after he refuses to rule out Trump as a target in the Russia investigation, and one day after Yates likewise refuses to do so—will tell Congress what happened between him and Trump the day after Flynn's February 13 firing. According to Comey, he went to the Oval Office the day after Flynn's firing for a scheduled briefing, after which the president asked him to stay behind. Comey was hoping Sessions would prevent Trump from seeking a one-on-one audience with the FBI director, but Sessions left the room when Trump asked him to do so. Thereafter, Trump said to Comey (in Comey's paraphrase), " 'I want to talk about Mike Flynn.' . . . The President began by saying Flynn hadn't done anything wrong in speaking with the Russians, but he had to let him go because he had misled the Vice President. He added that he had other concerns about Flynn, which he did not then specify. . . . 'He is a good guy and has been through a lot.' . . . He then said, 'I hope you can see your way clear to letting this go, to letting Flynn go. He is a good guy. I hope you can let this go.' "[39] Comey will add that, because of "the setting and the fact that Trump asked to see him alone, he took the president's words as a directive."[40]

Trump's attempts to derail the FBI investigation into his campaign's ties with Russia are unusually direct, forceful, and persistent. In addition to his effort to stop any further investigation of Flynn and his inappropriate contact with Flynn post-firing, he asks Comey four times to declare that the Russia investigation is not and will not be looking at him; commands White House counsel Don McGahn to try to get Sessions to "un-recuse" himself from the Russia investigation and then personally lobbies Sessions himself, while also, according to the *New York Times*, "complain[ing] to friends about how much he would like to get rid of Mr. Sessions" because of his decision to recuse himself; and unsuccessfully tries to convince both his director of national intelligence and his NSA director to "help him push back against the FBI investigation . . . and publicly deny the existence of any evidence of collusion during the 2016 election," requests that both men deem inappropriate and refuse.[41] Trump had earlier made the same request of Obama's director of national intelligence, James Clapper, asking him to directly refute the Steele dossier—and had been denied then, too.[42] Clapper will observe, in a May 2018 interview on MSNBC, that in his interactions with the president-elect, Trump's focus "seemed to be . . . [on] the dossier."[43] All of these actions beg the question of what it was in the Steele dossier Comey shared with Trump on January 6 that initiated Trump's intense concern about federal law enforcement's ongoing consideration of Russia's ties to his presidential campaign.

The day after Trump fires Comey, he hosts Sergey Kislyak and Russian foreign minister Sergei Lavrov in the Oval Office. The latter features prominently in the Steele dossier as one of the Russian officials aware of the Kremlin's interference campaign; the former had met secretly with many of Trump's national security aides. As the *Washington Post* will report, while Lavrov and Kislyak are in the Oval, "Trump brag[s] about the intelligence he receives and share[s] highly classified information from a U.S. partner" with Lavrov and Kislyak; it will later be revealed that the "U.S. partner" is Israel and the "intelligence" is the classified details of a February 2017 military action against ISIS in Syria.[44] Worse still, writes *Newsweek*, "Trump is alleged to have revealed the name of the city where the operation took place, leading to fears that the source who alerted the Israelis to ISIS's intentions may be compromised."[45] Trump also brags to the two Russian officials about firing Comey, calling the former FBI director "crazy" and a "nut job" and saying that with Comey gone the "great pressure" he had been facing "because of Russia" has been "taken off."[46]

The next night Trump tells a national television audience, via an interview with NBC News's Lester Holt, that he fired Comey because of "this Russia thing."[47] He also confirms that he had been planning to fire Comey "regardless of [the] recommendation[s]" he solicited and received from Attorney General Jeff Sessions and Deputy Attorney General Rod Rosenstein—both of which supported Comey's firing.[48]

Annotated History

In the final few days of Flynn's tenure as National Security Advisor, the Kremlin attempts to pass a sanctions relief proposal to Flynn—framed as a "peace deal" for Ukraine—through a Kremlin-allied Ukrainian politician, Andrii V. Artemenko. Artemenko meets with Trump business partner Felix Sater and Trump attorney and fixer Michael Cohen. At the meeting, he hands them an envelope with the Kremlin-approved anti-sanctions proposal inside. The envelope later ends up on Flynn's desk. Cohen at first acknowledges bringing the envelope to the White House and giving it to Flynn, and then changes his story and says he had no interest in what Artemenko was "selling" and told the Ukrainian to mail his proposal to the White House by regular mail if he wanted to contact President Trump.

According to a February 2017 *New York Times* article, on February 6, 2017, Michael Flynn, just a week from his resignation as Trump's National Security Advisor, received a "sealed proposal . . . hand-delivered to his office."[49] Inside was a plan for "President Trump to lift sanctions against Russia."[50] The *Times* reported that the plan was being "pushed" by Michael Cohen and Felix Sater in cooperation with a Ukrainian politician who had proudly informed Cohen and Sater that the plan "had received encouragement . . . from top aides to Mr. Putin."[51] That Sater should again be attempting to connect Putin and Trump on what he euphemistically called "peace"—and indeed, the *Times* categorized Artemenko's proposal as a "peace plan for Ukraine and Russia"—is not surprising given his astounding level of access to Putin as far back as Ivanka Trump's 2006 foray into Putin's office.[52] That by "peace" Sater meant peace for *three* countries—Russia and Ukraine, but also the United States—was confirmed by his February 19, 2017, statement to the *Washington Post* on the Artemenko proposal: "I got excited about trying to stop a war. I thought if this could improve conditions in three countries, good, so be it."[53] And to the *Times*, Sater said, in justification of his actions, "I want to stop a war, number one. Number two, I absolutely believe that the U.S. and Russia need to be allies, not enemies."[54] As ever, though, the improvement of relations between America and Russia depended, in the Russian view, on the lifting of U.S. sanctions.

It is difficult to believe Cohen's representations about his handling of the proposal from Artemenko. Just days after the *New York Times* scoop on the "peace deal," the *Washington Post* asked Cohen about the allegation that he had delivered a sealed envelope to Flynn, Trump's National Security Advisor. Cohen responded that he had taken the envelope from Artemenko but had done nothing with it and had never discussed it—with anyone—ever again.[55] He added that he had advised Artemenko, even as he was taking the sealed envelope from the Ukrainian politician, to mail his envelope (the very one Cohen had just taken) to the White House at 1600 Pennsylvania Avenue via regular mail.[56] Reached for comment by the *Post*, the *Times* stood by its more plausible account of events, which it said had been sourced from Cohen himself just days earlier: "Mr. Cohen told the *Times* in no uncertain terms that he delivered the Ukraine proposal to Michael Flynn's office at the White House," *Times* deputy manager editor Matt Purdy told the *Washington Post*.[57]

In fact, Cohen had said quite a bit more than that, telling the *Times* that he brought the Artemenko proposal with him to the White House on a day he was scheduled to meet with President Trump himself; he left the proposal in Flynn's office while there, he said.[58] His implication that he brought a Kremlin-backed sanctions deal into the White House—on a day he was meeting with the president himself—and never raised the matter of the document in his possession with Trump directly strains credulity. That he would later claim to have left the White House without giving the documents to Flynn is also hard to believe. Cohen's narrative is especially improbable given that, as the nation was learning that very month, Flynn had been the presidential transition's covert point man on sanctions negotiations with Russia. Artemenko's proposal would therefore have been of enormous interest to the Trump administration generally and to Trump and his National Security Advisor specifically.

Speaking to the *Huffington Post* six months later, Cohen changed his story once again: he now suggested that his friend Sater hadn't told him in advance whom he would be meeting with, and that at the meeting Artemenko handed him a "long brown envelope," which he both "never opened" and yet could reliably report contained "one or two pages."[59] He went so far as to confirm his knowledge of the length of the document by saying, "When was the last time you saw a peace proposal on one piece of paper? SAT computations for algebraic equations take at least two pages or more."[60] He added that he rejected Artemenko's request to pass along the proposal because, for reasons he did not clarify, he "had no interest in what he was selling." This explanation might be difficult for investigators to accept, given that Artemenko had represented to Cohen that the proposal came with the Kremlin's imprimatur and that Artemenko had gone to the 2016 Republican National Convention, attended Trump's inauguration, and visited Congress as part of his lobbying efforts in Washington.[61]

All of these actions beg the question of what it was in the Steele dossier Comey shared with Trump on January 6 that initiated Trump's intense concern about federal law enforcement's ongoing consideration of Russia's ties to his presidential campaign.

Following the Steele dossier's January 10, 2016, publication by *Buzz-Feed*, conversation about its veracity began. Andrei Soldatov, writing for the *Guardian*, argued that—based on his experience "covering the Russian secret services since 1999 and hav[ing] spent the last five years researching Russian cyber activities"—Steele's dossier "rings frighteningly true." "[O]verall it reflects accurately the way decision-making in the Kremlin looks to close observers," wrote Soldatov, adding, "[T]he Trump dossier is a good reflection of how things are run in the Kremlin—the mess at the level of decision-making and increasingly the outsourcing of operations, combined with methods borrowed from the KGB and the secret services of the lawless 1990s [in Russia]."[62]

A review of the dossier's key claims suggests that a great many of them have been confirmed.[63] CBS News wrote that "investigations and criminal cases are revealing some truth" in the dossier and "have begun to resolve at least some of the questions surrounding the memos"; *Newsweek* reported that former director of national intelligence James Clapper had concluded that "more and more of the infamous Steele Dossier is turning out to be true"; CNN wrote, in early February 2017, that "U.S. investigators [have] corroborate[d] some aspects of the Russia dossier"; and in the United Kingdom, the *Independent* observed that "Trump denounced the document as fake, but much of [the dossier's] contents have turned out to be true."[64]

As individual claims in the dossier have been confirmed, the media has taken note—such as when the pension scheme described in the dossier (by which the Kremlin made clandestine payments to its agents) was confirmed as still in existence.[65] At the time, the BBC wrote that a "key claim" in the dossier had just been "verified."[66] After Carter Page's congressional testimony, *Business Insider* wrote that the former Trump national security adviser's testimony was "filled with bombshells—and supports key portions of the Steele dossier," particularly with respect to whom Page met with in Moscow in July 2016 and the fact that he did indeed discuss the privatization of Rosneft with at least one executive from the company, Andrey Baranov.[67]

Former FBI director James Comey concluded in 2018 that the dossier came "from a credible source, someone with a track record, someone who was a credible and respected member of an allied intelligence service during his career."[68] Moreover, the dossier gained credibility with both American and foreign journalists when one of its suspected sources, Oleg Erovinkin—a former KGB chief turned top aide to Rosneft CEO Igor Sechin—was found dead in Moscow in the backseat of a car on December 26, 2016, not long after the FBI took possession of a copy of the dossier.[69] According to Christo Grozev, an expert on Russian security threats interviewed by the *Telegraph*, Erovinkin was

likely the source Steele mentioned in his dossier as being a "close associate of Sechin." According to Grozev,

> Insiders have described Erovinkin to me alternately as "Sechin's
> treasurer" and "the go-between between Putin and Sechin." One
> thing that everyone seems to agree [on]—both in public and
> private . . . is that Erovinkin was Sechin's closest associate. I
> have no doubt that at the time Erovinkin died, Mr. Putin had
> Mr. Steele's Trump dossier on his desk. He would—arguably—
> have known whether the alleged . . . story is based on fact or
> fiction. Whichever is true, he would have had a motive to seek—
> and find the mole. . . . He would have had to conclude that
> Erovinkin was at least a person of interest.[70]

The *Daily Beast* concurred with Grozev's judgment that Erovinkin's
death might have been dossier-related: "The notorious dossier on
Trump that Republicans want to discredit may well have been credible enough in Russian President Vladimir Putin's eyes to get at least
one person [Erovinkin] killed," wrote the digital news outlet in January
2018.[71] It noted, too, that initial reports on Erovinkin's death announced
that he had been "killed"—but the reports were subsequently altered,
without explanation, to read that Erovinkin had simply "died." [72]

The possibility that Erovinkin was a Steele source was aired officially when Glenn Simpson, the head of the firm that hired Steele,
was asked a question about the dossier during a Senate Judiciary Committee hearing and his attorney, Joshua Levy, suddenly interjected,
"Somebody's already been killed as a result of the publication of this
dossier." [73]

Erovinkin's death was one in a string of suspicious deaths of influential Russian figures, CNN noted in March 2017. Andrey Malanin, a
senior diplomat at the Russian embassy in Athens, Greece—the city
where Papadopoulos sought to make clandestine contacts with Russians or Russian allies in 2016—"died suddenly of natural causes" less
than two weeks after Erovinkin.[74] On Election Day in November 2016,

Sergei Krivov, the Russian consulate's duty commander for security affairs in New York City, was found dead; Russian officials first told investigators that Krivov fell from a roof and then that he died of a heart attack, but the police report ultimately filed that day identifies the apparent cause of death as "an unknown trauma to the head."[75] In March 2017, Nikolai Gorokhov, the former lawyer for Sergei Magnitsky—after whom the sanctions Putin wanted so urgently for Trump to drop were named—"fell" from the fourth floor of his Moscow apartment and nearly died; he had been continuing his old client's fight against corruption in the Kremlin.[76] In all, nine prominent Russian officials died under suspicious circumstances (often a "heart attack") in the nine months after Trump's election victory.[77]

Broadly, the Steele dossier alleges that the Russian regime had been "cultivating, supporting and assisting Trump for at least five years"—from 2011 to 2016—a claim supported by Kremlin-connected Russian nationals' repeated outreach to Trump for business deals, including overpayment for his properties in the United States.[78] This outreach began at least five years before the 2016 presidential election, and possibly even fifteen years before Trump's November 2016 victory (see chapter 1). The dossier says Putin's aim between 2011 and 2016 was to "encourage splits and divisions in [the] western alliance"—an ambition that has been confirmed many times over by Putin's attacks on NATO and the European Union, his government's meddling in the Brexit vote, and his attempts to sow discord within America via social media in the run-up to the 2016 election.[79] Of still graver concern, however, is that Trump—perhaps because of cultivation, support, and assistance from Russia—has put forward since 2011 a foreign and domestic policy that dovetails with Putin's designs on Western democracy, particularly with respect to the NATO alliance. Trump has declined to affirm NATO's Article 5—its mutual defense clause—and more recently scrapped the trilateral NAFTA agreement between the United States, Canada, and Mexico.[80]

The dossier correctly notes that Trump has not followed through on any proffered deals from Russia this decade; it would have been more salacious for the dossier's sources to claim otherwise, but the dossier is sober on this point. The dossier does indicate that Trump has received a "regular flow of intelligence" from the Kremlin—a claim that now seems prescient, as it was recorded by Steele six months before the FBI interviewed Papadopoulos about his back channel to the Kremlin. This was a back channel that, in April 2016, led to his discovery that the Russians were stealing emails from Americans, or at least claiming to have done so.[81] The dossier points to Manafort as a key "manager" of Trump-Russia coordination, which tracks with both Manafort's past work on behalf on Russian interests and the discovery, in September 2017, that Manafort had offered a close associate of Putin, Russian oligarch Oleg Deripaska, "private briefings" on the internal machinations of the Trump campaign.[82]

There is substantial support for the dossier's claims about Russian *kompromat* collected in November 2013 (see chapter 3). CIA officers who spoke to the BBC on this issue through an intermediary confirmed the dossier's core contention: that there are compromising videos of Trump.[83] The dossier also makes the explosive allegation that Putin personally oversaw the recent Kremlin operations interfering with America's political process; in January 2017, a consensus report from the nation's three foremost intelligence agencies confirmed that Putin directly ordered the 2016 "influence campaign" that helped Trump secure victory at the polls.[84] Part of Putin's plan, says the dossier, was to "sow discord and disunity within . . . the United States itself" through an "extensive program of state-sponsored offensive cyber operations"; certainly, Special Counsel Mueller's 2018 indictments of Russian nationals connected to Russia's GRU (military intelligence) and its so-called Internet Research Agency confirm that segment of the Steele dossier.[85]

The dossier's depiction of the Kremlin's power structure tracks with what is presently known of it, from the centrality of Dmitry Peskov and Sergei Lavrov to the Kremlin's use of "people who ha[ve] family and ethnic ties to Russia and/or ha[ve] been incentivized financially to cooperate." The description of recruiting such people by incentivizing them financially "to cooperate" seems to explain the actions of Felix Sater, Michael Cohen, Trump's two Trump SoHo partners, and many other Americans in Trump's orbit from the mid-2000s onward.[86] The dossier's reference to Putin's reliance on Jewish Americans with a Russian ethnic background matches the unusual number of Israeli persons and organizations—like Joel Zamel and his firm Wikistrat, Black Cube, and the mysterious Israeli who met George Papadopoulos in Tel Aviv—who connected with Trump's aides and advisers in the United States and abroad. Indeed, Israeli newspaper *Haaretz* observed that "of ten billionaires with Kremlin ties who funneled political contributions to Donald Trump and a number of top Republican leaders, at least five are Jewish."[87] The dossier contends that Michael Cohen traveled to Prague in late August or early September 2016 to assist Trump in coordinating with the Russian government; in April 2018, McClatchy reported that Special Counsel Mueller indeed has evidence that the trip occurred.[88] While some of the allegations in the dossier are unverifiable—and so may, due to their nature, remain unverified—as former director of national intelligence James Clapper said in May 2018, none of the dossier has been disproven.[89]

CHAPTER THIRTEEN

TESTIMONY AND PLEA

June to December 2017

Summary

ONCE FBI DIRECTOR JAMES COMEY IS FIRED AND DEPUTY Attorney General Rod Rosenstein appoints Robert Mueller special counsel, the investigation into Trump-Russia collusion continues with even greater vigor than before. As Mueller and his team—which includes forty of the top attorneys and investigators in the country—request or subpoena large numbers of potentially inculpatory documents, including Trump's personal banking records and all Russia-related documents in the possession of the Trump Organization, there are major developments on the testimonial side of the Trump-Russia case as well: key witnesses in the investigation either disappear, become unavailable, get arrested, or are successfully corralled into hours of testimony before Congress that reveals, in many instances, that they have not been telling the truth.[1]

In Europe, George Papadopoulos's primary conduit to the Kremlin, Joseph Mifsud, suddenly disappears without even telling his fiancée where he's gone; in the United States, Papadopoulos himself is arrested.[2] Mueller's team meets with Christopher Steele to debrief him on his dossier, and even as Steele continues to refuse to testify before Congress, Trump advisers Erik Prince and Donald Trump Jr. do so—but when both men testify extensively before Congress, their interrogations reveal substantial holes in their accounts of what they did during the presidential campaign.[3] In October 2017, Trump's campaign manager Paul Manafort and his deputy campaign manager Rick Gates are indicted on twelve federal charges, including conspiracy against the United States.[4] Later in the month, Papadopoulos pleads guilty to lying to the FBI—an event that seems to presage Trump's former National Security Advisor Michael Flynn being charged with the same offense, cutting a cooperation deal with Special Counsel Mueller, and pleading guilty to one count of making false statements in December 2017.[5]

Meanwhile, the congressional investigation of Trump-Russia collusion moves ahead, even if progress is slow and the results unclear. Sessions and Comey testify again before Congress in June 2017; in July, Jared Kushner meets with Senate investigators and Paul Manafort with the Senate Select Committee on Intelligence. In August, Mueller's grand jury interviews June 2016 Trump Tower meeting participant and former Soviet intelligence officer Rinat Akhmetshin, and the Senate Judiciary Committee interviews Fusion GPS founder Glenn Simpson, the man who hired Christopher Steele to compile raw intelligence about Trump's business dealings abroad. Donald Trump Jr. testifies before the Senate Judiciary Committee in September and the House and Senate intelligence committees in December. Mueller's team interviews former White House chief of staff Reince Priebus, former Trump campaign national cochair Sam Clovis, and former White House press secretary Sean Spicer in October 2017, as well as current Trump domestic policy adviser Stephen Miller in November. The Senate Select Committee on Intelligence interviews Corey Lewandowski in October, and the House Permanent Select Committee on Intelligence questions both Carter Page and Erik Prince in November.

With each new indictment, plea, and transcript of testimony—as well as new reports on Russia's social media meddling from Facebook and Twitter and on Russia's electoral-infrastructure hacking campaign from the Department of Homeland Security—the breadth and depth of Russia's attack on the United States in the run-up to the 2016 presidential election becomes clearer. This clarity stands in stark contrast to two puzzling events that cast a long shadow over the second half of 2017: Trump's insistence, in July, on meeting Putin face-to-face— and multiple times—under highly unusual circumstances during the G20 summit, and his inexplicable delay in carrying out new sanctions against Putin and his oligarchs that are overwhelmingly passed by Congress the same month.

The Facts

AS THE FIRST YEAR OF TRUMP'S PRESIDENCY WEARS ON, the beleaguered president becomes more and more erratic. He floats the possibility that he has secretly recorded James Comey, before retracting that claim; he brags about his ability to pardon whomever he wants, including himself; he attacks his own attorney general in the media, suggesting that he wouldn't have nominated him had he known Sessions wouldn't protect him against investigations of his conduct; he signs into law new Russia sanctions passed by a stunning 517–5 vote in Congress but fails to carry out the sanctions by the deadline required by the legislation. Throughout 2017—and beyond—he pays more than $200,000 in legal fees to his personal attorney Michael Cohen out of his campaign coffers, despite Cohen being a witness in a federal criminal investigation Trump has reason to believe is looking into his own actions. And after Putin cuts U.S. diplomatic staff in Moscow in retaliation for President Obama's December 2016 cuts to Russian diplomatic staff in the United States, Trump thanks Putin for saving the United States money, telling Americans in August 2017 that he is "very thankful" for Putin's decision.[6]

Throughout the latter half of the year, the scope of Russian interference in the 2016 presidential election becomes clear. In September, Facebook admits that Russian troll farms purchased thousands of ads on the popular social media platform, turning over more than three thousand of them to Congress.[7] Later that month, the Department of Homeland Security informs twenty-one U.S. states that they were hacked by the Russians prior to the election; in subsequent months, DHS will amend the number of states hacked to thirty-nine and admit that seven states' election systems were in fact "compromised" by Russian hacking.[8] September also sees Twitter joining Facebook in acknowledging the role social media played in Russia's election-year operations, with the company's confessing that just that month it shut down hundreds of accounts run by Russian operatives—accounts that spent, in total, hundreds of thousands of dollars to spread Kremlin propaganda in the United States.[9]

Having declared, on June 9, 2017, from the Rose Garden at the White House, that he is "100 percent" willing to be interviewed by Mueller and would be "glad" to do so, Trump has nevertheless taken no steps to do so by December 2017—and by the end of the year he will have called Mueller's investigation a "witch hunt" fourteen times on Twitter.[10] Behind the scenes, Trump is raging, threatening to fire Jeff Sessions, Rod Rosenstein, and/or Robert Mueller, should the Trump-Russia investigation continue; indeed, in the very month he says he'd be happy to be interviewed by the special counsel, he orders his White House counsel Don McGahn to fire Mueller—backing off only when McGahn threatens to quit his job.[11] Having failed to rid himself of Mueller, less than a week after stating his willingness to cooperate with the former FBI director he will imply on Twitter that Mueller and the other attorneys leading the Trump-Russia investigation are "very bad" people whose conflicts of interest (he alleges) disqualify them from working on the case.[12]

On August 30, 2018, Trump will say "I'll see what happens" when asked by the media whether he will even honor a judge-issued subpoena from the special counsel—adding that the special counsel's investigation is "illegal."[13]

Meanwhile, the several ongoing congressional investigations, marked by fierce partisan infighting, continue. From Emin Agalarov's publicist Rob Goldstone, Senate Judiciary investigators learn a great deal about how "the participants [of the June 2016 Trump Tower meeting] scrambled to square their stories in July 2017 after public scrutiny began of the Trump Tower meeting," with Goldstone messaging both Emin Agalarov and Ike Kaveladze, a vice president at the Agalarovs' Crocus Group, after news of the meeting broke to ask "how to respond." [14] One result of these contacts appears to be Goldstone changing his story as to who he believed was at the meeting he attended; whereas in June 2016 he had told Trump Jr. he was bringing a "Russian government attorney" to Trump Tower as part of "Russia and its government's support" for Trump, after he corresponds with the Russians he will say the meeting was "in no way connected with the Russian Government or any of its officials." [15] The Senate Judiciary Committee discovers, too, that Donald Trump Jr.'s lawyer sent Goldstone a statement for him to issue after the meeting was made public, which Goldstone then forwarded to Kaveladze. *Bloomberg* calls this "an apparent effort to keep their stories consistent." [16] Trump Jr.'s attorney asks Goldstone to begin his statement with the claim that "the statements I have read by Donald Trump Jr. are 100 percent accurate." [17]

Investigators also learn that when Goldstone emailed Trump Jr. and Trump himself (via Rhona Graff) in January 2016 to offer "massive exposure for Mr. Trump on the [Russian equivalent of Facebook] site—and it will be covered in Russian media also—where . . . your campaign is covered positively almost daily . . . [with] extremely gracious comments from President Putin," Graff did in fact respond to this offer of foreign assistance to Trump's presidential campaign.[18] Though the proffered "massive exposure" on a Russian social media site called "VK" had high in-kind value and might therefore be construed as an illegal campaign contribution, Graff wrote Goldstone in response to the offer—whether on her own initiative or on Trump's behalf is unclear—that it was a "terrific opportunity" and that Goldstone should follow up with Dan Scavino, the Trump campaign's social media director.[19] By the time Goldstone wrote Scavino about receiving this assistance from the Agalarovs and VK, he was able to represent that "Don [Jr.] and Paul [Manafort]" had told him they were, in CNN's description of the email, "on board with the idea." [20] While a source will tell CNN that Goldstone brought up the idea for a Trump page on VK to Trump Jr. and Manafort at the end of the Trump Tower meeting in June 2016, Trump Jr. will insist that he has no recollection of it when he testifies before Congress.[21]

Investigators also learn that, just five days after the June 2016

Trump Tower meeting—when news dropped that Russian hackers had accessed Democratic National Committee emails—Goldstone emailed Emin Agalarov that that news was "eerily weird" in light of the meeting Goldstone had just attended at Trump Tower.[22] In the same tranche of emails, congressional investigators also find an email to Ike Kaveladze from his son George, in which George asks his father, of Donald Trump Jr.'s decision to release his emails to and from Emin Agalarov, "Why did he release this email admitting to collusion?"[23] The email's subject line is "dt jr."[24]

From Corey Lewandowski, the Senate Intelligence Committee learns that Donald Trump Sr. does indeed use a blocked number—suggesting that Trump's son may have called him when, after discussing a prospective June 2016 Trump Tower meeting with Emin Agalarov for the first time, he called a blocked number whose owner he insists to Congress he cannot recall.[25] Lewandowski does not answer all the questions asked of him, however, and by January 2018, he is refusing to answer any "questions about events that took place during the campaign and his conversations with President Donald Trump since then," though his legal rationale for either refusal is unclear.[26] Steve Bannon will later attempt to do the same. As it turns out, however, campaign conversations are not privileged, and former campaign advisers who do not work in the White House as presidential advisers cannot assert executive privilege or adopt a president's assertion of executive privilege.[27] Bannon will later say that the White House told him to invoke executive privilege.[28] The result of his stonewalling is a subpoena from both the House Permanent Select Committee on Intelligence and Special Counsel Mueller; after a brief negotiation, Mueller allows Bannon to interview voluntarily with his office instead.[29]

Another witness who cooperates with Mueller but not Congress—albeit for very different reasons—is former MI6 agent and dossier author Christopher Steele, who speaks with Mueller's team in the summer of 2017.[30] Shortly thereafter, in August 2017, Fusion GPS founder Glenn Simpson's testimony to the Senate Judiciary Committee includes some startling new revelations about Steele. Simpson recounts how Steele withdrew his cooperation with the FBI one week before the 2016 election because he believed the FBI "was being 'manipulated' by Trump insiders."[31] The timing of Steele's withdrawal from his partnership with the FBI is noteworthy, as it coincides with Trump advisers and allies Rudy Giuliani, Erik Prince, Donald Trump Jr., Michael Flynn, Joe diGenova, and Steve Bannon working (see chapter 10) to get leaks from active FBI agents into the media—with the apparent aim of getting FBI director James Comey to focus on the closed Clinton email investigation rather than the still-pending Trump-Russia investigation.[32] Steele's suspicions about pro-Trump factions within the FBI were heightened when, on October 31, 2016, the *New York Times* cited FBI officials for the proposition that no "conclusive or direct link between Mr. Trump and the Russian government" had been found.[33] Steele considered the FBI's representation false and withdrew from cooperation with the Bureau on that basis, Simpson testifies.[34] Before their partnership ended, however, Steele "[got] into [with the FBI] who his sources were, how he knew certain things," according to Simpson.[35] Even more startling, Simpson testifies that the FBI told Steele it had "a source inside the Trump campaign": "an internal Trump campaign source. . . . [whose] intelligence . . . indicated the same thing [as the dossier] and one of those pieces of intelligence was a human source from inside the Trump organization."[36] Simpson declines to say who the source is, citing "security" reasons. Whether those security concerns involve him or someone else is unclear.[37]

Months later, in a January 2018 op-ed in the *New York Times*, Simpson will publicly stand by his 2017 testimony, underscoring that Fusion GPS never told Steele whom he was working for, that Fusion was not the entity that leaked Steele's dossier to *BuzzFeed* in January 2017, and that the commercial research firm never spoke to the FBI about Steele's work at any time. Simpson will add that "our sources said the dossier was taken so seriously [by the FBI] because it corroborated reports the bureau had received from other sources, including one inside the Trump camp. The intelligence committees have known for months that credible allegations of collusion between the Trump camp and Russia were pouring in from independent sources during the campaign."[38] Simpson's op-ed appears to reject a popular Republican conspiracy theory, which supposes that the FBI used a "mole"—someone not native, or ever adopted into, the Trump campaign—to report on the campaign's activities through sporadic engagement with it in 2016.[39] The *Guardian* will quote "a person close to the matter" as saying that Simpson was referring to George Papadopoulos as the source inside the Trump camp, but this will remain unclear even after Simpson's *New York Times* op-ed.[40] The ongoing mystery of the Simpson-cited "human source" is fueled by a letter from Senate Judiciary Committee Republicans to Simpson in which they highlight a phrase from Simpson's testimony that seems to describe neither George Papadopoulos nor University of Cambridge fellow Stefan Halper—the subject of the right-wing conspiracy theory about an FBI "mole."[41] Halper had only intermittent contact with three Trump advisers as an outside observer of the Trump campaign; Simpson's testimony clearly refers to "a human source from *inside* the Trump organization. . . . who decided to pick up a phone and report something" (emphasis added).[42]

In August 2018, the *New York Times* will reveal that U.S. law enforcement and the U.S. intelligence community have lost nearly all their human sources of information in Russia, in part because Trump and his congressional allies insisted on "burning" Stefan Halper as a confidential informant on Russia by naming him publicly.[43] According to the *Times*, among other potential factors, "officials also [raise] the possibility that the outing of an F.B.I. informant under scrutiny by the House intelligence committee—an examination encouraged by President Trump—has had a chilling effect on intelligence collection [in Russia]."[44]

Investigators also make some unexpected discoveries involving Michael Cohen. From January through August 2017, an American company controlled by Russian oligarch Viktor Vekselberg paid Michael Cohen $500,000—depositing the money, the purpose of which remains unknown, into the same shell corporation (Essential Consultants, LLC) that Cohen had set up for the exclusive purpose of paying off Trump's ex-mistresses. The news raises the possibility of Trump receiving illegal campaign contributions—or other illicit payments—from a foreign national through Cohen.[45] *Slate*, noting that Essential

Consultants is a single-member LLC that was created just a month before the 2016 presidential election, and that Vekselberg's company indeed stood to be "affected by Trump administration decisions," will call explanations for the payments given by Vekselberg's company and others "ridiculous"—and speculate that a more likely explanation is either "bribery" or "a cash-for-access contribution to a sleazy hush-money slush fund."[46] That Cohen also receives payments from other companies into the same account, and that the services he is ostensibly being paid for do not match up with his areas of expertise, further suggests, *Slate* will argue, that these payments are not on the level.[47] The *New York Times* will note that "Cohen also used the company [Essential Consultants, LLC] to collect $250,000 after arranging payments in 2017 and 2018 by a major Republican donor, Elliott Broidy, to a former Playboy model he allegedly impregnated"; notably, Trump named Cohen and Broidy co-deputy finance chairs of the Republican National Committee in April 2017, as Cohen was still collecting money from Broidy to cover up his alleged affair.[48] That during this period Broidy—alongside Mueller cooperating witness George Nader—was selling access to Trump for $1 billion to the governments of Saudi Arabia and the United Arab Emirates makes Broidy's payments into Trump's ex-mistress slush fund even more problematic.[49] *New York Magazine* will write that Broidy was likely giving Trump more than money for his lobbying access. Basing its conjecture on knowledge of the backgrounds and known behaviors of Broidy, who has has been accused of paying off the girlfriend of a friend before, and Trump, who has a "well-documented history of having unprotected sex with women in the adult-entertainment industry," the magazine contends that Playboy Playmate Shera Bechard became pregnant not by Broidy, but by Trump.[50] The magazine cites as part of its evidence the fact that Bechard was paid off through a contract that used Trump's longtime alias for such "hush money" payments, "David Dennison."[51]

Among the persons and entities contributing to the $4.4 million Cohen received through Essential Consultants in 2017, Viktor Vekselberg is a particularly troubling example. Vekselberg attended Trump's inauguration—as did Kremlin agent Natalia Veselnitskaya, former So-

viet intelligence officer Rinat Akhmetshin, and accused Russian spy
Maria Butina—and is subject to U.S. sanctions on Russian persons and
entities. These are the sanctions that Putin was pushing in 2017 (and
even now) to have repealed.[52] Even more strikingly, Vekselberg sat next
to Putin at the same 2015 RT gala that Michael Flynn attended while he
was advising then candidate Trump on national security issues.[53] According to *Business Insider*, Vekselberg is "closely aligned with Putin,
with whom he frequently meets to discuss business"; moreover, "two
of Vekselberg's American associates donated a combined $1.25 mil-
lion to Trump's inaugural committee."[54] These donations, coming as
they did from Russia-connected Americans rather than Russian nationals, might have gone unnoticed but for the fact that, as of January
2018, tens of millions of dollars are missing from the inaugural fund
Vekselberg's associates donated to—raising the possibility they were
steered to private individuals.[55] Trump's inaugural committee collected
approximately twice the amount (and for a relatively modest inaugural
celebration) that President Obama did for the more expensive of his two
inaugurations; the man in charge of Trump's inaugural organizing committee was his good friend Thomas Barrack, who at the time was lobbying him on nuclear reactor sales to Saudi Arabia alongside Michael
Flynn, Rick Gates, and Bud McFarlane.[56] This confluence of facts will
lead Mueller's team to, in March 2018, "[stop] Mr. Vekselberg . . . at
a New York–area airport . . . [search] his electronic devices and [ques-
tion] him."[57] All told, in the first year of Trump's presidency, the total
payments to Cohen's shell corporation—$4.4 million—will dwarf the
payout to Trump's mistress Stormy Daniels ($130,000) for which the
corporation was ostensibly originally created.[58]

When Senate investigators interview Jared Kushner in July 2017,
they discover that his defense to accusations of untoward conduct is his
own inexperience.[59] Kushner tells investigators that the reason he had
to update his federal security clearance forms so many times—with officials discovering more than a hundred errors or omissions, a record of
nondisclosure Charles Phalen, director of the National Background Investigations Bureau, will call the worst he's ever seen—was that he had
"thousands" of meetings and exchanges during the campaign and that

some, including the many Russian contacts he left off his SF-86 form, were not "impactful or memorable."[60] In saying "I have never seen that level of mistakes" on an SF-86 form, Phalen will note that Kushner's initial SF-86 form "did not mention any foreign contacts" and that his subsequent update of the form added "100 contacts" but still did not mention the June 2016 Trump Tower meeting.[61] In his July 2017 statement to congressional investigators, Kushner will claim to have never initiated contact with any foreign officials—though he will concede that he set up Trump's April 2016 Mayflower Hotel speech and that at the VIP event beforehand he did communicate separately with each ambassador, including Sergey Kislyak. Kushner will further say that he did tell Kislyak—as he told the other three ambassadors when he met with them, according to his statement—that he hoped they would be interested in Trump's "fresh approach" to foreign policy.[62] Oddly, Kushner tells investigators that he doesn't remember speaking on the phone to Kislyak even once, though Reuters reports he has done so at least twice.[63] Despite Reuters having "six sources" who are "U.S. officials" saying that Kushner had "multiple" contacts with Kislyak by telephone, Kushner will tell investigators he is "highly skeptical" any such calls occurred.[64] And although sanction relief for Russia is critical to the "good deal" Trump spoke of during his speech at the Mayflower Hotel, Kushner tells investigators that when Natalia Veselnitskaya brought up the Magnitsky Act sanctions in Trump Tower, "I had no idea why that topic was being raised." He will add that he "thought nothing more" of the meeting after he left it and believes "[n]o part of the meeting I attended included anything about the campaign."[65]

As for his meetings with Kislyak and VEB chairman Sergei Gorkov during the transition, Kushner says he solicited neither meeting. Furthermore, Kushner asserts that it was Kislyak who wanted to discuss Syria with him and Flynn rather than the reverse. He makes this assertion even though he was the architect of Flynn being brought aboard the transition team, Flynn had been in contact with Kislyak prior to the election, and, after the election, Flynn immediately moved to get involved in Syria policy—possibly as part of a "grand bargain" to simultaneously end U.S. sanctions on Russia and Russian support for the

Iranian militants aiding Syrian President Bashar al-Assad.[66] As for his meeting with Gorkov, Kushner will denounce Gorkov's description of the event—just as he had, in the same statement, denounced the intelligence community's description of his contacts with Kislyak—and insist that "at no time was there any discussion [with Gorkov] about my companies, business transactions, real estate projects, loans, banking arrangements, or any private business of any kind."[67]

Just two months after Kushner says, following his two-hour interview with Senate investigators, "Hopefully, this [interview] put these matters to rest," the Senate Select Committee on Intelligence will discover—not from Kushner, but from TV—that Kushner has a secret private email server he never disclosed to the committee.[68] Moreover, the only reason Kushner's private server makes the news is that his attorney Abbe Lowell accidentally sent an email to a prankster who was pretending to be Kushner; Lowell thereby revealed the existence of an email server his client had not disclosed to investigators.[69] In November 2017, a bipartisan letter from the Senate Judiciary Committee to Kushner will accuse Trump's son-in-law of providing—even after the revelation of his private email server—"incomplete" information to Congress.[70] The letter will accuse Kushner of not disclosing "emails related to WikiLeaks and Kushner's security clearance form that originally omitted certain contacts with Russian officials."[71]

While Kushner, in the statement he issues after his congressional interview, will present himself (as summarized by *Rolling Stone*) as having been "out of place, confused, and polite" during the June 2016 Trump Tower meeting—as well as arriving late and leaving early—Goldstone's testimony to Congress will paint an entirely different picture.[72] According to the British publicist, Kushner became "agitated and infuriated" when the Russians didn't provide the dirt on Clinton that Kushner had apparently anticipated—suggesting also that, contrary to Trump Jr.'s testimony to Congress, Kushner had foreknowledge of what the meeting was about.[73]

Little is known about Rinat Akhmetshin's August 2017 appearance before the grand jury convened by Mueller, as grand jury proceedings are secret. In an interview not long after his testimony, however, Akhmetshin will tell the *Financial Times* that Veselnitskaya told Trump Jr., Manafort, and Kushner about "bad money end[ing] up in Manhattan and . . . [being] put into supporting political campaigns." Akhmetshin's implication is that the campaign in question was Hillary Clinton's.[74] It is unclear what legally obtained "official documents and information"—to use Goldstone's characterization of Veselnitskaya's evidence—the Russians intended to provide (or did provide) the Trump campaign to establish that allegation as true. However, Akhmetshin will be clear on one point over the course of his media interviews: Veselnitskaya did indeed give documents to the Trump campaign during the June 2016 meeting.[75]

One additional note about Akhmetshin's conduct in Trump Tower will come not from Akhmetshin but from Agalarov employee Ike Kaveladze, who testifies to the Senate Judiciary Committee about the former Soviet intelligence officer's " 'highly inappropriate' pink attire" at the meeting—a significant observation given that Trump Jr. will cite Akhmetshin as the one Russian in the room whose presence he couldn't thereafter remember at all.[76]

While little is known of Priebus's mid-October interview with Mueller's team, the *Washington Examiner* reports in March 2018 that Trump attempted to get Priebus to tell him what Mueller's agents had asked him.[77] One likely topic of discussion was the contemporaneous memos Comey wrote in early 2017 about his interactions with President Trump and his staff; according to an April 2018 report in the *Washington Post*, Comey wrote, shortly after a February 8, 2017, meeting with Priebus, that Priebus had asked to have a "private conversation" with the FBI director and then requested a key piece of information from him: whether there was a FISA order on then National Security Advisor Michael Flynn, who had attended Trump's August 17, 2016, classified security briefing with the candidate and then New Jersey governor Chris Christie. Comey answered at the time that the question was inappropriate—it needed to be "asked and answered through established channels"—but gave Priebus the information he was looking for anyway (though his answer is redacted from his memo before it is made public).[78] Priebus's question is curious, because any FISA order on Flynn might have picked up conversations Flynn had in December 2016 with other Trump officials about his conversations with Sergey Kislyak—and Priebus was one of the officials K. T. McFarland kept in the loop about Flynn's ongoing sanctions negotiations with the Russians. In fact, Priebus was scheduled to be on a call with the president-elect and his whole national security team on the day Flynn conducted his negotiations with Kislyak. If Flynn were to have been on that call while under a FISA warrant, both Priebus and the president-elect might well have had their statements about negotiating with the Russians captured. As the *Washington Post* notes, "The fact that [Priebus] asked Comey on February 8 about whether Flynn was under surveillance suggests [Priebus] may have had reason to believe that Flynn's transgressions were more serious than just lying to Pence. If that's true, the chances that Trump didn't know that Flynn had done something extremely serious are shrinking."[79]

In October 2017, Sam Clovis, the man who hired both George Papadopoulos and Carter Page—one of whom has already pleaded guilty to a federal felony, and the other of whom invoked his Fifth Amendment right against self-incrimination before the House Permanent Select Committee on Intelligence—is interviewed by Mueller's investigators. He then testifies before Mueller's grand jury in October 2017.[80] Within seventy-two hours of his cooperation with Mueller being revealed to the public, Clovis withdraws from Trump's nomination of him to be the chief scientist at the Department of Agriculture.[81] One of the senior members of the Senate Agriculture Committee, Senator Patrick Leahy (D-VT), says at the time that at Clovis's confirmation hearings he would have asked the former Air Force colonel about his knowledge of Papadopoulos's back-channel communications with the Russians; after Clovis's withdrawal, Leahy will call Clovis "almost a comically bad nominee, even for this administration."[82] According to Reuters, one of the key topics Mueller's team had asked Clovis about under oath was whether Trump knew of Papadopoulos's back-channel communications with the Russians. Papadopoulos—one of Mueller's cooperating witnesses—has said that Trump did indeed know about his communications with the Russians, with *Newsweek* noting that, according to Papadopoulos, "[Trump] met with [him] one-on-one . . . [and he] told Trump about his ongoing efforts to set up a meeting between Trump and Russian President Vladimir Putin."[83] Papadopoulos will later change his story and say that the first time he ever met Trump was at the Trump International Hotel in D.C. on March 31, 2016—ten days after Trump singled him out as an "excellent guy" in an interview with *The Washington Post*.[84]

That Flynn's December 2017 plea deal requires him to plead guilty to only a single count of making false statements to the FBI confuses many who have followed the Flynn headlines. As *Lawfare* writes, "[Flynn's] behaviors raised a raft of substantial criminal law questions. . . . His problems include, among other things, an alleged kidnapping plot [to capture and extradite a dissident Turkish cleric to Turkey], a plan to build nuclear power plants all over the Middle East, alleged violations of the Foreign Agents Registration Act (FARA) involving at least two different countries [Turkey and Russia], and apparent false statements to the FBI."[85] Flynn's deal is based on stipulated facts that add little to the public's understanding of what he did, given that his actions (discussing ending U.S. sanctions on Russia with the Russian ambassador and then lying to the FBI about doing so) have already been widely reported. New, however, is the information in the Flynn plea affidavit that when he called K. T. McFarland at Mar-a-Lago to ask for advice on how to conduct his negotiations with Kislyak, McFarland was with "other senior members of the Presidential Transition Team." Given this, it would have been difficult for McFarland not to share the content of her phone call with Flynn with her superiors on the transition.[86] That McFarland communicated to Flynn, during at least one of their calls, that "the Presidential Transition Team at Mar-a-Lago did not want Russia to escalate the situation [regarding sanctions]" suggests that McFarland was passing on information from her superiors to Flynn—also difficult to do if the superiors were not aware that Flynn was both on the phone and asking for guidance from above him in the chain of command rather than from his deputy, McFarland.[87] The affidavit also establishes that Flynn didn't discuss just Obama's sanctions with Kislyak but also "the incoming administration's foreign policy goals" writ large, which, as would later be reported by Yahoo News in June 2017, included "secret efforts to ease Russia sanctions" upon Trump taking office.[88] The affidavit also notes that when Flynn's course of negotiations was complete, he "spoke with" not just one but multiple "senior members of the Presidential Transition Team" to brief them on Russia's decision not to retaliate against the United States for Obama's imposition of new sanctions. It is unclear whether Flynn merely told these senior officials of the outcome of his conversations or also what he had said to Kislyak during those conversations to achieve that outcome.[89] Finally, Flynn's plea deal establishes that Kushner asked him to find out various nations' position on a UN resolution related to Israeli settlements; Mueller's court filings assert that Flynn did more than merely ask countries' representatives for their position on the resolution, but also requested that the nations he spoke to vote a certain way on it. The affidavit gives no indication of whether all of Flynn's actions were sanctioned by Kushner.[90]

Papadopoulos's late October plea documents are rather more detailed and revealing than Flynn's.[91] They establish, as discussed here in previous chapters, that Papadopoulos was in touch with top officials on the Trump campaign to keep them perpetually apprised of his progress in negotiating, with several Kremlin agents, a Trump-Putin summit.[92] The affidavit also establishes that Papadopoulos tried to destroy evidence that would have confirmed his Russian ties; in February 2017, he shut down a Facebook account that, when searched by the FBI, revealed "communications . . . with Russian nationals and other foreign contacts."[93] The affidavit does not say which other countries' nationals Papadopoulos was in contact with, though separate reporting suggests, at a minimum, Israel, Greece, and Egypt as likely answers to that question (see chapters 5, 6, and 7).

The affidavit does not establish which Trump campaign officials Papadopoulos told about the Russians having "thousands" of Clinton emails. But it does contend that his claim that he never told *anyone* on the campaign what Mifsud had told him about Clinton "dirt" was a "false statement."[94] The affidavit further indicates that Papadopoulos had an "extensive talk" with Russian deputy foreign minister Ivan

Timofeev, and that the result of this talk was Papadopoulos learning that the Russians were indeed "open to cooperation."[95] Papadopoulos also revealed to Timofeev that a meeting between top Trump campaign officials and Russian government officials ("members of President Putin's office") had been "approved" on the Trump side, and that the purpose of such a meeting would be "a day of consultations."[96]

The Papadopoulos affidavit states that, on April 11, 2016, Papadopoulos received an email from Olga Polonskaya (née Vinodagrova) offering—as she eventually makes clear, on behalf of both her contacts at "the [Russian] Embassy in London" and the "Russian Federation" as a whole—to "support your initiatives between our two countries."[97] Finally, the affidavit confirms that Papadopoulos wanted Russian government officials to see his late September 2016 interview with Russian media outlet Interfax; in that interview, Papadopoulos stated that Trump opposed all sanctions on Russia.[98]

The most explosive Trump-Russia testimonies of 2017 are those of Carter Page, Erik Prince, and Donald Trump Jr. The most startling revelation from the last of these is Trump Jr.'s September 2017 concession that he cannot recall whether he told his father about the June 2016 Trump Tower meeting at the time it was happening—a question he has answered in the negative on other occasions.[99] As *USA Today* notes, "Interviews with the Senate Judiciary Committee" could not answer the question of whether Trump Jr. told his father about the June 2016 meeting, "as Trump Jr. said he couldn't remember whether he talked to his father about it."[100] *Rolling Stone* offers a longer account of this critical segment of Trump Jr.'s testimony:

> The biggest question hanging over the June 9th meeting is whether Donald Trump had any knowledge of it. . . . As the testimony lays out, after being contacted by Goldstone, Trump Jr. received a call from Emin Agalarov to discuss the meeting. Following the call, Trump Jr. placed a call to a blocked number, and, after that call concluded, dialed Agalarov back. Speculation has swirled that Trump was on the other end of the unknown call, and Trump Jr.'s amnesia-ridden testimony doesn't exactly

quash suspicion that Trump knew of the meeting. When asked who he called between the two calls with Agalarov, Trump Jr. replied, "I have no idea." Corey Lewandowski testified separately that Trump's primary residence uses a blocked number, but Trump Jr.—who one would assume would also possess this information—didn't seem so sure. When asked if his father uses a blocked number "on his cellphone or on any phones that you call him on," Trump Jr. replied, "I don't know." When asked to clarify that he doesn't know if the call to the blocked number was to his father, Trump Jr. replied, "I don't."[101]

In January 2018, Democratic members of the Senate Judiciary Committee will demand that Trump Jr.'s three transcribed testimonies from 2017 be turned over to Special Counsel Mueller, on the argument that "President Donald Trump's oldest son made false statements to members of the committee," a federal crime.[102]

Erik Prince will face similar allegations after his November 2017 testimony before the House Permanent Select Committee on Intelligence, with one crucial difference: media reports will indicate that Special Counsel Mueller already has evidence to confirm that Prince lied to Congress. According to a breaking news report on April 6, 2018, by ABC News:

> Special Counsel Robert Mueller has obtained evidence that calls into question Congressional testimony given by Trump supporter and Blackwater founder Erik Prince last year, when he described a meeting in Seychelles with a Russian financier close to Vladimir Putin as a casual chance encounter "over a beer". . . . Well-connected Lebanese-American businessman George Nader, a key witness given limited immunity by Mueller, has been interviewed seven times by prosecutors on a wide range of subjects. He told investigators that he set up a meeting in the Seychelles between Prince and Russian sovereign wealth fund CEO Kirill Dmitriev, mere days before Trump was inaugurated. . . . Documents obtained by Mueller suggest

that before and after Prince met Nader in New York a week before the trip to the Seychelles, Nader shared information with Prince about Dmitriev . . . which appears to be inconsistent with Prince's sworn testimony before a U.S. House of Representatives investigative panel. "I didn't fly there to meet any Russian guy," Prince told the House Permanent Select Committee on Intelligence in November. He testified that he travelled to the Seychelles for a meeting with United Arab Emirates officials about possible business opportunities, and they introduced him—unexpectedly—to Dmitriev.[103]

Prince will make a number of statements on equally significant topics—such as whether he ever had formal communications or contacts with the Trump campaign in 2016—that likewise will come under scrutiny as possible perjuries. For instance, Prince's claim to have had no formal communication or contact with Trump's campaign is contradicted by revelations about an August 3, 2016, Trump Tower meeting Prince set up between himself, Donald Trump Jr., George Nader, and Joel Zamel.[104]

In November 2017, Mueller interviews Stephen Miller, called by CNN "the highest-level aide still working at the White House known to have talked to investigators."[105] According to CNN, Miller can speak not only to Trump's thinking as he decided whether and when to fire James Comey, but also to a "March 2016 meeting where foreign policy adviser George Papadopoulos said that he could arrange a meeting between Trump and Russian President Vladimir Putin through his connections."[106] It is unclear whether this is the March 31, 2016, meeting Trump held with his entire National Security Advisory Committee or a smaller meeting between Trump, Papadopoulos, and Miller. Miller is known to be one of the first Trump campaign aides Papadopoulos told of his contact with Mifsud (see chapter 5), and he authored an early draft of Trump's letter firing Comey. The New York Times reports that White House counsel Don McGahn blocked the letter because of its "angry, meandering tone."[107]

Perhaps the most problematic event of the latter half of 2017 comes at the G20 summit in Hamburg, Germany, where Trump not only meets with Putin multiple times and for longer than scheduled each time, but also manages to hold his talks with the Russian president without a full complement of witnesses and notetakers present—only Putin friend Rex Tillerson, Sergei Lavrov, and two interpreters are allowed to attend. At one of the G20's several joint meals, Trump orchestrates a second meeting with Putin that is disclosed to the media only when leaked to the press by a concerned summit attendee.[108]

Annotated History

In January 2018, Democratic members of the Senate Judiciary Committee will demand that Trump Jr.'s three transcribed testimonies from 2017 be turned over to Special Counsel Mueller, on the argument that "President Donald Trump's oldest son made false statements to members of the committee," a federal crime.

On September 7, 2017, Donald Trump Jr. testified before the Senate Judiciary Committee.[109] He maintained that he did not collude with "any foreign government"—a statement covering, therefore, not just Russia but Saudi Arabia, the United Arab Emirates, Israel, Turkey, Hungary, and other governments known to have reached out to the Trump campaign pre-election—and also that he "did not know of anyone who did."[110]

The focus of Trump Jr.'s testimony was his June 9, 2016, meeting with several Russian nationals at Trump Tower. A few minutes after being told that "although [this] interview is not under oath, by law you are required to answer questions truthfully," Trump Jr. said, "I don't remember much from the meeting because I didn't give it much credence."[111] He did remember, however, that the Russians told him "U.S. or Russian based . . . business people who were supporters of the DNC and perhaps Hillary Clinton were in some sort of tax scheme to avoid paying taxes in both the United States and Russia."[112] The second time he described Veselnitskaya's narrative to the committee he was even clearer: "[P]eople who had some connections or dealings in Russia and the United States who were big funders of the DNC and/or Hillary Clinton were perhaps avoiding paying taxes in both of those markets through some sort of scheme."[113] He added, "[It] didn't really seem all that relevant to me."[114] Noteworthy here is that on the day of the meeting Trump Jr.'s father was just ninety-six hours from a planned speech on a single subject: misconduct by the Clintons and those connected to the Clintons.[115] Asked about what Manafort, Trump's campaign manager, and Kushner, one of Trump's top advisers, were doing during the "20 minutes, maybe 30" of the meeting, Trump Jr. replied that both were on their phones—the implication being that neither man was particularly interested in the meeting.[116]

Though Trump Jr. told investors at a Manhattan conference in 2008 that he'd made "half a dozen trips to Russia *in the last 18 months* [March 2007 to September 2008]," Trump Jr. testified before Congress that he'd been to Russia only "four or five" times over the course of his life (emphasis added).[117] He said there were no discussions about "real estate projects" between Trump and the Agalarovs at the Miss Universe pageant in Moscow in November 2013, as it was only "following the pageant" that the parties began "preliminarily discussing" the topic.[118] He added that the Trump Organization "has not . . . made investments in Russia"—ever.[119] Though Paul Manafort had taken over the day-to-day operations of the Trump campaign from Corey Lewandowski by mid-April 2016, Trump Jr. claimed that "as of June 2016 . . . we were . . . in the process of replacing our campaign manager [Lewandowski]. It was an extraordinarily intense period of time. . . . [a] maelstrom." [120]

Despite having told Goldstone "I love it" in response to his offer of Clinton-incriminating "official documents and information," Trump Jr. told Congress that his first reaction to Goldstone's offer was a "skeptical" one.[121] He said that Kushner and Manafort attended the meeting with no idea what it was about or who would attend and were invited "on a moment's notice." [122] He added that he had told no one else about the meeting.[123] With respect to the information that Kremlin agent Natalia Veselnitskaya provided to him, Kushner, and Manafort, he said that it was very general and "difficult to understand"; moreover, he said it had no "point" because as a "private citizen" no one on the campaign could negotiate foreign policy.[124] Trump Jr. returned to this same detail several times, at one moment saying to his questioners, "[W]e made [the Russians] aware that we [he himself, Kushner, and Manafort] were private citizens, this isn't something we're doing about adoption." [125] He added that the Magnitsky Act sanctions were "not a campaign issue and [weren't] going to be a campaign issue, wasn't something we were talking about [in the campaign]."[126]

Trump Jr. said that after the meeting was over he never spoke of it again—to anyone.[127] He insisted that he had no information whatsoever as of June 3, 2016—the day Rob Goldstone emailed him about setting up a meeting at Trump Tower—that "the Russian government supported then-candidate Trump."[128]

As to the phone calls and emails of June 6, 2016, just three days before the meeting, Trump Jr. told the Senate Judiciary Committee that he couldn't remember whether he received a call from Emin after Rob Goldstone emailed him to say Emin was about to call—indeed, he couldn't remember any call he had made or received that day.[129] He said it was possible that, after the Miss Universe pageant, he went "back and forth by phone or e-mail [with Emin Agalarov] because . . . we were looking at a potential deal in Moscow. . . . We've met face to face [on] two or three occasions and we looked at [doing] a deal once."[130] Tellingly, when asked about whether Emin Agalarov has ties to the Russian government, Trump responded that he knew of no "specific" ties; when asked, on follow-up, if there were any "general" ties Trump Jr. was aware of, he responded that there were no "official" ties; when then asked, as part of a further follow-up, if there were any ties at *all* between Emin and the Russian government, Trump Jr. responded simply, "I would only speculate."[131]

Asked if, on June 9, 2016, "anyone . . . offer[ed] to release hacked e-mails to aid the Trump campaign," Trump Jr. said "no"; however, June 9, 2016—the very day the Russian government had promised the Trump campaign, through the Agalarovs, it would hand over Clinton "dirt"—was the first full day of the website and social media operation for DCLeaks, a Russian entity whose sole purpose was to "release hacked emails to aid the Trump campaign," per the congressional record.[132]

Asked if, on June 9, 2016, "anyone offer[ed] to manufacture and distribute fake news to aid the Trump campaign," Trump Jr. responded "no"; he did not note his August 3, 2016, Trump Tower meeting with

Joel Zamel, at which Zamel did exactly what Trump Jr. had just been asked about: "offer[ed] to manufacture and distribute fake news to aid the Trump campaign." Nor did he note that, after the election, Zamel's Psy Group formed a partnership with Cambridge Analytica.[133]

Asked if there was "any discussion of anything that might reasonably be considered collusion between the Trump campaign and the Russian government," Trump Jr. said "no"; yet he later revealed, in the same testimony, that within minutes of being offered detrimental information about Clinton by Veselnitskaya, he told her that Trump would take another look at the Magnitsky Act if he were elected president.[134]

Trump Jr. claimed he had no recollection of Rinat Akhmetshin being at the meeting.[135] Akhmetshin has been called by the *New York Times* a man with "[deep] ties to the Russian government and Kremlinback oligarchs . . . [and] an association with a former deputy head of a Russian spy service, the F.S.B., and a history of working for close allies of Vladimir V. Putin."[136] Akhmetshin was indeed at the meeting, as he has confirmed.

Trump Jr. summarized his feelings about the meeting by saying that it was immediately "pretty apparent that this [meeting] wasn't going anywhere and we were all looking to get back to our daily lives."[137] On the crucial question of whether he spoke to his father by telephone about the meeting before it happened, Trump Jr. had amnesia—not just for any calls he made that week to his father or to Emin Agalarov, but even on the subject of whether his father, whom he indicated he spoke with daily, used a phone number that came up blocked on Trump Jr.'s phone.[138] The rest of Trump Jr.'s testimony revealed many additional issues that could, as the committee Democrats subsequently noted, open Trump Jr. up to legal liability.

Prince will make a number of statements on equally significant topics—such as whether he ever had formal communication or contact with the Trump campaign in 2016—that likewise will come under scrutiny as possible perjuries.

Much of Erik Prince's testimony appeared at first blush to be false.[139] He told the House Permanent Select Committee on Intelligence, for instance, that he played no "official . . . or unofficial" role in Trump's bid for the presidency; that Steve Bannon was "the only guy in the campaign I knew pretty well"; that when he met Kirill Dmitriev he had no idea Dmitriev ran the Russian government's direct investment fund; and that he was in no way representing the Trump campaign in meeting with Dmitriev.[140] Prince even claimed not to have received the committee's pre-testimony letter requesting documents from him; according to the committee, the letter had been sent to him, on a bipartisan basis, by "certified mail, electronic mail, and facsimile."[141] Later, Prince said that he had received from the Senate the same sort of letter he said that he had not received from the House; the only known difference between the two entreaties was that Prince had met beforehand with Devin Nunes, the Republican chair of the House Permanent Select Committee on Intelligence.[142] Indeed, Prince revealed that he had had multiple private meetings with either Nunes or his staff prior to his testimony before Nunes's committee—a notable fact, given that Prince was active in assisting the Trump team during the transition, Nunes was a member of Trump's transition team, and many of the allegations of improper conduct that were raised during Prince's testimony arose from events that allegedly occurred during the transition.[143]

Prince's answers at times changed in midstream. After telling Congressman Schiff under oath that he didn't "recall specifically speaking to anyone about a meeting that happened [during the transition] with any Emirati officials in New York," additional questioning forced a concession: "I think I remember Steve Bannon saying they [members of the transition team] had met with . . . Mohammed bin Zayed . . . and that he was a great guy."[144] Pressed further, he admitted that Bannon "characterized the meeting for him" in addition to complimenting bin Zayed.[145] Likewise, in August 2016 Prince set up a meeting between an emissary of the crown prince of the United Arab Emirates, George Nader, and the Trump campaign, yet told Congress that not one of the policy papers he gave to Bannon had anything to do with the UAE.[146] He also admitted to Congress having multiple interactions with Michael Flynn in 2015 and 2016, including at least one face-to-face interaction; the UAE was at the time central to the lobbying work on nuclear energy that Flynn was engaged in with Thomas Barrack, Bud McFarlane, Rick Gates, and others.[147] Prince also said he had spoken with Bannon about Russia during the transition; at the time, a significant issue before the Trump team was whether Russian construction firms would be able to get contracts for nuclear-reactor construction projects in the Middle East, including in the UAE (see chapter 11).[148]

Prince's description of his meeting with Dmitriev likewise strained credulity. He indicated that the meeting was a "by the way" afterthought at the end of his meetings with the Emiratis and Mohammed bin Zayed.[149] Prince said the Emiratis indicated he should meet with Dmitriev only "if" he wanted to, and that the only reason to do so was because Prince happened to be in the Seychelles (Prince used the phrase "while you're here" multiple times to describe the Emiratis' passive endorsement of a Prince-Dmitriev meeting).[150] Minutes before the meeting, Prince said he googled Dmitriev to try to find out something about him and could discover only that he was a "Russian hedge fund manager"; Mueller's information is that Nader had fully briefed Prince on Dmitriev even before Prince flew to the Seychelles.[151] According to ABC News, Nader told prosecutors that he set up a meeting in the Seychelles between Prince and Dmitriev just days before Trump was inaugurated.[152] In short, if Nader's account is true, it means that almost nothing Erik Prince told Congress in November 2017 was.

CHAPTER FOURTEEN

A NATION IN SUSPENSE

2018

Summary

IN THE SECOND YEAR OF TRUMP'S PRESIDENCY, THE TRUMP-Russia scandal explodes, extending out in so many different directions simultaneously, it is difficult to track them all, especially as all but one congressional investigation goes dark and Special Counsel Mueller begins collecting cooperating witnesses from Trump's orbit through ancillary indictments rather than Russia-related ones. As other scandals not directly related to Trump-Russia collusion begin to rock the Trump administration, from the resignations of cabinet secretaries to illicit hush-money payoffs to ex-mistresses, from a bungled North Korea summit to the president's ongoing attacks on dying war hero John McCain, tracing the shape of the Trump-Russia investigation becomes more a matter of identifying nodes of activity than charting a single through-line. This is made especially difficult by the increasing number of seeming wrong turns or dead ends—leads that appear to promise the exposure of critical components of the Trump-Russia quid pro quo, only to remain frustratingly unresolved. Ultimately, the innumerable narrative tendrils of the Trump-Russia affair become so varied in their contours and trajectory in 2018 that the current state of the Trump-Russia investigation, inasmuch as it is visible to the public, can be described only as one of perpetual suspense.

Trump's increasingly mercurial behavior characterizes the second year of near-daily controversy in the White House. He floats pardons for both convicted associates and those under investigation; he re-

mains in secretive contact with potential witnesses against him, raising concerns about possible witness tampering; he works both behind
the scenes and publicly, on his Twitter feed, to see punished, demoted,
fired, or otherwise disgraced any member of the law enforcement or intelligence community investigating him or his aides, allies, and associates; he maneuvers himself into a position to fire Attorney General Jeff
Sessions, Deputy Attorney General Rod Rosenstein, Special Counsel
Robert Mueller, or all three, darkly intimating his intention to do so in
daily tweets and statements to the media; he uses Twitter as a weapon,
alleging wild "deep state" conspiracies against him at the highest levels of his own government; he plays a public relations game with his
self-proclaimed, but perpetually elusive, willingness to cooperate with
investigators; he issues declarations of innocence that become propaganda in Russia almost instantaneously. "From the United States, we
hear there was not any [Russian] meddling in the elections," says Putin's right-hand man and Kremlin spokesman Dmitry Peskov in August 2018, referring to statements made by the president of the United
States.[1]

In all, the state of not only the Trump presidency but the Union itself comes to seem in doubt in 2018, with the path back to normalcy
and good order in government for either law enforcement, Congress, or
concerned Americans treacherous at best—and perhaps even impassable.

The Facts

IN JULY 2017, CONGRESS BUCKS YEARS OF EVER-INCREASING
partisan rancor to agree almost unanimously on a single subject: the
need to punish the Russian government for its interference in the 2016
presidential elections. The result is CAATSA (Countering America's Adversaries Through Sanctions Act), which passes through both

houses of Congress with a total vote of 517–5.[2] The bill mandates that the White House submit for congressional approval any proposal to terminate or waive Russian sanctions; that current sanctions against Russia be maintained; and that the executive branch identify new targets for sanctions in ten sectors of Russian activity. Trump signs CAATSA in August 2017, yet declares that the bill is "seriously flawed" and "encroaches on the executive branch's authority to negotiate [with the Kremlin]."[3] When the October 2017 deadline for the White House to identify new sanction targets arrives, the White House ignores it; indeed, Secretary of State Rex Tillerson, an "old friend" of Putin's according to *Vanity Fair*, has shut down the State Department office that oversees sanctions.[4] At the very end of November, the White House finally issues a preliminary list of new targets upon whom sanctions will be leveled in January.[5]

In January 2018, the Trump administration grudgingly meets CAATSA's six-month deadline for new sanctions to be announced, identifying twenty-one new persons and nine new companies to be sanctioned, but announces that it will go no further, reasoning that "the threat of sanctions [is] already acting as a deterrent" against continued Russian cyberattacks on the United States and that Russia's defense industry is "already suffering" to a sufficient degree under the existing sanctions.[6] While the White House does release, consistent with CAATSA's reporting requirements, an unclassified list of 114 senior Russian politicians and 96 businesspeople considered Russian "oligarchs," it does not impose any penalties on them.[7]

Trump's hostility to legally mandated sanctions after signing off on a new round is not the only mixed signal coming out of his administration. Mike Pompeo, Trump's hand-picked CIA director, declares in January that he "fully expects" the Russians to interfere in the midterm elections—even though the administration has soft-pedaled the CAATSA sanctions on the grounds that they cannot deter Russian cyber-aggression any more than current U.S. countermeasures are.[8] Less than seventy-two hours later, news breaks that Pompeo has secretly met with the chief officers of Russia's foreign intelligence agency and internal security agency, both men barred from entering the

United States under the sanctions imposed on Russia in 2014.[9] Pompeo is said to have followed a "multi-agency legal process" to get the two Russian intelligence officers into the United States.[10]

Meanwhile, Mueller continues his interrogations of key figures in the Trump-Russia case. In January, he strikes an agreement with former Trump campaign CEO Steve Bannon to interview him out of court rather than subpoena him to appear before a grand jury.[11] Around the same time, Jeff Sessions becomes the fifteenth member of the Trump administration to be interviewed by Mueller; the attorney general's voluntary interview lasts "several hours," according to confirmation by the Justice Department.[12] In March, investigators from Mueller's team question Trump national security adviser Erik Prince and subsequently seize his phones and a computer.[13] Media reports note that one of Mueller's many possible areas of inquiry for Prince is the means by which Prince's January 2017 meeting in the Seychelles was arranged. While Prince claims it was merely a fortuitous event, other reporting, most notably from the *Washington Post*, suggests otherwise:

> The United Arab Emirates arranged a secret meeting in January between Blackwater founder Erik Prince and a Russian close to President Vladimir Putin as part of an apparent effort to establish a back-channel line of communication between Moscow and President-elect Donald Trump, according to U.S., European and Arab officials. . . . [T]he UAE agreed to broker the meeting in part to explore whether Russia could be persuaded to curtail its relationship with Iran, including in Syria, a Trump administration objective that would be likely to require major concessions to Moscow on U.S. sanctions. Though Prince had no formal role with the Trump campaign or transition team, he presented himself as an unofficial envoy for Trump.[14]

In his November 2017 testimony before Congress, Prince had grudgingly admitted to being told of a single meeting involving Steve Bannon and the crown prince of Abu Dhabi, but according to the *Post* there were multiple such "discussions." They also involved Michael Flynn and Jared Kushner, and the crown prince decided to assist the Trump transition team in setting up a back channel to Putin only after "[meeting] twice with Putin in 2016 . . . and urg[ing] the Russian leader to work more closely with the Emirates and Saudi Arabia—an effort to isolate Iran." [15]

In April, Special Counsel Mueller asks Dana Boente, the FBI's general counsel, to testify before the Trump-Russia grand jury. The request is significant because Boente is one of Comey's corroborating witnesses, fellow FBI officials to whom Comey related his conversations with Trump shortly after they were completed and who kept their own contemporaneous notes. While Trump has successfully cast doubt on Comey and his deputy, Andrew McCabe (another Comey confidant), in the minds of many Republicans in Washington, Boente remains undiscussed and untouched by Trump and his allies thus far. Boente's testimony also underscores that Mueller is considering obstruction of justice charges in the Trump-Russia affair—if brought against Trump, an impeachable offense—and not merely Trump-Russia collusion, which would in the first instance be charged as aiding and abetting or conspiracy.[16]

In June, Mueller's team questions Ukrainian politician Andrii V. Artemenko for "several hours" before a grand jury. Artemenko will later say that most of the questions were focused on Michael Cohen, confirming that Mueller retains significant interest in Trump's personal attorney and fixer on the Russia collusion question, even as federal prosecutors in Manhattan are investigating Cohen for white-collar financial crimes.[17] This interest is confirmed when it is revealed that Mueller's agents have also detained and questioned Viktor Vekselberg, the Russian oligarch who paid Cohen hundreds of thousands of dollars in alleged consulting fees, at a New York airport.[18]

In August, prosecutors in the Southern District of New York grant immunity to Allen Weisselberg, the chief financial officer of the Trump Organization. While the grant is a "limited" one that is allegedly focused on the ongoing investigation of Michael Cohen, the deal with Weisselberg raises the specter of Mueller sometime soon piercing the Trump Organization's corporate veil to get information on

Trump's own financial dealings and tax returns.[19] According to CNN, Weisselberg is "so much more than [the Trump Organization CFO]. Hired first by Trump's father, Weisselberg has been the money man in Trump's orbit for decades. And, he didn't just handle finances for the Trump Organization but also for Trump's personal accounts."[20] According to *Bloomberg*, "Nobody knows the Trump Organization like Allen Weisselberg."[21] The *Atlantic*, writing on the grant of immunity to Weisselberg, concluded that "New York prosecutors may pose a bigger threat to Trump than Mueller."[22] Mueller's relationship with New York prosecutors is procedurally a two-way street, however; just as Mueller can, in August, refer three individuals for prosecution by the Southern District of New York for failing to register as foreign lobbyists, the Southern District is presumed to be willing to share with Mueller any information from its own investigations.[23] *Slate* will even speculate that Mueller's intention in "spread[ing] [his] work around" to other prosecutors is to hedge his bets against his own eventual firing, making the investigation of Trump's business dealings impossible to derail even if Jeff Sessions, Rod Rosenstein, and Mueller himself are all fired by the president.

In late February, the House Permanent Select Committee on Intelligence interviews Hope Hicks in a closed session. Hicks reportedly refuses to answer any questions about events post-inauguration— while admitting she may have lied for Trump on occasion, although she insists none of the lies were "substantive."[24] The next day, she announces that she will be resigning her position at the White House.[25] Within twelve days, the committee has ended its investigation. It will later issue a report—endorsed only by its Republican members— concluding that there was no collusion whatsoever between the Trump campaign and Russia.[26]

In March, federal agents detain self-described Trump adviser Ted Malloch—also a known associate of Roger Stone's—and seize his cell phone. Their subsequent questioning of him focuses on Stone, WikiLeaks, Julian Assange, Nigel Farage, and Malloch's repeated contacts with both Stone and the Trump campaign in 2016.[27]

Throughout 2018, Mueller proceeds expeditiously with his work,

periodically issuing indictments that rock America's political ecosys-
tem before returning to the necessary secrecy and opacity of his ongoing investigation. While some of the major advancements in Mueller's
federal criminal probe are attributable to charges brought by Mueller
and his D.C. team, others are the result of Mueller's referrals to federal prosecutors elsewhere. Into this latter category falls one particularly critical set of Trump-related convictions: eight convictions for
Trump's former personal attorney Michael Cohen, for offenses including tax fraud, bank fraud, causing an unlawful corporate contribution, and making an excessive campaign contribution.[28] While there is
no direct link between these convictions and the Trump-Russia case,
other than them comprising additional evidence that Trump is easily
blackmailed—a perpetual concern if Putin holds *kompromat* on him—
they do directly implicate Trump in a crime for the first time since he
has taken office.

At his in-court allocution, Cohen unambiguously identifies Trump
(using a euphemistic appellation required by Department of Justice
protocols) as the man who directed him to commit a number of his
crimes.[29] Because the prevailing wisdom in the Department of Justice
and the legal community more broadly is that a sitting president cannot be indicted—or, if indicted, cannot be tried in a criminal court—
Cohen's accusation does not lead to immediate legal jeopardy for
Trump.[30] But it adds evidence of criminality to any future impeachment proceedings and, perhaps as important, puts Cohen at the mercy
of Special Counsel Mueller. Cohen's plea deal in Manhattan all but en-
sures he will spend at least four or five years in prison. But cooperation
with Mueller could potentially shorten that sentence, or any sentence
Mueller might seek on collusion-related conspiracy charges down the
line—though at the time of Cohen's plea all parties agree no such deal
yet exists.[31]

Cohen faces additional legal liability for his clandestine negotiations
with Russian nationals during the campaign; for ferrying a policy proposal by a foreign power to the White House, which would violate the
Logan Act; and for possibly selling access to Trump prior to Trump's
inauguration. He was also paid $400,000 by Ukrainian nationals to set

up a back channel between Trump and Ukrainian president Petro Poro-
shenko in June 2017, according to the BBC. The timing of the payment
is significant, because shortly afterward, the Ukrainian government
halted its domestic criminal investigations of Paul Manafort.[32]

Another case Mueller hands off to other prosecutors that likewise
could, in time, become significant to the Trump-Russia investigation is
Maria Butina's indictment in the District of Columbia in July for conspiracy to act as an agent of a foreign government and failing to register
as a foreign agent.[33] While the very fact of Butina's arrest (and the continued freedom of her boyfriend, Paul Erickson) suggests that Erickson may be a cooperating witness in the case against her, her youth,
vulnerability as a Russian national caught in a nation not her own, and
apparently substantial knowledge of Russian intelligence activities and
capabilities within the United States suggest she, too, could be susceptible to a cooperation agreement.[34] Certainly, the information Mueller
appends to her indictments suggests that she has substantial knowledge to offer Mueller on the subject of illicit Russian activities from the
same period of time the Trump-Russia investigation is focused upon:
2012 to 2016.[35]

Of course, Mueller also remains busy in 2018, continuing his prosecution of Trump associates while adding to his prosecutorial brief new
charges against Russian nationals directly involved in Russian interference in the 2016 presidential election. In February, he indicts thirteen
Russian nationals and three Russian organizations on charges of conspiracy to defraud the United States, conspiracy to commit wire fraud
and bank fraud, and six counts of aggravated identity theft.[36] Because
the special counsel uses what is called a "speaking indictment"—an
indictment that not only lays out charges but discusses in some detail the inculpatory facts undergirding them—his indictment of participants in Russia's Internet Research Agency gives Americans their
first look at the Russian propaganda operation from the inside. What
Americans learn is that Russia's election influence and interference
campaign began in May 2014, approximately six months after Trump
returned from his November 2013 Miss Universe Moscow trip. Putin's
anger over the American response to his 2014 annexation of Crimea

is more likely to have prompted his initiation of such a complex, hostile, and geopolitically dangerous operation in May 2014 than Trump's still-incipient presidential campaign, but it is nevertheless clear—given Trump's December 2013 conversations with New York politicians and Trump aide Sam Nunberg's observations of when Trump decided to run for president—that for those in the know, particularly those in personal or business partnerships with Trump, his plans for 2016 were evident in late 2013. Mueller's indictment of the Internet Research Agency and a number of its participants also establishes that several Russian nationals traveled to the United States to conduct reconnaissance before the operation began, raising the possibility that they were in contact with American political operatives during their travels.[37] As NPR notes, Mueller's indictment does confirm that Trump campaign workers corresponded with "Russian influence-mongers . . . [who] even paid some Americans to show up for protests they organized," but "none of the Americans knew they were dealing with Russian operatives," despite their actions offering "important help" to the Russian operation.[38] Russian interactions with unwitting Republican political operatives even aided the Russians in determining which states to target their activities toward for maximum impact during the 2016 election cycle.[39]

While both Mueller and his Russian defendants are aware the case will never be prosecuted—the DOJ and FBI have no expectation the Kremlin will extradite the men and women charged—the indictment does have the unanticipated side effect of briefly forcing Trump to acknowledge Russian malfeasance. On February 16, 2018, Trump tweets, "Russia started their anti-US campaign in 2014, long before I announced that I would run for President. The results of the election were not impacted. The Trump campaign did nothing wrong—no collusion!"[40] Trump's erroneous statement of when information about his anticipated 2016 presidential run became common knowledge in select political and corporate circles aside, his reference to an "anti-US campaign" by Russia will be one of the only times he ever recognizes Russian criminality during the 2016 election as a certainty rather than one possible scenario among many.

In July 2018, Mueller charges twelve spies from Russia's military intelligence agency, the GRU, as key culprits behind the Russian hacking operation that attacked America's electoral infrastructure in 2015 and 2016. The GRU—the same Russian outfit with which Michael Flynn was unusually enamored in 2013 and 2014—is accused by Mueller, per *Vox*, of "hacking the computer networks of members of Hillary Clinton's campaign, the Democratic National Committee, and the Democratic Congressional Committee . . . [and] coordinat[ing] to release damaging information to sway the election under the names 'DCLeaks' and 'Guccifer 2.0.' "[41] The former of these two entities, a website, had its first full day of operation on June 9, 2016, the very day the Kremlin promised to give the Trump campaign materials damaging to Clinton, while the latter, a persona, was in contact with Trump adviser Roger Stone on more than one occasion. Mueller's indictment is silent on whether the actions of these GRU spies affected the outcome of the 2016 election, and indeed it takes the same non-position on that question that Mueller's February indictments did. But in mid-July, Trump will nevertheless tweet that the special counsel's investigation is intended as merely a "Democrat excuse for losing the '16 Election."[42] In all, Mueller's July indictment charges eleven Russians with conspiracy to commit computer crimes, eight counts of aggravated identity theft, and conspiracy to launder money, while two defendants are charged with a separate count of conspiracy to commit computer crimes.[43]

In between these two sets of indictments, the first person to serve time as a result of the Trump-Russia investigation, Belgian-born lawyer Alex van der Zwaan, reports to prison for a thirty-day sentence.[44] Van der Zwaan had, according to his plea deal, lied to Mueller's team in November 2017 about his phone calls and emails with Trump deputy campaign manager (and later Trump-RNC liaison) Rick Gates.[45] Special Counsel Mueller will announce, in March 2018, that Gates had "repeated contacts during the final weeks of the 2016 presidential race with a business associate tied to Russian intelligence . . . a person the F.B.I. believes had active links to Russian spy services at the time. . . . [Gates] told an associate the person 'was a former Russian Intelligence Officer with the G.R.U.,' the Russian intelligence agency."[46]

After his February 2018 plea to one count of making false state-ments, Alex van der Zwaan begins serving his prison time in April.[47] The case is considered significant, not because someone closely con-nected to a top Trump associate is imprisoned or because the lies van der Zwaan told and evidence he destroyed stemmed from Gates's and Manafort's actions in Ukraine in the aughts, but because van der Zwaan told "a knowing lie during an investigation of international impor-tance," according to Judge Amy Berman Jackson, and hence deserved his sentence. The facts already publicly known in the Trump-Russia investigation suggest that before Mueller's investigation is complete, a similar allegation may be leveled at several Americans in Trump's im-mediate orbit.

In August 2018, Paul Manafort is convicted of eight federal felo-nies, including five counts of tax fraud, two counts of bank fraud, and one count of failure to disclose a foreign bank account.[48] The jury hangs—11 to 1 for conviction—on ten additional charges.[49] While the trial does not directly implicate Trump's 2016 campaign, the facts re-vealed during the course of the prosecution's case in chief underscore that Manafort had no intention of being Trump's campaign manager for free; instead, he was deeply in debt and hoping to use his work for Trump as a means of settling his debts with Russian oligarch Oleg Deripaska. The trial thereby establishes a motive for collusion for the man running Trump's presidential campaign from early April to mid-August 2016. Moreover, it gives Mueller enough leverage over Manafort to get Manafort's cooperation in prosecuting other defen-dants in the Trump-Russia investigation, despite Trump's dangling of a presidential pardon for Manafort in the press.[50] As an op-ed in the New York Times will note after Manafort's trial, "by speculating about [a Trump pardon of Manafort], the president and his surrogates have al-ready acted improperly."[51]

Later in August, W. Samuel Patten, an associate of Paul Manafort's longtime Russian business partner Konstantin Kilimnik, pleads guilty to acting as an unregistered foreign lobbyist, admits to lying to Con-gress, and acknowledges facilitating the transfer of money from a Ukrainian oligarch to Trump's inaugural fund.[52] The case brings into even greater relief a growing controversy surrounding the tens of millions of dollars missing from the inaugural fund; $26 million of the more than $100 million raised for Trump's inauguration was paid out to a firm run by Melania Trump's top adviser, and a significant percentage of that $26 million went to a team run by Mark Burnett, creator of the program that made Trump a television celebrity, *The Apprentice*.53 According to the *New York Times*, Trump personally requested Burnett's involvement with the inaugural festivities, a significant fact, given that multiple Trump associates have alleged that Burnett is still today protecting Trump from the disclosure of *Apprentice* outtakes in which Trump can be heard uttering misogynistic and racist slurs.54 Should Mueller's investigation extend to possible corruption in the form of bribery or money laundering in the inaugural activities coordinated by Trump friend Thomas Barrack, who was lobbying Trump on Middle Eastern energy issues while managing the money for Trump's inauguration, it could open the door to a more robust public consideration of both Trump's pre-election payoffs to bury damaging information and his receipt of funds from foreign nationals during and after the 2016 presidential campaign.

Whether it is these indictments and convictions that rile Trump or something else, 2018 sees the president expressing increasing desperation in his public remarks on the Trump-Russia case, calling it (or, variously, individual elements of it) "rigged" 44 times on Twitter between January and August 2018, a "witch hunt" 106 times, and "illegal" 24 times.55

In an April 2018 interview, former FBI director James Comey implies that he perceives "consciousness of guilt" in certain of Trump's actions since allegations he and his team colluded with the Russian government became public.56 The *Washington Post* has been even more forceful, publishing an article by Pulitzer Prize–winning columnist Eugene Robinson alleging that "Trump seems to be staging a cover-up."57

Trump's actions in 2018 will do much to further this impression among his critics and others in law enforcement. His fury at his enemies and anxiety over the loyalty of his allies lead to an erratic course of conduct that sees Trump courting potential allies and persecuting perceived enemies throughout the year in ways that may eventually produce criminal liability for him or, in the short term, hurt him politically. When former CIA director John Brennan becomes a vocal critic of Trump—calling Trump's claims that he did not collude with the Russians "hogwash"—Trump revokes his lifetime national security clearance, an act of vengeance against a political critic that is unprecedented in American politics.[58] He threatens to do the same to several other officials who have disagreed with him publicly, including former director of national intelligence James Clapper.[59] As Brennan himself observes, writing in the *New York Times* in August, Trump began "[s]tep by step, from the moment 10 days into his administration that he fired the acting attorney general, Sally Q. Yates . . . [to oversee] the removal of top national security officials who have defied him or worked at senior levels of the Russia investigation. They include James B. Comey, the former F.B.I. director; Andrew G. McCabe, the former F.B.I. deputy director; and Peter Strzok, the former F.B.I. counterintelligence agent who helped oversee . . . the Russia investigation."[60]

In February 2018, the FBI also loses David Laufman, whom the *New York Times* calls "the top Justice Department official overseeing espionage investigations, as well as cases involving foreign lobbying and leaks of classified information," for "personal reasons." His exit is deemed "surprising"; the fact that he is mentioned in controversial anti-Trump text messages sent by Peter Strzok to former FBI attorney Lisa Page, and was in charge of "aspects of the investigation into Russian interference in the 2016 election," raises the possibility that he is another victim of the president's withering public critiques.[61] Other significant personnel developments at the FBI and DOJ from April 2017 through 2018, all involving individuals connected in some way to the Russia investigation, include Lisa Page, who resigns in May 2018 after being accused of texting controversial messages about Trump to and receiving controversial messages about Trump from FBI agent Peter Strzok; James Baker, the FBI's general counsel, who is demoted in 2017 and then resigns in 2018, and is known to be a "close friend and longtime associate" of Trump enemy Comey (this fact leads to complaints, according to *Business Insider*, by "national-security experts and former intelligence officials," who question the timing of Baker's departure and "whether it was a politically motivated decision in response to pressure from President Donald Trump and his allies"); James Rybicki, also a close associate of Comey—in fact, his former chief of staff—who quits the Bureau in January 2018; Bill Priestap, the head of the FBI counterintelligence division and in a "pivotal leadership position," per the *Hill*, in the Russia probe, who is called to testify before the House and remains "under fire from conservatives" throughout 2018, in part because of a "trip to London . . . in May 2016 . . . [that may be] connected to the Russia case"; and Mary McCord, the Justice Department's lead attorney on the Russia investigation, who announces her resignation in April 2017, in the midst of her work, offering no public reason for leaving besides telling her staff that "the time is now right for me to pursue new career opportunities."[62]

In August 2018, Bruce Ohr's name is added to the above list of federal officials hounded or punished by Trump, when the president, having already successfully pushed for Ohr's demotion at the Department of Justice, engages in a public campaign to have him fired, even as he is also threatening to revoke Ohr's security clearance—which, were it to happen, would make it impossible for Ohr to do his job. That Ohr's role at the Department of Justice has long been to investigate and prosecute Russian organized crime, and that the Russia investigation has at certain points connected Trump to Russian organized crime, is difficult to ignore. Indeed, in September 2018, the *New York Times* will report that Ohr was at the head of an effort at the Department of Justice to "flip" Oleg Deripaska against Russian organized crime and expose "possible Russian aid to President Trump's 2016 campaign."[63] The effort Trump launches to oust Ohr—tweeting about him and sometimes his wife, a Fusion GPS employee, thirteen times over the final three weeks of August 2018—must be understood in this context.[64]

In addition to investigating Russian organized crime and seeking to turn Russian oligarchs into informants, Ohr was also Christopher Steele's primary contact at the FBI when Steele wanted to turn his raw intelligence over to federal law enforcement during the 2016 campaign. The two men had known each other for more than a decade before Steele was asked to research Trump's Russian business ties by an anti-Trump Republican in 2015.[65] According to CNN, when Steele gave Ohr the first few entries in what would become the "Steele dossier" at a breakfast in July 2016, the former MI6 agent told the Justice Department lawyer that "Russian intelligence thought they had the then-candidate [Trump] 'over a barrel' during the 2016 campaign."⁶⁶

Even DOJ and FBI officials much higher in the ranks than Ohr, and even those higher in the ranks and nominated by Trump himself, face Trump's ire as he attempts to purge both institutions of those who persist in investigating his ties to Russia. *Axios* reports in January 2018 that Trump's replacement for Comey at the FBI, Christopher Wray, "threatened to resign" if Attorney General Sessions fired Andrew McCabe, a plan of action the digital news outlet notes came "at the public urging of President Donald Trump."⁶⁷ Sessions fires McCabe anyway, doing so less than forty-eight hours before McCabe's scheduled retirement.⁶⁸ The decision denies the FBI's second-in-command his early retirement benefits and a portion of his anticipated pension, and is now the subject of a lawsuit.⁶⁹

Trump's triumphant tweet after McCabe's firing is characteristic of his public statements on social media throughout 2018 regarding the DOJ and FBI officials he most associates with the investigations of his conduct: "Andrew McCabe FIRED," writes the president on March 17, "a great day for the hard working men and women of the FBI—A great day for Democracy. Sanctimonious James Comey was his boss and made McCabe look like a choirboy. He knew all about the lies and corruption going on at the highest levels of the FBI!"⁷⁰

Trump's pick for deputy attorney general, Rod Rosenstein, also spends 2018 in professional uncertainty, with Trump "threaten[ing] to 'get involved' [in the Russia investigation] and fire [him]," according to the *Daily Beast*, and "considering firing" him, according to CNN.⁷¹ The threat comes as Trump's closest allies in the House are preparing articles of impeachment against Rosenstein for what they say is his failure to turn over documents to them in a timely fashion; the documents they seek aim to prove a "deep state" conspiracy at the FBI and DOJ to frame Trump for impeachable offenses using fraudulent intelligence.⁷² Impeachment of the personal or political sort is not enough of a punishment for Christopher Steele, however, in the judgment of Trump's congressional allies; in January 2018, Republicans on the Senate Judiciary Committee unilaterally refer Steele to the Department of Justice for criminal prosecution on the allegation that Steele misled federal investigators on whether he'd spoken to the media about the raw intelligence he'd compiled on Trump.[73] While the referral does not lead to a prosecution, it successfully keeps Steele from testifying before Congress or traveling to the United States to assist federal investigators working on the Trump-Russia case.

These attacks come in the context of all the Republican-led congressional investigations of possible Trump-Russia ties shutting down, with the exception of one: the Senate Select Committee on Intelligence, which, per the *New York Times*, Trump spends the last few months of 2017 lobbying to have end its work as well.[74] Moreover, Trump's attacks are by and large against individuals who are likely witnesses against him in a federal investigation; his tweets apparently seek to intimidate them into silence, threaten them with professional punishment, or impugn their character following demotions or firings he encouraged—and may ultimately be regarded as witness tampering under federal law.[75]

Friendly witnesses can be tampered with also, of course, and Trump's 2018 record of conduct on this score likewise requires some consideration. Knowing that Hope Hicks is an almost certain federal witness in any future legal or political proceeding against him, Trump in early August 2018 invites Hicks to travel to Ohio with him; during the trip the two have several private meetings.[76] Soon afterward, it is revealed that Hicks has been offered a paying job on Trump's 2020 reelection campaign.[77] Hicks is not the only Trump associate or employee Trump offers a job. The Republican National Committee signs a $15,000 per month contract for "security services" with Trump's former bodyguard Keith Schiller after he leaves the White House. That deal comes under scrutiny when former Trump adviser Omarosa Manigault Newman alleges that the White House is systematically pushing former aides to sign agreements of exactly this sort—and at exactly this pay scale—to silence them, even knowing that many of these aides will have to testify before Congress, Mueller's grand jury, or both.[78] And by 2018, the Republican National Committee is paying not just for the services of Keith Schiller, but at least half a million dollars in legal fees for Hope Hicks and others, according to the *Washington Post*.[79]

At various moments in the strange, chaotic sequence of events marking Trump's second year in office, he will be accused of using pardons not just for political purposes, but to send a message to potential government collaborators among his set—most notably Roger Stone and Paul Manafort—that the reward for keeping quiet is a future presidential pardon and effective immunity for their past actions. After Trump pardons conservative firebrand Dinesh D'Souza for making illegal campaign contributions in 2014, Stone announces that the pardon is a message to Robert Mueller: "indict people for crimes that don't pertain to Russian collusion and this [a pardon] is what could happen."[80] Stone has since said that he believes Mueller will indict him, but not for a crime pertaining to Russian collusion, which makes him part of a group that would benefit from what he perceives to be Trump's largesse with pardons.[81] Stone has made the same prediction with respect to Donald Trump Jr. as well.[82] Meanwhile, in late August, *Bloomberg* will accuse Trump attorney Rudy Giuliani of being on "thin ice" legally—perhaps even guilty of obstruction—for "hinting at a presidential pardon for a key witness" in the Trump-Russia case, namely, Paul Manafort.[83] Giuliani aside, many news outlets, and even some Republican politicians, hint or plainly assert in 2018 that Trump's own public comments on the presidential pardon power could constitute new acts of obstruction.[84]

Throughout this bizarre, possibly illegal course of conduct, Trump vacillates publicly on whether he will cooperate with the Mueller investigation, though many in the media concluded from the beginning that he would not.[85] Even so, he says twice in January 2018, "I am looking forward to it," when asked about being interviewed by Mueller, adding—also twice—"I would do it under oath."[86] The result of these misdirections is that by August 2018, media outlets are writing articles with titles like "Trump's Lawyers Can't Talk Him Out of Talking with Mueller," although Trump's initial promise to do so had come fourteen months earlier, and in the meantime he has secured the demotion, firing, or resignation of many of those he considered enemies at the DOJ and FBI and has even attempted to fire Mueller on two occasions.[87] By

mid-2018, Trump's attorneys have outstripped even the president's re-
luctance to speak to Mueller, arguing that Trump will have every right
to ignore a Mueller *subpoena* as well as an interview request should he
wish to do so.[88]

Whether Trump will speak to Mueller ranks, in 2018, as a mystery
with little real mystery at all: the seemingly universal presumption is
that Trump will not speak to Mueller voluntarily, possibly not even
if compelled by a subpoena, whatever he may say on occasion about
being willing to do so.

But many other 2018 mysteries remain unresolved. One of them
is so significant yet unknowable that even top U.S. officials—on both
sides of the political aisle—want to resolve it but cannot: what Donald
Trump and Vladimir Putin said to each other at their hastily arranged
"summit" in Helsinki in July.[89] Only interpreters were present for the
two-hour private conversation between the two men, which was then
followed by a press conference. That conversation is cause for concern
if what Trump said publicly at the post-summit press conference is in-
dicative of what he said to Putin behind closed doors. As the *Washington Post* noted at the time,

> American foreign-policy officials were stunned by Trump's
> behavior [in Helsinki], which ranged from rejecting his intel-
> ligence community's assessment that the Kremlin interfered in
> the 2016 election to considering, albeit briefly, handing over a
> number of current and former American diplomats for ques-
> tioning by Russian authorities. His performance earned rebukes
> from lawmakers and former officials, and even a retort from his
> own Director of National Intelligence.[90]

In August, that director of national intelligence, Dan Coats, will say
that he still doesn't "fully understand" what happened in Helsinki, as
he is "not in a position" to "know what happened in that meeting."[91]
He will add that it is the "President's prerogative" to have private conversations with foreign leaders without informing his top intelligence
officials of any of the contents of those conversations.[92]

On September 14, 2018, Trump's former campaign manager, Paul Manafort, pleads guilty in D.C. to one count of conspiracy against the United States and one count of conspiracy to obstruct justice; Manafort's plea deal could land him in federal prison for seventeen to twenty-one years—with the incarceration to run concurrent to any prison time he receives in the Eastern District of Virginia—but his sentence can be reduced if he offers full cooperation to Mueller across all areas of the Trump-Russia probe.[93]

News of Manafort's plea sends shockwaves through U.S. politics, given NBC News' January 2018 reporting that Trump considers Manafort the one person who could place him in legal peril should he "flip." "Trump is telling friends and aides in private that things are going great—for him," NBC News wrote at the time. "Some reasons: He's decided that a key witness in the Russia probe, Paul Manafort, isn't going to 'flip' and sell him out."[94]

As America nears the 2018 midterms, the popular political speculation is that voters will rebuke Trump's excesses and malfeasance with a "blue wave": a Democratic takeover of the House of Representatives. The Republicans' Senate majority is considered safe; in any case, should the Democrats by some significant electoral surprise take the Senate, the sixty-seven votes needed to convict a president who has been impeached by the House means that any removal of Trump from the Oval Office would have to be bipartisan.

If the Democrats take the House, however, they can push on their own for significant progress in the investigation of the president—an investigation that might culminate in impeachment proceedings. Witnesses who previously were not subpoenaed and therefore were not compelled to testify before Congress could be subpoenaed; witnesses who appeared voluntarily but refused to answer certain questions could be required by either subpoenas or threats of being held in contempt of Congress to answer those questions; documents Congress never sought that would normally have been the subject of investigative inquiry and eventually, if not produced, subpoenaed—such as Trump's tax returns—could now be demanded. Should the midterm elections indeed result in a "blue wave," by mid- to late 2019 many of the questions that remain unresolved in the Trump-Russia investigation may be close to a resolution, as may be the entire affair—whether the final chapter is impeachment and removal, a dramatic resignation from office, or some unforeseen and unpredictable machination relating to Trump's criminal liability for actions taken both before and after Russian interference in the 2016 election. In one way or another, the chaos of 2018 will be resolved, although perhaps not before it has deepened, widened, and put even more pressure on America's public institutions and culture.

Until then, what the citizenry has is a public record of the Trump-Russia investigation that comes, for now, from the results of investigative journalism by reporters and enterprising citizens and perhaps, at some point in the future, from what Mueller himself has referred to in court filings as an "ongoing criminal investigation with multiple lines of non-public inquiry."[95]

Annotated History

But many other 2018 mysteries remain unresolved.

For instance, the lasting importance of the strange saga of twenty-one-year-old Belarusian escort Nastya Rybka (real name: Anastasia Vashukevich) remains difficult to determine. In February 2018, Rybka claimed to have audio recordings of Paul Manafort's former boss, Russian oligarch and Putin confidant Oleg Deripaska, that would, she said, confirm that Russian government officials colluded with the Trump campaign.[96] At the time she made this claim, Rybka had just been arrested in Thailand, along with a number of others, on allegations of working without a work permit—specifically, conducting a "sex workshop." As she was being transported to jail, she recorded and released a video indicating that if American officials would come rescue her from incarceration, she would give them hard evidence establishing connections between top Kremlin officials, Paul Manafort, and Trump himself.[97] Her evidence was teased in a February video by Putin critic Alexei Navalny, who does not know Rybka, but used public records research to reveal that the young escort had long boasted on her social media feeds of "seducing some oligarch." Her claim seemed to be supported by the fact that she'd posted online many pictures and videos of herself and Deripaska spending time together.[98] In one video, Deripaska is heard and seen saying to Sergey Eduardovich Prikhodko, a longtime Putin adviser who at the time of the video was a deputy prime minister and top adviser to Russian prime minister Dmitry Medvedev, "We've got bad relations with America, because the friend of Sergey Eduardovich, [then U.S. assistant secretary of state for European and Eurasian affairs Victoria] Nuland . . . is responsible for them. When she was your age, she spent a month on a Russian whaling boat. She hates our country after this."[99] Navalny, seeking to discover more about this secretly recorded but publicly published conversation, learned that Rybka had written a book in which she detailed exactly when the con-

versation on the boat—Deripaska's yacht *Elden*—occurred: August
2016. Moreover, pictures on Rybka's social media feed established the
location of her yacht trip with Deripaska as the coastline of Norway. In
her book, Rybka referred to Deripaska as "Ruslan" and Prikhodko as
"Daddy." [100]

Navalny thereafter contended, in a video posted online that now
has nearly eight million views on YouTube, that Deripaska's invitation to Prikhodko to take a trip on his yacht and—as Rybka's video
makes clear—Deripaska's purchase of multiple escorts for Prikhodko's
entertainment and enjoyment constituted a bribe; Navalny laid out
evidence that Deripaska had also arranged for Prikhodko to be transported by private jet to a remote area of Norway for their meeting.[101]
Navalny alleged that one of Prikhodko's many surprisingly luxurious
homes—surprising, as he is ostensibly merely a government minister,
albeit a powerful one who is "responsible for Russian foreign policy,"
per Navalny—was in the same building as the family of Igor Sechin,
Rosneft's CEO, and that Prikhodko was friendly with the Sechins.[102]
Navalny theorized that Paul Manafort's offer of private briefings for
Deripaska was made as part of a slightly longer back channel intended
to lead from Manafort to Deripaska, Deripaska to Prikhodko, and Prikhodko to both Putin and Medvedev. Navalny's implication that Prikhodko's astounding personal wealth and landholdings are the product
of graft—bribes from oligarchs like Deripaska—is unverifiable. But
in Rybka's book and social media accounts and in Navalny's investigation, there is evidence that Deripaska was briefing Prikhodko on
goings-on in American politics as part of a secretive meeting on a yacht
off Norway.[103] Within six months of his video's going viral, Navalny
was jailed for thirty days by Putin's government for a January 2018
protest. In the meantime, Rybka's arrest, which began as a deportable
status offense, has suddenly turned into more serious crimes, such as
indecency and solicitation, for which Rybka now faces ten years' imprisonment in Thailand.[104]

In March 2018, the *New York Times* quoted the chief of Thailand's
Immigration Bureau, Suttipong Wongpin, as saying of Rybka, "She
will be deported. Her immigration offense is working without a work

permit."[105] Once word of her offer to American officials became international news, however, her circumstances changed: her charges were amended from immigration offenses to indecency, conspiracy, and belonging to a secret society, charges that carry, with conviction, a significant prison sentence in Thailand.[106] While the *New York Times* quoted Rybka and her codefendants as "claim[ing] they are facing [increased charges] because of the intervention of a foreign power [Russia] they angered," the *Times* also noted Rybka now was "coy about the content of her recordings—and said she now has no plan to make them public."[107] Her coyness and change of heart were easily explained: she gave the tapes to Deripaska, the Associated Press reported, after she "promised Deripaska she would no longer speak on the matter, and . . . he had . . . promised her something in return for not making that evidence public."[108] As she changed her plea to guilty in a Thai court— she will be sentenced for soliciting (prostitution) and conspiracy to solicit at a sentencing hearing in late summer 2018—she told the Associated Press, "He [Deripaska] promised me a little something already. If he do that [what he promised] then there will be no problem, but if he don't . . ." Then she shrugged and smiled. The Associated Press reported her having the same reaction to a question on whether she still held copies of the audio and video she previously offered to American law enforcement.[109] Prior to making an arrangement with Rybka, Deripaska had been so concerned about her allegations that in February he had sought and received an injunction from a Russian court against Instagram and YouTube; the injunction, demanding the immediate removal of all Rybka-Deripaska-Prikhodko material from the two sites, threatened to block access to both sites in Russia if the two companies did not comply. Russia's Federal Service for Supervision of Communications, Information Technology and Mass Media, or Roskomnadzor, backed the order and promised to punish both YouTube and Instagram for any noncompliance.[110]

Rybka was not the only potential Trump-Russia witness whose silence in 2018 spoke as loudly as her words. In August 2018, George Papadopoulos's attorneys filed a sentencing memo in advance of Papadopoulos's sentencing hearing, the defendant and the government having experienced enough of a breakdown in their relationship that Mueller's team was now insisting on incarceration for Papadopoulos, while Papadopoulos, through his attorney, was requesting probation. In the affidavit accompanying his sentencing request, Papadopoulos revealed five facts heretofore unknown to the public: that he had unsuccessfully sought a job with Trump in mid-2015 before suddenly being hired in early March 2016, just days before traveling to Italy; that he was hired to assist with "the [Trump] campaign's foreign policy focus," which he was told was "Russia," despite the campaign's knowing he had "no experience in dealing with Russian policy or its officials"; that then candidate Trump "nodded with approval" when Papadopoulos told him, on March 31, 2016, at the Trump International Hotel in D.C., that he was a Kremlin intermediary tasked with setting up a secret meeting and back channel between Trump and Putin; that then senator Sessions's reaction to the proposal was to "like the idea and [state] that the campaign should look into it"; and that Papadopoulos told the Greek foreign minister, whom he met on a campaign-approved trip to Greece in late May 2016, that the Russians had "dirt" on Hillary Clinton—even as he maintained, still, that "he [did] not recall ever passing the information on to the campaign."[111]

What is still unclear is what Mueller's decision to recommend imprisonment for Papadopoulos was primarily based on: it could be based on the impact of Papadopoulos's lies on federal law enforcement's ability to question and apprehend Mifsud; on Papadopoulos's decision to begin speaking to the media in December 2017; or, most tellingly if so, on Mueller's conclusion that "the defendant did not provide 'substantial assistance' [to prosecutors], and much of the information provided by the defendant came only after the government confronted him with his own emails, text messages, internet search history, and other information it had obtained via search warrants and subpoenas."[112] While Mueller's team cited all three aggravating factors in its sentencing memorandum, only the last of these suggests that prosecutors do not believe Papadopoulos is telling them the entire truth and that he may still be trying to protect Trump officials, through whom, the memorandum notes, Papadopoulos was seeking full-time employment in either the State Department, the Department of Energy, or the National Security Council at the time of his questioning by FBI agents.[113] Regardless, that Papadopoulos put in his sentencing memo that his back-channel communications with the Russians were approved by both Trump and Sessions—who have since denied giving any such approval—raises the possibility that Papadopoulos and the three other March 2016 meeting attendees who have spoken with Mueller concur with Papadopoulos's version of events and are telling the truth, while Trump and Sessions are not.

Among the events that followed the March 31 meeting is another mystery: the matter of the electronic "pinging" detected throughout 2016 between a server in Trump Tower and two servers at Alfa Bank in Russia. During the months-long period available to data analysts, 87 percent of all pings to Trump Tower came from Alfa Bank, with nearly all the remainder coming from a server in Michigan under the control of Erik Prince's brother-in-law.[114] However, no expert has yet been able to conclusively determine what the pings mean—whether they indicate a transfer of information, some sort of signal, or nothing at all.[115] *Slate* will note, however, that "[t]he conversation between the Trump and Alfa servers appeared to follow the contours of political happenings in the United States. 'At election-related moments, the traffic peaked,' according to [Indiana University computer scientist L. Jean] Camp."[116] The FBI is now examining the evidence, but no conclusion has yet been revealed.[117] The key intersections of the Trump-Russia case with Alfa Bank, pings aside, are these two: the man who helped write Trump's "Mayflower Speech," Richard Burt, was at the time on the advisory board of Alfa Bank, and Maria Butina, the accused Russian spy now idling in a D.C. jail, had an account at Alfa Bank that exchanged hundreds of thousands of dollars with her boyfriend's bank account at Wells Fargo in the years leading up to the 2016 election.[118] What, if anything, any of this means remains unclear.

Equally unclear is what role Cambridge Analytica will have in the Trump-Russia saga when its full history is written. In May 2018, the data-collection firm shut down permanently, even as questions still abound about its founder, Steve Bannon; about Jared Kushner, the man who contracted it to control the Trump campaign's data operation; about its CEO, Alexander Nix, who reached out to WikiLeaks during the 2016 campaign and was caught on undercover video implying that the company engaged in domestic psychological operations, "honey-pot" operations, and other unsavory tactics in order to win elections; and about the Soviet-born data scientist Aleksandr Kogan, who, while receiving funding from a Moscow university, not only compiled fifty million Facebook profiles, but then left that data accessible to unknown Russian nationals, possibly giving Russian propagandists the tools they needed to better target their election interference campaign.[119]

Finally, we cannot know what the effect of whistle-blowers will be on the Trump-Russia investigation. Tell-all books like Omarosa Manigault Newman's *Unhinged*, Bob Woodward's *Fear*, or Michael Wolff's *Fire and Fury*—the last of which gave Steve Bannon an opportunity to opine about the Trump White House, including a claim that there was "zero" chance Trump Jr. didn't tell his father about the June 2016 Trump Tower meeting beforehand—could yet lead to revelations otherwise inaccessible to Congress, the special counsel, or public journalism. While Trump has tried to gag former staffers with nondisclosure agreements (NDAs) or seduce them into silence with do-little "jobs" that pay handsomely, the legality of such NDAs is in dispute and future staffers may, like Manigault Newman—who now says she will "blow the whistle" on what she calls Trump's "corruption"—opt for transparency rather than complicity in Trump's still-opaque machinations.[120]

THE DEATH AND REBIRTH
OF AMERICA

A REVIEW OF EVERYTHING DONALD TRUMP HAS DONE
since deciding to run for president shortly after the 2012 presidential
election, as well as everything we have learned about what he, those
of his children working in the Trump Organization, and his closest associates did in the decade prior, should cause profound unease in the
heart of every American. The picture that emerges is of a man whose
venality and solipsism have left him vulnerable to being compromised
by the Kremlin.

Since the 1980s, Trump has shown a commitment to his own self-
interest over any other consideration. As he hopes for more business
opportunities to develop in Moscow and St. Petersburg, his views on
Russia bear more similarity to Kremlin propaganda than anything we
would expect to hear from the mouth of an American, let alone our
president. When Trump was just a businessman, it was possible to find
those views, which nearly always castigated our allies and heartened
our enemies, odious but ultimately irrelevant. Now, all of America
can see what the Kremlin long ago saw: Trump was always headed
for a life in politics. The only question was what the consequences for
America would be. We now have an answer to that question: the result
of elevating such a man to international prominence and authority is a

foreign policy that Trump implicitly surrendered to foreign interests thirty years ago and explicitly traded for continued access to foreign money and influential foreign leaders in 2013 or shortly thereafter. It was in that year that the Kremlin made it abundantly clear how much Trump, his family, and his business stood to gain if he threw over U.S. interests in favor of a policy portfolio that echoed the public statements of the Russian government—or, more simply, those of Vladimir Putin.

From his campaign to transition to administration, there have been dozens of clandestine meetings between those in his inner circle and hostile foreign actors, all of which were subsequently lied about to the media, to voters, to law enforcement, and to Congress. Throughout it all, Trump and those voluntarily sheltered in his strange milieu have exhibited an unwillingness to change course, even after it became clear that Russian interests were poised to threaten Western-style democracy.

The volume and scope of Trump's deceit, along with his indefensible domestic and foreign policies, could well produce, in short order, the crashing of the American economy, multiple costly military adventures abroad, and a continued degradation of American cultural and political discourse that will take many years to heal. Ironically, the chances that Trump will cause dramatic harm to the very party that elevated him to the presidency are far higher than many suppose; we cannot expect that Trump will go quietly into the good night while he retains his hold on power or at any time thereafter. He will pursue vengeance against anyone he perceives as having been an instrument of his accountability, whether those in his sights are Democrats or, as he might see it, disloyal Republicans.

What Americans—Democrats and Republicans alike—have learned in the Trump era is what nations around the globe learned long ago: autocrats are poisonous to any nation in which they take root. Many civil societies collapse under the weight of their autocrats' corruption and moral turpitude. That said, in America we have the benefit and shield of a democracy most of us believe in and would fight to protect, a rule of law that is long-standing and broadly just, and a history of surviving tragedy and periods of shame with our optimism and our moral ambitions mostly intact. America will survive this period; to do so, however, it will have to finally accept the unthinkable: it elected a man capable of corporate crime, astonishing greed, and personal cruelty. What ties together the dizzying number of lies, misdirections, and degradations endemic to this era is quite simply that this presidency is not an American presidency but a *Trump* presidency: a course of ill governance that is *for* Trump, *about* Trump, and inextricably tethered to the interests *of* Trump.

The penchant for dubious associations Trump has historically pursued is, if not matched, at least dwarfed in size and scope by the collective perfidy of the more than a dozen Trump family members, aides, allies, and associates who in some cases for years have enabled his behavior in business and now in politics. Never has a presidential campaign birthed so many lies from so many different mouths: lies of indifference, lies of carelessness, lies of callousness, lies of pique, lies of strategic advantage, lies of ignorance, lies of malicious intent, lies of ulterior motive. The rogues' gallery produced by the Trump campaign, then Trump transition, now Trump administration will encompass a number of men and women—including many who had little inkling of Trump's quid pro quo with the Kremlin. These ancillary figures will be accounted in history as mere adjuncts to Trump's deceit; they flew too close to a dark sun.

But this is only one version of the future. It is equally probable that history will deem even minor Team Trump figures—spokesmen and -women, high-level administrative assistants, and second-tier family members—willing accomplices in Trump's monstrous accomplishment: perverting American government and culture. They may be blamed, too, for having left America, in their wake, unable to recognize truth from fiction, benign intent from malice, courage from cowardice, patriotism from self-interest.

It will take many years, perhaps even more than a decade, for America to fully recover from the Trump presidency.

If America's rule of law remains fully intact, and if there are still men and women of abiding conscience on both sides of the political aisle, Trump will be impeached by the House of Representatives in 2019 and convicted of impeachable offenses by the U.S. Senate in

2019 or 2020. To avoid the embarrassment—an offense to his vanity, not his dignity—of being the first president to be removed from office, it is equally possible Trump will resign in 2019 shortly before he is impeached or shortly before he is convicted. This rather obvious plan of escape is complicated by the fact that the moment Trump is no longer president he can be indicted by his former Department of Justice.

The menu of federal offenses from which the roster of indictments against Trump and his closest associates may be drawn includes the following (as well as conspiracy to commit any or all of these offenses): various campaign finance violations, election fraud, wire fraud, bribery, bank fraud, computer crimes, extortion, identity theft, obstruction of justice, witness tampering, perjury, making false statements to Congress, making false statements to law enforcement, failure to register as a foreign agent, money laundering, tax evasion, and RICO charges. No one Trump administration official, Trump included, would ever face more than a handful of these, but several are likely to tick a number of the boxes here. If Robert Mueller is a typical prosecutor, he will propose as many charges and as serious a set of charges against each defendant (provided he or she is not cooperating with the government) that he reasonably can, assuming—as prosecutors do—that negotiations will occur down the line to limit the number and severity of any given defendant's charges and exposure to prison time.

Special Counsel Mueller has thus far exhibited an extraordinary willingness to under-charge those who can assist him in establishing that the president of the United States is compromised. That Michael Flynn, an evident bad actor in the events described in this book, should face only a single charge is either a testament to Mueller's uncommon mercy, Flynn's value to the investigation of the president, or Mueller's choice to focus on other targets he considers more culpable than even the disgraced former National Security Advisor. These other targets could include, in addition to the president, Erik Prince, Steve Bannon, Donald Trump Jr., Jared Kushner, Sam Clovis, Roger Stone, Joseph Schmitz, J. D. Gordon, Carter Page, a number of Russian nationals (whose prosecutions would be difficult to pursue because of the unlikelihood of their being extradited to the United States), and, because lawyers tend to take misconduct by other lawyers particularly seriously, Jeff Sessions. Naive dupes and cutouts like George Papadopoulos who cooperate will face minimal jail or prison time. Mueller could also decide to view the conspiracy question through a narrow lens, concluding that while many people assisted Trump with his plans and particularly with the cover-up of his misdeeds, few beneath Trump and his family in the campaign and administration hierarchies stood to directly benefit from the graft above their heads and therefore had little reason to fully appreciate its scope. One imagines that in the Trump-Russia investigation, as in many conspiracy investigations, a core group of bad actors is surrounded by a large number of men and women responsible for after-the-fact offenses like obstruction of justice, perjury, witness tampering, making false statements, or participation in a conspiracy whose ambitions they knew were criminal but whose breadth they did not understand.

Those who predict widespread violence should Trump be impeached and convicted or resign are being reactionary. Americans are as a national community more noble than that, and most have much more instinctive faith in our legal and political institutions than our often poisonous discourse would suggest. Violence is for those who have given up on America completely. While it is true that the tens of millions of Americans who voted for this president are not yet prepared to give up the way he makes them feel and the self-respect they had in the moment they cast a ballot in his name, they did not support him because they'd given up on America. Rather, in a particular way that can be difficult for the rest of America to appreciate, they voted for him because they love America.

Perhaps a more pressing question is the fate of the Republican Party should Trump maintain his cultish appeal and position himself as a martyr after his impending fall from grace. Were he not likely to face imprisonment—an eventuality only a "grand bargain" involving his voluntary resignation could avoid—one would expect him to found a television network the way he'd planned to do if he lost the 2016 election. One would further expect that the television network would promote a new slate of right-wing populists whose Trump-inspired "grab-bag" of policy positions would eventually sever the GOP in two. The odds that the Republican Party exists in its current state ten years after Trump leaves the White House are longer than many believe. Should Trump feel the GOP has betrayed him, he will stop at nothing to destroy it in whatever years he has left. The hardened core of "strong" Trump supporters within the party, comprising about 30 percent or so of voting-age Republicans, will follow Trump wherever he leads. If he bolts the party following whatever happens in 2019, he will lead these voters into political irrelevance, and the splintered Republican Party will guarantee an America in which the Democratic Party is the long-term majority in all branches of federal government. That prospect alone should convince Trump and his followers to try to remake rather than unmake the Republican Party.

Oddly, for all Trump's railing against federal law enforcement and the American intelligence community, the FBI, DOJ, CIA, and other now-maligned government agencies are likely to emerge from the Trump presidency unscathed. The Republican Party has too much to gain by continuing to steer debate over the criminal justice system with "law-and-order" rhetoric to remain the would-be executioners of that system for long.

A greater question is how we will all live with one another going forward—that is to say, love one another. It is hard to imagine many proud Trump voters feeling any goodwill toward those who helped en-gineer his political downfall in the years ahead. How one stood on the question of Donald J. Trump at this moment in American history will be the defining feature of many Americans' self-identity as citizens for years to come.

There is, of course, one remaining possibility that could alter the equation as laid out here: America may be invited to witness the com-plete, utter, monstrously loud self-disassembly of Donald J. Trump in the public square. Should Trump attempt to effectively suspend the rule of law in America by firing Jeff Sessions, Rod Rosenstein, and/or Rob-ert Mueller; should he seek to pardon any person believed by half or more of the country to be one of his coconspirators at the time he par-dons them; or should he so dissociate from the reality of America as a democracy that his increasingly mercurial Twitter feed and undignified public presence become unsustainably obscene, then a spectacular self-implosion like this could so embarrass his allies and a sizable percentage of his backers that support for his administration craters in a way modern polling has never seen. In that case, America might yet awake from this presidency as from a bad dream. This future becomes increasingly likely with each Trump tweet baselessly calling the Mueller investigation "rigged" or ominously signing off "stay tuned!" after declaring that any investigation of his actions before his presidency or while he is in office is "illegal." Having represented more than two thousand accused criminals and seeing, in several of the worst of them, many of the same traits evident in this president, I cannot help but anticipate at least one illegal firing and at least one illegal pardon—obstruction in the guise of leniency—before the curtain falls on the Trump era. Any such action would of course be accompanied by a legion of pundits and politically minded attorneys assuring Trump and his supporters that a president can execute any of his constitutional functions for an illegal purpose. But he cannot.

If the Democrats do take the House of Representatives in the fall of 2018, it will happen in part because Trump cannot help himself from committing political and cultural atrocities on a near-daily basis. In that, and in his inability to tell the truth or value any cause or person more than he values himself, he is apparently pathological. He will not, one would expect, ever agree to be interviewed by Robert Mueller; he will fight any subpoena issued to him in court, and he will lose if his case reaches the Supreme Court. By the same token, Trump's allies in Congress may continue to obstruct the investigations into his administration, even mounting a doomed campaign to impeach Rod Rosenstein or terminate the special counsel's authority. But I predict cooler heads among the Republican leadership—with a longer vision, if not necessarily a more expansive understanding of civic duty—will prevail.

If Rod Rosenstein is still the acting attorney general for the Trump-Russia investigation when Mueller issues his final report sometime in 2019 or 2020, he will release the report to the public over the objections of fellow Republicans in Congress. If they somehow temporarily block him from making the report public, it will leak; it will be longer, more comprehensive, and more damning than any public consideration of Trump's misdeeds could have anticipated. Mueller's access to Trump's financial records, for a start, will have opened for the special counsel an entire landscape of graft Americans can't now contemplate. Unfortunately, far-right media—in many cases, personalities on the right who simultaneously advise Trump as they analyze his presidency—have done so much to inure a subsection of Trump supporters to a sober, professional, rational analysis of the hard and circumstantial evidence in the Trump-Russia investigation that a notable bloc of voting Americans will reject whatever Mueller writes in his report simply because he was the one to write it.

Whatever happens, America—which has been spiritually, psychologically, and politically paralyzed by Trump's toxic insinuation into its culture—will continue in a state of paralysis that won't be broken until Trump's exit from American life. And when that happens, America is likely to find that the president's unprincipled and narcissistic reality could not be sustained at home or under the gaze of the entire world. That gaze will reveal, even more than is already evident, that the world Donald J. Trump inhabits isn't the one most of the rest of us do.

ACKNOWLEDGMENTS

The list of people without whom this book would have been impossible is nearly as long as the list of people whose names appear in its index.

I am, first and before all, fortunate beyond deserving for the love and support of my wife, whose wisdom, temperament, and perspective was a compass in this endeavor as it has been in so many others.

This book draws together the research of hundreds of investigative journalists from around the world, whose articles and employers are cited in the book's endnotes and whose names and other contributions to journalism could readily fill a book several times this size. In networking and synthesizing the knowledge and hard work of a large number of these professionals as a curatorial journalist, I was always in awe of their fearlessness, ambition, perspicacity, and candor. The information matrix we call the Trump-Russia investigation is impassable without the work, work ethic, and nodes of data these journalists have provided.

I'd like to particularly thank Natasha Bertrand, Paul Wood, David Corn, Michael Isikoff, Luke Harding, Craig Unger, Julia Ioffe, Bill Moyers, Virginia Heffernan, Caroline Orr, Ryan Goodman, Asha Rangappa, Jeffrey Toobin, Carl Bernstein, Jim Sciutto, Steve Schmidt, Laurence Tribe, Isaac Arnsdorf, Matt Apuzzo, Carol Cadwalladr, Sharon LaFraniere, Kenneth Vogel, Carol Leonnig, Rosalind Helderman, Tom Hamburger, Mark Mazzetti, Annette Schatzle, Jos Van Dongen, Manon Blaas, Marianna Kakaounaki, Alex Papchelas, Katie Benner, Adam Goldman, and the members of the Channel 4 News (UK) investigative team for their excellent reporting and analysis. The employers of these journalists and all those whose work appears in *Proof of Collusion* also deserve thanks for sponsoring the sort of journalism that daily acts as a guiding star in times of confusion and anxiety.

Closer to home, the team that worked on this book—including Jonathan Karp, Priscilla Painton, Megan Hogan, Jonathan Evans, Ed Klaris, Alexia Bedat, Keith Schneider, Kristina Rebelo, Julie Tate, Elise Ringo, Marie Florio, Felice Javit, Kristen Lemire, Tom Spain, and Jeff Wilson—improved a project whose scope could easily have become unwieldy. The commitment of the whole team to telling this story was inspiring.

Throughout each stage of the process, my agent Jeff Silberman has been far more than that: he has been an advisor, mentor, and erudite discussion partner whose contributions run throughout the book and are no less valuable for being seamlessly interwoven into the text. I feel incredibly lucky to have had him as a partner on this journey.

Finally, I want to acknowledge perhaps the largest and most diverse class of participants in this project: the family members, friends, co-workers, social media acquaintances, Twitter readers, rescue hounds, peer curatorial journalists, and passionately engaged fellow citizens whose enthusiasm, advice, and encouragement helped sustain me throughout. Their efforts reminded me, at a time I definitely needed the reminder, that there is no storm that cannot be weathered when those of courage, integrity, and kindness stand together.

NOTES

INTRODUCTION: A THEORY OF THE CASE

1. Emma Loop and Jason Leopold, "Senate Intel Wants to Follow the Money in the Russia Probe," *BuzzFeed News*, August 14, 2018, https://www.buzzfeednews.com/article/emmaloop/senate-intel-wants-to-follow-the-money-in-the-russia-probe.
2. Craig Unger, "Trump's Russian Laundromat," *New Republic*, July 13, 2017, https://newrepublic.com/article/143586/trumps-russian-laundromat-trump-tower-luxury-high-rises-dirty-money-international-crime-syndicate.

CHAPTER ONE: RUSSIA AND THE TRUMPS

1. Oren Dorell, "Donald Trump's ties to Russia go back 30 years," *USA Today*, February 15, 2017, https://www.usatoday.com/story/news/world/2017/02/15/donald-trumps-ties-russia-go-back-30-years/97949746/.
2. The Moscow Project, "Banks refuse to lend to Trump, citing 'the Donald risk.'" https://themoscowproject.org/collusion/banks-refuse-lend-trump-citing-donald-risk/.
3. Susanne Craig and David W. Chen, "Donald Trump Considered Path to Presidency Starting at Governor's Mansion in New York," *New York Times*, March 5, 2016, https://www.nytimes.com/2016/03/06/nyregion/donald-trump-new-york-governor.html.
4. Conor Friedersdorf, "When Donald Trump Became a Celebrity," *Atlantic*, January 2016, https://www.theatlantic.com/politics/archive/2016/01/the-decade-when-donald-trump-became-a-celebrity/422838/; Jonathan Chait, "Will Trump Be Meeting with His Counterpart—Or His Handler?" *New York*, July 2018, http://nymag.com/daily/intelligencer/2018/07/trump-putin-russia-collusion.html.
5. Ibid.
6. Ibid.
7. Ilan Ben-Meir, "That Time Trump Spent Nearly $100,000 On An Ad Criticizing U.S. Foreign Policy," *BuzzFeed News,* July 2015, https://www.buzzfeednews.com/article/ilanbenmeir/that-time-trump-spent-nearly-100000-on-an-ad-criticizing-us.
8. Michael Kruse, "The True Story of Donald Trump's First Campaign Speech—In 1987," *Politico,* February 2016, https://www.politico.com/magazine/story/2016/02/donald-trump-first-campaign-speech-new-hampshire-1987-213595.

9. David Ignatius, "A history of Donald Trump's business dealings in Russia," *Washington Post*, November 2, 2017, https://www.washingtonpost.com/opinions /a-history-of-donald-trumps-business-dealings-in-russia/2017/11/02/fb8eed22 -ba9e-11e7-be94-fabb0f1e9ffb_story.html?utm_term=.72af02b3fd8c.

10. Bryan Hood, "4 Times Donald Trump's Companies Declared Bankruptcy," *Vanity Fair*, June 29, 2015, https://www.vanityfair.com/news/2015/06/donald-trump -companies-bankruptcy-atlantic-city.

11. Ignatius, "A history of Donald Trump's business dealings in Russia."

12. Megan Twohey and Steve Eder, "For Trump, Three Decades of Chasing Deals in Russia," *New York Times*, January 16, 2017, https://www.nytimes.com/2017/01 /16/us/politics/donald-trump-russia-business.html.

13. David Ignatius, "A history of Donald Trump's business dealings in Russia."

14. Twohey and Eder, "For Trump, Three Decades of Chasing Deals in Russia."

15. Susanne Craig, "Trump Boasts of Rapport With Wall St., but the Feeling Is Not Quite Mutual," *New York Times*, May 23, 2016, https://www.nytimes.com/2016 /05/24/business/dealbook/donald-trump-relationship-bankers.html.

16. Mark Singer, "Trump Solo," *New Yorker*, May 19, 1997, https://www.newyorker .com/magazine/1997/05/19/trump-solo.

17. Ibid.

18. "Five prime minsters sacked in Yeltsin's reshuffles," *Irish Times*, August 10, 1999, https://www.irishtimes.com/news/five-prime-ministers-sacked-in-yeltsin-s -many-reshuffles-1.215145.

19. Marcus Warren, "Putin 'rigged Miss Russia contest as policewoman's secret admirer,'" *Telegraph*, April 22, 2001, https://www.telegraph.co.uk/news/world news/europe/russia/1317002/Putin-rigged-Miss-Russia-contest-as-policewomans -secret-admirer.html.

20. Ibid.

21. Ibid.

22. Ibid.

23. Francie Grace, "Russia Wins 1st Miss Universe Title," CBS News, May 30, 2002, https://www.cbsnews.com/news/russia-wins-1st-miss-universe-title/.

24. "Russia Gangster knocks up Miss Universe," *Pravda*, October 1, 2002, http:// www.pravdareport.com/news/russia/01-10-2002/13864-0/.

25. "Vladimir Putin's girl became miss universe," *Pravda*, May 30, 2002, http:// www.pravdareport.com/news/russia/30-05-2002/43486-0/.

26. Personal communication with author, November 2, 2017.

27. Lisa Respers France, "Pageant coordinator quoted as saying Trump picks finalists," CNN, September 2, 2009, http://www.cnn.com/2009/SHOWBIZ/09/02 /trump.pageant.selection/index.html?iref=nextin.

28. Personal communication with author, November 2, 2017.

29. Ibid.

30. Sue Chan, "Deposed Miss Couldn't Give The Time," CBS News, September 23, 2002, https://www.cbsnews.com/news/deposed-miss-couldnt-give-the-time/.

31. Personal communication with author, November 2, 2017.

32. Hazel Heyer, "Executive Talk: Donald Trump Jr. bullish on Russia and few

emerging markets," ETN, September 15, 2008, https://www.eturbonews.com /9788/executive-talk-donald-trump-jr-bullish-russia-and-few-emerging-ma.

33. Caleb Melby and Keri Geiger, "Behind Trump's Russia Romance, There's a Tower Full of Oligarchs," *Bloomberg Businessweek*, March 16, 2017, https://www.bloomberg.com/news/articles/2017-03-16/behind-trump-s-russia-romance -there-s-a-tower-full-of-oligarchs.

34. Lachian Markay and Dean Sterling Jones, "Inside the Online Campaign to Whitewash the History of Donald Trump's Business Associates," *Daily Beast,* July 15, 2018, https://www.thedailybeast.com/inside-the-online-campaign-to -whitewash-donald-trumps-russian-business-ties.

35. Greg Price, "Ivanka Trump Sat In Vladimir Putin's Chair And Spun Around When At Kremlin, President's Former Associates Say,"*Newsweek*, May 17, 2018, https://www.newsweek.com/ivanka-putin-chair-spun-kremlin-931754.

36. Mark Abadi, "Former Trump adviser says in email that he 'arranged for Ivanka to sit in Putin's private chair' during a trip to Moscow,"*Business Insider,* August 28, 2017, https://www.businessinsider.com/ivanka-trump-putin-chair-felix -sater-russia-2017-8.

37. Michael Koenigs, "The controversial residents of Trump Tower," ABC News, February 23, 2018, https://abcnews.go.com/Politics/controversial-residents -trump-tower/story?id=52577191.

38. Jeff Horwitz and Chad Day, "AP Exclusive: Before Trump job, Manfort worked to aid Putin," Associated Press, March 22, 2017, https://www.apnews.com /122aeob5848345faa88108a03de40c5a/Manafort's-plan-to-'greatly-benefit-the -Putin Government?utm_campaign=SocialFlow&utm_source=Twitter&utm_me dium=AP_Politics.

39. Ibid.

40. Rosalind S. Helderman and Tom Hamburger, "Former Mafia-linked figure de-scribes association with Trump," *Washington Post*, May 17, 2016, https://www .washingtonpost.com/politics/former-mafia-linked-figure-describes-association -with-trump/2016/05/17/cec6c2c6-16d3-11e6-aa55-670cabef46eo_story.html ?utm_term=.62c25be47c39.

41. Ibid.

42. Timothy O'Brien, "Trump, Russia and a Shadowy Business Partnership," Bloomberg, June 21, 2017, https://www.bloomberg.com/view/articles/2017-06-21 /trump-russia-and-those-shadowy-sater-deals-at-bayrock.

43. Ibid.

44. Rosalind S. Helderman and Tom Hamburger, "Former Mafia-linked figure de-scribes association with Trump."

45. Tom Hamburger, Rosalind S. Helderman, and Michael Birnbaum, "Inside Trump's financial ties to Russia and his unusual flattery of Vladimir Putin," *Washington Post*, June 17, 2016, https://www.washingtonpost.com/politics/inside -trumps-financial-ties-to-russia-and-his-unusual-flattery-of-vladimir-putin/2016 /06/17/dbdcaac8-31a6-11e6-8ff7-7b6c1998b7ao_story.html?utm_term=.df008 fod1033.

46. Twohey and Eder, "For Trump, Three Decades of Chasing Deals in Russia."

47. Ibid.
48. Ibid.
49. Russ Choma, "The Trump Files: Watch the Trump Vodka Ad Designed for a Russian Audience," *Mother Jones,* July 29, 2016, https://www.motherjones.com /politics/2016/07/trump-files-watch-trump-vodka-ad-designed-russian-audience/.
50. Tony Wong, "Priciest condo in tallest tower goes to youngest billionaire," *Toronto Star*, August 11, 2011, https://www.thestar.com/business/2007/08/11/priciest_condo_in_tallest_tower_goes_to_youngest_billionaire.html.
51. Heidi Brown and Nathan Vardi, "Man of Steel," *Forbes*, March 28, 2005 https:// www.forbes.com/forbes/2005/0328/132.html#3990004e2fc0.
52. Robert Cribb et al., "How every investor lost money on Trump Tower Toronto, but Donald Trump made millions anyway," *Toronto Star*, October 21, 2017, https://www.thestar.com/news/world/2017/10/21/how-every-investor-lost -money-on-trump-tower-toronto-but-donald-trump-made-millions-anyway.html.
53. Rob Barry, Christopher S. Stewart, and Brett Forrest, "Russian State-Run Bank Financed Deal Involving Trump Hotel Partner," *Wall Street Journal*, May 17, 2017, https://www.wsj.com/articles/russian-state-run-bank-financed-deal-involving -trump-hotel-partner-1495031708.
54. Alec Luhn, "Who is Sergei Gorkov, the powerful Russian banker who met Jared Kushner," *Guardian*, June 3, 2017, https://www.theguardian.com/world/2017 /jun/03/sergei-gorkov-russian-banker-jared-kushner.
55. David Filipov et al., "Explanations for Kushner's meeting with head of Kremlin-linked bank don't match," *Washington Post*, June 1, 2017, https://www.washingtonpost.com/politics/explanations-for-kushners-meeting-with-head-of-kremlin -linked-bank-dont-match-up/2017/06/01/dd1bdbb0-460a-11e7-bcde-624ad9417 0ab_story.html?utm_term=.438970db7b77.
56. Ibid.
57. Bob Dreyfuss, "Unpacking a Strange, Violent Connection Between Trump and Putin," *Rolling Stone*, May 11, 2018, https://www.rollingstone.com/politics/pol itics-features/unpacking-a-strange-violent-connection-between-trump-and-putin -630690/.
58. Ibid.
59. Heyer, "Executive Talk: Donald Trump Jr. bullish on Russia and few emerging markets."
60. Ibid.
61. Ibid.
62. Ibid.
63. Ibid.
64. Emily Stewart, "Read: Donald Trump Jr.'s congressional testimony about the Trump Tower Meeting," *Vox,* May 16, 2018, https://www.vox.com/policy-and-pol itics/2018/5/16/17360484/donald-trump-jr-transcript-senate-judiciary-committee.
65. Heyer, "Executive Talk: Donald Trump Jr. bullish on Russia and few emerging markets."
66. Ibid.

67. Ibid.

68. Ibid.

69. Melby and Geiger, "Behind Trump's Russia Romance, There's a Tower Full of Oligarchs."

70. Craig Unger, "Trump's Russian Laundromat," *New Republic*, July 13, 2017, https://newrepublic.com/article/143586/trumps-russian-laundromat-trump-tower -luxury-high-rises-dirty-money-international-crime-syndicate.

71. Michael Crowley, "Trump and the Oligarch," *Politico,* July 28, 2016, https:// www.politico.com/magazine/story/2016/07/donald-trump-2016-russian-ties-21 4116.

72. Ibid.

73. Ibid.

74. Ibid.

75. Kevin G. Hall et al., "Trump, Russian billionaire say they've never met, but their jets did—in Charlotte," *Charlotte Observer*, March 7, 2017, https://www.char lotteobserver.com/news/politics-government/article136940273.html.

76. Ibid.

77. Ibid.

78. Ibid.

79. Ibid.

80. Nathan Layne et al., "Special Report: Russian elite invested nearly $100 million in Trump buildings, records show," Reuters, March 17, 2017, https://www.reu ters.com/article/us-usa-trump-property-specialreport-idUSKBN16O2F6.

81. Z. Byron Wolf, "Russia's oligarchs are different from other billionaires," CNN, April 6, 2018, https://www.cnn.com/2018/04/06/politics/oligarch-russia-billion aires-government-putin-sanctions/index.html.

82. Howard Adelman, "Two More Eastern Israeli Billionaires: Mashkevich and Rabinovich," Howardadelman.com, June 5, 2006, https://howardadelman.com /2013/05/06/two-more-eastern-european-israeli-billionaires-mashkevich-and-rabino vich-02-05-13/.

83. Marc Champion, "How a Trump Soho Partner Ended Up With Toxic Mining Riches From Kazakhstan," Bloomberg, January 11, 2018, https://www.bloom berg.com/news/features/2018-01-11/how-a-trump-soho-partner-ended-up-with -toxic-mining-riches-from-kazakhstan.

84. Jesse Eisenger et al., "Ivanka and Donald Trump Were Close to Being Charged With Felony Fraud," *ProPublica*, October 4, 2017, https://www.propublica.org /article/ivanka-donald-trump-jr-close-to-being-charged-felony-fraud.

85. Tina Nguyen, "Eric Trump Reportedly Bragged About Access to $100 million in Russian Money," *Vanity Fair*, May 8, 2017, https://www.vanityfair.com/news /2017/05/eric-trump-russia-investment-golf-course.

86. Unger, "Trump's Russian Laundromat."

87. FBI, https://www.fbi.gov/wanted/topten/topten-history/hires_images/FBI-494-Se mionMogilevich.jpg/view, retrieved August 16, 2018.

88. Singer, "Trump Solo."

89. Kevin Hall and Ben Weider, "Trump dreamed of his name on towers across former Soviet Union," *McClatchy*, June 28, 2017, https://www.mcclatchydc.com/news/nation-world/national/article158518589.html.

90. Shane Harris, "Signs of Trump-Putin collaboration, starting years before the campaign?" *Washington Post*, August 17, 2018, https://www.washingtonpost.com/outlook/is-there-a-case-for-trump-putin-collaboration-years-before-the-campaign/2018/08/16/00578f1e-9440-11e8-80e1-00e80e1fdf43_story.html?utm_term=.04a8ad6b2b6a.

91. Ibid.

92. Jessica Durando, "Trump says 'I have nothing to do with Russia.' That's not exactly true," *USA Today*, January 11, 2017, https://www.usatoday.com/story/news/world/2017/01/11/donald-trump-russia-vladimir-putin/96444482/.

93. Ben Protess et al., "Mueller Wants Trump's Business Records. What's the Russia Connection?" *New York Times*, March 17, 2018, https://www.nytimes.com/2018/03/17/business/trump-organization-russia-mueller.html.

94. Ibid.

95. Ignatius, "A history of Trump's business dealings in Russia."

96. Amy Cheng and Humza Jilani, "Trump on Putin:The U.S. President's View, In His Own Words," *Foreign Policy,* July 18, 2018, https://foreignpolicy.com/2018/07/18/trump-on-putin-the-u-s-president-in-his-own-words/.

97. Jill Colvin, "Have Trump and Putin met before? It depends when you asked," Associated Press, July 7, 2017, https://www.apnews.com/ff6f1043180d490bb1f3c3d07fa26d45.

98. Ibid.

99. Ibid.

100. Ibid.

101. Charlotte Alter, "Here's the Deal with That *60 Minutes* Episode Trump Mentioned," *Time,* November 11, 2015, http://time.com/4108198/donald-trump-60-minutes-putin/.

102. Colvin, "Have Trump and Putin met before? It depends when you asked."

103. Ibid.

104. Ibid.

105. Ibid.

106. "Trump Rule—Hot Chicks Required in Miss USA," TMZ, November 12, 2009, http://www.tmz.com/2009/11/12/trump-rule-hot-chicks-required-in-miss-usa/; Tessa Stuart, "A Timeline of Donald Trump's Creepiness While H Owned Miss Universe," *Rolling Stone*, October 12, 2016, https://www.rollingstone.com/politics/politics-features/a-timeline-of-donald-trumps-creepiness-while-he-owned-miss-universe-191860/.

107. Ibid.

108. Joshua Cinelli, "Donald Trump's hand-picked Miss Universe: Choreographer spills on "rigged" selection process," *New York Daily News*, September 2, 2009, http://www.nydailynews.com/news/national/donald-trump-hand-picked-universe-choreographer-spills-rigged-selection-process-article-1.403667.

109. Jessica Kwong, "Trump Eliminated Miss Universe Finalists Who Were 'Too

Ethnic' or 'Snubbed His Advances,' Pageant Staff Claim," *Newsweek,* March 8, 2018, https://www.newsweek.com/trump-miss-universe-women-ethnic-837139.

110. Stuart, "A Timeline of Donald Trump's Creepiness While He Owned Miss Universe."

111. Ibid.

112. Jenna Johnson, "Trump attacks former Miss Universe who 'gained a massive amount of weight' and had 'attitude'" *Washington Post,* September 17, 2016, https://www.washingtonpost.com/news/post-politics/wp/2016/09/27/trump-attacks-former-miss-universe-who-gained-a-massive-amount-of-weight-and-had-attitude/?utm_term=.895fd5ac86ae.

113. "I'm not married, says dethroned Miss Universe," *Sydney Morning Herald,* September 25, 2002, https://www.smh.com.au/lifestyle/fashion/im-not-married-says-dethroned-miss-universe-20020925-gdfnw7.html.

114. Ibid.

115. Ibid.

116. Ibid.

117. Ibid.

118. Ibid.

119. Andrew Rice, "The Original Russia Connection," *New York,* August 7, 2017, http://nymag.com/daily/intelligencer/2017/08/felix-sater-donald-trump-russia-investigation.html; Bob Dreyfuss, "Who Is Felix Sater, and Why Is Donald Trump So Afraid of Him?" *Nation,* September 8, 2017, https://www.thenation.com/article/who-is-felix-sater-and-why-is-donald-trump-so-afraid-of-him/.

120. Ibid.

121. "Trump picked Mafia-linked stock fraud felon as senior adviser," *Chicago Tribune,* December 4, 2015, http://www.chicagotribune.com/news/nationworld/politics/ct-trump-felix-sater-felon-adviser-20151204-story.html.

122. Richard Behar, "Donald Trump and the Felon: Inside His Business Dealings with a Mob-Connected Hustler," *Forbes,* October 25, 2016, https://www.forbes.com/sites/richardbehar/2016/10/03/donald-trump-and-the-felon-inside-his-business-dealings-with-a-mob-connected-hustler/.

123. Ibid.

124. Luke Harding, *Collusion* (New York: Vintage Books, 2017), p. 292.

125. Ibid., pp. 291–92.

126. Ibid.

127. O'Brien, "Trump, Russia and a Shadowy Business Partnership."

128. Martin Longman, "Trump's Soho Project, The Mob, and Russian Intelligence," *Washington Monthly,* February 20, 2017, https://washingtonmonthly.com/2017/02/20/trumps-soho-project-the-mob-and-russian-intelligence/; Martin Longman, "The Odd Chabad Connection Between Trump and Putin," *Washington Monthly,* November 27, 2017, https://washingtonmonthly.com/2017/11/27/the-odd-chabad-connection-between-putin-and-trump/.

129. Konrad Putzier, "Hotel trio aims to bring Manhattan to Moscow," *Real Estate Weekly,* November 12, 2013, https://rew-online.com/hotel-trio-aims-to-bring-manhattan-to-moscow/.

130. Behar, "Donald Trump and the Felon."

131. Carol D. Leonig et al., "Trump's business sought deal on a Trump Tower in Moscow while he ran for president," *Washington Post*, August 27, 2017, https://www .washingtonpost.com/politics/trumps-business-sought-deal-on-a-trump-tower-in -moscow-while-he-ran-for-president/2017/08/27/d6e95114-8b65-11e7-91d5-ab 4e4bb76a3a_story.html?utm_term=.17a015b794cd.

132. Abadi, "Former Trump adviser says in email that he 'arranged for Ivanka to sit in Putin's private chair' during a trip to Moscow."

133. Michael Kranish et al., "Michael Cohen, once at pinnacle of Trump's world, now poses threat to it," *Washington Post*, April 21, 2018, https://www.washing tonpost.com/politics/michael-cohen-once-at-pinnacle-of-trumps-world-now-poses -threat-to-it/2018/04/21/efb1c9c6-3cd4-11e8-974f-aacd97698cef_story.html?no redirect=on&utm_term=.50d4d5024384.

134. Ibid.

135. Pete Madden and Meghan Keneally, "Soviet-born Donald Trump adviser Felix Sater: 'Send 'em to jail' if Robert Mueller finds collusion," ABC News, March 16, 2018, https://abcnews.go.com/Politics/soviet-born-donald-trump-ad viser-felix-sater-send/story?id=53790920.

136. Ibid.

137. Alec Luhn, "15 years of Vladimir Putin: 15 ways he has changed Russia and the world," *Guardian*, May 6, 2015, https://www.theguardian.com/world/2015/may /06/vladimir-putin-15-ways-he-changed-russia-world.

138. Marial Synan, "What is the largest country in the world?" The History Channel (retrieved September 10, 2018), https://www.history.com/news/what-is-the-larg est-country-in-the-world.

139. Linda Qiu, "Does Vladimir Putin kill journalists?", PolitiFact, January 2016, https://www.politifact.com/punditfact/article/2016/jan/04/does-vladimir-putin-kill -journalists/.

140. Ibid.

141. "Vladimir Putin condemns 'tragedy' of Soviet-era political repression," *Irish Independent,* October 30,2017, https://www.independent.ie/world-news/vladimir -putin-condemns-tragedy-of-sovietera-political-repression-36274601.html.

142. Moritz Pfeiffer, "Confessions of a Witness," *East European Film Bulletin* 86 (Summer 2018), https://eefb.org/perspectives/vitaly-manskys-putins-witnesses -svideteli-putina-2018/; Sarah Rainsford, "Boris Nemtsov murder: Five Chechens jailed for attack," BBC News, July 13, 2017, https://www.bbc.com/news /world-europe-40592248.

143. Ibid., BBC News; Ivan Nechepurenko, "5 Who Killed Boris Nemtsov, Putin Foe, Sentenced in Russia," *New York Times,* July 13, 2017, https://www.nytimes.com /2017/07/13/world/europe/boris-nemtsov-putin-russia.html; David M. Herszenhorn, "Chechen's Ties to Putin Are Questioned Amid Nemtsov Case," *New York Times,* March 9, 2015, https://www.nytimes.com/2015/03/20/world/europe /chechens-ties-to-putin-are-questioned-amid-nemtsov-murder-case.html.

144. Max Bearak, "Who did Manafort and Gates work for in Ukraine and Rus-

sia?" Washington Post, October 30, 2017, https://www.washingtonpost.com news/worldviews/wp/2017/10/30/who-did-manafort-and-gates-work-for-in -ukraine-and-russia/?utm_term=.e6dcff68d831; Sophie Pinkham, "How annexing Crimea allowed Putin to claim he had made Russia great again," *Guardian*, March 22, 2017, https://www.theguardian.com/commentisfree/2017/mar/22/an nexing-crimea-putin-make-russia-great-again.

145. Edward Hunter Christie, "Sanctions after Crimea: Have they worked?" NATO Review, 2015, https://www.nato.int/docu/review/2015/russia/sanctions-after -crimea-have-they-worked/EN/index.htm.

146. John W. Schoen, "U.S. sanctions have taken a big bite out of Russia's economy," CNBC, July 25, 2017, https://www.cnbc.com/2017/07/25/us-sanctions-have -taken-a-big-bite-out-of-russias-economy.html.

147. Ibid.

148. Layne et al., "Special Report: Russian elite invested nearly $100 million in Trump buildings, records show."

149. Eileen Kinsella, "Why Did the Firm Behind the Trump-Russia Dossier Implicate Art Collector Dmitry Rybolovlev in Its Testimony?" *ArtNet News*, January 23, 2018, https://news.artnet.com/art-world/why-did-fusion-gps-drag-russian-bil lionaire-dmitry-rybolovlev-into-trump-testimony-1204088.

150. Marcus Warren, "Putin 'rigged Miss Russia contest as policewoman's secret admirer.' "

151. Ibid.

152. Ibid.

153. Braden Kell, "Behind The 'Miss' Fire Booted Beauty's Moscow's Mysteries," *New York Post*, September 29, 2002, https://nypost.com/2002/09/29/behind-the -miss-fire-booted-beautys-moscow-mysteries/.

154. Ibid.

155. Ibid.

156. Chan, "Deposed Miss Couldn't Give The Time."

157. Ibid.

158. Ibid.

159. Ibid.

160. Ursula Hirschkorn, "Death threats to drug busts: Top ten dethroned beauty queens," *Daily Mail*, November 29, 2009, http://www.dailymail.co.uk/femail/ar ticle-1231484/Death-threats-drug-busts-Top-dethroned-beauty-queens.html.

161. Daniel Tovrov, "Miss Universe Scandal: Could Leila Lopes Lose the Crown?" *International Business Times*, September 18, 2011, https://www.ibtimes.com /miss-universe-scandal-could-leila-lopes-lose-crown-314898.

162. *The Howard Stern Show*, YouTube (at 3:10), https://www.youtube.com/watch ?v=zR_ysGc-Aas&t=.

163. Ibid.

164. Ibid.

165. Aletha Adu, "Russian Miss Universe slams Western media for 'harassing her to DERAIL Trump's campaign,' " *Express*, November 10, 2016, https://www.ex

press.co.uk/news/world/730704/Russia-Miss-Universe-Vladimir-Putin-Donald
-Trump-Western-media-President-Oxana-Fedorova.
166. Ibid.
167. Pomah Kytysob, "Sellers of Vodka and Toilets Became Kings of Real Estate of
St. Petersburg," *Forbes Russia*, February 13, 2013, http://www.forbes.ru/kom
panii/potrebitelskii-rynok/234215-kak-prodavtsy-vodki-i-unitazov-stali-korolyami
-nedvizhimosti-sa.
168. Ibid.
169. Ibid.
170. Ibid.
171. "Russia Gangster knocks up Miss Universe."
172. Ibid.
173. France, "Pageant coordinator quoted as saying Trump picks finalists."
174. Ibid.
175. 47 U.S.C. § 509, https://www.law.cornell.edu/uscode/text/47/509.
176. Ibid.
177. Gary Kasparov, "Putin's Sochi and Hitler's Berlin: The Love Affair Between
Dictators and the Olympic Games," *Daily Beast,* February 7, 2014, https://www
.thedailybeast.com/putins-sochi-and-hitlers-berlin-the-love-affair-between-dic
tators-and-the-olympic-games.
178. Bill Powell, "Donald Trump Associate Felix Sater Is Linked to the Mob and the
CIA—What's His Role in the Russia Investigation?" *Newsweek*, June 7, 2018,
https://www.newsweek.com/2018/06/15/sater-963255.html.
179. Dreyfuss, "Who Is Felix Sater, and Why Is Donald Trump So Afraid of Him?"
180. Rice, "The Original Russia Connection."
181. Helderman and Hamburger, "Former Mafia-linked figure describes association
with Trump"; Stephanie Kirchgaessner and Julian Borger, "Felix Sater: the enig-
matic businessman at the heart of the Trump-Russia inquiry," *Guardian,* August
31, 2017, https://www.theguardian.com/us-news/2017/aug/31/felix-sater-trump
-russia-investigation.
182. Madden and Keneally, "Soviet-born Donald Trump adviser Felix Sater."
183. Paul Wood, "Forget Charlottesville—Russia is still the true Trump scandal,"
Spectator, August 19, 2017, https://www.spectator.co.uk/2017/08/forget-charlot
tesville-russia-is-still-the-true-trump-scandal/.
184. Ibid.
185. Ibid.
186. Ibid.
187. Ben Wieder and Kevin G. Hall, "Colorful Trump associate Sater will cooperate with Feinstein request," *McClatchy*, November 15, 2017, https://www.mc
clatchydc.com/news/nation-world/national/article184887318.html.
188. Rice, "The Original Russia Connection."
189. Nguyen, "Eric Trump Reportedly Bragged About Access to $100 million in Rus-
sian Money."
190. Ibid.
191. Mark Moore, "Eric Trump said dad's golf courses funded by Russia: report,"

New York Post, May 7, 2017, https://nypost.com/2017/05/07/eric-trump-said
-dads-golf-courses-were-funded-by-russia.

192. Nguyen, "Eric Trump Reportedly Bragged About Access to $100 million in Russian Money."

193. Layne et al., "Special Report: Russian elite invested nearly $100 million in Trump buildings, records show."

CHAPTER TWO: TRUMP AND THE AGALAROVS

1. Noah Kirsch, "The Full Exclusive Interview: Emin Agalarov, Russian Scion at Center of Trump Controversy," *Forbes*, July 12, 2017, https://www.forbes.com/sites/noahkirsch/2017/07/12/the-full-exclusive-interview-emin-agalarov-russian-donald-trump-jr-controversy/#40ccf15e69d0.

2. Andrew Roth, "The Man Who Drives Trump's Russia Connection," *Washington Post*, July 22, 2017, https://www.washingtonpost.com/world/europe/the-man-who-drives-trumps-russia-connection/2017/07/21/43485a0e-6c98-11e7-abbc-a53480672286_story.html?utm_term=.35742516ba1f.

3. David Corn and Hannah Levintova, "How Did an Alleged Russian Mobster End Up on Trump's Red Carpet?" *Mother Jones*, September 14, 2016, https://www.motherjones.com/politics/2016/09/trump-russian-mobster-tokhtakhounov-miss-universe-moscow/; Nataliya Vasilyeva, "Russian Real Estate Deals Never Materialized for Trump," *Morning Journal*/Associated Press, March 4, 2017, http://www.morningjournal.com/article/MJ/20170304/NEWS/170309725.

4. "2012. EMIN - AMOR ft. Miss Universe 2012 Olivia Culpo (Official Video)," YouTube, https://www.youtube.com/watch?v=r-O8XR060_E.

5. Kirsch, "The Full Exclusive Interview."

6. Mark Hosenball and Jonathan Landay, "U.S. Lawmakers Question Businessman at 2016 Trump Tower Meeting: Sources," Reuters, December 26, 2017, https://www.reuters.com/article/us-usa-trump-russia-kaveladze/u-s-lawmakers-question-businessman-at-2016-trump-tower-meeting-sources-idUSKBN1EL009; Isaac Chotiner, "What Happened in Vegas," *Slate*, March 15, 2018, https://slate.com/news-and-politics/2018/03/david-corn-and-michael-isikoff-on-their-las-vegas-revelations.html; Jon Swaine and Shaun Walker, "Trump in Moscow: What Happened at Miss Universe in 2013," *Guardian*, September 18, 2017, https://www.theguardian.com/us-news/2017/sep/18/trump-in-moscow-what-happened-at-miss-universe-in-2013.

7. Swaine and Walker, "Trump in Moscow."

8. Ibid.

9. Raymond Bonner, "Laundering of Money Seen as 'Easy,'" *New York Times*, November 29, 2000, https://www.nytimes.com/2000/11/29/business/laundering-of-money-seen-as-easy.html?referer=https://t.co/kVU9K2qVHO%3famp=1.

10. Swaine and Walker, "Trump in Moscow."

11. Yulya Alferova, "Trump and Agalarov Agree," LiveJournal, June 17, 2013, https://alferova-yulya.livejournal.com/169017.html.

12. Swaine and Walker, "Trump in Moscow."

13. Ibid.

14. David Corn and Michael Isikoff, "What Happened in Moscow: The Inside Story of How Trump's Obsession with Putin Began," *Mother Jones*, March 8, 2018, https://www.motherjones.com/politics/2018/03/russian-connection-what-happened-moscow-inside-story-trump-obsession-putin-david-corn-michael-isikoff/.

15. Mollie Simon and Jim Zarroli, "Timeline of Events: The 2013 Miss Universe Pageant," NPR, July 17, 2017, https://www.npr.org/2017/07/17/536714404/timeline-of-events-the-2013-miss-universe-pageant.

16. Michael Crowley, "When Donald Trump Brought Miss Universe to Moscow," *Politico,* May 15, 2016, https://www.politico.com/story/2016/05/donald-trump-russia-moscow-miss-universe-223173.

17. Cheyenne Roundtree, "Donald Trump hand-picked finalists for Miss Universe from countries he targeted to swing deals and hosted the contest in cities where he already had a financial stake, former contestants claim," *Daily Mail*, February 19, 2018, http://www.dailymail.co.uk/news/article-5409329/Trump-chose-Miss-Universe-finalists-based-business.html; Jeffrey Toobin, "Trump's Miss Universe Gambit," *New Yorker*, February 26, 2018, https://www.newyorker.com/magazine/2018/02/26/trumps-miss-universe-gambit?reload=true.

18. Roundtree, "Donald Trump hand-picked."

19. Toobin, "Trump's Miss Universe Gambit."

20. Katie Rogers, "How Trump's Miss Universe in Russia Became Ensnared in a Political Inquiry," *New York Times*, July 11, 2017, https://www.nytimes.com/2017/07/11/us/politics/how-trumps-miss-universe-in-russia-became-ensnared-in-a-political-inquiry.html; Shane Harris et al., "In a Personal Letter, Trump Invited Putin to the 2013 Miss Universe Pageant," *Washington Post*, March 3, 2018, https://www.washingtonpost.com/world/national-security/in-a-personal-letter-trump-invited-putin-to-the-2013-miss-universe-pageant/2018/03/09/a3404358-23d2-11e8-a589-763893265565_story.html?utm_term=.45f15b7697a4.

21. Ibid.

22. Ibid.

23. Ibid.

24. Swaine and Walker, "Trump in Moscow."

25. Ibid.

26. Ibid.

27. Tea Party Patriots, American Conservative Union, "CPAC 2014—Donald Trump, Chairman and President of the Trump Organization, speaks at CPAC 2014 on March 6, 2014," YouTube, https://www.youtube.com/watch?v=3nzaemPHSU0.

28. Michal Kranz, "Trump Received a Mysterious Letter from Putin in 2013—and No One Knows What Was in It," *Business Insider,* March 8, 2018, https://www.businessinsider.com/trump-2013-letter-from-putin-2018-3; Harris et al., "In a Personal Letter, Trump Invited Putin"; Kevin Sullivan, "Trump's Foreign Network," *Washington Post*, January 13, 2017, https://www.washingtonpost.com/sf/world/2017/01/13/trumps-foreign-network/?utm_term=.9e608b8d9af9.

29. Kranz, "Trump Received a Mysterious Letter from Putin in 2013."

30. Erica R. Hendry, "The Many Different Ways Trump Has Described Putin and

Russian Election Interference," PBS, July 16, 2018, https://www.pbs.org/news
hour/politics/the-many-different-ways-trump-has-described-putin-and-russian
-election-interference.

31. Tom Arnold (@TomArnold), "Wrong. Putin called Trump at Moscow Ritz Nov
2013. Trump put on speakerphone for everyone to hear. Putin congratulated
Trump on Trump Tower Moscow & encouraged Trump to run for President &
offered Russia's support. It's all on tape dude. #MuellerIsComing," Twitter, February 22, 2018, 4:28 a.m., https://twitter.com/tomarnold/status/966832062132
080642?lang=en.

32. Swaine and Walker, "Trump in Moscow."

33. Svetlana Reiter, "Exclusive: Putin's Ex-Wife Linked to Multi-Million-Dollar
Property Business," Reuters, May 19, 2017, https://www.reuters.com/article/us
-russia-putin-foundation-idUSKCN18F0QX?u.

34. Michael Isikoff and David Corn, *Russian Roulette: The Inside Story of Putin's
War on America and the Election of Donald Trump* (New York: Twelve, 2018).

35. Vicky Ward, "Michael Cohen Speaks: Trump Exec Admits Russia Dealings
Were Gross, but Not Illegal," *Huffington Post,* August 30, 2017, https://www.huff
ingtonpost.com/entry/michael-cohen-trump-lawyer-russia_us_59a71a28e4b010
ca2899e933.

36. Kranz, "Trump Received a Mysterious Letter from Putin in 2013."

37. Corn and Levintova, "How Did an Alleged Russian Mobster End Up on Trump's
Red Carpet?"

38. Ibid.

39. Ibid.

40. Ibid.

41. "Donald Trump Planning Skyscraper in Moscow," *Moscow Times*, November 12,
2013, https://themoscowtimes.com/articles/donald-trump-planning-skyscraper
-in-moscow-29441; "Sberbank Funds $2.4 Billion Construction at Crocus City,"
Moscow Times, November 19, 2013, https://themoscowtimes.com/articles/sber
bank-funds-24-billion-construction-at-crocus-city-29740.

42. Swaine and Walker, "Trump in Moscow"; Vasilyeva, "Russian Real Estate Deals
Never Materialized for Trump."

43. Alex Pfeiffer, "Former Trump Adviser Tells a Story about the President-Elect
and Prostitutes," *Daily Caller,* January 14, 2017, http://dailycaller.com/2017/01
/14/former-trump-adviser-tells-a-story-about-the-president-elect-and-prostitutes/;
Chuck Ross, "Trump Bodyguard Testifies Russian Offered 'Five Women' to
Trump, Was Rejected," *Daily Caller,* November 9, 2017, http://dailycaller.com
/2017/11/09/report-trump-bodyguard-testifies-russian-offered-five-women-to
-trump-was-rejected/.

44. Donald J. Trump (@realDonaldTrump), "I just got back from Russia-learned lots
& lots. Moscow is a very interesting and amazing place! U.S. MUST BE VERY
SMART AND VERY STRATEGIC," Twitter, November 10, 2013 6:44 p.m.,
https://twitter.com/realdonaldtrump/status/399729261684490240?lang=en.

45. Donald J. Trump (@realDonaldTrump), "@AgalarovAras I had a great weekend
with you and your family. You have done a FANTASTIC job. TRUMP TOWER

-MOSCOW is next. EMIN was WOW!" Twitter, November 11, 2013, 8:39 a.m., https://twitter.com/realdonaldtrump/status/399939505924628480?lang=en.

46. Susanne Craig and David W. Chen, "Donald Trump Considered Path to Presidency Starting at Governor's Mansion in New York," *New York Times*, March 6, 2016, https://www.nytimes.com/2016/03/06/nyregion/donald-trump-new-york -governor.html.

47. Michael Isikoff, "Inside Bannon's next campaign: Keep the House to save Trump," *Skullduggery*, August 3, 2018, https://www.yahoo.com/lifestyle/inside -bannons-next-campaign-keep-house-save-trump-090037613.html.

48. Yulya Alferova (@Yulya AlferovaE), "'@ell7654321: @realDonaldTrump If u run for president u have my vote' Remember that!" Twitter, March 30, 2014, 1:17 a.m., https://twitter.com/AlferovaYulyaE?lang=en&lang=en.

49. Yulya Alferova (@Yulya AlferovaE), retweet from Donald J. Trump (@realDonaldTrump), "The situation with Russia is much more dangerous than most people may think - and could lead to World War III. WE NEED GREAT LEADERSHIP FAST," Twitter, March 22, 2014 6:23 a.m., https://twitter.com /AlferovaYulyaE?lang=en&lang=en.

50. Alferova, Twitter, March 30, 2014, 1:17 a.m.

51. Kirsch, "The Full Exclusive Interview"; Emily Stewart, "Read: Donald Trump Jr.'s Congressional Testimony about the Trump Tower Meeting," *Vox,* May 16, 2018 (Donald Trump Jr. testimony, pg. 32), https://www.vox.com/pol icy-and-politics/2018/5/16/17360484/donald-trump-jr-transcript-senate-judi ciary-committee; Ivanka Trump (Ivankatrump), "ivankatrump Moscow," Instagram photo, February 3, 2014, https://www.instagram.com/p/j9eJV4ikAI/.

52. Damien Sharkov, "Neither Vladimir Putin Nor His Staff Have Ever Spoken to Trump: Kremlin," *Newsweek*, August 3, 2016, https://www.newsweek.com/nei ther-putin-nor-his-staff-have-ever-spoken-trump-kremlin-486712.

53. Corn and Isikoff, "What Happened in Moscow."

54. Eugene Robinson, "Is Donald Trump Just Plain Crazy?" *Washington Post*, August 1, 2016, https://www.washingtonpost.com/opinions/is-donald-trump-just -plain-crazy/2016/08/01/cd171e86-581d-11e6-831d-0324760ca856_story.html ?utm_term=.bec6910faab3.

55. Donald Trump, "Building the Trump Brand," speech, Washington, D.C., May 27, 2014, National Press Club, https://www.press.org/events/npc-luncheon-donald -trump-chairman-and-president-trump-organization; Transcript: C-Span https:// www.c-span.org/video/?319570-1/donald-trump-national-press-club-speech.

56. Pfeiffer, "Former Trump Adviser Tells a Story about the President-Elect and Prostitutes."

57. Scott Shane et al., "How a Sensational, Unverified Dossier Became a Crisis for Donald Trump," *New York Times*, January 11, 2017, https://www.nytimes.com /2017/01/11/us/politics/donald-trump-russia-intelligence.html?rref=collection %2Fbyline%2Fnicholas-confessore&action=click&contentCollection=unde fined&region=stream&module=stream_unit&version=latest&contentPlacement =2&pgtype=collection.

58. Adam Entous et al., "Clinton campaign, DNC paid for research that led to Russia dossier," *Washington Post*, October 24, 2017, https://www.washingtonpost.com/world/national-security/clinton-campaign-dnc-paid-for-research-that-led-to-rus sia-dossier/2017/10/24/226fabf0-b8e4-11e7-a908-a3470754bbb9_story.html?utm_term=.20253e4063af.

59. Donald J. Trump (@realDonaldTrump), "Workers of firm involved with the discredited and Fake Dossier take the 5th. Who paid for it, Russia, the FBI or the Dems (or all)?" Twitter, October 19, 2017, 4:45 a.m., https://twitter.com/real donaldtrump/status/920981920787386368.

60. Ken Bensinger et al., "These Reports Allege Trump Has Deep Ties to Russia," *BuzzFeed News,* January 10, 2017, https://www.buzzfeednews.com/article/ken bensinger/these-reports-allege-trump-has-deep-ties-to-russia.

61. Ibid.

62. Ibid.

63. "Russians abandon plans for Trump Tower construction in Moscow region," Construction.ru, February 17, 2017, http://russianconstruction.com/news-1/26505-russians-abandon-plans-for-trump-tower-construction-in-moscow-region.html.

64. Ibid.

65. Kirsch, "The Full Exclusive Interview."

66. Emily Stewart, "Trump is 'definitely still involved' in his hotel business, a new report says," *Vox,* December 30, 2017, https://www.vox.com/2017/12/30/168329 64/trump-business-washington-hotel.

67. Page Six Team, "Trump Researching 2016 Run," *New York Post*, May 27, 2013, https://pagesix.com/2013/05/27/trump-researching-2016-run/.

68. Kevin Robillard, "Report: Trump spends $1M on 2016 research," *Politico*, May 27, 2013, https://www.politico.com/blogs/click/2013/05/report-trump-spends-1m-on-2016-research-164818.

69. Page Six Team, "Trump Researching 2016 Run."

70. Yulya Alferova (@AlferovaYulyaE), "I'm tweeting, Donald Trump @real DonaldTrump is talking . . . Again and again about Obama))," Twitter, November 9, 2013, 7:24 a.m. Moscow, https://twitter.com/alferovayulyae/status/39919 5775185731584?lang=en.

71. Anna Nemtsova, "She Met Donald Trump at the Moscow Ritz (Not That Way!)," *Daily Beast,* January 20, 2017, https://www.thedailybeast.com/she-met-donald-trump-at-the-moscow-ritz-not-that-way.

72. Will Stewart, "Exclusive: the oligarch who brings Putin 'solutions not problems'—how billionaire tycoon at center of meeting with Don Jr is Russian leader's go-to for tough projects (like wooing Trump)," *Daily Mail*, July 13, 2017, http://www.dailymail.co.uk/news/article-4690806/Agalarov-s-relationship-Trump-manna-Putin.html.

73. Ibid.

74. Ibid.

75. Roth, "The Man Who Drives Trump's Russia Connection."

76. Neil MacFarquhar, "A Russian Developer Helps Out the Kremlin on Occasion. Was He a Conduit to Trump?" *New York Times*, July 16, 2017, https://www.nytimes.com/2017/07/16/world/europe/aras-agalarov-trump-kremlin.html.

77. Ibid.

78. Ibid. The "outside" header on the main page of the *Times* has additional text for the same article: https://archive.nytimes.com/www.nytimes.com/indexes/2017/07/17/todayspaper/index.html.

79. Stewart, "Exclusive: The oligarch who brings Putin 'solutions not problems.'"

80. "Azerbaijan Corruption Report," GAN Business Anti-Corruption Portal, July 2016, https://www.business-anti-corruption.com/country-profiles/azerbaijan/; Adam Davidson, "Donald Trump's Worst Deal," *New Yorker*, March 13, 2017, https://www.newyorker.com/magazine/2017/03/13/donald-trumps-worst-deal; Adam Davidson, "Trump's Business of Corruption," *New Yorker*, August 21, 2017, https://www.newyorker.com/magazine/2017/08/21/trumps-business-of-corruption; Veronika Bondarenko, "Donald Trump's Hotel in Azerbaijan Linked with Corruption, Iran's Revolutionary Guard," *Business Insider,* March 6, 2017, https://www.businessinsider.com/donald-trumps-azerbaijan-hotel-linked-with-corruption-iran-2017-3; Andrew E. Kramer, "Former Trump Tower in Azerbaijan, Dogged by Controversy, Is Engulfed by Fire," *New York Times*, April 28, 2018, https://www.nytimes.com/2018/04/28/world/asia/fire-trump-tower-azerbaijan.html.

81. Davidson, "Donald Trump's Worst Deal"; Davidson, "Trump's Business of Corruption"; Bondarenko, "Donald Trump's Hotel in Azerbaijan"; Kramer, "Former Trump Tower in Azerbaijan."

82. Matthew Yglesias, "Donald Trump's fishy behavior on Russia is bigger than possible email collusion," *Vox*, July 11, 2017, https://www.vox.com/policy-and-politics/2017/7/11/15947434/something-weird-donald-trump-russia.

83. Crowley, "When Donald Trump Brought Miss Universe to Moscow."

84. "Donald Trump's Tweet About "Best Friend Putin" Is Most Retweeted From Final Debate," *Hollywood Reporter*, October 19, 2016, https://www.hollywoodreporter.com/news/donald-trumps-tweet-best-friend-939986.

85. Stewart, "Exclusive: The Oligarch Who Brings Putin Solutions."

86. Ibid.

87. Corn and Isikoff, "What Happened in Moscow."

88. Ibid.

89. Ibid.

90. Ibid.

91. Kirsch, "The Full Exclusive Interview."

92. Harris et al., "In a Personal Letter, Trump Invited Putin."

93. Evgenia Pismennaya, "The Day Trump Came to Moscow: Oligarchs, Miss Universe and Nobu," Bloomberg, December 21, 2016, https://www.bloomberg.com/news/articles/2016-12-21/the-day-trump-came-to-moscow-oligarchs-miss-universe-and-nobu.

94. Andrew Kaczynski, "80 Times Trump Talked about Putin," CNN, March 21, 2017, https://www.cnn.com/interactive/2017/03/politics/trump-putin-russia-timeline/.

95. Megan Twohey and Steve Eder, "For Trump, Three Decades of Chasing Deals in Russia," *New York Times*, January 16, 2017, https://www.nytimes.com/2017/01/16/us/politics/donald-trump-russia-business.html; "Excerpts From The Times' Interview with Trump," *New York Times*, July 19, 2017, https://www.nytimes.com/2017/07/19/us/politics/trump-interview-transcript.html.

96. Twohey and Eder, "For Trump, Three Decades of Chasing Deals in Russia."

97. Martin Longman, "The Odd Chabad Connection Between Putin and Trump," *Washington Monthly*, November 27, 2017, https://washingtonmonthly.com/2017/11/27/the-odd-chabad-connection-between-putin-and-trump/.

98. David B. Green, "Who Is Lev Leview, the Israeli Billionaire with Ties to Jared Kushner and Putin," *Haaretz*, July 25, 2017, https://www.haaretz.com/us-news/who-is-the-israeli-billionaire-with-ties-to-kushner-and-putin-1.5435007.

99. Konrad Putzier, "Hotel Trio Aims to Bring Manhattan to Moscow," *Real Estate Weekly*, November 12, 2013, http://rew-online.com/2013/11/12/hotel-trio-aims-to-bring-manhattan-to-moscow/.

100. Ibid.

101. Trump Twitter, November 10, 2013, 6:44 p.m.

102. Trump Twitter, November 11, 2013, 8:39 a.m.

103. Bensinger et al., "These Reports Allege Trump Has Deep Ties to Russia."

104. Angel Au-Yeung, "World Cup 2018 Exclusive: The 15 Russian Billionaires Connected to the Games," *Forbes*, June 30, 2018, https://www.forbes.com/sites/angelauyeung/2018/06/11/world-cup-2018-fifa-russia-billionaires-putin-sanction-trump/#4b7b283e11d2.

105. Vasilyeva, "Russian Real Estate Deals Never Materialized for Trump."

106. Sarah Fitzpatrick et al., "Daniels' Lawyer: Cohen Got $500,000 from Russian Oligarch Viktor Vekselberg," NBC News, May 8, 2018, https://www.nbcnews.com/news/us-news/daniels-lawyer-cohen-got-500k-russian-oligarch-viktor-vekselberg-n872481; Au-Yeung, "World Cup 2018 Exclusive."

107. Ibid.; Ben Schreckinger and Julie Ioffe, "Lobbyist Advised Trump Campaign While Promoting Russian Pipeline," *Politico*, October 7, 2016, https://www.politico.com/story/2016/10/donald-trump-campaign-lobbyist-russian-pipeline-229264.

108. Tom Hamburger et al., "Inside Trump's financial ties to Russia and his unusual flattery of Vladimir Putin," *Washington Post*, June 17, 2016, https://www.washingtonpost.com/politics/inside-trumps-financial-ties-to-russia-and-his-unusual-flattery-of-vladimir-putin/2016/06/17/dbdcaac8-31a6-11e6-8ff7-7b6c1998b7a0_story.html?noredirect=on&utm_term=.164960a98173.

109. Ibid.

110. Ibid.

111. Vernon Silver and Evgenia Pismennaya, "Trump's Two Nights of Parties in Moscow Echo Two Years Later," Bloomberg, July 13, 2017, https://www.bloomberg.com/news/articles/2017-07-13/trump-s-two-nights-of-parties-in-moscow-reverberate-years-later.

112. Yulya Alferova (@AlferovaYulyaE), "Waiting for your business to start in Russia, Mr. Trump @realDonaldTrump! @eminofficial #Russia #Moscow," Twit-

ter, November 11, 2013, 3:51 a.m., https://twitter.com/alferovayulyae/status/399
867018725568512?lang=en.

113. Scott Glover and Sara Sidner, "Trump's lawyer referred a client to Stormy Daniels' former lawyer, raising new questions about collaboration," CNN, April 6,
2018, https://www.cnn.com/2018/04/06/politics/michael-cohen-referred-keith
-davidson-client-invs/index.html; Tom Arnold (@TomArnold), "RT THREAD
Final Chuck LaBella tweets: Heard from his new high-powered lawyer who
repped Trumps Playmate GF & others with DJT dirt & handles," Twitter, October 21, 2017, 11:37 a.m., https://twitter.com/TomArnold/status/92180770809
2710912.

114. Vice Staff, "VICELAND Is Sending Tom Arnold on a Hunt for More Trump
Tapes," *VICE News,* May 2, 2018, https://www.vice.com/en_us/article/gym4y3
/viceland-is-sending-tom-arnold-on-a-hunt-for-more-trump-tapes.

115. Tracy Connor and Brandy Zadrozny, "Tom Arnold tweets picture with Michael
Cohen, says he has all the tapes,'" NBC News, June 21, 2018, https://www.nbc
news.com/news/us-news/trump-lawyer-michael-cohen-mugs-trump-critic-tom
-arnold-n885611.

116. Jimmy Geurts, "Tom Arnold Was Talking Trump Sex Tape Last Week," *International Herald Tribune*, January 11, 2017, http://www.heraldtribune.com/news
/20170111/tom-arnold-was-talking-trump-sex-tape-last-week.

117. Glover and Sidner, "Trump's lawyer referred a client to Stormy Daniels' former
lawyer."

118. Sara Sidner and Scott Glover, "Hush money deals business as usual for Stormy
Daniels' ex-attorney," CNN, April 27, 2018, https://www.cnn.com/2018/04/27
/politics/stormy-daniels-attorney-hush-agreements-invs/index.html.

119. Kendra Becker, "NBC Boss Shocked That Arnold Schwarzenegger Agreed to
Celebrity Apprentice," *Irish Examiner*/Goss.ie (Ireland), September 14, 2016,
http://goss.ie/uncategorized/nbc-boss-shocked-arnold-schwarzenegger-agreed
-celebrity-apprentice-80557.

120. Trump, "Building the Trump Brand."

121. Tom Arnold (@TomArnold), "Trump LOVES Chuck LaBella. I'd kill if a reporter asked DJT about him. Chuck can confirm pee pee tape & Putin call &
Apprentice Miss U filth," October 16, 2017, 9:39 a.m., https://twitter.com/tomar
nold/status/920146901651116032?lang=en.

122. Tom Arnold (@TomArnold), "Not in my control. Mark Burnett has all. Mark's
most loyal man in town, his son was DJT's ring bearer, Trump boned him. He
should fight back Tom Arnold added, Robert Jolley @bj95432geemale," Twitter, March 28, 2017, 11:11 a.m., https://twitter.com/tomarnold/status/84678677
2197507072; Katie Kilkenny, "Tom Arnold Slams Mark Burnett for Protecting
Trump in Rambling 'Live' Appearance," *Hollywood Reporter,* August 16, 2018,
https://www.hollywoodreporter.com/live-feed/tom-arnold-slams-mark-burnett
-protecting-trump-rambling-live-appearance-1135353; Chris Cillizza, "Katrina
Pierson's explanations of the alleged 'n-word' tape make no sense," CNN, August 14, 2018, https://www.cnn.com/2018/08/14/politics/katrina-pierson-donald
-trump-omarosa/index.html.

123. Tim Mak, "How Did Steven Seagal and Vladimir Putin Become BFFs? Bob Van Ronkel Introduced Them," NPR, July 3, 2018, https://www.npr.org/2018/07/03/624059365/how-did-steven-seagal-and-vladimir-putin-become-bffs-bob-van-ronkel-introduced-t; Kyle Swenson, "The Putin-Seagal Bromance: The Backstory," *Washington Post*, August 8, 2018, https://www.washingtonpost.com/news/morning-mix/wp/2018/08/08/meet-the-la-dealmaker-who-helped-bring-steven-seagal-and-vladimir-putin-together/?utm_term=.3616dda53d0d; Greg Walters, "It's Entirely Possible Putin Used a Pop Star to Get to Trump Jr.," *VICE News,* July 14, 2017, https://news.vice.com/en_ca/article/eva8dj/is-it-possible-putin-used-a-pr-rep-and-pop-star-to-get-to-trump-jr; Corn and Isikoff, "What Happened in Moscow."

124. Mak, "How Did Steven Seagal and Vladimir Putin Become BFFs?"; Swenson, "The Putin-Seagal Bromance"; Walters, "It's Entirely Possible Putin Used a Pop Star to Get to Trump Jr." ; Corn and Isikoff, "What Happened in Moscow"; Bob Van Ronkel (website), photos of Van Ronkel with Vladimir Putin et al., http://bobvanronkel.ru/bvr#/en/.

125. Mak, "How Did Steven Seagal Vladimir Putin Become BFFs?"; Swenson, "The Putin-Seagal Bromance"; Walters, "It's Entirely Possible Putin Used a Pop Star to Get to Trump Jr."; Corn and Isikoff, "What Happened in Moscow?"

126. AFIO (website), "POSSIBLE KGB TELEVISION SERIES: Producer Bob Van Ronkel is currently putting together a multimillion-dollar television series tentatively titled 'Files From the KGB,'" August 13, 2001, https://www.afio.com/sections/wins/2001/2001-32.html.

127. Van Ronkel website.

128. Melissa Gomez, "Steven Seagal Appointed by Russia as Special Envoy to the U.S.," *New York Times*, August 5, 2018, https://www.nytimes.com/2018/08/05/world/asia/steven-seagal-putin-russia.html; Emma Stefansky, "Steven Seagal Receives Official Russian Citizenship from Vladimir Putin," *Vanity Fair*, November 26, 2016, https://www.vanityfair.com/hollywood/2016/11/steven-seagal-vladimir-putin-russian-citizenship.

129. Chuck LaBella, Internet Movie Database biography entry for Chuck LaBella, https://www.imdb.com/name/nm1238132/.

130. Ibid.

131. Ibid.

132. Arnold Twitter, October 16, 2017, 9:39 a.m.

133. Max Seddon and Rosie Gray, "Putin's Action Hero: How Steven Seagal Became the Kremlin's Unlikeliest Envoy," *BuzzFeed News,* April 20, 2015, https://www.buzzfeednews.com/article/maxseddon/putins-action-hero-how-steven-seagal-became-the-kremlins-unl.

134. Ibid.

135. Ibid.

136. Ibid.

137. Walters, "It's Entirely Possible Putin Used a Pop Star to Get to Trump Jr."

138. Van Ronkel website.

139. Demetri Sevastopulo and Max Seddon, "Trumps Keep Controversy in the Fam-

ily," *Financial Times*, July 14, 2017, https://www.ft.com/content/3397e9f8-6874
-11e7-8526-7b38dcaef614.

140. Walters, "It's Entirely Possible Putin Used a Pop Star to Get to Trump Jr."

141. Ollie Gillman, "Putin 'begged to meet Trump at 2013 Miss Universe but was
left disappointed after the billionaire arrived late—so the Russian had an oligarch's daughter deliver a gift instead,'" *Daily Mail*, July 29, 2016, http://www
.dailymail.co.uk/news/article-3714527/Putin-begged-meet-Trump-2013-Miss
-Universe-left-disappointed-billionaire-arrived-late-Russian-oligarch-s-daughter
-deliver-gift-instead.html.

142. Swaine and Walker, "Trump in Moscow."

143. Corn and Isikoff, "What Happened in Moscow"; Rosalind S. Helderman, "Putin
dismisses question about whether Russia has compromising information on
Trump," *Washington Post*, July 16, 2018, https://www.washingtonpost.com/pol
itics/putin-dismisses-question-about-whether-russia-has-compromising-infor
mation-on-trump/2018/07/16/19e29f90-8915-11e8-85ae-511bc1146b0b_story
.html?utm_term=.06ed2052952b.

144. Trump, "Building the Trump Brand"; Katherine Faulders, "Donald Who? Putin
Doesn't Remember Trump in Moscow," ABC News, July 17, 2018, https://abc
news.go.com/Politics/donald-putin-remember-trump-moscow/story?id=56652016.

145. Craig and Chen, "Donald Trump Considered Path to Presidency Starting at Governor's Mansion in New York."

146. Ibid.

147. Ibid.

148. Ibid.

149. Ibid.

150. Donald J. Trump (@realDonaldTrump), "Funny how the Fake News Media
doesn't want to say that the Russian group was formed in 2014, long before my
run for President. Maybe they knew I was going to run even though I didn't
know!" Twitter, February 17, 2018, 11:46 a.m., https://twitter.com/realdonald
trump/status/964949269374529538.

151. Construction.ru, February 17, 2017, http://russianconstruction.com/news-1/26
505-russians-abandon-plans-for-trump-tower-construction-in-moscow-region.html.

152. Hunter Walker and Brett Arnold, "Michael Cohen's efforts to build a Trump
Tower in Moscow went on longer than he has previously acknowledged," Yahoo!
News, May 16, 2018, https://ca.news.yahoo.com/michael-cohens-efforts-build
-trump-tower-moscow-went-longer-previously-acknowledged-232845349.html.

153. Kirsch, "The Full Exclusive Interview."

154. Ibid.

155. Ibid.

156. Ibid.

157. Ibid.

158. Nolan D. McCaskill, "Trump Tells Wisconsin: Victory Was a Surprise," *Politico*,
December 13, 2016, https://www.politico.com/story/2016/12/donald-trump-wis
consin-232605.

159. Michael Wolff, *Fire and Fury: Inside the Trump White House* (New York: Henry Holt, 2018).

160. Ibid.

161. Rebecca Savransky, "Scarborough: Trump didn't think he would win, campaign was 'money-making scam,'" *Hill,* August 29, 2017, http://thehill.com/home news/media/348370-scarborough-trump-never-thought-he-was-going-to-win -campaign-was-a-money; Chase Peterson-Withorn, "Trump Refuses to Divest Assets, Passes Control to Sons," *Forbes,* January 11, 2017, https://www.forbes .com/sites/chasewithorn/2017/01/11/donald-trump-will-hand-over-business/#4e 1697636od7.

162. Jennifer Rubin, "The Emoluments Case is the Nightmare Trump Has Long Feared," *Washington Post*, July 25, 2018, https://www.washingtonpost.com /blogs/right-turn/wp/2018/07/25/trump-loses-big-in-emoluments-case/?utm_term =.df858faoff5e.

CHAPTER THREE: *KOMPROMAT*

1. Todd Franklin, "Multiple Sources Corroborate Trump 'Pee-Pee' Tape— Additional Tapes Alleged," IR.Net, September 4, 2017, http://ir.net/news/politics /127232/multiple-sources-corroborate-trump-pee-pee-tape-additional-tapes-al leged/.

2. John Swain and Shaun Walker, "Trump in Moscow: what happened at Miss Universe in 2013," *Guardian*, September 18, 2017, https://www.theguardian.com/us -news/2017/sep/18/trump-in-moscow-what-happened-at-miss-universe-in-2013.

3. Martin Longman, "A #TrumpRussia Confession in Plain Sight," *Washington Monthly*, November 24, 2017, https://washingtonmonthly.com/2017/11/24/a -trumprussia-confession-in-plain-sight/; Martin Longman, "Does a Russian's Confession Fit What We Know?" *Washington Monthly*, November 28, 2017, https://washingtonmonthly.com/2017/11/28/does-a-russians-confession-fit-what -we-know/; Scott Stedman, "Hacking Efforts, Strongly Implied Colluding With Trump Team in Facebook Posts," *Medium,* November 21, 2017, https://medium .com/@ScottMStedman/kremlin-propagandist-boasted-of-his-hacking-efforts -strongly-implied-colluding-with-trump-team-in-a905104965a1.

4. Patrick Hopwell O'Neill, "This dark net brothel makes finding sex as easy as hailing an Uber," *Daily Dot,* June 24, 2016, https://www.dailydot.com/layer8 /dosung-dark-net-russian-brothel/.

5. Alex Pfeiffer, "Former Trump Adviser Tells A Story About The President-Elect and Prostitutes," *Daily Caller,* January 14, 2017, http://dailycaller.com/2017 /01/14/former-trump-adviser-tells-a-story-about-the-president-elect-and-prosti tutes/; Chuck Ross, "Report: Trump Bodyguard Testifies Russian Ordered 'Five Women' To Trump, Was Rejected," *Daily Caller,* November 9, 2017, http://daily caller.com/2017/11/09/report-trump-bodyguard-testifies-russian-offered-five -women-to-trump-was-rejected/.

6. Adam Goldman and Nicholas Fandos, "Keith Schiller, Trump's Ex-Bodyguard,

Says He Turned Down Offer of Women in Moscow," *New York Times*, November 10, 2017, https://www.nytimes.com/2017/11/10/us/politics/trump-keith-schiller-russia.html.

7. DiLanian and Allen, "Trump Bodyguard Keith Schiller Testifies Russian Offered Trump Women, Was Turned Down," NBC News, November 9, 2017, https://www.nbcnews.com/news/us-news/trump-bodyguard-testifies-russian-offered-trump-women-was-turned-down-n819386.

8. James West, "This Is One of the Most Surreal Bits from Donald Trump's Bizarre Press Conference," *Mother Jones*, January 11, 2017, https://www.motherjones.com/politics/2017/01/trump-russia-hotel-bugging-um-what-weird/.

9. DiLanian and Allen, "Trump Bodyguard Keith Schiller Testifies Russian Offered Trump Women, Was Turned Down."

10. Ken Bensinger et al., "These Reports Allege Trump Has Deep Ties to Russia," *BuzzFeed News*, January 10, 2017, https://www.buzzfeednews.com/article/kenbensinger/these-reports-allege-trump-has-deep-ties-to-russia; Jane Mayer, "Christopher Steele, The Man Behind The Trump Dossier," *New Yorker*, March 12, 2018, https://www.newyorker.com/magazine/2018/03/12/christopher-steele-the-man-behind-the-trump-dossier; Howard Blum, "How Ex-Spy Christopher Steele Compiled His Explosive Trump-Russia Dossier," *Vanity Fair*, March 30, 2018, https://www.vanityfair.com/news/2017/03/how-the-explosive-russian-dossier-was-compiled-christopher-steele.

11. Natasha Bertrand, "Fusion GPS testimony brings alleged dossier source Sergei Millian back into the spotlight," *Business Insider*, January 19, 2018, https://www.businessinsider.com/sergei-millian-michael-cohen-glenn-simpson-fusion-gps-2018-1.

12. Bensinger et al., "These Reports Allege Trump Has Deep Ties to Russia."

13. Kevin Drum, "BBC's Paul Wood: There are Four Sourcs For Claims of Possible Trump-Russia Blackmail," *Mother Jones*, January 12, 2017, https://www.motherjones.com/kevin-drum/2017/01/bbcs-paul-wood-there-are-four-sources-possible-trump-russia-blackmail/; Paul Wood, "Forget Charlottesville—Russia is still the true Trump scandal," *Spectator*, August 17, 2017, https://www.spectator.co.uk/2017/08/forget-charlottesville-russia-is-still-the-true-trump-scandal/.

14. Wood, "Forget Charlottesville—Russia is still the true Trump scandal."

15. Twitter communication with author, October 7, 2017.

16. Rosalind S. Helderman and Tom Hamburger, "Who is Source D? The man said to be behind the Trump-Russia dossier's most salacious claim," *Washington Post*, March 29, 2017, https://www.washingtonpost.com/politics/who-is-source-d-the-man-said-to-be-behind-the-trump-russia-dossiers-most-salacious-claim/2017/03/29/379846a8-0f53-11e7-9d5a-a83e627dc120_story.html?utm_term=.ea33cad824cb; Brian Ross and Matthew Mosk, "US-Russian Businessman Said to Be Source of Key Trump Dossier Claim," ABC News, January 30, 2017, https://abcnews.go.com/Politics/us-russian-businessman-source-key-trump-dossier-claims/story?id=45019603.

17. Paul Wood, "Trump 'compromising' claims: How and why did we get here?" BBC, January 12, 2017, https://www.bbc.com/news/world-us-canada-38589427.

18. Ibid.

19. "Russia says Trump intel claims a 'fabrication and utter nonsense,'" CBS News, January 11, 2017, https://www.cbsnews.com/news/russia-vladimir-putin-com promising-intelligence-donald-trump-fabrication/; Twitter (Donald Trump verified account), https://twitter.com/realDonaldTrump/status/8191553117937 0 0865?ref_src=twsrc%5Etfw%7Ctwcamp%5Etweetembed%7Ctwterm%5E819 155311793700865&ref_url=https%3A%2F%2Fwww.cbsnews.com%2Fnews%2 Frussia-vladimir-putin-compromising-intelligence-donald-trump-fabrication%2F; Twitter (Donald Trump verified account), https://twitter.com/realDonald Trump/status/819159806489591809?ref_src=twsrc%5Ettwitter-are-we-living-in -nazi-germany.html fw%7Ctwcamp%5Etweetembed%7Ctwterm%5E81915980 6489591809&ref_url=https%3A%2F%2Fwww.cbsnews.com%2Fnews%2Frus sia-vladimir-putin-compromising-intelligence-donald-trump-fabrication%2F.

20. Jacob Pramuk, "Trump melts down on Twitter: 'Are we living in Nazi Germany?'" CNBC, January 11, 2017, https://www.cnbc.com/2017/01/11/trump-melts -down-on-twitter-are-we-living-in-nazi-germany.html.

21. Ben Guarino, "Shaking hands is 'barbaric': Donald Trump, the germaphobe in chief," *Washington Post*, January 12, 2017, https://www.washingtonpost.com /news/morning-mix/wp/2017/01/12/shaking-hands-is-barbaric-donald-trump-the -germaphobe-in-chief/?utm_term=.09ad9aadd7d6 is a germaphobe.

22. Michael Isikoff, "Trump told Comey he never slept in Moscow. But he did." Yahoo.com, April 20, 2018, https://www.yahoo.com/news/trump-told-comey -never-slept-moscow-185535745.html; Adam Lusher, "Flight records appear to disprove Donald Trump's Moscow prostitutes alibi," *Independent,* April 24, 2018, https://www.independent.co.uk/news/world/americas/us-politics/trump -russia-dossier-pee-tape-prostitutes-flight-records-moscow-christopher-steele -james-comey-memos-a8319731.html.

23. Guarino, "Shaking hands is 'barbaric.'"

24. West, "This Is One of the Most Surreal Bits from Donald Trump's Bizarre Press Conference."

25. "Donald Trump's News Conference: Full Transcript and Video," *New York Times*, January 11, 2017, https://www.nytimes.com/2017/01/11/us/politics/trump-press -conference-transcript.html.

26. Ibid.

27. Alex Eriksen, "Who Is Kata Sarka? This Hungarian Beauty Claims Donald Trump Made a Pass at Her," Yahoo.com, January 14, 2017, https://www.yahoo .com/lifestyle/who-is-kata-sarka-this-hungarian-beauty-claims-donald-trump -made-a-pass-at-her-212728724.html.

28. Eli Watkins, "Karen McDougal tells CNN Trump once tried to pay her after sex," CNN, March 22, 2018, https://www.cnn.com/2018/03/22/politics/karen-mcdou gal-donald-trump/index.html.

29. Pfeiffer, "Former Trump Adviser Tells a Story about the President-Elect and Prostitutes."

30. Carol D. Leonig, "Former security chief says he rejected offer of women for Trump during Moscow trip," *Washington Post*, November 9, 2017, https://www

.washingtonpost.com/politics/former-security-chief-says-he-rejected-offer-of
-women-for-trump-during-moscow-trip/2017/11/09/55531270-c585-11e7-aaeo
-cb18a8c29c65_story.html?utm_term=.828eod5ae410.

31. "Emin Agalarov denies allegation he offered to send women to Trump's hotel
room," ABC News, July 2018, https://abcnews.go.com/Politics/video/emin-aga
larov-denies-allegation-offered-send-women-trumps-56494402; Aaron Blake,
"The Trump Russia story reaches a ridiculous new zenith, in a Russian music
video," *Washington Post*, June 26, 2018, https://www.washingtonpost.com/news
/the-fix/wp/2018/06/26/trumps-russian-pop-star-ally-releases-a-music-video
-trump-will-hate/?utm_term=.60546c13484c; Elahe Izadi, "How Trump ended
up in a 2013 Europop video connected to the latest Russia controversy," *Washington Post*, July 10, 2017, https://www.washingtonpost.com/news/arts-and
-entertainment/wp/2017/07/10/how-trump-ended-up-in-a-2013-europop-video
-connected-to-the-latest-russia-controversy/?utm_term=.bc33bf01c4b3.

32. Lydia Ramsey, "Trump's doctor says he only sleeps 4-5 hours each night—
and there could be a scientific reason why," *Business Insider,* January 16, 2018,
https://www.businessinsider.com/some-people-only-need-a-few-hours-of-sleep
-2016-12.

33. Anna Nemtsova, "She Met Donald Trump at the Moscow Ritz (Not That Way!),"
Daily Beast, January 20, 2017, https://www.thedailybeast.com/she-met-donald
-trump-at-the-moscow-ritz-not-that-way?ref=scroll.

34. Anna Nemtsova, "The Untold Tale of Colbert's Hunt for Trump 'Pee Tape,'"
Daily Beast, July 29, 2017, https://www.thedailybeast.com/colbert-takes-on-the
-kremlinand-russians-love-it.

35. Andrew Higgins and Andrew E. Kramer, "Russia's Sexual Blackmail Didn't Die
With the Soviets," *New York Times*, January 11, 2017, https://www.nytimes.com
/2017/01/11/world/europe/donald-trump-russia.html.

36. Ibid.

37. Matthew Rosenberg, "Ex-Chief of C.I.A. Suggests Putin May Have Compromising Information on Trump," *New York Times*, March 21, 2018, https://www.ny
times.com/2018/03/21/us/politics/john-brennan-trump-putin.html.

38. Veronica Stracqualursi, "Comey: 'I don't know if Trump was with prostitutes
in Moscow,'" CNN, April 13, 2018, https://www.cnn.com/2018/04/13/politics
/james-comey-trump-dossier/index.html.

39. Matthew Yglesias, "Asked directly, Putin does not deny possessing 'compromising material,' on Trump," *Vox,* July 16, 2018, https://www.vox.com/2018/7/16
/17576784/trump-putin-pee-tape.

40. Ibid.

41. Justin Criado, "Bob Baer shares scoop on Trump and Russia," *Telluride Daily
Planet*, August 10, 2018, https://www.telluridenews.com/news/article_fe60e776
-9cf7-11e8-8d94-7f6e5cd044d1.html.

42. Ibid.

43. Scott Stedman, "Kremlin Propagandist who claimed he coordinated with Trump
team, was previously appointed as Putin's 'trusted confidant,'" *Medium*, Febru-

ary 26, 2018, https://medium.com/@ScottMStedman/kremlin-propagandist-who
-claimed-he-coordinated-with-trump-team-was-previously-appointed-as-putins
-2dc5f83298e5; Martin Longman, "A #TrumpRussia Confession in Plain Sight."

44. Molly Schwartz, "The man who taught the Kremlin how to win the internet,"
Public Radio International, May 7, 2018, https://www.pri.org/stories/2018-05-07
/man-who-taught-kremlin-how-win-internet.

45. O'Neill, "This dark net brothel makes finding sex as easy as hailing an Uber."

46. Scott Stedman, Artem Lyushin Attended 2015 Trump Speech in Iowa," *Medium*,
November 21, 2017, https://web.archive.org/web/20180101154942/https://me
dium.com/@ScottMStedman/artem-klyushin-attended-2015-trump-speech-in
-iowa-6b4619af7420.

47. Andrew Osborn, "From Russia with love: why the Kremlin backs Trump,"
Reuters, March 24, 2016, https://www.reuters.com/article/us-usa-election
-trump-russia/from-russia-with-love-why-the-kremlin-backs-trump-idUSKCN0
WQ1FA.

48. Higgins and Kramer, "Russia's Sexual Blackmail Didn't Die With the Soviets."

49. "Putin Bragged about Russian Hookers . . . According to Comey Memo," *TMZ*,
April 19, 2018, http://www.tmz.com/2018/04/19/donald-trump-vladimir-putin
-russian-hookers-comey-memo/.

50. Shane Harris et al., "In a personal letter, Trump invited Putin to the 2013 Miss
Universe pageant," *Washington Post*, March 9, 2018, https://www.washington
post.com/world/national-security/in-a-personal-letter-trump-invited-putin-to
-the-2013-miss-universe-pageant/2018/03/09/a3404358-23d2-11e8-a589-76389
3265565_story.html?utm_term=.dc8f6cd8db13.

51. *The Late Show With Stephen Colbert,* YouTube video, July 21, 2017, https://
www.youtube.com/watch?v=Lk1uBMZOaXc.

52. *Conan,* YouTube video, November 7, 2017, https://www.youtube.com/watch
?v=yyNkvEts8K8.

53. Adam Gopnik, "Trump and Obama: A Night to Remember," *New Yorker*, September 12, 2015, https://www.newyorker.com/news/daily-comment/trump-and
-obama-a-night-to-remember.

54. Roxanne Roberts, "I sat next to Donald Trump at the infamous 2011 White
House correspondents' dinner," *Washington Post*, April 28, 2016, https://www
.washingtonpost.com/lifestyle/style/i-sat-next-to-donald-trump-at-the-infamous
-2011-white-house-correspondents-dinner/2016/04/27/5cf46b74-0bea-11e6-8ab
8-9ad050f76d7d_story.html?utm_term=.416908506726.

55. Wood, "Forget Charlottesville—Russia is still the true Trump scandal."

56. Wood, "Trump 'compromising' claims: How and why did we get here?"

57. Bensinger et al., "These Reports Allege Trump Has Deep Ties to Russia."

58. Will Stewart, "Putin 'solutions not problems'—how billionaire tycoon at center
of meeting with Don Jr is Russian leader's go-to for tough projects (like wooing Trump)," *Daily Mail*, July 13, 2017, http://www.dailymail.co.uk/news/article
-4690806/Agalarov-s-relationship-Trump-manna-Putin.html.

59. Michele Neubert et al., "Christopher Steele, Trump Dossier Author, Is a Real

-Life James Bond," NBC News, January 13, 2017, https://www.nbcnews.com /news/us-news/christopher-steele-trump-dossier-author-real-life-james-bond -n706376.

60. Adam Davidson, "A Theory of Trump Kompromat," *New Yorker*, July 19, 2018, https://www.newyorker.com/news-desk/swamp-chronicles/a-theory-of-trump -kompromat.
61. Swaine and Walker, "Trump in Moscow."
62. Ibid.

CHAPTER FOUR: THE CAMPAIGN BEGINS

1. Sarah Wheaton, "NRA Facing Member Backlash over Trump Endorsement," *Politico*, May 21, 2016, https://www.politico.com/story/2016/05/nra-donald-trump -endorsement-backlash-223442.
2. Fred Barnes, "Gunning for Hillary," *Weekly Standard,* February 24, 2017, https:// www.weeklystandard.com/fred-barnes/gunning-for-hillary.
3. Andrew Prokop, "Maria Butina, Explained: the accused Russian spy who tried to sway US politics through the NRA," *Vox,* July 19, 2018, https://www.vox.com /2018/7/19/17581354/maria-butina-russia-nra-trump.
4. Philip Bump, "Timeline: The odd overlap of Maria Butina, the gun-rights movement and the 2016 election," *Washington Post,* July 16, 2018, https://www .washingtonpost.com/news/politics/wp/2018/07/16/timeline-the-odd-overlap-of -maria-butina-the-gun-rights-movement-and-the-2016-election/?utm_term=.c86 179bb0c52.
5. Tim Dickinson, "Inside the Decade-Long Russian Campaign to Infiltrate the NRA and Help Elect Trump," *Rolling Stone,* April 2, 2018, https://www.rolling stone.com/politics/politics-features/inside-the-decade-long-russian-campaign-to -infiltrate-the-nra-and-help-elect-trump-630054/.
6. Ibid.
7. Ibid.
8. Esteban Duarte et al., "Mobster or Central Banker? Spanish Cops Allege This Russian Both," Bloomberg, August 8, 2016, https://www.bloomberg.com/news /articles/2016-08-09/mobster-or-central-banker-spanish-cops-allege-this-russian -both.
9. Sonam Sheth, "The FBI has obtained wiretaps of a Putin ally tied to the NRA who met with Trump Jr. during the campaign," *Business Insider*, May 26, 2018, https://www.businessinsider.com/fbi-obtains-alexander-torshin-wiretaps-from -spanish-police-2018-5; Jose Maria Irujo and John Carlin, "The Spanish Connection with Trump's Russia Scandal," *El Pais*, April 3, 2017, https://elpais.com /elpais/2017/03/31/inenglish/1490984556_409827.html.
10. Mark Follman, "The NRA Has Deep Ties to Accused Russian Spy Maria Butina," *Mother Jones,* July 19, 2018, https://www.motherjones.com/politics /2018/07/nra-maria-butina-spying-charges-trump-campaign/; Jessica Schladebeck, "A Look at Paul Erickson, Alleged Contact of Accused Russian Agent Maria Butina," *New York Daily News,* July 18, 2018, http://www.nydailynews

.com/news/national/ny-news-maria-butina-paul-erickson-russia-ties-20180718
-story.html.

11. Follman, "The NRA Has Deep Ties to Accused Russian Spy Maria Butina."
12. Ibid.
13. Ibid.
14. Ibid.
15. "Here's a Timeline of Every Time Donald Trump Ran for President," *TV Guide,* July 28, 2015, https://www.tvguide.com/news/donald-trump-presidential-campaign-timeline/.
16. Susanne Craig and David W. Chen, "Donald Trump Considered Path to Presidency Starting at Governor's Mansion in New York," *New York Times,* March 6, 2016, https://www.nytimes.com/2016/03/06/nyregion/donald-trump-new-york-governor.html.
17. Follman, "The NRA Has Deep Ties to Accused Russian Spy Maria Butina"; DOJ affidavit accompanying indictments, July 17, 2018, https://www.justice.gov/opa/press-release/file/1080766/download.
18. Ilya Arkhipov and Evgenia Pismennaya, "Putin Loyalists Are Invading Washington," Bloomberg, April 6, 2017, https://www.bloomberg.com/news/articles/2017-04-06/trump-s-russian-fans-won-t-take-nyet-for-an-answer-in-washington.
19. Tim Mak, "Depth of Politician's Cultivation of NRA Ties Revealed," NPR, March 1, 2018, https://www.npr.org/2018/03/01/590076949/depth-of-russian-politicians-cultivation-of-nra-ties-revealed.
20. Michael Isikoff, "White House Pulled Out of Meet and Greet with 'Conservatives' Favorite Russian' Over Suspected Mob Ties," Yahoo!, April 2, 2017, https://www.yahoo.com/news/white-house-pulled-out-of-meet-and-greet-with-conservatives-favorite-russian-a-suspected-mobster-060026495.html.
21. Mak, "Depth of Politician's Cultivation of NRA Ties Revealed."
22. Christopher Brennan, "Russian Banker Said He Met Trump Through NRA," New York *Daily News,* March 2, 2018, http://www.nydailynews.com/news/national/russian-banker-met-trump-nra-article-1.3850535.
23. Philip Bump, "The Subtle Evolution of Trump's Views on Putin and Russia," *Washington Post,* July 17, 2018, https://www.washingtonpost.com/news/politics/wp/2018/07/17/the-subtle-evolution-of-trumps-views-on-putin-and-russia/?utm_term=.5ebd2b282183; Andrew Kaczynski et al., "80 Times Trump Talked About Putin," CNN, March 21, 2017, https://www.cnn.com/interactive/2017/03/politics/trump-putin-russia-timeline/.
24. Bump, "Timeline."
25. DemoCast, "Donald Trump Handles Questions at FreedomFest July 11, '15 Las Vegas," YouTube, https://www.youtube.com/watch?v=nP8x0gCIGXw&t=9m3s.
26. Ibid.
27. Emily Stewart, "Read: Donald Trump Jr.'s Congressional Testimony about the Trump Tower Meeting," *Vox,* May 16, 2018 (Trump Jr. testimony, p. 31), https://www.vox.com/policy-and-politics/2018/5/16/17360484/donald-trump-jr-transcript-senate-judiciary-committee.
28. Carol D. Leonnig et al., "Trump's business sought deal on a Trump Tower in

Moscow while he ran for president," *Washington Post,* August 27, 2017, https://www.washingtonpost.com/politics/trumps-business-sought-deal-on-a-trump-tower-in-moscow-while-he-ran-for-president/2017/08/27/d6e95114-8b65-11e7-91d5-ab4e4bb76a3a_story.html?utm_term=.e5ad8751f181.

29. Natasha Bertrand, " 'Help world peace and make a lot of money': Here's the letter of intent to build a Trump Tower Moscow," *Business Insider,* September 8, 2017, https://www.businessinsider.com/trump-tower-moscow-letter-of-intent-2017-9.

30. Alexander Sazonov et al., "Trump's Would-Be Moscow Partner Faces Homebuyers' Ire," Bloomberg, September 1, 2017, https://www.bloomberg.com/news/articles/2017-09-01/trump-s-would-be-moscow-partner-faces-ire-of-homebuyers.

31. CBS News, "Trump Moscow Letter of Intent Divulged," CBS News, September 8, 2017, https://www.cbsnews.com/news/trump-moscow-letter-of-intent-divulged/.

32. Brian Ross and Matthew Mosk, "Trump signed letter of intent for Russian tower during campaign, lawyer says," ABC News, August 28, 2017, https://abcnews.go.com/Politics/trump-knew-moscow-tower-proposal-campaign-lawyer/story?id=49472342.

33. Tom Hamburger et al., "Trump's company had more contact with Russia during campaign, according to documents turned over to investigators," *Washington Post,* October 2, 2017, https://www.washingtonpost.com/politics/trumps-company-had-more-contact-with-russia-during-campaign-according-to-documents-turned-over-to-investigators/2017/10/02/2091fe5e-a6c0-11e7-850e-2bdd1236be5d_story.html?utm_term=.3f429ce5ad7e.

34. Ibid.

35. Ibid.

36. Bertrand, " 'Help world peace and make a lot of money.' "

37. Ibid.

38. Matt Apuzzo and Maggie Haberman, "Trump Associate Boasted that Moscow Business Deal 'Will Get Donald Elected,' " *New York Times,* August 28, 2017, https://www.nytimes.com/2017/08/28/us/politics/trump-tower-putin-felix-sater.html.

39. Sonam Sheth, "Russian-born businessman Felix Sater has confirmed a bombshell detail in the Russia investigation," *Business Insider,* March 17, 2018, https://www.businessinsider.com/felix-sater-confirms-trump-pursued-deal-with-sanctioned-russian-bank-2018-3.

40. Press Center, "Treasury Sanctions Individuals and Entities for Sanctions Evasion and Other Activities Related to Russia and Ukraine," Department of the Treasury, December 22, 2015, https://www.treasury.gov/press-center/press-releases/Pages/jl0314.aspx.

41. Apuzzo and Haberman, "Trump Associate Boasted that Moscow Business Deal 'Will Get Donald Elected.' "

42. Donie O'Sullivan, "Russians targeted Senate and conservative think tanks, Microsoft says," CNN, August 21, 2018 (for Peskov as "Kremlin spokesman"), https://www.cnn.com/2018/08/21/politics/microsoft-russia-american-politicians

/index.html; Rosalind S. Helderman et al., "Top Trump organization executive asked Putin aide for help on business deal," *Washington Post*, August 28, 2017, https://www.washingtonpost.com/politics/top-trump-organization-execu tive-reached-out-to-putin-aide-for-help-on-business-deal/2017/08/28/095aebac -8c16-11e7-84c0-02cc069f2c37_story.html?utm_term=.96ea0599bbbb.

43. "The NRA Has Deep Ties to Accused Russian Spy Maria Butina."

44. Tim Mak, "Top Trump Ally Met with Putin's Deputy in Moscow," *Daily Beast,* March 7, 2017, https://www.thedailybeast.com/top-trump-ally-met-with-putins -deputy-in-moscow.

45. Peter Stone and Greg Gordon, "FBI investigating whether Russian money went to NRA to help Trump," *McClatchy*, January 18, 2018, https://www.mc clatchydc.com/news/nation-world/national/article195231139.html.

46. Robert Windrem, "Guess Who Came to Dinner with Flynn and Putin," NBC News, April 18, 2017, https://www.nbcnews.com/news/world/guess-who-came -dinner-flynn-putin-n742696; Robert Windrem, "Mike Flynn's RT Headache Won't Go Away," NBC News, April 27, 2017, https://www.nbcnews.com/news /us-news/mike-flynn-s-rt-headache-won-t-go-away-n752216.

47. Windrem, "Mike Flynn's RT Headache Won't Go Away."

48. Ibid.

49. James Kitfield, "How Mike Flynn Became America's Angriest General," *Polit- ico*, October 16, 2016, https://www.politico.com/magazine/story/2016/10/how -mike-flynn-became-americas-angriest-general-214362.

50. Linley Sanders, "George Papadopoulos Lied on His Résumé to Get Trump Campaign Foreign Policy Job, Former Employer Says," *Newsweek,* Novem- ber 1, 2017, https://www.newsweek.com/george-papadopoulos-lied-his-resume -698409.

51. Nicholas Fandos, "Operative Offered Trump Campaign 'Kremlin Connection' Using NRA Ties," *New York Times*, December 3, 2017, https://www.nytimes .com/2017/12/03/us/politics/trump-putin-russia-nra-campaign.html.

52. Ibid.

53. Ibid.

54. Matt Apuzzo et al., "Top Russian Official Tried to Broker 'Backdoor' Meeting Between Trump and Putin," *New York Times*, November 17, 2017, https://www .nytimes.com/2017/11/17/us/politics/trump-russia-kushner.html.

55. Ibid.

56. Arkhipov and Pismennaya, "Putin Loyalists Are Invading Washington"; Chris Smith, "'Coincidence Number 395': The NRA Spent $30 Million to Elect Trump. Was It Russian Money?" *Vanity Fair,* June 21, 2018, https://www.van ityfair.com/news/2018/06/the-nra-spent-dollar30-million-to-elect-trump-was-it -russian-money; Stone and Gordon, "FBI investigating whether Russian money went to NRA to help Trump."

57. Fandos, "Operative Offered Trump Campaign 'Kremlin Connection'"; Smith, "'Coincidence Number 395'"; Stone and Gordon, "FBI investigating whether Russian money went to NRA to help Trump."

58. Peter Stone and Ben Weider, "NRA Spent More than Reported During 2016

election," *McClatchy*, October 5, 2017, https://www.mcclatchydc.com/news/pol itics-government/article177312006.html; Stone and Gordon, "FBI investigating whether Russian money went to NRA to help Trump."

59. Ibid.

60. Jeremy W. Peters and Rachel Shorey, "Trump Spent Far Less than Clinton, but Paid His Companies Well," *New York Times*, December 9, 2016, https://www .nytimes.com/2016/12/09/us/politics/campaign-spending-donald-trump-hillary -clinton.html.

61. David A. Graham, "The Lie of Trump's 'Self-Funding' Campaign," *Atlantic,* May 13, 2016, https://www.theatlantic.com/politics/archive/2016/05/trumps -self-funding-lie/482691/; Ian Mount, "Trump Decides He's Not Rich Enough to Self-Fund His Campaign," *Fortune,* May 5, 2016, http://fortune.com/2016/05 /05/trump-big-donors-super-pacs/.

62. Smith, "'Coincidence Number 395'"; Stone and Gordon, "FBI investigating whether Russian money went to NRA to help Trump"; Greg Gordon et al., "Sanctioned Russians include dossier figure and banker linked to NRA," *McClatchy*, April 6, 2018, https://www.mcclatchydc.com/news/nation-world/na tional/article208180169.html.

63. Bump, "Timeline."

64. Michael Birnbaum and Jose A. DelReal, "Trump tells Ukraine conference their nation was invaded because 'there is no respect for the United States,'" *Washington Post*, September 11, 2015, https://www.washingtonpost.com/news/post-pol itics/wp/2015/09/11/trump-tells-ukraine-conference-their-nation-was-invaded -because-there-is-no-respect-for-the-united-states/?utm_term=.eadc51f992dc.

65. Kaczynski, "80 Times Trump Talked About Putin."

66. Ibid.

67. Ibid.

68. Ibid.

69. Ibid.

70. Ibid.

71. Ibid.

72. Ibid.

73. Ibid.

74. Tim Mak, "Documents Reveal How Russian Official Courted Conservatives in US Since 2009," NPR, May 2018, https://www.npr.org/2018/05/11/610206357 /documents-reveal-how-russian-official-courted-conservatives-in-u-s-since -2009.

75. Ibid.

76. Ibid.

77. Ibid.

78. Bob Dreyfuss, "Who Is Felix Sater, and Why Is Donald Trump So Afraid of Him?" *Nation,* September 2017, https://www.thenation.com/article/who-is-felix -sater-and-why-is-donald-trump-so-afraid-of-him/.

79. Brennan Weiss, "Inside the close relationship between Trump and his 'pit bull' lawyer Michael Cohen, who paid Stormy Daniels, says he'd 'take a bul-

let' for Trump, and was raided by the FBI," *Business Insider*, April 10, 2018, https://www.businessinsider.com/michael-cohen-history-with-trump-2018-3?r =UK&IR=T.

80. Ibid.; Emily Jane Fox, "Michael Cohen Would Take a Bullet for Donald Trump," *Vanity Fair,* September 6, 2017, https://www.vanityfair.com/news/2017/09/mi chael-cohen-interview-donald-trump.

81. Philip Shenon, "Trump's Lawyer Went to the Worst Law School in America," *Politico*, May 2018, https://www.politico.com/magazine/story/2018/05/04/trump -michael-cohen-lawyer-cooley-law-school-218318; Weiss, "Inside the close relationship"; Alan Feuer et al., "Sean Hannity Is Named as Client of Michael Cohen, Trump's Lawyer," *New York Times*, April 16, 2018, https://www.nytimes .com/2018/04/16/business/media/sean-hannity-michael-cohen-client.html.

82. Lachlan Markay and Asawin Suebsaeng, "Sean Hannity Has Been Advising Donald Trump on the Nunes Memo because of Course He Has," *Daily Beast,* February 1, 2018, https://www.thedailybeast.com/sean-hannity-has-been-advis ing-donald-trump-on-the-nunes-memo-because-of-course-he-has; Jim Rutenberg, "Sean Hannity Turns Adviser in the Service of Donald Trump," *New York Times*, August 22, 2016, https://www.nytimes.com/2016/08/22/business/media /sean-hannity-turns-adviser-in-the-service-of-donald-trump.html; Alex Isenstadt, "RNC Fundraiser Resigns after Report of $1.6 Million Playmate Payoff," *Politico*, April 13, 2018, https://www.politico.com/story/2018/04/13/rnc-deputy -finance-chair-broidy-resigns-522867; Jim Rutenberg and Jaclyn Peiser, "The Path of Stormy Daniels's $130,000 Payment to Keep Quiet," *New York Times*, May 3, 2018, https://www.nytimes.com/2018/05/03/us/politics/stormy-dan iels-trump-payment.html; RNC Announcements, "RNC Announces Additions to RNC Finance Leadership Team," GOP.com press statement, April 3, 2017, https://gop.com/rnc-announces-additions-to-rnc-finance-leadership-team/.

83. David D. Kirkpatrick and Mark Mazzetti, "How 2 Gulf Monarchies Sought to Influence the White House," *New York Times*, March 21, 2018, https://www.ny times.com/2018/03/21/us/politics/george-nader-elliott-broidy-uae-saudi-arabia -white-house-influence.html.

84. Kyle Cheney, "Trump Jr. cites attorney-client privilege in not answering panel's questions about discussions with his father," *Politico*, December 6, 2017, https:// www.politico.com/story/2017/12/06/donald-trump-privilege-questions-284841.

85. Ross and Mosk, "Trump signed letter of intent for Russian tower."

86. Ibid.

87. Ibid.

88. Bertrand, " 'Help world peace and make a lot of money.' "

89. Ross and Mosk, "Trump signed letter of intent for Russian tower."

90. Bertrand, " 'Help world peace and make a lot of money.' "

91. Vicky Ward, "Michael Cohen Speaks: Trump Exec Admits Russia Dealings Were Gross, but Not Illegal," *Huffington Post,* August 30, 2017; updated September 1, 2017, https://www.huffingtonpost.com/entry/michael-cohen-trump -lawyer-russia_us_59a71a28e4b010ca2899e933.

92. Ibid.

93. Hunter Walker and Brett Arnold, "Michael Cohen's efforts to build a Trump Tower in Moscow went on longer than he has previously acknowledged," Yahoo! News, May 16, 2018, https://www.yahoo.com/news/michael-cohens-efforts -build-trump-tower-moscow-went-longer-previously-acknowledged-232845349 .html.

94. Ward, "Michael Cohen Speaks."

95. Ken Dilanian, "Former Diplomats: Trump Team Sought to Lift Sanctions on Russia," NBC News, June 1, 2017, https://www.nbcnews.com/politics/white -house/former-diplomats-trump-team-sought-lift-sanctions-russia-n767406.

96. Twitter (Yulia Alferova, November 12, 2015), https://twitter.com/alferovayulyae /status/664932169240956928?lang=en.

97. Twitter (Yulia Alferova, November 11, 2013), https://twitter.com/alferovayulyae /status/399867018725568512?lang=en.

98. Ibid.

99. Windrem, "Guess Who Came to Dinner with Flynn and Putin"; Windrem, "Mike Flynn's RT Headache Won't Go Away."

100. Michael D. Shear and Adam Goldman, "Michael Flynn Pleads Guilty to Lying to the FBI and Will Cooperate with Russia Inquiry," New York Times, December 1, 2017, https://www.nytimes.com/2017/12/01/us/politics/michael-flynn-guilty -russia-investigation.html.

101. Matt Novak, "Trump Says He Didn't Know Michael Flynn in 2015, which Is a Big Fucking Lie," Gizmodo, May 12, 2017, https://gizmodo.com/trump-says-he -didnt-know-michael-flynn-in-2015-which-i-1795153990.

102. Dana Priest, "Trump adviser Michael T. Flynn on his dinner with Putin and why Russia Today is just like CNN," Washington Post, August 15, 2016, https://www .washingtonpost.com/news/checkpoint/wp/2016/08/15/trump-adviser-michael-t -flynn-on-his-dinner-with-putin-and-why-russia-today-is-just-like-cnn/.

103. Nicholas Schmidle, "Michael Flynn, General Chaos," New Yorker, February 27, 2017, https://www.newyorker.com/magazine/2017/02/27/michael-flynn-general -chaos.

104. Ibid.

105. Priest, "Trump adviser Michael T. Flynn on his dinner with Putin."

106. "Michael Flynn, General Chaos."

107. Ibid.

108. Ibid.

109. Ibid.

110. Luke Harding et al., "Michael Flynn: New evidence spy chiefs had concerns about Russia ties," Guardian, March 31, 2017, https://www.theguardian.com /us-news/2017/mar/31/michael-flynn-new-evidence-spy-chiefs-had-concerns -about-russian-ties.

111. Ibid.

112. Ibid.

113. Ibid.

114. Zembla, "The Dubious Friends of Donald Trump: The Russians," YouTube,

posted on May 11, 2017, https://www.youtube.com/watch?v=1bEdMuKq3oI&t
=208s.

115. John Santucci, "Trump Says 'Great Honor' to Get Compliments from 'Highly Respected' Putin," ABC News, December 17, 2015, https://abcnews.go.com /Politics/trump-great-honor-compliments-highly-respected-putin/story?id=358 29618.

116. Robert Windrem, "Senate Russia Investigators Are Interested in Jill Stein," NBC News, December 19, 2017, https://www.nbcnews.com/news/us-news/why-are -senate-russia-investigators-interested-jill-stein-n831261.

CHAPTER FIVE: THE NATIONAL SECURITY ADVISORY COMMITTEE

1. Tom Hamburger et al., "Trump campaign emails show aide's repeated efforts to set up Russia meetings," Washington Post, August 14, 2017, https://www.wash ingtonpost.com/politics/trump-campaign-emails-show-aides-repeated-efforts-to -set-up-russia-meetings/2017/08/14/54d08da6-7dc2-11e7-83c7-5bd5460f0d7e _story.html?utm_term=.0d5f53a7a22a; John Bowden, "Papadopoulos Was in Regular Contact with Stephen Miller," Hill, November 10, 2017, http://thehill .com/blogs/blog-briefing-room/news/359891-nyt-papadopoulos-was-in-regular -contact-with-stephen-miller.

2. Natasha Bertrand, "It looks like another Trump adviser has significantly changed his story about the GOP's dramatic shift on Ukraine," Business In- sider, March 3, 2017, https://www.businessinsider.com/jd-gordon-trump-adviser -ukraine-rnc-2017-3; Michael Krantz, "3 witnesses have contradicted a key por- tion of Jeff Sessions' Russia testimony—and it could intensify scrutiny on him," Business Insider, March 19, 2018, https://www.businessinsider.com/jeff-ses sions-perjury-trump-russia-meeting-papadopoulos-2018-3

3. Josh Rogin, "Trump Campaign Guts GOP's Anti-Russia Stance on Ukraine," Washington Post, July 18, 2016, https://www.washingtonpost.com/opinions /global-opinions/trump-campaign-guts-gops-anti-russia-stance-on-ukraine/2016/07 /18/98adb3b0-4cf3-11e6-a7d8-13d06b37f256_story.html?utm_term=.8a690c633 7a3; Bertrand, "It looks like another Trump adviser."

4. Philip Rucker, "Trump: 'I don't remember much' about meeting with Papado- poulos, campaign adviser who has pleaded guilty," Washington Post, Novem- ber 3, 2017, https://www.washingtonpost.com/news/post-politics/wp/2017/11 /03/trump-i-dont-remember-much-about-meeting-with-papadopoulos-campaign -adviser-who-has-pleaded-guilty/?utm_term=.80839efdd05d.

5. "Three witnesses contradict Sessions account of Trump campaign meet- ing,"Guardian, March 18, 2018, https://www.theguardian.com/us-news/2018 /mar/18/jeff-sessions-trump-campaign-meeting-witnesses-contradict.

6. Rucker, "Trump: 'I don't remember.'"

7. Jeremy Diamond and Nicole Gaouette, "Donald Trump unveils foreign policy advisers," CNN, March 3, 2016, https://www.cnn.com/2016/03/21/politics/don ald-trump-foreign-policy-team/index.html.

8. David Rutz, "Donald Trump Refuses to Say Who Will Be on His Foreign Policy Team," *Washington Free Beacon*, March 14, 2016, https://freebeacon.com /politics/trump-refuses-foreign-policy-team/; Wilson Andrews et al., "2016 Delegate Count and Primary Results," *New York Times,* July 5, 2016, https://www .nytimes.com/interactive/2016/us/elections/primary-calendar-and-results.html.

9. Glenn Thrush, "To Charm Trump, Paul Manafort Sold Himself as an Affordable Outsider Image," *New York Times*, April 8, 2017, https://www.nytimes.com/2017 /04/08/us/to-charm-trump-paul-manafort-sold-himself-as-an-affordable-outsider .html

10. Kenzi Abou-Sabi et al., "What Did Ex-Trump Aide Paul Manafort Really Do in Ukraine," NBC News, June 27, 2017, https://www.nbcnews.com/news/us -news/what-did-ex-trump-aide-paul-manafort-really-do-ukraine-n775431; Andrew Roth, "Paul Manafort Went to Kyrgyzstan to Strengthen Russia's Position," *Guardian*, August 22, 2018, https://www.theguardian.com/us-news/2018/aug/22 /paul-manafort-went-to-kyrgyzstan-to-strengthen-russias-position.

11. Michael Kranish, "He's Better than This,' Says Thomas Barrack, Trump's Loyal Whisperer," *Washington Post*, October 10, 2017, https://www.washingtonpost .com/politics/hes-better-than-this-says-thomas-barrack-trumps-loyal-whisperer /2017/10/10/067fc776-a215-11e7-8cfe-d5b912fabc99_story.html?utm_term =.902a2b7bd069; "Read the Job Application Memo Manafort Sent to Trump," *New York Times*, October 31, 2017, https://www.nytimes.com/interactive/2017 /10/31/us/politics/document-manafort-trump-application.html.

12. "Read the Job Application Memo Manafort Sent to Trump."

13. Thrush, "To Charm Trump."

14. Ibid.

15. Katy Tur et al., "Trump Campaign Manager Corey Lewandowski Ousted," NBC News, June 20, 2016, https://www.nbcnews.com/politics/2016-election/trump -campaign-manager-corey-lewandowski-ousted-n595581; Meghan Keneally, "Timeline of Paul Manafort's Role in the Trump Campaign," ABC News, October 30, 2017, https://abcnews.go.com/Politics/timeline-paul-manaforts-role -trump-campaign/story?id=50808957; Alexander Burns and Maggie Haberman, "Donald Trump Hires Paul Manafort to Lead Delegate Effort," *New York Times*, March 28, 2016, https://www.nytimes.com/politics/first-draft/2016/03/28/don ald-trump-hires-paul-manafort-to-lead-delegate-effort/.

16. John King et al., "Donald Trump Meeting Suggests Campaign Changes," CNN, April 7, 2016, https://www.cnn.com/2016/04/06/politics/trump-campaign-over haul-manafort-lewandowski/index.html.

17. Tur, "Trump Campaign Manager Corey Lewandowski Ousted"; Keneally, "Timeline of Paul Manafort's Role in the Trump Campaign"; Burns and Haberman, "Donald Trump Hires Paul Manafort to Lead Delegate Effort."

18. Ibid.

19. Kenneth P. Vogel and Ben Schreckinger, "Trump campaign rift gets personal," *Politico*, May 25, 2016, https://www.politico.com/story/2016/05/trump-cam paign-manafort-lewandowski-223532.

20. Senate Judiciary Committee documents (pp. 6–7), https://www.judiciary.sen

ate.gov/imo/media/doc/Trump%20Jr%20Exhibits_redacted.pdf; Thrush, "To
Charm Trump."

21. Emily Stewart, "Read: Donald Trump Jr.'s Congressional Testimony about the
Trump Tower Meeting," *Vox*, May 16, 2018 (Trump Jr. testimony, pp. 34–35),
https://www.vox.com/policy-and-politics/2018/5/16/17360484/donald-trump-jr
-transcript-senate-judiciary-committee; Senate Judiciary Committee documents.

22. Ibid.

23. Keneally, "Timeline of Paul Manafort's Role in the Trump Campaign"; Matt
Apuzzo et al., "Former Trump Aides Charged as Prosecutors Reveal New Campaign Ties with Russia," *New York Times*, October 30, 2017, https://www.ny
times.com/2017/10/30/us/politics/paul-manafort-indicted.html.

24. Kate Brannen, "A Timeline of Paul Manafort's Relationship with Donald
Trump," *Slate*, October 30, 2017, http://www.slate.com/articles/news_and_pol
itics/jurisprudence/2017/10/a_timeline_of_paul_manafort_s_relationship_with
_the_trump_world.html.

25. Caitlin Oprysko, "Trump: Manafort Trial Is a 'Very Sad Day for Our Country,' "
Politico, August 17, 2018, https://www.politico.com/story/2018/08/17/paul
-manafort-trial-trump-pardon-783133.

26. Tom McCarthy, "Sean Spicer Contradicts Trump's Manafort Claims in New
Book," *Guardian*, July 12, 2018, https://www.theguardian.com/us-news/2018
/jul/12/sean-spicer-contradicts-trumps-manafort-claims-in-new-book; Kenneth P.
Vogel, "Manafort Advised Trump Team on Russian Scandal," *Politico*, May 25,
2017, https://www.politico.com/story/2017/05/25/manafort-trump-russia-advise
-238803.

27. Vogel, "Manafort Advised Trump Team on Russian Scandal."

28. Darren Samuelson and Josh Gerstein, "Manafort Trial Day 9: Witness Suggests
Trump Role Helped Manafort Nab Loans," *Politico*, August 10, 2018, https://
www.politico.com/story/2018/08/10/manafort-trial-day-9-judge-ts-ellis-772518.

29. Jennifer Rubin, "Why Trump Is So Freaked Out by the Manafort Trial," *Washington Post*, August 1, 2018, https://www.washingtonpost.com/blogs/right-turn
/wp/2018/08/01/how-the-manafort-trial-may-hurt-trump/?utm_term=.9a4341b6
5fa7.

30. Mike McIntire, "Manafort Was in Debt to Pro-Russia Interests, Cyprus Records
Show," *New York Times*, July 19, 2017, https://www.nytimes.com/2017/07/19/us
/politics/paul-manafort-russia-trump.html; Tom Hamburger et al., "Manafort Offered to Give Russian Billionaire 'Private Briefings' on 2016 Campaign," *Washington Post*, September 20, 2017, https://www.washingtonpost.com/politics
/manafort-offered-to-give-russian-billionaire-private-briefings-on-2016-campaign
/2017/09/20/399bba1a-9d48-11e7-8ea1-ed975285475e_story.html?utm_term
=.166af7bf895c.

31. Nick Gass, "Trump Names Sessions Chairman of National Security Committee,"
Politico, March 3, 2016, https://www.politico.com/blogs/2016-gop-primary-live
-updates-and-results/2016/03/donald-trump-jeff-sessions-chairman-of-national
-security-committee-220220.

32. Artin Afkhami, "A Timeline of Carter Page's Contacts with Russia," *Slate*, No-

vember 7, 2017, http://www.slate.com/articles/news_and_politics/jurisprudence
/2017/11/a_timeline_of_carter_page_s_contacts_with_russia.html.

33. "FBI Releases Carter Page's Surveillance Records," CBS News, July 22, 2018,
https://www.cbsnews.com/news/carter-page-fisa-documents-released-today-2018
-07-21/; HPSCI documents (Carter Page testimony, November 2017, p. 45),
https://www.documentcloud.org/documents/4176248-Carter-Page-Hpsci-Hearing
-Transcript-Nov-2-2017.html.

34. "FBI Releases Carter Page's Surveillance Records"; Tom Hamburger and Rosalind S. Helderman, "'Anyone . . . with a Pulse': How a Russia-friendly adviser
found his way into the Trump campaign," *Washington Post*, May 25, 2017, https://
www.washingtonpost.com/politics/anyone—with-a-pulse-how-a-russia-friendly
-adviser-found-his-way-into-the-trump-campaign/2017/05/25/32438f72-4014
-11e7-8c25-44d09ff5a4a8_story.html?utm_term=.c8a4131f7d4d;HPSCIdocuments;
January 26, 2015, https://www.justice.gov/opa/pr/attorney-general-holder-announces
-charges-against-russian-spy-ring-new-york-city.

35. Jeremy Diamond and Jeremy Herb, "Who Is Michael Flynn?" CNN, December 1, 2017, https://www.cnn.com/2017/12/01/politics/who-is-michael-flynn
/index.html.

36. Ali Watkins, "A Former Trump Adviser Met with a Russian Spy," *BuzzFeed
News*, April 3, 2017, https://www.buzzfeednews.com/article/alimwatkins/a-former
-trump-adviser-met-with-a-russian-spy.

37. Ibid.

38. Massimo Calabresi and Anna Abramson, "Carter Page Touted Kremlin Contacts
in a 2013 Letter," *Time*, February 4, 2018, http://time.com/5132126/carter-page
-russia-2013-letter/.

39. HPSCI documents.

40. Hamburger and Helderman, "'Anyone . . . with a Pulse.'"

41. Ibid.

42. Mark Hosenball and Steven Holland, "Trump Being Advised by ex-U.S. Lieutenant General Who Favors Closer Russia Ties," *Reuters,* February 26, 2016,
https://www.reuters.com/article/us-usa-election-trump-advisor/trump-being-ad
vised-by-ex-u-s-lieutenant-general-who-favors-closer-russia-ties-idUSMTZSA
PEC2Q6G3JRH.

43. Josh Marshall, "Why did Clovis say Russia was a principal focus of the campaign," *Talking Points Memo,* November 1, 2017, https://talkingpointsmemo
.com/edblog/why-did-clovis-say-russia-was-a-principal-focus-of-the-campaign;
Allegra Kirkland, "Trump Adviser Who Pleaded Guilty Met Russian-Linked
Prof About Clinton 'Dirt,'" *Talking Points Memo*, October 30, 2017, https://
talkingpointsmemo.com/muckraker/george-papadopoulos-pleads-guilty-lying
-to-fbi.

44. Pamela Brown and Jeremy Herb, "Papadopoulos' fiancée says he didn't act
'without campaign approval," CNN, December 8, 2017, https://www.cnn.com
/2017/12/08/politics/george-papadopoulos-fiancee/index.html.

45. Ibid.

46. Jake Tapper, "The Mysterious Case Of George Papadopoulos: George Papado-

poulos Ignited the Russia Conspiracy Investigation," CNN, September 7, 2018, http://www.cnn.com/TRANSCRIPTS/1809/07/csr.01.html.

47. Kirkland, "Trump Adviser Who Pleaded Guilty."

48. Papadopoulos affidavit, CNN, October 30, 2017, https://www.cnn.com/2017/10 /30/politics/george-papadopoulos-offense-affidavit-complaint/index.html; Tapper, "The Mysterious Case of George Papadopoulos."

49. Ibid.; Ali Watkins, "Mysterious Putin 'Niece' Has a Name," *Politico*, November 9, 2017, https://www.politico.com/story/2017/11/09/putin-niece-olga-vinogra dova-george-papadopoulos-russia-probe-244758.

50. Papadopoulos affidavit.

51. Ibid.

52. Sharon LaFraniere et al., "A London Meeting of an Unlikely Group: How a Trump Adviser Came to Learn of Clinton 'Dirt,'" *New York Times*, November 10, 2017, https://www.nytimes.com/2017/11/10/us/russia-inquiry-trump.html.

53. Ibid.

54. Ibid.

55. Linley Sander, "Trump Knew Papadopoulos Would Meet with Foreigners, Ex-Aide Claims," *Newsweek*, November 17, 2017, https://www.newsweek.com /papadopoulos-says-trump-authorized-him-meet-foreign-leaders-714644.

56. Ibid.

57. Ibid.

58. "A transcript of Donald Trump's meeting with the *Washington Post* editorial board," *Washington Post*, March 21, 2016, https://www.washingtonpost.com /blogs/post-partisan/wp/2016/03/21/a-transcript-of-donald-trumps-meeting-with -the-washington-post-editorial-board/?utm_term=.5d8482216abe; direct Twitter message from Marianna Kakaouani, the Kathimerini reporter who interviewed Papadopoulos and is cited in the *Newsweek* article: "That[']s the story he told me—that that picture [from March 31] was not from [then] but from [March] 21st. That it was that day that he got invited [to] his [Trump's] Washington hotel for a speech and [at the] last minute he got invited upstairs in[to] one of the rooms [for a one-on-one meeting]. . . . right after that the [March 21, 2016] *Washington Post* interview happened. That[']s what he told me [in] December [2016]. He might have been mixed up but seemed quite certain about the sequence of events." Trump did indeed give a "speech" at his "Washington hotel" on March 21, 2016, just as Papadopoulos says he did, and he also did give his *Washington Post* interview that day. For the March 21, 2016, Trump speech, see https://www.c-span.org/video/?407049-1/donald-trump-news-conference-wash ington-dc.

59. Dion Nissenbaum, "Private Group Sought to Arm Syrian Rebels," *Wall Street Journal*, May 18, 2014, https://www.wsj.com/articles/private-group-sought-to -arm-syrian-rebels-1400464766.

60. Adam Serwer, "Top Romney Adviser Tied to Militia That Massacred," *Mother Jones*, October 27, 2011, https://www.motherjones.com/politics/2011/10/walid -phares-mitt-romney-lebanese-forces/; Southern Poverty Law Center, March 2016, https://www.splcenter.org/hatewatch/2016/03/28/meet-anti-muslim-lead

ers-advising-donald-trump-and-ted-cruz; Jennifer Williams, "How to get a top national security job in Trump's administration: Be afraid of Muslims," *Vox*, November 16, 2016, https://www.vox.com/world/2016/11/16/13638606/trump-sec retary-state-defense-giuliani-bolton-islam-terrorism.

61. Michael A. Memoli, "Trump's national security advisor, Michael Flynn, resigns over contacts with Russia," *Los Angeles Times*, February 13, 2017, http://www .latimes.com/politics/washington/la-na-essential-washington-updates-keith-kel logg-is-trump-s-new-national-1487051920-htmlstory.html; White House press release, April 23, 2018, https://www.whitehouse.gov/briefings-statements/vice -president-mike-pence-announces-lieutenant-general-ret-keith-kellogg-national -security-advisor/.

62. Jeremy Scahill, "Notorious Mercenary Erik Prince Is Advising from the Shadows," *Intercept*, January 17, 2017, https://theintercept.com/2017/01/17/notorious -mercenary-erik-prince-is-advising-trump-from-the-shadows/; Bryan Bender, "Trump Names Mike Flynn National Security Adviser," *Politico*, November 17, 2016; Spencer S. Hsu and Victoria St. Martin, "Four Blackwater Guards Sentenced in Iraq shootings of 31 Unarmed Civilians," *Washington Post*, April 13, 2015, https://www.washingtonpost.com/local/crime/four-blackwater-guards -sentenced-in-iraq-shootings-of-31-unarmed-civilians/2015/04/13/55b777e0 -dee4-11e4-be40-566e2653afe5_story.html.

63. Ryan Hutchins, "Christie: Warning About Flynn Among Reasons I Was Fired from Trump Transition," *Politico*, December 6, 2017, https://www.politico.com /states/new-jersey/story/2017/12/06/christie-warning-about-flynn-among-reasons-i -was-fired-from-trump-transition-136432.

64. Matthew Rosenberg and Matt Apuzzo, "Flynn Is Said to Have Talked to Russians about Sanctions Before Trump Took Office," *New York Times*, February 9, 2017, https://www.nytimes.com/2017/02/09/us/flynn-is-said-to-have-talked-to-russians -about-sanctions-before-trump-took-office.html; Matthew Mosk et al., "Putin ally suggests Seychelles meeting with Erik Prince more than chance encounter over a beer," ABC News, May 2018, https://abcnews.go.com/Politics/putin-ally-sey chelles-meeting-erik-prince-chance-encounter/story?id=55408942.

65. Alexandra Wilts, "Trump says he can't 'remember much' about his 2016 meeting with adviser who pleaded guilty in Russia probe," *Independent,* November 3, 2017, https://www.independent.co.uk/news/world/americas/us-politics/trump -russia-investigation-meeting-george-papadopoulos-latest-response-comments -a8036231.html.

66. Robert Farley and Eugene Kiely, "Was Papadopoulos a 'Low-Level Volunteer," FactCheck.org, October 31, 2017, https://www.factcheck.org/2017/10/papado poulos-low-level-volunteer/.

67. HPSCI documents; "Carter Page at a Meeting with Tulsi Gabbard in Hawaii on April 1, 2016," Daily Kos, June 26, 2018, https://www.dailykos.com/stories /2018/6/26/1775668/-Carter-Page-at-a-Meeting-with-Tulsi-Gabbard-in-Hawaii -on-April-1-2016.

68. Karin Freifeld et al., "Exclusive—Sources Contradict Sessions' Testimony He

Opposed Russia Outreach," Reuters, March 18, 2018, https://af.reuters.com/arti
cle/worldNews/idAFKBN1GUoNE.

69. Andrew Prokop, "Jeff Sessions's Russia Testimony Problem Keeps Getting Worse," *Vox,* November 14, 2017, https://www.vox.com/policy-and-politics /2017/11/3/16599426/jeff-sessions-russia-testimony.

70. Freifeld et al., "Exclusive—Sources Contradict Sessions' Testimony He Opposed Russia Outreach."

71. Ibid.

72. Ibid.

73. Scott Shane, "Trump Campaign Got Early Word Russia Had Democrats' Emails," *New York Times*, October 30, 2017, https://www.nytimes.com/2017/10 /30/us/politics/trump-russia-mueller-indictment.html.

74. Chuck Ross, "Trump Adviser Proposed Meeting with Russians During Campaign but Was Shot Down by Sessions," *Daily Caller*, August 17, 2017, http:// dailycaller.com/2017/08/17/trump-adviser-proposed-meeting-with-russians-during -campaign-but-was-shot-down-by-sessions/.

75. Freifeld et al., "Exclusive."

76. Catherine Herridge, "Special Counsel Investigators Start Questioning White House Staffers," Fox News, September 29, 2017, http://www.foxnews.com /politics/2017/09/29/special-counsel-investigators-start-questioning-white-house -staffers.html; Matthew Rosenberg et al., "Ongoing Trump Migraine: His Initial Foreign Policy Team," *New York Times*, October 31, 2017, https://www.nytimes .com/2017/10/31/us/trump-foreign-policy-advisers.html.

77. Mikhaila Fogel, "Document: George Papadopoulos Defense Team Sentencing Memo," *Lawfare*, September 1, 2018, https://www.lawfareblog.com/document -george-papadopoulos-defense-team-sentencing-memo.

78. Ken Dilanian et al., "FBI Told Trump Russians Would Try to Infiltrate His Campaign," NBC News, December 19, 2017, https://www.nbcnews.com/news /us-news/fbi-warned-trump-2016-russians-would-try-infiltrate-his-campaign-n83 0596.

79. John Bowden, "Papadopoulos was in regular contact with Stephen Miller, helped edit Trump speech: Report," *Hill*, November 10, 2017, http://thehill.com/blogs /blog-briefing-room/news/359891-nyt-papadopoulos-was-in-regular-contact -with-stephen-miller.

80. Brianne Pfannenstiel, "Reports: Iowan Sam Clovis Encouraged Papadopoulos Russia Meeting," *Des Moines Register,* October 31, 2017, https://www.des moinesregister.com/story/news/politics/2017/10/31/sam-clovis-encouraged-papa dopoulos-russia-meeting/817054001/.

81. Rosalind S. Helderman and Tom Hamburger, "Top Campaign Officials Knew of Trump Adviser's Outreach to Russia," *Washington Post*, October 30, 2017, https://www.washingtonpost.com/politics/trump-campaign-adviser-pleaded -guilty-to-lying-about-russian-contacts/2017/10/30/d525e712-bd7d-11e7-97d9 -bdab5a0ab381_story.html?utm_term=.cb347272de62.

82. Ellen Nakashima, "Russian government hackers penetrated DNC, stole oppo-

sition research on Trump," *Washington Post*, June 14, 2016, https://www.wash ingtonpost.com/world/national-security/russian-government-hackers-penetrated -dnc-stole-opposition-research-on-trump/2016/06/14/cf006cb4-316e-11e6-8ff7 -7b6c1998b7a0_story.html?utm_term=.bbd72169d749.

83. Evan Perez, "Sources: US Officials Warned DNC of Hack Months Before the Part Acted," CNN, July 26, 2016, https://www.cnn.com/2016/07/25/politics /democratic-convention-dnc-emails-russia/index.html.

84. "Transcript: Donald Trump Expounds on His Foreign Policy Views," *New York Times*, March 27, 2017, https://www.nytimes.com/2016/03/27/us/politics/don ald-trump-transcript.html; Rosalind S. Helderman, "Mueller was investigat- ing Trump adviser as unregistered agent of Israel, his wife says," *Washington Post*, June 5, 2018, https://www.washingtonpost.com/politics/mueller-was-in vestigating-trump-adviser-as-unregistered-agent-of-israel-his-wife-says/2018/06 /05/8a30b258-68ec-11e8-bea7-c8eb28bc52b1_story.html?utm_term=.a99614c72 191; Luke Harding, "Why Carter Page Was Worth Watching," *Politico*, February 3, 2018, https://www.politico.com/magazine/story/2018/02/03/carter-page-nunes -memo-216934; Rosenberg et al., "Ongoing Trump Migraine.

85. "Transcript: Donald Trump Expounds on His Foreign Policy Views"; Helder- man, "Mueller was investigating Trump adviser"; Harding, "Why Carter Page Was Worth Watching."

86. Rosalind S. Helderman, "Who's Who in the George Papadopoulos Court Docu- ments," *Washington Post*, November 2, 2017, https://www.washingtonpost.com /politics/whos-who-in-the-george-papadopoulos-court-documents/2017/10/30 /e131158c-bdb3-11e7-97d9-bdab5a0ab381_story.html?utm_term=.cf33cbfed723.

87. Asha Rangappa, "What the FISA Warrants Against Paul Manafort Tell Us About Mueller's Investigation," Just Security, September 23, 2017, https://www.justse curity.org/45255/fisa-warrants-paul-manafort-muellers-investigation/.

88. Evan Perez et al., "Exclusive: US Government Wiretapped Former Trump Cam- paign Chairman," CNN, September 19, 2017, https://www.cnn.com/2017/09/18 /politics/paul-manafort-government-wiretapped-fisa-russians/index.html.

89. Department of Justice, indictment against employees of the Internet Research Agency, February 16, 2018, https://www.justice.gov/file/1035477/download.

90. Juliet Eilperin, " Trump agriculture nominee Sam Clovis confirms he has no hard-science credentials, withdraws over ties to Russia probe," *Washington Post*, November 2, 2017, https://www.washingtonpost.com/news/energy-environment /wp/2017/11/02/sam-clovis-trumps-nominee-for-usdas-top-scientist-confirms-he -has-no-hard-science-credentials/?utm_term=.8b82ba417a09.

91. Bryon York, "Trump Campaign Vet: Informant Used Me to Get to Papadopou- los," *Washington Examiner*, May 28, 2018, https://www.washingtonexaminer .com/news/trump-campaign-vet-sam-clovis-says-informant-used-him-to-get-to -papadopoulos.

92. Ibid.

93. Ben Schreckinger, "GOP Researcher Who Sought Clinton Emails Had Alt-right Help," *Politico*, July 11, 2017, https://www.politico.com/magazine/story/2017 /07/11/gop-researcher-who-sought-clinton-emails-had-alt-right-help-215359.

94. Ibid.

95. Catherine Boudreau and Josh Dawsey, "Clovis Said to Be 'Cooperative Witness' in Senate Russia Probe," *Politico*, October 31, 2017, https://www.politico.com /story/2017/10/31/sam-clovis-senate-russia-investigation-244370.

96. Department of Justice, October 5, 2017, https://www.justice.gov/file/1007346 /download; Boudreau and Dawsey, "Clovis Said to Be 'Cooperative Witness.'"

97. Ibid.

98. Borzou Daragahi, "Papadopoulos And Flynn Client Both Tied To Israeli Energy Consortium," *BuzzFeed News*, November 3, 2017, https://www.buzzfeednews .com/article/borzoudaragahi/papadopoulos-and-flynn-client-both-tied-to-israeli -energy.

99. Ibid.

100. Ibid.

101. Darren Samuelsohn, "Forget Rudy: Here Are Trump's Fiercest Defenders," *Politico*, June 9, 2018, https://www.politico.com/story/2018/06/09/trump-lawyers -joseph-digenova-victoria-toensing-634996.

102. Aaron Blake, "Sam Clovis's really bad excuse for greenlighting a Trump campaign meeting with Russians," *Washington Post*, October 31, 2017, https://www.washing tonpost.com/news/the-fix/wp/2017/10/31/sam-cloviss-really-bad-excuse-for-green lighting-a-trump-campaign-meeting-with-russians/?utm_term=.80edb367da0e.

103. Alan Rappeport, "Top Experts Confounded by Advisers to Donald Trump," *New York Times*, March 22, 2016, https://www.nytimes.com/2016/03/23/us/politics /donald-trump-foreign-policy-advisers.html.

104. Ibid.

105. Ibid.

106. Diamond and Gaouette, "Donald Trump Unveils Foreign Policy."

107. Dion Nissenbaum, "Private Group Sought to Arm Syrian Rebels."

108. Ibid.

109. "Donald Trump's Top Foreign Adviser, Joseph Schmitz, Is a Former Blackwater Executive," Democracy Now, March 25, 2016, https://www.democracynow.org /2016/3/25/donald_trumps_top_foreign_adviser_joseph.

110. Southern Poverty Law Center, March 2016.

111. Helderman, "Mueller Was Investigating."

112. Ibid.

113. Sharon LaFraniere et al., "How the Russia Inquiry Began: A Campaign Aide, Drinks and Talk of Political Dirt," *New York Times*, December 30, 2017, https:// www.nytimes.com/2017/12/30/us/politics/how-fbi-russia-investigation-began -george-papadopoulos.html.

114. Helderman, "Mueller Was Investigating."

115. Ibid.

116. David M. Weinberg, "Know Comment: The Donald's Foreign Policy," *Jerusalem Post*, April 7, 2016, https://www.jpost.com/Opinion/Know-Comment-The -Donalds-foreign-policy-450602.

117. Amir Tibon and Allison Kaplan Sommer, "Trump Campaign Adviser Who Pled Guilty to Lying to FBI Has Surprising Ties to Israeli Settlers," *Haaretz*, Octo-

ber 30, 2017, https://www.haaretz.com/us-news/george-papadopoulos-has-sur prising-ties-to-israeli-settlers-1.5461531; *Politico*, March 2016, https://www.po litico.com/blogs/2016-gop-primary-live-updates-and-results/2016/03/trump-for eign-policy-team-221049.

118. Bertrand, "It looks like another Trump adviser has significantly changed his story"; Wilts, "Trump says he can't 'remember much.' "

119. Weinberg, "Know Comment."

120. Mark Mazzetti et al., "Trump Jr. and Other Aides Met with Gulf Emissary Offering Help to Win Election," *New York Times*, May 19, 2018, https://www.nytimes .com/2018/05/19/us/politics/trump-jr-saudi-uae-nader-prince-zamel.html.

121. Alexander Murinson, "The Ties Between Israel and Azerbaijan," BESA Center, October 2014, https://besacenter.org/wp-content/uploads/2014/10/MSPS110 -web.pdf

122. Ken Klippenstein, "Inside the Mysterious Intelligence Firm Now in Mueller's Sights," *Daily Beast,* June 4, 2018, https://www.thedailybeast.com/inside-the -mysterious-intelligence-firm-now-in-muellers-sights.

123. Daragahi, "Papadopoulos and Flynn Client"; ECFR website, https://www.ecfr.eu.

124. Margot Cleveland, "Here's What We Can Glean from What George Papadopoulos's Wife Is Telling Media," *Federalist*, June 13, 2018, http://thefederalist.com /2018/06/13/heres-can-glean-george-papadopouloss-wife-telling-media/.

125. Ibid.

126. "Embattled ex Trump Adviser's Cyprus Connection," *Cyprus Mail*, November 5, 2017, https://cyprus-mail.com/2017/11/05/embattled-ex-trump-advisers-cyprus -connection/; Daragahi, "Papadopoulos And Flynn Client."

127. Quineta Jurecic, "Document: George Papadopoulos Sentencing Memo," *Lawfare*, August 17, 2018, https://www.lawfareblog.com/document-george-papado poulos-sentencing-memo.

128. Sue Surkes, "Ex-Trump adviser was reportedly accused of being unregistered Israeli agent," *Times of Israel*, June 7, 2018, https://www.timesofisrael.com/ex -trump-adviser-was-reportedly-accused-of-being-unregistered-israeli-agent/; Tibon and Sommer, "Trump Campaign Adviser."

129. Surkes, "Ex-Trump Adviser."

130. Helderman, "Mueller Was Investigating."

131. Ibid.; Twitter (Simona Mangiante account), August 16, 2018, https://twitter.com /simonamangiante/status/1030325912007585792; GoFundMe, August 2018, https://www.gofundme.com/rmjtv-legal-fees.

132. Katelyn Polantz and Caroline Kelly, "George Papadopoulos gets 14 days in prison," CNN, September 8, 2018, https://www.cnn.com/2018/09/07/politics /george-papadopoulos-sentencing-hearing/index.html.

133. Mikhaila Fogel, "Document: George Papadopoulos Defense Team Sentencing Memo," *Lawfare*, September 1, 2018, https://www.lawfareblog.com/document -george-papadopoulos-defense-team-sentencing-memo.

134. Ibid.

CHAPTER SIX: THE MAYFLOWER HOTEL

1. James Kirchick, "Donald Trump's Russia Connection," *Politico* (Europe), April 27, 2016, https://www.politico.eu/article/donald-trumps-russia-connections-for eign-policy-presidential-campaign/.
2. "Donald Trump Delivers Foreign Policy Speech," hosted by Center for the National Interest's magazine, *The National Interest*, April 27, 2016, https://cftni.org /recent-events/donald-trump-delivers-foreign-policy-speech/.
3. Meghan Keneally, "A Closer Look at the Meetings with Russians the Trump Team Failed to Disclose," ABC News, October 12, 2017, https://abcnews.go .com/Politics/closer-meetings-russians-trump-team-failed-disclose/story?id=50 397154.
4. Robert C. McFarlane, "The Global Oil Rush," *National Interest*, June 1, 2006, https://nationalinterest.org/article/the-global-oil-rush-302?page=0%2C1.
5. Transcript of Trump's Foreign Policy Speech, *New York Times,* as transcribed by Federal News Service, April 27, 2016, https://www.nytimes.com/2016/04/28/us /politics/transcript-trump-foreign-policy.html.
6. Ibid.
7. Ibid.
8. John Bowden, "Papadopoulos was in regular contact with Stephen Miller, helped edit Trump speech: report," *Hill*, November 10, 2017, http://thehill.com /blogs/blog-briefing-room/news/359891-nyt-papadopoulos-was-in-regular-contact -with-stephen-miller.
9. Caleb Melby et al., "Kushner Foreign Policy Role Grew After Kissinger Lunch," Bloomberg, August 13, 2018, https://www.bloomberg.com/news/articles/2018 -08-13/kushner-s-ties-to-russia-linked-group-began-with-kissinger-lunch.
10. Maria Butina, "The Bear and the Elephant," *National Interest*, June 12, 2015, https://nationalinterest.org/feature/the-bear-the-elephant-13098.
11. Melby et al., "Kushner Foreign Plicy Role Grew After Kissinger Lunch."
12. Ibid.
13. Ibid.
14. Ibid.
15. Mark Hosenball, "Former Reagan Aide Helped Trump Write Foreign Policy Speech," Reuters, June 8, 2016, https://www.reuters.com/article/us-usa-election -trump-adviser-idUSKCN0YU2I9.
16. Stephanie Kirchgaessner, "Lobbyist for Russian Interests Says He Attended Dinners Hosted by Sessions," *Guardian*, June 15, 2017, https://www.theguardian .com/us-news/2017/jun/15/lobbyist-russian-interests-jeff-sessions-testimony.
17. Sharon LaFraniere et al., "A London Meeting of an Unlikely Group: How A Trump Adviser Came to Learn of Clinton Dirt," *New York Times*, November 10, 2017, https://www.nytimes.com/2017/11/10/us/russia-inquiry-trump.html.
18. Jonathan Martin and Jeremy W. Peters, "Donald Trump to Reshape Image, New Campaign Chief Tells G.O.P.," *New York Times*, April 21, 2016, https://www.ny times.com/2016/04/22/us/politics/donald-trump-to-reshape-image-new-campaign -chief-tells-gop.html.

19. Kenneth P. Vogel and David Stern, "Authorities Looked into Manafort Protégé," *Politico*, March 8, 2017, https://www.politico.com/story/2017/03/trump-russia -manafort-235850.

20. Ibid.

21. Aaron Blake, " 'How do we use [this] to get whole?': The most intriguing new Paul Manafort-Russia email," *Washington Post*, September 20, 2017, https://www .washingtonpost.com/news/the-fix/wp/2017/09/20/paul-manaforts-ominous-email -to-an-aide-how-do-we-use-this-to-get-whole/?utm_term=.dc24a252f363.

22. Aggelos Petropoulos and Richard Engel, "Manafort Had $60 million Relation- ship with a Russian Oligarch," NBC News, October 13, 2017, https://www.nbc news.com/news/world/manafort-had-60m-relationship-russian-oligarch-n810541.

23. Vogel and Stern, "Authorities Looked into Manafort Protégé."

24. Ibid.

25. Sonam Sheth, " A Putin Ally's Jet Arrived in the US Within Hours of a Meeting Between Trump Campaign Chairman Paul Manafort and a Russian Operative," *Business Insider*, March 30, 2018, https://www.businessinsider.com/oleg-deri paska-jet-arrived-in-us-after-manafort-kilimnik-meeting-2018-3.

26. Isaac Arnsdorf and Benjamin Oreskes, "Putin's Favorite Congressman," *Polit- ico*, November 23, 2016, https://www.politico.com/story/2016/11/putin-con gress-rohrabacher-trump-231775; CNN Staff, "Trump Tower Russia Meeting: At Least Eight People in the Room," CNN, July 17, 2017, https://www.cnn.com /2017/07/14/politics/donald-trump-jr-meeting/index.html.

27. Ibid.

28. Nicholas Fandos, "He's a Member of Congress. The Kremlin Likes Him So Much, It Gave Him a Code Name," *New York Times*, November 21, 2017, https:// www.nytimes.com/2017/11/21/us/politics/dana-rohrabacher-putin-trump-kremlin -under-fire.html.

29. Arnsdorf and Oreskes, "Putin's Favorite Congressman."

30. Jeremy Scahill, "Notorious Mercenary Erik Prince Is Advising Trump from the Shadows," *Intercept,* January 17, 2017, https://theintercept.com/2017/01/17/no torious-mercenary-erik-prince-is-advising-trump-from-the-shadows/.

31. Jeremy Herb et al., "Democrats Grilled Erik Prince About Meeting Bannon Be- fore Seychelles Trip," CNN, December 6, 2017,https://www.cnn.com/2017/12 /06/politics/erik-prince-steve-bannon-seychelles-meeting/index.html; House tes- timony of Erik Prince, U.S. House of Representatives, Permanent Select Com- mittee on Intelligence, November 30, 2017, https://docs.house.gov/meetings/IG /IG00/20171130/106661/HHRG-115-IG00-Transcript-20171130.pdf.

32. Ned Parker and Jonathan Landay, "Exclusive: Trump Son-in-Law Had Undis- closed Contacts with Russian Envoy—Sources," Reuters, May 26, 2017, https:// www.reuters.com/article/us-usa-trump-fbi-kushner-exclusive-idUSKBN18N018.

33. Ibid.

34. "Jared Kushner's Statement on Russia to Congressional Committees," CNN, July 24, 2017, https://www.cnn.com/2017/07/24/politics/jared-kushner-state ment-russia-2016-election/index.html; Melby et al., "Kushner Foreign Policy Role Grew after Kissinger Lunch."

35. Philip Bump, "Timeline: How a Trump Adviser Tried to Work with the Russian Government," *Washington Post*, October 30, 2017, https://www.washingtonpost .com/news/politics/wp/2017/10/30/timeline-how-a-trump-adviser-tried-to-work -with-the-russian-government/?utm_term=.b869dfa4de32.

36. Ibid.

37. Ibid.

38. Ibid.

39. Ibid.

40. Ibid.

41. Natasha Bertrand, "Clinton 'Dirt,' " *Business Insider*, November 13, 2017, https://www.businessinsider.com/george-papadopoulos-stephen-miller-trump -russia-clinton-2017-11.

42. "Timeline."

43. Sharon LaFraniere et al.,"How the Russia Inquiry Began: A Campaign Aide, Drinks and Talk of Political Dirt," *New York Times*, December 30, 2017, https:// www.nytimes.com/2017/12/30/us/politics/how-fbi-russia-investigation-began -george-papadopoulos.html.

44. Bump, "Timeline."

45. Ibid.

46. Donald Trump, "The National Interest: Donald Trump Foreign Policy Speech," National Press Club, April 27, 2016, https://www.press.org/events/national -interest-donald-trump-foreign-policy-speech-invitation-only; Jonathan Easley "Trump Changes Location of Foreign Policy Speech," *Hill,* April 22, 2016, http://thehill.com/blogs/ballot-box/277308-trump-to-give-foreign-policy-speech -at-national-press-club; "Event Facilities Description," National Press Club, https://www.press.org/services/event-facilities/main-level; "Event Space Chart," Mayflower Hotel, https://www.historichotels.org/hotels-resorts/the-mayflower -hotel-autograph-collection/meetings.php.

47. Shadow Governance Intel, "The Mysterious Rosneft Deal and Its Conse-quences," OilPrice.com, May 31, 2017, https://oilprice.com/Geopolitics/Interna tional/The-Mysterious-Rosneft-Deal-And-Its-Consequences.html.

48. "The Steele Dossier," Moscow Project, December 13, 2006, full Steele Dossier transcript, https://themoscowproject.org/dossier/.

49. Shadow Governance Intel, "The Mysterious Rosneft Deal And Its Conse-quences."

50. Melby et al., "Kushner Foreign Policy Role Grew after Kissinger Lunch."

51. MSNBC, "Donald Trump Lied About His Relationship With Vladimir Putin," October 25, 2016, YouTube video, posted November 2, 2016, https://www.you tube.com/watch?time_continue=32&v=ZqCo8e459Vo.

52. Adam Entous et al., "Sessions Met With Russian Envoy Twice Last Year, En-counters He Later Did Not Disclose," *Washington Post*, March 1, 2017, https:// www.washingtonpost.com/world/national-security/sessions-spoke-twice-with -russian-ambassador-during-trumps-presidential-campaign-justice-officials-say /2017/03/01/77205eda-feac-11e6-99b4-9e613afeb09f_story.html?utm_term= .d5b7accbc783.

53. Manu Raju et al., "Comey Told Senators Sessions May Have Met Russia's Ambassador a Third Time," CNN, June 8, 2017, https://www.cnn.com/2017/06/08/politics/jeff-sessions-kislyak-meeting/.
54. Ibid.
55. "Jeff Sessions' Prepared Remarks to Intelligence Committee," Fox News, June 13, 2017, http://www.foxnews.com/politics/2017/06/13/jeff-sessions-prepared-remarks-to-intelligence-committee.html.
56. Ibid.
57. Alice Ollstein, "What Really Happened at the Mayflower? Sessions Gives Conflicting Answers," *Talking Points Memo*, June 13, 2017, https://talkingpointsmemo.com/dc/sessions-mayflower-hotel-trump-kislyak-russia-senate.
58. Julia Ioffe, "Why Did Jeff Sessions Really Meet with Sergey Kislyak?" *Atlantic*, June 13, 2017, https://www.theatlantic.com/politics/archive/2017/06/why-did-jeff-sessions-really-meet-sergey-kislyak/530091/.
59. Ibid.
60. Melby et al., "Kushner Foreign Policy Role Grew after Kissinger Lunch."
61. Nicholas Fandos and Michael S. Schmidt, "Tantalizing Testimony From a Top Trump Aide Sets Off a Search for Proof," *New York Times*, May 15, 2018, https://www.nytimes.com/2018/05/15/us/politics/john-mashburn-trump-russia-email-papadopoulos.html.
62. Kirchick, "Donald Trump's Russia Connection."
63. Ibid.
64. Fred Pleitgen, "Donald Trump's Foreign Policy Speech Earns Praise in Russia," CNN, April 28, 2016, https://www.cnn.com/2016/04/28/politics/donald-trump-russia-putin/index.html.
65. Ibid.
66. LaFraniere et al., "How the Russia Inquiry Began."
67. Ibid.
68. Kirchick, "Donald Trump's Russia Connection."
69. Ibid.
70. "Transcript: Donald Trump's Foreign Policy Speech," *New York Times*, April 27, 2016, https://www.nytimes.com/2016/04/28/us/politics/transcript-trump-foreign-policy.html.
71. Jonathan Chait, "Trump Is Fulfilling Russia's Dream of Splitting the Western Alliance," *New York*, June 8, 2018, http://nymag.com/daily/intelligencer/2018/06/trump-is-fulfilling-russias-dream-of-splitting-the-west.html.
72. Eric Lipton et al., "The Perfect Weapon: How Russian Cyberpower Invaded the U.S.," *New York Times*, December 13, 2016, https://www.nytimes.com/2016/12/13/us/politics/russia-hack-election-dnc.html?hp&action=click&pgtype=Homepage&clickSource=story-heading&module=a-lede-package-region&region=top-news&WT.nav=top-news&_r=0.
73. Martin and Peters, "Donald Trump to Reshape Image, New Campaign Chief Tells G.O.P."; Reuters, "Inside Donald Trump's Image Makeover," *Newsweek*, April 22, 2016, https://www.newsweek.com/donald-trump-image-makeover-foreign-policy-general-election-voters-popularity-451660.

74. Frank Jacobs, "How Donald Trump Sees the World—in Three Maps," Big Think, April 25, 2016, https://bigthink.com/strange-maps/the-world-according-to-trump.

75. Easley, "Trump Changes Location of Foreign Policy Speech"; "Event Facilities Description," National Press Club; "Event Space Chart," Mayflower Hotel.

76. Martin and Peters, "Donald Trump to Reshape Image, New Campaign Chief Tells G.O.P."

77. Ben Schreckinger and Nick Gass, "Trump Vows to Make America Strong Again," *Politico*, April 27, 2016, https://www.politico.com/story/2016/04/trump-foreign-policy-222537.

78. Ibid.

79. Ibid.

80. Ioffe, "Why Did Jeff Sessions Really Meet with Sergey Kislyak?"

81. Bertrand, "Clinton 'Dirt.' "

82. Ibid.

83. Jacqueline Thomsen, "Ex-Trump Staffer at Center of Mueller Probe Sat Next to Sessions at Campaign Dinner: Report," *Hill,* October 31, 2017, http://thehill.com/homenews/administration/358152-ex-trump-staffer-sat-next-to-sessions-at-campaign-dinner-report.

84. LaFraniere et al., "How the Russia Inquiry Began."

85. Ibid.

86. Francis Elliott, "Say Sorry to Trump or Risk Special Relationship, Cameron Told," *Times* of London, May 4, 2016, https://www.thetimes.co.uk/article/say-sorry-to-trump-or-risk-special-relationship-cameron-told-h6ng0r7xj.

87. LaFraniere et al., "How the Russia Inquiry Began."

CHAPTER SEVEN: THE BACK CHANNELS

1. Andrew Prokop, "The Michael Cohen, CNN, and Trump-Russia Controversy, Explained," *Vox*, August 30, 2018, https://www.vox.com/2018/8/30/17795674/michael-cohen-trump-russia-mueller-cnn-lanny-davis.

2. Ibid.

3. Jim Sciutto, Carl Bernstein, and Marshall Cohen, "Cohen claims Trump knew in advance of 2016 Trump Tower meeting," CNN, July 26, 2019, updated July 27, 2018, https://www.cnn.com/2018/07/26/politics/michael-cohen-donald-trump-june-2016-meeting-knowledge/index.html; Jim Sciutto and Carl Bernstein, "Attorney for Michael Cohen keeps changing his story on Trump Tower meeting," CNN, August 28, 2018, https://www.cnn.com/2018/08/28/politics/lanny-davis-trump-tower-michael-cohen/index.html.

4. "George Papadopoulos and the Secret Visit to Athens," *To Vima* (in Greek), November 13, 2016, http://www.tovima.gr/politics/article/?aid=843919; Linley Sanders, "Trump Knew Papadopoulos Would Meet with Foreigners, Ex-Aide Claims," *Newsweek*, November 17, 2017, https://www.newsweek.com/papadopoulos-says-trump-authorized-him-meet-foreign-leaders-714644; Bill Whitaker, "When Russian Hackers Targeted the U.S. Election Infrastructure," CBS News,

July 17, 2018, https://www.cbsnews.com/news/when-russian-hackers-targeted-the-u-s-election-infrastructure/; Sarah D. Wire, "House Majority Leader Kevin McCarthy in 2016: 'There's two people I think Putin pays: Rohrabacher and Trump,'" *Los Angeles Times*, May 17, 2017, http://www.latimes.com/politics/essential/la-pol-ca-essential-politics-updates-year-old-mccarthy-comment-that-trump-1495063901-htmlstory.html; Sharon LaFraniere et al., "How the Russia Inquiry Began: A Campaign Aide, Drinks and Talk of Political Dirt," *New York Times*, December 30, 2017, https://www.nytimes.com/2017/12/30/us/politics/how-fbi-russia-investigation-began-george-papadopoulos.html; Aaron Blake, "Rod Rosenstein and Robert Mueller officially repudiate a major Trump conspiracy theory," *Washington Post*, July 13, 2018, https://www.washingtonpost.com/news/the-fix/wp/2018/07/13/rod-j-rosenstein-and-robert-s-mueller-iii-officially-rebuke-a-major-trump-conspiracy-theory/?utm_term=.25be2a757e46.

5. Seth Abramson (@SethAbramson), "BREAKING NEWS: Deripaska Mistress Nastya Rybka Was in Athens on the Same Day as George Papadopoulos and Vladimir Putin (Papadopoulos was there on a secret, as-yet unexplained trip for the Trump campaign, and Putin was there to talk sanctions with men we know Papadopoulos met)" {Post includes screenshot of Nastya Rybka Instagram account, Twitter, March 6, 2018, https://twitter.com/sethabramson/status/971205101846188032; Mike Eckel, "The Deputy PM, the Oligarch, and His Lover: New Navalny Exposé Highlights Tycoon's Ties to Kremlin Bigwig," Radio Free Europe/Radio Liberty, February 8, 2018, https://www.rferl.org/a/russia-deripaska-prikhodko-rybka-nuland-yacht/29028148.html.

6. Seth Abramson (@SethAbramson), Twitter, March 6, 2018; Mark Mazzetti et al., "Trump Jr. and Other Aides Met With Gulf Emissary Offering Help to Win Election," *New York Times*, May 19, 2018, https://www.nytimes.com/2018/05/19/us/politics/trump-jr-saudi-uae-nader-prince-zamel.html.

7. Adam Entous, "House majority leader to colleagues in 2016: 'I think Putin pays' Trump," *Washington Post*, May 17, 2017, https://www.washingtonpost.com/world/national-security/house-majority-leader-to-colleagues-in-2016-i-think-putin-pays-trump/2017/05/17/515f6f8a-3aff-11e7-8854-21f359183e8c_story.html?utm_term=.57efe14abdbf.

8. Steve Reilly, "Timeline: The many times George Papadopoulos tried to connect the Trump campaign with Russia," *USA Today*, November 2, 2017, https://www.usatoday.com/story/news/2017/11/02/timeline-many-times-george-papadopoulos-tried-connect-trump-campaign-russia/820951001/; Association of Accredited Public Policy Advocates to the European Union, "Russian Sanctions and EU Member States Stance," November 9, 2017, http://www.aalep.eu/russian-sanctions-and-eu-member-states-stance; "Russian President Meets with Greek Leaders on First Trip to EU This Year," RadioFreeEurope, by Interfax, Reuters, AFP, and AP, May 27, 2016, https://www.rferl.org/a/russia-putin-visit-greece/27761430.html.

9. Kalyeena Makortoff, "Putin courts Athens ahead of vote on sanctions extension," CNBC, May 2016, https://www.cnbc.com/2016/05/27/putin-courts-athens-ahead-of-vote-on-sanctions-extension.html.

10. Alexis Papachelas, "The Ambitious George Papadopoulos," *Kathimerini*, November 6, 2017, http://www.ekathimerini.com/222996/article/ekathimerini/news/the-ambitious-george-papadopoulos.

11. "George Papadopoulos," *To Vima*; Daniel Halper, "National Security Leaders to Congress: 'Stop Sequestration Now,'" *Weekly Standard*, February 11, 2013, https://www.weeklystandard.com/daniel-halper/national-security-leaders-to-congress-stop-sequestration-now; Michael Warren, "Foreign Policy Experts to Congressional Leaders: Enforce Iranian Compliance With Nuclear Deal," *Weekly Standard*, January 9, 2014, https://www.weeklystandard.com/michael-warren/foreign-policy-experts-to-congressional-leaders-enforce-iranian-compliance-with-nuclear-deal; Daniel Halper, "'Secure Ukraine, Isolate Russia, and Strengthen NATO,'" *Weekly Standard*, March 21, 2014, https://www.weeklystandard.com/daniel-halper/secure-ukraine-isolate-russia-and-strengthen-nato.

12. "George Papadopoulos," *To Vima*.

13. Meghan Clyne, "Reagan Aides Try To Remember KT McFarland," *New York Sun*, March 7, 2006, https://www.nysun.com/national/reagan-aides-try-to-remember-kt-mcfarland/28643/; Adam Entous, "The Agonizingly Slow Downfall of K. T. McFarland," *New Yorker*, January 29, 2018, https://www.newyorker.com/news/news-desk/the-agonizingly-slow-downfall-of-k-t-mcfarland; "Seth Cropsey, Director, Center for American Seapower," Hudson Institute, https://www.hudson.org/experts/530-seth-cropsey.

14. Marianna Kakaounaki, "Trump's Pre-Election Trip to Greece That Never Happened," *Kathimerini*, November 6, 2017, http://www.ekathimerini.com/222995/article/ekathimerini/news/trumps-pre-election-trip-to-greece-that-never-happened.

15. Ibid.

16. Griff Witte, "For Trump adviser at center of Russia probe, a rapid rise and dramatic fall in his ancestral land," *Washington Post*, December 10, 2017, https://www.washingtonpost.com/world/europe/for-trump-adviser-at-center-of-russia-probe-a-rapid-rise-and-dramatic-fall-in-his-ancestral-land/2017/12/10/91bb696a-d390-11e7-9ad9-ca0619edfa05_story.html?utm_term=.7de3b3cfe36b.

17. "Russian President Meets with Greek Leaders on First Trip to EU This Year."

18. Witte, "For Trump adviser at center of Russia probe."

19. Sanders, "Trump Knew Papadopoulos Would Meet with Foreigners, Ex-Aide Claims."

20. Ibid.

21. Tom Dreisbach and Kelly McEvers, "Former Trump Campaign Adviser Was More than a Coffee Boy, Fiancée Says," NPR, February 12, 2018, https://www.npr.org/2018/02/12/584855759/former-trump-campaign-adviser-was-more-than-a-coffee-boy-fiancee-says.

22. Witte, "For Trump adviser at center of Russia probe."

23. Kakaounaki, "Trump's Pre-Election Trip to Greece."

24. Ibid.

25. "Kammenos 'Confident of Close Cooperation' with Trump Administration," *Kathimerini*, January 20, 2017, http://www.ekathimerini.com/215454/article

/ekathimerini/news/kammenos-confident-of-close-cooperation-with-trump-admini stration.

26. Ibid.

27. "Kammenos Congratulates Trump on Twitter," *Kathimerini*, November 9, 2016, http://www.ekathimerini.com/213536/article/ekathimerini/news/kammenos -congratulates-trump-on-twitter.

28. Paul Owen, "Full Text of the Emails Between Donald Trump Jr. and Rob Gold-stone," *Guardian*, July 11, 2017, https://www.theguardian.com/us-news/2017/jul /11/donald-trump-jr-emails-full-text-russia-rob-goldstone.

29. Max Seddon, "Did Russia's Top Prosecutor Yuri Chaika Want to help Donald Trump?" *Financial Times*, July 12, 2017, https://www.ft.com/content/3b7146fc -6706-11e7-8526-7b38dcaef614.

30. 52 U.S. Code § 30121, "a provision of the Federal Election Campaign Act (FECA), 52 U.S.C. 30121(a)(2), which prohibits any person from soliciting a contribution or donation from a foreign national (as defined)," http://uscode .house.gov/view.xhtml?req=(title:52%20section:30121%20edition:prelim).

31. Ibid.

32. Zack Beauchamp, "Donald Trump Jr. is digging himself a big legal hole," *Vox*, July 10, 2017, https://www.vox.com/world/2017/7/10/15948078/donald-trump -jr-russia-illegal.

33. Owen, "Full Text of the Emails."

34. Ibid.

35. Ibid.

36. Allan Smith, " 'You're going to find it very, very interesting': Donald Trump an-nounces he will make 'major' speech about the Clintons," *Business Insider*, June 7, 2016, https://www.businessinsider.com/donald-trump-announced-speech-hil lary-bill-clinton-2016-6.

37. Ibid.

38. Owen, "Full Text of the Emails."

39. Dan Merica, "Recreating June 9: A Very Consequential Day in the 2016 Cam-paign," CNN, July 12, 2017, https://www.cnn.com/2017/07/11/politics/trump -campaign-june-9/index.html.

40. Ibid.

41. Ibid.

42. Eli Stokols, "Trump Prepares Charge Sheet Against Clinton," *Politico*, June 9, 2016, https://www.politico.com/story/2016/06/donald-trump-hillary-clinton-at tacks-224094.

43. Ibid.

44. Ibid.

45. Rosalind S. Helderman and Tom Hamburger, "Eighth Person in Trump Tower Meeting Is Identified," *Washington Post*, July 18, 2017, https://www.washington post.com/politics/eighth-person-in-trump-tower-meeting-is-identified/2017/07/18 /e971234a-6bce-11e7-9c15-177740635e83_story.html?utm_term=.10f33976fb8c; Andrew Higgins and Andrew E. Kramer, "Soviet Veteran Who Met With Trump Jr. Is a Master of the Dark Arts," *New York Times*, July 15, 2017, https://

www.nytimes.com/2017/07/15/world/europe/rinat-akhmetshin-donald-trump-jr
-natalia-veselnitskaya.html; Sonam Sheth, "Trump may have let something slip
about the Russian lawyer from the Trump Tower meeting," *Business Insider*,
April 2018, https://www.businessinsider.com/trump-rally-natalia-veselnitskaya
-putin-trump-tower-meeting-2018-4; Keir Simmons, "Russian Lawyer Veselnitskaya Says She Didn't Give Trump Jr. Info on Clinton," NBC News, July 11,
2017, https://www.nbcnews.com/news/world/russian-lawyer-who-met-trump-jr
-i-didn-t-have-n781631; Ken Dilanian and Natasha Ledeveda, "Donald Trump Jr.
Asked Russian Lawyer for Info on Clinton Foundation," NBC News, December 5, 2017, https://www.nbcnews.com/news/us-news/donald-trump-jr-asked
-russian-lawyer-info-clinton-foundation-n826711; Emily Stewart, "Read: Donald Trump Jr.'s Congressional Testimony About the Trump Tower Meeting," *Vox*,
May 16, 2018, https://www.vox.com/policy-and-politics/2018/5/16/17360484
/donald-trump-jr-transcript-senate-judiciary-committee; Sonam Sheth and Ellen
Cranley, "The Russian lawyer who met with Trump campaign says she is a
Kremlin 'informant,'" *Business Insider*, April 27, 2018, https://www.businessin
sider.com/natalia-veselnitskaya-russia-informant-trump-tower-meeting-2018-4.

46. Ibid., Trump Jr. transcript, pp. 19 and 46.
47. Ibid.
48. Ibid., p. 43.
49. Ibid.
50. Stephan Dinan, "Trump Jr. Says He Never Told His Father About Russia Meeting," *Washington Times*, May 16, 2018, https://www.washingtontimes.com
/news/2018/may/16/trump-jr-says-he-never-told-father-russia-meeting/; Marshall
Cohen, "20 times Trump and his allies denied he knew of the 2016 Trump Tower
meeting," CNN, July 27, 2018, https://www.cnn.com/2018/07/27/politics/trump
-denials-trump-tower-2016-meeting/index.html; Jeremy Herb and Marshall
Cohen, "The Trump Tower Meeting: A Timeline," CNN, July 31, 2018, https://
www.cnn.com/2018/07/31/politics/trump-tower-meeting-timeline/index.html.
51. Donald J. Trump (@realDonaldTrump), "How long did it take your staff of 823
people to think that up—and where are your 33,000 emails that you deleted?"
Twitter, June 9, 2016, 4:40 p.m., http://www.trumptwitterarchive.com/archive.
52. Tom Hamburger et al., "Trump maintains not knowing in advance about meeting
with Russians, disputing Cohen claim," *Washington Post*, July 27, 2018 (updated
August 26, 2018), https://www.washingtonpost.com/politics/trump-maintains
-not-knowing-in-advance-about-meeting-with-russians-disputing-cohen-claim
/2018/07/27/5e18f57a-9143-11e8-bcd5-9d911c784c38_story.html?utm_term=
.66cc6be6f19d; Joe Tacopino, "Cohen Willing to Testify That Trump Approved
2016 Meeting with Russians," *New York Post*, July 26, 2018, https://nypost.com
/2018/07/26/cohen-trump-approved-2016-trump-tower-meeting-with-russians/.
53. David Cloud, "Mueller calls back at least one participant in key meeting with
Russians at Trump Tower," *Los Angeles Times*, January 6, 2018, http://www.la
times.com/politics/la-na-pol-trump-probe-20180106-story.html#.
54. Michael Wolff, *Fire and Fury: Inside the Trump White House* (New York: Henry
Holt, 2018).

55. Ibid.

56. Josh Dawsey, "Spokesman for Trump's legal team resigns just two months after starting," *Politico*, July 20, 2017, https://www.politico.com/story/2017/07/20/spokesman-for-trumps-legal-team-resigns-just-two-months-after-starting-240783.

57. Rosalind S. Helderman et al., "Russian social media executive sought to help Trump campaign in 2016, emails show," *Washington Post*, December 7, 2017, https://www.washingtonpost.com/politics/russian-social-media-executive-sought-to-help-trump-campaign-in-2016-emails-show/2017/12/07/31ec8d90-db9a-11e7-b859-fb0995360725_story.html?utm_term=.066f1fc3efcd.

58. Stewart, Trump Jr. transcript, pp. 47–48.

59. Ibid., p. 48.

60. Philip Bump, "Timeline: How a Trump adviser tried to work with the Russian government," *Washington Post*, October 30, 2017, https://www.washingtonpost.com/news/politics/wp/2017/10/30/timeline-how-a-trump-adviser-tried-to-work-with-the-russian-government/?utm_term=.b869dfa4de32; Jenna Johnson, "Veteran Strategist Paul Manafort Becomes Trump's Campaign Chairman," *Washington Post*, May 19, 2016, https://www.washingtonpost.com/news/post-politics/wp/2016/05/19/veteran-strategist-paul-manafort-becomes-trumps-campaign-chairman/?utm_term=.fd49375b16f8.

61. Brian Whitaker, "The George Papadopoulos File: A Timeline," *Medium*, November 19, 2017, https://medium.com/@Brian_Whit/the-george-papadopoulos-file-a-timeline-5c699c3aae4b.

62. Ibid.; John Sweeney and Innes Bowen, "Joseph Mifsud: The mystery professor behind Trump Russia inquiry," BBC, March 21, 2018, https://www.bbc.com/news/world-us-canada-43488581.

63. Witte, "For Trump adviser at center of Russia probe."

64. Tim Dickinson, "Was Jeff Sessions Aware of a Proposed Trump-Putin Back Channel?" *Rolling Stone*, April 27, 2018, https://www.rollingstone.com/politics/politics-news/was-jeff-sessions-aware-of-a-proposed-trump-putin-back-channel-628043/; Nicholas Fandos, "Operative Offered Trump Campaign 'Kremlin Connection' Using N.R.A. Ties," *New York Times*, December 3,2017, https://www.nytimes.com/2017/12/03/us/politics/trump-putin-russia-nra-campaign.html.

65. Denise Clifton and Mark Follman, "The Very Strange Case of Two Russian Gun Lovers, the NRA, and Donald Trump," *Mother Jones*, March 2018, https://www.motherjones.com/politics/2018/03/trump-russia-nra-connection-maria-butina-alexander-torshin-guns/.

66. Ken Dilanian and Carol E. Lee, "Kushner failed to disclose outreach from Putin ally to Trump campaign," NBC News, November 2017, https://www.nbcnews.com/news/us-news/kushner-failed-disclose-outreach-putin-ally-trump-campaign-n822021.

67. Fandos, "Operative Offered Trump Campaign 'Kremlin Connection."

68. Peter Stone and Greg Gordon, "FBI Investigating Whether Russian Money Went to NRA to Help Trump," *McClatchy*, January 18, 2018, https://www.mcclatchydc.com/news/nation-world/national/article195231139.html.

69. Steven Mufson and Tom Hamburger, "Trump's adviser's public comments, ties

to Moscow stir unease in both parties," *Washington Post*, August 5, 2016, https://www.washingtonpost.com/business/economy/trump-advisers-public-comments-ties-to-moscow-stir-unease-in-both-parties/2016/08/05/2e8722fa-5815-11e6-9aee-8075993d73a2_story.html?utm_term=.12a1f7b2c91b.

70. Ibid.

71. Michael S. Schmidt, "Major Takeaways from Carter Page's Congressional Interview on Russian Election Meddling," *New York Times*, November 7, 2017, https://www.nytimes.com/2017/11/07/us/politics/trump-adviser-carter-page-transcript-meeting-2016-campaign-russia.html.

72. Ibid.

73. Manu Raju and Jeremy Herb, "Exclusive: Carter Page Testifies He Told Sessions About Russia Trip," CNN, November 3, 2017, https://www.cnn.com/2017/11/02/politics/carter-page-testimony-russia-trip/index.html; Manu Raju et al., "Sessions Under Renewed Scrutiny on Capitol Hill," CNN, November 2, 2017, https://www.cnn.com/2017/11/02/politics/jeff-sessions-congress-russia-trump-campaign/index.html.

74. Ben Schreckinger and Julia Ioffe, "Lobbyist Advised Trump Campaign While Promoting Russian Pipeline," *Politico*, October 7, 2016, https://www.politico.com/story/2016/10/donald-trump-campaign-lobbyist-russian-pipeline-229264.

75. Ibid.; Nicholas Fandos, "Hope Hicks Acknowledges She Sometimes Tells White Lies for Trump," *New York Times*, February 27, 2018, https://www.nytimes.com/2018/02/27/us/politics/hope-hicks-house-intelligence-committee-testimony.html.

76. Sean Illing, "Cambridge Analytica, the shady data firm that might be a key Trump-Russia link, explained," *Vox,* April 4, 2018, https://www.vox.com/policy-and-politics/2017/10/16/15657512/cambridge-analytica-facebook-alexander-nix-christopher-wylie.

77. Ibid.

78. Ibid.

79. Associated Press, "Michael Flynn to Disclose Advisory Role Linked to Cambridge Analytica," August 4, 2017, *Guardian,* https://www.theguardian.com/us-news/2017/aug/04/michael-flynn-cambridge-analytica-disclosure; Illing, "Cambridge Analytica"; Donie O'Sullivan, "Cambridge Analytica's Facebook Data Was Accessed from Russia, MP Says," CNN, July 17, 2018, https://money.cnn.com/2018/07/17/technology/cambridge-analytica-data-facebook-russia/index.html; Eli Watkins and Carol Jordan, "Cambridge Analytica Suspends CEO Alexander Nix After Undercover Recordings air," CNN, March 20, 2018, https://www.cnn.com/2018/03/20/politics/alexander-nix-cambridge-analytica/index.html.

80. Philip Bump, "A new undercover video raises significant questions about Cambridge Analytica's elections work," *Washington Post*, March 20, 2018, https://www.washingtonpost.com/news/politics/wp/2018/03/20/a-new-undercover-video-raises-significant-questions-about-cambridge-analyticas-elections-work/?utm_term=.e00c341101c6; Sheth and Cranley, "The Russian lawyer who met with Trump campaign says she is a Kremlin 'informant.'" *Insider*, April 27, 2018, https://www.businessinsider.com/natalia-veselnitskaya-russia-informant-trump-tower-meeting-2018-4.

81. Ibid.

82. Kyle Swenson, "Rebekah Mercer, the billionaire backer of Bannon and Trump, chooses sides," *Washington Post*, January 5, 2017, https://www.washingtonpost .com/news/morning-mix/wp/2018/01/05/rebekah-mercer-the-billionaire-backer -of-bannon-and-trump-chooses-sides/?utm_term=.8f950711f69f; Curt Devine et al., "How Steve Bannon Used Cambridge Analytica to Further His Alt-right Vision for America," CNN, March 2018, https://www.cnn.com/2018/03/30/politics /bannon-cambridge-analytica/index.html.

83. Carole Cadwalladr and Peter Jukes, "Arron Banks 'met Russian officials multiple times before Brexit vote,'" *Guardian*, June 9, 2018, https://www.theguard ian.com/politics/2018/jun/09/arron-banks-russia-brexit-meeting.

84. Ibid.

85. William Booth and Karla Adam, "Arron Banks: The brash British millionaire who backed Brexit, befriended the Russian ambassador and loves Trump," *Washington Post*, June 30, 2018, https://www.washingtonpost.com/world/eu rope/arron-banks-the-brash-british-millionaire-who-backed-brexit-befriended -the-russian-ambassador-and-loves-trump/2018/06/30/077d7204-78bb-11e8-ac4e -421ef7165923_story.html?utm_term=.ca1d3ffc679e.

86. Cadwalladr and Jukes, "Arron Banks."

87. Joey Millar, "'We STUFFED the establishment!' Farage receives OVATION as Trump fans praise 'Mr. Brexit,'" *Express*, February 24, 2018, https://www.ex press.co.uk/news/world/923263/donald-trump-cpac-nigel-farage-speech-brexit -referendum.

88. Stephanie Kirchgaessner, "Trump-Russia Inquiry is told Nigel Farage may have given Julian Assange data," *Guardian*, January 19, 2018, https://www.theguard ian.com/politics/2018/jan/19/trump-russia-inquiry-is-told-nigel-farage-may-have -given-julian-assange-data.

89. Lydia O'Connor, "Nigel Farrage Just Made a Very Bizarre Visit to the Ecuadorian Embassy," *Huffington Post,* March 9, 2017, https://www.huffingtonpost.com /entry/nigel-farage-julian-assange_us_58c1a73ae4b0d1078ca50e2e.

90. Jon Stone, "Brexit: Nigel Farage is a 'fifth columnist' Putin cheerleader, says Guy Verhofstadt," *Independent*, June 13, 2018, https://www.independent.co.uk /news/uk/politics/brexit-nigel-farage-putin-cheerleader-eu-russia-guy-verhofstadt -erdogan-a8396476.html.

91. Robert Midgley, "Watch: How Nigel Farage became friends with Donald Trump," *Telegraph*, November 22, 2016, https://www.telegraph.co.uk/news /2016/11/16/watch-how-nigel-farage-became-friends-with-donald-trump/.

92. "Farage flattered by Trump's call for him to be US ambassador—video," *Guardian*, November 22, 2016, https://www.theguardian.com/politics/video/2016/nov /22/farage-flattered-trump-call-us-ambassador-video; Christopher Hope, "Donald Trump must not meet Nigel Farage: Downing St. accused of laying down red line ahead of UK visit," *Telegraph*, July 3, 2018, https://www.telegraph.co.uk /politics/2018/07/03/donald-trump-must-not-meet-nigel-farage-downing-st-ac cused-laying/.

93. Rosalind S. Helderman, "Who's Who in the George Papadapoulos Court Docu-

ments," *Washington Post*, November 2, 2017, https://www.washingtonpost.com
/politics/whos-who-in-the-george-papadopoulos-court-documents/2017/10/30
/e131158c-bdb3-11e7-97d9-bdab5a0ab381_story.html?utm_term=.acf4ac75004d.

94. Ibid.

95. Papachelas, "The Ambitious George Papadopoulos."

96. Ibid.

97. Ibid.

98. Ibid.

99. "Greek Government Mulls Repercussions of Trump Election," *Kathimerini*,
November 9, 2016, http://www.ekathimerini.com/213560/article/ekathimerini
/news/greek-government-mulls-repercussions-of-trump-election.

100. Mark Mazzetti, "Excerpts From the New York Times Interview With George
Papadopoulos," *New York Times*, September 7, 2018, https://www.nytimes.com
/2018/09/07/us/politics/george-papadopoulos-interview-trump.html.

101. Papachelas, "The Ambitious George Papadopoulos."

102. Margot Cleveland, "Here's What We Can Glean from What George Papadopoulos's Wife Is Telling Media," *Federalist*, June 13, 2018, http://thefederalist.
com/2018/06/13/heres-can-glean-george-papadopouloss-wife-telling-media;
Jake Tapper, "The Mysterious Case of George Papadopoulos; George Papadopoulos Ignited the Russia Conspiracy Investigation," CNN Transcripts, aired
September 7, 2018, http://www.cnn.com/TRANSCRIPTS/1809/07/csr.01.html.

103. Quinta Jurecic, "Document: George Papadopoulos's Sentencing Memo," *Lawfare*, August 17, 2018, https://www.lawfareblog.com/document-george-papado
poulos-sentencing-memo.

104. "ND demands answers over Saudi defense deal," *Kathimerini*, November 6,
2017, http://www.ekathimerini.com/222984/article/ekathimerini/news/nd-demands
-answers-over-saudi-defense-deal.

105. Tara Palmeri, "Need to Reach Trump? Call Rhona," *Politico* (Europe), March
26, 2017, https://www.politico.eu/article/need-to-reach-donald-trump-call-rhona
-graff-assistant/.

106. Ibid.

107. Stewart, Trump Jr. transcript, p. 83.

108. Palmeri, "Need to Reach Trump? Call Rhona."

109. Ibid.

110. Helderman, "Who's Who in the George Papadopoulos Court Documents."
Reilly, "Timeline."

111. Ibid.

112. William Saletan, "Blurred Line: The Papadapoulos plea deal in the Russian
meddling probe suggests both collusion and cover-up," *Slate,* October 30, 2017,
http://www.slate.com/articles/news_and_politics/politics/2017/10/papadopoulos
_plea_blurs_the_line_between_collusion_and_cover_up.html.

CHAPTER EIGHT: THE REPUBLICAN NATIONAL CONVENTION

1. Andrew Prokop, "Carter Page, the Star of the Nunes Memo, Explained," *Vox*, February 2, 2018, https://www.vox.com/policy-and-politics/2018/2/2/16956014 /nunes-memo-carter-page.

2. Ibid.

3. Donald Trump (@realDonaldTrump), "In politics, and in life, ignorance is not a virtue. This is a primary reason that President Obama is the worst president in U.S. history!" Twitter, May 16, 2016, 6:08 p.m., https://twitter.com/realdonal dtrump/status/732377163505225728.

4. Prokop, "Carter Page, the Star of the Nunes Memo, Explained."

5. *Washington Post*, October 30, 2017, https://www.washingtonpost.com/news /the-fix/wp/2017/10/30/7-big-questions-about-the-russia-probe-from-trump-aide -george-papadopouloss-plea-deal/?utm_term=.4ec80211257d.

6. Ibid.

7. Franklin Foer, "The Astonishing Tale of the Man Mueller Just Indicted," *Atlantic*, June 6, 2018, https://www.theatlantic.com/politics/archive/2018/06/the-as tonishing-tale-of-the-man-mueller-calls-person-a/562217/.

8. Ibid.

9. Cristiano Lima, "Lewandowski: 'My Memory Has Been Refreshed' on Carter Page Moscow Trip," *Politico*, November 8, 2017, https://www.politico.com /story/2017/11/08/corey-lewandowski-carter-page-email-244689.

10. Ken Meyer, "Lewandowski Fiercely Denied Russia Trip Knowledge; Carter Page Testimony Says Otherwise," *Mediaite*, November 7, 2017, https://www .mediaite.com/online/lewandowski-vehemently-denied-knowledge-of-russia-trips -carter-page-testimony-says-otherwise/.

11. Lima, "Lewandowski: 'My Memory Has Been Refreshed.' "

12. Natasha Bertrand, "Trump Campaing Adviser: Carter Page 'Went Around Me' to Get Permission for Moscow Trip," *Business Insider*, November 7, 2017, https:// www.businessinsider.com/jd-gordon-carter-page-trump-russia-moscow-trip-2017-11.

13. Ibid.

14. Ryan Lucas, "Carter Page Tells House Intel Panel He Spoke to Sessions About Russia Contacts," NPR, November 7, 2017, https://www.npr.org/2017/11/07 /562537269/inquiry-widens-following-disclosure-of-trump-aides-told-about-rus sia-contacts.

15. John Kelly and Steve Reilly, "Trump Team Issued at Least 20 Denials of Contacts with Russia," *USA Today*, March 2, 2017, https://www.usatoday.com/story /news/politics/2017/03/02/trump-teams-many-many-denials-contacts-russia/986 25780/; Artin Afkhami, "A Timeline of Carter Page's Contacts With Russia," *Slate*, November 11, 2017, http://www.slate.com/articles/news_and_politics /jurisprudence/2017/11/a_timeline_of_carter_page_s_contacts_with_russia.html.

16. Ruptly.tv, Russia's propaganda station, RT, "Live: Former Trump Adviser Carter Page Holds Presentation in Moscow," Streamed live on December 12, 2016, https://www.youtube.com/watch?v=MEmg4DNVFSE.

17. Benjamin Segal et al., "After months of public denials, Carter Page admits he

told public officials about meeting with Russia," ABC News, November 7, 2017, https://abcnews.go.com/Politics/carter-page-told-trump-campaign-officials -moscow-trip/story?id=50977310.

18. Mark Mazzetti and Adam Goldman, "Trump Campaign Adviser Met with Russian Officials in 2016," *New York Times*, November 3, 2017, https://www.ny times.com/2017/11/03/us/politics/trump-campaign-page-russian.html.

19. "The Steele Dossier," OilPrice.com, May 31 2017, https://oilprice.com/Geo politics/International/The-Mysterious-Rosneft-Deal-And-Its-Consequences.html; Steele Dossier, Moscow Project, https://themoscowproject.org/dossier/.

20. Lucas, "Carter Page Tells House Intel Panel He Spoke to Sessions About Russia Contacts."

21. Ibid.

22. Ibid.

23. David Corn, "Top Hill Democrat Says Mueller Should Consider Perjury Charges Against Trump-Russia Witnesses," *Mother Jones*, June 7, 2018, https://www .motherjones.com/politics/2018/06/mueller-schiff-perjury/.

24. Tom Hamburger et al., "Manafort Offered to Give Russian Billionaire 'Private Briefings' on 2016 Campaign," *Washington Post*, September 20, 2017, https:// www.washingtonpost.com/politics/manafort-offered-to-give-russian-billionaire -private-briefings-on-2016-campaign/2017/09/20/399bba1a-9d48-11e7-8ea1-ed9 75285475e_story.html?utm_term=.a5476a430a28.

25. Ibid.

26. Ibid.

27. Tom Hamburger et al., "Trump's Company Had More Contact With Russia During Campaign, According to Documents Turned Over to Investigators," *Washington Post*, October 2, 2017, https://www.washingtonpost.com/politics /trumps-company-had-more-contact-with-russia-during-campaign-according-to -documents-turned-over-to-investigators/2017/10/02/2091fe5e-a6c0-11e7-850e -2bdd1236be5d_story.html?utm_term=.ae19f7819c5e.

28. Ibid.

29. Ibid.

30. Ibid.

31. Jonathan Vankin, "Michael Cohen Mystery: Donald Trump 'Fixer' Said He Was Going to Moscow in 2016, Report Says—Where Was He?" *INQUISITR,* May 21, 2018, https://www.inquisitr.com/4908791/michael-cohen-donald-trump -moscow/.

32. Anthony Cormier, "This Is The Inside Of Trump's Lawyer's Passport," *BuzzFeed News,* May 5, 2017, https://www.buzzfeednews.com/article/anthonycormier /trumps-lawyer-showed-you-the-cover-of-his-passport-heres#.kcGZWqoxLA.

33. Roger Friedman, "Exclusive: Trump Lawyer Michael Cohen's Alibi Blown—He Lied About July 2016 Capri Vacation with Rock Star Steve van Zandt," *Showbiz 411,* April 13, 2018, http://www.showbiz411.com/2018/04/13/exclusive-michael -cohen-alibi-blown-he-lied-about-july-2016-capri-vacation-with-rock-star-steve -van-zandt.

34. Cormier, "This Is the Inside of Trump's Lawyer's Passport."

35. "Trump attorney Cohen on intelligence dossier: 'I've never been to Prague and I've never been to Russia,'" Fox News, January 12, 2017, http://www.foxnews .com/politics/2017/01/12/trump-attorney-cohen-on-intelligence-dossier-ive-never -been-to-prague-and-ive-never-been-to-russia.html.

36. Philip Bump, "Yes, Sean Hannity Was a Legal Client of Michael Cohen's," *Washington Post*, April 17, 2018, https://www.washingtonpost.com/news/politics /wp/2018/04/17/yes-sean-hannity-was-a-legal-client-of-michael-cohens/?utm _term=.47a576d10468.

37. Luke Harding et al., "British Spies Were First to Spot Trump Team's Links with Russia," *Guardian*, April 13, 2017, https://www.theguardian.com/uk-news/2017 /apr/13/british-spies-first-to-spot-trump-team-links-russia.

38. Josh Meyer, "Investigators Probe European Travel of Trump Associates," *Politico*, December 6, 2017, https://www.politico.com/story/2017/12/06/trump-eu rope-russia-travel-281134.

39. Peter Stone and Greg Gordon, "Sources: Mueller Has Evidence Cohen Was in Prague in 2016 Confirming Part of Dossier," *McClatchy*, April 13, 2018, https://www.mcclatchydc.com/news/politics-government/white-house/article 208870264.html.

40. Cormier, "This Is the Inside of Trump's Lawyer's Passport."

41. Ibid.; Artin Afkhami, "Timeline of Carter Page's Contacts With Russia Updated," Just Security, February 5, 2018, https://www.justsecurity.org/46786 /timeline-carter-pages-contacts-russia/.

42. *Politico* staff, "Transcript: Jeff Sessions' Testimony on Trump and Russia," *Politico*, June 13, 2017, https://www.politico.com/story/2017/06/13/full-text-jeff-ses sion-trump-russia-testimony-239503.

43. Allan Smith, "We now know more about why Jeff Sessions and a Russian ambassador crossed paths at the Republican convention," *Business Insider*, March 2, 2017, https://www.businessinsider.com/why-jeff-sessions-spoke-to-russian-am bassador-rnc-2017-3; Adam Entous et al., "Sessions discussed Trump campaign -related matters with Russian ambassador, U.S. intelligence intercepts show," *Washington Post*, July 21, 2017, https://www.washingtonpost.com/world/na tional-security/sessions-discussed-trump-campaign-related-matters-with-russian -ambassador-us-intelligence-intercepts-show/2017/07/21/3e704692-6e44-11e7-9c 15-177740635e83_story.html?utm_term=.cace22b6c753.

44. Manu Raju and Evan Perez, "Russia meetings in security clearance form, DOJ says," CNN, May 25, 2017, https://www.cnn.com/2017/05/24/politics/jeff-ses sions-russian-officials-meetings/index.html.

45. Entous et al., "Sessions discussed Trump campaign-related matters with Russian ambassador."

46. Julia Ioffe, "Why Did Jeff Sessions Really Meet with Sergey Kislyak?" *Atlantic*, June 13, 2007, https://www.theatlantic.com/politics/archive/2017/06/why-did -jeff-sessions-really-meet-sergey-kislyak/530091/.

47. Natasha Bertrand, "It looks like another Trump adviser has significantly changed his story about the GOP's dramatic shift on Ukraine," *Business Insider*, March 3, 2017, https://www.businessinsider.com/jd-gordon-trump-adviser-ukraine-rnc

-2017-3; Carrie Johnson, "2016 RNC Delegate: Trump Directed Change to Party Platform on Ukraine Support," NPR, December 4, 2017, https://www.npr.org/2017 /12/04/568310790/2016-rnc-delegate-trump-directed-change-to-party-platform -on-ukraine-support.

48. Ibid.
49. Ibid.
50. Ibid.
51. Kenneth P. Vogel and David Stern, "Authorities Looked into Manafort Protégé," *Politico*, March 8, 2017, https://www.politico.com/story/2017/03/trump-russia -manafort-235850.
52. Natasha Bertrand, "A Trump adviser gave the campaign 'the chance to intervene' in controversial Ukraine platform change — and lawmakers want to know why," *Business Insider*, November 8, 2017, https://www.businessinsider.com /congressional-russia-investigators-are-now-examining-the-gops-ukraine-platform -change-2017-11; Kaitlan Collins, "Bannon ally leaves the National Security Council after less than six months," CNN, July 6, 2017, https://www.cnn.com /2017/07/06/politics/tera-dahl-bannon-ally-national-security-council/index.html.
53. Sara Murray et al., "More Trump advisers disclose meetings with Russia's ambassador," CNN, March 4, 2017, https://www.cnn.com/2017/03/02/politics/rus sia-donald-trump-meetings-ambassador/index.html.
54. Kelly and Reilly, "Trump Team Issued at Least 20 Denials of Contacts with Russia."
55. Ibid.
56. Prokop, "Carter Page, the Star of the Nunes Memo, Explained."
57. Michael C. Butz, "AJC Panel dissects American role in global affairs," *Cleveland Jewish News*, July 21, 2016, https://www.clevelandjewishnews.com/news /politics/rnc/ajc-panel-dissects-america-s-role-in-global-affairs/article_7d91f20a -4f3f-11e6-97b6-ab6586eff87a.html.
58. Tapper, "The Mysterious Case of George Papadopoulos."
59. Ibid.
60. Carole Cadwalladr and Stephanie Kirchgaessner, "Cambridge Analytica director 'met Assange to discuss US election,'" *Guardian,* June 7, 2018, https://www .theguardian.com/uk-news/2018/jun/06/cambridge-analytica-brittany-kaiser-julian -assange-wikileaks.
61. Ibid.
62. Ken Stern, "Exclusive: Stephen Bannon, Trump's New C.E.O., Hints at His Master Plan," *Vanity Fair*, August 17, 2016, https://www.vanityfair.com/news /2016/08/breitbart-stephen-bannon-donald-trump-master-plan.
63. Mark Tait, "The Time I Got Recruited to Collude with the Russians," *Lawfare*, June 30, 2017, https://www.lawfareblog.com/time-i-got-recruited-collude-rus sians.
64. Ibid.
65. CNN Library, "2016 Presidential Election Investigation Fast Facts," CNN, October 10, 2017, https://www.cnn.com/2017/10/12/us/2016-presidential-election -investigation-fast-facts/index.html; David E. Sanger and Eric Schmitt, "Spy

Agency Consensus Grows That Russia Hacked D.N.C.," *New York Times*, July 26, 2016, https://www.nytimes.com/2016/07/27/us/politics/spy-agency-consen sus-grows-that-russia-hacked-dnc.html; Michael S. Schmidt, "Trump Invited the Russians to Hack Clinton. Were They Listening?" *New York Times*, July 13, 2018, https://www.nytimes.com/2018/07/13/us/politics/trump-russia-clinton-emails .html.

66. Alex Gangitano, "DCCC Hacked in Series of Cyberattacks Against Democratic Groups," *Roll Call,* July 29, 2016, https://www.rollcall.com/news/politics/dccc -hacked-in-series-of-cyber-attacks-against-democratic-groups.

67. Meghan Keneally, "Timeline leading up to Jeff Sessions' recusal and the fall-out," ABC News, July 26, 2017, https://abcnews.go.com/Politics/timeline-lead ing-jeff-sessions-recusal-fallout/story?id=45855918.

68. "Transcript: Jeff Sessions' Testimony on Trump and Russia," *Politico*.

69. Ibid.

70. Ibid.

71. Ibid.

72. Matthew Yglesias, "The other 25 senators on Sessions's committee say they had no meetings with Russian ambassador in 2016," *Vox*, March 2, 2017, https:// www.vox.com/2017/3/2/14794646/sessions-kislyak-senate-armed-services.

73. Ioffe, "Why Did Jeff Sessions Really Meet with Sergey Kislyak?"

74. Bertrand, "It looks like another Trump adviser."

75. Ibid.

76. Philip Rucker, "Trump: 'I don't remember much' about meeting with Papado-poulos, campaign adviser who has pleaded guilty," *Washington Post*, Novem-ber 11, 2017, https://www.washingtonpost.com/news/post-politics/wp/2017/11/03 /trump-i-dont-remember-much-about-meeting-with-papadopoulos-campaign-ad viser-who-has-pleaded-guilty/?utm_term=.235236858f4f.

77. Bertrand, "It looks like another Trump adviser."

78. Ibid.

79. Ibid.

80. Johnson, "2016 RNC Delegate."

81. Ibid.

82. Bertrand, "Former Trump adviser: I gave the campaign 'the chance to inter-vene.'"

83. "Full text of "Carter Page November 2, 2017 HPSCI Testimony," Internet Ar-chive (digital library), November 2, 2017, https://archive.org/stream/Carter PageNovember22017HPSCITestimony/carter_page_hpsci_hearing_transcript _nov_2_2017_djvu.txt.

84. Steve Reilly, "Exclusive: Two other Trump advisers also spoke with Russian envoy during GOP convention," *USA Today*, March 2, 2017, https://www.usato day.com/story/news/2017/03/02/exclusive-two-other-trump-advisers-also-spoke -russian-envoy-during-gop-convention/98648190/.

85. Jeff Zeleny and Kevin Liptak, "Inside Mar-a-Lago for 48 hours critical to the Russia investigation," CNN, December 2017, https://www.cnn.com/2017/12/08 /politics/michael-flynn-donald-trump-mar-a-lago/index.html.

86. "Carter Page in Budapest," *Hungarian Spectrum*, November 13, 2017, http:// hungarianspectrum.org/tag/u-s-house-intelligence-committee/; "J. D. Gordon, Paul Behrends, Hungary and the Russian connection," *Hungarian Free Press*, August 12, 2017, http://hungarianfreepress.com/2017/08/12/j-d-gordon-paul -behrends-hungary-and-the-russian-connection/.

87. Emily Stewart, "Alleged Russian spy Maria Butina chatted with former Trump campaign aide ahead of the 2016 election," *Vox*, August 4, 2018, https://www .vox.com/policy-and-politics/2018/8/4/17651234/maria-butina-jd-gordon-russia -trump.

CHAPTER NINE: THE HUNT FOR HER EMAILS

1. Rosalind S. Helderman and Tom Hamburger, " 'You should do it': Trump of-ficials encouraged George Papadopoulos's foreign outreach, documents show," *Washington Post*, March 23, 2018, https://www.washingtonpost.com/politics /you-should-do-it-trump-officials-encouraged-george-papadopouloss-foreign-out reach-documents-show/2018/03/23/2dae8c8e-2d38-11e8-8688-e053ba58f1e4_ story.html?utm_term=.c94a97ee206e.

2. Michael Shear and Michael S. Schmidt, "President Admits Trump Tower Meet-ing Was Meant to Get Dirt on Clinton," *New York Times*, August 5, 2018, https:// www.nytimes.com/2018/08/05/us/politics/trump-tower-meeting-donald-jr.html.

3. "George Papadopoulos: Sanctions have done little more than to turn Russia to-wards China," *Interfax*, September 30, 2016, http://www.interfax.com/interview .asp?id=704556.

4. Steve Reilly, "Trump Campaign Gave Page Permission for Moscow Trip," *USA Today*, March 7, 2017, https://www.usatoday.com/story/news/2017/03 /07/campaign-granted-page-permission-moscow-trip/98874648/; Byron Tau, "Ex-Adviser Carter Page Told Trump Campaign of Moscow Trip," *Wall Street Journal*, November 7, 2017, https://www.wsj.com/articles/adviser-told-trump -campaign-of-moscow-trip-1510031679; Steele dossier.

5. Benjamin Siegel, "After months of public denials, Carter Page admits he told Trump officials about meeting with Russians," ABC News, November 7, 2017, https://abcnews.go.com/Politics/carter-page-told-trump-campaign-officials -moscow-trip/story?id=50977310.

6. Ibid.

7. Josh Meyer, "Investigators probe European travel of Trump associates," *Politico*, November 6, 2017, https://www.politico.com/story/2017/12/06/trump-europe -russia-travel-281134; Artin Afkhami, "Timeline of Carter Page's Contacts with Russia," Just Security, February 5, 2018, https://www.justsecurity.org/46786 /timeline-carter-pages-contacts-russia/.

8. Ibid.

9. Jenna McLaughlin et al., "Exclusive: Trump adviser played key role in pursuit of possible Clinton emails from dark web before election," CNN, April 7, 2018, https://www.cnn.com/2018/04/06/politics/joseph-schmitz-trump-adviser-clinton -emails/index.html.

10. Ibid.

11. Ibid.

12. Ibid.

13. Ibid.

14. Matt Tait, "The Time I Got Recruited to Collude with the Russians," *Lawfare*, June 30, 2017, https://www.lawfareblog.com/time-i-got-recruited-collude-russians.

15. Ibid.

16. Ibid.

17. Katherine Skiba et al., "Peter W. Smith, GOP operative who sought Clinton's emails from Russian hackers, committed suicide, records show," *Chicago Tribune,* July 13 2017, http://www.chicagotribune.com/news/local/politics/ct-peter-smith-death-met-0713-20170713-story.html.

18. Michael S. Schmidt, "Trump Invited the Russians to Hack Clinton. Were They Listening?" *New York Times*, July 13, 2018, https://www.nytimes.com/2018/07/13/us/politics/trump-russia-clinton-emails.html.

19. Ibid.

20. Shimon Prokupecz et al., "Trump received first classified intelligence briefing Wednesday," CNN, August 16, 2016, https://www.cnn.com/2016/08/16/politics/donald-trump-intelligence-briefing/index.html.

21. David E. Sanger and Eric Schmitt, "Spy Agency Consensus Grows That Russia Hacked D.N.C.," *New York Times*, July 27, 2016, https://www.nytimes.com/2016/07/27/us/politics/spy-agency-consensus-grows-that-russia-hacked-dnc.html.

22. Ken Dilanian et al., "FBI warned Trump in 2016 Russians would try to infiltrate his campaign," NBC News, December 18, 2017, https://www.nbcnews.com/news/us-news/fbi-warned-trump-2016-russians-would-try-infiltrate-his-campaign-n830596.

23. Gabrielle Healy, "Did Trump really mention WikiLeaks over 160 times in the last month of the election cycle?" *PolitiFact*, April 21, 2017, https://www.politifact.com/truth-o-meter/statements/2017/apr/21/jackie-speier/did-trump-really-mention-wikileaks-over-160-times-/; Julia Ioffe, "The Secret Correspondence Between Donald Trump, Jr. and WikiLeaks," *Atlantic,* November 13, 2017, https://www.theatlantic.com/politics/archive/2017/11/the-secret-correspondence-between-donald-trump-jr-and-wikileaks/545738/; Natasha Bertrand, "Roger Stone's Secret Messages with Wikileaks," *Atlantic,* February 17, 2018, https://www.theatlantic.com/politics/archive/2018/02/roger-stones-secret-messages-with-wikileaks/554432/; Benjamin Siegel and James Gordon Meek, "WikiLeaks Says Senate Intelligence Committee Wants to Question Julian Assange," ABC News, August 9, 2018, https://abcnews.go.com/Politics/wikileaks-senate-intelligence-committee-question-julian-assange/story?id=57117270.

24. Greg Miller, "CIA director alerted FBI to pattern of contracts between Russian officials and Trump campaign associates," *Washington Post*, May 23, 2017, https://www.washingtonpost.com/world/national-security/cia-director-warned-russian-security-service-chief-about-interference-in-election/2017/05/23/ebff2a7e-3fbb-11e7-adba-394ee67a7582_story.html?utm_term=.70fc0838f92b.

25. Philip Elliott, "How Donald Trump Fired and Hired Paul Manafort," *Time,* October 31, 2017, http://time.com/5003298/paul-manafort-indictment-donald-trump.

26. Andrew E. Kramer et al., "Secret Ledger in Ukraine Lists Cash for Donald Trump's Campaign Chief," *New York Times*, August 15, 2016, https://www.nytimes.com/2016/08/15/us/politics/paul-manafort-ukraine-donald-trump.html.

27. *Daily Beast,* October 2017, https://www.thedailybeast.com/trump-data-guru-i-tried-to-team-up-with-julian-assange.

28. Franklin Foer, "Was a Trump Server Communicating with Russia?" *Slate,* October 31, 2016, http://www.slate.com/articles/news_and_politics/cover_story/2016/10/was_a_server_registered_to_the_trump_organization_communicating_with_russia.html.

29. Pamela Brown and Jose Pagliery, "Sources: FBI investigation continues into 'odd' computer link between Russia bank and Trump Organization," CNN, March 9, 2017, https://www.cnn.com/2017/03/09/politics/fbi-investigation-continues-into-odd-computer-link-between-russian-bank-and-trump-organization/index.html.

30. Matthew Cole et al., "Top-Secret NSA Report Details Russian Hacking Effort Days Before 2016 Election," *Intercept*, June 5, 2017, https://theintercept.com/2017/06/05/top-secret-nsa-report-details-russian-hacking-effort-days-before-2016-election/.

31. Ibid.

32. Andy Greenberg, "The FBI Has Been Investigating Trump's Russia Ties Since July," *Wired,* March 2017, https://www.wired.com/2017/03/fbi-director-comey-confirms-investigation-trump-campaigns-russia-ties/; *Washington Post*, September 2017, https://www.washingtonpost.com/politics/manafort-offered-to-give-russian-billionaire-private-briefings-on-2016-campaign/2017/09/20/399bba1a-9d48-11e7-8ea1-ed975285475e_story.html?utm_term=.09be971476f7.

33. Sharon LaFraniere et al., "How the Russia Inquiry Began: A Campaign Aide, Drinks and Talk of Political Dirt," *New York Times*, December 30, 2017, https://www.nytimes.com/2017/12/30/us/politics/how-fbi-russia-investigation-began-george-papadopoulos.html.

34. Elizabeth Weise, "Tech Crowd Goes Wild for Trump's '400-Pound Hacker,'" *USA Today,* September 27, 2016, https://www.usatoday.com/story/tech/news/2016/09/27/tech-crowd-goes-wild-trumps-400-pound-hacker/91168144/.

35. George Papadopoulos, "Sanctions have done little."

36. Manu Raju and Jeremy Herb, "Email pointed Trump campaign to WikiLeaks documents," CNN, December 8, 2017, https://www.cnn.com/2017/12/08/politics/email-effort-give-trump-campaign-wikileaks-documents/index.html.

37. Artin Afkhami, "Timeline of Carter Page's Contacts with Russia [Updated]," Just Security, February 5, 2018, https://www.justsecurity.org/46786/timeline-carter-pages-contacts-russia/.

38. Andras Gollner, "The Budapest Bridge: Hungary's Role in the Collusion Between the Trump Campaign and the Russian Secret Service," *Hungarian Free Press,* April 13, 2017, http://hungarianfreepress.com/2017/04/13/the-budapest

-bridge-hungarys-role-in-the-collusion-between-the-trump-campaign-and-the
-russian-secret-service/.

39. Luke Harding et al., "British spies were first to spot Trump team's links with Russia," *Guardian,* April 13, 2017, https://www.theguardian.com/uk-news/2017 /apr/13/british-spies-first-to-spot-trump-team-links-russia.

40. *New York Times* staff, "Former CIA Chief Tells of Concern Over Possible Russia Ties to Trump Campaign," *New York Times,* May 23, 2017, https://www.nytimes .com/2017/05/23/us/politics/congress-testimony-john-brennan-russia-budget.html.

41. Department of Justice, October 5, 2017, https://www.justice.gov/file/1007346 /download.

42. AALEP, November 2017, http://www.aalep.eu/russian-sanctions-and-eu-mem ber-states-stance.

43. John Hayward, "Erik Prince: NYPD Ready to Make Arrests in Anthony Weiner Case," *Breitbart News,* November 4, 2016, https://www.breitbart.com/radio /2016/11/04/erik-prince-nypd-ready-make-arrests-weiner-case/.

44. Amanda Robb, "Anatomy of a Fake News Scandal," *Rolling Stone,* November 16, 2017, https://www.rollingstone.com/politics/politics-news/anatomy-of-a-fake-news -scandal-125877/.

45. Erik Prince, Congressional Testimony, November 30, 2017, https://docs .house.gov/meetings/IG/IG00/20171130/106661/HHRG-115-IG00-Transcript-20 171130.pdf.

46. Ibid.

47. Philip Bump, "Donald Trump's falsehood-laden press conference, annotated," *Washington Post,* July 27, 2016, https://www.washingtonpost.com/news/the-fix /wp/2016/07/27/donald-trumps-falsehood-laden-press-conference-annotated/?ut m_term=.3f6d219ff5c4.

48. Tim Fernholz, "Why Donald Trump, Jr's meeting with a Russian lawyer wasn't just typical 'opposition research,'" *Quartz,* July 12, 2017, https://qz.com/1026 780/did-hillary-clinton-collude-with-ukraine-in-the-2016-presidential-election/.

49. Ken Dilanian, "Former Diplomats: Trump Team Sought to Lift Sanctions on Russia," NBC News, June 1, 2017, https://www.nbcnews.com/politics/white -house/former-diplomats-trump-team-sought-lift-sanctions-russia-n767406.

CHAPTER TEN: THE OCTOBER SURPRISE

1. Amanda Robb, "Anatomy of a Fake News Scandal," *Rolling Stone,* November 16,2017,https://www.rollingstone.com/politics/politics-news/anatomy-of-a-fake -news-scandal-125877/; Nicholas Confessore and Daisuke Wakabayashi, "How Russia Harvested American Rage to Reshape U.S. Politics," *New York Times,* October 9, 2017, https://www.nytimes.com/2017/10/09/technology/russia-elec tion-facebook-ads-rage.html.

2. "General Election: Trump vs. Clinton vs. Johnson vs. Stein," *RealClearPolitics,* October 18, 2016, https://realclearpolitics.com/epolls/2016/president/us/gen eral_election_trump_vs_clinton_vs_johnson_vs_stein-5952.html.

3. Nate Silver, "The Comey Letter Probably Cost Clinton the Election," *FiveThirty-Eight*, May 3, 2017, https://fivethirtyeight.com/features/the-comey-letter-proba bly-cost-clinton-the-election/.

4. Alex Isenstadt et al., "Inside Trump's Stunning Upset Victory," *Politico*, November 9, 2016, https://www.politico.com/magazine/story/2016/11/donald-trump -wins-2016-214438-.

5. Jonathan Chait, "Mueller's New Indictment Points to Collusion With Russia," *New York*, July 13, 2018, http://nymag.com/daily/intelligencer/2018/07/mueller -indictment-suggests-trump-colluding-with-russia.html; Andrew Prokop, "Roger Stone, explained: the longtime Trump adviser and dirty trickster is in Mueller's sights," *Vox*, July 16, 2018, https://www.vox.com/2018/7/16/17149324/roger -stone-mueller-trump-russia.

6. Prokop, "Roger Stone, explained"; Emily Birnbaum, "Roger Stone preemptively denies upcoming report on Trump's knowledge of WikiLeaks dump," *Hill*, August 27, 2018, http://thehill.com/homenews/administration/403884-roger-stone -preemptively-denies-upcoming-report-that-will-say-he-told.

7. Marc Caputo, "Sources: Roger Stone quit, wasn't fired by Trump in campaign shakeup," *Politico*, August 8, 2015, https://www.politico.com/story/2015 /08/sources-roger-stone-quit-wasnt-fired-by-donald-trump-in-campaign-shakeup -121177; Martin Longman, "The Story of Roger Stone, Paul Manafort and Donald Trump," *Washington Monthly*, February 23, 2018, https://washingtonmonthly .com/2018/02/23/the-story-of-roger-stone-paul-manafort-and-donald-trump/; Jonathan Chait, "Roger Stone Knew in Advance About the Stolen Emails. Did He Tell Trump?" *New York*, March 13, 2018, http://nymag.com/daily/intelligencer/2018 /03/roger-stone-knew-about-the-stolen-emails-did-he-tell-trump.html.

8. Chait, "Roger Stone knew."

9. Ibid.

10. Manuel Roig-Franzia and Rosalind S. Helderman, "Trump associate Roger Stone reveals new contact with Russian national during 2016 campaign," *Washington Post*, June 17, 2018, https://www.washingtonpost.com/politics/trump -associate-roger-stone-reveals-new-contact-with-russian-national-during-2016-cam paign/2018/06/17/4a8123c8-6fd0-11e8-bd50-b80389a4e569_story.html?utm_ term=.e7d5dca207be.

11. Ibid.

12. Ibid.; David Smiley and Glenn Garvin, "Mystery Miamian tied to Trump probe had many names, foul mouth, 2 DUI busts," *Miami Herald*, June 19, 2018, https:// www.miamiherald.com/news/politics-government/article213359854.html.

13. Ibid.

14. Ibid.

15. Ibid.

16. Gideon Resnick, "Roger Stone Convinced Trump to Hire Paul Manafort, Former Officials Say," *Daily Beast,* April 21, 2017, https://www.thedailybeast.com/roger -stone-convinced-trump-to-hire-paul-manafort-former-officials-say.

17. Gabrielle Healy, "Did Trump really mention WikiLeaks over 160 times in the

last month of the election cycle?" *PolitiFact*, April 21, 2017, https://www.politi
fact.com/truth-o-meter/statements/2017/apr/21/jackie-speier/did-trump-really
-mention-wikileaks-over-160-times-/.

18. Staff, "Roger Stone Confirms That He's In Communication With Julian Assange," Media Matters, August 9, 2016, https://www.mediamatters.org/video
/2016/08/09/roger-stone-confirms-hes-communication-julian-assange/212261.

19. Andrew Kaczynski et al.,"Trump adviser Roger Stone repeatedly claimed to
know of forthcoming WikiLeaks dumps," CNN, March 20, 2017, https://www
.cnn.com/2017/03/20/politics/kfile-roger-stone-wikileaks-claims/index.html.

20. Ibid.

21. Ibid.

22. Ibid.

23. Ibid.

24. Ibid.

25. Natasha Bertrand, "Roger Stone's Secret Messages with Wikileaks," *Atlantic*,
February 27, 2018, https://www.theatlantic.com/politics/archive/2018/02/roger
-stones-secret-messages-with-wikileaks/554432/; Sara Murray, "Mueller subpoenas Randy Credico, who Roger Stone says was his WikiLeaks back channel,"
CNN, August 10, 2018, https://www.cnn.com/2018/08/10/politics/randy-credico
-roger-stone-wikileaks/index.html.

26. Martin Longman, "Inside the Dirty Tricks of Roger Stone," *Washington Monthly*,
April 19, 2018, https://washingtonmonthly.com/2018/04/19/inside-the-dirty
-tricks-of-roger-stone/.

27. Sara Murray and Caroline Kelly, "Stone's alleged Assange conduit expects to
be subpoenaed," CNN, June 25, 2018, https://www.cnn.com/2018/06/25/politics
/stone-credico-assange-wikileaks-expects-subpoena/.

28. Kaczynski et al.,"Trump adviser Roger Stone repeatedly claimed to know."

29. Bertrand, "Roger Stone's Secret Messages with Wikileaks."

30. Ibid.

31. Kaczynski et al., "Trump adviser Roger Stone repeatedly claimed to know."

32. Jessie Hellman, "Roger Stone: Wednesday will be end of Clinton's campaign,"
Hill, October 2, 2016, http://thehill.com/blogs/ballot-box/presidential-races
/298883-roger-stone-threatens-wednesday-will-be-end-of-clinton.

33. Kaczynski et al., "Trump adviser Roger Stone repeatedly claimed to know."

34. Jenna McLaughlin, "Wikileaks Turned Down Leaks on Russian Government
During US Presidential Campaign," *Foreign Policy*, August 17, 2017, https://
foreignpolicy.com/2017/08/17/wikileaks-turned-down-leaks-on-russian-govern
ment-during-u-s-presidential-campaign/.

35. Bob Dreyfuss, "Was the Trump Campaign Working With WikiLeaks and the
Russians to Undermine the Clinton Campaign?" *Nation*, November 17, 2017,
https://www.thenation.com/article/was-the-trump-campaign-working-with-wiki
leaks-and-the-russians-to-undermine-the-clinton-campaign/.

36. Micah Lee and Cora Currier, "In Leaked Chats, Wikileaks Discusses Preference for GOP Over Clinton, Russia, Trolling, and Feminists They Don't Like,"

Intercept, February 2018, https://theintercept.com/2018/02/14/julian-assange
-wikileaks-election-clinton-trump/.

37. Michal Kranz, "Over 10,000 private Twitter messages from WikiLeaks founder Julian Assange have been leaked—read Assange's thoughts on Hillary Clinton, Russia, and Chelsea Manning," *Business Insider*, February 14, 2018, https:// www.businessinsider.com/highlights-from-julian-assanges-leaked-twitter-messages -2018-2.

38. Ibid.

39. Alex Isenstadt et al., "Inside Trump's Stunning Upset Victory," *Politico*, November 9, 2016, https://www.politico.com/magazine/story/2016/11/donald-trump -wins-2016-214438.

40. Ibid.

41. Kenneth P. Vogel, "Manafort advised Trump team on Russia scandal," *Politico*, May 25, 2017, https://www.politico.com/story/2017/05/25/manafort-trump-rus sia-advise-238803.

42. Evan Perez et al., "Exclusive: US government wiretapped former Trump campaign chairman," CNN, September 19, 2017, https://www.cnn.com/2017/09/18 /politics/paul-manafort-government-wiretapped-fisa-russians/index.html.

43. Howard Fineman, "The 'state' of Donald Trump? He thinks it couldn't be better," NBC News, January 30, 2018, https://www.nbcnews.com/storyline/2018 -state-of-the-union-address/state-donald-trump-he-thinks-it-couldn-t-be-better-n8 42501.

44. Sharon LaFraniere, Paul Manafort, Trump's Former Campaign Chairman, Guilty of 8 Counts," *New York Times*, August 21, 2018, https://www.nytimes.com/2018 /08/21/us/politics/paul-manafort-trial-verdict.html; Sarah Fitzpatrick et al., "Michael Cohen pleads guilty, says he paid hush money at Trump's direction," NBC News, August 22, 2018, https://www.nbcnews.com/news/crime-courts/ex-trump -lawyer-michael-cohen-discussing-plea-deal-prosecutors-n902571.

45. David A. Fahrenthold et al., " 'He can't get rid of any of this': Trump's wall of secrecy erodes amid growing legal challenges," *Washington Post*, August 25, 2018, https://www.washingtonpost.com/politics/he-cant-get-rid-of-any-of-this -trumps-wall-of-secrecy-is-eroding-amid-mounting-legal-challenges/2018/08/25 /93d417dc-a7c6-11e8-8fac-12e98c13528d_story.html?utm_term=.367ae6a49005.

46. Katelyn Polantz and Stephen Collinson, "12 Russians indicted in Mueller investigation," CNN, July 14, 2018, https://www.cnn.com/2018/07/13/politics/russia -investigation-indictments/index.html.

47. Ibid.

48. Jen Kirby, "Poll: only 32 percent of Republicans think Russia interfered in the 2016 election," *Vox*, July 19, 2018, https://www.vox.com/2018/7/19/17586390 /poll-russia-trump-election-interference-republicans.

49. "Debate Fact-Check: Reviewing What Donald Trump and Hillary Clinton Said During the Dabate," ABC News, October 10, 2016, https://abcnews.go.com/Politics /debate-fact-check-reviewing-donald-trump-hillary-clinton/story?id=42686581.

50. Andy Greenberg, "A Timeline of Trump's Strange, Contradictory Statements on

Russian Hacking," *Wired*, January 2017, https://www.wired.com/2017/01/time line-trumps-strange-contradictory-statements-russian-hacking/.

51. Evan Perez et al., "Feds believe Russians hacked Florida election—systems vendor," CNN, October 12, 2016, https://www.cnn.com/2016/10/12/politics/florida -election-hack/index.html.

52. Brian Bennett, "CIA Chief calls Wikileaks 'non-state hostile intelligence service,'" *Los Angeles Times*, April 13, 2017, http://www.latimes.com/politics /washington/la-na-essential-washington-updates-pompeo-are-you-sure-trump-149 2114120-htmlstory.html; Twitter, January 4, 2017, https://twitter.com/realDon aldTrump/status/816620855958601730.

53. Matt Zapotosky, "Rudy Guiliani is claiming to have insider FBI knowledge. Does he really?" *Washington Post*, November 4, 2016, https://www.washington post.com/news/post-nation/wp/2016/11/04/rudy-giuliani-is-claiming-to-have -insider-fbi-knowledge-does-he-really/?utm_term=.f114181068b9.

54. Debbie Lord, Cox Media Group National Content Desk, "Conway accused of Hatch Act violation; what is the Hatch Act?" *Atlanta Journal-Constitution*, March 2, 2018, https://www.ajc.com/news/national/conway-accused-hatch-act -violation-what-the-hatch-act/i7n7IThB8MSO7zQbdnAThN/; Christina Manduley and Eugene Scott, "Giuliani changes story on FBI," CNN, November 5, 2016, https://www.cnn.com/2016/11/04/politics/rudy-giuliani-hillary-clinton-email-fbi/.

55. Ibid.

56. Zapotosky, "Rudy Guiliani is claiming to have insider FBI knowledge."

57. Manduley and Scott, "Giuliani changes story on FBI," CNN, November 5, 2016.

58. Ibid.

59. Ibid.

60. Chuck Ambrose, "5 reasons Comey should have recommended Clinton's indictment," *Hill*, October 6, 2016, http://thehill.com/blogs/pundits-blog/crime /299661-5-reasons-comey-should-have-recommended-clintons-indictment.

61. Darren Samuelsohn, "Forget Rudy: Here are Trump's fiercest defenders," *Politico*, June 9, 2018, https://www.politico.com/story/2018/06/09/trump-lawyers-jo seph-digenova-victoria-toensing-634996.

62. Jim Stinson, "Former US Attorney: James Comey Is 'A Dirty Cop,'" *LifeZette*, October 13, 2016, https://www.lifezette.com/2016/10/former-u-s-attorney-fbi -director-comey-dirty-cop/.

63. Samuelsohn, "Forget Rudy."

64. Kerry Picket, "Exclusive: FBI Agents Say Comey 'Stood in the Way' of Clinton Email Investigation," *Daily Caller*, October 17, 2016, https://dailycaller.com /2016/10/17/exclusive-fbi-agents-say-comey-stood-in-the-way-of-clinton-email -investigation/; Hadas Gold, "Canadian billionaire's company buys Laura Ingraham's site *Lifezette*," News 4 Jacksonville, January 30, 2018, https://www .news4jax.com/news/canadian-billionaires-company-buys-laura-ingrahams-site -lifezette; John Bonazzo, "Trump's Campaign Secretly Paid Tucker Carlson's *Daily Caller* $150k for Email Blasts," *Observer*, June 2, 2017, http://observer .com/2017/06/trump-tucker-carlson-daily-caller/.

65. Picket, "FBI Agents Say Comey 'Stood in the Way.'"

66. Ibid.

67. Ibid.

68. Ibid.

69. Bonazzo, "Trump's Campaign Secretly Paid Tucker Carlson's *Daily Caller*."

70. Larry O'Connor, "Joe DiGenova on the FBI Reopening the investigation into Hillary Clinton," WMAL 105.9 FM DC, October 28, 2016, http://www.wmal.com/2016/10/28/joe-digenova-on-the-fbi-reopening-the-investigation-into-hillary-clinton/.

71. Samuelsohn, "Forget Rudy."

72. Michael Goodwin, "Evidence suggests a massive scandal is brewing at the FBI," *New York Post*, January 23, 2018, https://nypost.com/2018/01/23/evidence-suggests-a-massive-scandal-is-brewing-at-the-fbi/.

73. Michael D. Shear and Michael S. Schmidt, "Trump, Offering No Evidence, Says Obama Tapped His Phones," *New York Times*, March 4, 2017, https://www.nytimes.com/2017/03/04/us/politics/trump-obama-tap-phones.html; Robert Mackey, "In Plots to Smear Obama Aides and George Soros, Israeli Spies for Hire Attack Netanyahu's Enemies," *Intercept*, May 7, 2018, https://theintercept.com/2018/05/07/effort-israeli-spies-smear-obama-aides-echoes-attack-critics-hungarys-leader/.

74. Matt Apuzzo et al., "Justice Dept. Strongly Discouraged Comey on Move in Clinton Email Case," *New York Times*, October 29, 2016, https://www.nytimes.com/2016/10/30/us/politics/comey-clinton-email-justice.html?_r=1.

75. "Judicial Watch: New FBI Records Show FBI Leadership's Conflicts of Interest Discussions on Clinton Email Investigation," Judicial Watch, November 21, 2017, https://www.judicialwatch.org/press-room/press-releases/judicial-watch-new-fbi-records-show-fbi-leaderships-conflicts-interest-discussions-clinton-email-investigation/.

76. "FBI Director Lobbied Against Criminal Charges For Hillary After Clinton Insider Paid His Wife $700,000," *True Pundit*, October 24, 2016, https://truepundit.com/fbi-director-lobbied-against-criminal-charges-for-hillary-after-clinton-insider-paid-his-wife-700k/.

77. Peter Hasson, "Growing Evidence of a Politically Tainted Clinton Investigation," *Daily Caller*, December 14, 2017, https://dailycaller.com/2017/12/14/fbi-hillary-clinton-email-investigation-peter-strzok-lisa-page-james-comey/.

78. Ibid.

79. Matt Apuzzo, "Comey Tried to Shield the F.B.I. From Politics. Then He Shaped an Election," *New York Times*, April 22, 2017, https://www.nytimes.com/2017/04/22/us/politics/james-comey-election.html.

80. "A Review of Various Actions by the Federal Bureau of Investigation and Department of Justice in Advance of the 2016 Election," Office of the Inspector General, US Department of Justice, June 2018, p. 344, https://www.justice.gov/file/1071991/download.

81. Ibid., p. x.

82. Ibid., p. xii.

83. Ibid., p. 82.

84. Ibid., p. 242.

85. Miles Parks et al., "The James Comey Saga, in Timeline Form," WBUR News, May 15, 2017, http://www.wbur.org/npr/527773206/what-just-happened-the-james-comey-saga-in-timeline-form.

86. Thomas Paine, "FBI Raid Thomas Paine's House, Point Guns at His Young Children; How an Award-Winning Reporter Became Thomas Paine," *True Pundit*, August 27, 2018, https://truepundit.com/fbi-raid-thomas-paines-house-point-guns-at-his-young-children-how-an-award-winning-reporter-became-thomas-paine/.

87. Kathryn Alfisi, "A Conversation With Joseph diGenova," *Washington Lawyer*, February 2013, https://www.dcbar.org/bar-resources/publications/washington-lawyer/articles/february-2013-legends-in-the-law.cfm.

88. Robb, "Anatomy of a Fake News Scandal," *Rolling Stone*, November 16, 2017.

89. Ibid.

90. Ibid.; Jonathan Tilove, "Roger Stone Tangos in Austin. Will Anchor Infowars by Night. May Let a Flat," Austin radio show, *Austin American Statesman*, June 1, 2017, http://politics.blog.mystatesman.com/2017/06/01/roger-stone-tangos-in-austin-will-anchor-infowars-by-night-may-let-a-flat/.

91. Ibid.

92. Ibid.

93. Ibid.

94. Ibid.

95. Ibid.

96. Ibid.

97. Ibid.

98. Ibid.

99. Ibid.

100. Ibid.

101. Ibid.

102. Ibid.

103. Ibid.

104. Mark Mazzetti et al., "Trump Jr. and Other Aides Met With Gulf Emissary Offering Help to Win Election," *New York Times*, May 19, 2018, https://www.nytimes.com/2018/05/19/us/politics/trump-jr-saudi-uae-nader-prince-zamel.html.

105. Ibid.

106. Ibid.

107. Robb, "Anatomy of a Fake News Scandal."

108. Craig Silverman et al., "Macedonia's Pro-Trump Fake News Industry Had American Links And Is Under Investigation For Possible Russia Ties," *BuzzFeed News*, July 18, 2018, https://www.buzzfeednews.com/article/craigsilverman/american-conservatives-fake-news-macedonia-paris-wade-libert.

109. Ibid.

110. Ibid.

111. Ibid.

112. Ibid.

113. Ibid.

114. "Paris Wade discusses his 'Liberty Writers' website," *Las Vegas Review Journal*,

May 18, 2018, https://www.reviewjournal.com/videos/paris-wade-discusses-his
-liberty-writers-website/.

115. Craig Timberg, "Russian propaganda effort helped spread 'fake news' during
election, experts say," *Washington Post*, November 24, 2016, https://www.washin
gtonpost.com/business/economy/russian-propaganda-effort-helped-spread-fake
-news-during-election-experts-say/2016/11/24/793903b6-8a40-4ca9-b712-716af6
6098fe_story.html?utm_term=.729ca2638c95; http://www.propornot.com/p/the
-list.html.

116. Ibid.

117. "United States of America v. Internet Research Agency LLC, et al.," Criminal
number (18 U.S.C. §§ 2, 371, 1349, 1028A), Case 1:18-cr-00032-DLF, filed on
February 16, 2018, https://www.justice.gov/file/1035477/download.

118. Silverman et al., "Macedonia's Pro-Trump Fake News Industry Had American
Links."

119. Robb, "Anatomy of a Fake News Scandal."

120. Ibid.

121. Doug Hagman, "What FBI Has Found in Weiner's Laptop? Doug Hagman and
Alex Jones," YouTube, InfoWars, published on November 2, 2016, https://www
.youtube.com/watch?v=BRGOlgZS4tw.

122. Graham Rayman, "NYPD sex crimes chief donated thousands to Trump after
video scandal on grabbing women 'by the p——y,' " *New York Daily News*, April
2018, http://www.nydailynews.com/new-york/nypd-sex-crimes-donated-trump
-p-video-scandal-article-1.3911144.

123. Hagman, "What FBI Has Found in Weiner's Laptop?"

124. Ibid.

125. Ibid.

126. "Breaking Bombshell: NYPD Blows Whistle on New Hillary Emails: Money
Laundering, Sex Crimes with Children, Child Exploitation, Pay to Play, Perjury,"
True Pundit, November 2, 2016, https://truepundit.com/breaking-bombshell
-nypd-blows-whistle-on-new-hillary-emails-money-laundering-sex-crimes-with
-children-child-exploitation-pay-to-play-perjury/. Nov 2, 2016 09:18:47 PM

127. Michael Flynn (@GenFlynn), "U decide - NYPD Blows Whistle on New Hillary Emails: Money Laundering, Sex Crimes w Children, etc . . . MUST READ!
Twitter, November 2, 2016, 6:47 p.m., http://www.trumptwitterarchive.com/.

128. Donald Trump Jr. (@DonaldJTrumpJr), "@GenFlynn: U decide - NYPD Blows
Whistle on New Hillary Emails: Money Laundering, Sex Crimes w Children,
etc . . . MUST READ! https://t.co/O," Twitter, November 4, 2016, 12:15 p.m.,
http://www.trumptwitterarchive.com/.

129. Paul Szoldra, "Trump's national security adviser has promoted tweets alleging Hillary Clinton was involved in 'sex crimes,' " *Business Insider*, November 18, 2016,
https://www.businessinsider.com/michael-flynn-tweets-hillary-clinton-2016-11.

130. Ibid.

131. Ben Schreckinger, "Inside Donald Trump's Election Night War Room," *GQ*, November 7, 2017, https://www.gq.com/story/inside-donald-trumps-election-night
-war-room.

132. *Politico*, May 19, 2018, https://www.politico.com/story/2018/05/19/erik-prince -congressional-testimony-trump-tower-meeting-598052.

133. Ari Melber, "Sam Nunberg: I expect Roger Stone to be indicted," MSNBC, August 3, 2018, https://www.msnbc.com/the-beat-with-ari-melber/watch/sam-nun berg-i-expect-roger-stone-to-be-indicted-1292041795756?v=raila.

134. Sara Murray, "The pot-farming, house-painting Roger Stone aide who's resisting Robert Mueller," CNN August 25, 2018, https://www.cnn.com/2018/08/24/poli tics/andrew-miller-roger-stone-aide-defies-robert-mueller/index.html.

135. Ibid.

136. Justin Wise, "Roger Stone predicts he'll be indicted next in Mueller probe," *Hill,* August 27, 2018, http://thehill.com/blogs/blog-briefing-room/news/403838 -roger-stone-predicts-hell-be-indicted-next-in-mueller-probe.

137. Dan Friedman, "Roger Stone to Associate, 'Prepare to Die,'" *Mother Jones*, May 25, 2018, https://www.motherjones.com/politics/2018/05/roger-stone-to -associate-prepare-to-die/.

138. Ibid.

139. Ibid.

140. Ibid.

141. Ibid.

142. Ibid.

143. Ibid.

144. Dan Friedman, "Mueller Is Examining Roger Stone's Emails," *Mother Jones*, August 13, 2018, https://www.motherjones.com/politics/2018/08/roger-stone -randy-credico-mueller-assange-wikileaks/.

145. Ibid.

146. Chris Sommerfeldt, "President Trump is so eager to pardon Paul Manafort he's reportedly considering hiring a new White House counsel," *New York Daily News*, August 27, 2018, http://www.nydailynews.com/news/politics/ny-news -trump-pardon-manafort-donald-mcgahn-20180827-story.html.

147. Nancy Cook, "Aides expect Trump to go rogue on Manafort pardon," *Politico*, August 24, 2018, https://www.politico.com/story/2018/08/24/trump-manafort -pardon-white-house-aides-795712; Gabriel Sherman, "'Trump Is Nuts. This Time Really Feels Different': Trump Rejects 'War Council' Intervention, Goes It Alone," *Vanity Fair*, August 27, 2018, https://www.vanityfair.com/news/2018/08 /donald-trump-nuts-rejects-war-council-intervention-goes-it-alone.

148. Sherman, "'Trump Is Nuts.'"

149. *Los Angeles Times*, "A National Enquirer safe is said to have held damaging Trump stories," (Associated Press), http://www.latimes.com/politics/la-na-pol -national-enquirer-trump-vault-20180823-story.html.

CHAPTER ELEVEN: THE TRANSITION

1. Daniel Hemel and Eric Posner, "Why the Trump Team Should Fear the Logan Act," *New York Times*, December 4, 2017, https://www.nytimes.com/2017/12/04 /opinion/trump-team-flynn-logan-act.html.

2. David Filipov and Andrew Roth, "Moscow had contacts with Trump during campaign, Russian diplomat says," *Washington Post*, November 10, 2016, https://www.washingtonpost.com/world/moscow-had-contacts-with-trump-team-during-campaign-russian-diplomat-says/2016/11/10/28fb82fa-a73d-11e6-9bd6-184ab22d218e_story.html?utm_term=.fafoobff7f60; Reuters, "Russia says it was in touch with Trump campaign during election," CNBC, November 10, 2016, https://www.cnbc.com/2016/11/10/russian-diplomat-there-were-contacts-with-trumps-campaign.html; Luke Harding et al., "British spies were first to spot Trump team's links with Russia," *Guardian*, April 13, 2017, https://www.theguardian.com/uk-news/2017/apr/13/british-spies-first-to-spot-trump-team-links-russia.

3. Filipov and Roth, "Moscow had contacts with Trump"; Reuters, "Russia says it was in touch."

4. Ibid.

5. Nicholas Fandos, "Hope Hicks Acknowledges She Sometimes Tells White Lies for Trump," *New York Times*, February 27, 2018, https://www.nytimes.com/2018/02/27/us/politics/hope-hicks-house-intelligence-committee-testimony.html.

6. Reuters, "Russia says it was in touch."

7. Thuy Ong, "Obama personally warned Mark Zuckerberg to take the threats of fake news 'seriously,'" *Verge*, September 25, 2017, https://www.theverge.com/2017/9/25/16360482/obama-mark-zuckerberg-fake-news-facebook.

8. Abby Ohlheiser, "Mark Zuckerberg denies that fake news on Facebook influenced the elections," *Washington Post*, November 11, 2016, https://www.washingtonpost.com/news/the-intersect/wp/2016/11/11/mark-zuckerberg-denies-that-fake-news-on-facebook-influenced-the-elections/?utm_term=.926660306ea7; Adam Entous et al., "Obama tried to give Zuckerberg a wake-up call over fake news on Facebook," *Washington Post*, September 24, 2017, https://www.washingtonpost.com/business/economy/obama-tried-to-give-zuckerberg-a-wake-up-call-over-fake-news-on-facebook/2017/09/24/15d19b12-ddac-4ad5-ac6e-ef909e1c1284_story.html?utm_term=.51cf68a4e3c1; John Shinal, "Mark Zuckerberg responds to Trump, regrets he dismissed election concerns," CNBC, September 27, 2017, https://www.cnbc.com/2017/09/27/mark-zuckerberg-says-facebook-impact-on-2016-election-went-beyond-ads.html.

9. Michael S. Schmidt, "Emails Dispute White House Claims That Flynn Acted Independently on Russia," *New York Times*, December 2, 2017, https://www.nytimes.com/2017/12/02/us/russia-mcfarland-flynn-trump-emails.html.

10. Ibid.

11. Marcy Wheeler, "Putting a Face (Mine) to the Risks Posed by GOP Games on Mueller Investigation," *Emptywheel* (website of independent national security/civil liberties journalist Marcy Wheeler), July 3, 2018, https://www.emptywheel.net/2018/07/03/putting-a-face-mine-to-the-risks-posed-by-gop-games-on-mueller-investigation/.

12. Ryan Hutchins, "Christie: Warning about Flynn among reasons I was fired from Trump transition," *Politico*, December 6, 2017, https://www.politico.com/states/new-jersey/story/2017/12/06/christie-warning-about-flynn-among-reasons-i

-was-fired-from-trump-transition-136432; Summer Meza, "Jared Kushner and Ivanka Trump Pushed to put Flynn in Office, Ignored Warnings," *Newsweek,* August 2, 2017, https://www.newsweek.com/ivanka-trump-jared-kushner-wanted -michael-flynn-white-house-729379.

13. Hutchins, "Christie."
14. Matthew Nussbaum, "Pence Pleads Ignorance as Russia Probe Deepens," *Politico*, December 4, 2017, https://www.politico.com/story/2017/12/04/pence-russia -probe-flynn-mueller-278785.
15. Ibid.
16. Ned Parker and Jonathan Landay, "Exclusive: Trump son-in-law had undisclosed contacts with Russian envoy—sources," Reuters, May 26, 2017, https://www .reuters.com/article/us-usa-trump-fbi-kushner-exclusive/exclusive-trump-son-in -law-had-undisclosed-contacts-with-russian-envoy-sources-idUSKBN18N018; "Read: Jared Kushner's statement on Russia to congressional committees," CNN, July 24, 2017, https://edition.cnn.com/2017/07/24/politics/jared-kushner -statement-russia-2016-election/index.html.
17. Michael S. Schmidt et al., "Kushner and Flynn Met with Russian Envoy in December, White House Says," *New York Times*, March 2017, https://www.nytimes .com/2017/03/02/us/politics/kushner-flynn-sessions-russia.html.
18. Carrie Cordero, "How to Understand Kushner's 'Back-Channel,'" *Politico*, June 6, 2017, https://www.politico.com/magazine/story/2017/06/06/how-to-understand -kushners-back-channel-215232.
19. Ibid.
20. Noah Feldman, "Trump's Wiretap Tweets Raise Risk of Impeachment," Bloomberg, March 6, 2017, https://www.bloomberg.com/view/articles/2017-03 -06/trump-s-wiretap-tweets-raise-risk-of-impeachment.
21. Hutchins, "Christie"; "Read: Jared Kushner's statement."
22. Hemel and Posner, "Why the Trump Team."
23. Tom Kertscher, "Did Russian officials go in back door of Trump Tower to meet Donald Trump son-in-law Jared Kushner," *PolitiFact*, March 8, 2017, https:// www.politifact.com/wisconsin/statements/2017/mar/08/mark-pocan/russian-of ficials-went-back-door-trump-tower-meet-/.
24. Adam Entous, "The agonizingly slow downfall of K. T. McFarland," *New Yorker*, January 29, 2018, https://www.newyorker.com/news/news-desk/the-agonizingly -slow-downfall-of-k-t-mcfarland.
25. Siddhartha Mahanta, "K. T. McFarland: A Reagan Veteran in Trumpworld," *Atlantic*, December 12, 2016, https://www.theatlantic.com/international/archive /2016/12/mcfarland-trump-reagan-weinberger-flynn-washington-fox/510323/.
26. Rosalind S. Helderman et al., "'She was like a novelty': How alleged Russian agent Maria Butina gained access to elite conservative circles," *Washington Post*, July 17, 2018, https://www.washingtonpost.com/politics/she-was-like-a -novelty-how-alleged-russian-agent-maria-butina-gained-access-to-elite-conser vative-circles/2018/07/17/1bb62bbc-89d2-11e8-a345-a1bf7847b375_story.html ?utm_term=.62ebd9a29437; Kristen Welker and Adam Howard, "Trump Taps K. T. McFarland for National Security Post, Donald McGahn for White House

Counsel," NBC News, November 2016, https://www.nbcnews.com/politics /2016-election/trump-taps-k-t-mcfarland-national-security-post-donald-mcgahn -n688341.

27. Michael S. Schmidt and Sharon LaFraniere, "McFarland's Testimony About Russian Contacts Is Questioned," *New York Times*, December 4, 2017, https:// www.nytimes.com/2017/12/04/us/politics/kt-mcfarland-flynn-russia-emails -congressional-testimony.html.

28. Ibid.
29. Ibid.
30. Ibid.
31. Ibid.

32. Natasha Bertrand, "Top Trump transition official in private email: Russia 'has just thrown' the election to Trump," *Business Insider*, December 2, 2017, https:// www.businessinsider.com/emails-kt-mcfarland-russia-thrown-election-to-trump -flynn-2017-12.

33. Tara Palmeri, "Need to reach Trump? Call Rhona," *Politico* (Europe), March 26, 2017, https://www.politico.eu/article/need-to-reach-donald-trump-call-rhona -graff-assistant/.

34. Jeremy Herb, "Russians followed up on Trump Tower meeting after election, Democrats say," CNN, April 27, 2018, https://www.cnn.com/2018/04/27/politics /russians-trump-team-magnitsky-act/index.html; Tucker Higgins, "Emails show follow-up to June 2016 Trump Tower meeting: Reports," CNBC, December 7, 2017, https://www.cnbc.com/2017/12/07/cnn-emails-show-follow-up-to-june -2016-trump-tower-meeting.html.

35. Amanda Holpuch, "Timeline: Trump and associates denied Russian involvement at least 20 times," *Guardian*, July 11, 2017, https://www.theguardian.com /us-news/2017/jul/11/donald-trump-russia-timeline-campaign-denials; Marshall Cohen, "Trump lawyers say he 'dictated' statement on Trump Tower meeting, contradicting past denials," CNN, June 2, 2018, https://www.cnn.com/2018/06 /02/politics/trump-lawyers-statement-trump-tower-russians/index.html.

36. Cohen, "Trump lawyers say he 'dictated.'"

37. Alex Horton, "The Magnitsky Act, Explained," *Washington Post*, July 14, 2017, https://www.washingtonpost.com/news/the-fix/wp/2017/07/14/the-magnitsky -act-explained/?utm_term=.a0e1e2ef287d.

38. David Kocieniewski, "Russian Lawyer Who Met Trump Jr. Saw a Clinton Scandal in Tax Inquiry," Bloomberg, July 2017, https://www.bloomberg.com/news /articles/2017-07-12/russian-at-trump-tower-is-said-to-have-gathered-details-on -ziffs.

39. Emily Stewart, "Read: Donald Trump Jr.'s congressional testimony about the Trump Tower meeting," *Vox*, May 16, 2018 (Trump Jr. transcript, p. 53), https:// www.vox.com/policy-and-politics/2018/5/16/17360484/donald-trump-jr-tran script-senate-judiciary-committee.

40. Ibid.
41. Ibid.

42. Amie Ferris-Rotman, "Why Did Russia Send Sergei Gorkov to Meet with Jared

Kushner?" *Foreign Policy*, July 25, 2017, https://foreignpolicy.com/2017/07/25/why-did-russia-send-sergei-gorkov-to-meet-with-jared-kushner/.

43. Ibid.

44. David Filipov, "Explanations for Kushner's meeting with the head of the Kremlin-linked bank don't match up," *Washington Post*, June 1, 2017, https://www.washingtonpost.com/politics/explanations-for-kushners-meeting-with-head-of-kremlin-linked-bank-dont-match-up/2017/06/01/dd1bdbb0-460a-11e7-bcde-624ad94170ab_story.html?utm_term=.39779e3f480e.

45. Ibid.

46. Ibid.

47. Filipov, "Explanations"; Chad Day, "Fynn timeline: It all began with a UN resolution condemning Israeli settlements," *Times of Israel*, December 2017, https://www.timesofisrael.com/flynn-timeline-it-all-began-with-a-un-resolution-condemning-israeli-settlements/.

48. Greg Miller et al., "National security adviser Flynn discussed sanctions with Russian ambassador, despite denials, officials say," *Washington Post,* February 9, 2017, https://www.washingtonpost.com/world/national-security/national-security-adviser-flynn-discussed-sanctions-with-russian-ambassador-despite-denials-officials-say/2017/02/09/f85b29d6-ee11-11e6-b4ff-ac2cf509efe5_story.html?utm_term=.164bf18fd274.

49. "Former Trump adviser Page speaking about fake news, security threats & economy in Moscow," RT, YouTube (RT official account, 28:30 mark), December 12, 2016, https://www.youtube.com/watch?v=E4gkf-7rGn8.

50. Ibid.

51. Ken Bensinger, "These Reports Allege Trump Has Deep Ties to Russia," *BuzzFeed News,* January 10, 2017, https://www.buzzfeednews.com/article/kenbensinger/these-reports-allege-trump-has-deep-ties-to-russia; The Steele Dossier (pp. 9 and 30–31), June 20, 2016, https://www.documentcloud.org/documents/3259984-Trump-Intelligence-Allegations.html.

52. "Former Trump adviser Page speaking about fake news," (30:30 mark).

53. Ibid. (22:15 mark).

54. Ibid.

55. Bensinger, "These Reports Allege"; Steele Dossier, pp. 9 and 30–31.

56. Ibid.

57. Ibid.

58. Ibid.

59. Katya Golubkova et al., "How Russia sold its oil jewel: Without saying who bought it," Reuters, January 24, 2018, https://www.reuters.com/article/us-russia-rosneft-privatisation-insight/how-russia-sold-its-oil-jewel-without-saying-who-bought-it-idUSKBN1582OH.

60. Isaac Arnsdorf, "White House May Share Nuclear Power Technology with Saudi Arabia," ProPublica, November 29, 2017, https://www.propublica.org/article/white-house-may-share-nuclear-power-technology-with-saudi-arabia.

61. Reuters, "Saudi Arabia Says It Has Options if U.S. Walks Away from Nuclear Power Deal," *Haaretz*, March 25, 2018, https://www.haaretz.com/middle-east

-news/saudi-arabia-says-it-has-options-if-u-s-walks-from-nuclear-power-deal
-1.5938599; Warren Strobel, "Exclusive: Mideast nuclear plan backers bragged
of support of top Trump aide Flynn," Reuters, December 1, 2017, https://www
.reuters.com/article/us-usa-trump-flynn-nuclear-exclusive/exclusive-mideast
-nuclear-plan-backers-bragged-of-support-of-top-trump-aide-flynn-idUSKB
N1DV5Z6.

62. Arnsdorf, "White House May Share."

63. Chas Danner, "Beyond Russia: Understanding the New Trump Campaign Collu-
    sion Story," *New York*, May 20, 2018, http://nymag.com/daily/intelligencer/2018
    /05/understanding-the-new-trump-campaign-collusion-story.html.

64. Ibid.

65. Ibid.

66. Ibid.

67. James Gordon Meek, "Special Counsel Obtains Trump Ally Erik Prince's
    Phones, Computer," ABC News, June 25, 2018, https://abcnews.go.com/Politics
    /special-counsel-obtains-trump-ally-erik-princes-phones/story?id=56143477.

68. Jesse Drunker et al., "Kushner's Family Business Received Loans after White
    House Meeting," *New York Times*, February 28, 2018, https://www.nytimes.com
    /2018/02/28/business/jared-kushner-apollo-citigroup-loans.html; Portia Crowe,
    "The US just sanction a fund that was connected to some of the biggest names in
    finance," *Business Insider*, July 30, 2015, https://www.businessinsider.com/rus
    sian-investment-fund-connected-to-us-investors-sanctioned-2015-7.

69. Meek, "Special Counsel Obtains."

70. Ibid.

71. Ibid.

72. Ibid.

73. Arnsdorf, "White House May Share."

74. Ibid.

75. Sharon LaFraniere et al., "How the Russia Inquiry Began: A Campaign Aide,
    Drinks and Talk of Political Dirt," *New York Times*, December 2017, https://
    www.nytimes.com/2017/12/30/us/politics/how-fbi-russia-investigation-began
    -george-papadopoulos.html; Maegan Vazquez, "Ex-Trump campaign adviser
    Papadopoulos was just a coffee boy," CNN, October 31, 2017, https://www
    .cnn.com/2017/10/31/politics/caputo-papadopoulos-coffee-boy-cnntv/index
    .html.

76. Brian Whitaker, "What George Papadopoulos did before joining the Trump cam-
    paign: A chronology," Medium, August 24, 2018, https://medium.com/@Brian
    _Whit/what-george-papadopoulos-did-before-joining-the-trump-campaign-a
    -chronology-eaf0e4a59b5d.

77. Arnsdorf, "White House May Share."

78. Rosie Perper, "Saudi Arabia's crown prince reportedly bragged about having
    Jared Kushner 'in his pocket' after being told classified information meant for
    Trump," *Business Insider*, March 2018, https://www.businessinsider.com/saudi
    -crown-prince-jared-kushner-relationship-2018-3; Alex Emmons, "Saudi Crown
    Prince Boasted That Jared Kushner Was 'In His Pocket,'" Intercept, March 21,

2018, https://theintercept.com/2018/03/21/jared-kushner-saudi-crown-prince -mohammed-bin-salman/.

79. Jessica Kwong, "Lawsuit Claims Saudis Bought Out Jared Kushner, White House Is Compromised," *Newsweek*, April 4, 2018, https://www.newsweek.com /trump-administration-sued-after-saudi-prince-bragged-jared-kushner-was-his -872401.

80. Emmons, "Saudi Crown Prince Boasted."

81. Ibid.

82. Carol E. Lee et al., "Mueller team asking if Kushner foreign business ties influenced Trump policy," NBC News, March 2, 2018, https://www.nbcnews.com/ politics/white-house/mueller-team-asking-if-kushner-foreign-business-ties-in fluenced-trump-n852681.

83. Drucker, "Kushner's Family Business Received"; "White House investigating loans to Kushner's business: Official," Reuters, March 26, 2018, https://www .reuters.com/article/us-usa-trump-kushner/white-house-investigating-loans-to -kushners-business-official-idUSKBN1H301A.

84. Drucker, "Kushner's Family Business Received."

85. Clayton Swisher and Ryan Grim, "Jared Kushner's Real-Estate Firm Sought Money Directly from Qatar Government Weeks Before Blockade," *Intercept*, March 2, 2018, https://theintercept.com/2018/03/02/jared-kushner-real-estate -qatar-blockade/; Felix Salmon, "The Most Important Questions to Ask About the Kushner 666 Fifth Ave. Deal," *Slate*, May 17, 2018, https://slate.com/busi ness/2018/05/kushner-666-fifth-ave-deal-brookfield-and-qatar-what-questions -need-answering.html; Bess Levin, "Did Jared Kushner Punish Qatar Because It Wouldn't Lend His Family Money?" *Vanity Fair*, March 2, 2018, https:// www.vanityfair.com/news/2018/03/did-jared-kushner-punish-qatar-because-it -wouldnt-lend-his-family-money#~o.

86. Ibid.

87. Scott Deveau, "Kushners Unload 666 Fifth Ave. to Brookfield in 99-Year Lease," Bloomberg, August 3, 2018, https://www.bloomberg.com/news/articles/2018-08 -03/brookfield-acquires-99-year-lease-on-nyc-tower-from-kushner-cos.

88. Jed Handelsman Shugerman, "L'Affaire Kushner," *Slate,* March 2, 2018, https:// slate.com/news-and-politics/2018/03/a-series-of-revelations-about-jared-kush ner-have-added-further-credence-to-a-key-claim-of-the-steele-dossier.html.

89. Hassan Hassan, "Qatar Won the Saudi Blockade," *Foreign Policy*, June 4, 2018, https://foreignpolicy.com/2018/06/04/qatar-won-the-saudi-blockade/.

90. Irana Slav, "Will Rosneft Move Forward in the Arctic Without Exxon," OilPrice, March 11, 2018, https://oilprice.com/Energy/Energy-General/Will-Rosneft -Move-Forward-In-The-Arctic-Without-Exxon.html.

91. Ibid.; Google search, "How much is a ton of oil worth," (current cost of a ton of oil as of August 2018), https://www.google.com/search?q=how+much +is+a+ton+of+oil+worth&oq=how+much+is+a+ton+of+oil+worth&aqs= chrome..69i57j0.3806j1j4&sourceid=chrome&ie=UTF-8.

92. "Donald Trump Names Rex Tillerson as Secretary of State," *Morning Joe/*

MSNBC YouTube channel, December 13, 2016, https://www.youtube.com
/watch?v=HCK8ck-Y8es.

93. Zeeshan Aleem, "Saudi Arabia's Controversial Quest for Nuclear Power,
Explained," *Vox*, March 26, 2018, https://www.vox.com/world/2018/3/26
/17144446/saud-arabia-nuclear-weapons-trump-iran-deal.

94. Chuck Freilich, "Opinion: Trump's Mayhem Allows Putin's Russia to Take Over
the Middle East, One Country at a Time," *Haaretz*, July 19, 2018, https://www
.haaretz.com/us-news/.premium-how-putin-s-russia-is-taking-over-the-middle
-east-one-country-at-a-time-1.6290146.

95. Ibid.

96. Mark N. Katz, "Balancing Act: Russia between Iran and Saudi Arabia," London
School of Economics and Political Science, Middle East Centre Blog, May 7,
2018, http://blogs.lse.ac.uk/mec/2018/06/26/balancing-act-russia-between-iran
-and-saudi-arabia/.

97. Mark Mazzetti et al., "Trump Jr. and Other Aides Met with Gulf Emissary Offering Help to Win Election," *New York Times*, May 19, 2018, https://www.nytimes
.com/2018/05/19/us/politics/trump-jr-saudi-uae-nader-prince-zamel.html.

98. Adam Entous, "Israeli, Saudi, and Emirati Officials Privately Pushed for Trump
to Strike a 'Grand Bargain' with Putin," *New Yorker*, July 9, 2018, https://www
.newyorker.com/news/news-desk/israeli-saudi-and-emirati-officials-privately
-pushed-for-trump-to-strike-a-grand-bargain-with-putin.

99. Ibid.; Clifford Krauss, "United States, Saudi Arabia and Russia Find Agreement
on Oil Policy," *New York Times*, June 13, 2018, https://www.nytimes.com/2018
/06/13/business/energy-environment/russia-saudi-arabia-oil-prices.html.

100. Steve Mufson, "Pompeo: Saudis must not enrich uranium if it seeks civilian
nuclear cooperation," *Washington Post*, May 24, 2018, https://www.washing
tonpost.com/business/economy/pompeo-saudis-must-not-enrich-uranium-if
-it-seeks-civilian-nuclear-cooperation/2018/05/24/714c5e30-5f92-11e8-a4a4
-c070ef53f315_story.html?utm_term=.13d5782b6cf8.

101. Andrew Prokop, "The secret Seychelles meeting Robert Mueller is zeroing in
on, explained," *Vox*, April 10, 2018, https://www.vox.com/2018/3/7/17088908/
erik-prince-trump-russia-seychelles-mueller; Erin Banco, "Trump Envoy Erik
Prince Met with CEO of Russian Direct Investment Fund in Seychelles," Intercept, November 28, 2017, https://theintercept.com/2017/11/28/blackwaters-erik
-prince-met-with-ceo-of-russian-direct-investment-fund/.

102. Banco, "Trump Envoy Erik Prince."

103. Ibid.

104. Ibid.

105. "Erik Prince testimony transcript," US House of Representatives, November 30,
2017, https://docs.house.gov/meetings/IG/IG00/20171130/106661/HHRG-115
-IG00-Transcript-20171130.pdf.

106. Ibid.

107. Lisette Partelow and Meg Benner, "(Betsy DeVos) Unqualified and Dangerous," *U.S. News and World Report*, February 7, 2017, https://www.usnews

.com/opinion/knowledge-bank/articles/2017-02-07/5-reasons-to-reject-donald -trumps-education-pick-betsy-devos; Helaine Olen, "Betsy Devos's disastrous interview shows the limitations of being rich," *Washington Post*, March 12, 2018, https://www.washingtonpost.com/blogs/plum-line/wp/2018/03/12/betsy -devos-disastrous-interview-shows-the-limitations-of-being-rich/?utm_term =.12686600e7a6; Joy Resmovits, "Betsy DeVos 'is unprepared and unqualified' to be Education secretary, charter school booster Eli Broad says," *Los Angeles Times*, February 1, 2017, http://www.latimes.com/local/education/la-me-eli -broad-opposes-devos-20170201-story.html.

108. BBC, "Why is Betsy DeVos, Trump's pick for education secretary, so unpopular?" February 7, 2017, https://www.bbc.com/news/world-us-canada-38875924.

109. Michael D. Shear and Maggie Haberman, "Rex Tillerson, Exxon C.E.O., Chosen as Secretary of State," *New York Times*, December 12, 2016, https://www.ny times.com/2016/12/12/us/politics/rex-tillerson-secretary-of-state-trump.html.

110. Mike Murphy, "Trump lobbied for Sessions to protect him from investigation, report says," *MarketWatch,* January 4, 2018, https://www.marketwatch.com/ story/trump-lobbied-for-sessions-to-protect-him-from-investigation-report-says -2018-01-04.

111. Adam Entous et al., "Sessions met with Russian envoy twice last year, encounters he later did not disclose," *Washington Post*, March 2017, https://www .washingtonpost.com/world/national-security/sessions-spoke-twice-with-rus sian-ambassador-during-trumps-presidential-campaign-justice-officials-say /2017/03/01/77205eda-feac-11e6-99b4-9e613afeb09f_story.html?utm_term =.e3c9ad3327be.

112. Mark Landler and Eric Lichtblau, "Jeff Sessions Recuses Himself from Russian Inquiry," *New York Times*, March 2, 2017, https://www.nytimes.com/2017/03/02 /us/politics/jeff-sessions-russia-trump-investigation-democrats.html.

113. Miller, "National Security Adviser Flynn."

114. Karoun Demirjian, "Trump praises Putin's response to sanctions, calls Russian leader 'very smart!'" *Washington Post*, December 30, 2016, https://www.wash ingtonpost.com/news/powerpost/wp/2016/12/30/trump-praises-putins-response -to-sanctions-calls-russian-leader-very-smart/?utm_term=.128a6cb3288d.

115. Graham Lanktree, "Trump White House Made Secret Efforts to Remove Russia Sanctions," *Newsweek*, June 2, 2017, https://www.newsweek.com/trump-white -house-secret-efforts-lift-russia-sanctions-putin-619508; Jonathan Landay and Arshad Mohammad, "Trump adviser had five calls with Russian envoy on day of sanctions: sources," Reuters, January 13, 2017, https://www.reuters.com/article /us-usa-trump-russia-idUSKBN14X1YX; Matthew Kahn, "Michael Flynn Plea Agreement Documents," *Lawfare*, December 1, 2017, https://www.lawfareblog .com/michael-flynn-plea-agreement-documents.

116. Howard Blum, "Exclusive: What Trump Really Told Kislyak After Comey Was Canned," *Vanity Fair*, November 22, 2017, https://www.vanityfair.com/news /2017/11/trump-intel-slip?link_success=true.

117. "Assessing Russian Activities and Intentions in Recent US Elections: The Ana-

lytic Process and Cyber Incident Attribution," DNI.gov, January 6, 2017, https://www.dni.gov/files/documents/ICA_2017_01.pdf.

118. Marshall Cohen, "Everything Trump has said about who tried to hack the US election," CNN, June 21, 2017, https://www.cnn.com/2017/06/21/politics/trump-russia-hacking-statements/index.html.

119. Nick Hopkins and Luke Harding, "Donald Trump dossier: Intelligence sources vouch for author's credibility," *Guardian*, January 12, 2017, https://www.theguardian.com/us-news/2017/jan/12/intelligence-sources-vouch-credibility-donald-trump-russia-dossier-author.

120. Bensinger, "These Reports Allege."

121. Adam Levine, "Comey's response to Trump's claim of not being under investigation," CNN, June 7, 2017, https://www.cnn.com/2017/06/07/politics/donald-trump-james-comey-conversations/index.html.

122. Cohen, Everything Trump has said."

123. Ibid.

124. Ibid.

125. Michael S. Schmidt et al., "Intercepted Russian Communications Part of Inquiry into Trump Associates," *New York Times*, January 19, 2019, https://www.nytimes.com/2017/01/19/us/politics/trump-russia-associates-investigation.html.

126. Ibid.

127. Hutchins, "Christie"; Meza, "Jared Kushner andIvanka Trump."

128. Byron York, "Jared Kushner's Grudge Against Chris Christie," *Washington Examiner*, April 16, 2017, https://www.washingtonexaminer.com/byron-york-the-sordid-case-behind-jared-kushners-grudge-against-chris-christie.

129. Julie Hirschfeld Davis, "Firings and Discord Put Trump Transition Team in a State of Disarray," *New York Times*, November 16, 2016, https://www.nytimes.com/2016/11/16/us/politics/trump-transition.html.

130. Ibid.

131. Michael Kranish, "Kushner companies finalizes deal on troubled office tower," *Washington Post*, August 3, 2018, https://www.washingtonpost.com/politics/kushner-companies-finalizes-deal-on-troubled-office-tower/2018/08/03/89cb5eb0-9756-11e8-810c-5fa705927d54_story.html?utm_term=.9b9b3f023f55; Ken Dilanian et al., "Was Kushner Seeking a Russian Bailout for Manhattan Building? Congress Will Ask," NBC News, June 5, 2017, https://www.nbcnews.com/news/us-news/was-kushner-seeking-russian-bailout-manhattan-building-congress-will-ask-n766801; Cristina Alesci, "Charles Kushner: 'I Pushed Jared to Do the Deal' for 666 Fifth Ave.," CNN, April 2018, https://www.cnn.com/2018/04/23/politics/charles-jared-kushner-666-fifth-avenue/index.html.

132. Kranish, "Kushner companies finalizes deal"; Dilanian, "Was Kushner Seeking"; Alesci, "Charles Kushner"; Michelle Mark, "Charles Kushner explains his meeting with Qatar's finance minister, says it was 'a wrong thing to do,' but 'none of us knew the rules of government,'" *Business Insider*, June 2018, https://www.businessinsider.com/charles-kushner-qatar-finance-minister-meeting-666-fifth-ave-2018-6.

133. "Michael Flynn: Timeline of his rise, fall and guilty plea," NBC News, February 14, 2017, https://www.nbcnews.com/news/us-news/mike-flynn-timeline-his-rise -fall-russia-call-n720671.

134. Jessica Taylor, "White House Press Secretary Says Trump Fired Flynn as National Security Adviser," NPR, February 14, 2017, https://www.npr.org/2017/02 /14/515215088/white-house-press-secretary-says-trump-fired-flynn-as-national -security-adviser.

135. Peter Nicholas et al., "Trump Open to Shift on Russia Sanctions, One China Policy," *Wall Street Journal*, January 2017, https://www.wsj.com/articles/donald -trump-sets-a-bar-for-russia-and-china-1484360380.

136. Robert Windrem and William M. Arkin, "Trump Told Russia to Blame for Hacks Long Before 2016 Debate," NBC News, October 10, 2016, https://www.nbc news.com/news/us-news/trump-was-told-russia-was-blame-hacks-long-debate -n663686.

137. Donald J. Trump (@realDonaldTrump), "The 'Intelligence' briefing on so-called 'Russian hacking' was delayed until Friday, perhaps more time needed to build a case. Very strange!" Twitter, January 3, 2017, 5:14 p.m., https://twitter.com/real DonaldTrump/status/816452807024840704.

CHAPTER TWELVE: THE FIRINGS OF FLYNN AND COMEY

1. Bryan Bender and Shane Goldmacher, "Trump's Favorite General," *Poilitco*, July 8, 2016, https://www.politico.com/story/2016/07/donald-trump-general-mi chael-flynn-vp-225253.

2. John Haltiwanger, "John McCain describes how he received the Steele dossier that contains the most salacious allegations about Trump and Russia," *Business Insider*, May 22, 2018, https://www.businessinsider.com/how-john-mccain-re ceived-steele-dossier-trump-russia-2018-5.

3. Tom Hamburger and Rosalind S. Helderman, "Hero or hired gun? How a British former spy became a flash point in the Russia investigation," *Washington Post*, February 6, 2018, https://www.washingtonpost.com/politics/hero-or-hired -gun-how-a-british-former-spy-became-a-flash-point-in-the-russia-investiga tion/2018/02/06/94ea5158-0795-11e8-8777-2a059f168dd2_story.html?utm_ter m=.6129890f680a; Amy Knight, "Was This Russian General Murdered over the Steele Dossier," *Daily Beast*, January 23, 2018, https://www.thedailybeast.com/ was-this-russian-general-murdered-over-the-steele-dossier.

4. Department of Justice release, May 17, 2017, https://www.documentcloud.org/ documents/3726396-Order-3915-2017-Special-Counsel-0.html.

5. Glenn Kessler, "President Trump vs. James B. Comey: A Timeline," *Washington Post*, March 23, 2017, https://www.washingtonpost.com/news/fact-checker /wp/2017/05/23/president-trump-versus-james-comey-a-timeline/?noredi rect=on&utm_term=.e77c4f07d28c.

6. Ibid.

7. Ibid.

8. Ibid.

9. Ibid.

10. Carol E. Lee, "Flynn Kept FBI Interview Concealed from White House, Trump," NBC News, January 24, 2018, https://www.nbcnews.com/politics/donald-trump/flynn-kept-fbi-interview-concealed-white-house-trump-n840491.

11. Emily Schultheis, "Mike Pence Says Trump Adviser's Contact with Russia Was 'Strictly Coincidental,'" CBS News, January 15, 2017, https://www.cbsnews.com/news/mike-pence-michael-flynn-russia-contact-strictly-coincidental/.

12. Kessler, "President Trump vs. James B. Comey."

13. Ibid.

14. Ibid.

15. Ibid.

16. Ibid.

17. Edward-Isaac Dovere and Matthew Nussbaum, "Obama Warned Trump About Flynn, Officials Say," *Politico,* May 8, 2017, https://www.politico.com/story/2017/05/08/obama-warn-trump-michael-flynn-238116.

18. Eric Bradner et al., "Trump Offers Flynn Job of National Security Advisor," CNN, November 18, 2016, https://www.cnn.com/2016/11/17/politics/trump-offers-flynn-job-of-national-security-adviser/index.html.

19. Maureen George, "Pence, Flynn and the Russia Investigation: A Timeline of Key Events," *USA Today*, December 10, 2017, https://www.usatoday.com/story/news/politics/2017/12/10/pence-flynn-and-russia-investigation-timeline-key-events/935046001/.

20. Chad Day and Eric Tucker, "Michael Flynn didn't disclose Mideast trip for security clearance, top Dems say," Associated Press, September 13, 2017, https://www.twincities.com/2017/09/13/top-dems-say-flynn-left-mideast-trip-off-security-clearance/.

21. Megan Twohey and Scott Shane, "A Back-Channel Plan for Ukraine and Russia, Courtesy of Trump Associates," *New York Times*, February 19, 2017, https://www.nytimes.com/2017/02/19/us/politics/donald-trump-ukraine-russia.html.

22. Vicky Ward, "Michael Cohen Speaks: Trump exec admits Russia dealings were gross, but not illegal," *Huffington Post*, September 1, 2017, https://www.huffingtonpost.com/entry/michael-cohen-trump-lawyer-russia_us_59a71a28e4b010ca2899e933.

23. Adam Entous et al., "Justice department warned White House that Flynn could be vulnerable to Russian blackmail, officials say," *Washington Post*, February 13, 2017, https://www.washingtonpost.com/world/national-security/justice-department-warned-white-house-that-flynn-could-be-vulnerable-to-russian-blackmail-officials-say/2017/02/13/fc5dab88-f228-11e6-8d72-263470bf0401_story.html?utm_term=.2ad9d7219690; Carol D. Leonnig et al., "Trump lawyer says president knew Flynn had given FBI the same account he gave to vice president," *Washington Post*, December 3, 2017, https://www.washingtonpost.com/politics/trump-lawyer-says-president-knew-flynn-had-given-fbi-the-same-account-he-gave-to-vice-president/2017/12/03/5c59a620-d849-11e7-a841-2066faf731ef_story.html?utm_term=.77576596808a.

24. Glenn Kessler, "Trump Pointing of the Finger at Obama for Failing to Vet

Flynn," *Washington Post*, May 9, 2017, https://www.washingtonpost.com/news/fact-checker/wp/2017/05/09/trumps-pointing-of-the-finger-at-obama-for-failing-to-vet-flynn/?utm_term=.4727c5b99e7c.

25. Ibid.

26. George, "Pence, Flynn and the Russia Investigation."

27. Ibid.

28. Sari Horwitz and Adam Entous, "Flynn in FBI interview denied discussing sanctions with Russian ambassador," *Washington Post*, February 16, 2017, https://www.washingtonpost.com/world/national-security/flynn-in-fbi-interview-denied-discussing-sanctions-with-russian-ambassador/2017/02/16/e3e1e16a-f3d5-11e6-8d72-263470bf0401_story.html?utm_term=.31f996e40396.

29. "Trump fully briefed on Flynn's calls with Russian ambassador, source says," Fox News, February 16, 2017, http://www.foxnews.com/politics/2017/02/16/trump-fully-briefed-on-flynns-calls-with-russian-ambassador-source-says.htm.html.

30. Mark Mazzetti and Matthew Rosenberg, "Michael Flynn Offers to Testify Before Congress in Exchange for Immunity," *New York Times*, March 30, 2017, https://www.nytimes.com/2017/03/30/us/politics/michael-flynn-congress-immunity-russia.html.

31. Ibid.

32. Ken Dilanian and Kasie Hunt, "Michael Flynn's Immunity Request Rejected by Senate Intelligence Committee," NBC News, April 1, 2017, https://www.nbcnews.com/news/us-news/senate-intelligence-committee-rejects-immunity-michael-flynn-n741061.

33. Michael Isikoff, "As investigators circled Flynn, he got a message from Trump: Stay strong," Yahoo! News, May 18, 2017, https://www.yahoo.com/news/investigators-circled-flynn-got-message-trump-stay-strong-145442727.html?soc_src=mail&soc_trk=ma.

34. Doug G. Ware, "Senate Intel Head: Flynn Won't Comply with Subpoena," UPI, May 18, 2017, https://www.upi.com/Senate-intel-head-Flynn-wont-comply-with-subpoena/9991495123468/.

35. Catherine Herridge, "Carter Page, Former Trump Adviser, Says He's Cooperating with the Senate Russian Probe," Fox News, May 2, 2017, http://www.foxnews.com/politics/2017/05/02/former-trump-adviser-says-hes-cooperating-with-senate-russian-probe.html.

36. Ibid.

37. Senate Judiciary Committee interview of Donald J. Trump, Jr., September 7, 2017, https://www.judiciary.senate.gov/imo/media/doc/Trump%20Jr%20Transcript_redacted.pdf.

38. "Full Transcript: Sally Yates and James Clapper Testify on Russia Election Interference," *Washington Post*, May 8, 2017, https://www.washingtonpost.com/news/post-politics/wp/2017/05/08/full-transcript-sally-yates-and-james-clapper-testify-on-russian-election-interference/?utm_term=.c526a6e37537.

39. Kessler, "President Trump vs. James B. Comey."

40. Ibid.

41. Ibid.; Michael S. Schmidt and Julie Hirschfield Davis, "Trump Asked Sessions to Retain Control of Russia Inquiry After His Recusal," *New York Times*, May 29, 2018, https://www.nytimes.com/2018/05/29/us/politics/trump-sessions-ob struction.html.

42. MSNBC broadcast, https://www.youtube.com/watch?v=hmuKwCfb8fo.

43. Ibid.

44. Philip Rucker and Karen DeYoung, "Inside the Oval Office with Trump and the Russians: Broad Smiles and Loose Lips," *Washington Post*, May 16, 2017, https://www.washingtonpost.com/politics/inside-the-oval-office-with-trump -and-the-russians-broad-smiles-and-loose-lips/2017/05/16/2e8b0d14-3a66-11e7 -8854-21f359183e8c_story.html?utm_term=.ba6bb089abfe.

45. Jack Moore, "Trump Revealed Israel's Secret Syria Raid to Russian Diplomats," *Newsweek*, November 23, 2017, https://www.newsweek.com/trump-revealed-se cret-israeli-mission-northern-syria-russian-diplomats-720600.

46. Matt Apuzzo et al., "Trump Told Russians that Firing 'Nut Job' Comey Eased Pressure from Investigation," *New York Times*, May 19, 2017, https://www.ny times.com/2017/05/19/us/politics/trump-russia-comey.html.

47. "Lester Holt's Extended Interview with President Trump," NBC News, May 11, 2017, https://www.nbcnews.com/nightly-news/video/pres-trump-s-extended-ex clusive-interview-with-lester-holt-at-the-white-house-941854787582?v=railb.

48. Ibid.

49. Twohey and Shane, "A Back-Channel Plan."

50. Ibid.

51. Ibid.

52. Ibid.

53. Tom Hamburger and Rosalind S. Helderman, "Amid Russian scrutiny, Trump as sociates received informal Ukraine policy proposal," *Washington Post*, February 19, 2017, https://www.washingtonpost.com/politics/amid-russia-scrutiny-trump -associates-received-informal-ukraine-policy-proposal/2017/02/19/72b0b264 -f6eb-11e6-be05-1a3817ac21a5_story.html?utm_term=.fb02c96be975.

54. Twohey and Shane, "A Back-Channel Plan."

55. Hamburger and Helderman, "Amid Russian Scrutiny."

56. Ibid.

57. Ibid.

58. Twohey and Shane, "A Back-Channel Plan."

59. Ward, "Michael Cohen Speaks."

60. Ibid.

61. Ibid.; Twohey and Shane, "A Back-Channel Plan."

62. Andreii Soldatov, "The Leaked Trump-Russia Dossier Rings Frighteningly True," *Guardian*, January 12, 2017, https://www.theguardian.com/commentis free/2017/jan/12/donald-trump-russia-dossier-frighteningly-true?CMP=share_ btn_tw.

63. *BuzzFeed News*, January 10, 2017, https://www.documentcloud.org/documents /3259984-Trump-Intelligence-Allegations.html.

64. "Some Questions in Trump-Russia Dossier Now Finding Answers," CBS News,

June 29, 2018, https://www.cbsnews.com/news/some-questions-in-trump-russia
-dossier-now-finding-answers/; William Mansell, "James Clapper says more and
more of the Trump Dossier has turned out to be true," *Newsweek*, May 27, 2018,
https://www.newsweek.com/james-clapper-steele-dossier-donald-trump-spygate
-fbi-946058; Kim Sengupta, "Steele Dossier: Donald Trump denounced the document as fake, but much of its contents have turned out to be true," *Independent*,
April 20, 2018, https://www.independent.co.uk/news/world/americas/us-poli
tics/trump-russia-dossier-christopher-steele-fake-true-mi6-putin-moscow-hotel
-cohen-a8315046.html; Jim Sciutto and Evan Perez, "US Investigators Corroborate Some Aspects of the Russia Dossier," CNN, February 10, 2017, https://
www.cnn.com/2017/02/10/politics/russia-dossier-update/index.html.

65. Greg Gordon et al., "Russia's pension money for its veterans escapes scrutiny as
it flows into US," *McClatchy*, Feburary 21, 2017, https://www.mcclatchydc.com
/news/nation-world/national/article133879684.html.

66. Paul Wood, "Trump Russia Dossier Key Claim 'Verified,'" BBC News, March
30, 2017, https://www.bbc.com/news/world-us-canada-39435786.

67. Natasha Bertrand, "Carter Page's testimony is filled with bombshells—and supports key portions of the Steele dossier," *Business Insider*, November 6, 2017,
https://www.businessinsider.com/carter-page-congressional-testimony-tran
script-steele-dossier-2017-11; Knight, "Was This Russian General Murdered
Over the Steele Dossier."

68. Meghan Keneally, "Comey says he believes the source of the Steele 'dossier'
to be 'credible,'" ABC News, April 15, 2018, https://abcnews.go.com/Politics/
comey-believes-source-steele-dossier-credible/story?id=54488781.

69. Shannon Vavra, "Russian diplomats keep dying unexpectedly," *Axios*, August
24, 2017, https://www.axios.com/russian-diplomats-keep-dying-unexpectedly
-1513303951-de0183f3-7f77-400e-b9a2-45fb8ed7dfbd.html; Knight, "Was This
Russian General Murdered Over the Steele Dossier"; "Report: Death of Former
Russian Spy Chief Linked to Dossier on Trump," Haaretz, June 30, 2017, https://
www.haaretz.com/us-news/report-death-of-russian-spy-chief-linked-to-dossier
-on-trump-1.5491949; Gareth Davies, "Former KGB general who helped MI6
spy compile the Donald Trump dirty dossier has been found dead in the back
of his car amid claims of a Kremlin cover up," *Daily Mail*, January 28, 2017,
https://www.dailymail.co.uk/news/article-4166610/Kremlin-covered-murder
-former-KGB-chief.html; Charlotte England, "Unexpected deaths of six Russian
diplomats in four months triggers conspiracy theories," *Independent*, February
27, 2017.

70. Robert Mendick and Robert Verkaik, "Mystery death of ex-KGB chief linked to
MI6 spy's dossier on Donald Trump," *Independent*, January 27, 2017, https://
www.telegraph.co.uk/news/2017/01/27/mystery-death-ex-kgb-chief-linked-mi6
-spys-dossier-donald-trump/.

71. Knight, "Was This Russian General Murdered Over the Steele Dossier."

72. Ibid.

73. Ibid.

74. Marshall Cohen and Jose Pagliery "Nine Months, Nine Prominent Russians

Dead," CNN, August 24, 2017, https://www.cnn.com/2017/03/24/europe/dead
-russians/index.html

75. Ibid.
76. Ibid.; Richard Engel and Aggelos Petropoulos, "Lawyer Probing Russian Corruption Says His Balcony Fall Was 'No Accident,'" NBC News, July 7, 2017,
https://www.nbcnews.com/news/world/lawyer-probing-russian-corruption-says
-his-balcony-fall-was-no-n780416.
77. Cohen and Pagliery, "Nine months."
78. Glenn Kessler, "What you need to know about Christopher Steele, the FBI and
the Trump 'dossier,'" *Washington Post*, January 9, 2018, https://www.washing
tonpost.com/news/fact-checker/wp/2018/01/09/what-you-need-to-know-about
-christopher-steele-the-fbi-and-the-dossier/?utm_term=.b25ccd6dbf01
79. Ibid.
80. Rosie Gray, "Trump Declines to Affirm NATO's Article 5," *Atlantic*, May 25,
2017, https://www.theatlantic.com/international/archive/2017/05/trump-declines
-to-affirm-natos-article-5/528129/; David Leonhardt, "Trump Tries to Destroy
the West," *New York Times*, June 10, 2018, https://www.nytimes.com/2018/06/10
/opinion/g7-trump-quebec-trudeau.html; Susan B. Glasser, "Trump National Security Team Blindsided by NATO Speech," *Politico*, June 5. 2017, https://www
.politico.com/magazine/story/2017/06/05/trump-nato-speech-national-security
-team-215227; Eric Martin et al, "Trump Says U.S. to Pursue Mexico Trade Deal
to Replace NAFTA," Bloomberg, August 27, 2018, https://www.bloomberg.com
/news/articles/2018-08-27/nafta-breakthrough-seems-imminent-after-year-of
-fractious-talks.
81. Mikayla Bouchard and Emily Cochrane, "How We Got Here: A Timeline of
Events Leading Up to the Charges," *New York Times*, October 30, 2017, www
.nytimes.com/2017/10/30/us/politics/timeline-charges-special-counsel-mueller
.html.
82. Tom Hamburger et al., "Manafort offered to give Russian billionaire 'private
briefings' on 2016 campaign," *Washington Post*, September 20, 2017, https://
www.washingtonpost.com/politics/manafort-offered-to-give-russian-billionaire
-private-briefings-on-2016-campaign/2017/09/20/399bba1a-9d48-11e7-8ea1
-ed975285475e_story.html?utm_term=.cc92bce52d4f.
83. Wood, "Trump Russia Dossier Key Claim 'Verified.'"
84. David E. Sanger, "Putin Ordered 'Influence Campaign' Aimed at U.S. Election,
Report Says," *New York Times*, January 6, 2017, https://www.nytimes.com/2017
/01/06/us/politics/russia-hack-report.html?login=email&auth=login-email.
85. David Voreacos and Chris Strohm, "Mueller Shows How Russians Sowed Discord with Dirty Tricks," Bloomberg, February 16, 2018, https://www.bloomberg
.com/news/articles/2018-02-16/mueller-shows-how-russians-sowed-discord
-with-dirty-tricks.
86. *BuzzFeed News*, January 10, 2017, https://www.documentcloud.org/documents
/3259984-Trump-Intelligence-Allegations.html.
87. Ron Kampeas, "Know Your Oligarch: A Guide to the Jewish Billionaires in
the Trump-Russia Probe," *Haaretz*, May 23, 2018, https://www.haaretz.com/us

-news/know-your-oligarch-a-guide-to-the-jewish-machers-in-the-russia-probe
-1.6113189.

88. Peter Stone and Greg Gordon, "Sources: Mueller has evidence Cohen was
in Prague in 2016, confirming part of dossier," McClatchy, April 13, 2018,
https://www.mcclatchydc.com/news/politics-government/white-house/arti
cle208870264.html.

89. MSNBC, https://www.youtube.com/watch?v=hmuKwCfb8fo.

CHAPTER THIRTEEN: TESTIMONY AND PLEA

1. Michelle Mark, "Meet the all-star team of lawyers Robert Mueller has working
on the Trump-Russia investigation," *Business Insider,* May 17, 2018, https://
www.businessinsider.com/lawyers-robert-mueller-hired-for-the-trump-russia
-investigation-2017-6; Ken Dilanian, "Mueller subpoenas Trump campaign for
Russia documents," NBC News, November 17, 2017, https://www.nbcnews
.com/news/us-news/mueller-subpoenas-trump-campaign-russia-documents
-n821776; Stephanie Kirchgaessner, "Deutsche Bank hands bank records of
Trump affiliates to Robert Mueller," *Guardian,* December 5, 2017, https://
www.theguardian.com/us-news/2017/dec/05/donald-trump-bank-records
-handed-over-robert-mueller.

2. James Risen, "The Absent Professor," *Intercept,* April 12, 2018, https://theinter
cept.com/2018/04/12/trump-russia-intermediary-joseph-mifsud-missing-case
-for-collusion/; *U.S. v. George Papadopoulos,* October 5, 2017, https://www.jus
tice.gov/file/1007346/download.

3. Evan Perez et al, "Exclusive: Mueller's team met with Russia dossier author,"
CNN, October 25, 2017, https://www.cnn.com/2017/10/05/politics/special
-counsel-russia-dossier-christopher-steele/index.html.

4. Aaron Blake, "The 12-count Manafort and Gates indictment, annotated," *Washington Post,* October 30, 2017, https://www.washingtonpost.com/news/the-fix/
wp/2017/10/30/the-paul-manafort-and-rick-gates-indictment-annotated/?utm_
term=.522f8aa729ce.

5. *U.S. v. George Papadopoulos.*

6. Manuela Tobias, "A timeline of Donald Trump's talk about nonexistent James
Comey tapes," *PolitiFact,* June 22, 2017, https://www.politifact.com/truth-o
-meter/article/2017/jun/22/timeline-donald-trumps-talk-about-nonexistent
-jame/; Sean Illing, "President Trump says he can pardon himself. I asked 15
experts if that's legal," Vox, July 4, 2017, https://www.vox.com/policy-and-pol
itics/2017/7/21/16007934/trump-president-pardon-himself-limits-power-con
stitution; Eileen Sullivan, "Trump Attacks Sessions Again, This Time Over the
Acting F.B.I. Director," *New York Times,* July 26, 2017, https://www.nytimes
.com/2017/07/26/us/politics/jeff-sessions-trump-mccabe.html; Peter Baker
et al., "Citing Recusal, Trump Says He Wouldn't Have Hired Sessions," *New
York Times,* July 26, 2017, https://www.nytimes.com/2017/07/19/us/politics/
trump-interview-sessions-russia.html; Zeeshan Aleem, "It's official: Congress

has handcuffed Donald Trump on Russia," *Vox,* August 2, 2017, https://www
.vox.com/policy-and-politics/2017/7/28/16055630/congress-trump-russia
-sanctions-veto; Tom Embury-Dennis, "Trump refuses to impose new Russia
sanctions despite law passed by US Congress over election hacking," *Independent,* January 30, 2018, https://www.independent.co.uk/news/world/americas
/us-russia-sanctions-trump-no-new-congress-law-election-hacking-interven
tion-putin-kremlin-a8184866.html; Katherine Faulders et al., "Trump campaign has paid portions of Michael Cohen's legal fees: Sources," ABC News,
April 30, 2018, https://abcnews.go.com/Politics/trump-campaign-paid-por
tions-michael-cohens-legal-fees/story?id=54831269; Warren Strobel and Jonathan Landy, "Trump thanks Putin for slashing US diplomatic staff," Reuters,
August 10, 2017, https://www.reuters.com/article/us-usa-trump-russia-diplo
mats-idUSKBN1AQ2IW.

7. Scott Shane and Mike Isaac, "Facebook to Turn Over Russian-Linked Ads to
Congress," *New York Times,* September 21, 2017, https://www.nytimes.com
/2017/09/21/technology/facebook-russian-ads.html.

8. Sari Horwitz et al, "DHS tells states about Russian hacking during 2016 election," *Washington Post,* September 22, 2017, https://www.washingtonpost.com
/world/national-security/dhs-tells-states-about-russian-hacking-during-2016
-election/2017/09/22/fd263a2c-9fe2-11e7-8ea1-ed975285475e_story.html
?utm_term=.0ea051789d7d; Michael Riley and Jordan Robertson, "Russian
Hacks on U.S. Voting System Wider Than Previously Known," Bloomberg, June
13, 2017, https://www.bloomberg.com/news/articles/2017-06-13/russian-breach
-of-39-states-threatens-future-u-s-elections; Cynthia McFadden et al., "U.S.
intel: Russia compromised seven states prior to 2016 election," NBC News,
February 28, 2018, https://www.nbcnews.com/politics/elections/u-s-intel-russia
-compromised-seven-states-prior-2016-election-n850296.

9. Elizabeth Dwoskin, "Twitter finds hundreds of accounts tied to Russian operatives," *Washington Post,* September 28, 2017, https://www.washingtonpost.com/
business/economy/twitter-finds-hundreds-of-accounts-tied-to-russian-operatives
/2017/09/28/6cf26f7e-a484-11e7-ade1-76d061d56efa_story.html?utm_term=
.d8e068fb0f9d.

10. *Time,* YouTube account, June 9, 2017, https://www.youtube.com/watch?v=h
gR4SlEjFeQ; Trump Twitter Archive, http://www.trumptwitterarchive.com/ar
chive.

11. Dara Lind, "Trump wants Robert Mueller gone. He needs to get rid of Jeff Sessions first," *Vox,* July 28, 2017, https://www.vox.com/policy-and-politics/2017/7
/28/16050148/trump-fire-sessions-recess-appointment; Michael S. Schmidt and
Maggie Haberman, "Trump Ordered Mueller Fired, but Backed Off When White
House Counsel Threatened to Quit," *New York Times,* January 25, 2018, https://
www.nytimes.com/2018/01/25/us/politics/trump-mueller-special-counsel-rus
sia.html.

12. Donald Trump verified account, Twitter, June 15, 2017, https://twitter.com/real
donaldtrump/status/875321478849363968.

13. David Alexander, "Trump says Sessions safe in job at least until November elections: Bloomberg," Reuters, August 30, 2018, https://www.reuters.com/article/us-usa-trump-sessions/trump-says-sessions-safe-in-job-at-least-until-november-elections-bloomberg-idUSKCN1LF2JJ.

14. Kevin Whitelaw et al., "Trump Tower Meeting: Key Moments From the Senate Documents," Bloomberg, May 16, 2018, https://www.bloomberg.com/news/articles/2018-05-16/trump-tower-meeting-key-moments-from-senate-probe-documents.

15. Ibid.

16. Ibid.

17. Ibid.

18. Ibid.

19. Ibid.

20. Jim Sciutto et al., "Exclusive: Previously undisclosed emails show follow-up after Trump Tower meeting," CNN, December 7, 2017, https://www.cnn.com/2017/12/07/politics/previously-undisclosed-emails-after-trump-tower-meeting/index.html.

21. Ibid.

22. Ibid.

23. Philip Ewing, "What You Need To Know About The New Documents On The 2016 Trump Tower Meeting," NPR, May 16, 2018, https://www.npr.org/2018/05/16/611678188/what-you-need-to-know-about-the-new-documents-on-the-2016-trump-tower-meeting.

24. Kevin Whitelaw et al., "Trump Tower Meeting."

25. Ibid.

26. Sonam Sheth, "Another key Trump campaign official is stonewalling the House Intelligence Committee amid the Trump-Russia investigation," *Business Insider,* January 18, 2018, https://www.businessinsider.com/corey-lewandowski-stonewalls-house-intel-committee-in-russia-testimony-2018-1.

27. Dylan Matthews, "A brief guide to executive privilege, and why it won't save the Trump administration," *Vox,* June 19, 2017, https://www.vox.com/policy-and-politics/2017/6/19/15795986/executive-privilege-explained.

28. Manu Raju et al., "Bannon stonewalls House panel after WH advised him to invoke executive privilege," CNN, February 15, 2018, https://www.cnn.com/2018/02/14/politics/bannon-contempt-hearing/index.html.

29. Michael S. Schmidt, "Bannon Is Subpoenaed in Mueller's Russia Investigation," *New York Times,* January 16, 2018, https://www.nytimes.com/2018/01/16/us/politics/steve-bannon-mueller-russia-subpoena.html; Kyle Cheney, "Schiff: Bannon, Lewandowski defy committee's requests in Russia probe," *Politico,* February 7, 2018, https://www.politico.com/story/2018/02/07/bannon-lewandowski-russia-probe-testimony-397412.

30. Adam K. Raymond, "Robert Mueller's Team Has Interviewed the Guy Behind the Infamous 'Pee Tape' Dossier," *New York,* October 6, 2017, http://nymag.com/daily/intelligencer/2017/10/muellers-team-spoke-to-the-guy-behind-the-pee-tape-dossier.html.

31. Alan Yuhas et al., "Source inside Trump campaign reported concerns to FBI, new transcript suggests," *Guardian*, January 9, 2018, https://www.theguardian.com/us-news/2018/jan/09/trump-russia-dossier-senator-dianne-feinstein-glenn-simpson.

32. Ibid.

33. Eric Lichtblau and Steven Lee Myers, "Investigating Donald Trump, F.B.I. Sees No Clear Link to Russia," *New York Times*, October 31, 2016, https://www.nytimes.com/2016/11/01/us/politics/fbi-russia-election-donald-trump.html.

34. Yuhas et al., "Source inside Trump campaign."

35. Byron York, "What Glenn Simpson said about that 'human source' inside the Trump campaign," *Washington Examiner*, May 30, 2018, https://www.washingtonexaminer.com/news/what-glenn-simpson-said-about-that-human-source-inside-the-trump-campaign.

36. Ibid.

37. Ibid.

38. Glenn R. Simpson and Peter Fritsch, "The Republicans' Fake Investigations," *New York Times*, January 2, 2018, https://www.nytimes.com/2018/01/02/opinion/republicans-investigation-fusion-gps.html.

39. York, "What Glenn Simpson said."

40. Yuhas et al., "Source inside Trump campaign."

41. Grassley letter, United States Senate Committee on the Judiciary, January 11, 2018, https://www.judiciary.senate.gov/imo/media/doc/2018-01-11%20CEG%20to%20Fusion%20GPS%20(accuracy%20of%20interview)%20(003).pdf.

42. Amber Phillips, "4 surprising facts about Stefan Halper, a professor and top-secret informant on Russia," *Washington Post*, May 22, 2018, https://www.washingtonpost.com/news/the-fix/wp/2018/05/22/4-surprising-facts-about-stefan-halper-the-professor-and-top-secret-informant-on-russia/?utm_term=.cb0c322b3590.

43. Julian E. Barnes and Matthew Rosenberg, "Kremlin Sources Go Quiet, Leaving C.I.A. in the Dark About Putin's Plans for Midterms," *New York Times*, August 24, 2018, https://www.nytimes.com/2018/08/24/us/politics/cia-russia-midterm-elections.html.

44. Ibid.

45. Mike McIntire et al., "Firm Tied to Russian Oligarch Made Payments to Michael Cohen,"*New York Times,* May 8, 2018, https://www.nytimes.com/2018/05/08/us/politics/michael-cohen-shell-company-payments.html; Ben Mathis-Lilley, "We're Supposed to Believe Michael Cohen's One-Person Shell Company Provided 'Consulting' Services Worth Millions of Dollars," *Slate,* May 9, 2018, https://slate.com/news-and-politics/2018/05/michael-cohen-essential-consultants-corporate-explanations-fail-laugh-test.html.

46. Mathis-Lilley, "We're Supposed to Believe."

47. Ibid.

48. McIntire et al., "Firm Tied to Russian Oligarch"; Republican National Committee, April 3, 2017, https://gop.com/rnc-announces-additions-to-rnc-finance-leadership-team/.

49. Elliot Hannon, "Trump Fundraiser Reportedly Secured $1 Billion in Contracts from Saudi Arabia and UAE to Push Anti-Qatar Policies With Trump," *Slate,* May 21, 2018, https://slate.com/news-and-politics/2018/05/top-trump-fundraiser -broidy-reportedly-secured-usd1-billion-in-contracts-from-saudi-arabia-and-uae -in-return-for-pushing-anti-qatar-policies-to-administration.html.

50. Paul Campos, "Hey, Look: More Evidence That Broidy May Have Been Covering for Trump in That Playmate Affair," *New York*, May 8, 2018, http://nymag .com/daily/intelligencer/2018/05/more-evidence-that-broidy-was-covering-for -trump-in-affair.html.

51. Ibid.

52. Adam Goldman et al., "Viktor Vekselberg, Russian Billionaire, Was Questioned by Mueller's Investigators," *New York Times*, May 4, 2018, https://www .nytimes.com/2018/05/04/us/politics/viktor-vekselberg-mueller-investigation. html; Sonam Sheth, " 'It was Moscow's victory, after all': At least 6 Putin-allied Russians reportedly attended Trump's inaugural celebrations," *Business Insider,* January 20, 2018, https://www.businessinsider.com/veselnitskaya-akhmetshin -russians-attended-trump-inauguration-2018-1.

53. Goldman et al., "Viktor Vekselberg, Russian Billionaire."

54. Sonam Sheth, " 'It was Moscow's victory, after all.' "

55. Linley Sanders, "Trump's Inauguration money is still missing one year later after his administration took control of the White House," *Newsweek*, January 18, 2018, https://www.newsweek.com/trump-inauguration-money-still-missing -783934.

56. Ibid.; Isaac Arnsdorf, "White House May Share Nuclear Power Technology With Saudi Arabia," *ProPublica*, November 29, 2017, https://www.propublica.org/ar ticle/white-house-may-share-nuclear-power-technology-with-saudi-arabia.

57. Goldman et al., "Viktor Vekselberg, Russian Billionaire."

58. Ibid.; Philip Bump, "We may soon learn a lot more about that $130,000 payment to Stormy Daniels," *Washington Post,* April 10, 2018, https://www.washington post.com/news/politics/wp/2018/04/10/we-may-soon-learn-a-lot-more-about -that-130000-payment-to-stormy-daniels/?utm_term=.dfdc949dd5f7.

59. Jared C. Kushner's Statement to Congressional Committee, *New York Times*, July 24, 2017, https://www.nytimes.com/interactive/2017/07/24/us/politics/docu ment-Read-Jared-Kushner-s-Statement-to-Congressional.html.

60. Kara Scannell, "Background check chief has 'never seen' mistakes and omissions at level of Jared Kushner forms," CNN, October 12, 2017, https://www .cnn.com/2017/10/12/politics/jared-kushner-background-check-form/index .html.

61. Ibid.

62. Jared C. Kushner's statement to Congressional committee.

63. Ibid.

64. Ned Parker and Jonathan Landay, "Exclusive: Trump son-in-law had undisclosed contacts with Russian envoy - sources," Reuters, May 26, 2017, https://www.reu ters.com/article/us-usa-trump-fbi-kushner-exclusive/exclusive-trump-son-in-law -had-undisclosed-contacts-with-russian-envoy-sources-idUSKBN18N018.

65. Ibid.

66. Josh Barro, "Why are Russians so bothered by Mike Flynn's departure?" *Business Insider,* February 14, 2017, https://www.businessinsider.com/michael
-flynn-russia-resignation-2017-2; Summer Meza, "Jared Kushner and Ivanka
Trump pushed to put Flynn in office, ignored warnings," *Newsweek,* December 2, 2017, https://www.newsweek.com/ivanka-trump-jared-kushner-wanted
-michael-flynn-white-house-729379; Adam Entous, "Israeli, Saudi, and Emirati
Officials Privately Pushed for Trump to Strike a 'Grand Bargain' with Putin,"
New Yorker, July 9, 2018, https://www.newyorker.com/news/news-desk/israeli
-saudi-and-emirati-officials-privately-pushed-for-trump-to-strike-a-grand-bar
gain-with-putin.

67. Jared C. Kushner's statement to Congressional committee.

68. Jonathan Schieber, "Senate investigators learned about Jared Kushner's private email server from the news," *TechCrunch*, September 28, 2017, https://tech
crunch.com/2017/09/28/senate-investigators-learned-about-jared-kushners-pri
vate-email-server-from-the-news/.

69. Ibid.

70. Mary Clare Jalonick, "Senators press Kushner for more documents in Russia
investigation," *PBS NewsHour,* November 16, 2017, https://www.pbs.org/new
shour/politics/senators-press-kushner-for-more-documents-in-russia-investiga
tion.

71. Ibid.

72. Ryan Bort, "Newly Released Documents Only Raise More Questions About
Don Jr. and Russia," *Rolling Stone*, May 16, 2018, https://www.rollingstone.com
/politics/politics-news/newly-released-documents-only-raise-more-questions
-about-don-jr-and-russia-628277/.

73. Ibid.

74. Katrina Manson, "Russian lobbyist testifies to Mueller grand jury," *Financial
Times*, August 30, 2017, https://www.ft.com/content/eb36aed6-8d87-11e7-a352
-e46f43c5825d.

75. Allan Smith, "Russian-American lobbyist says Russian lawyer presented documents in Trump Jr. meeting," *Business Insider,* July 14, 2017, https://www.busi
nessinsider.com/rinat-akhmetshin-trump-jr-meeting-russia-documents-2017-7.

76. Bort, "Newly Released Documents."

77. Diana Stancy Correll, "Trump asked Reince Priebus about his interview with
Robert Mueller: Report," *Washington Examiner*, March 7, 2018, https://www
.washingtonexaminer.com/trump-asked-reince-priebus-about-his-interview-with
-robert-mueller-report#.

78. Paul Waldman, "Here's another telling revelation in the Comey memos," *Washington Post*, April 20, 2018, https://www.washingtonpost.com/blogs/plum-line/
wp/2018/04/20/heres-another-telling-revelation-in-the-comey-memos/?utm_ter
m=.55891cfb6fa7.

79. Ibid.

80. Ken Dilanian and Mike Memoli, "Top Trump Campaign Aide Clovis Spoke to
Mueller Team, Grand Jury" NBC News, October 31, 2017, https://www.nbc

news.com/news/us-news/top-trump-campaign-aide-clovis-spoke-mueller-team -grand-jury-n816106.

81. Eileen Sullivan, "Trump Nominee Sam Clovis Withdraws From Consideration for Agriculture Department Post," *New York Times*, November 2, 2017, https:// www.nytimes.com/2017/11/02/us/politics/trump-nominee-sam-clovis-with draws-from-consideration-for-agriculture-department-post.html.

82. Ibid.

83. Mark Hosenball and John Walcott, "Investigators probe Trump knowledge of campaign's Russia dealings: sources," Reuters, November 11, 2017, https:// www.reuters.com/article/us-usa-trump-russia-investigation/investigators -probe-trump-knowledge-of-campaigns-russia-dealings-sources-idUSKB N1DB04J; Linley Sanders, "Trump knew Papadopoulos would meet with for eigners, ex-aide claims," *Newsweek,* November 17, 2017, https://www.news week.com/papadopoulos-says-trump-authorized-him-meet-foreign-leaders -714644.

84. Philip Rucker and Robert Costa, "Donald Trump names foreign policy advi-sors," Boston Globe, March 21,2016, https://www.bostonglobe.com/news/ politics/2016/03/21/donald-trump-names-foreign-policy-advisors/zoneTaCS lynydDc1WgMjqK/story.html; Jake Tapper, "The Mysterious Case of George Papadopoulos; George Papadopoulos Ignited the Russia Conspiracy Investiga-tion," CNN transcripts, aired September 7, 2018, http://www.cnn.com/TRAN SCRIPTS/1809/07/csr.01.html.

85. Julian Borger, "Ex-Trump aide Flynn investigated over plot to kidnap Turkish dissident—report," *Guardian*, November 10, 2017, https://www.theguardian. com/us-news/2017/nov/10/michael-flynn-trump-turkish-dissident-cleric-plot; Susan Hennessey et al., "The Flynn Plea: A Quick and Dirty Analysis," *Lawfare*, December 1, 2017, https://www.lawfareblog.com/flynn-plea-quick-and-dirty -analysis.

86. *U.S. v. Michael Flynn,* December 1, 2017, https://www.justice.gov/file/1015126/ download.

87. Ibid.

88. Ibid.

89. Ibid.

90. Ibid.

91. Statement of offense, affidavit against George Papadopoulos, CNN, October 30, 2017, https://www.cnn.com/2017/10/30/politics/george-papadopoulos-offense -affidavit-complaint/index.html.

92. Ibid.

93. Ibid.

94. Ibid.

95. Ibid.

96. Ibid.

97. Ibid.

98. Ibid.

99. Gregory Korte and John Fritze, "Trump Jr. told investigators he can't recall if he discussed Russian meeting with his father," *USA Today*, May 16, 2018, https://www.usatoday.com/story/news/politics/2018/05/16/trump-jr-cant-recall-if-he-spoke-father-russians/614773002/.

100. Ibid.

101. Bort, "Newly Released Documents."

102. Grace Guarnieri, "Democrats want to turn over Trump, Jr. transcripts to Mueller, suggesting he made false statements to committee," *Newsweek*, January 25, 2018, https://www.newsweek.com/domocrats-trump-jr-testimony-mueller-false-statements-790575.

103. Pierre Thomas and James Gordon Meek, "Mueller has evidence that Trump supporter's meeting with Putin ally may not have been a chance encounter: Sources," ABC News, April 6, 2018, https://abcnews.go.com/Politics/mueller-evidence-raising-questions-prince-testimony-meeting-russian/story?id=54277090.

104. Dan Friedman, "Report Suggests Blackwater Founder Erik Prince May Have Lied to Congress," *Mother Jones*, May 19, 2018, https://www.motherjones.com/politics/2018/05/report-suggests-blackwater-founder-erik-prince-may-have-lied-to-congress/.

105. Pamela Brown et al, "Mueller interviews top White House aide," CNN, November 2017, https://www.cnn.com/2017/11/09/politics/stephen-miller-interviewed-special-counsel-russia-investigation/index.html.

106. Ibid.

107. Michael S. Schmidt and Maggie Haberman, "Mueller Has Early Draft of Trump Letter Giving Reasons for Firing Comey," *New York Times*, September 1, 2017, https://www.nytimes.com/2017/09/01/us/politics/trump-comey-firing-letter.html?_r=0.

108. Patrick Wintour and Anushka Asthana, "Trump-Putin meeting dominates G20 as Russia denies interfering in US election," *Guardian*, July 7, 2017, https://www.theguardian.com/world/2017/jul/07/trump-putin-meeting-dominates-g20-as-russia-denies-interfering-in-us-election; Eli Watkins and Jeremy Diamond, "Trump, Putin met for nearly an hour in second G20 meeting," CNN, July 18, 2017, https://www.cnn.com/2017/07/18/politics/trump-putin-g20/index.html; "At G20 dinner, Trump appeared to gesture to Putin," CNN, July 2017, https://www.cnn.com/videos/politics/2017/07/20/trump-appears-to-gesture-at-putin-orig-tc.cnn; Steve Holland, "Trump, Putin held a second, undisclosed meeting at G20 summit," Reuters, July 18, 2017, https://www.reuters.com/article/us-usa-trump-russia-putin-idUSKBN1A32H5.

109. Emily Stewart, "Read: Donald Trump Jr.'s congressional testimony about the Trump Tower meeting," *Vox,* May 16, 2018 https://www.vox.com/policy-and-politics/2018/5/16/17360484/donald-trump-jr-transcript-senate-judiciary-committee.

110. Ibid., p.12.

111. Ibid., p. 45.

112. Ibid., pp. 45–46.

113. Ibid., p. 104.

114. Ibid., p. 46.

115. Allan Smith, " 'You're going to find it very, very interesting': Donald Trump announces he will make 'major' speech about the Clintons," *Business Insider,* June 7, 2016, https://www.businessinsider.com/donald-trump-announced-speech-hillary-bill-clinton-2016-6.

116. Stewart, "Read: Donald Trump Jr.'s congressional testimony."

117. Hazel Heyer, "Executive Talk: Donald Trump Jr. bullish on Russia and few emerging markets," ETN, September 15, 2008, https://www.eturbonews.com/9788/executive-talk-donald-trump-jr-bullish-russia-and-few-emerging-ma; Stewart, "Read: Donald Trump Jr.'s congressional testimony."

118. Stewart, "Read: Donald Trump Jr.'s congressional testimony."

119. Ibid.

120. Ibid., pp. 15, 36; "DCLeaks And Russian Hackers: 5 Fast Facts You Need to Know," *Heavy,* July 13, 2018, https://heavy.com/news/2018/07/dcleaks-russian-hackers/; Senate Judiciary Committee, Rob Goldstone transcript, https://www.judiciary.senate.gov/imo/media/doc/Goldstone%201%20Transcript_redacted.pdf; Jacqueline Thomsen, "Mueller: Russian officers launched leaks website in June 2016," *Hill,* July 13, 2018, http://thehill.com/policy/cybersecurity/396947-mueller-russian-officers-launched-leaks-website-in-june-2016.

121. Stewart, "Read: Donald Trump Jr.'s congressional testimony."

122. Ibid., p. 18.

123. Ibid., p. 29.

124. Ibid., pp. 19–20.

125. Ibid., p. 43.

126. Ibid.

127. Ibid., p. 20.

128. Ibid., p. 23.

129. Ibid., pp. 26–28.

130. Ibid., p. 32.

131. Ibid., pp. 33–34.

132. Ibid., p. 36.

133. Ibid.

134. Ibid., p. 37.

135. Ibid., p. 38.

136. Sharon LaFraniere et al., "Lobbyist at Trump Campaign Meeting Has a Web of Russian Connections," *New York Times*, August 21, 2017, https://www.nytimes.com/2017/08/21/us/rinat-akhmetshin-russia-trump-meeting.html.

137. Stewart, "Read: Donald Trump Jr.'s congressional testimony," p. 39.

138. Ibid., pp. 26–27.

139. House Permanent Select Committee on Intelligence, testimony of Erik Prince, November 30, 2017, https://docs.house.gov/meetings/IG/IG00/20171130/106661/HHRG-115-IG00-Transcript-20171130.pdf.

140. Ibid., pp. 5–7.

141. Ibid., pp. 11–12.

142. Ibid., pp. 12, 14, 32.

143. Ibid., pp. 11–12; Sarah D. Wire, "California Rep. Devin Nunes named to Trump's transition team," *Los Angeles Times,* November 11, 2016, http://www .latimes.com/politics/essential/la-pol-ca-essential-politics-updates-rep-devin -nunes-named-to-trump-s-1478893307-htmlstory.html.

144. Prince testimony, p. 14.

145. Ibid., p. 15.

146. Ibid., pp. 17, 30.

147. Ibid., pp. 19–20.

148. Ibid., pp. 20–21.

149. Ibid., pp. 24–27.

150. Ibid., p. 32.

151. Ibid., pp. 35–36.

152. Thomas and Meek, "Mueller has evidence."

CHAPTER FOURTEEN: A NATION IN SUSPENSE

1. "Microsoft Thwarts New Russia Attacks Ahead of Midterms; President Trump Asserts He Could Run the Russia Probe," CNN, August 21, 2018, http://tran scripts.cnn.com/TRANSCRIPTS/1808/21/cnr.03.html.

2. "US senators vote overwhelmingly for new sanctions on Russia," *Independent*, July 28, 2017, https://www.independent.co.uk/news/world/americas/us-politics /us-senate-vote-russia-sanctions-donald-trump-vladimir-putin-retaliate-latest -crimea-a7864041.html.

3. Alexandra Wilts, "Deadline looms for Trump to issue further sanctions against Russia over election meddling," *Independent*, January 29, 2018, https://www .independent.co.uk/news/world/americas/us-politics/donald-trump-russia-sanc tions-deadline-presidential-election-meddling-vladimir-putin-a8184391.html.

4. Abigail Tracy, "Vladimir Putin Sours on His Old Friend Rex Tillerson," *Vanity Fair*, September 7, 2017, https://www.vanityfair.com/news/2017/09/vladimir -putin-rex-tillerson.

5. Darya Korsunskaya et al., "For Some Russian Oligarchs, Sanctions Risk Makes Putin Awkward to Know," Reuters, November 30, 2017, https://www.reuters .com/article/russia-sanctions-oligarchs/for-some-russian-oligarchs-sanctions -risk-makes-putin-awkward-to-know-idUSL8N1NU356.

6. Wilts, "Deadline looms"; Tom Embury-Dennis, "Trump refuses to impose new Russia sanctions despite law passed by US Congress over election hacking," *Independent*, January 30, 2018, https://www.independent.co.uk/news/world/ americas/us-russia-sanctions-trump-no-new-congress-law-election-hacking-in tervention-putin-kremlin-a8184866.html.

7. Korsunskaya et al., "For Some Russian Oligarchs"; Embury-Dennis, "Trump refuses to impose."

8. Eli Meixler, "CIA Director Mike Pompeo Says He 'Fully Expects' Russia Will Try to Interfere in U.S. Midterms," *Time*, January 30, 2018, http://time.com /5124313/cia-mike-pompeo-russia-midterm-elections/.

9. Jim Sciutto and Nicole Gaouette, "CIA chief met with sanctioned Russian spies, officials confirm," CNN, February 2, 2018, https://www.cnn.com/2018/02/01/politics/pompeo-russian-spies-meeting/index.html.

10. Ibid.

11. Ariane de Vogue, "Mueller's Office Spoke with Sessions, Comey in Russia Investigation," CNN, January 23, 2018, https://www.cnn.com/2018/01/23/politics/jeff-sessions-robert-mueller-interview/index.html; Carrie Johnson, "Sessions Sits for Voluntary Interview with Mueller," NPR, January 23, 2018, https://www.npr.org/2018/01/23/579952874/sessions-sits-for-voluntary-interview-with-mueller; Michael S. Schmidt and Maggie Haberman, "Sessions Is Questioned as Russia Inquiry Focuses on Obstruction," *New York Times,* January 23, 2018, https://www.nytimes.com/2018/01/23/us/politics/jeff-sessions-special-counsel-russia.html?rref=collection%2Fbyline%2Fmichael-s.-schmidt&action=click&contentCollection=undefined&region=stream&module=stream_unit&version=latest&contentPlacement=1&pgtype=collection.

12. Ibid.

13. Betsy Woodruff, "Special Counsel Mueller's Team Questioned Blackwater Founder Erik Prince," *Daily Beast,* May 9, 2018, https://www.thedailybeast.com/special-counsel-muellers-team-questioned-blackwater-founder-erik-prince; James Gordon Meek, "Special counsel obtains Trump ally Erik Prince's phones, computer," ABC News, June 2018, https://abcnews.go.com/Politics/special-counsel-obtains-trump-ally-erik-princes-phones/story?id=56143477.

14. Adam Entous, "Blackwater founder held secret Seychelles meeting to establish Trump-Putin back channel," *Washington Post*, April 2017, https://www.washingtonpost.com/world/national-security/blackwater-founder-held-secret-seychelles-meeting-to-establish-trump-putin-back-channel/2017/04/03/95908a08-1648-11e7-ada0-1489b735b3a3_story.html?utm_term=.3cab3e2cc8f9.

15. Ibid.

16. Alex Johnson, "FBI general counsel says in letter that Mueller asked him to testify in Russia probe," NBC News, April 10, 2018, https://www.nbcnews.com/politics/national-security/fbi-general-counsel-says-letter-mueller-asked-him-testify-russia-n864886.

17. Rosalind S. Helderman and Tom Hamburger, "Pressure on Michael Cohen intensifies as Mueller stays focused on the Trump attorney," *Washington Post*, June 13, 2018, https://www.washingtonpost.com/politics/pressure-on-michael-cohen-intensifies-as-mueller-stays-focused-on-trump-attorney/2018/06/13/00a207fe-6f12-11e8-bf86-a2351b5ece99_story.html?utm_term=.f43137c08ca8.

18. Adam Goldman et al., "Viktor Vekselberg, Russian Billionaire, Was Questioned by Mueller's Investigators," *New York Times*, May 2018, https://www.nytimes.com/2018/05/04/us/politics/viktor-vekselberg-mueller-investigation.html.

19. Chris Cillizza, "Why the Allen Weisselberg immunity deal may be the biggest news of this bananas week," CNN, August 24, 2018, https://www.cnn.com/2018/08/24/politics/allen-weisselberg-trump/index.html.

20. Ibid.

21. Shahien Nasiripour and Caleb Melby, "Nobody Knows the Trump Organization Like Allen Weisselberg," Bloomberg, August 30, 2018, https://www.bloomberg.com/news/articles/2018-08-30/nobody-knows-the-trump-organization-like-allen-weisselberg.

22. Natasha Bertrand, "New York Prosecutors May Pose a Bigger Threat to Trump than Mueller," *Atlantic*, August 24, 2018, https://www.theatlantic.com/politics/archive/2018/08/new-york-prosecutors-allen-weisselberg-trump/568516/.

23. Colby Hamilton, "Former Skadden Partner, 2 Others Referred to SDNY by Mueller," *New York Law Journal*, August 1, 2018, https://www.law.com/newyorklawjournal/2018/08/01/former-skadden-partner-2-others-referred-to-sdny-by-mueller/?slreturn=20180802000242; Jed Shugerman, "Why Robert Mueller Handed Off the Michael Cohen Raid," *Slate,* April 2018, https://slate.com/news-and-politics/2018/04/why-robert-mueller-handed-off-the-michael-cohen-raid.html.

24. Manu Raju and Jeremy Herb, "Hicks acknowledges white lies, but won't talk White House in testimony," CNN, February 2018, https://www.cnn.com/2018/02/26/politics/hope-hicks-house-intelligence-committee/index.html.

25. Maggie Haberman, "Hope Hicks to Leave Post as White House Communications Director," *New York Times*, February 2018, https://www.nytimes.com/2018/02/28/us/politics/hope-hicks-resign-communications-director.html?smid=tw-share.

26. Philip Ewing, "House Intelligence GOP Releases Full Report Clearing Trump in Russia Imbroglio," NPR, April 27, 2018, https://www.npr.org/2018/04/27/606351800/house-intelligence-gop-releases-full-report-clearing-trump-in-russia-imbroglio.

27. Tom Winter, "Trump ally detained, served with Mueller subpoena at Boston airport," NBC News, March 30, 2018, https://www.nbcnews.com/politics/white-house/trump-ally-detained-served-mueller-subpoena-boston-airport-n861456.

28. Veronica Rocha et al., "Michael Cohen Pleads Guilty to 8 Counts," CNN, August 22, 2018, https://www.cnn.com/politics/live-news/michael-cohen-trump-lawyer-plea-deal-fbi/index.html; Jenni Fink, "Will Michael Cohen Go to Prison? How Much Jail Time Is Former Trump Attorney Facing?" *Newsweek*, August 21, 2018, https://www.newsweek.com/will-michael-cohen-go-prison-how-much-jail-time-former-trump-attorney-facing-1084211.

29. Adam Liptak and Jim Rutenberg, "Cohen Implicates President Trump. What Do Prosecutors Do Now?" *New York Times*, August 21, 2018, https://www.nytimes.com/2018/08/21/us/politics/cohen-trump-indicted.html.

30. Salvadore Rizzo, "Can the President Be Indicted or Subpoenaed?" *Washington Post*, May 22, 2018, https://www.washingtonpost.com/news/fact-checker/wp/2018/05/22/can-the-president-be-indicted-or-subpoenaed/?utm_term=.d07acdad9c42.

31. Fink, "Will Michael Cohen Go to Prison?"

32. "Ukraine Allegedly Paid Michael Cohen $400,000 for Trump Meeting," BBC,

May 23, 2018, https://www.bbc.com/news/av/world-us-canada-44233864/ukraine-allegedly-paid-michael-cohen-400000-for-trump-meeting.

33. Quinta Jurecic, "Document: Indictment against Maria Butina," *Lawfare*, July 17, 2018, https://www.lawfareblog.com/document-indictment-against-mariia-butina.

34. Ibid.

35. Ibid.; Sean Rossman, "Sex and schmoozing are common Russian spy tactics. Publicity makes Maria Butina different," *USA Today*, August 28, 2018, https://www.usatoday.com/story/news/investigations/2018/08/28/maria-butina-accused-russian-spy-nra-networking-old-russian-spy-tactic-not-being-public-figure/1002964002/.

36. Philip Ewing, "The Russia Investigations: Mueller Indicts the 'Internet Research Agency,'" NPR, February 17, 2018, https://www.npr.org/2018/02/17/586698361/the-russia-investigations-mueller-indicts-the-internet-research-agency; Chantal Da Silva, "What Is a Speaking Indictment? Mueller Deploys Key Tool in Russia Investigation," *Newsweek*, August 24, 2018, https://www.newsweek.com/what-speaking-indictment-muellers-key-tool-russia-investigation-1089564; DOJ indictments, Case 1:18-cr-00032-DLF, *United States of America v. Internet Research Agency LLC et al.*, filed February 16, 2018, https://www.justice.gov/file/1035477/download.

37. Ewing, "The Russia Investigations."

38. Ibid.

39. Ibid.

40. Donald J. Trump (@realDonaldTrump), "Russia started their anti-US campaign in 2014, long before I announced that I would run for President. The results of the election were not impacted. The Trump campaign did nothing wrong - no collusion!" Twitter, February 16, 12:18 p.m., https://twitter.com/realDonaldTrump/status/964594780088033282?ref_src=twsrc%5Etfw%7Ctwcamp%5Etweetem bed%7Ctwterm%5E964594780088033282%7Ctwgr%5E373939313b73706563696669635f73706f7274735f616374696f6e&ref_url=https%3A%2F%2

41. Alex Ward, "Read: Mueller Indictment Against 12 Russian Spies for DNC Hack," *Vox*, July 13, 2018, https://www.vox.com/2018/7/13/17568806/mueller-russia-intelligence-indictment-full-text/.

42. Donald J. Trump (@realDonaldTrump), "The Rigged Witch Hunt, headed by the 13 Angry Democrats (and now 4 more have been added, one who worked directly for Obama W.H.), seems intent on damaging the Republican Party's chances in the November Election. This Democrat excuse for losing the '16 Election never ends!" Twitter, July 21, 2018, 3:40 p.m., https://twitter.com/realdonaldtrump/status/1020800615226793986.

43. Ward, "Read: Mueller Indictment."

44. Pete Williams, "Attorney Alex van der Zwaan, first person sentenced in Mueller probe, gets 30 days in prison," NBC News, April 3, 2018, https://www.nbcnews.com/politics/justice-department/attorney-alex-van-der-zwaan-first-person-sentenced-mueller-probe-n862186.

45. Mark Mazzetti, "Trump Aide Spoke During Campaign to Associate Tied to Russian Intelligence," *New York Times*, March 28, 2018, https://www.nytimes.com /2018/03/28/us/politics/rick-gates-trump-campaign-russian-intelligence.html.

46. Ibid.

47. Williams, "Attorney Alex van der Zwaan."

48. Sharon LaFraniere, "Paul Manafort, Trump's Former Campaign Chairman, Guilty of 8 Counts," *New York Times*, August 21, 2018, https://www.nytimes .com/2018/08/21/us/politics/paul-manafort-trial-verdict.html.

49. Ibid.

50. Lydia Wheeler, "Manafort Faces Maximum of 80 Years in Prison," *Hill*, August 21, 2018, http://thehill.com/homenews/administration/402935-manafort-faces -maximum-of-80-years-in-prison.

51. Alex Whiting and Ryan Goodman, "Will Trump Pardon Manafort?" *New York Times*, August 30, 2018, https://www.nytimes.com/2018/08/30/opinion/trump -manafort-pardon-mueller.html.

52. Katelyn Polantz, "Lobbyist pleads guilty, says he helped steer foreign money to Trump inaugural and lied to Congress," CNN, August 31, 2018, https://www .cnn.com/2018/08/31/politics/w-samuel-patten-plea-russia-ukraine/index .html.

53. Maggie Haberman and Kenneth P. Vogel, "Trump's Inaugural Committee Paid $26 Million to Firm of First Lady's Adviser," *New York Times*, February 15, 2018, https://www.nytimes.com/2018/02/15/us/politics/trumps-inaugural-com mittee-paid-26-million-to-first-ladys-friend.html.

54. Maria Puente, "Trump 'Apprentice' Slur Tapes: A who's who of people associated with alleged recording," *USA Today*, August 16, 2018, https://www.us atoday.com/story/life/people/2018/08/16/trump-apprentice-slur-tape-whos-who -people-associated/996532002/.

55. Donald J. Trump (@realDonaldTrump), Trump Twitter Archive, search terms "rigged," "witch hunt," and "illegal," January 1, 2018, to August 2018, http:// www.trumptwitterarchive.com/.

56. Toby Harnden, "Comey on Trump's 'Consciousness of Guilt,'" *RealClearPolitics*, April 25, 2018, https://www.realclearpolitics.com/articles/2018/04/25/ comey_on_trumps_consciousness_of_guilt_136899.html.

57. Eugene Robinson, "Trump seems to be staging a cover-up. So what's the crime?" op-ed, *Washington Post*, May 2017, https://www.washingtonpost.com/ opinions/trump-seems-to-be-staging-a-coverup-so-whats-the-crime/2017/05/11 /d728c58a-3681-11e7-b4ee-434b6d506b37_story.html?noredirect=on&utm_ter m=.01efd1869444.

58. Julie Hirschfeld Davis and Michael D. Shear, "Trump Revokes Ex-C.I.A. Director John Brennan's Security Clearance," *New York Times*, August 15, 2018, https://www.nytimes.com/2018/08/15/us/politics/john-brennan-security-clear ance.html; Jeremy Diamond and Betsy Klein, "Trump revokes ex-CIA director John Brennan's security clearance," CNN, August 2018, https://www.cnn.com /2018/08/15/politics/john-brennan-security-clearance/index.html.

59. Hirschfeld Davis and Shear, "Trump Revokes."

60. Ibid.

61. Josh Gerstein, "Two More Officials Cited in FBI Texts Step Down," *Politico,* February 8, 2018, https://www.politico.com/story/2018/02/08/fbi-texts-officials-resign-400533.

62. Eliza Relman, "James Comey's Former Chief of Staff Quit the FBI," *Business Insider,* January 23, 2018, https://www.businessinsider.com/james-comey-former-chief-of-staff-quit-the-fbi-2018-1; Laura Jarrett and Josh Campbell, "FBI Officials Lisa Page and James Baker Resign," CNN, May 2018, https://edition.cnn.com/2018/05/04/politics/fbi-officials-lisa-page-james-baker-resign/index.html; Natasha Bertrand, " 'Trump fears them': Former officials defend FBI leaders swept up in the Trump-Russia firestorm," *Business Insider,* December 24, 2017, https://www.businessinsider.com/fbi-general-counsel-james-baker-reassigned-amid-trump-russia-firestorm-2017-12; Samuel Chamberlain and Catherine Herridge, "Demoted FBI agent Peter Strzok had larger role in Clinton, Russia probes than previously known," Fox News, June 2018, http://www.foxnews.com/politics/2018/06/05/demoted-fbi-agent-peter-strzok-had-larger-role-in-clinton-russia-probes-than-previously-known.html; Carrie Johnson, "Leader of Justice Department National Security Division on the Way Out," NPR, April 20, 2017, https://www.npr.org/2017/04/20/524905899/leader-of-justice-department-national-security-division-on-the-way-out.

63. Kenneth P. Vogel and Matthew Rosenberg, "Agents Tried to Flip Russian Oligarchs. The Fallout Spread to Trump," *New York Times*, September 1, 2018, https://www.nytimes.com/2018/09/01/us/politics/deripaska-ohr-steele-fbi.html.

64. Donald J. Trump (@realDonaldTrump), "Wow, Nellie Ohr, Bruce Ohr's wife, is a Russia expert who is fluent in Russian. She worked for Fusion GPS where she was paid a lot. Collusion! Bruce was a boss at the Department of Justice and is, unbelievably, still there!" Trump Twitter Archive, August 30, 2018, 5:54 a.m., http://www.trumptwitterarchive.com/archive.

65. Associated Press, "Trump Target in Russia Probe Questioned by Republicans," *New York Times*, August 28, 2018, https://www.nytimes.com/aponline/2018/08/28/us/politics/ap-us-trump-russia-probe-congress.html.

66. Jeremy Herb, "Ohr says Steele told him Russian intel believed they had Trump 'over a barrel,' " CNN, August 31, 2018, https://www.cnn.com/2018/08/31/politics/bruce-ohr-christopher-steele-donald-trump/index.html.

67. Jonathan Swan, "Scoop: FBI director threatened to resign amid Trump, Sessions pressure," *Axios,* January 23, 2018, https://www.axios.com/scoop-sessions-fbi-trump-christopher-wray-877adb3e-5f8d-44a1-8a2f-d4f0894ca6a7.html.

68. Laura Jerrett and Pamela Brown, "Ex-FBI Deputy Director Andrew McCabe is fired—and fires back," CNN, March 17, 2018, https://www.cnn.com/2018/03/16/politics/andrew-mccabe-fired/index.html.

69. Ibid.

70. Donald J. Trump (@realDonaldTrump), "Andrew McCabe FIRED, a great day

for the hard working men and women of the FBI - A great day for Democracy. Sanctimonious James Comey was his boss and made McCabe look like a choirboy. He knew all about the lies and corruption going on at the highest levels of the FBI!" Twitter, March 16, 2018, 9:08 p.m., https://twitter.com/realDonald Trump/status/974859881827258369.

71. "Trump Threatens to 'Get Involved' and Fire Rosenstein," *Daily Beast,* April 2018, https://www.thedailybeast.com/trump-threatens-to-get-involved-and-fire -rosenstein; Pamela Brown et al., "Trump considering firing Rosenstein to check Mueller," CNN, April 2018, https://www.cnn.com/2018/04/10/politics/trump -rod-rosenstein-robert-mueller/index.html.

72. Ibid.

73. Jeremy Herb, "GOP Senators Send Criminal Referral to Justice Department for Dossier Author," CNN, January 2018, https://www.cnn.com/2018/01/05/politics /dossier-judiciary-committee-investigations/index.html.

74. Jonathan Martin et al., "Trump Pressed Top Republicans to End Senate Russian Inquiry," *New York Times*, November 2017, https://www.nytimes.com/2017/11 /30/us/politics/trump-russia-senate-intel.html.

75. 18 U.S.C. § 1512. 1729. Protection of Government Processes—Tampering With Victims, Witnesses, or Informants—18 U.S.C. 1512, United States Department of Justice, https://www.justice.gov/usam/criminal-resource-manual-1729-pro tection-government-processes-tampering-victims-witnesses-or.

76. Jacqueline Thomsen, "Trump Officials Pushing Hope Hicks to Join 2020 Campaign: Report," *Hill*, August 9, 2018, http://thehill.com/homenews/administra tion/401130-trump-officials-pushing-hope-hicks-to-join-2020-campaign-report.

77. Ibid.

78. Josh Dawsey and Ashley Parker, " 'Everyone signed one': Trump is aggressive in his use of nondisclosure agreements, even in government," *Washington Post*, August 13, 2018, https://www.washingtonpost.com/politics/everyone-signed-one -trump-is-aggressive-in-his-use-of-nondisclosure-agreements-even-in-govern ment/2018/08/13/9d0315ba-9f15-11e8-93e3-24d1703d2a7a_story.html?utm_ term=.b782c8ee0284.

79. Michelle Ye Hee Lee and Anu Narayanswamy, "RNC paid nearly half a million dollars to law firm representing Hope Hicks and others in Russia probes," *Washington Post*, May 20, 2018, https://www.washingtonpost.com/news/post-politics /wp/2018/05/20/rnc-paid-nearly-half-a-million-dollars-to-law-firm-representing -hope-hicks-and-others-in-russia-probes/?utm_term=.cfee1d0661e3.

80. Justin Wise, "Roger Stone: Trump Pardon of D'Souza Was a Signal to Mueller," *Hill*, June 1, 2018, http://thehill.com/policy/national-security/390220-stone -calls-pardon-of-dsouza-a-sign-for-mueller-trump-has-awesome.

81. Ken Dilanian, "Ex-Trump adviser Roger Stone says he expects Mueller to charge him with a crime," NBC News, August 30, 2018, https://www.nbcnews.com/ politics/donald-trump/ex-trump-adviser-roger-stone-says-he-expects-mueller -charge-n905091.

82. Joshua Caplan, "Roger Stone Predicts Mueller Will Indict Donald Trump Jr. on

Process Crime," Breitbart, August 24, 2018, https://www.breitbart.com/big
-government/2018/08/24/roger-stone-donald-trump-jr-mueller-indict-process
-crime/.

83. Noah Feldman, "Giuliani the Prosecutor Would've Called This Obstruction,"
Bloomberg News, August 24, 2018, https://www.bloomberg.com/view/articles
/2018-08-24/rudy-giuliani-is-on-thin-ice-with-paul-manafort-pardon-quote.

84. Jonathan Chait, "Trump, Obstructing Justice Again, Asked Lawyers About
Manafort Pardon," *New York*, August 23, 2018, http://nymag.com/daily/intel
ligencer/2018/08/trump-obstructing-justice-manafort-pardon.html; Joe Lock-
hart, "President Donald Trump issuing pardons during special counsel Robert
Mueller's investigation could be considered obstruction of justice," CNN, June
1, 2018, https://www.cnn.com/videos/politics/2018/06/01/joe-lockhart-trump
-pardons-obstruction-of-justice-newday.cnn; Steven T. Dennis, "Republican
Senators Warn Trump Not to Obstruct Justice or Pardon Himself," Bloomberg,
June 5, 2018, https://www.bloomberg.com/news/articles/2018-06-05/key-sen
ate-republicans-warn-trump-on-obstruction-pardon-powers; "Former Federal
Prosecutor: A Pardon Can Equal Obstruction of Justice," *Hardball with Chris
Matthews*, "MSNBC, August 21, 2018, https://www.msnbc.com/hardball
/watch/fmr-federal-prosecutor-a-pardon-can-equal-obstruction-of-justice
-1303730755624?v=railb; Abigail Tracy, " 'That's Obstruction of Justice': What
Pardoning Manafort Would Mean for Trump," *Vanity Fair*, August 24, 2018,
https://www.vanityfair.com/news/2018/08/donald-trump-paul-manafort-pardon;
Sean Illing, "10 legal experts on why Trump can't pardon his way out of the
Russia investigation," *Vox,* August 21, 2017, https://www.vox.com/2017/8/29
/16211784/paul-manafort-charged-guilty-trial-trump-pardon-power.

85. Randall D. Eliason, "Trump Won't Talk to Mueller. Here's Why," Opinion,
Washington Post, February 2018, https://www.washingtonpost.com/opinions
/trump-shouldnt-talk-to-mueller-heres-why/2018/02/14/0be8a8c2-11a5-11e8
-9570-29c9830535e5_story.html?utm_term=.4a6b47b294fe; Kellan Howell,
"Legal Experts: Almost No Upside for Trump to Speak to Mueller," NewsChan-
nel5, August 2018, https://www.newschannel5.com/newsy/legal-experts-almost
-no-upside-for-trump-to-speak-to-mueller.

86. Dan Merica and Pamela Brown, "Trump says he wants to talk to Mueller, would
do so under oath," CNN, January 25, 2018, https://www.cnn.com/2018/01/24/
politics/robert-mueller-donald-trump/index.html.

87. Jonathan Chait, "Trump's Lawyers Can't Talk Him Out of Talking to Mueller,"
New York, August 6, 2018, http://nymag.com/daily/intelligencer/2018/08/trumps
-lawyers-cant-stop-mueller-interview.html.

88. Laura King, "Giuliani: Trump wouldn't 'have to' obey a Mueller subpoena,
could take the 5th," *Los Angeles Times*, May 6, 2018, http://www.latimes.com/
politics/la-na-pol-giuliani-trump-20180506-story.html.

89. Ishaan Tharoor, "What happened in Helsinki? We Still Don't Know," *Washington Post*, July 23, 2018, https://www.washingtonpost.com/news/worldviews
/wp/2018/07/23/what-happened-in-helsinki-we-still-dont-know/?utm_ter
m=.21cb8dba2893.

90. Ibid.

91. Zachary Cohen, "Trump's intel chief still doesn't 'fully understand' what happened in Putin meeting," CNN, August 2, 2018, https://www.cnn.com/2018/08/02/politics/dni-coats-trump-putin-helsinki-meeting/index.html.

92. Ibid.

93. Del Quentin Wilbur, "Paul Manafort pleads guilty to reduced charges and agrees to cooperate with special counsel's probe," September 14, 2018, *Los Angeles Times*, http://www.latimes.com/politics/la-na-pol-manafort-plea-20180914-story.html; Paul J. Manafort, Jr. "Complete Plea Offer," Case 1:17-cr-00201, *U.S. v. Paul J. Manafort*, Crim. No. 17-201-1, U.S. Department of Justice, The Special Counsel's Office, September 14, 2018, https://www.justice.gov/file/1094151/download.

94. Howard Fineman, "The 'state' of Donald Trump? He thinks it couldn't be better," NBC News, News analysis, January 30, 2018, https://www.nbcnews.com/storyline/2018-state-of-the-union-address/state-donald-trump-he-thinks-it-couldn-t-be-better-n842501.

95. "Robert Mueller coolly reminds everyone that the Trump-Russia investigation is still happening, with 'multiple lines of non-public inquiry,'" *Week*, May 23, 2018, http://theweek.com/speedreads/774925/robert-mueller-coolly-reminds-everyone-that-trumprussia-investigation-still-happening-multiple-lines-nonpublic-inquiry.

96. Richard C. Paddock, "Seeking Asylum, an Escort Has a Tale of Trump and Russia to Offer," *New York Times*, March 2, 2018, https://www.nytimes.com/2018/03/02/world/asia/nastya-rybka-trump-putin.html.

97. Ibid.

98. Aleksei Navalny, YouTube, February 8, 2018, https://www.youtube.com/watch?v=RQZr2NgKPiU.

99. Ibid.

100. Ibid.

101. Ibid.

102. Ibid.

103. Ibid.

104. Lincoln Pigman, "Aleksei Navalny, Kremlin Critic, Is Jailed Ahead of Russian Pension Protests," *New York Times*, August 27, 2018, https://www.nytimes.com/2018/08/27/world/europe/russia-navalny.html.

105. Paddock, "Seeking Asylum, an Escort Has a Tale."

106. Richard C. Paddock, "She Gambled on Her Claim to Link Russians and Trump. She Is Losing," *New York Times*, August 31, 2018, https://www.nytimes.com/2018/08/31/world/asia/escort-anastasia-vashukevich-nastya-rybka-trump.html.

107. Ibid.

108. Kaweewit Kaewjinda, "Escort Says Oligarch Now Has Tapes on Russia Interference," Associated Press, August 20, 2018, https://apnews.com/78eef0ecec49412b816ac5169d63279a.

109. Ibid.

110. Marc Bennetts, "Russian watchdog orders YouTube to remove Navalny luxury yacht video," *Guardian*, February 13, 2013, https://www.theguardian.com/world /2018/feb/13/russian-watchdog-orders-youtube-to-remove-navalny-video.

111. "Defendants Sentencing Memorandum," *United States of America v. George Papadopoulos,* pp. 5–12, filed August 31, 2018, https://www.documentcloud.org/ documents/4807546-Papadopoulos-defense-sentencing-memo.html.

112. Quint Forgey and Kyle Cheney, "Mueller Recommends Sentence Up to 6 Months for Papadopoulos," *Politico,* August 17, 2018, https://www.politico.com /story/2018/08/17/papadopoulous-mueller-sentencing-trump-campaign-russia -787835.

113. Ibid.

114. Franklin Foer, "Was a Trump Server Communicating with Russia?" *Slate,* October 31, 2016, http://www.slate.com/articles/news_and_politics/cover_story /2016/10/was_a_server_registered_to_the_trump_organization_communicat ing_with_russia.html.

115. Sam Biddle, "Russian Bank Accused of Trump Connection Tries to Clear Name by Pressuring U.S. Computer Researcher," Intercept, October 26, 2017, https:// theintercept.com/2017/10/26/russian-bank-accused-of-trump-connection-tries -to-clear-name-by-pressuring-u-s-computer-researcher/.

116. Foer, "Was a Trump Server."

117. Natasha Bertrand, "The FBI is reportedly examining why a Russian bank with ties to Putin wanted to reach the Trump Organization during the campaign," *Business Insider*, March 10, 2017, https://www.businessinsider.com/fbi-alfa -bank-trump-organization-servers-2017-3.

118. Tina Nguyen, "The Spy Story of Maria Butina Keeps Getting Stranger," *Vanity Fair*, August 1, 2018, https://www.vanityfair.com/news/2018/08/maria-butina -russia-spy-financial-investigation.

119. Sara Salinas, "Cambridge Analytica is shutting down, says the 'siege of media coverage' drove away clients," CNBC, May 2018, https://www.cnbc.com/2018 /05/02/cambridge-analytica-is-shutting-down-wsj.html; James Vincent, "Academic who collected 50 million Facebook profiles: 'We thought we were doing something normal,'" *Verge,* March 21, 2018, https://www.theverge.com/2018 /3/21/17146342/facebook-data-scandal-cambridge-analytica-aleksandr-kogan -scapegoat; Channel 4 News, six-part YouTube video, Channel "Cambridge Analytica: Undercover Secrets of Trump's Data Firm," published March 20, 2018, https://www.youtube.com/watch?v=cy-9iciNF1A; "Cambridge Analytica Uncovered: Secret filming reveals election tricks," YouTube, published March 19, 2018, https://www.youtube.com/watch?v=mpbeOCKZFfQ&t=2s; "Cambridge Analytica finally speak to Channel 4 News (interview)," YouTube, published April 26, 2018, https://www.youtube.com/watch?v=qRuUX6fsPVg; "Cambridge Analytica boss under fire from MPs," YouTube, published March 18, 2018, https://www.youtube.com/watch?v=u5aQgS2Uh1M; "Cambridge Analytica: Whistleblower reveals data grab of 50 million Facebook profiles," YouTube, published March 17, 2018, https://www.youtube.com/watch?v=zb6-xz-geH4;

"Cambridge Analytica: how big data shaped the US election," YouTube, published October 24, 2016, https://www.youtube.com/watch?v=CgYvf3Ckdso.

120. Jill Colvin and Catherine Lucey, "Omarosa Says She Will 'Blow the Whistle' on White House Corruption," *Time*, August 13, 2018, http://time.com/5365352/omarosa-white-house-trump-corruption/; Esha Bhandari, "No, the President Can't Legally Gag White House Staffers," ACLU, March 20, 2018, https://www.aclu.org/blog/free-speech/employee-speech-and-whistleblowers/no-president-cant-legally-gag-white-house.

ABOUT THE AUTHOR

SETH ABRAMSON is a former criminal defense attorney and criminal investigator who teaches digital journalism, legal advocacy, and cultural theory at the University of New Hampshire. A regular political and legal analyst on CNN and the BBC during the Trump presidency, he is the author of eight books and editor of five anthologies. Abramson is a graduate of Dartmouth College, Harvard Law School, the Iowa Writers' Workshop, and the PhD program in English at the University of Wisconsin-Madison. He lives in New Hampshire with his wife and two one-year-old rescue hounds, Quinn and Scout.